DATE DUE

	NOV 9 2001
APR - 6 1995	OCT 1 3 2003
APR 27 1995	
OCT 1 9 1995	
DEC 1 8 1995	
FEB 1 1996	
FEB 1 7 1996	
MAY - 3 1996	
JUL 2 5 1996	
OCT 2 8 1996	
MAR - 6 1997	
SEP 2 7 1997	
APR 1 4 1998	
JAN 3 0 1999	
MAY 2 8 1999	
MAR - 9 2000	
APR 2 2 2000	

BRODART   Cat. No. 23-221

TRAUMA VICTIM

Theoretical Issues

and

Practical Suggestions

Lee Hyer

and

Associates

Accelerated Development Inc.

Publishers

Muncie, Indiana

TRAUMA VICTIM
Theoretical Issues and Practical Suggestions

Technical Development: Cynthia Long
                          Marguerite Mader
                          Janet Merchant
                          Shaeney Pigman
                          Sheila Sheward

Library of Congress Cataloging-in-Publication Data

Hyer, Lee, 1944-
    Trauma victim : theoretical issues and practical suggestions / Lee Hyer and associates.
        p.   cm.
    Includes bibliographical references and index.
    ISBN:1-55959-047-5
    1.   Post-traumatic stress disorder--Treatment.   I.   Title.
RC552.P67H94   1993
616.85'21--dc20   93-14158
                                                                              CIP

LCN: 93-14158
ISBN: 1-55959-047-5

Order additional copies from: **ACCELERATED DEVELOPMENT INC.,**

PUBLISHERS
3808 West Kilgore Avenue
Muncie, Indiana 47304-4896
Toll Free Order Number 1-800-222-1166

FOREWORD

At one point in this comprehensive, thoughtful, and clinically sound review of PTSD therapy and treatment, Dr. Hyer laments that "trauma has a way of preventing other issues from being considered." I also agree that clinicians working with trauma victims need a "theory-driven and hypothesis-checked plan of intervention" and a way to monitor the progress of treatment. Hyer has provided such a conceptual and clinical framework in this book. His model is complementary to approaches that start with the severity of trauma and end with a focus on PTSD symptoms. Hyer instead starts with the person rather than the trauma. His focus is on the impact of trauma on the person as an entity. Although relief of specific PTSD symptoms remains important, it is never the primary goal of treatment.

Acknowledging his debt to Adler, Millon, and cognitive behavioral therapy (CBT), Hyer provides a model by which trauma is best understood through its impact on the overall constellation of the person. In order to understand the person we need to assess each individual's "schemas" and "personality styles." Schemas provide the essential structural base for the cognitive/affective/behavioral components "of each individual." "Personality style" consists of "model styles and selfperpetuating patterns" that are stable aspects of a given individual's characteristic mode of engaging the world. Together schemas and personality styles influence the expression of beliefs and symptoms.

Different people have different core schemas and personality styles. They appraise stressful situations differently and exhibit different patterns of adaptive behavior. Schemas, personality styles and coping behaviors provide the ongoing psychological context through which individuals integrate ongoing experience.

Trauma disrupts this process and may lead to a number of dysfunctional beliefs and symptoms—sometimes to PTSD, sometimes to personality disorders and other psychiatric syndromes, and sometimes to PTSD and comorbid diagnoses.

Dr. Hyer keeps reminding us that symptoms and diagnoses need not be the starting point for clinical assessment, nor should they be the end point of treatment. In that regard, his approach challenges more standard PTSD therapies. Hyer's starting point is the careful assessment and evaluation of how the client's central "affective, cognitive, and behavioral processes develop and interact in an interpersonal context." From this perspective, the therapist can conceptualize a wide array of psychopathological manifestations that may erupt when the seeds of trauma penetrate the various soils of different personalities.

In addition to his scholarly and comprehensive review of the trauma literature and his presentation of the Adlerian model, Dr. Hyer devotes a great deal of this book to treatment issues from a theoretical and practical perspective. This is a major contribution, as the trauma literature has become long on theory and assessment but woefully short on practical matters concerning treatment. Many useful sections and tables detailing assessment and therapeutic strategies derived from his conceptual model are presented. Also included are excellent sections on the therapeutic relationship which spell out appropriate tasks and expectations that therapist and client should have for each other. In these sections, the reader gets more than a glimpse of Dr. Hyer as a well-seasoned therapist and eloquent humanist who brings both compassion and a wry sense of humor to his work.

Besides its theoretical and practical usefulness, Lee Hyer's conceptual approach lends itself easily to several important issues that are of concern to clinicians and controversial to experts. These include high rates of comorbid diagnoses among PTSD patients, post-traumatic syndromes that do not meet DSM-III-R criteria for PTSD, and the clinical expression of post-traumatic syndromes cross-culturally.

A conceptual and clinical vexation has been that PTSD is often accompanied by affective disorders, other anxiety disorders, alcoholism, personality disorders, and other diagnosable entities. If only we could separate out the "pure PTSD" from the rest of the complex and often confusing diagnostic picture, we think, we might have a chance to understand and treat this disorder more effectively. But among treatment seeking trauma survivors, "impure" PTSD seems to be the rule rather than the exception. Some of us are just beginning to ask whether the high prevalence of cormorbidity among PTSD patients indicates something fundamental about the psychopathology of post-traumatic stress syndromes. As I have argued elsewhere from a biological and pathophysiological perspective, diagnosable affective or anxiety disorders detected among PTSD patients may be inherent parts of the syndrome itself rather than separate and distinct clinical entities (Friedman, 1990.)

Hyer's perspective is that the question of "pure" versus "impure" PTSD from a DSM-III-R perspective is moot. The discrete diagnostic chips and symptoms will fall as they may. What really matters are the individual's pre-traumatic schemas and personality styles because they determine the post-traumatic clinical picture. In some cases PTSD will be accompanied by other DSM-III-R diagnosable disorders. Practically speaking, whether it is "pure" or "impure" PTSD, treatment will always focus preferentially on schemas and personality styles rather than on specific symptoms or diagnoses.

A second issue is what to do about people who have been significantly affected by trauma but who do not meet PTSD diagnostic criteria. Such people have partial PTSD— recognizable PTSD symptoms but not enough to qualify for the full PTSD diagnosis, or they may be rape/incest or torture victims who meet criteria for a "non-approved" diagnosis such as DESNOS (Disorders of Extreme Stress Not Otherwise Specified, Herman, 1992). Although these examples represent problems from a DSM-III-R perspective, they are easily accommodated by Dr. Hyer's conceptual and clinical approach.

Concern is growing about the applicability of the PTSD model to individuals from traditional non-Western societies.

This group includes refugees and other survivors of torture, rape, natural disasters and war. It appears that although such individuals have unquestionably been exposed to catastrophic stress, their overall clinical presentation may deviate from the PTSD cluster of symptoms (Friedman & Jaransen, in press; Marsella, et al., in press). Again, an approach that focuses on schemas and personality styles provides a conceptual and clinical framework in which to conduct treatment. To utilize Hyer's model in this context, however, the therapist must have the necessary cross-cultural skills to assess accurately the schemas and personality styles of non-Western clientele.

Although Lee Hyer has written most of this book, important contributions were made by other authors. Pat Boudewyns provides an excellent chapter on Direct Therapeutic Exposure, a behavioral technique for which he has been a leading exponent. Brett Litz and Diana Hearst have contributed a lucid description of clinical information processing in PTSD. Francine Schapiro offers a comprehensive description of the treatment she has originated, Eye Movement Desentization and Reprocessing. Finally, Mary Summers and Lee Hyer provide a useful chapter on the effects of trauma on older people.

In my opinion this book provides a conceptual umbrella under which many discrete theoretical and clinical approaches easily can fit. Theory is only useful if it helps us look in different places for new knowledge or if it helps us understand why some clinical approaches may be more useful than others. Dr. Hyer's model does both. It is an important contribution, and I recommend it enthusiastically.

Matthew J. Friedman, M.D., Ph.D.

REFERENCES

Friedman, M. J. (1990). Interrelationships between biological mechanisms and pharmacotherapy of posttraumatic stress disorder. In M.E. Wolfe & E.D. Mosnaim (Eds.), *Postraumatic stress disorder: biological mechanisms and clinical aspects.* Washington, DC: American Psychiatric Press.

Friedman, M. J., & Jaransen, J. M. (in press). The applicability of the PTSD concept to refugees. In A. J. Marsella, T. H. Borneman, S. Ekblad, & J. Orley (Eds.), *Amidst peril and pain: the mental health and well-being of the world's refuge.* Washington, DC: American Psycological Association.

Herman, J. L. (1992). Complex PTSD: A syndrome in survivors of prolonged and repeated trauma. *Journal of Trumatic Stress, 5,* 372-392.

Marsella, A. J., Friedman, M. J., & Spain, E. H. (in press). Ethnocultural aspects of PTSD: an overview of issues, research, and directions. In J.M. Oldham, A. Tasman, & M. Riba (Eds.), *American Psychiatric Press Review of Psychiatry, 12.* Washington, DC: American Psychiatric Press.

PREFACE

Cezanne noted that by being a painter he became more lucid when confronted by nature. By writing this book, we too have become more lucid in our understanding of the effects of trauma. We are painfully aware that care of victims (as a result of trauma) is tough business. We have come to know that to fully understand anyone's response to trauma is a luxury indeed. Yet we also know that information on this topic is exploding before our professional eyes. In a sense we have become multiepistomologists—seekers of the truth and meaning from many sources. And, through the course of these efforts we have been both excited and humbled by these happenings. We have developed instincts for moving toward truth, but only instincts.

We explicate the thesis and plan of this book in Chapter 1. Before we get started on our odyssey, however, we are compelled to specify several ideas that have guided our deliberating. In no particular order they are listed as six propositions.

Proposition One: **Any model of trauma must include roles for individual vulnerability (and resilience), for characteristics of the stressor, and for post-exposure mediating variables, especially coping and social support.** Reactions to trauma are complex; a careful analysis of each victim's problem is most important. People respond poorly to trauma over time because of some personal vulnerability, of something unique about the stressor (e.g., excessive or continuous), of some deficit in adjustment resources, and of the interaction among these components. It is now clear, for example, that a trauma problem beyond six months is influenced by variables different than those for acute victims (less than six months). In fact, it pains us to note that chronic trauma victims are singularly unable to habituate to stressor cues (often other stressors). Clinicians must now attend to both elements of trauma causation and elements of trauma maintenance.

Proposition Two: **Individuals respond to trauma events by their own interpretation and by the perceived implications of the trauma events. The official psychiatric nosology recognizes this fact.** We base much of this book on this fact. The argument is easily made that no definition of trauma exists except by reference to the person who experiences it. The initial unconditioned response gives way to a massive and embedded array of triggers that are anchored to the person's own meaning and individuality. This core memory connection has even been labeled "superconditioning." Further, all nonconditioned areas of the person are "emotionally biased" toward this conditioning, thereby creating a whole trauma response. The disorder, Post-traumatic Stress Disorder (PTSD), may be phasic (intrusion and avoidance) in appearance, but it is "at the ready" and at the dictates of the person.

Proposition Three: **Core expectations about self (schemas and personality) are disrupted during trauma, resulting in a distortion of cognitive/emotional processing, not an objective representation of reality.** The most annoying fallout is a protective and biased apperception of incoming stimuli. This trauma-influenced, tacit knowledge results in an unfriendly inner dialogue and a compromised accommodation to the environment. An understanding of the key dispositional factors is required for care.

Proposition Four: **The first response of the victim is to reexperience the trauma and to adapt through avoidance/ arousal, all of which is directed by the "person" of the victim.** Trauma is experienced by "everyman" and can be expressed in an infinite number of ways. Implications are that adjustment to trauma is normal and commonplace and that adaptation is best considered eugenic. At the risk of an obvious oxymoron, "normal deviant" reactions (as a result of trauma) are distinctly different due to both the person and the specific trauma. If PTSD problems develop, the influence of the "person" of the victim has organized the adaptation beyond the assimilation/ accommodation skills of the person. In time something wrong evolves—the deregulation of the victim's neurobiology (at molecular, synaptic, and brain system levels) and of the victim's psychological and behavioral functioning. Clearly, avoidant and intrusive symptoms are just starting points for analysis.

Proposition Five: **Treatment of the trauma victim requires an integrated approach, a considered attack on two components—the victim's self (schemas) and symptoms (trauma based emotions and cognitions).** Each trauma victim possesses self-referent schemas that are disrupted. Sometimes these are accessible, sometimes not. The trauma victim who is open to these experiences has been labeled an integrator, open to the continuity of thoughts and feelings throughout life and likely to benefit from a holistic treatment regimen; self-constructionist therapies are most apt for this patient. The trauma victim who isolates thoughts and feelings and reacts in an encapsulated, alien way to the victimization experience is likely to require different therapies; supportive, educative, or symptom based therapies are in order. This style of victimization has been called sealing over. Over time, the integrator is likely to adjust better. Once again, an understanding of the continuity process of self and how to distinguish between these states is important.

Proposition Six: **An integrated, multimodel treatment program is required that addresses the real and symbolic reenactment of the person's trauma response (first, if possible) with a judicious melding of symptom-based therapies—cognitive and exposure components, stress management, and education.** As noted in several of the previous propositions, the trauma victim possesses a generic representation of self that dictates the trauma response. The "person" of the trauma victim determines the form of the reenactment of trauma. What now appears is that the necessary curative components of the treatment drama involve a "just right" mixture of an empathic and neutral relationship, exposure of the trauma elements, and cognitive\emotional\interpersonal meaning alteration. In fact, traditional psychotherapies address differing amounts of these components and, as such, attack distinct symptoms;

psychodynamic therapy, for example, achieves a greater reduction in avoidance and character symptoms, exposure based therapies impact reexperiencing symptoms, and desensitization therapies address hyperarousal symptoms. Trauma work demands that the therapist understand this *and* experience the victim's phenomenology, so that trauma can be "conjointly solved."

These "essential tensions" have served as sediment for the book. Through a mixture of trial and error and science we have developed our position and an armamentarium of treatments. Sometimes these are effective, sometimes not. Our belief is that we do have a better road map and better technologies.

Finally, in writing this book we have noticed something quite simple that arose from our work with older adults. We have discovered that integrity or self-actualization in life, the "realized self," appears to be more easily accessed and dialogued at later life; the time when there is no future, subject and object are easily blurred, and the balance of "doing" and "being" is tipped toward the latter. The "wisdom of the body" is less blocked at later life. This is not as easy at other ages.

This task, it strikes us, is the goal of the trauma conflict, the inner psychological reordering of personal issues. Trauma victims, too, are attempting to make sense of self with all the confusions of life. At rock bottom then, the victim's struggle is the balance of dedicated energy toward core goals, the person's own unique meaning (the daimon), and the person's needs in life, the necessary preoccupations of living that include trauma. As a result of trauma the "examined life" is no longer transacted. Large segments of experience become stuck, "free radicals" corrupting where they should not. Victims of trauma stop being biographers of self, lacking the ability to "unstick" the past, "be" in the present, or "remember" the future. To borrow from Eric Fromm, the person of the victim accepts a "moratorium" on living and a "foreclosure" on life.

In this book our task is to turn "happenings into meanings." This is the narrative of change of one's inner assumptive world or schema to the realities of the external world. This is the pursuit of the healing theory of one's stuck life. The victim has a chronic indwelling, a tacit knowledge of being a victim, and has no avenue out. This "always felt" body memory inhabits the person and chronically spurts to the foreground. How the transformation of this victim position to a whole person unfolds and how it can be moved along constitutes our undertaking.

Hopefully, the reader will become a active spectator, one who creates.

TABLE OF CONTENTS

LIST OF FIGURES

LIST OF TABLES

Chapter **1**

INTRODUCTION: AN OVERVIEW

Fantasy
I am flying, I am soaring,
    I am floating high and free;
Now I'm swimming in the ocean,
    and the waters cover me.

I have cast aside material things
    and all reality;
I am totally submerged in make believe,
    in a world of fantasy.   (James Martin, circa 1985)

Arguably the most intriguing construct to evolve in mental health during the past decade is trauma and its effects. With advances in knowledge it has become unreasonable to expect that victims of trauma, any trauma, are able to walk away from the experience as whole people. Since virtually all humans experience trauma in various forms, we are constantly being intruded upon and aspects of our personhood eroded. The good news is that trauma seems to affect measurably only a small percentage of us in any long-term negative way. The residuals of an intense stressor may cause minor difficulties in many of us; major symptoms result in a substantially smaller group. The bad news, on the other hand, is that trauma symptoms are sufficiently prevalent and intrusive as to become a major concern for mental health practitioners. Additionally, trauma gives rise to a variety of disorders, some of which may affect the victim at a subclinical level, whereas others are full-blown and more seriously affect psychological adaptation. The most noxious disorder resulting from trauma is **post-traumatic stress disorder (PTSD).** How this disorder develops, under what circumstances, and with what types of people are major questions yet to be fully elaborated.

ASPECTS OF EFFECTS OF TRAUMA

This book addresses a variety of aspects of the effects of trauma on the person of the trauma victim. Its thesis is that the human experience is an unfolding of core processes or schemas that construct, order, and foster one's identity, goals, and actions. These processes most parsimoniously organize and direct the individual's response to trauma. Mahoney (1991) labeled this concept **core ordering processes**. They constitute activities whereby individuals derive meaning, identity, and a sense of control out of life. Appropriate attention to the parts and mechanics of these core schemas will maximize an understanding of the human change process in therapy. Clinical formulation and treatment of trauma victims, then, are most accurate and effective when based on a conceptualization of the individual that is informed by core principles or schemas. Adler "summed" these core processes or schemas under the concept **life-style (LS)**, a unique functional and structural entity that makes the individual who he or she is.

This is certainly not a radical notion. Previous writers on the treatment of trauma victims, ranging from Freud to, more recently, Horowitz, and Pearlman and McCann placed a heavy emphasis on the schema structure of the trauma victim. In this book, we borrow heavily from these authors, as well as from the ideas of Adler and Millon, to provide a flexible paradigm and framework for assessment and treatment of the trauma victim. Our goal is an integrated approach to the person of the victim.

We also borrow liberally from two other paradigms. The first, **information processing**, provides a theoretical framework and methodology to disaggregate a person's cognitive/affective/behavioral makeup for greater clinical understanding. The second, **Cognitive Behavioral Therapy (CBT)**, also allows for a differentiation of the person processes. CBT is noteworthy for distinctive treatment methods and a careful emphasis on cognitive processes as a source of the person's response patterns. CBT also has differentiated the treatment process into **schema therapy** and **symptom therapy**. This distinction will prove important in our formulation.

An implied message of this book is that the person of the victim is often given "short shrift" or often not recognized due to the excessive emphasis on objectification, assessment, and specific trauma-related techniques by the health care providers. Both information processing and CBT have been accused of this failing. The basic belief of this book is that the human change process is highly individualized, but understandable within an integrated formulation of the person. Our professions have become too focused on the stressor, and too committed to depersonalized, expeditious care, and professional canons. All theories of human change contain implicit conceptual stowaways; we seek different canons and generative constructs. The way forward then depends on both systemic solutions and the personal experience of the unmeasurable person.

Perhaps this is best expressed by Millon (1969, 1981). Utilizing the polythetic model of the psychiatric nosology, he proposed an integrated system of treatment. Under our current nosology, differential features of syndromes are not considered to be singularly necessary or jointly sufficient for membership in a category; rather, a heterogeneity exists among symptoms and an overlap of boundaries exists between diagnostic categories. Clients possess various mixtures of character problems, symptoms, and situational stressors. Millon has devised a theory-driven paradigm based on the importance of personality. The person's responses ultimately evolve from personality. The structure and style of the various information and affective processes of the person are thereby directed and strongly influenced by these learned patterns of behavior. This is the personality. Based on these enduring strategies the individual interacts with the world, is influenced by it, and responds to both internal and external stressors in predictable patterns, even when decompensation occurs. These patterns are logical if understood from the perspective of personality patterns. All roads lead outward from the person.

Corollaries

Several corollaries follow. The presenting symptoms or syndromes (Axis I) are understood best from the core learnings of schemas and personality (Axis II), which give expression to the trauma response. Schemas and personality are central to the person. Schemas especially are defining features, the core strategies that give rise to the personality (Axis II). The functional and structural attributes of the personality styles, therefore, represent the expressive modes of regulation that are deeply imbedded within the person. From here the action unfolds.

Unfortunately, reality makes for a messy corollary here. Real clients rarely are pure textbook prototypes. In each is always a complex mixture of schemas or personality styles. An individual can exhibit behavioral features of one, interpersonal features of another, and affective features of yet a third style. The clinician's role, therefore, is to understand and help arrange this interactive mix. To address only clinical symptoms of Axis I or schema and personality features of Axis II alone is insufficient; addressing either level requires an ongoing awareness of the other level.

A second corollary is that clients with the same diagnosis do not display the same set of problems. Taxonomic categories must be conceived as both types and dimensions, permitting unique characteristics of clients to be displayed in their full complexity. The multiaxial paradigm of the current nosology endorses this. As has already been expressed, underlying schemas and personality styles of the person are prepotent in any assessment and treatment of the person.

The third corollary is that schema or personality patterns are highly learned and deeply entrenched and therefore resistant to change. Borrowing from the CBT perspective, schemas can be assessed and treated in three different ways according to their availability for treatment. They may be reconstructed, modified, or reinterpreted. **Reconstruction** involves a new organization of the schemas, a long-term pursuit of these enduring strategies of the person. **Modification** entails maintenance of certain aspects of the existing schemas with alteration of their more negative components to allow for better quality of life. **Reinterpretation,** the least involved alteration of the schema process, involves maintenance of the schema but reframes them in more functional ways. Choosing the most apt approach for a particular patient with an awareness of the schema's influence on Axis I problems is a clinical decision that is key in this integrated approach.

Finally, an important corollary is that the treating clinician should conceive of the treatment of the trauma victim as a configuration of strategies and tactics selected not only for their resolving symptom features, but also for their contribution to the overall constellation of the person. The therapist, therefore, views the treatment of the trauma victim from an integrated therapeutic model, as emphasized by Millon. This is similar to a conductor of an orchestra, whose task is to bring a harmonious balance among all the instruments, accentuating some, attenuating others, and in the end allowing for full expression of the composition. The elements of meaningful integration are an understanding of the "person" parts, a plan for intervention, and the execution of this plan in a coordinated fashion.

SIMPLE MODEL

At the risk of hubris, a loose consensus seems to prevail in the psychodynamic and information processing literature on how people handle anxiety or trauma. Again taking liberties, a **homunculus** exists within each of us that becomes activated to frustrations or to a trauma. At the moment of trauma, normal procedures of this small sub-being are suspended, and it begins to do what any system would do under stress: it self-protects by overdoing what it knows and underdoing what is risky. The homunculus knows immediately what to do in this situation: evade anxiety wherever it exists. Goleman (1986) viewed this process as a diversionary goal to produce a **lacuna** (a gap or black hole of the mind that diverts attention from anxiety, thus creating a defense). In effect, a lacuna is a blind spot. The result is a shortcircuiting of awareness due to pain or anxiety that is far from a random act. With a particular irritant, like a noxious mother, the homunculus learns to shut her out, to daydream, or to hide. In the moment of severe trauma, this little organism has to work harder, but quickly learns where not to be focused. This homunculus knows how to keep the system's integrity.

We will develop a model following the work of the homunculus. As we enter it, Figure 1.1 pictures this covert operation. This little organism is expert at arranging things to occur smoothly and effectively for one purpose: reduction of pain/anxiety. This model portrays how the homunculus alters the world of the trauma victim, forms a person, and eventually leads to problems with a poor resolution. If the first victim of trauma is **innocence,** the ongoing victims are **distortions** and **stagnation.**

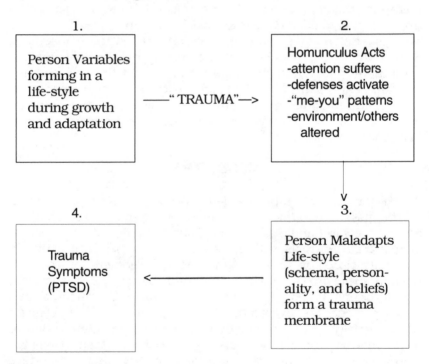

Figure 1.1. Simple trauma model.

Prices have to be paid for keeping the system integrated. First, blind spots occur, so the individual, while protected, is ever watchful of pain stimuli and, by dint of this effort, ever unobservant to portions of life. The more anxious the person, the greater the effort and the more the gaps in life. This default mode of processing eventually leads to false idols or at the least an inquietude in life. The first victim, then, is attention.

The second problem is repression. Within a person an unassimilated painful experience (that is repressed) naturally does one thing: it repeats. When there is a lacuna, threatening stimuli abound and the homunculus seeks safety—safety in distortion, safety in confusion, safety in dulling affect, safety in any defensive operation that gets the job done. Always the homunculus has or develops its favorite safety styles. The homunculus, for example, directs the avoidant style cognitively to disrupt or blank out potentially troubling information. In time, this person suffers in hundreds of ways, ultimately missing out on much of life.

Third, rigidity sets in. Favored tactics become the only tactics. Through developed self-structures (e.g., self image and intrapsychic processes) and self-functions (e.g., interpersonal styles and behaviors), the homunculus demands conformity and allegiance, establishing set ways of numbing/avoiding. For trauma victims, numbing and avoidance are especially seductive to the victim's self-reward system, since these processes provide temporary relief from intrusions of trauma. Play has no room here; the prices are too high. Eventually, the homunculus has created rigid patterns, modal styles, and self-defeating strategies—in short, an armored person. The person who was formerly adaptive and resilient is now trapped and overdetermined.

Further, this process is not complete. Not only do many slights occur to balance this cauldron of unassimilated information and negative emotions (lacunae), but a collusion process occurs with others. The homunculus knows that the victim is required to live with others as well as feel safe, so it orchestrates a "dance." "Me-you" patterns evolve with significant and non-significant others to keep harmony. Again, the homunculus seeks safe "frames" of interaction within which to operate. Soon, everyday patterns are overlearned and see to it that business is taken care of safely. Over time, the issues of safety seek prepotent recognition and the commerce of life suffers, depending on stress and circumstances. Now the homunculus has come full circle—safety inside, safety outside. Subtle distortions have become accepted reality.

Emerged Truths

Two rather important "truths" emerge from the simple model, one bad news and one good news. First, the bad news: "every man is in certain respects (a) like all other men, (b) like some other men, (c) like no other man" (Kluckholn & Murray, 1965, p.53). The person is ultimately unique. The bad news then is that no way is known to measure or understand a person adequately. With a reliance on the proto-typical model of understanding people (e.g., DSM), we can at best know how a person is like others or perhaps "some men," but certainly not like "no other man." A construct-like life-style, which tries to incorporate all facets of the person (idiographic and nomothetic), may provide a better understanding of the person, but it too is wanting.

Second, the good news: we are not totally "at sea." Based on early caregiving learnings, nurtured through early and middle childhood, "identified" more vigorously in adolescence, added and subtracted across one's busy twenties and thirties, nervously assessed at mid-life, and accepted or rejected at later life, the person forms habits, styles, patterns, and ways of being that persist and are recordable. They are tinkered with, struggled over, and often resolved. But at the level of traits, at least some measure of consistency exists. Traits represent then, the substance from which to understand a person and, although limited, we can know something of them. Perhaps, from the human perspective it is important that we cannot know and measure all the variance of a person; to know something fully serves only to diminish it.

SCHEMA VERSUS SYMPTOM

We have advocated a requirement for trauma work: to know the person of the victim, including his or her core and self-referential modes of expression. CBT has provided a distinction that nicely organizes this process. Assessment of the person starts with information about schemas. The principled pursuit of the core organizing processes or schemas of the person has been labeled **schema therapy.** This involves the careful assessment and evaluation of the client's central cognitive processes. Schemas are the "Grand Central Station" of the person's actions and behaviors, and an understanding of these is necessary for change. From the CBT perspective, **symptom therapy** addresses other issues. Whereas schema therapy attends to core person issues, symptom therapy addresses the various symptoms or syndromes that are present. For trauma victims the most notable syndrome is PTSD. Symptom therapy includes different techniques used to treat symptoms and should be employed in conjunction with schema therapy to treat the person of the victim.

An understanding of this process and its decision rules is important. Unfortunately an adequate dividing line does not exist between schema therapy and symptom therapy. Both must be considered. Treatment that is intended solely to understand, isolate, expose, and provide alternatives to the person's schemas can lead to symptom changes, but almost always in less than efficient ways. Structured schemas are hard to alter. Similarly, treatment intended solely for symptom removal is often shortsighted, as negative schemas remain intact and virulent. Dye and Roth (1991) noted that clinicians treat trauma victims by combining elements of both **approach** and **avoidance psychotherapies**. Approach strategies emphasize the trauma experience of the victim by addressing, exploring, and reframing person issues around key elements of the trauma pain. The effort is to integrate the trauma experience into the person. Conversely, avoidance is a psychological activity that directs focus away from the trauma. Here, the effort is to reduce symptoms. The clinician then will be variously faced with distinct schema or symptom problems and must utilize both approach and avoidance strategies.

An ideal therapeutic regimen may not be possible, as different victims are variously open and vulnerable to the dangers of approach or are unable to apply many avoidance techniques. In fact, some traumas may be so deeply buried that existential schemas are disrupted; meaningful human integration may not be possible. Vietnam veterans who committed atrocities, for example, may never be able to integrate such an experience into their person. Consequently, at various times a schema or symptom therapy focus can be either helpful or harmful. The idea that the treating clinician should perform pure schema therapy or pure symptom therapy is quixotic.

What has occurred in recent years in the treatment of the trauma victim has been an excessive emphasis on symptoms, on objectification, and on approaches that endorse the "quick fix." Our position is that issues of the person require consideration, contextualization, and care, first. From this personologic perspective, information is processed, and from this perspective, affective, cognitive, and behavioral processes develop and interact in an interpersonal context. In this effort, symptoms must be integrated and commingled with schemas. These issues are two sides of the same coin. Symptom therapy can be just as crucial to the treatment of the trauma victim as schema therapy.

This book is divided into sections with emphasis on the CBT constructs, schema and symptom. The first seven chapters are devoted to a discussion of trauma and, most importantly, to articulation of characteristic cognitive constructs and the manner in which these give rise to symptoms. Trauma is discussed, therefore, in the context of the schema (Part I). When perturbed sufficiently, the schema filtering process gives way to symptoms. The trauma response (PTSD and its variants) is considered the most serious symptom complex exhibited by the victim. While Part II considers some of the unique sources of trauma, Part III is devoted to the symptom therapies. Part IV attempts to highlight the incompatibility between the pressure of society and the person's need for self-understanding and meaning.

LS=Sc+P+(B)+Sy

This equation stands for "Life-Style equals Schema, plus Personality Style, plus Belief, plus Symptom." This represents our case formulation of the person. The LS is Adler's concept of the essential workings of the person. The LS is the person. Philosophically we never really can know the person and fully formulate the LS. This then is an evolving construct that pushes the boundaries of the epistemological limits of psychology. We are allowed only glimpses of the workings of person processes. As outsiders, clinicians "muddle through" understanding the infinitely unique individual perspectives of the person, never fully satisfied with one formulation.

The Sc+P+(B)+Sy equation is an effort to account for this complexity by identification of selected and reasonably known psychological processes. This equation is considered a "good enough" approximation of the LS. It possesses necessary features of meaningful clinical science. These variables embody information from several theoretical positions which allow for clinical inferences regarding the care of the victim. They also imply tools or instruments from which to measure or quantify status and progress. Finally, these disaggregated constructs suggest change-oriented interventions that are therapeutically specific. From these propositions a case formulation grows, the complexity of the trauma victim can be understood, and a treatment plan ordered.

If this book has one credo, it is that *an understanding of the core parts* (Sc + P) of this equation and process facilitates an understanding of the less important [(B) + Sy] parts and allows for a better treatment perspective. This knowledge is fluid, changing with the needs of the schemas, the current situation, and the reciprocal determination among these variables. In effect, an internal network of beliefs, assumptions, formulas, and rules are hierarchically arranged and interact to form the person's actions. Their independent and joint contributions require some map so the clinician can tear "nature at the joints" to better know and appreciate the person [i.e., Sc+P+(B)+Sy]. There is no worse source of error than to pursue absolute truth; these punctuations help us with a less certain, but friendly understanding.

We start our understanding with the person's schemas(Sc). They provide the essential structural base for the cognitive/

affective/behavioral components. This eventually translates into modal styles and self-perpetuating patterns, called personality (P). These two structures, in turn, influence the expression of the last two parts of the equation. Beliefs (B) provide a monitoring or appraisal mechanism of the person. They assist in governing the person's stability and consistency. The (B) is in parentheses because these surface beliefs and appraisals, while important and therapeutically "knowable," are inseparably connected to both schemas and the cognitive constructs of personality styles. Beliefs represent the top level, the knowable level, of this (cognitive) paradigm. In turn, these three emergent person patterns may deteriorate or decompensate in the form of symptoms (Sy). To date, very little research has been assessed in the relationship between specific core schemas or personality styles and the adapting behaviors that result in success (or failure). Nonetheless, our position is that this process occurs: core schemas assisted by the personality styles, and to some extent by beliefs, account for the organization and actions of the person. Symptoms represent an attempt towards adaption to the environment.

This formulation posits that schemas and, to a large extent, personality serve to integrate the activity of the person under a given set of rules. Normally this proceeds smoothly. Trauma, however, disrupts this process. In the previous section we described the difference between schema and symptom formulation. The person of the trauma victim [normal Sc+P+(B)+Sy rules] becomes subverted for periods of time, as the person is influenced by the overwhelming pull of symptoms. Beck (1991) described how anxiety and depression have their own symptom rules, and for a time take over. This also appears to occur during trauma. The person is disrupted to such an extent that the clinician must treat (or intervene upon) this crisis before normal person schema rules return.

Fortunately, occasions of symptom disruption are short-lived and, even when operative, influenced to a large extent by the logic of the person formulation [Sc+P+(B)+Sy]. But, even when symptoms are chronic (in chronic PTSD), the trauma victim appears to display a "logic" to the symptom pathology, thereby allowing for both a prediction of a behavior and appropriate interventions.

A further argument is that this case formulation provides the necessary therapeutic stimuli to assist in the human change process. This conceptualization empowers the clinician with an adequate representation of the trauma victim. This product in turn can be evaluated for its clinical utility. Eventually, other inductive and empirical procedures can be utilized and refined. Use of these constructs also allows for a collaborative empiricism between the treating professional and the victim, where the agency of the person is always encouraged. The goal is to provide both for an understanding of the person of the victim and for the development of choice in the victim's life. This process provides a model for healing and prevents "predigested thinking" or the oversimplification of complex issues into simple formulas (Gambrill, 1990).

The reader has no doubt noticed the reduced emphasis on trauma. When trauma is excessive, the victim's thinking is intruded upon or numb for periods of time, often masking any understanding of his or her person. Despite this, trauma at its heart disrupts schemas, which in turn leads to inflexible personality styles, dysfunctional beliefs, and eventually trauma symptoms, often in the form of PTSD. So, from our formulation, the trauma response starts with disrupted schemas, often resulting in PTSD. What is central to this Sc+P+(B)+Sy conceptualization, then, is that the parameters of the trauma response are reasonably discernable and even predictable, given information about the person and information about the nature of the trauma itself. Trauma infects all parts of the Sc+P+(B)+Sy sequence, but the expression and variety of infection emanates from the core person strategies (schemas). The trauma response, while complicated, has boundaries, and these are adequately provided by the information of the Sc+P+(B)+Sy sequence and the nature of the trauma. With knowledge of both the Sc+P+(B)+Sy sequence and the nature of the trauma, we can devise plans of care. This mini-model then assists in closing the gap between theory and clinical practice.

TREATMENT

The purpose for understanding of the person of the victim is to guide treatment. In fact, treatment is never far from the case formulation of the trauma victim. While difficult to encapsulate, treatment embodies the struggle against internal and external hopelessness and pain due to a disruption of the continuity of the person. How another human being can assist a trauma victim in this curative procedure is a most fascinating and powerful mystery. Through a combination of client and therapist factors, the client comes to accept another internal story, one less influenced by trauma. With trauma victims, however, this search for competence (self empowerment) requires careful clinical consideration and care.

Therapist's Role

We have previously suggested that the human change process of the trauma victim demands a collaborative undertaking with both schema and symptom issues. The ultimate goal of therapy is to be able to *jointly cooperate and problem solve in the observation and evaluation of experiences related to the trauma in the ongoing drama of the therapy.* For this to occur the therapist's role is as a "therapy manager," not just with schemas and symptoms, but with direction and influence on behalf of healing, behavior change, and skill enhancement. The therapist thereby validates, teaches, and presents alternatives to the trauma reality established by the trauma victim. Often the operative tasks are basic: keeping the trauma victim in treatment, being supportive during difficult periods, maintaining appropriate arousal levels, and in general assuring commitment to the goals of therapy. The more the victim is influenced by symptoms (Axis I), the more these therapeutic tasks are required. Most often, however, the operative focus of treatment involves schemas and personality. As already noted, the influence of both of these is present to varying degrees at all times. The more the individual is motivated by person components, the more the clinician is required to provide schema and Axis II structure, education, and interpersonal feedback.

For those who have never experienced intense trauma, being able to imagine its effects is extremely difficult. Trauma disrupts all core ordering processes. The trauma response devastates a person and changes ensue (a destructuring process). If the individual has one task in this process, it is to make sense of the trauma, to answer the question, "Why me?" Developmental theorists hold that trauma prevents the normal processes of assimilation and accommodation. Intense trauma compromises meaning and selfhood in all trauma victims. As a result, the victim oscillates through cycles of intrusion and numbing with regard to the trauma material. Some (e.g., Horowitz, 1986) consider this the central dynamic of trauma. As the trauma victim seesaws through this, he or she often adapts to intense stressors in dysfunctional ways, partially effective and partially ineffective at resolving the trauma experiences. Avoidance and numbing, however, become seductive and deceptive friends, serving to provide only a temporary peace at the cost of long-term harmony. Over time, the cycle of disequilibrium can easily become entrenched into the personality.

Victim's Role

In this book we argue that treatment involves three central tasks, an *understanding of the Sc+P+(B)+Sy process, development of the relationship,* and the *implementation of schema and symptom psychotherapy.* The victim has an important role in each of these tasks. These interdependent functions are punctuated only in writing. Nevertheless, we believe they provide conceptual clarity and boundaries that describe and guide therapeutic goals and interactions with trauma victims. Some plan is needed.

Understanding of Self [Sc+P+(B)+Sy]. We already have addressed briefly the first task, the complex understanding of human change unfolding at the direction of the person [Sc+P+(B)+Sy]. In fact, the argument can be made that human beings epigenetically unfold in a life span sequence at the behest of the schema. These core ordering processes construct and foster ongoing stabilities in their own way, presenting new requirements of mastery at each stage of growth. But schemas are so constructed that they are given special protection against changing, and this protection becomes most manifest in therapy. The individual's ability to evaluate these schemas critically and to alter his/her internal relationship to them constitutes the most powerful determinant of change.

During this phase as well as the other two phases of therapy, one effort above all others is required of the client—to be a collaborator. This role of collaborator creates the task environment. A meaningful cooperative experience is a human commitment to be open as a person and to experience the unfolding process. Just as the clinician needs to have a working paradigm for the trauma victim, the trauma victim needs to have a clear understanding of this process. Although it may seem obvious, trauma victims need to be aware of their maladaptive schemas and how these unfold in their interpersonal fields. Entrenched schemas are by definition rigid, self-fulfilling, and accompanied by a faulty cognitive construction of the environment. One might say that abused schemas (as a result of trauma) foster the worst of person behavior. In addition, trauma victims often approach therapy with less than optimal motivation, less than optimal skills, a "press" for secondary gain, and schema rigidity. A collaborative commitment permits a fair hearing of these issues. Often under such an understanding, these issues can be outlined, redirected, and reseated. Therefore, empowering clients to become "personal scientists" in the understanding of their own information processing is paramount.

Also implied is that the trauma victim know the "rules of the game," what he or she must do in therapy. In a safe setting, an understanding of and commitment to the tasks should be established. Education about his/her Sc+P+(B)+Sy process, his/her trauma, his/her commitment to the therapy process, and his/her contract to the task of self-discovering (his/her own self-change work), must be provided. The end result of what the client must do is not only an understanding of his/her map, his/her Sc+P+(B)+Sy profile, but also knowledge of how to attack his/her own constructs or schemas. *Only then can active engaging occur in selected rituals of schema and symptom therapy.* Again, optimal helping respects the agency of victims as the primary directors in actions. Optimal helping also encourages self-caring and self-responsibility.

From this "conceptual base camp," the witnessing process in the psychotherapeutic experience can unfold.

The Sc+P+(B)+Sy process works in therapy when the focus is on the corrective recognition of the self: "Can I be an observer of my therapeutic experience?" and "Can I remain open in this therapeutic context to my perceptions as hypotheses?" The trauma victim learns the reality of the Sc+P+(B)+Sy influence and what being "outside" and making choices about one's life is like. The victim learns how he or she influences problems. In this sense the person of the victim becomes reowned. The therapist is there to guide the client, to provide a set of tools that empower the victim not to fear his/her lost boundaries due to trauma, and, of course, to remain committed to this task. This is the essence of what others have said is important in trauma therapy—experiential learning through nonjudgmental exploration, the "correct amount" of affect arousal and behavior change techniques. The victims, then, become part of the human change process, oscillating between experiences in the therapeutic hour, observations and evaluations of this, and attempted new behaviors. Perceived constraints indeed become artificial.

Development of Relationship. This therapy phase allows phases one and three to work. Bugental (1987) stated that a working relationship consists of "two energy systems being brought into concert to accomplish purposes important to both" (p. 219). Virtually every writer on PTSD has endorsed the need for a therapeutic alliance in trauma work. The problem with this view is that the victim can't hold up his/her side of the bargain. The client cannot be a true collaborator if empty or in turmoil. The victim's response of dispiritedness and pain often mandates further feelings of neediness, making commitment nominal and "cheap." If the concept of relationship means anything to the trauma victim, it implies a minimal level of commitment for shared intimacy and struggle. This compliance contract serves not just to reduce pain, but also to increase motivation and curiosity in the pursuit of the inward journey. A carefully worked relationship then is one that nurtures the right amount of "optimal frustration," insuring both human care (support) and human struggle (work). On the one hand, there is the work of empathy; "The heart of empathy is imagined possibility" (Nettler, 1970, p.34). On the other hand, there are the stratagems for change; the facilitative confrontation that unblocks comfortable patterns. Ultimately, a balance must be negotiated.

Often the relationship involves something more than interpersonal glue; *often it is the intervention.* The victim of trauma eventually responds very much as he or she does in other situations. Quite simply, as the victim seeks confirmation, he or she indulges in redundant patterns of interaction that are observable and usable in the clinical setting. The "me-you" patterns are what reveal schemas and personality styles (and symptoms). Redundancy is both usual and usable in treatment. While the attention by the therapist to identify core cognitions (schemas), interpersonal patterns (personality and beliefs), and symptoms represents the central task of therapy, this always plays out within the relationship. The evoking style of the client meets the decoding activity of the clinician. The clinician's task here is to do more than the analytic goal of "staying out of the way" as much as possible. Initially, the clinician hooks into the process and lets things go. Later, the therapist unhooks from this process and becomes a "working" therapist. Success in therapy depends on the way in which this is done. The relationship provides the interpersonal and collaborative cement for this to occur. Kahn (1991) noted, that of all the therapeutic activities, the relationship is least understood, requires the most time to appreciate, and in the end "is the therapy" (p. 2).

Implementation of Schema and Symptom Therapy. How "schema friendly" the victim becomes is a sensitive measure of the entire process. This is understood through the first task of treatment (understanding and education), allowed to be during the second task (relationship), and hopefully altered during the third (schema or symptom therapy). This third task of psychotherapy represents a major emphasis of the book. Once the trauma victim knows roughly who he or she is and what to do, and appreciates the importance of collaboration and the tasks of the therapy, then therapy begins the changing process of schemas and symptoms. Naturally, this process is well underway as a result of the first two tasks. By becoming aware of his/her Sc+P+(B)+Sy process and experiencing the relationship, schema or symptom tasks are implied. In this sense the third treatment task simply iterates the continual pursuit of the first two tasks, the repetitive and judicious unearthing of constructs and interpersonal patterns for purposes of self choice.

Symptoms may have brought the client to treatment, but the reduction of turmoil ultimately is not the goal. Symptoms must be treated initially both because they are important by themselves, and because only by a reduction of symptoms can other, longer-term treatment (schema treatment) occur. The major work of therapy, however, involves the person of the victim, and personality styles.

Both clients and therapists may resist this formulation. Clients especially, have vested interests in focusing on problems "out there" and in avoiding any personal contribution to their situation. Often the therapist can easily be seduced into maintaining a crisis or symptom focus to obscure more primary concerns. Therapists too often treat "bad" symptoms or even "bad" clients at the expense of the person of the victim. More is required of both. The client needs (1) to understand that what is occurring is acceptable and knowable, (2) to experience safety and trust, and (3) to commit to the struggle of self change. Significant psychological change is rarely easy or fast. Psychotherapists need to know that change in an absolute sense rarely occurs. The format of the human struggle is too messy. This book attempts to elucidate the messiness of trauma by walking the line between objectivity and subjectivity and by specifying an assessment and treatment process.

As noted, these three therapy tasks overlap. Some part of each session is devoted to all three, thereby paying respect to their importance. However, the careful titration by the clinician to all three—reading the client, respecting the client, and working with reasonable consistency in the tasks of therapy—is what constitutes better therapy. In the literature of psychotherapy are pointed out times for effort and challenge, and also times for acceptance and reflection. The more the trauma has disrupted the person of the victim, the closer to the person's experiences of self and world has been the insult. In such situations, our belief is that the only way to wholeness is through psychotherapy.

PLAN OF THE BOOK

"Science is spectrum analysis: art is photosynthesis." This aphorism points to the quandary of this book: not to stray too far from either mooring. Our intent is to present a model of assessment and care of trauma victims: the reader's odyssey must continue with other readings and other experiences. We seek an understanding of the person and a balance in treatment between person and symptom issues. Our bias, by now evident, turns away from the quick fix approaches. Hopefully, readers will assimilate our central thesis, improve on their own theory-driven ideas, develop personal checks and balances, and respond to the human condition in the most empathic and clinically curious ways possible.

Too often we have heard clinicians who treat trauma victims lament that change is difficult or excessively slow. This position comes from at least two clinical stances. First, trauma has a way of preventing other issues from being considered. The person is viewed only as a trauma victim with symptoms. As a consequence, the clinician is forced to treat a most resistant trauma victim, a person who has adapted in such a way as to prevent a meaningful reaccounting of pain. This is his/her only story.

Second, clinicians often treat the weakest link in the complex chain of the client's experience. If the trauma victim presents with a combination of character problems, situational issues, and trauma specific pain, then to order clinical responses may prove difficult. Nothing is so practical as a good theory, as Kurt Lewin noted over 60 years ago. Clinicians require a plan. This plan should allow for a reasonable disaggregation of the trauma victim's parts, a theory-driven and hypothesis-checked plan of intervention (an optimistic set), and a fair monitoring of the procedure.

We have divided the book into four sections. In the next six chapters (Part I) information about trauma as well as the knowledge and care of the person of the victim are emphasized. We describe the importance of trauma and our central formulation, the Sc+P+(B)+Sy model. In Chapter 2 is described the trauma literature from the perspective of the intractability of the problem. Chronic trauma victims represent a challenge for any clinician; an overview of the effects of chronic trauma is given. In Chapter 3 are considered theories relevant to the development of our formulation. This includes works of several key authors whose creative musings have advocated for the care of the person of the trauma victim. Chapters 4 and 5 contain information that represents the core concepts for understanding the client. In Chapter 4 is described the "big picture" from the formulation of Adler, with a focus on LS, personality, private logic (beliefs), and symptoms. These are conceptually anchored to our formulation. In Chapter 5 these Adlerian concepts are iterated, but this time according to the specifics of the Sc+P+(B)+Sy model. Measurement is emphasized. In Chapter 6 is discussed treatment according to the formulation described in this Introduction. The therapeutic relationship is discussed in Chapter 7. Issues unique to trauma victims are highlighted. As relationship is such a central feature of care, our effort is to specify its components, strengths, and weaknesses.

Part II includes two chapters on unique issues of trauma. In these chapters are discussed the two positions that are always implied in psychotherapy, cognition and emotion. In Chapter 8 "clinical" information processing, a disaggregation of the trauma experience, as well as therapeutic rubrics specific to trauma victims' mode of thinking, are discussed. In Chapter 9 the focus is on emotions, highlighting guilt as a most resistant affective experience. How this emotion can be better addressed in this population has been a special problem.

In Part III four types of symptom therapies are described. Also, a chapter is included on trauma as experienced by victims who now are older. In Chapter 10 is discussed a newer technique, *Eye Movement Desensitization and Reprocessing (EMDR)*. This is a most compelling technique that directly tracks the spontaneous generation of the trauma experience and provides closure. In Chapter 11 is discussed *Direct Therapeutic Exposure (DTE)*, a technique with which we have had a good amount of experience. This procedure involves the essence of the curative feature of trauma: exposure. Chapter 12 is one that advocates a short-term grief model. Traumatic grief, trauma preventing the work of mourning, is universal for trauma victims but has not been widely discussed. Chapter 13 is a most important one. In it are described techniques based on a stress reduction model that has proven helpful with chronic victims. Chapter 14 describes the effects of trauma on victims who are now older. This involves distinctive assessment and care issues and represents a long overdue topic.

We close this book (Part IV) with a chapter (15) on the social psychological perspective of trauma for combat related PTSD. How trauma victims reduce the dissonance resulting from trauma and the culture by developing beliefs and behaviors is a topic in need of clarification. There may be no answers for ways to reduce the moral or personal antinomy of trauma, but its explication is badly needed.

As we end at the beginning, certain "apologies" are in order. We shall outline these with little explanation. First, we view PTSD, the trauma response, chronic victims, trauma victims as conceptually similar, differing only in frequency and intensity. We use these terms and others in functionally equivalent ways. Whether a person has full PTSD or subclinical problems as a result of trauma is less important than a consideration of the person of the victim and the particular symptom experience. Second, the concern of what to label the subject of our writings is at issue. Our writings address mostly chronic victims. The word victim, therefore, represents this group. Our belief, however, is that knowledge of the group is generalizable to all levels and types of trauma problems. We realize the debate around this issue and address it at various points in this book. In this regard we also variously use the words client and patient to refer to the trauma victim. All these labels, then, are considered coequal. Third, we use the personal pronouns "we" and "our" according to the dictionary's first meaning—I and the rest of the group (at the Augusta Veterans Administration Medical Center and Medical College of Georgia). While this work represents the major author's writings (largely), it is reflective of the general thinking of our group and, most especially, the authors in this book. Finally, this book is largely based on war trauma. In other writings a case is made for equality of the impact of trauma on victims (Dye & Roth, 1991). We concur with this view. Our experience with this most difficult of populations is that informational value extends to all victims. We challenge the reader to see this as otherwise.

REFERENCES

Beck, A. (1991). Cognitive therapy: A 30 year retrospective. *American Psychologist*, 46, 368-375.

Bugental, J. (1987). *The art of the psychotherapist.* New York:Norton Press.

Dye, E., & Roth, S. (1991). Psychotherapy with Vietnam veterans and rape and incest survivors. *Psychotherapy*, 28, 103-120.

Gambrill, E., (1990). *Critical thinking in clinical practice.* San Francisco: Jossey-Bass.

Goleman, D. (1986). *Vital lies, simple truths.* New York: Simon & Schuster.

Horowitz, M. J. (1986). *Stress response syndromes.* New York: Jason Aronson.

Kahn, M. (1991). *Between therapist and client: The new relationship.* New York: Freeman.

Kluckholn, C., & Murray, H. (1965). Personality formation: The determinants. In C. Kluckholn, H. Murray, & D. Scheneider (Eds.), *Personality in nature, society and culture* (2nd ed.) (pp. 53-67). New York: Alfred Knoff.

Mahoney, M. C. (1991). *Human change processes: The scientific foundations of psychotherapy.* Delran, NJ: Basic Books.

Millon, T. (1969). *Modern psychopathology.* Philadelphia: Sanders.

Millon, T. (1981). *Disorders of personality: DSM-III Axis II.* New York: Wiley.

Nettler, G. (1970). *Explanations.* New York: McGraw-Hill.

PART I

Schema Therapy
PTSD
and the Person

Chapter **2**

THE TRAUMA RESPONSE: ITS COMPLEXITY AND DIMENSIONS

"We have to change the truth a little in order to remember it." Santayana

For many years the scientific interest in the consequences of traumatic stress has been small. One can even argue that massive denial has occurred regarding this issue. After various efforts to translate combat trauma into the clinical domain (e.g., shell shock, war memories, soldiers' heart, combat fatigue, physioneurosis, etc.) not until 1980 in the DSM-III were the effects of stress legitimated (American Psychiatric Association, 1980). This form of the nosology became official only after considerable concern and suffering as a result of combat in Vietnam. Given our history with this disorder, maybe each generation has to rediscover post-traumatic stress disorder (PTSD) "for the first time" (Rozynko & Dondershine, 1991). That engagement and all its ramifications presented society and the scientific community with problems, confusion, and splintered solutions that are just now beginning to be better understood.

Our focus is combat trauma. An understanding of this type of stressor, singularly devastating and unforgiving, generalizes to the effects of other stressors. To paraphrase Kipling, "A look at the best deserves a look at the worst"; an understanding of combat related trauma has application to other stressors. Much can be said for the common landscaping of responses of trauma due to different stressors. Along with rape and the holocaust the literature on this stressor is further advanced than that regarding any other form of trauma.

Of course, no benefit is gained in a competition among stressors. The awkward but common sense truth, however, is that trauma is most noxious if it is intense, persistent, or "unexpected." Combat or war trauma meets these criteria. It leaves an "indelible image" on all (Lifton, 1979). Solomon (1990a) wrote:

> War is the ultimate in human aggression. In addition to the destruction of life and limb, property and culture, it often exacts a fearful, though less visible, toll in psychological damage (Milgram, 1986). Combatants are not only in constant danger themselves, but they also bear forced witness to the injury and deaths of friends and enemy and to all the gruesome sights and sounds of slaughter. They struggle with loneliness and isolation and with the more tangible deprivations of food, drink, and sleep. The enormous destructive power of modern weapons and the uncertainties of modern guerrilla warfare, where fire can come at any time and from any direction, add to the already massive stress. While most soldiers cope adequately, for some the stress becomes so overwhelming that the person's defenses are unable to withstand the strain and 'psychological breakdown' occurs (p. 1733).

War trauma is so excessive that during the past few decades research increasingly documents biological anomalies, including a dysynchrony of neurohormones and excessive morbidity and even mortality (Boyle, Decoufle, & O'Brien, 1989; Kormos, 1978). Recently, for example, several authors (e.g., van der Kolk & Greenberg, 1987; ver Ellen & van Kammen, 1990) have documented that the neurologic based "on and off" switches have been refitted causing hyperarousal. Mason, Kosten, Southwick and Giller (1990) showed hormonal differences due to stressors between two combat trauma groups and others. van der Kolk and Greenberg (1987) and Friedman (1988) have independently suggested that kindling is a neurological model that applies to PTSD. **Kindling** is a process by which neuroanatomic structures become "hot" following repeated exposure; this results in chronic central sympathetic arousal. War trauma is distinctive and possibly "deeply" altering, even biologically.

Of trauma-related problems, two sets of questions have been proposed. This first is **nomothetic**; the focus is on principles or generalized rubrics of traumatic stress reactions. This concerns those pieces of information reasonably common to the stressor and to the response that are helpful in the categorization of the disorder for its assessment and treatment. As we will see, extrapolating consistent, valid, and usable information about this question is important but not always easy and not the only issue. Nomothetic concerns will represent the bulk of the content of this chapter.

A second and more important question involves the **idiographic approach**, individual differences in the adaptation to stressful life-events. This involves the person of the victim and will be dealt with most directly in Part I of this book (Chapters 4 through 7). The argument is that "better" trauma formulation is a deliberative marriage between assessment and treatment, consisting of a case specific formulation and theory driven treatment. This information is derived from the particulars of the client's presenting problem and a reasonable model of human care. The therapist's task is to understand as best he/she can the workings of the person, guided in turn by the development of hypotheses about the person and a plan for change.

This book attempts to dissect the grammar of trauma, but only as it evolves from the person: the individual conducts and orchestrates the impact of his/her trauma. This transcoding process becomes important in the calculus of care. *The psychological processing of the trauma event involves three important basics: the role of the long-standing characteristics of the individual, the trauma itself, and the mediating influences of the recovery process.* Trauma sequelae or symptoms are responses, the result of a calculated destructuring process whose principal player is the person. This is the most important element in the equation: the person is the fulcrum for the unfolding of the trauma response. Perhaps, as has been suggested (Briere, 1992), the "first wave" of trauma research has passed; now a developmental perspective is required to fully understand the variability of symptoms ("sleeper effects").

The emphasis of the book, then, is "away" from the stressor. The impact of clinical maneuvers comes from an understanding of the person, the information processing of trauma. If **trauma as response** is emphasized instead of trauma as a stressor, a reasonable conclusion is that the person of the victim must be studied. From this perspective trauma is secondary and its course has multiple trajectories. The clinician, therefore, must know the distinctive "maladaptive resolutions" (Epstein, 1990) and apply considered health care interventions. It will be argued that this is best conceptualized according to a disaggregation procedure composed of core identity (life-style) and its various "protectors" (personality style, beliefs, and symptoms). A formulation of these modular features allows for an integrated treatment that can focus on any of the parts with a better conceptual focus and improved treatment efficacy.

Several issues are covered in this chapter. First, we discuss PTSD and the current nosology. An insidious terminological confusion regarding the constructs of PTSD exists; the opponent process of "over" and "under" symptoms is chronically confusing, resulting in an unnecessary array of clinical problems. Next, we contextualize this state within the Anxiety Disorders. Some consider the chronic trauma response a strange stepchild under their designation. Nonetheless, PTSD may be one disorder where exact classification placement is helpful therapeutically. Next, **comorbidity**, a major problem of PTSD, is considered. Rarely is a victim of chronic trauma, especially combat related, without other diagnoses. Coincident with this issue is the phase or cycle of trauma, as well as the mediating influences of the person. These issues are so important that any cross sectional study on PTSD is limited; only longitudinal studies are helpful. A brief section is also devoted to the epidemiology of PTSD. A view of the "big picture" is important. Finally, this chapter closes with a brief overview of outcome research in this area.

POST-TRAUMATIC STRESS DISORDER (PTSD)
THE TIP OF THE ICEBERG

Definition

As yet, no satisfactory answer has been developed to the most logical question regarding trauma, "Why some and not others." As a result, no clinical or epistemological comfort can be obtained in the various designations of trauma-related problems. The fact of trauma is but a starting point for a specific inquiry on its potential negative effects. The nosology proceeds, however, with two premises: (1) a stressor event outside the range of human experience; and (2) one that impacts markedly and negatively on a person. The final common pathway that allows for some sanctuary of understanding is, of course, PTSD. This starting point represents a best guess for the present about the more serious effects of trauma. Where the effects of war trauma are concerned, only now are these becoming apparent to many clinicians as being pervasive. Careful study has indicated that many more war trauma victims have problems than was suspected (Kulka, Schlenger, Fairbank, Hough, Jordan, Marman, & Weiss, 1988). Also becoming apparent are many varieties of PTSD along various dimensions. The role of how unique clusters of PTSD symptoms attach themselves to particular kinds of victims (or particular kinds or amounts of stressors) is also relevant. Final validation of any current reality of the effects of trauma is far from complete.

In Table 2.1 are listed the DSM-III-R criteria for PTSD: three categories encompassing 17 symptoms in addition to the trauma (American Psychiatric Association, 1987). For the most part these symptoms have been endorsed and validated by studies interested in symptom formulation. The centerpiece, however, is trauma. Chronic PTSD sufferers fail to habituate despite persistent imagined reexposure in the form of reexperiencing, intrusion, flashbacks, and the like. Category B, therefore, receives the most interest as these symptoms are painful and disturbing to normal living. "Reexperience of trauma" symptoms are considered more pronounced than "avoidance/numbing" (Category C), according to many studies

(continued on page 34)

TABLE 2.1
DSM-III-R Criteria for PTSD

A. The person has experienced an event that is outside the range of usual human experience and that would be markedly distressing to almost anyone, e.g., serious threat to one's life or physical integrity; serious threat or harm to one's children, spouse, or other close relatives and friends; sudden destruction of one's home or community; or seeing another person who has recently been, or is being seriously injured or killed as the result of an accident or physical violence.

B. The traumatic event is persistently reexperienced in at least one of the following ways:

   1. Recurrent and intrusive distressing recollections of the event (in young children, repetitive play in which themes or aspects of the trauma are expressed)
   2. Recurrent distressing dreams of the event
   3. Sudden acting or feeling as if the traumatic event were recurring (includes a sense of reliving the experience, illusions, hallucinations, and dissociative (flashback) episodes, even those that occur upon awakening or when intoxicated)
   4. Intense psychological distress at exposure to events that symbolize or resemble an aspect of the traumatic event, including anniversaries of the trauma.

C. Persistent avoidance of stimuli associated with the trauma or numbing of general responsiveness (not present before the trauma), as indicated by at least three of the following:

   1. Efforts to avoid thoughts or feelings associated with the trauma
   2. Efforts to avoid activities or situations that arouse recollections of the trauma
   3. Inability to recall an important aspect of the trauma (psychogenic amnesia)

(continued)

TABLE 2.1 (continued)

4. Markedly diminished interest in significant activities (in young children, loss of recently acquired developmental skills such as toilet training or language skills)
5. Feeling of detachment or estrangement from others
6. Restricted range of affect, e.g., unable to have loving feelings
7. Sense of a foreshortened future, e.g., does not expect to have a career, marriage, or children, or a long life.

D. Persistent symptoms of increased arousal (not present before the trauma), as indicated by at least two of the following:

1. Difficult falling or staying asleep
2. Irritability or outbursts of anger
3. Difficulty concentrating
4. Hypervigilance
5. Exaggerated startle response
6. Physiologic reactivity upon exposure to events that symbolize or resemble an aspect of the traumatic event (e.g., a woman who was raped in an elevator breaks out in a sweat when entering any elevator)

E. Duration of the disturbance (symptoms in B, C, and D) of at least 1 month.

Specify delayed onset if the onset of symptoms was at least 6 months after the trauma.

(Pitman, Orr, Forgue, deJong, & Claiborn, 1987; Weisenberg, Solomon, Schwarzwald, & Mikulincer 1987; Woolfolk & Grady, 1988).

Unfortunately, Category C perpetuates the trauma state. In fact, the style of avoidance and constriction seems to represent adaptation and continuance of the trauma responses; sufferers avoid/escape in the most creative of ways. In so doing, they perpetuate the resistant and noxious components of the disorder; the trauma is never fully reexperienced and is periodically reconditioned, thus reinforcing the status quo. Like Plato's shadows in the cave, the sufferer never fully reexperiences the stressor. Category D, increased arousal, bears further testimony to avoidance, by its "frozen in time" quality. Lifton and Olson (1976) noted that individuals "surrender" in the face of the traumatic event.

Overall Problems

Many excellent reviews are available on the status of the research on PTSD (e.g., King & King, 1991; Lyons, Gerardi, Wolfe, & Keane, 1988). From a perspective of the nosology, however, two problems are especially troubling. The first regards trauma. "Traumatic" has no established definitional or conceptual context. According to the DSM-III-R, the stressor is one that would "evoke significant symptoms of distress in almost everyone." In the DSM-III and DSMIII-R, the types of stressors that would be markedly distressing to almost anyone have been expanded to include rape, assault, military combat, floods, fires, or receiving threats to one's life or physical integrity (children, partners, etc.), suffering the loss of one's home or community, viewing another person who has been killed or harmed, and learning about serious threats or harm to someone close, among others. Presumably, any stressor that qualifies is high in intensity, unexpected, infrequent, but can vary in duration from minutes to years. While a war stressor clearly applies, considerable evidence suggests that this type of stressor is far from unidimensional (Green, Wilson, & Lindy, 1985). We shall address elements of war stress later.

Second, in the DSM-III-R the advice to the clinician is to be sensitive to the extent of change in the person's life as well as uncontrolled aspects and number of stressors.

According to the nosology, this determination should be based on the stressor and not on the person's vulnerability. Unfortunately, the longer the delay from the onset of problems, the more confusing any evaluation of the stressor becomes. The compromise is poor, therefore, for the treating professional to be required to be detective and health care provider at the same time, especially regarding criteria that are both part of the etiology and symptom picture of the disorder.

An uneasy truce exists regrading the parameters of PTSD. While the symptoms of this disorder have been largely corroborated in factor analytic studies, the psychiatric nosology is not intended to represent any disorder fully, but rather to provide clinicians with symptoms that allow for maximal differences from other disorders. Multimodal evaluations that include "ancillary" symptoms are required. Typically, this is not what is done. In one study, McFall, Murburg, Smith, and Jensen (1991) used DSM-III-R criteria and surveyed 448 psychiatrists and psychologists on their opinions of the criteria most utilized to assign a diagnosis of PTSD to combat veterans (Table 2.2). Evidence of exposure to stress and symptoms of reexperiencing were consistently rated as more influential than criteria of avoidance/numbing or increased arousal. In addition, symptoms that are directly ascribed to the trauma event were rated more influential than others. Certain items were not important at all—rage, sleep disturbances, or possession of weapons. While the study is only a perceptional assessment of clinical use, it does suggest that clinician differentiated diagnostic judgments are made according to a traditional trauma-related PTSD prototype.

The role of symptoms in PTSD is unclear; no one-to-one relationship exists between this disorder and the stressor. The nature of the stressor and the person have a strong influence on the existence and type of PTSD. In acute disasters, for example, those who experience intrusions often have little numbing or avoidance. This may be as much an indicator of normal stress due to exposure as it is a marker of PTSD (McFarlane, 1990). In the chronic form of this disorder, victims tend to endorse all criteria, but actually develop maladaptive patterns around only selected symptoms. In addition, although all 17 PTSD symptoms correlate highly with PTSD as a whole (indicating each's contribution), the actual role of intrusion or avoidance, as well as their actual expression for any one person is highly variable.

TABLE 2.2

Percentage of Respondents Identifying DSM-III-R and Non-DSM-III-R Characters as an Aid to Differential Diagnosis*

Criteria	Percentage Identifying Item
Exposure to traumatic event	93
Traumatic event recurring	78
Dreams of trauma	77
Intrusive recollections	75
Symbolic reminders of trauma	73
Physiologic reactivity	66
Avoidance of thoughts of trauma	57
Survival guilt	50
Guilt over actions	48
Avoidance of reminders of trauma	45
Startle response	42
Psychic numbing	39
Deterioration of psychosocial functioning	35
Hypervigilance	33
Distress exhibited during interviews	31
Ability to vividly retell trauma	30
Restricted range of affect	28
Compulsion to repeat trauma	25
Negative self-image	22
Inability to sustain intimacy	20
Possession of weapons	19
Chronic depression	17
Psychogenic amnesia	15
Detachment and estrangement	14
Intolerance of groups	14
Fears of losing control	10
Preoccupation with war	10
Disturbed sleep	9
Diminished interest	9
Foreshortened future	9
Recurrent rage	8
Irritability and anger	7
Explosive behavior	6
Pervasive distrust	5
Concentration difficulties	4

*From "An analysis of the criteria used by VA clinicians to diagnose combat related PTSD" by McFall, Murburg, Smith, & Jensen in *Journal of Traumatic Stress (1991)*. Reproduced by permission.

Reexperiencing and Numbing: A Closer Look

A brief look at the "opponent process" of PTSD, reexperiencing and numbing, is in order. Available data on natural disasters indicate that self report-ratings of intrusion and avoidance account for only 25% of the variance each of a carefully considered DSM-III-R diagnosis of PTSD (Green, 1991). Interestingly, other self-report scales (e.g., SCL-90-R) do about the same. While an accurate determination of caseness increases with the use of multiple measures, reliable self-reports and interviewer-rated scales (anchored to the DSM-III-R), the correlations between the two central symptoms and PTSD are not very different in community samples of combat-related PTSD (Kulka, Schlenger, Fairbank, Jordan, Hough, Marmar, & Weiss, 1991). Unfortunately, symptom clusters leave clinicians ignorant as to their etiology, expression, and influence on PTSD. Reexperiencing especially is confusing. Many reasons conspire for this state of affairs; fears of the client of being labeled psychotic or crazy, a professional bias or confusion avoiding this area, and conceptual confusion of the construct, among others. Furthermore, in the DSM-III-R is provided little information to assist in its clarity. In the long run, reexperiencing symptoms may turn out to be exactly like that of obsessive compulsives (increased physiological arousal) or hypochondriacs (selective attention to bodily sensations and behavior aimed at avoidance to defuse anxiety).

Peralme (1991) noted that reexperiencing requires careful disaggregation for adequate understanding. Each of the four components of the DSM-III-R will be briefly discussed. The first one, **reexperiencing**, largely refers to trauma memories that intrude on conscious activity. While that degree of combat exposure is directly related to reexperiencing (Brett & Mangine, 1985), several issues remain unclear: whether type of combat differentially affects reexperiencing symptoms; whether the events experienced are reexperienced or "screen memories" (Breslau & Davis, 1987); whether recalled events are reflective of anxiety, hyperarousal, or other emotions (Pitman, Orr, Forgue, Altman, deJong, & Herz, 1990); whether reexperienced events are fragmented or whole (thereby influencing treatment);

whether increased physiological arousal is concordant with all reexperienced memories or only selected ones; and which reexperienced events are recurrent (Peralme, 1991).

Trauma memories themselves have not been assessed with any rigor. Generally evaluations take two forms. First, the phenomenon is parsed apart, as in the evaluation of central or peripheral details (Christianson & Loftus , 1990), or separating observer and field memories (Nigro & Neisser, 1983). Trauma memories have not undergone this scrutiny. Second, global relationships with key PTSD symptoms have occurred. Pitman et al. (1990), for example, found a relationship between the presence of trauma memories and physiological indices. This too is a rare study.

Similar confusion applies to the second component, distressing *dreams*. A universal symptom of combat related PTSD among Vietnam veterans is sleep problems. This includes frequency of nightmares, their content and characteristics, and sleep architecture. While agreement exists that rapid eye movement (REM) patterns are altered (decreased in length, increased latency, etc.), little agreement exists on many other features, chiefly on the existence and phenomenology of nightmares or night terrors. Alterations of dreams over time, degree of recurrence, whether dreams represent a conditional emotional response (CER) to be avoided (Inman, Silver, & Doghramji, 1990; Kramer & Kinney, 1988), and whether a disturbed sleep pattern results in PTSD symptoms or vice versa, are issues in doubt among PTSD victims.

Flashback (third component) is a term used to refer to the sudden acting or feeling as if the event were recurring. This is a rather amorphous area. Peralme (1991) wrote:

> Historically, the adoption of the term "flashback" was based on combat veterans' use of the term to describe their experiences to others. In other words, the term was not generated by psychiatrists or psychologists to describe clinical phenomena they were observing. Given that the term was essentially experientially derived and then adopted by professionals in order to communicate with combat veterans, the question is raised as to whether this term is the best clinical descriptor (p. 49).

As clinicians know, the flashback can be all things to all people. Solursh (1989) even reported this to be positively reinforcing. However, whether these experiences are a distortion of reality, are related to other disorders (like schizophrenia), are a dissociative experience, are reflective of event-specific content, are a behavioral reenactment, are substance abuse related, have a constant or variable course, or are influenced by the environment is unclear (Peralme, 1991). In addition, Brende (1987), Blank (1985), Mellman and Davis (1985), and Hendin and Haas (1984) all have attempted taxonomies of this construct. One can only guess that the construct flashback is so troubling as to be a monitor of long-term symptoms of stress, but careful evaluation of this symptom only results in lower prevalence rates. Perhaps, characteristics of the person influence this kind of symptom formed, as we as its expression and intensity.

Finally, **distress at stimuli related to trauma** (last component), fall under this umbrella of puzzlement. The principle concern is with the triggers of the startle or hyperarousal response. Numerous external stimuli have been identified covering all the senses. Internal potentiators include mood, fatigue, and drugs among many others. The plethora of studies notating excessive physiological reactions to combat veterans (but not other trauma victims) with PTSD also applies. (See Chapter 3 under psychophysiological theories.) Symbolic triggers have included losses of all kinds; acts of commitment, love, or responsibility; or any theme related to intense feelings of combat. The problem is the wide path of these stimuli, their immediate and generalizing effects, and of course their resistance to extinction.

Numbing, the counterpart of reexperiencing, is an unknown symptom entity also. For example, is numbing the result of chronic avoidance or the result of emotional reactions that are unavailable or even the poor offspring of an exhausted effort at dealing with intrusion? We have already implied that this symptom and all its forms mask PTSD; substance abuse, for example, may appear as the only problem in a trauma victim. The relation of "ancillary symptoms" of numbing, including guilt and cognitive interference (Watson, Juba, Manifold, Kucala, & Anderson, 1991), also is unclear. At present we seem to know only that numbing is related to trauma intensity (Woolfolk & Grady, 1988) and, if developed early (after trauma), becomes a predictor of chronic PTSD. Not until the nature of these emotional deficits is more clearly specified will better measures be developed and better care provided. Effective diagnostic thinking may even require the removal of rigid and exclusive categories.

Information regarding the trait versus state status of numbing, proximal versus distal influencing elements, and defensive "reasons" for this coping style, will assist in treatment. In addition, a further refinement of the measurement of numbing is required—use of multiple response mechanisms, of many stimulus conditions, of primed versus unprimed states, and the manipulation of person variables. Fortunately the C criteria is extracted in one factor solutions (in factor analyses), Unfortunately, we do not know what "causes" its make-up, or, more accurately, what makes this construct "hang together." Thus, while avoidance congeals as a construct, we do not know why or how. In one study Schlenger, Fairbank, and Caddell (1992) presented preliminary data of the National Vietnam Veterans Readjustment Study (NVVRS) regarding the question, what predicts avoidance criteria? (C4, C5, and C6; see Table 2.1). Using logistic regression equations with selected B and D criteria, demographic information, affective status and substance abuse status as predictors, only one variable significantly accounted for these numbing symptoms—hyperarousal. In other words, victims who are hyperaroused tend to avoid, or avoidance is a tiger in sheep's clothing.

Finally, note needs to be made that among the major efforts to organize symptoms of combat related PTSD (e.g., Laufer, Brett, & Gallops, 1985; Horowitz, 1976; Watson et al., 1991), as well as the DSM standards, all have been based on rational deliberation and not research data. The clinician, therefore, should be sensitive to both the primary and secondary symptoms of PTSD. The clinician is entasked with the role of a detective to pursue leads that help explain the nature/ purpose of this symptom in this person. While consensus exists on the symptom clusters of intrusion, numbing, and increased arousal, confusion prevails around the makeup of each. As can be seen, symptoms can be so bizarre (e.g., illusions, hallucinations, or flashbacks), so distancing (e.g., emotional deadness), so embedded (e.g., hyperarousal even to stimuli remotely connected to the trauma), or so pervasive and recalcitrant to change (e.g., intrusions or sleeplessness), that the diagnosis of PTSD easily extends to other disorders and its treatment is an imposing task. Nonetheless, one feature of PTSD seems firm: as the psychiatric community "traveled through" the DSMs since 1952 (DSM-I), the idea of a stress reaction changed from one emphasizing its transient nature to the current view that extreme stress has long and lasting sequelae.

PTSD AND ANXIETY

During PTSD's short existence, it has been lobbied as a dissociative disorder, stress disorder, affective disorder, and a non-disorder, as well as a social phenomena. In the literature, special problems have been noted with the diagnosis of PTSD relative to the adjustment disorders, schizophrenia, factitious disorders, malingering, personality disorders, chiefly antisocial and borderline, as well as the depressive and anxiety disorders (Peterson, Prout, & Schwartz, 1991). Conceptually, each disorder has a "place" either singly or in conjunction with others. The clinical process is usually straightforward. A threshold of suffering titrated to the current DSM specifies the worst area, and this is called the primary diagnosis. Unfortunately, this may not be the most important problem or the only one that should be addressed.

Anxiety: The Needed Platform

Currently, the features of anxiety have been sufficiently persuasive to keep it categorized under the Anxiety Disorders in the DSM-III-R and soon the DSM-IV. Therefore, a worthwhile procedure would be to look at Anxiety Disorders to contextualize PTSD.

Jones and Barlow (1990) explicated how PTSD is a result of readiness of low-grade anxieties. They stated:

> Anxiety in the final analysis contributes substantially to the prediction of who will develop PTSD and who will not. Without the development of anxiety, individuals undergoing severe trauma may occasionally experience a nonclinical

learned alarm or flashback to the trauma when encountering triggering stimuli without the overwhelming negative affective burden associated with the development of PTSD. (p. 320)

Anxiety is a diffuse cognitive-affective conglomeration composed of various levels and combinations of activation, perception of lack of control over future events, and shifts in attention to a self-focused evaluation. The distinctive feature of an Anxiety Disorder is not the unique quality of its principal components (physiologic arousal, cognitive processes, and avoidant coping strategies), but its excessiveness (Gelder, 1991). The presence of trauma problems is connected to the intensity and severity of the person's experience with the trauma. The trauma that leads to problems appears to start with a platform of anxiety and multiple associations that are deeply stored in the form of stimulus, response, and meaning propositions (Lang, 1977, 1979). Other anxiety features, like a chronic action readiness, lack of control, self-focused attention, and presence of hot cognitions, probably contribute. What seems to exist is that, as in other Anxiety Disorders, a person must possess this ready-state of anxiety, as well as a sense of unpredictable/uncontrollable reactions, to join with the stressor for a chronic victim status to result. Perhaps the reason that the severity of the trauma is so highly related to PTSD is that stress potentiates this "ready" state as one would an addict, always waiting to act.

Model

No etiological model of PTSD adequately accounts for its formation, and no model even addresses treatment. Below, we present Barlow's formulation of PTSD based on anxiety and the influence of "hard core" meditating variables. Importantly too, Foy (Foy, Osato, Houskamp, & Neumann, 1992) noted that for acute PTSD, initial unconditioned stimuli are associated with trauma cues and develop into conditioned stimuli and responses, but for chronic PTSD other vaiables mediate its development and maintain symptoms. Vulnerability or resiliency factors, therefore, seem different for acute or chronic PTSD. A model of PTSD is provided in Figure 2.1, (Barlow 1989). Symptoms of PTSD develop from a complex interaction of biological and psychological predispositions. The components are the occurrence of a stressor, the ready availability of an anxious state (vulnerable and unpredictable), and an absence or excessive dependence on coping and social support. A real trauma (true alarm) intrudes on the biological and psychological vulnerability eventuating in continuous anxiety specific apprehension. In fact, Barlow asserts a genetic predisposition of both biological and psychological substrates exists giving form to anxiety problems. Basically, this involves a chronic autonomic overarousal as well as an emotional hypersensitivity to feedback in most any situation. The principal components of PTSD then are anxiety over unpredictable alarm responses that "may come" and often enough "do come" in the form of intrusions. In turn, this may be moderated by supportive resources, both internal and external. Eventually, the person develops anxiety signs and symptoms (DSM-III-R) and may even extend the trauma response to other Anxiety Disorders. It will come as no surprise that treatment involves a focus on these internal interoceptive emotional or somatic cues (as in Panic Disorder).

A major point needs to be made: the occurrence of stressor(s) or trauma event(s) is not sufficient for the disorder PTSD. Rather, one also must experience anxiety (emotional distress) which serves as a stimulant to consequent problems for PTSD. By definition, anxiety involves anxiety specific reactions— uncontrollability, vulnerability, self-focused attention, and action centeredness. Without this presence, individuals experiencing a stressor may occasionally sense subclinical problems but not the consistent overwhelming affective burden associated with PTSD.

Paradoxically, the experience of anxiety and its associate henchmen (hypervigilance, attentional narrowing, avoidance) virtually guarantee the reexperience of trauma memories. The partial experience of the trauma memory assures its continuance. Negative reinforcement in the form of avoidance, that is, the individual's partially effective and partially ineffective attempts at dealing with the trauma experience, perpetuates the problem. As the individual attempts to avoid stimuli or recollection of trauma related material, these efforts result in temporary successes. Learning theory, mostly classical and operant conditioning, explains the self-defeating connections

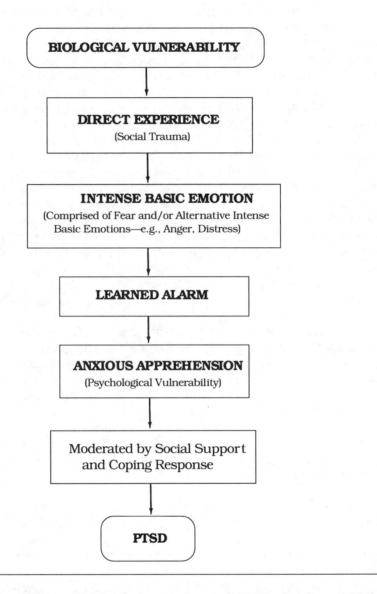

Figure 2.1. A model of the etiology of PTSD (Barlow, 1989). Reproduced by permission.

made during these times. Over time, the fear of memories, images, thoughts, and feelings associated with the traumatic event often result in obsessive-like cognitions (to avoid intrusions). Also, a vigilance for stimuli develops that might elicit them. At the same time, avoidance blocks any recognition that trauma memories are not dangerous. Avoidance reinforces the occurrence of future avoidance and further cements PTSD. Peterson et al. (1991) noted that the end state of avoidance is psychic numbing. Initially the client tries to avoid thoughts, images, and feelings directly related to the disorder (first-order associations). However, different internal stimuli may remind the person of this first-order association. They are also avoided. Eventually, via this process, the world is narrowed and anxiety is "controlled."

Other Anxiety Disorders and Trauma

PTSD also bears much in common to other Anxiety Disorders. Starting with a Generalized Anxiety Disorder, PTSD shares chronic anxiety, tonic arousal, hypervigilance, and poor concentration, among other hyperarousal symptoms. PTSD shares fear-based avoidance with Simple and Social Phobias as well as Agoraphobia. PTSD shares many features with Panic Attacks including flashbacks, nightmares, and the actual experience of the panic attacks. PTSD shares persistent, recurrent, intrusive, and unwelcome thoughts or images with Obsessive Compulsive Disorder. In addition, PTSD shares with the Anxiety Disorders common treatments (e.g., exposure) and a moderately efficacious response pattern to antidepressant drugs (Davidson & Foa, 1991). Unless classification is regarded as a function of etiology (a recommendation of the DSM-IV), PTSD is probably best situated under the Anxiety Disorders. Note is made, however, that anxiety is not an essential feature for the diagnosis of PTSD.

Perhaps a strong relationship seems to exist between trauma and the components of anxiety. When researchers have carefully assessed histories among various diagnostic groups, prevalence rates of physical or sexual abuse or both are alarmingly high. This is especially characteristic of the Anxiety Disorders. One recent study (Solomon & Canino, 1990) found that PTSD was not the sole or even the major outcome of victims exposed to traumatic events. Therefore, results suggest that trauma may be more associated with Anxiety Disorders, not necessarily PTSD. In addition, Burnam, Stein, Golding, Siegel, Sorenson, Forsythe, & Telles (1988) showed that sexual assault predicted later onset of other Anxiety Disorders–Phobia, Panic Disorder, and Obsessive-Compulsive Disorder. Interestingly, trauma at early ages is not associated with or PTSD. Finally, Davidson, Swartz, Storck, Krishnan, & Hammett (1985) examined the issue of family history of psychiatric disorders and revealed that the relative prevalence of the Anxiety Disorders in families of PTSD probands was reasonably high suggesting that PTSD is from this group and not other diagnostic groups.

The "punch" of PTSD as an Anxiety Disorder seems to evolve from psychophysiological and cognitive symptoms. The hyperarousal pattern of the person has been labeled a conditioned emotional response (CER) (Kolb, 1987). Chronic victims are hyperaroused, most notably during presentation of trauma-related stimuli, but also at other times. This is an insidious symptom that is unrelenting and the probable initiator of panic attacks. It is also a symptom that may prove diagnostic of the disorder itself (Keane & Kolb, 1988).

Cognitions represent those beliefs or styles of thinking anchored to the trauma. In Lang's (1979) formulation, these provide meaning to the stimuli and response elements, creating a fear structure. Eventually, these "overvalued" ideas also must be addressed—both the exaggerated thoughts associated with the feared consequences and the valence of stimuli or responses (the structural features of trauma). Various theories, including expectancy, attribution, and cognitive appraisal, among others, have identified more typical cognitions or cognitive styles in the trauma victim (e.g., Hyer, Woods, & Boudewyns, 1991). Also, several studies (e.g., Fairbank, Hansen, & Fitterberg, 1991) have documented that PTSD victims utilize poorer coping techniques for trauma memories than for other stressors.

Both hyperarousal and cognitive selectivity of a trauma victim require therapeutic intervention. In this sense trauma is a perceptual problem; threat infects information processing by altering basic patterns that organize data and their consequent affects. Both cognitions and hyperarousal patterns are involved. Ultimately, both must be addressed therapeutically and integrated within the person. Several treatment programs (e.g., Foa, Rothbaum, Riggs, & Murdock, 1991) utilize both exposure and cognitive methods.

Finally, PTSD is different from the other Anxiety Disorders. In fact, it may be that the development of PTSD is forewarned in most cases by an initial debilitating response in some form (Foy, et al., 1992). Beyond this, however, a linear relationship appears to exist between trauma intensity and reaction intensity. Some axioms are (1) that the more extreme the stressor, the greater the severity of PTSD; (2) that the longer the duration or greater the intensity (or both) of the stressor, the stronger the learning (conditioning); and (3) that the stronger the avoidance post-trauma, the greater the resistance to extinction, and in all probability the greater the generalization. It also may be that the more intense the stressor, the less the need for "input" regarding the individual influences of biological or psychological vulnerabilities. The new conditioned stimuli are everywhere. What is worse, the new conditioned response (PTSD) is deep, broad, and readily accessible. The resulting fear structures are pervasive and deep. These structures have more "parts" (stimuli, meaning, and response propositions), and are hierarchically arranged and interconnected. Very little is required of the external environment to match these fear propositions. The trauma victim develops a "trauma membrane," a self-protective shell that partially or negatively reinforces the trauma. In discussing the salient features of PTSD, Foa, Steketee, and Rothbaum (1989) wrote:

> Three factors appear to be central: the intensity of the responses; the size of the structure, and the ready accessibility of the structure. The change in rules of safety lead to inclusion of a plethora of stimuli in the fear structure (e.g., home, men, darkness). The pervasiveness of the stimuli, the intensity of the responses (both physiological and behavioral), and the low threshold for activation of the fear structure renders PTSD more disruptive to daily functioning. Many stimuli activate this structure, resulting in frequent bursts of arousal (e.g. startle) and re-experiencing of the events (e.g., nightmares, flashbacks), alternating with attempts to avoid or escape fear (e.g., numbness, behavioral avoidance, depersonalization). The latter are at

best only temporarily successful, as evidenced by the frequent flashbacks, nightmares and startle responses. (p. 167)

At the risk of redundancy, this process prevents the integration of trauma. As soon as a minimal amount of information matches the fear memory, it is activated. At this time (if not already), avoidance starts. For treatment to be successful, these components must be held at a reasonable arousal level until extinction occurs. In addition to regaining a sense of control over one's emotions via exposure, "abused" core cognitions must be identified and altered. This combination is quite an imposing task for the health care provider.

Emotional Complexity

The emotional topography of a trauma victim often appears like a puzzle. Heitler (1990), for example, noted that anxiety is one state that immobilizes the person (in response to a trauma) and collides with all other emotions. In fact, she notes that this emotion represents a constant approach-avoidance dilemma, the frozen response of two opposing impulses. Since this always occurs in the response to trauma, anxiety is always present. This result is a perplexing confluence of emotions with the homogenized "anxiety" reaction omnipresent.

Loo (1933) also addressed this problem. She, however, attempted a systematic integration of the treatment of PTSD based on client readiness to change and type of symptom. No longer was anxiety everywhere. Treatment should address key symptoms (emotions) first according to an "ordering," the more important symptoms influencing others. The symptom that reduces the greatest amount of variance gets the nod for treatment. For the first time, therefore, someone tried to clarify PTSD symptoms and their treatment: alleviate detachment or isolation first, followed by avoidance, then self-blame, shame or guilt, rage/anger, and eventually symptoms "deep" inside the person, perceived vulnerability and loss of control. Perhaps this is quixotic at our current level of understanding, but, with such emotional and symptom confusion, it is good "bad science."

COMORBIDITY

An old saying is appropriate here: if you ask for trouble you will find it. PTSD is a problem not simply because of its avoidance patterns, changing symptoms, and intensity, but also it is the "victim" of its own system, both DSM and health care.

Moving Target

How PTSD found its niche among the 290 plus psychiatric disorders is hard to understand. Kendall (1982) noted the best in classification systems: categories are mutually exclusive and jointly exhaustive. Target members would possess features that define one category and one only. The DSM-III-R is quite different. It is devised as a multiaxial and polythetic system where categories share symptoms from other disorders and do not necessarily include features that are solely representative. The current nosology also is based on a hierarchal exclusionary principle. It establishes that a diagnostic entity is discrete and thereby coexisting, unless it has "associated features" and is functionally related to another disorder. Since conceptual similarity and symptom overlap occur between PTSD and other disorders, it is not surprising that syndromes based on emotional turmoil (e.g., Anxiety Disorder or Major Affective Disorder) or acting out (e.g., substance abuse) are often comorbid. Disconcerting but true, DSM-III-R is not intended to be a complete or thorough description of a disorder. This polythetic model of psychopathology is intended to provide a bandwidth fidelity to outline criteria, empirically and clinically established, that maximally differentiate one disorder from all others (Lyons, 1991). Little convergent validity exists between depression, anxiety, and substance abuse, and PTSD. In fact, none of the PTSD criteria are unique to that disorder (except the trauma). This is intended chaos of an imperfect, evolving system. Given this state of affairs, it may be best to employ "clinical empiricism," to develop orienting concepts or local clinical rules based on response to treatment or confirmed external correlates of care (e.g., employment).

Specific to PTSD and the DSM, this problem is evident when various criteria or threshold levels are debated. Schwartz and Kowalski (1991) investigated the effects of symptom threshold and criteria selection for PTSD. Using DSM-III, DSM-III-R, and proposed DSM-IV criteria for PTSD for liberal (occurring at least a little of the time), moderate (occurring at least some of the time), and conservative (occurring at least much or most of the time) symptom thresholds, differences were found for both the DSM criteria (DSM-III diagnosed fewest cases) and threshold levels (liberal threshold allowed for the greatest number of cases). Results showed then that troublesome and confusing diagnostic incongruities of criteria sets resulted from complex interactions among threshold and revisions of items within clusters. We have a moving target.

The DSMs were developed by "psychologic" understanding of pathological disorders, logical rules of quasi-philosophical deliberation at classification. O'Donahue and Elliott (1992), among others, have picked at this "system" from a logical perspective. They playfully challenge: Does not PTSD constitute an expected response or is it rightly a non-normative response? Or more aptly, what is normal for one who is violently abused? Either an agreement is established that "normal" excessive responses to trauma can exist (in which case PTSD does not exist) or all "excessive" responses are abnormal ones. These authors recommend several options; V Code ("conditions not attributable to a mental disorder"), independent disorder (not an Anxiety Disorder), or subtyping by stressor (e.g., PTSD-war, PTSD-rape, etc.), including the trauma subtyping by other disorders (e.g., Major Depression-war). Due to the heterogeneity of response to trauma in general and the paradoxical similarity of response to a specific kind of trauma, this last suggestion is most appealing. One other author (Herman, 1992) noted that at least a distinction between acute and prolonged stressors should exist; the latter showing a "pleomorphic symptom picture, enduring personality changes, and a high risk of repeated harm, either self-inflicted or at the hands of others." (p. 387).

A preliminary report on the DSM-IV (Resnick & Kilpatrick, 1992) has released its recommendations. Criterion A (see Table 1) will reflect both the objective and subjective, internal and external aspects of the trauma; Criterion B (with the addition of D6) and Criterion C are settled and will remain largely as is; and Criterion E will stay at one month (prevalence rates change too drastically when other time periods are entertained). (Also a recommendation was made for the health care provider to screen for multiple trauma events, as trauma event histories are both complex and pervasive). As we move from the DSM-III through the DSM-III-R and eventually to DSM-IV, certain principles seem to apply: (1) the definition of the stressor is both broad and expanding; (2) "common sense" and behaviorally anchored criteria (with higher thresholds) are in evidence; (3) few core and discriminating features exist for many disorders; and (4) the polythetic model is established, allowing for various mixtures of symptoms for a given disorder (Frances, Pincus, Widiger, Wakefield, & First, 1990). In the "real world" of trauma victims, a heterogeneity of disorder possibilities are present with no pathognomonic signs to identify the disorder. In fact, *no other disorder in the DSM appears to share more symptoms with other disorders or is as conceptually related to other disorders than PTSD.* This overlap highlights the inherent variability among trauma victims and reflects the inadequacies of current nosologic systems.

Health Care Model

Related to the health care system itself, other problems also prevail. Health care in our culture developed due to the medical model. This traditional model allows for signs and symptoms to be directly related to a specific disease. This level of parsimony, however, belies the reality of multiple symptom pictures, multiple etiologies, and multiple treatments. Older or chronic populations especially require different care models to make sense of the type and levels of disability. Figure 2.2 provides five health care models of disease used in geriatrics (Fried, Stores, King, & Lodden, 1991). Models 2 through 5 are more reflective of difficulties with chronic trauma victims, all for different reasons with different victims. In Model 2 is specified that often multiple chronic processes are present, each of which contributes to a common cumulative morbidity. In combination, these trends cause functional decline. In Model 3, clients may sense a decline and attribute this to previously diagnosed chronic problems. In fact, another cause may be present. Model 4 is reflective of a sequential process, one factor causing another. The chief complaint,

1. Medical—Patient's symptoms and signs correspond directly to disease.

Symptoms

2. Synergistic Morbidity—Patient has multiple chronic problems, each contributes to a common, cumulative morbidity.

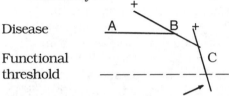

3. Attribution—Unrecognized problems "cause" a worsening of chronic problems.

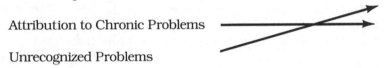

4. Causal Chain Model — One problem causes another as well as functional decrement

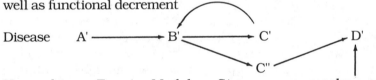

5. Unmasking Event Model — Stressor unmasks an underlying, stable or slowly progressive premorbid condition, previously handled event

Figure 2.2. Models of "illness." Extrapolated from "Diagnosis of illness presentations in the elderly" by Fried, Stores, King, and Lodden (1991), *Journal of the American Geriatrics Society.*

however, is often the "last straw." One physical ailment (A) precipitates a chain of subsequent events and results in functional decline (B), which causes C (and exacerbates B and causes problem C and D). Finally, in Model 5 a stressful event may unmask an underlying stable or slowly progressing condition previously compensated. When this goes, either the event is blamed or some symptom takes center stage. Many PTSD victims would fall under Model 5.

These latter four models expand the identification of medical illness beyond the pathology of a single disease. Their biopsychosocial emphasis is the real world of chronic victimization. They also recognize the importance of a more in-depth and multiaxial view toward psychopathology, as displayed by trauma victims. Both internal and external stimuli are able to potentiate the stressor response. In these models also is endorsed the many variables of stress models, including the role of the environment, the phases of the disorder, and most importantly, the complex person influencing the disorder. Finally, we know that the longer the effects of trauma persist, the greater the likelihood that the residual or delayed categories of the stressor problems become part of the character structure of the victim. As such, no simple model applies.

Range of Symptoms

The very nature of the disorder is also a concern. Since trauma stress is external and intense, victims necessarily show a range of symptoms. How this plays out with comorbid disorders is largely unclear. First, virtually no data are available on the relationship between comorbidity type and symptom presentation with other variables, stressor related or person related. Information on symptom clusters of PTSD and their relationship to outcome measures is also woefully underrepresented. Second, it is often unclear which symptoms or disorders are primary and which are secondary. The frequency of comorbid disorders is so high that to find "pure culture" PTSD is a rarity. Rates of comorbidity range from a high of almost 98% of males who reach criteria for PTSD (also reach criteria for another disorder at some previous time) (Kulka et al., 1988), to rates below 50% (Helzer, Robins, &

McEvoy, 1987). These data apply independent of data collecting method, training of interviewer, clinical/non-clinical status, or method of study (clinical studies or survey data) (Keane, 1991). Some evidence suggests that comorbidity is more likely in PTSD as a function of increased combat exposure (Penk & Robinowitz, 1987), difficult premorbid patterns or experiences (Foy, Sipprelle, Rueger, & Carroll, 1984), presence of depression (Forfar, 1992), or perhaps the nature of the combat experience itself (Helzer, 1984). As Keane (1991) implied, comorbidity may be an integral part of PTSD itself.

To date, over a dozen studies have provided data on this issue. At this center, Boudewyns, Woods, Hyer, and Albrecht (1991) carried out a systematic prospective assessment of the relationship between comorbidity as determined by the Diagnostic Interview Schedule (DIS) with PTSD. In Table 2.3 are listed these results along with common secondary symptoms of PTSD. By far the most common comorbid condition was substance abuse/dependence. Other popular co-existing syndromes included the Anxiety Disorders, Affective Disorders, and Schizophrenia. Evidence is increasing that these comorbid conditions influence treatment and adjustment. In the same study, sufferers with co-diagnoses of Schizophrenia or Affective Disorder with Psychotic Features were shown to be less likely to complete the treatment program than nonpsychotic victims and more likely to be rehospitalized within a year of discharge. Lower completion rates of treatment also applied to substance abuse/dependence. If these studies are any indicator of PTSD, comorbidity appears to be the rule rather than the exception, and these coexisting problems lead to increased treatment difficulties.

Currently, the phrase dual diagnosis—the coinfluencing effects of two psychiatric disorders—is popular. In most instances, this designation refers to PTSD and substance abuse (most often alcohol). Given such high co-morbidity rates, perhaps no more accurate statement regarding the interface between PTSD and alcohol problems exists than that they are "inextricably intertwined" (Boudewyns, et al., 1991). One emerging truth is that higher levels of combat exposure are related to increases in both PTSD and alcohol problems (see Boudewyns et al., 1991). While a "dose related" effect seems to exist among

TABLE 2.3
Comorbid Axis I Diagnoses and Secondary Symptoms

I. Comorbid Diagnosis	Current (%)	Lifetime (%)
Alcohol Abuse	65	83
Substance Abuse	64	56
Anxiety Disorder	42	66
Affective Disorder	36	79
Schizophrenia	25	28

II. Secondary Symptoms of PTSD*

Depression	feeling dysphoric, low energy, suicidal ideation, worthlessness
Panic Reactions	related to trauma cues or distinctive panic features most represented around crowds, public places, performance anxiety
Generalized Anxiety Disorder	constant tension readiness in distinct life areas, multiple physical problems
Acting Out	poor anger management, fights, difficulties with authority, jobs, or low frustration tolerance
Substance Abuse	virtually universal, begun in combat and used as an avoidance mechanism (self-medication)
Somatization	exhaustion, multiple pains, gastric distress, cardiac symptoms, hoarseness, allergic reactions
Sexual Dysfunction	erectile dysfunction, loss of interest, avoidance
Chronic Victim/ Killer Image	common "bottom line" response to any stress, feelings of "poor me" or "bad me"

Extropolated from Peterson, Prout, & Schwartz (1991).

the principal players here (of combat, PTSD, and alcohol abuse), the strength of the relationship varies as does the role of vulnerability and personality factors of the individual.

Traditionally three formulations have guided the managed care of PTSD victims who abuse alcohol. Hyer, McCranie, and Peralme (in press) discussed these. The first and most popular is the self *medication model* which holds that alcohol or other substances relieve PTSD symptoms (at least initially) and induce sleep. Accordingly, anxiety, irritability, and depression (sometimes) are suppressed. Over time of course, alcohol tolerance works in the other direction; PTSD symptoms are not quelled, and increased alcohol use occurs leading to alcoholism (Miller & Gold, 1991). Substantial support exists for this position based largely on clinical common sense, noting the primacy and prepotency of PTSD symptoms, and two PTSD dynamics, avoidance from pain and being "turned on" or rewarded for abuse (see Hyer et al., 1991).

The second model is that *alcoholism is primary*. Evidence for this position shows that drinking existed before combat (Helzer, 1984), that drinking started while in combat and continued (see Boudewyns et al., 1991), that risk factors related to alcohol abuse, such as family history of abuse (Davidson, Smith, & Kudler, 1989), are present, that drinking typically begins before trauma problems (Davidson, Kudler, Saunders, & Smith, 1990), or that substance abuse is the first priority in any treatment (Nace, 1988).

Last, the *comorbid model* is considered. This position has appeal because it does not offend previous positions and requests that the safest road be traveled; treat both. Sometimes the recommendation is that substance abuse be treated first (Nace, 1988), but most often integrated care is endorsed (Boudewyns et al., 1991). Proponents of this model, Jelinek and Williams (1984), divided patients into three categories: those free of substance abuse; those who started alcohol use in combat (to relieve stress) and continued to self-medicate; and primary alcoholics, whose abuse predated combat. Not surprisingly, the first two groups received PTSD care (the alcohol group presumably eliminating this habit after treatment) and the last group was given primary alcohol treatment, then PTSD treatment.

Regardless of which slot a trauma victim falls, treatment will not be simple and will not follow "clean" nosological rules (e.g., treat condition A, then B; treat both conditions simultaneously; treat the primary condition only; etc.). Treatment must be individualized and developed through an understanding of the person (Bolo, 1991). Hyer et al. (in press) strongly recommended that personality measures, psychotherapy indices, and tests sensitive to substance abuse patterns be considered.

At the risk of gilding the lily here, one other area related to comorbidity is a concern—and with each passing year, an increasing concern—physical health. Among combat veterans, very little data are available on the physical problems or complaints related to PTSD. Kulka et al. (1988) noted that non-help seeking veterans exposed to higher levels of combat reported more physical health problems and used medical services more than their counterparts. Recently Litz, Keane, Fisher, Marx, and Manaco (1992) showed that among a group of treatment-seeking combat veterans (of Vietnam) with PTSD, more self-reported health problems resulted, but not physician-diagnosed disorders (than a matched group). While little evidence of health complaints or problems related to a particular PTSD symptom is reported, this group did reveal at least one noteworthy relationship: the relationship between the psychophysiological measure, baseline heart rate, and reported heart problems and rapid breathing. Cardiovascular concerns *will* be a problem in coming years.

As we lead into our next section on the cyclic nature of PTSD and its moderating factors, two other points are made. Recent evidence has pointed to difficulty and challenge in the accuracy of a PTSD diagnosis (Eldridge, 1991). Problems related to the training and experience of the assessor, secondary gains of the victims, race and culture of the survivor, social economic and personal resources of the survivor, time elapsed since the stress, and coping related to other psychiatric disorders, among other factors, have been highlighted. Beliefs and actions of the assessor also may influence this process. Finally, due to resistance of the disorder to change, to the litigation focus of many evaluations, and to a compensation emphasis (especially among combat veterans), no "evaluation free" zone of objectivity may exist.

Second, the next generation of research is now hard at work identifying salient dimensions for trauma subtypes. These include personality, response to treatment, and various trauma-related variables, as well as comorbidity. Currently, evidence is accumulating that the influence of individual differences, especially early learnings and personality variables, "predicts" the existence and type of trauma response and may even influence whether one is exposed to trauma or how one responds to the stressor (Frank, Elliott, Corcoran, & Wonderlich 1987; Lyons, 1991). In the child sexual abuse literature, for example, Miller-Perrin and Wurtele (1990) noted a relationship between characteristics of the sexual experience (e.g., duration and frequency, relationship of victim to abuser, etc.) and the distinct type of psychological effect on the victim. Epstein (1990) further differentiated PTSD beyond the DSM-III-R criteria, specifying distinctive "maladaptive resolutions" (of PTSD) based on the generalization of the fear response, of the anger response, of the withdrawal response, as well as dissociation, and embracing the trauma. The notion of "maladaptive resolution" highlights the unique adaptation of chronic PTSD victims as each comes to terms with self, others, the world, and stress. As this information unfolds, a refinement of the PTSD construct will occur along with a refinement in treatment. Comorbidity and subtyping will become increasingly clear also. PTSD is not of one form, even for chronic victims.

PTSD is comorbid with other disorders for many reasons but perhaps mostly because of how it is defined, global and non-specific given a stressor. Davidson and Foa (1991) stated:

> Although the frequency of anxiety is elevated, so are a wide range of other disorders, which means that almost any statement about the relation of PTSD to other psychiatric categories can be supported. For example, these data can support the claim that PTSD is a form of anxiety and is properly placed, or on the other hand, PTSD can be shown to be a dissociative or somatoform disorder. Also, because of PTSD's close connection to depression in terms of comorbidity, then it can perhaps be classified as a

depressive variant. One can also take the position that because no consistent pattern emerges from the comorbidity data, PTSD must be viewed as a condition *sui generis*. (p. 352)

PHASES AND MODERATORS OF PTSD

Two "unclean" components of chronic trauma are considered: the cyclical nature of the disorder and moderating factors. The hope is that this section, along with the ones just covered, will lead to the inevitable conclusion that the conceptualization of the trauma victim necessitates a case formulation centered around known person variables. These data also may painfully convince the reader that, as Keane (1988) noted, PTSD in combat veterans may be a lifelong disorder.

Stages of Trauma

Once trauma has an impact, stages of accomodation are not typical. Diagnostically, PTSD is divided into acute (onset of symptoms within six months of traumatic event) and chronic (greater than six months). It can also be delayed (symptoms emerging after a latency period of months or years following the trauma). This is only a starting point. For acute PTSD no pure form exists in the DSM-II-R. As clinicians know, however, acute reactions clearly do exist (Davidson & Foa, 1991). In fact, the ICD-10 proposes a diagnosis of "Acute Stress Reaction." This designation would involve the immediate onset of symptoms after exposure to a trauma. This is an important development not simply because the acute category is better represented, but it allows for a fuller understanding of the types of people who become victims: immediate with no later sequelae, immediate with later sequelae, delayed with no immediate reaction, delayed and chronic with no immediate reaction, etc. Other acute trauma are currently insufficiently developed, including pathological grief, chronic victimization disorder, and brief reactive dissociative disorders. Chronic victims, on the other hand, are often delayed as well as chronic. Symptoms often present after a six month period (PTSD delayed) and are maintained for a period of greater than six months before diagnosis (PTSD, chronic). These designations, however, are far from helpful except as global types.

Most authors (e.g., Burgess & Holmstrom, 1974; Frederick, 1985; Rangell, 1976) believe that trauma does have phases. For starters, little is known about the connection between the coping of the (potential) victim during the actual stressor and any eventual trauma response. After the stressor, however, the initial phase, usually short, is characterized by shock and disbelief, often blocking out most or all of the threat. Some variant of dissociation, depersonalization, and denial often occur. This can be most adaptive. This is followed by a second phase, which ushers in a variety of responses as the person either maintains initial defenses or engages the environment with more idiosyncratic coping patterns, such as numbing, identification with the aggressor, exercising a will to live, etc. In this second phase, often intrusions (nightmares, flashbacks, guilt) occur, and eventually an adaptive avoidance which causes its own problems results. If the trauma cycle of intrusion and numbing ensues, the victim may proceed on a distinctly downward trend in adjustment. Whatever the eventual pattern that develops, the person shows so much variability in patterns of coping and time to recovery (if ever), as to render these punctuated periods useless.

Resilience

Typically, coping is successful. The trauma victim copes well during trauma, and over time, doses himself/herself with tolerable amounts of the memory material. Symptoms eventually wane, and the trauma becomes integrated. Dye and Roth (1991) speculated on this ideal coping pattern. They noted:

> In the ideal situation, an individual is successfully able to recover from a trauma without psychotherapy over the course of time. Ideally, the trauma survivor is able to gradually 'dose her/himself with manageable amounts of emotionally charged material through alternately approaching and avoiding the trauma until she/he is able to integrate the trauma with pre-traumatic feelings and assumptions about her/himself (Horowitz, 1986). During this dosing process, the trauma survivors typically experience oscillating cycles of intrusion and denial which gradually become less intense. (p. 105)

This pattern may transpire for the majority of stressor victims; but how "empowered" self repair unfolds is unclear. Are those components or coping tools of the person most likely to be resilient in the face of trauma? Psychological resilience is the interaction of biological, psychological, and environmental factors that "steel" the person through stress. Such a person "perceives" less danger, copes, uses social supports, or even maladapts in extreme stress so as to adapt later. Hendin and Haas (1984) suggested that the central issue is not the objectivity of trauma but its perception. In their study of 10 functioning veterans, they argued that variables, like calmness under pressure, intellectual control, and acceptance of fear, provided protection. These authors speculated that the person of the victim (individual differences) interacts with the trauma to provide distinct patterns of adjustment. Bruner (1990) labeled this critical period (shortly after trauma), "meaning making." Other authors (e.g., Ursano, Wheatley, Sledge, Rahe, & Carlson 1986; Quarantelli, 1985) have noted that selected types of victims even benefit from intense war stressors (e.g., POW status). It can be said, however, that these issues are understudied: how acute transits into chronic PTSD, what constitutes positive (or negative) coping at or after trauma, and what person variables provide "protection" from the effects of trauma.

Individual Differences

Individual differences are paramount and next to impossible to measure and understand fully. Once trauma has occurred and the assimilation or accommodation of the stressor is prevented, various permutations of coping and adaptation occur. Responses, both at the time of stress and subsequently, intermix with the many situational and supportive variables to produce some form of adaptation. Pictorially this is represented in Figure 2.3. Person A appears especially vulnerable to trauma, maintains high levels of tension readiness, and eventually habituates. Persons B and C appear somewhat resilient initially, but show problems in different ways as time passes. At any point in time, the sufferer can appear different from previous times. Again, the DSM-III-R designation of acute, chronic, or delayed is not helpful.

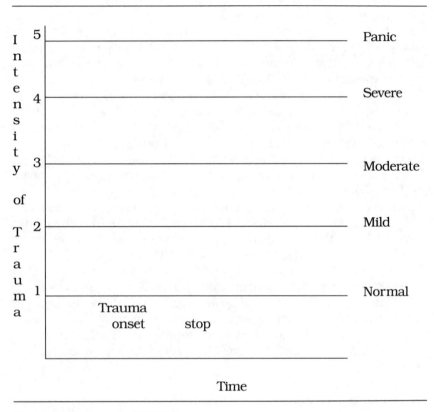

Figure 2.3. Course of PTSD.

The person of the victim takes some time to "readjust" to the exact form of PTSD acceptable. Weisaeth (1984) followed victims of a Norwegian fire over time. He found that the prevalence of acute PTSD was related mostly to the initial intensity of the exposure. After four years, however, pre-accident psychological functioning was a higher predictor than accident intensity to adjustment. McFarlane (1990) also found that in an acute group of fire victims, no vulnerability factors of importance were noted; but in a chronic group, several of these, including a concurrent psychiatric disorder, a positive family history of problems, avoidance as a personality trait, as well as being older and having panicked during the disaster itself, were related. Several authors (e.g., Benedek, 1985; Black, 1982) also have noted that over time the ability to request social support is related both to adjustment and to one's identity. Similarly, Solomon, Benbenishty, and Mikulincer (1991) identified changes over time in soldiers with combat stress reaction in regards to symptoms and self efficacy. Psychic umbing, for example, showed a strong relationship to self efficacy during the war and less after. Also, in the first two years post combat, symptoms specific to trauma events remained robust, but not in the third year, when more "general psychopathological" symptoms were more highly related.

Known Moderators

The second problem, moderating factors, is implied in this discussion. In fact, moderating factors *are* the person of the victim. These factors, perhaps influenced by the culture, provide a sense of control and meaning for the person. Already, we have discussed how victims who become prone to problems possess a biological vulnerability to stress (showing itself in physiological hyperarousal) and a psychological vulnerability (often with a sense of uncontrollability and unpredictability). If one's early environment has sensitized the person to specific foci of anxiety, the probability is that these very features will be recapitulated during stress periods. Exactly what the factors are that mediate between trauma and its emotional impact is the objective of considerable research effort. Denny, Robinowitz, and Penk (1987) discussed combat victims and outlined many of the influences that interact between the person and stressor. These authors noted dispositional characteristics, but direct special attention to concurrent living patterns, such as other psychiatric problems, intervening trauma, personality styles, social support, and secondary gains, among others.

Gibbs (1989) more directly discussed many mediating factors of trauma, drawing special attention to "obvious" person variables. Among these are gender, age, sex, and race. Women, for example, are more likely than men to internalize their emotional reactions to disaster. They may be more likely to experience stress from the demands of the support system, but they also may be better able to obtain support from their environment. The influence of age is less clear. Being older, for example, has been shown both to help or to hinder the trauma process. Being younger may actually be a negative, leading to a less adaptive capacity. Older victims may experience more "on time" stressors and have more realistic expectations.

Just as older age can act as a sort of "chronological maturity," so high income and education have been found to correlate with fewer psychological effects in a disaster. Race also has been a differentiator in trauma, especially combat related trauma. For example, Blacks experienced more war trauma in Vietnam and showed greater amounts of psychopathology than Whites (Penk & Allen, 1991). One other background variable is noteworthy: a positive family history of an Anxiety Disorder (Breslau, Davis, & Andreski, 1990) or a psychiatric disorder (Davidson, et al., 1989) has been shown to be a positive risk factor in the development of PTSD. Finally, other psychologically based variables, variously assessed, such as locus of control, coping styles, use of religion, and problem solving methods, influence adaptations to trauma. Researchers and clinicians, assessing adjustment among trauma victims, may need to incorporate premorbid variables considered to covary with measures of adjustment into these studies in routine ways. Any variables may have direct, indirect, or interactive influences on adjustment.

One variable that asserts a special influence is support. In the trauma literature, one axiom is that positive adjustment is at risk with an unsupportive environment for any stressor victim, especially directly after the stressor. Erickson (1976) stated, "It is difficult for people to recover from the effects of individual trauma when the community on which they have depended remains (or becomes) fragmented" (page 302). During and after the Vietnam era, society was anything but supportive. The "second wound" or "sanctuary trauma" was universally felt among combat veterans of Vietnam. During this time frame also, the American culture changed at a rapid rate. Issues related to authority, gender, goals, race, sexual practices, tradition, and education, among others, metamorphized before the victim's eyes. The result was a constant role strain from many perspectives, a perpetual identity diffusion. Vietnam veterans may have been victims of the cultural revolution as much as war trauma.

Finally, note is made that current stressors (large or small) appear to have as much an influence on the presence and intensity of PTSD problems as anything. In an earlier study Hyer, Boudewyns O'Leary, and Harrison (1987) showed that the majority of the variance of a PTSD self report measure was accounted for by current interpersonal stressors. Several researchers have reported that interpersonal criticism from significant others is a predictor of problems of relapse for depression or schizophrenia, as well as medical conditions (Meichenbaum & Fitzpatrick, 1991). Specific to Vietnam veterans, data are convincing that wives (of veterans with PTSD) experience increased levels of stress. Other family members also described elevated levels of problems—violence, negative behaviors, poorer parenting skills (Fairbank, Schlenger, Caddell, & Woods, in press). Psychiatric problems in general have a greater chance of success, given a helping environment. PTSD is no different.

Longitudinal View of Trauma

An understanding of the longitudinal course of this disorder, an understanding of the variables that potentiate symptoms before, during, and after trauma, and an understanding of how to predict/obviate cycles of pathology are important. What is not known is whether responses that predict the reoccurrence or course of this disorder are the same as those present at onset (Monroe, Bromet, Connell, & Steiner 1986). In both war victims and rape victims especially, a varied latency exists before the disorder "spontaneously generates."

In one study on combat trauma, Solomon (1990b) used a longitudinal design to show that those with combat stress reactions retained their problems at later times at rates greater than soldiers who showed no initial combat stress. This group (Solomon, 1990b) followed Israeli soldiers since the Yom Kipper War in 1973. Solomon showed some interesting findings in an evaluation of 382 Lebanon War (1982) soldiers who were diagnosed with a **Combat Stress Reaction (CSR)** against 334 matched control soldiers who had participated in the same frontline combat units as the CSR soldiers. CSR rates were increased as a function of prior combat or a previous CSR. Therefore, both exposure and a previous episode (PTSD) "influenced" later problems. Also, soldiers with a later CSR (in Lebanon War) showed differences *during* combat (feeling more lonely, guilty, threatened, and less prepared) and *subsequently* (feeling more lonely, perceiving less social support, viewing their family as less cohesive and expressive, and more conflicted). Previous trauma begets more trauma even 10 years later.

The longitudinal design allows for a unique perspective on trauma victims, permitting clinicians to inspect the trauma response in distinctive ways. In this case a number of different factors (age, education, economic status, battle experiences, previous war-related psychological problems, the extent of the combat stress reaction, as well as post war experiences) made independent and differential contributions to the development of PTSD across time. More vulnerable soldiers (due to moderating factors) suffered more severe PTSD. Assessing rape victims over a three month period, Rothbaum, Foa, Riggs, Murdock, and Walsh (1992) showed that, although PTSD rates declined over time, women at three months who had problems showed no improvement after that time. Conversly, those who did show early improvement continued to do so. Patterns were predictable at an early time post trauma. In this country, however, very few studies have used prospective or longitudinal designs to assess the effects of trauma. Where this has been done, using either early grade school data (Card, 1987) or premorbid college data (Schnurr, Friedman, & Rosenberg, 1991), results indicate that early "personality problems" were noted with Vietnam combat veterans with a lifetime prevalence of PTSD symptoms relative to those who had no symptoms.

The reactivation of stress is a common experience. This can happen at "lower" levels of stress (e.g., grief) as well as in intense stressor situations. An objective is a working model of the trauma response applicable to all stressor levels. Resultant models almost certainly will prove helpful, even in error, because they force clinicians into critical thinking, unpacking person variables as they interact with the trauma. One earlier psychosocial model that encapsulates many of these variables is that of Green, Wilson, and Lindy (1985). In this model (Figure 2.4) is suggested that an adaptive or maladaptive response is a result of the interaction of the trauma experience, individual characteristics, and the recovery environment. The core of the response occurs in the information processing of the event. For these authors, the individual characteristics included the many premorbid and current coping variables of the person. The environment involves perceived social support, and intactness of community and the culture. Outcome refers to good or bad adjustment. Although no confirmatory analyses have been performed yet, results of many studies have generally supported the relationship of the "input" factors with each other and with outcome. A related model, that of Wilson (1989), also emphasized central variables in trauma processing— person (e.g., motives, values, and coping styles), environment (dimensions of the trauma, experience of the trauma, structure of the trauma, and post-trauma milieu), individual subjective response to trauma (emotional, cognitive, motivational, neurophysiological, and coping), and the post-trauma adaptation (acute, chronic, and life course). Interestingly, Wilson included resilience in his model, emphasizing positive person input to trauma resolution. Both are highly interactive models but one element is paramount, the position of the person in the influence of the outcome. Although helpful, these models are almost simple, largely linear (and studies have been quasi-experimental) and assess only one measure at a time, leaving the imagination (and the future) to provide new "truths." The collective whole is not necessarily understandable from the properties of its parts. We require, therefore, multiplicative models and longitudinal designs.

PREVALENCE

Most studies on the incidence of adjustment problems following trauma hold firm to a narrow bandwidth. As a function

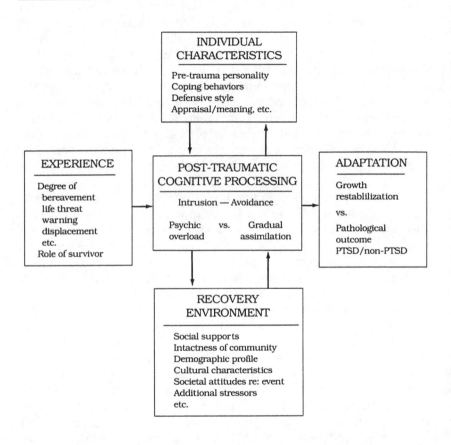

Figure 2.4. Psychosocial framework for understanding post-traumatic stress disorder. (Green, Wilson, & Lindy, 1985, p. 73) Reprinted with permission.

of the kind of trauma, definition of adjustment, the sample used, and the overall methodology, a range of current morbidity has evolved among combat veterans of Vietnam from a low of 1.8% in one community based sample (Snow, Stellman, Stellman, & Sommer, 1988) to over 25% in Legacies of Vietnam (Egendorf, Kadushin, Laufer, Rothbart, & Sloan, 1981). Other studies using other samples have found even higher rates. In one study Breslau, Davis, Andreski, and Peterson (1991) assessed a random community sample regarding the prevalence of PTSD and its risk factors. Lifetime prevalence rates of exposure to traumatic events was 39.1%; rate of PTSD in those who were exposed was 23.6%. Davidson and Smith (1990) found even higher rates in a psychiatric sample. Interestingly, Snow et al. (1988) had varying prevalence rates of PTSD (1.8% to 15%) depending on how strictly trauma was operationalized. A meta-analysis of 67 studies of Vietnam combat veterans appearing in the literature from 1972 through 1985 (Kaylor, King, & King, 1987) showed this group to be more dysfunctional on adjustment factors than both era veterans not in Vietnam and non-veterans.

Finally, Boyle et al. (1989) documented other lingering problems. In a large survey performed at the Center for Disease Control noted that most Vietnam veterans are generally similar to their veteran peers in economic and social functions. Regarding psychiatric concerns, this group wrote:

> Posttraumatic stress disorder and symptoms that resemble those of this disorder are more prevalent among Vietnam veterans and are strongly associated with the extent of combat experience. Subgroups of Vietnam veterans may be at especially high risk of this condition because of certain predisposing factors and particular military experiences. Current rates of depression, anxiety, and heavy alcohol use are higher among Vietnam veterans than among other Vietnam-era veterans. Current use of drugs does not appear to be more frequent among Vietnam veterans; but an early post service excess of drug-related mortality may have occurred. Deaths from unintentional injuries (mostly motor vehicle crash deaths) were more frequent among Vietnam veterans in the first five to 10 years after discharge. This excess may be related to the development of risk-taking characteristics resulting from the service in the Vietnam

War zone (6). It is unclear whether suicide and homicide were also elevated during this early post service period, but there is a suggestion from one study of an excess of both in the first five years after discharge.(p.22)

As combat veterans now negotiate the fourth and fifth decades of their lives, the residues of living may take their toll, especially those modal for males (cardiac, cerebrovascular, etc.) or accumulative for the group (effects of alcohol or drugs).

"The" Study

Unfortunately most of these studies are victims of measures that did not easily link mental and emotional problems or stress to diagnostic category. This was not the problem for the National Vietnam Veteran Readjustment Study (NVVRS) (Kulka et al., 1988). This survey was a very carefully undertaken and now popular epidemiological study. The focus of this undertaking was prevalence and incidence of a psychiatric problems among this population. Mandated by Congress in 1983 and carried out between 1984 and 1988 by the Research Triangle Institute in Raleigh, North Carolina, on a non-treatment seeking sample, this study used state-of-the-art techniques. Face-to-face interviews with a nationally representative sampling (3,016) of Vietnam theater veterans, Vietnam Era veterans, and non-veterans or civilian counterparts were held. The non-veterans or civilian counterparts were matched to the theater veterans in age, sex, race (ethnicity for men), and by occupation (for women only). Minorities and other underrepresented samples were oversampled. This study also conducted preliminary validation of all measures of PTSD used. Therefore, it used multiple measures in carefully devised samples in its assessment of PTSD.

Highlight data of the findings are in Table 2.4. As background to these findings, this study clearly demonstrated that combat intensity increases PTSD problems. Current point prevalence rates are at about 15 percent. Interestingly most of the studies noted on the epidemiology of PTSD (several cited above being "outliers") lie within 95% confidence interval of the NVVRS estimate (13.0% to 17.4%) for combat related PTSD (Fairbank, Schlenger, Caddell, & Woods, in press). Roughly

TABLE 2.4
Statistical Data from the National Vietnam Veterans Readjustment Study

- 15.2% of male theater veterans (479,000) currently suffer from PTSD.

- 11.1% have significant symptoms of the disorder but do not meet DSM-III-R criteria (Partial PTSD).

- 30% of male Vietnam veterans have had PTSD at some time since the end of the war.

- 50% have had at least one other diagnosable psychiatric disorder in the past six months.

- 27.9% of Hispanic Vietnam theater veterans currently have PTSD.

- 20.6% of Black male theater veterans have the disorder.

- 8.5% of female theater veterans currently have PTSD.

- 7.8% of female theater veterans have Partial PTSD.

Extrapolated from Kulka et al. (1988).

one in two combat veterans will experience some form of psychiatric syndrome or PTSD symptoms over his/her lifetime. Adding to this, Weiss, Marmar, Schlenger, Fairbank, Jordan, Hough, and Kulka (1992) reported the prevalence rates of partial PTSD: 22.5% and 21.2% lifetime rates of partial PTSD for male theater and female veterans, respectively (current rates were 11.1% in males and 7.8% in females). These rates were above those of current PTSD. In the NVVRS, also, the variance accounted for by a set of over 80 pre-exposure variables that could render a victim more vulnerable was assessed and found to be small. However, this large study did confirm that PTSD is a chronic problem, more prevalent among veterans who experienced longer tours, were younger when in Vietnam, were wounded, were more decorated, and showed a slew of the "wrong" demographic factors, such as being separated or cohabitating, having less education, being unemployed, having a low income, living in a large city, and having no religious preference (Kulka et al., 1988). These variables have been largely confirmed by other studies (Card, 1987; Helzer et al., 1987; Snow et al., 1988).

As a result of these numbers, Kulka et al. (1988) reached six "truths" regarding this disorder's complexity and considerable needs for care. From these, *we can draw some simple truths. First*, residual problems of trauma at both clinical and sub-clinical levels are massive. This means that victims show trauma problems in different forms. *Second*, the variable that consistently "wins" in the battle for variance explanation is level of combat experience, and although this factor is not sufficient by itself, it is prepotent. This means that an etiologic linkage appears to exist between combat exposure and the emergence of subsequent problems that is driven by trauma and formed by the person. Validating this, a recent task force on war-related stress, as a result of Operation Desert Storm, concluded that two elements above all others placed people at risk: the greater the threat of loss or actual loss to which individuals were exposed and the fewer the coping resources of the individual (Hobfoll, Spielberger, Breznitz, Figley, Folkman, Lepper-Green, Meichenbaum, Milgram, Sandler, Sarason, & van der Kolk, 1991). These two risk factors were objective stressors or actual resources of the person. *Third*, many subtypes of trauma problems seem to exist, not just separated by clinical/subclinical or combat/noncombat dimensions, but other person dimensions. With some liberty, this means that the phenomenology of trauma comes from the person, an idiographic response at adaptation. *Fourth,* one can reasonably postulate that effects of this trauma are stubborn and resistant to change. This means that, as therapists, we must know the "right" person factors and trauma factors and intervene according to some plan. *Finally,* one other finding emerges (more so from other studies). Based on results obtained, the suggestion is that exposure to trauma potentiates other problems or disorders. This means that the sequela of trauma are rapacious in their quest for additional problems. This disorder not only does not habituate, it accentuates.

These "truths" are "essential tensions" that may take the scientist-practitioner beyond the data. Their common core is that trauma of the chronic intermittent or chronic continual variety impacts severely on the individual, setting in motion a trauma response that is unique for each person.

PSYCHOTHERAPY

In this final section, we address the importance of psychological healing of the trauma victims. At the outset it needs to be said that treatment of the chronic victim (to keep the metaphor of combat) necessitates more the strategies of trench warfare and less the quick strike mentality of a commando raid. To the serious student of psychotherapy outcome research with trauma victims, the need for any discussion does not exist, because only a few carefully controlled outcome studies have been done. Fortunately, the role of common sense or that of a friendly reading of these writings also applies. Most clinicians know that outcome research on psychotherapy is flawed: people are never really cured in any absolute or real sense. And, therapists know that the work of psychotherapy is bigger than efforts at evaluation. This is most apt with trauma victims as psychotherapy involves a deep healing process with efforts directed at change in self. Mahoney (1991) held that all psychotherapies are psychotherapies of the self. Psychotherapy must at some level be modulated through the self, and the person must be affected for change to occur.

No single treatment exists for PTSD, and outcome research has been disappointing. Most of the research in the treatment of PTSD concerns Vietnam veterans and is directed at symptoms. The use of behavioral and milieu inpatient programs, along with symptom specific medication, has proven helpful at various times (Hyer, Woods, & Boudewyns, 1991). Numerous other authors have espoused the merits of distinctive treatment types, including group, desensitization, flooding, cognitive restructuring, hypnotherapy, and family or couple therapy, among others (Fairbank & Nicholson, 1987; Peterson, Prout, & Schwartz, 1991). The integration of conjoined modalities, especially psychotherapeutic and psychopharmacologic, is also espoused (Fairbank et al., in press). These treatment offerings, however, were largely descriptive and based on poorly controlled clinical trials.

Where more careful efforts at the evaluation of psychotherapy with PTSD victims have been done, results have supported the specific and intended focus of the treatment. The effect on the symptom cluster intrusions have been especially contradictory. Keane, Fairbank, Caddell, and Zimering (1989), using a flooding technique on combat-related PTSD veterans, did show some symptom removal, largely on intrusions. In two controlled outcome studies at this center (Boudewyns, Hyer, Woods, Harrison, & McCranie, 1990; Boudewyns & Hyer, 1990), flooding (direct therapeutic exposure) was used and found to be only slightly better than milieu or psychotherapy, the major changes occurring in the symptom area of intrusions. Other outcome studies (e.g., Hyer, Woods, Bruno, & Boudewyns, 1989; Scurfield, Kenderline, & Pollard, 1990) have found that only selected symptoms remit, but rarely the intrusive experiences.

In a summary analysis of psychotherapy, Solomon, Gerrity and Muff (1992) also discovered the value of the effects of focused treatment. This group identified 255 treatment studies on various trauma populations (with PTSD). Only 11 studies qualified for their sample. The qualifications were a confirmed PTSD diagnosis and a random assignment to a treatment condition (with an alternative or no treatment control). Five of these studies involved pharmacotherapy and six psychotherapy. Of interest were two features. One involved the specific effects of treatment: exposure based therapy reduced intrusive symptoms; pharmacological agents specific to depression or anxiety showed effects in these areas only; and (in one study) a psychotherapy directed at avoidance was sensitive to this symptom only. Second, while change often occurred, the specifics were unclear—issues of how long, timing of measurement, best candidates for care, individual versus group therapy, combined versus single treatments, effects of comorbidity, acute versus chronic victims, etc. In effect, a trauma victim is not a trauma victim. The authors noted that the "assumption that all traumatized populations share important similarities that allow for meaningful generalizability of findings" (p. 637) may not apply. So, a good deal of individuality exists in how this process unfolds.

Components

Based on this literature, helpful information on treatment efficacy is lacking. What does appear, however, are three components of the trauma experience that require some therapeutic response (at least). The first is *exposure* to the trauma. The reexperiencing of the trauma experience is a highly individual process that is involuntary and often intensely intrusive. Unfortunately, most reexperiencing of trauma "breaks off" when it becomes intense. Components of the experience are not deconditioned (Lyons & Keane, 1989) or cognitively integrated (Garmezy & Rutter, 1985) due to the persistence of the person's avoidance response repertoire. Since avoidance prevents a "satisfactory absorption" of the trauma, some type of clinician directed exposure should be considered as part of the therapist's armamentarium.

One carefully controlled study, Foa et al. (1991), examined the relative efficacy of three treatments—stress inoculation training, exposure, and supportive counseling (as well as a control) on rape victims. Interestingly, stress inoculation training produced significantly more improvement on PTSD symptoms than the other groups immediately after treatment, but exposure was superior at follow-up. Presumably, exposure disrupts the integrating processes of the victim in the short run but is more curative given more time. A recent study at this center corroborated this finding, finding that combat-related victims tended to hold their treatment gains if they received exposure therapy one year after discharge (Boudewyns, Albrecht, & Hyer, 1992).

The **search for meaning** also must occur. Attribution theory holds that a natural "need" develops to discover meaning in something that is incomplete. How does the victim cognitively appraise trauma? Eventually in treatment the unacknowledged experiences are to be accessed, exposed, and reintegrated into the meaning structures of the person. How the individual reattributes or reworks trauma is a very personal and complex process. A central theme of Frankl's (1959) work has always been the extent to which a person extends self on behalf of meaning. The pain of the trauma experience must be transformed into meanings and meaning potentials (not repressed) for growth. Interestingly, this occurs best by a renewed connection to one's fellow man (Frankl, 1959).

With chronic trauma victims this process is rather difficult. According to Lyons (1991), several distortions may occur in this process, such as self-blame or "bad" attributions (e.g., internal, global, and stable). At some point, however, the person's cognitive appraisal of the trauma event must change in personal meaning, which almost certainly involves an individual struggle and rearrangement of self. Shafer (1981) labeled this process, "narrative repair." This is most apt to happen when the victim is "engaged"—the meaning of the therapeutic interaction is currently in process and the arousal level is high. We can surmise with Mahoney (1991) that what is happening in any trauma victim's inner life is only partially understandable, but is intimately involved with self and other lives. Waxing poetic, what might be said is that the experience of intrusive ideation is not necessarily psychopathological. A healing resolution may not be a function of its absence. Rather, resolution occurs when meaning is provided or, when little is left to be learned (Epstein, 1990). Hidden pain gives way to understood pain and eventually extinction. Regardless, one's cognitions need to be considered.

Unfortunately, this may be only a positive reframe on an ugly situation. Using grief (as a result of loss) as a model, Fleming and Robinson (1991) argue that the loss can rarely be integrated when meaning is sought; resolution is found in the meaning of the life that was lived—an appreciation of the legacy of the deceased. This is a very personal process. Through a mix of affective (processing the emotion) and cognitive (attacking distortions at peripheral and core evils), the person of the survivor extends beyond the death to life and formulates personal meaning in his/her own growth and future. For trauma victims, moving on is difficult. In this regard too, Project Koach in Isreal was developed to avoid "chronic care": the emphasis is away from "why me" or meaning issues, and a concentration is placed on the present and future (Solomon, Bleich, Shoham, Nardi, & Kotler, 1992).

The last therapeutic component of treatment of the trauma victim entails the related combination of *coping* and *social support.* An argument even may be that success of post-trauma processing of social support is related to the degree of discrepancy between the client and other's perception of the trauma, who believes it to be more serious. If the client feels that others believe the trauma is less consequential, problems are likely to develop as a repetitive need for validation ensues. As noted, a virtual truism is that, if the trauma is intense and if the social support and coping mechanisms are inadequate following the trauma, the risk of pathological adjustment is high. Social support is a multidimensional construct that involves the social skills of both the recipient and the caretaker. How people perceive the social support is related to their own identity and social view of self (Sarason, Shearin, Pierce, & Sarason, 1987).

Note should be made that social support is not just social support. Implied is an active stance toward life, where social skills are required that must be applied continuously and are best done with a coping repertoire of great latitude (Hobfoll et al., 1991). How effectively support is used then is probably moderated by how one uses these qualities as well as his/her own personal resources (personality). In addition, trauma events serve to disrupt helpful social networks during these very important times (Solomon, 1986). Supporting this, Freedy, Shaw, Jarrell, and Masters (1992) assessed the "total" resources of victims (social roles, possessions, self and world views, and energy) and found that resource loss was directly related to psychological distress. In effect, resource loss (coping and social support) can actually be another trauma and extend beyond the acute episode. We shall discuss this and the other two treatment variables further in later chapters.

Results

Psychotherapy results are disappointing. Chronic trauma victims often remain stuck in their patterns. Perhaps a self-referent care has only a small "window" of time within which to act. In a war setting, if psychiatric principles of centrality, immediacy, brevity, proximity, simplicity, and expectancy are applied, psychiatric casualties are kept at low levels. In the Persian Gulf War, for example, ninety-nine percent of soldiers treated in this fashion were returned to duty after a brief intervention (McDuff & Johnson, 1992). In grief responses, also, a person who is unable to find meaning soon afterwards may be unlikely to find it later. In fact, it is beginning to appear that either intrusive experiences early in the trauma cycle or lack of meaning (or both) forebode distress for the victim. With chronic trauma victims especially, the removal or reduction of these symptoms (intrusions) is most difficult. Scurfield et al. (1990) noted that, even after considerable treatment, Vietnam veterans with PTSD possess raw or sensitive reactions to memories. With chronic victims, change tends to take place in interpersonal relationships, in better acceptance of self, and in a reduction of intrusive or avoidant symptoms (but not both). Perhaps this occurs because trauma can never really be integrated. Over time victims simply rearrange their condition: the passive "victim" moves to become a better coping "survivor" (Figley, 1988). The trauma experience may even be reworked again and again at each new developmental stage (Beardslee, 1989). Worse, adaptation may take downwardly mobile forms. When this occurs, the victim becomes so preoccupied with the press of symptomological relief that normal life span issues are smothered (Scaturo & Hayman, 1992).

Through these efforts, too little attention has been devoted to the primacy of the person. If so, our task is to know this entity and to disaggregate the processes carefully. We also should not expect equal reactivity in the human change process for each of these "person" parts. In fact, we may need different goals for each. An empowered person, however, may be enough to initiate change just as he/she made "some" input to the initial trauma response.

CONCLUSION

No one model of PTSD is accurate. Trauma symptoms develop because "something occurs" between the stimuli representative of the trauma (conditioned stimuli) and the on-going efforts at adaptation. If this "something" is reflective of risk factors (intra- or interpersonal), then maladaptation results; if reflective of resiliency, then adaptation evolves. In the PTSD research literature, various models are currently placing their bets on which vulnerability factors lead to the formation of the trauma response. The search is only about a decade old.

We have addressed several contenders in this process. However, throughout this chapter two issues were examined: the importance of the individual and the complexity and heterogeneity of the chronic trauma response. The reader is encouraged to appreciate the subjective objectivity of this disorder and perhaps to "disidentify" somewhat with traditional offerings of human care directed at trauma. Just as the trauma victim has to reintegrate the trauma into a new wholeness, clinical caregivers also may approach this disorder and their self/professional role with a curious epistemology and considered hope.

A paradigm shift is required. The trauma response is not only a biological disease or so many units of a stressor, but also is an experience that is physiological and psychological and mediated by very selective person variables. The critical thinking is in the experimental prerequisites for the cognitive schemas and their influence in the expression of the trauma response. The next chapter starts us on the theories most important for understanding the "person" of the victim.

REFERENCES

American Psychiatric Association. (1980). *Diagnostic and statistical manual of mental disorders* (3rd ed.). Washington, DC: Author.

American Psychiatric Association (1987). *Diagnostic and statistical manual of mental disorders* (3rd ed. revised). Washington, DC: Author.

Barlow, D. (1989). *Anxiety and its disorders.* New York: Guilford Press.

Beardslee, W. (1989). The role of self-understanding in resilient individuals: The development of a perspective. *Orthopsychiatry, 59,* 266-278.

Benedek, E. P. (1985). Children and disaster: Emerging issues. *Psych. Annuals, 15*(3), 168-172.

Black, D. (1982). Children and disaster. *British Medical Journal, 285:* 989-990.

Blank, A. S. (1985). The unconscious flashback to the war in Vietnam veterans: Clinical mystery, legal defense, and community problems. In S. M. Sonnenberg, A. S. Blank, & J. A. Talbott (Eds.), *The trauma of war: Stress and recovery in Vietnam veterans* (pp. 295-308). Washington, DC: American Press.

Bolo, P. (1991). Substance abuse and anxiety disorders. In M. Gold & A. Slaby (Eds.), *Dual diagnosis in substance abuse* (pp. 45-56). New York: Marcel Dekker.

Boudewyns, P. A., Albrecht, J., & Hyer, L. (1992, August). Long-term effects of direct therapeutic exposure in PTSD. Poster Session presented at the One Hundredth Annual Meeting of the American Psychological Association. Washington, DC.

Boudewyns, P. A., & Hyer, L. (1990). Physiological response to combat memories and preliminary treatment outcome in Vietnam veteran PTSD patients treated with direct therapeutic exposure. *Behavior Therapy, 21,* 63-87.

Boudewyns, P. A., Hyer, L., Woods, M. G., Harrison, W. R., & McCranie, E. (1990). PTSD among Vietnam veterans: An early look at treatment outcome using direct therapeutic exposure. *Journal of Traumatic Stress, 3,* 359-368.

Boudewyns, P. A., Woods, G., Hyer, L., & Albrecht, J. (1991). Chronic combat related PTSD and concurrent substance abuse: Implications for treatment of this frequent "dual diagnosis." *Journal of Consulting and Clinical Psychology.*

Boyle, C. A., Decoufle, P., & O'Brien, T. R. (1989). Long-term health consequences of military service in Vietnam. *Epidemiologic Reviews, 11,* 1-27.

Brende, J. O. (1987). Dissociative disorders in Vietnam combat veterans. *Journal of Contemporary Psychotherapy, 17*(2), 77-86.

Breslau, N., & Davis, G. C. (1987). Posttraumatic stress disorder: The etiologic specificity of wartime stressors. *American Journal of Psychiatry, 144*(5), 578-583.

Breslau, N., Davis, G. C. & Andreski, P. (1990). PTSD: Risks for event exposure, and syndrome. American Psychiatric Association Annual Meeting. New York.

Breslau, N., Davis, G., Andreski, P., & Peterson, E. (1991). Traumatic events and posttraumatic stress disorder in an urban population of young adults. *Achives of General Psychiatry, 48,* 216-222.

Brett, E. A., & Mangine, W. (1985). Imagery and combat stress in Vietnam Veterans. *Journal of Nervous and Mental Disease, 173*(5), 309-311.

Briere, J. (1992). Methodological issues in the study of sexual abuse effects. *Journal of Consulting and Clinical Psychology, 60,* 196-203.

Bruner, J. (1990). *Acts of meaning.* Cambridge, Mass.: Harvard University Press.

Burgess, A. W., & Holmstrom, L. L. (1974). Rape trauma syndrome. *American Journal of Psychiatry, 131,* 981-986.

Burnam, M., Stein, J., Golding J., Siegel, J., Sorenson, S., Forsythe, A., & Telles, C. (1988). Sexual assault and mental disorders in a community population. *Journal of Consulting and Clinical Psychology, 56,* 843-850.

Card, J. J. (1987). Epidemiology of PTSD in a national cohort of Vietnam veterans. *Journal of Clinical Psychology, 43,* 6-17.

Christianson, S., & Loftus, E. (1990). Some characteristics of people's traumatic memories. *Bulletin of the Psychonomic Society, 28*(3), 195-198.

Davidson, J., & Foa, E. (1991). Diagnostic issues to posttraumatic stress disorder: Consideration for the DSM-IV. *Journal of Abnormal Psychology, 100,* 3, 346-355.

Davidson, J., & Smith, R. (1990). Traumatic experiences in psychiatric outpatients. *Journal of Traumatic Stress, 3,* 459-474.

Davidson, J. R., Kudler, H. S., Saunders, W. S., & Smith, R. D. (1990). Symptom and comorbidity patterns in World War II and Vietnam veterans with posttraumatic stress disorder. *Comprehensive Psychiatry, 31,* 162-170.

Davidson, J., Smith, R. & Kudler, H. (1989). Familial psychiatric illness in chronic post-traumatic stress disorder. *Comprehensive Psychiatry, 30,* 1-7.

Davidson, J., Swartz, M., Storck, J., Krishnan, R. R., & Hammett, E. (1985). A diagnostic and family study of posttraumatic stress disorder. *The American Journal of Psychiatry, 142,* 90-93.

Denny, N., Robinowitz, R., & Penk, W. (1987). Conducting applied research on Vietnam combat-related posttraumatic stress disorder. *Journal of Clinical Psychology, 43,* 56-66.

Dye, E., & Roth, S. (1991). Psychotherapy with Vietnam veterans and rape and incest survivors. *Psychotherapy, 28,* Spring, 103-120.

Egendorf, A., Kadushin, C., Laufer, R. S., Rothbart, G., & Sloan, L. (1981). *Leagacies of Vietnam: Comparative adjustment of veterans and their peers.* Washington, DC: U.S. Government Office.

Eldridge, G. (1991). Contextual issues in the assessment of posttraumatic stress disorder. *Journal of Traumatic Stress, 4*(1), 7-24.

Epstein, S. (1990). Beliefs and symptoms in maladaptive resolutions of the traumatic neurosis. In D. Ozer, J. M. Healy, & A. J. Stewart (Eds.), *Perspectives on personality, Vol. 3.* London: Jessica Kingsley, Publishers.

Erickson, K. (1976). Loss of communicability at Buffalo Creek. *American Journal of Psychiatry, 133,* 302-305.

Fairbank, J. A., Hansen, D. J., & Fitterberg, J. M. (1991). Patterns of appraisal and coping across different stressor conditions among former prisoners of war with and without posttraumatic stress disorder. *Journal of Consulting and Clinical Psychology, 59,* 274-281.

Fairbank, J. A., & Nicholson, R. A. (1987). Theoretical and empirical issues in the treatment of posttraumatic stress disorder in Vietnam veterans. *Journal of Clinical Psychology, 43,* 44-55.

Fairbank, J., Schlenger, W., Caddell, J., & Woods, G. (in press). Post-traumatic stress disorder. In P. Sutker & H. Adams (Eds.), *Comprehensive handbook of psychopathology* (2nd edition).

Figley, C. R. (1988). A five-phase treatment of posttraumatic stress disorder in families. *Journal of Traumatic Stress, 1,* 127-141.

Fleming, S., & Robinson, P. (1991). The application of cognitive therapy to the bereaved. In T. Vallis, J. Howes, & P. Miller (Eds.) *The challenge of cognitive therapy: Application to nontraditional populations* (pp. 35-1158). New York: Plenum Press.

Foa, E., Rothbaum, O., Riggs, D., & Murdock, C. (1991). Treatment of posttraumatic stress disorder in rape victims: Comparision between cognitive-behavioral procedures and counseling. *Journal of Consulting and Clinical Psychology, 59,* 715-723.

Foa, E., Steketee, G., & Rothbaum, B. (1989). Behavioral/cognitive conceptualizations of post-traumatic stress disorder. *Behavior Therapy, 20,* 155-176.

Forfar, C. S. (1992). *Keane's MMPI-PTSD scale: A false positive analysis.* Unpublished doctoral dissertation, The University of Alabama Graduate School.

Foy, D. W., Osato, S. S., Houskamp, B. M., Neumann, D. A. (1992). Etiology of Posttraumatic Stress Disorder. In A. P. Goldstein, L. Krasner, & S. L. Garfield (Eds.). *Posttraumatic Stress Disorder* (pp. 28-49). New York: Macmillan Publishing Company.

Foy, D. W., Sipprelle, R. C., Rueger, D. B., & Carroll, E. M. (1984). Etiology of posttraumatic stress disorder in Vietnam veterans: Analysis of premilitary, military and combat exposure influences. *Journal of Consulting and Clinical Psychology, 52,* 79-87.

Frances, A., Pincus, R., Widiger, T., Wakefield, D., & First, M. (1990). DSM-IV: Work in progress. *The American Journal of Psychiatry, 147,* 1439-48.

Frank, R. G., Elliott, T. R., Corcoran, J. R., & Wonderlich, S. A. (1987). Depression after spinal cord injury: Is it necessary? *Clinical Psychology Review, 7,* 611-630.

Frankl, V. (1959). *Man's search for meaning.* New York: Simon and Schuster.

Frederick, C. J. (1985). Selected foci in the spectrum of posttraumatic stress disorders. In S. Murphy & J. Laube (Eds.), *Perspective on disaster recovery.* New York: Appleton-Century-Crofts.

Freedy, J. R., Shaw, D. L., Jarrell, M. P. & Masters, C. R. (1992). Towards an understanding of the psychological impact of natural disasters: An application of the conservation resources stress model. *Journal of Traumatic Stress, 5,* 441-444.

Fried, L., Stores, D., King, D., & Lodden, F. (1991). Diagnosis of illness presentations in the elderly. *Journal of the American Geriatrics Society, 39,* 117-123.

Friedman, J. J. (1988). Toward rational pharmacotherapy for posttraumatic stress disorder: An interim report. *The American Journal of Psychiatry, 145,* 281-285.

Garmezy, N., & Rutter, M. (1985). Acute reactions to stress. In Rutter, M. & Hersov, L. (Eds.), *Child psychiatry: Modern approaches* (2nd ed.) (pp. 152-176). Blackwell: Oxford Press.

Gelder, M. (1991). Psychological treatment for Anxiety Disorder: Adjustment Disorders with Anxious Mood, Generalized Anxiety Disorders, Panic Disorders, Agoraphobia, and Avoidant Personality. In W. Coryell and G. Winokur (Eds.), *The clinical management of anxiety disorders*. New York: Oxford University Press.

Gibbs, M. (1989). Factors in the victim that mediate between disaster and psychopathology: A review. *Journal of Traumatic Stress, 2*(4), 489-514.

Green, B. (1991). Evaluating the effects of disasters. *Psychological Assessment: A Journal of Consulting and Clinical Psychology, 3*, 538-546.

Green, B. L., Wilson, J. P., & Lindy, J. D. (1985). Conceptualizing posttraumatic stress disorder: A psychosocial framework. In C. R. Figley (Ed.), *Trauma and its wake: The study and treatment of posttraumatic stress disorder*. New York: Brunner/Mazel.

Heitler, S. (1990). *From conflict to resolution: Strategies for diagnosis and treatment of distressed individuals, couples, and families*. New York: Norton.

Helzer, J. E., Robins, L. N., & McEvoy, L. (1987). Posttraumatic stress disorder in the general population: Findings of the Epidemiologic Catchment Area Survey. *The New England Journal of Medicine, 317*, 1630-1634.

Helzer, J. E. (1984). The impact of combat on later alcohol use by Vietnam veterans. *Journal of Psychoactive Drugs, 16*, 193-191.

Hendin, H., & Haas, A. (1984). Combat adaptation of Vietnam veterans without posttraumatic stress disorders. *American Journal of Psychiatry, 141*(8), 956-960.

Herman, J. L. (1992). Complex PTSD: A syndrome in survivors of prolonged and repeated trauma. *Journal of Traumatic Stress, 5*, 377-392.

Hobfoll, S., Spielberger, C., Breznitz, S., Figley, C., Folkman, S., Lepper-Green, B., Meichenbaum, D., Milgram, A., Sandler, I., Sarason, I., & van der Kolk, B. (1991). War related stress: Addressing the stress of war and other traumatic events. *American Psychologist, 46*, 848-855.

Horowitz, M. (1976). *Stress response syndrome*. New York: Aranson.

Hyer, L., Boudewyns, P., O'Leary, W., & Harrison, W. R. (1987). Key determinants of the MMPI-PTSD subscale: Treatment considerations. *Journal of Clinical Psychology, 43*, 337-340.

Hyer, L., McCranie, E., & Peralme, L. (in press). Dual diagnosis PTSD and alcohol abuse. *PTSD Newsletter.*

Hyer, L., Woods, M., & Boudewyns, P. (1991). A three tier evaluation of posttraumatic stress disorder. *Journal of Traumatic Stress, 4*(2), 165-194.

Hyer, L., Woods, M., Bruno, R., & Boudewyns, P. (1989). Treatment outcome of Vietnam veterans with PTSD and constance of MCMI. *Journal of Clinical Psychology, 45,* 547-552.

Inman, D. J., Silver, S. M., & Doghramji, K. (1990). Sleep disturbance in post-traumatic stress disorder: A comparison with non-PTSD insomnia. *Journal of Traumatic Stress, 3*(3), 429-437.

Jelinek, J. M., & Williams, T. (1984). Post-traumatic stress disorder and substance abuse in Vietnam combat veterans: Treatment problems, strategies and recommendations. *Journal of Substance Abuse Treatment, 1,* 87-97.

Jones, J. C., & Barlow, D. H. (1990). The etiology of post-traumatic stress disorder. *Clinical Psychology Review, 10*(3), 299-328.

Kaylor, J. A., King, D. W., & King, L. A. (1987). Psychological effects of military service in Vietnam: A meta-analysis. *Psychological Bulletin, 102,* 257-271.

Keane, T. (1991). The epidemiology of post-traumatic stress disorder. Some comments and concerns. *PTSD Research Quarterly, 1,* 1-7.

Keane, T. (1988). Trauma, Workshop presented at Association for Advancement of Behavior Therapy Conference, New York.

Keane, T. M., Fairbank, J. A., Caddell, J. M., & Zimering, R. T. (1989). Implosive (flooding) therapy reduces symptoms of PTSD in Vietnam combat veterans. *Behavior Therapy, 20,* 245-260.

Keane, T. M., & Kolb, L. (1988). The importance of psychophysiological measures in the determination of PTSD among combat related victims. *VA Cooperative Studies Grant.*

Kendall, R. (1982). The choice of diagnostic criteria for biological research. *Archives of General Psychiatry, 39,* 1134-39.

King, D., & King. L. (1991). Validity issues in research on Vietnam veterans adjustment. *Psychological Bulletin, 109,* 1, 107-124.

Kolb, L. (1987). A neuropsychological hypothesis explaining post-traumatic stress disorders. *American Journal of Psychiatry, 144,* 989-995.

Kormos, H. R. (1978). The nature of combat stress. In C. P. Figley (Ed.), *Stress Disorders Among Vietnam Veterans* (pp. 3-22). New York: Brunner/ Mazel.

Kramer, M., & Kinney, L. (1988). Sleep patterns in trauma victims with disturbed dreaming. *Psychiatric Journal of the University of Ottawa, 13*(1), 12-16.

Kulka, R., Schlenger, W., Fairbank, J., Jordan, K., Hough, R. Marmar, C., & Weiss, D. (1991). Assessment of posttraumatic stress disorder in the community: Prospects and pitfalls from recent studies of Vietnam veterans. *Psychological Assessment: A Journal of Counsulting and Clinical Psychology, 3,* 547-560.

Kulka, R. A., Schlenger, W. E., Fairbank, J. A., Hough, R. L., Jordan, B. K., Marmar, C. R., & Weiss, D. S. (1988). *Executive Summary: Contractual report of findings from the National Vietnam Veterans Readjustment Study.* Research Triangle Park, NC: Research Triangle Institute.

Lang, P. J. (1979). A bio-informational theory of emotional imagery. *Psychophysiology, 16,* 495-512.

Lang, P. J. (1977). The psychophysiology of anxiety. In H. Akiskal (Ed.), *Psychiatric diagnosis: Explanation of biological criteria.* New York: Spectrum.

Laufer, R. S., Brett, E., & Gallops, M. S. (1985). Symptom patterns associated with posttraumatic stress disorder in Vietnam veterans exposed to war trauma. *American Journal of Psychiatry, 142,* 1304-1311.

Lifton, R. J., & Olson, E. (1976). The human meaning of total disaster: The Buffalo Creek experience. *Psychiatry, 39,* 1-18.

Lifton, R. J. (1979). *The broken connection.* New York: Simon & Schuster.

Litz, B., Keane, T., Fisher, L., Marx, B., & Manaco, V. (1992). Physical health complainats in combat-related post-traumatic stress disorder: A preliminary report. *Journal of Traumatic Stress, 5,* 131-142.

Loo, C. (1993). An integrative-sequential treatment model for post-traumatic stress disorder: A case study of the Japanese-American internment and redress. *Clinical Psychology Review, 13,* 89-117.

Lyons, J. A. (1991). Strategies for assessing the potential for positive adjusting following trauma. *Journal of Traumatic Stress, 4*(1), 113-122.

Lyons, J. A., & Keane, T. M. (1989). Implosive therapy for the treatment of combat-related PTSD. *Journal of Traumatic Stress, 2,* 137-152.

Lyons, J. A., Gerardi, R. J., Wolfe, J., & Keane, T. M. (1988). Multidimensional assessment of combat-related PTSD: Phenomenological, psychometric, and psychophysiological considerations. *Journal of Traumatic Stress, 2,* 137-152.

Mahoney, M. (1991). *Human change process: The scientific foundation of psychotherapy.* New York: Basic Books.

Mason, J., Kosten, T., Southwick, S., & Giller, E. (1990). The use of psychoendocrine strategies in post-traumatic stress disorder. *Journal of Applied Social Psychology, 20*(21), 1822-1846.

McDuff, D. R., & Johnson, J. L. (1992). Classification and characteristics of army stress casualties during operation desert storm. *Hospital and Community Psychiatry, 43,* 812-815.

McFall, M. E., Murburg, M., Smith, D. E., & Jensen, C. (1991). An analysis of the criteria used by VA clinicians to diagnose combat related PTSD. *Journal of Traumatic Stress, 4*(1), 123-136.

McFarlane, A. C. (1990). Vulnerability to posttraumatic stress disorder. In M. Wolf & A. Mosnaim (Eds.), *Posttraumatic stress disorder: Etiology, phenomenology, and treatment.* Washington, DC: American Psychiatric Press.

Meichenbaum, D., & Fitzpatrick, D. (1991). A constructivist narrative perspective of stress and coping: Stress inoculation applications. In L. Goldberger & S. Breznitz (Eds.), *Handbook of stress.* New York: Free Press.

Mellman, T. A., & Davis, G. C. (1985). Combat-related flashbacks in posttraumatic stress disorder: Phenomenology and similarity to panic attacks. *Journal of Clinical Psychiatry, 46*(9), 379-382.

Miller, N., & Gold, M. (1991). Treatment of the dually diagnosed alcoholic. In M. Gold & A. Slaby (Eds.), *Dual diagnosis in substance abuse,* (pp. 223-236). New York: Marcel Dekker.

Miller-Perrin, C., & Wurtele, S. (1990). Reactions to childhood sexual abuse: Implications for post-traumatic stress disorders. In C. Meek (Ed.), *Post-traumatic stress disorder: Assessment, differential diagnosis and forensic evaluation.* Sarasota, FL: Professional Resources.

Monroe, S. M., Bromet, E. J., Connell, M. M., & Steiner, S. C. (1986). Social support, life events, and depressive symptoms: A 1-year prospective study. *Journal of Consulting and Clinical Psychology, 54,* 424-431.

Nace, E. P. (1988). Posttraumatic stress disorder and substance abuse: Clinical issues. In M. Galanter (Ed.) *Recent developments in alcoholism, Volume 6.* New York: Plenum.

Nigro, G. & Neisser, V. (1983). Point of view of personal memories. *Cognitive Psychology, 15,* 467-482.

O'Donahue, W., & Elliott, A. (1992). The current status of posttraumatic stress disorder as a diagnostic category: Problems and proposals. *Journal of Traumatic Stress, 5,* 421-440.

Penk, W. E., & Allen, I. (1991). Clinical assessment of posttraumatic stress disorder (PTSD) among American minorities who served in Vietnam. *Journal of Traumatic Stress, 4*(1), 41-66.

Penk, W. E., & Robinowitz, R. (1987). Posttraumatic stress disorders among Vietnam Veterans: Introduction. *Journal of Clinical Psychology, 43,* 3-5.

Peralme, L. (1991). *Empirical and theoretical analysis of reexperiencing of trauma in combat veterans: A critical review.* Florida State University, Department of Psychology. Tallahassee.

Peterson, K., Prout, M., & Schwartz, R. (1991). *Posttraumatic stress disorder: A clinician's guide.* New York: Plenum.

Pitman, R. K., Orr, S. P., Forgue, D. F., Altman, B., deJong, J. B., & Herz, L. R. (1990). Psychophysiologic responses to combat imagery of Vietnam veterans with posttraumatic stress disorder versus other anxiety disorders. *Journal of Abnormal Psychology, 99,* 49-54.

Pitman, R. K., Orr, S. P., Forgue, D. F., deJong, J. B., & Claiborn, J. (1987). Psychophysiologic assessment of posttraumatic stress disorder imagery in Vietnam combat veterans. *Archives of General Psychiatry, 44,* 970-975.

Quarantelli, E. L. (1985). An assessment of conflicting views of mental health: The consequences of traumatic events. In C. R. Figley (Ed.), *Trauma and Its Wake: The Study and Treatment of Post-traumatic Stress Disorder* (pp. 173-215). New York: Brunner/Mazel.

Rangell, L. (1976). Discussion of the Buffalo Creek disaster: The course of psychic trauma. *American Journal of Psychiatry, 133*(3), 313-316.

Resnick, H. S., & Kilpatrick, D. G. (1992, August). Posttraumatic stress disorder: Empirical evaluation of the stressor criterion. Presented at the One Hundredth Annual Meeting of the American Psychological Association. Washington, DC.

Rothbaum, B. O., Foa, E. B., Riggs, D. S., Murdock, T., & Walsh, W. (1992). A prospective examination of post-traumatic stress disorder in rape victims. *Journal of Traumatic Stress, 5*, 455-476.

Rozynko, V., & Dondershine, H. (1991). Trauma focus group therapy for Vietnam veterans with PTSD. *Psychotherapy, 28*, Spring 157-161.

Sarason, B. R., Shearin, E. N., Pierce, G. R., & Sarason, I. G. (1987). Interrelations of social support measures: Theoretical and practical implications. *Journal of Personality and Social Psychology, 52*, 813-832.

Scaturo, D., & Hayman, P.(1992). The impact of combat trama across the family life cycle: Clinical considerations. *Journal of Tramatic Stress, 5*, 273-288.

Schlenger, W., Fairbank, J., & Caddell J. (1992). Predictors of emotional numbing problems in combat-related PTSD: Data from the National Vietnam Veterans Readjustment Study. Paper presented at the One Hundredth Annual Meeting of the American Psychological Association. Washington, DC.

Schnurr, P., Friedman, M., & Rosenberg, S. (1991, August). *Premilitary MMPI scores as predictors of combat-related PTSD symptomatology.* Poster proposal submitted to Division 18 for the annual meeting of the American Psychological Association.

Schwartz, E., & Kowalski, J. (1991). Posttraumatic stress disorder after a school shooting: Effects of symptom threshold selection and diagnosis by DSM-III, DSM-III-R, or Popinel DSM-IV. *American Journal of Psychiatry, 148*(5), 592-597.

Scurfield, R., Kenderline S., & Pollard, R. (1990). Inpatient treatment for war-related posttraumatic stress disorder: Initial findings on a longer term outcome study. *Journal of Traumatic Stress, 3*(2), 185-202.

Shafer, R. (1981). Narration in the psychoanalytic dialogue. In W. J. Mitchell (Ed.), *On narrative.* Chicago: University of Chicago Press.

Snow, B. R., Stellman, J. M., Stellman, S. D., & Sommer, J. F. (1988). Posttraumatic stress disorder among American legionnaires in relation to combat experience in Vietnam: Associated and contributing factors. *Environmental Research, 47*, 175-192.

Solomon, S. D., Gerrity, E. T., Muff, A. M. (1992). Efficacy of treatments for posttraumatic stress disorder. *Journal of the American Medical Association, 268,* 633-638.

Solomon, Z. (1986). Mobilizing social support networks in times of disaster. In C. Figley (Ed.), *Trauma and Its Wake, Vol. II* (pp. 232-263). New York: Brunner/Mazel.

Solomon, Z. (1990a). Does the war end when the shooting stops? The psychological toll of war. *Journal of Applied Social Psychology, 20*(21), 1733-1745.

Solomon, Z. (1990b). Back to the front: Recurrent exposure to combat stress and reactivation of posttraumatic stress disorder. In M. Wolfe & A. Nosnaim (Eds.), *Posttraumatic Stress Disorder: Etiology, Phenomenology and Treatment* (pp. 114-126). Washington, DC: American Psychiatric Press.

Solomon, Z., Benbenishty, R., & Mikulincer, M. (1991). *The contribution of wartime pre-war, and post-war factors to self-efficacy: A longitudinal study of combat stress reaction, 4,* 345-362.

Solomon, Z., Bleich, A., Shoham, S., Nardi, C., & Kotler, M. (1992). The "Koach" project for treatment of combat-related PTSD: Rationale, aims, and methodology. *Journal of Traumatic Stress, 5,* 175-194.

Solomon, Z., & Canino, G. (1990). Appropriateness of DSM-III-R criteria for posttraumatic stress disorder. *Comprehensive Psychiatry, 31*(37), 227-237.

Solursh, L. (1989). Combat addiction: Overview of implications in symptom maintenance and treatment planning. *Journal of Traumatic Stress, 3*(4), 451-462.

Ursano, R. J., Wheatley, R., Sledge, W., Rahe, A., & Carlson, E. (1986). Coping and recovery styles in the Vietnam era prisoner of war. *Journal of Nervous and Mental Disorders, 174,* 707-714.

van der Kolk, B., & Greenberg, M. (1987). The psychobiology of the trauma response: hyperarousal, constriction, and addiction to traumatic reexposure. In B. van der Kolk (Ed.), *Psychological Trauma.* Washington, DC: American Psychiatric Press.

ver Ellen, P., & van Kammen, D. (1990). The biological findings in post-traumatic stress disorder: A review. *Journal of Applied Social Psychology, 20,* 1789-1821.

Watson, C., Juba, M., Manifold, V., Kucala, T., & Anderson, P. (1991). The PTSD interview: Rationale, description, rehabilitating and concurrent validity of a DSM-III based technique. *Journal of Clinical Psychology, 47*(2), 179-188.

Weisaeth, L. (1984). Stress reactions in an industrial accident. Unpublished doctoral dissertation. Oslo, Norway.

Weisenberg, M., Solomon, Z., Schwarzwald, J., & Mikulincer, M. (1987). Assessing the severity of posttraumatic stress disorder: Relation between dichotomous and continuous measures. *Journal of Consulting and Clinical Psychology, 55,* 432-434.

Weiss, D. S., Marmar, C. R., Schlenger, W. E., Fairbank, J. A., Jordan, B. K., Hough, R. L., & Kulka, R. A. (1992). The prevalence of lifetime and partial post-traumatic stress disorder in Vietnam theater veterans. *Journal of Traumatic Stress, 5,* 365-376.

Wilson, J. (1989). *Trauma transformation and healing: An integrative approach to therapy, research and post-traumatic therapy.* New York: Brunner/Mazel.

Woolfolk, R. L., & Grady, D. A. (1988). Combat-related post-traumatic stress disorder: Patterns of symptomatology in help-seeking Vietnam veterans. *The Journal of Nervous and Mental Disease, 176,* 107-111.

Chapter **3**

THEORETICAL
PERSPECTIVES OF PTSD

"The map appears to be more real than the land." Lawrence

Jeffrey Jay (1991), quoting Langer in his book *Holocaust Testimonies*, wrote:

> The woman answers that, in order to function, she still must make "a sort of schizophrenic division. . . . a compartmentalization" between her memories of the camp and what she described as "so-called normal life." Decades after her release, the terrible reality of the camp is still there for her, always, a dark wash permeating her daily life. "It's more a view of the world," she says, "a total world view of extreme pessimism. . . (a sense) of really knowing the truth in a way that other people don't know it. And all the truth is harsh and impossible to really accept, and yet you have to go on and function. So it's a complete lack of faith in human beings, in all areas you know, whether it's politics or whatever; you hear one thing and you believe something else. I mean you say, 'Oh, well, I know the truth.'" (pp. 18-20)

The influence of excessive trauma is powerful. Exactly how trauma affects normal information processing of the person, altering basic propositions of life, is unknown. Why are some trauma victims affected and others not? In the previous chapter we learned the basics of chronic trauma, its nature, its complexity, its prevalence, and its reach. We argued that trauma pathology involves more than a stressor. In this chapter we address directly the transaction between the stressor and the person in a different way. First, we consider the role of the stressor, then the role of the person. Our attention is next turned to the formative theories and positions in this area. Theory provides the understanding of key person variables (schema and personality) and the treatment decisions. Theory provides the logical foresight that allows the clinician to highlight just the right data, making it coherent, rule bound, and usable.

STRESSOR

Those involved with trauma victims seesaw regarding the importance of objective versus subjective features of the stressor. Elliott and Eisdorfer (1982) attempted to cover the area by differentiating four types of stressful events; acute and time limited (e.g., medical emergencies), stressor sequence (one stress triggering another), chronic intermittent (repeated exposures as in continual combat), and chronic continual (a debilitating chronic medical illness). *A stressor is not a stressor.* Meek (1990) noted over 20 DSM-III-R diagnoses compete with PTSD as a result of a stressor and several others not related to stressors (e.g., malingering, somatization, factitious disorders, antisocial personality, etc.). Davidson and Foa (1991) challenged any firm conviction regarding Criterion A (the stressor) as "markedly distressing to almost anyone" (American Psychiatric Association, 1987, pp. 247-248). Specifically, these authors have raised three questions: (1) Which events are outside usual experience and markedly distressing to almost everyone? (2) Can PTSD result from events that are within usual human experience? (3) Since even the most extreme events do not lead to PTSD, what characteristics of the stressor give rise to PTSD? Again, these authors have highlighted selected subjective factors that argue for a more perceptual position of the stressor. They (Davidson & Foa, 1991) wrote:

With respect to subjective response by the victim, the most critical determinants appear to be perception of life threat, perceived physical violence, experience of extreme fear, and a sense of helplessness. The importance of subjective perception is illustrated by a report from Pilowsky (1985) who described the emergence of PTSD-like symptoms in accident victims whose perception of danger far exceeded the actual risk once the facts had been assembled. Higher levels of perceived threat (Green, Grace, & Gleser, 1985), suffering (Speed, Engdahl, Schwaratz, & Eberley, 1989), perceived low level of controllability (Frye & Stockton, 1982; Mikulincer & Solomon, 1988), and the use of denial and avoidance (Green et al., 1985; Solomon, Mikulincer, & Plum, 1988) may also exacerbate PTSD or increase its likelihood. (p. 347)

Complexity

Among many clinicians who treat trauma victims no doubt a latent wish breeds that the stressor be considered an epiphenomenon. This applies because no definition of trauma is acceptable. We are very poor evaluators of this problem. The unfortunate truth is that the clinician is rendered both a clinician and historian of the trauma event. The psychiatric disorder PTSD is the only one that possesses an etiologic factor in its criteria. Very few circumstances exist in nature for which a particular etiologic agent is both necessary and sufficient for its occurrence. What this appears to mean is the influence of a stressor will rarely be known with certainty. For example, Othmer and Othmer (1989) have noted that a stressor can be related to a psychiatric disorder in various ways: time mark (problems occur at the time of the stressor), magnifier (stressor increases already existing problems), consequence (stressor is *the* result of a psychiatric disorder), pathological thought content (stressor leads to ruminations), trigger (as in a personality disorder eliciting problems chronically), or cause (PTSD). While these options may be more than any clinician would want, the clinician should approach the influence of a stressor conservatively, that it is not a true cause but just a "memorable event" that coincides with the psychiatric disorder. To accept the event as the cause of a disorder requires more.

If a "most" central problem exists with the concept of stressor, the dilemma arises of whether to give more respect to its objective or subjective value. Is the "power" of the experience in the event or in the person? Objective criteria of the DSM-III-R for PTSD are clear: the stressor must be excessive. Of course, good reasons can be identified for this. We know, for example, higher levels of stress (e.g., combat) lead to higher levels of symptoms and that many trauma victims have multiple traumas. In an effort to explain the function of this process, a sizable body of literature on the components of stress has developed that is operating in PTSD. Green (1990), Sowder (1985), and Bolin (1985), among others, have outlined various components of the stressor (e.g., degree of terror, duration, unexpectedness, ratio of loss to resources, natural or man-made, etc.). More specific to combat, several studies have found not only degree of combat exposure, but also involvement in atrocities, death of noncombatants, and being wounded were predictive of poorer adjustment (Lyons, 1991). King and King (1991) noted that three conditions of war trauma (of Vietnam) need to be addressed: the Vietnam environment, general military combat, and special features like atrocities. Distinctive measures have been developed to particularize trauma, such as the *War Zone Stress* inventory (WZS) (Kulka, Schlenger, Fairbank, Hough, Jordan, Marmar, & Weiss, 1990) and the *Adult Trauma Inventory* (Saigh, 1989). The WZS, for example, identified six first-order factors—Exposure to Combat, Exposure to Abusive Violence, Related Conflicts, Deprivation, Loss of Meaning and Control, and one individual item, Prisoner of War. Also, researchers increasingly see the merits of a more generic breakdown of stress. Linn (1986), for example, measured 41 different stressors, emphasizing the stressor experience of the person by addressing issues related to the person: perceived stress, unexpectedness of events, perceived responsibility, and degree of social support. Finally, Norris (1990) argued that six dimensions are required for all traumatic stress reactions: tangible loss, scope (others involved), threat to life and physical integrity, blame (self or others), familiarity, and post-traumatic reactions (cognitions and emotions tied to the event). Note also needs to be taken that Axis IV in the current DSM specifies the severity of the psychosocial stressor. This stressor, however, is to have occurred within the past year and to have contributed to the onset, recurrence, or exacerbation of a disorder (either Axis I or Axis II).

One other popular psychiatric disorder also requires a stressor (milder). This is an Adjustment Disorder, a maladaptive reaction within three months (and less than 6 months) of a stressor (and the exclusion of other disorders). This condition is deceivingly complicated, sharing many symptoms (six types in DSM-III-R) with other disorders. In addition, recent evidence indicates that the Adjustment Disorder tends to be chronic and relapsing (Othmer & Othmer, 1989). The so-called adjustment reaction, then, may really be the result of a coping deficit—a personality disorder. The clinical task of screening for similar past problems and stressors along with the identification of the coping deficits should be routine clinical tasks.

Characteristics

Table 3.1 presents several event characteristics found to have potential for traumatization. The top part of this table meets the needs of the DSM (and this book): what happened, what did you do, and what did/does it mean. The bottom part includes other objective factors that possess varying degrees of importance depending on the person and PTSD symptom clusters. These involve important features like type, degree, duration, and level of expectedness of the stressor, the resources available, and the post-trauma supports. These elements are not purely "objective" as they infringe on the barriers of the person and are encoded in unique ways. They are often cumulative and interactive. Any effort to evaluate all of these would take a hearty clinician. The point is, however, that all can be important, each in its own way.

Both clinically and empirically, the study of the stressor can be a "hall of mirrors." Not only are their objective issues of objective versus subjective apportionment, sequential components, other pre- or post-traumas, and daily hassles, but also subjective ones—what type of person issues and how to measure these. At present only the area of combat-related trauma has been broken apart with any degree of "precision" or accuracy in both qualitative and quantitative

TABLE 3.1
Assessment Factors of the Stressor

I. Necessary Components:

   1. Description of Stressor
     -single/multiple
     -man made/natural
     -occurs alone or in a group
     -time frame

   2. Role
     -acts of omission or commission
     -active/passive

   3. Meaning to Victim
     -current and past views of event

II. Comprehensive Factors*

   1. Assessment of stress
     Scope of stressor broad or narrow, modifiability, degree of threat to life, room for appraisal versus universal perception of trauma, secondary stresses created by trauma, intrusiveness of memories of trauma

   2. Context of stress
     Time frame; pretrauma, trauma,
     immediate post-trauma, long-term post-
     trauma
       Environment
       Culture
       History

   3. Motivation/arousal
     Will to live, survival as overriding motive, arousal/ hyperarousal, interpretation of threat.

(continued)

TABLE 3.1 (continued)

4. Coping
   Type, range, flexibility, appropriateness, traitlike versus situation-specific, problem versus emotion-focused

5. Process
   Time period as well as transaction with others

6. Coping resources
   Ego-strength, physical stamina, social supports, chance factors

7. Outcomes
   Physical health, mental health, personality, coping, achievements, social functioning, adjustment of aging

From Kahana, Kahana, Harel, & Rosner (1988). Reprinted by permission.

ways. Regarding this whole issue, Sutker, Uddo-Crane, and Allain (1991) stated:

> Available technologies for assessment of the stressor are also limited by failure to distinguish discrete, continuous, sequential, and multiple stressors, lack of relevance to an array of stressors from common to extraordinary events, meager attention to quantifying the stressor from objective and personalistic perspectives, and inadequate methodology for corroborating self-reported information. Additionally, most measures do not distinguish positive and negative events, or provide for positive event reporting, and stressor and response properties may be confounded by summary measures. (p. 523)

Clinical Truce

The question of the importance of the stressor will not easily resolve itself. It must be addressed, if only to gather "facts" about pre/post differences and the basic features of the stressor experience. In this instance, the argument is that a clinical truce be declared on the importance and place of the stressor within the victim. Ultimately a balance is required, one that shows respect to all parties, but most especially to the position of the person in this equation. On the importance of this component, Kasl (1990) wrote:

> The concept of 'trauma' may not be needed. What is needed, instead, is a detailed characterization of the exposure— in terms of both continuous dimensions and nominal scale characteristics—for each individual. A multivariate analysis of the additive and interactive influences of the various dimensions of exposures on a particular outcome—together with an analysis of vulnerability factors—will adequately describe the pathogenic components of the exposure. (p. 1656)

A refined understanding of how a stressor stresses awaits clarification. Meek (1990) noted that growing evidence exists that individuals with personality disorders are susceptible to stress-related disorders. She indicated that previous stress is likely to potentiate the effects of current stress. Evidence also is mounting that the accumulation of stressors along with pre-existing mental disorders (or personality factors) may predispose individuals to PTSD reactions or problems. Barlow (1988) in addition noted the possibility of a physiological resistance to stress, allowing some individuals to function well. Kolb (1986) identified the other side of the coin, neurological change (resulting from stress). Litz, Penk, Gerardi, and Keane (1991) considered that victims who seek help may have multiple traumas in their lives both before and after the index trauma event. In fact, the presence of a continuous severe trauma may potentiate person variables that initiate the occurrence of other trauma, or worse, victims may become victimizers. Finally, one study (an analog investigation) was even conducted to evaluate whether professionals could detect false reports of combat experience (Stegman & Blanford, 1992). The sample consisted of 312 mental health professionals who rated trauma scripts, some bogus. Results showed that most professionals were likely to judge false self reports as traumatic and did not question their veracity. A consensus on exactly what constitutes a trauma is lacking.

Finally, one other insidious twist on the stressor-person interaction is present. Reactions may not be just a function of the physical presence of the stressor and the information processing of the person of the victim. The duration of the traumatic stressor may be extended beyond its physical life. Baum, O'Keefe, and Davidson (1990) noted that this occurs as a function of:

> ...a person by situation interaction in which information processing and coping variables interact with the stressor to determine if and when reexperience may occur. When it does, and intrusive imagery or secondary events keep the trauma alive, chronic stress response may persist and habituation may not occur because cognitive processing may slightly alter each repetition or spacing of the event such that appropriate recovery is not possible. Regardless, these variables could cause a persistent response. Extreme cases of such chronic stress may be represented by victims suffering from post-traumatic stress syndromes. (p. 1652)

Truly, this is a frightening aspect of reexperiencing and a "gift that keeps on giving."

Interestingly, more than meets the eye does appear from a person perspective also. In Wilson's evaluation of the effects of person, combat, and environmental stress on symptom levels of PTSD (Wilson & Prabucki, 1989), an important finding turned up. The measure that was most associated with PTSD symptoms was environmental stress (stress sensitivity). This was an orthogonal measure of the entire stressor experience, assessing the degree to which an individual is sensitive to stress. This index was not related to any particular personality type or to any particular symptom. Therefore, the index is a general predispositional vulnerability factor of the person. Only time will tell how much this variable actually is part of the PTSD equation. Also, just as certain factors increase vulnerability, other factors increase resilience. These largely involve special training or preparedness, as well as a host of background factors related to higher functioning and health.

For more than three decades an extensive literature has itemized how everyday life stressors influences people. Explanatory models have exercised this construct in all possible ways: predictor, modifier, buffer, and outcome. This emphasis does not exist for extreme stressors, however. At present, the best we have is a hypothesis that a transaction between the person and stressor leads to a positive or negative outcome. This is certainly more appealing than a view of the stressor acting on its own or one that holds that person variables alone predict exposure to traumatic events rather than predict response to a stressor event (Dohrenwend & Shrout, 1985). Fortunately, in an increasing way, the subjective argument is gaining appeal in clinical use.

A low correlation exists between the amount and type of stress and any resulting psychopathology. Trauma is trauma because of its suddenness, its excess, and its ability to disrupt normal coping. Ultimately, trauma is trauma because the individual believes it to be so. It becomes "the" narrative of the person, unfolding in very special and unique ways. This narrative, unsympathetic and unyielding, becomes the person's story, the person's only internal stimulus that lives on.

For too long the importance of the stressor, its measurement and objectification, has held sway. Now, a "fair hearing" of all sides will allow for a greater understanding of the stressor and of the important person features, positive and negative coping, the active appraisal process, and the overall meaning that went into the making of the event. The balance struck, then, appreciates the shattering experience as well as the shattered person. The measurement and importance of the stressor justifies the DSM and a nomothetic understanding of the trauma experience. The measurement and importance of the person justify what is important in treatment.

WHITHER PERSONALITY?

The classification of most psychiatric disorders following trauma is intimately related to the role of personality or predisposing factors in the etiology of the stress responses. Several reasons can be listed, however, as to why this is not typically done. Table 3.2 outlines many of these. From the perspectives of the psychiatric classification system, confusion of the person's resilience or vulnerability, methodological problems, and political or secondary gain issues, the influence of personality in the determination of trauma has not received the attention other variables have. However, an increasing number of positions and data suggest the importance of the role of personality. The "distinct linear dose-relationship" (Snow, Stellman, Stellman, & Sommer, 1988) between level of trauma (e.g., combat) and PTSD may exist, but it does not speak to the strength of the relationship or, for that matter, the pattern of problems that result. Something else is involved. In fact, by studying data from a variety of trauma stressors, one would conclude that, even when extreme, only one-half the population develops PTSD (McFarlane, 1990). No one stressor necessarily leads to the disorder PTSD. Many authors have noted that the role of combat in PTSD formation is not large in other cultures (e.g., Andrews, Christensen, & Hadzi-Pavolovic, 1985). As if to set this issue straight, McFarlane (1990) noted:

> Thus the management of patients with PTSD requires a delicate balance between acknowledging the central role of the trauma in causing the intrusive thinking and avoidance and the part played by vulnerability factors in determining the meaning of the trauma and pattern of disordered mood and arousal. The consideration of premorbid vulnerability factors does not mean that the clinician either blames the patient or minimizes the importance of the trauma in molding the clinical picture. (p. 16)

Historically, when the effects of stress were first evaluated after WWII, the importance of premorbid problems was the prevailing view. Through the decades of the 70s and 80s, however, this position fell into disfavor. Only recently has a repositioning of views occurred. Reasons for these juxtaposing views are many, including a confluence of current science and the politics of the day. Maybe previous stress magnifies current stress. Maybe some personalities are "weaker" or more vulnerable than others. Nolen-Holksema and Morrow (1991), for example, documented that among earthquake victims the variables, elevated pre-depression levels *and* greater stressor intensity, were both predictive of greater depression and post-

TABLE 3.2
Variables that Confuse the Role of Personality in Formation
of PTSD Problems

Psychiatric History
  Role of psychoanalysis minimizes importance of adulthood variables (stressors).
  Early DSM's separated development of acute symptoms from personality patterns.
  Clarification of role of "normal" response to extreme trauma is cloudy.
  Confusion between levels of psychopathology (partial versus full) in DSM.
  Bias in criteria of PTSD-e.g. Category C mandates that avoidant personality characteristics be picked up.

Role of Individual Vulnerability
  Family history of psychiatric disorder especially Anxiety Disorders.
  Confusion of pre-trauma, trauma or post-trauma variables.
  Mental state or behavior at time of trauma.
    Stressor potentiators
    Participation in atrocity
    Stressor reaction at time of trauma
    Unexpectedness of event
    Intensity/direction of event
  Personal resilience
  Variance explained by various person factors vacillates (i.e., age, education, SES, previous war problems, etc.)

Methodology of Studies
  Unreliable or invalid instruments
  Recollections of trauma distorted (retrospective bias)
  Biased samples—often highly pathological as a result of trauma or not screened prior to trauma
  Assessment of marker variables that are the same ones used as screening variables.

Secondary Gains
  Compensation or financial agenda
  Political agendas
  Professional biases

traumatic stress symptoms at 10 days and seven weeks post trauma. Also, evidence exists that PTSD sufferers who have "more problems" pre-trauma are likely to have more problems post-trauma (perhaps being drawn to trauma) and perhaps may be more resistant to treatment (Lyons, 1991). In addition, previous victimization may lead to higher levels of continued victimization, especially where child or sexual abuse is concerned.

Competing Hypotheses

Two causal hypotheses have been offered to explain postwar maladjustment problems among combat veterans. The first, which can be labeled the *"personal characteristics" hypothesis,* maintains that persistent adverse psychological reactions following exposure to extreme trauma like combat are largely symptomatic manifestations of pre-existing social maladjustment and/or personality psychopathology (e.g., Hendin, Pollinger-Haas, Singer, Gold, Trigos, & Ulman, 1983; Worthington, 1978). Recently too, McFall, MacKay, and Donovan (1992) demonstrated that PTSD symptomatology was more predictive of substance abuse (among combat veterans) than was combat exposure. Combat, therefore, was less significant than clusters of symptoms were (presumably "person" influenced). The second hypothesis, which can be labeled the *"extreme event" argument,* (presumably "person" influenced) asserts that postwar maladjustment is largely a consequence of the nature of combat as an environmental stressor. According to this view, combat trauma, for example, represents an extraordinary stressor which is sufficiently traumatic to cause psychological readjustment problems irrespective of individual differences in premilitary life experiences (Figley, 1978).

Over the past decade, a growing body of research has examined variables related to both models in attempting to understand the development of PTSD among Vietnam combat veterans. Foy, Carroll, and Donahoe (1987) reviewed 12 studies that retrospectively examined both premilitary and military etiologic factors in combat-related PTSD among Vietnam veterans. That review, as well as other reviews (Boyle, Decoufle, & O'Brien, 1989; Kaylor, King, & King, 1987) and more recently published studies (Kulka et al., 1990; Resnick, Veronen, & Saunders, 1988; Snow et al., 1988; True, Goldberg, & Eisen, 1988) have consistently found that a diagnosis of PTSD and/or PTSD symptom intensity is most strongly associated with indices of high levels of exposure to combat and other war-zone stressors in Vietnam. In contrast, measures of various premilitary characteristics, including premilitary psychosocial adjustment, alcohol and drug problems, and family stability, have been found to exhibit no association or to be inconsistently or only weakly associated with PTSD in both clinical and nonclinical samples of Vietnam veterans. These findings have led some investigators to favor the extreme event argument as a model for explaining the origins of PTSD among Vietnam combat veterans, and to minimize the etiologic role of premilitary social and personality characteristics (Snow et al., 1988).

PERSON/EVENT MODEL

Increasingly, however, several researchers have argued for the position that personality factors predispose one to the development of PTSD (Andreasen & Noyes, 1972; Ettedgui & Bridges, 1985; McFarlane, 1988; Scrignar, 1984; Sudak, Martin, Corradi, & Gold, 1984; Wilson & Kraus, 1982; van der Kolk, 1987). As none of these were prospective studies, all that can be concluded is that negative personality changes have resulted some time after PTSD or that selected premorbid variables correlate with this disorder. Reich (1990) noted that one common denominator is present—PTSD subjects have had stability and fairness of their world so disrupted that each victim must reorganize the sense of self to adjust to the resulting emotional upheaval. He also laid the issue bare by exposing politics that may enter into the clinician's position; those who do not want to "blame the victim" tend to run from any conclusion that personality may be implicated in PTSD functions, and those who believe PTSD victims "would have had emotional problems anyway" tend to see it otherwise. Nonetheless, he (Reich, 1990) concluded:

> One observation seems fairly clear. Patients who suffer from PTSD, especially if it is chronic, will have some tendency toward deleterious personality change. The nature of this change, although not completely clear, may have a relationship to the meaning placed on the traumatic event

by the individual, although some could also be the deleterious effects of chronic illness." (p. 77)

The evidence for personality to predispose toward PTSD is fragmentary, but certainly shows a trend in a positive direction. Skilled clinicians point out that the meaning of a traumatic event is certainly involved in the pathogenesis of PTSD, and it is hard to believe that personality would not interact with the attribution of meaning. (p. 77)

This position prosecutes for a more comprehensive multicausal, etiologic model. Recently, Emery, Emery, Shama, Quiana, and Jassani (1991) conceived of the predisposition to PTSD along a continuum. At one end are intra-individual psychopathological factors (usually premorbid personality problems); in the middle are preexisting traits or characteristics considered within the range of normal (where a regression may occur due to stress); and at the other end are existing extra-individual factors, usually stressors in the family of origin. This "typology" is helpful because it represents the research thinking in predisposing person factors for PTSD. (The authors found support for the third option, extra-individual factors, where fully 90% of the PTSD group experienced significant stress compared to 20% of non-PTSD subjects.)

Again arguing for perspective, Wilson (1989) wrote:

Research in this area should attempt to identify the complex relationships between relevant dispositional and situation variables as they influence post-traumatic adaptation. Unfortunately, these complex interactional approaches have not, for the most part, been widely used in research paradigms on PTSD. For a variety of reasons many investigators have examined the relationship between stress and psychopathology through bivariate correlational procedures or simple group comparisons which do not tease out the more complex interactions between variables. Moreover, studies that use multivariate statistical procedures have primarily emphasized the main effects of important independent variables while giving less attention to interactive effects. Further, researchers have often pointed to studies that have found no relationship between dispositional variables and post-traumatic psychological problems to support interpretations that pre-trauma personality is unrelated to post-traumatic adaptation. However, there need not be a strong main effect of dispositional attributes for these variables to have an impact on psychosocial adaptation. Understanding the effects of pre-trauma disposition is quite likely to involve experimental designs that include various interactions between personality variables and severity of different types of stressors as added independent variables. (pp. 77-78)

A useful model which incorporates this synthetic view is the *person/event interaction model*. In this model, individual variability in response to extreme life events is viewed as a function of the interaction of both internal and external factors (Keane, 1989). This model assumes that extreme events may elicit significant psychological distress in everyone exposed, but, depending on the magnitude (e.g., intensity, duration) of the event and the individual's threshold for tolerating it, adverse reactions will either be maintained within tolerable limits or lead to an episode of disorder (Wilson, 1989). Accordingly, as the degree and intensity of extreme stress increase, the influence of personal characteristics in determining response diminishes in importance, "until extreme degrees of stress produce symptoms of psychologic disability in all who are exposed to them" (Hocking, 1970, p. 23). Conversely, at lower levels of stressor magnitude, "individual characteristics contribute to an understanding of why some people become ill and others do not" (Rabkin & Struening, 1976, p. 1018).

A few published studies have directly assessed the validity of this interactive or threshold model for understanding the etiology of PTSD among Vietnam combat veterans. Two studies serve as markers for different findings. In a large sample of U.S. Army enlisted men returning from Vietnam in 1971, Helzer (1981) attempted to assess the relative influence of various pre-service personal characteristics on current depressive symptoms at varying levels of combat exposure. Based on the interactive model, he hypothesized that antecedent factors would be less predictive under conditions of extreme stress. The results, however, indicated the exact reverse. At low levels of combat exposure, prevalence of depressive symptoms did not significantly differ between those with and without antecedent factors; whereas, at high levels of combat exposure, presence of certain antecedent factors (failure to graduate from high school, drug and alcohol use, parental arrest) did significantly predict depression—a result completely inconsistent with the threshold model. Helzer (1981) interpreted this finding as suggesting "a synergistic effect rather than an attenuation of predisposition in extreme situations" (p. 127).

Low Stress, High Influence

In a later replication study, Boulanger and Kadushin (1986) tested Helzer's "synergistic" hypothesis in a nationwide sample of 1,001 Vietnam veterans and nonveterans. The percentage of men with current PTSD-related stress reactions was compared by level of exposure to combat in Vietnam (no combat, low combat, high combat) in conjunction with level of stability in the family of origin (least stable, average, most stable). The composite index of family stability included variables "that would contribute toward a possibly unstable and unsupportive atmosphere in the family of origin, such as poverty, the separation from or death of the parents, the number of times the family moved during a given period (high school), and whether the father was frequently unemployed" (Boulanger & Kadushin, 1986, p. 41). In complete contrast to Helzer's findings, the predisposing factor of level of family stability was found to be unrelated to the prevalence of current stress reactions at *high levels of combat exposure*. That is, under the most extreme conditions, men from the most stable families were just as likely to exhibit such symptoms as men from the least stable family backgrounds. At low levels of combat exposure, however, men from the most stable families remained relatively free of stress reactions; whereas, men from less stable families were significantly more likely to report current stress reactions. Consistent with the threshold model Boulanger and Kadushin interpreted these results as indicating that under low or moderately stressful conditions predisposing factors play a role in producing PTSD-related stress reactions, but that "in the most extreme conditions everyone, even the least susceptible, is at risk to develop PTSD" (Boulanger & Kadushin, 1986, p. 50). Two additional studies (Foy et al., 1987; McCranie, Hyer, Boudewyns, & Woods, 1991) have recently confirmed these findings and advocated the person/event interaction or threshold model of PTSD etiology.

The person/event interaction model conforms to beliefs of many clinicians regarding the effect of stressors. Perhaps the results of a recent study by Green, Grace, Lindy, Gleser, and Leonard (1990) best summate the relative contribution of "causative" variables on PTSD: Premilitary factors accounted for 9%, military for 19%, and post-military for 12%. No personality measures were used, however. All three variables influence PTSD. Any position holding that trauma (combat) alone is causative of PTSD problems, or one holding that premorbid factors alone dictate symptoms, does not adequately reflect the facts. A more complete understanding of the unique adaptation to trauma involves an appreciation of known stressor variables along with person characteristics. Each person then creates his/her own representational models of the world, and the individual is the one who ultimately determines whether the experience is traumatic and, if so, how this is to be played out. Also logical is that, given a stressor of sufficient type and intensity, the individual contribution towards any disorder is lessened. Of course, the possibility exits that the person possesses a stress sensitivity—a generic predispositional vulnerability to stress (Wilson & Prabucki,1989). (As noted earlier, this variable does not correlate with any specific stressor or pattern of symptions.) The influence of the person, however, remains strong in the expression and course of trauma. This is central to the person/event interaction model.

THEORIES

An architectonic sense of larger issues allows for a meaningful sculpting of specialized knowledge. We borrow from several "larger" theories, as well as several specific to PTSD issues. The "larger" theories start with Adler, whose ideas have textured our reality in this and the next two chapters. Adler's concepts of care (holistic synthesis), individuality, and practicality (the psychology of use), are especially important. His views of the person are sharpened by the more nomothetic, theory-driven ideas of Millon (1969, 1981, 1983), as well as cognitive behavioral theory (CBT). Chiefly, these include the ideas of Beck (Beck & Freeman, 1990), Young (1990), and Safran and Segal (1990). Others include the personality work of Horowitz (Horowitz, Marmar, Krupnick, Wilner, Kaltreider, & Wallerstein, 1984) along with the constructionist self theory of McCann and Pearlman (1990), and information processing ideas of Foa (Foa, Steketee, & Rothbaum, 1989).

The concept of trauma evolved in psychiatry through the lens of psychoanalysis. Initially, trauma was associated with an actual external threat, changed in concept to an internal conflict or fantasy, and evolved to a compromise between internal and external events (at least for combat stresses). The idea was simple: too much stress overloaded the psychic apparatus, and the ego was overwhelmed. A "stronger" person, whose coping abilities or ego strengths were intact, would prevent the stimulus barrier and defense of repression, the two key modulators of trauma, from dissolution. For the weaker person, the result was a repetition compulsion which reactivated the trauma memory (but the victim was unknowing or amnestic).

In the last two decades, however, several other theories have helped to describe PTSD. These include behavioral (Keane, Wolfe, & Taylor, 1987; Kilpatrick, Veronen, & Resick, 1979), learned helplessness (Seligman, 1975), biological (e.g., Kolb 1983, 1984, 1988; van der Kolk, 1988), updated intrapsychic (e.g., Krystal, 1978), psychosocial (e.g., Lifton, 1979), self (e.g., Kohut, 1977; McCann & Pearlman, 1990; Mahoney, 1991), psychodynamic (e.g., Horowitz, 1990; Brende, 1983; Brende & McCann, 1984), and information processing (e.g., Chemtob, Roitblat, Hamada, Carlson, & Twentyman, 1988; Litz & Keane, 1989). Table 3.3 encapsulates many of these (plus others) important in the work on trauma victims. From this array, several will be described. (The work of Adler and Millon are presented in later chapters.) Several were chosen because of their significance in an understanding of trauma and their influence on the formulation of person variables, especially schema. They include behavioral theory and information processing along with the unique work emphasizing schemas by McCann and Pearlman (1990) (constructionist). Biological "theories" are also briefly addressed. Next, the CBT positions of Beck and Freeman are specially considered, as these authors emphasize the importance of both schema and personality. If trauma is anything, it is a shattering of the person. In the last section, this concept will be addressed as we borrow heavily from the work of Benyakar, Kutz, Dasberg, and Stern (1989), Janoff-Bulman (1985, 1989), and Epstein (1990).

(continued on page 114)

TABLE 3.3
Theoretical Positions

I. Learning Theory

Mowrer's two-factor theory as updated by Keane et al. (1985). Important constructs involve classical and instrumental conditioning as well as higher order conditioning and stimulus generalization. Learned helplessness also applies.

Rx: Desensitization or Flooding (Direct Therapeutic Exposure).

II. Information Processing

Information processing emphasizes impact of trauma on cognitive processing. Horowitz (1986b) and Foa et al. (1989) focus on disrupted meaning patterns. Also Janoff-Bulman (1985) and Epstein (1985) describe disequilibrium of world assumptions.

Rx: Horowitz model emphasizes titration of numbing/intrusion dynamic to complete information processing of trauma memory. Psychic overload is integrated.

III. Constructionism

McCann and Pearlman (1990) integrate clinical insight of object relations theory, self psychology and cognitive theory, and emphasize the construction-of-reality position of schemas (psychological or cognitive needs) as disrupted during trauma. As a function of the bruised schema, the social network and the person's ego/self skills, the trauma infects the system.

Rx: Schema balancing and trauma integration.

IV. Biological

Basic psychophysiological alterations (CER's) associated with trauma generalize to other cues and may become neurologically altering (Kolb, 1988). Biogenic markers of hyperarousal result in a dysynchrony of electrochemical systems. Norephinephine depletion especially can "cause" an analgesic response to subsequent stressors and "addiction to trauma" (van der Kolk, 1987).

Rx: Varies from exposure to psychopharmocologic agents.

(continued)

TABLE 3.3 (continued)

V. Psychodynamic

Classical analytic theory emphasizes the stimulus barrier broken by the stressor and a repetition compulsion to act out conflict. Object relations or self psychology emphasize unhealthy self objects and fragmentation of identity. Krystal (1978), Lifton (1976, 1979), and Brende (1983) described the catastrophic, symbolized or fragmented self pathology that extreme trauma produces.

Rx: Intrapsychic healing or transformation of the self by uncovering trauma memories.

VI. Psychosocial

Trauma cannot be integrated due to failure of ego defenses. Degree or level of trauma and lack of social support overcome individual defenses. A trauma response develops (Wilson & Krauss, 1982). Most affected among Vietnam veterans are the identity and past identity stages of psychosocial development (Wilson, 1989). Also, formative modes of thinking/symbolizing are altered (Lifton, 1976).

Rx: Resolution of psychosocial stages or reduction in disintegration of psychosocial stages.

VII. Ecosystem

Comprehensive PTSD paradigm elaborates on Green, Wilson, & Lindy (1985) psychosocial model. The experience of trauma directly influences cognitive processing, the nature of the environmental response, and nonconscious conditioning. Based on multiple appraisals, pretrauma strengths/weaknesses, and disruption of core schemas, the trauma victim adapts or maladapts. Also, a cybernetic circuit is set in motion which amplifies (or reduces) typical trauma patterns (e.g., numbing/contusion) (Peterson, Prout, & Schwartz, 1991).

Rx: Multimodal approach based on education and commitment.

Learning Theory

In recent years, the paradigm that has provided the most incentive for PTSD research and conceptual clarity is learning theory, chiefly the position of Mowrer (1960) as elaborated by Keane (Keane, Zimering, and Caddell, 1985). Mowrer's two-factor learning theory emphasizes the importance of both classical and instrumental learning in the development of psychopathology. The development of PTSD symptoms is thought to parallel the acquisition of classically conditioned psychological and behavioral fear responses. Traumatic combat stimuli act as unconditioned aversive stimuli that reflexively elicit extreme levels of automatic distress in the surviving individual (Fairbank & Keane, 1982). From a neurological perspective, hypersensitivity exists perhaps as a result of excessive involvement with the septal-hippocampal complex, adrenergic hypersensitivity, or a general heightened neurological sensitivity (Kolb, 1986). This hypersensitivity is believed to be potentially self-perpetuating and self-exacerbating and to be the substratum of a host of emotional and behavioral problems.

Psychophysiologically, the fact that PTSD combat veterans show heightened arousal has been proven. Several recent studies (e.g., Blanchard, Kolb, Pallmeyer, & Gerardi, 1982; Boudewyns & Hyer, 1990; Gerardi, Blanchard, & Kolb, 1989; Pitman, Orr, Forgue, de Jong, & Claiborn, 1987) found that PTSD combat veterans respond with heightened and excessive patterns of arousal when compared to matched groups that control for PTSD combat exposure in response to both generic (combat sites and sounds) or idiosyncratic (imaginal flooding of stressor) stimuli. Typically, patients are exposed to a variety of PTSD related stimuli as well as to non-PTSD related stimuli in a psychophysiological laboratory, while relevant physiological measures are administered. Heart rate, especially, has been shown to be a consistent and reliable measure in the identification of PTSD victims. Results have shown that psychophysiological responses are excessive and highly resistant to extinction (Boudewyns & Hyer, 1990). To date, flooding or direct therapeutic exposure has been one of only a few methods that have been mildly effective with PTSD patients (Keane, Fairbank, Caddell, & Zimering, 1989; Boudewyns & Hyer, 1990). (See chapter 11.)

The second factor of Mowrer's two-factor learning theory is instrumental learning: an organism will engage in whatever behavior necessary to avoid or escape exposure to conditional (CS) and unconditional (UCS) aversive stimuli. Escape and avoidance are reinforced by arousal or anxiety reduction and, hence, the subject is likely to attempt to avoid exposure to conditioned cues, i.e., cues associated in time and space with the unconditioned aversive stimuli. This avoidance tends to maintain the status quo, because it prevents deconditioning of aversive arousal through exposure to the now harmless CS complex (Fairbank & Nicholson, 1987). A PTSD sufferer, for example, often avoids sudden loud noises similar to those that were experienced in combat. Perhaps this explains why treatment models of PTSD patients often include reexamining and reexperiencing Vietnam experiences (desensitizing and preventing avoidance) in "rap" groups that seem to offer relief or release from hyperarousal.

Mowrer's theory represents an appealing paradigm in the formulation of PTSD. This disorder can actually be considered a maladaptation of approach/avoidance cycling of various conditioned and unconditioned stimuli representing trauma. Psychophysiological hyperarousal can be monitored during these vacillations. Treatment under this model primarily involves exposure. In the previous chapter we discussed the paucity of research on outcome, but noted that exposure did help some combat veterans. In addition to this overall "approach," several other learning methods (avoidance techniques) have been used. These entail methods that allow for distraction or escape and will be considered in later chapters. Information on their efficacy, however, is sketchy.

Finally, Keane and colleagues (Keane, Fairbank, Caddell, Zimering, & Bender, 1985) accounted for a number of problems in the speculation of PTSD by use of the two-factor theory. This group adapted this model by noting the importance of serial conditioned stimuli (many trauma cues), higher order conditioning and stimulus generalization (trauma cues are widespread and resistant to extinction), and even cognitions (as potential conditional stimuli). They acknowledged that it was wanting in its account of the persistence of avoidance and the lack of habituation of the victim. Also this group noted that PTSD is an Anxiety Disorder, but many of the principles of other Anxiety Disorders do not apply. The behavioral approach provides a tempting template to develop further theory but does not fully explain PTSD.

In effect, PTSD can be construed as a form of state-dependent learning, where "influences" are generated both internally and externally. In chronic situations, permanent psychobiological changes may result. Wilson and Walker (1989) extended learning theory and identified its interface biologically; the neurological program of PTSD is askew and the on and off switches of the ergotropic (sympathetic discharge) and trophotropic (parasympathetic discharge) subsystems, catecholamine and cholinergic secretions, neuropeptides (opiates), and their interaction in the brain are inadequate. Figure 3.1 portrays this. A model of inescapable shock and conditioned response depicts the neurophysiological processes of the intrusion cycle of PTSD leading to an avoidance/numbing reaction (Wilson, 1989). These latter reactions become elaborate defenses—overcontrol, isolation, and numbing—that deaden life. This biphasic response of the trauma victim cyclically alternates as the person struggles through life. Patterns become consistent, pervasive, and maladaptive. In fact, they *are a* whole mind-body operation. More of this is discussed under the biological section discussed later in this chapter.

Information Processing

If primary and secondary conditioning reinforce PTSD patterns, then other research during the decade of the 80s attempted to access and highlight cognitive processes of the disorder. The focus has been the isolation of key "structures" in the formation of information, their disaggregation, and eventually their intervention. Experiences are processed at sensory, perceptual, and cognitive levels. Horowitz (1990), Foa and Kozak (1991), Chemtob et al. (1988) and Litz and Keane (1989) have elaborated on information processing of PTSD based loosely on Lang's (1979) analysis of fear structures. Lang held that fear is stored as a network in memory and is essentially a program to escape danger. This network contained fear-relevant stimuli, responses (verbal, behavioral, psychological), and "meaning" information about the stimuli

Increased Autonomic Arousal
   Increased NE turnover
   Increased plasma catecholamine levels
   Depletion of brain NE
   Enhanced memory retention

PROLONGED   REPEATED

Catecholamine Use Exceeds Synthesis
   Depletion of Norepinephrine
      Decreased motivation
      Decreased functioning
      Decreased memory storage
   Depletion of Dopamine
      Decreased readiness to approach novel stimuli
   Decreased Level of Serotonin
      Anxiety
      Increased sensitivity to pain
      Enhanced reaction to incoming stimuli
Increased Levels of Acetylcholine
   May include dissociation
Escape deficits

Chronic Noradrenergic Hypersensitivity
   All-or-None Phenomena
   Decreased Tolerance for Arousal
      Hyperalert
      Difficulty modulating affect
      Re-experiencing
      Subjective sense of loss of control
      Compensatory symptoms:
         Estrangement
         Detachment
         Emotional constriction

Figure 3.1. Exposure to inescapable and unavoidable aversive events. From Wilson (1989). Used with permission.

and response data. The Foa group further maintained that the fear stimuli is not a memory and posited that PTSD is different from any other Anxiety Disorder because of the *intensity* of the response elements that produced psychophysiological arousal, the *size* of the fear structure (its generalizability), and the ready *accessibility* of the trauma-related network. Trauma violates assumptions and situations that previously were considered safe. Now these become cues for danger. As such, boundaries between safety and danger are blurred, resulting in less control. Regarding the Foa group, Peralme (1991) wrote:

> According to Foa and colleagues, a pathological or neurotic fear structure develops when neutral stimuli become associated with anxiety responses. The cognitive evaluations of such associations are faulty or erroneous; in other words, estimates of threat are unrealistic and a high negative valence is attached to the event. The associations are resistant to modification because they fail to extinguish or habituate due to insufficient exposure to the feared stimulus and corrective information fails to realign evaluations with reality (Foa & Kozak, 1985). Thus, they emphasize that deficits "lie in both stimulus-response association and their evaluations." (p. 124)

Thus, meaning propositions are incorporated into learning or associative elements.

Unfortunately, problems exist. The model does not decide what is unique regarding the stimulus, response, and meaning propositions of the fear structure that potentiates PTSD and not other Anxiety Disorders. Also, the focus on meaning is limited to safety and threat. Finally, the authors rely on exposure to all elements of the fear structure and do not account for cohesiveness of association or other stimulus proposition features. Virtually all stimuli become possible candidates as trigger stimuli and can activate the fear structure and its psychobiological, behavioral, cognitive, and affective components. The advantage of the model, however, is that it contains a focus "switch"; any therapeutic effort starts with an understanding of the fear structure (its meaning) within the person and applies experience judiciously.

In a similar, way Chemtob et al. (1988) described a "cognitive action" theory of PTSD. This group used a network to describe the development and maintenance of PTSD. Fear structures are comprised of hierarchically arranged and interconnected rules that separate all elements required for a specific act (e.g., fight, escape). These include information about neurochemical and muscular activity, thoughts and associate memories, behaviors, and emotions. The cognitive processing is influenced by internal as well as external factors. These authors contend further that individuals with PTSD not only continue to function and respond to their environment, but also perceive in a "survival mode." This pattern of responding easily activates fear memory structures. Since a level of activation always is present, individuals often apperceive problems where none exist. The fear network then acts as a feedback loop such that threat arousal potentiates threat behavior. In turn, the attention is re-aroused and ambiguous information is misrepresented. Once such a threat is activated, threat-related arousal further increases, causing another cycle through the feedback loop. What follows is that other networks in this process become inhibited, allowing the threat loop to receive complete neural attention. Like the Foa group, Chemtob allowed for flexibility of description. Activation of the trauma memory is not limited to stimulus properties or to the size of the network. The model is "closer" to actual brain functioning. PTSD fear networks alter the information processing symptoms, and this network is associated with behaviors and actions. Unfortunately this theory, rich in concept, is vague in practical explanation.

Horowitz Group. No one has described the process of PTSD or trauma problems more extensively or better than Mardi Horowitz (1986a). For two decades, he and his group have proposed an information-processing model which assumes that the major drive of cognitive processes is a "completion tendency," in which the "mind continues to process important new information until the situation or the models change, and reality and models reach accord" (Horowitz, 1979, p. 249). The basic idea is that trauma is never fully processed but seeks the "best fit" between itself in memory and incoming information. Until a traumatic life event can be assimilated and successfully integrated into existing schemas, the psychological elements of the event will remain active in memory storage. To handle this, an intrusion and numbing cycle is activated (Figure 3.2). This is conceived as a natural process, cyclic and repetitive, and one that differs over time only in a quantitative way from normal responses to trauma. Initially, unbidden images/thoughts intrude. To defend against this, a numbing phase is initiated preventing a breakthrough of the intrusive images. This part of the cycle serves the function of reducing cognitive processing, thus lowering anxiety but continuing the problem. Under a gradual and titrated dosing of the event by the therapist, assimilation and accommodation, the two basic developmental processes of change, occur. New representations (schemas) of the trauma eventually are established. This becomes part of a new long-term memory. The working through process involves the therapist reducing the controls of intrusion and numbing, thereby promoting self-regulation.

For purposes here, two points are pivotal. First, Horowitz described and depended heavily on the concept of schema. Schemas are conscious or unconscious self-representations used to organize inner mental processes. Generally, an individual has many self-schemas that are composed of a set of subordinate ones formatted in a hierarchical organization providing consistency. In fact, schemas provide mental forms specifying roles and scripts to be acted upon. Once a role-relationship model is set in motion as an organizer (of a state-of-mind), one tends to act according to the sequence contained within its script and to expect responses from others accordingly.

While Horowitz seemed to vacillate regarding exactly what a schema is or exactly what cognitive schemas are influenced by trauma, he had little difficulty describing its organizational role for action. He also had little difficulty in explicating its function. Schemas seek a "best fit" between themselves and the incoming stimuli. In trauma, assimilation and accommodation cannot occur. Consequently, the person must solidify, entrench, and excessively depend on extant schemas. After a trauma, schemas prevent the uncomplicated assimilation of threatened patterns. Individuals become stuck and chronically cycle through numbing and intrusion. Schemas then represent the explanatory mechanism for a person's needs, states of

Normal	Pathologic
Outcry	Panic, paralysis, exhaustion
Denial	Maladaptive avoidances; social withdrawl, suicide, drug or alcohol excesses, counterphobic impulsivity
Intrusion	Flooded, pressured, confused, distraught, or impulsive states, physiological disruptions
Working Through—Blocked	Anxiety and depressive states, hibernative frozen states, psychosomatic changes
Completion—Not reached	Inability to work, create, or love

Figure 3.2. Stress response states and pathological intensification. From Horowitz (1986b). Reproduced by permission.

mind, defenses, and role-relationship, and are organizers for patterns in the psychic infrastructure for coding and ignoring stimuli. They "take over," and after trauma become the key problem area.

Second, the concept of personality takes center stage. Horowitz (Horowitz et al., 1984) believed that each person has his/her own style for controlling the flow of ideas in order to avoid entering painful states. These are essentially personality styles of information processing. Personality styles and schemas function on autopilot, resulting in a whole person activation and defense of trauma. Processes include perceptions, cognitive styles, and imaging styles of problem solving, as well as defenses. Each person is unique—a mixture of dynamic patterns involving approach and avoidance. Schemas direct the methods of operation of the person: the processing of action within and outside the person. What this means is that schemas influence personality styles. Hysterical styles, for example, are vague and global, interpersonally dramatic and fickle, given to repression and denial, and fully ready to access emotions if necessary. The exact way schemas influence these styles is unclear; perhaps they lay dormant until the environment pulls them. The total person, however, is directing this process. Processing of trauma occurs at different levels, but the need for completion is not just a repetition compulsion. It represents a constant redoing of the information processing of schemas. Ultimately, phasic shifts occur in denial and intrusion.

The major advantage to an information processing approach is the provision of a conceptual framework for the trauma encapsulation process. The "throughput" process can be better outlined. This information processing model provides a framework to unpack the complex trauma network of cognitions and emotions. In Chapter 2 (Table 2.1), we noted how PTSD is a multivaried construct with hyper-activity (Categories B and D) and hypo-activity (Category C). Further, although factor analytic studies support these differing symptom complexes, how they coordinate their experience or pathology have never been made clear. Information processing assists in this understanding. In one explanation, Litz and Keane (1989) have outlined a broad range of information processing "parts" responsible for the formation of PTSD. They include storage (fear-related information in memory), activation (internal or external), relative accessibility (trauma information is available from memory but not readily accessible for recall), avoidance (overlearned response biases to threatening information), retrieval (high in mood dependent states or with arousal, low otherwise), attention (selective attention to trauma cues), arousal (increased sensitivity to combat cues when high), and symptom formation.

Since PTSD is attributable to an identifiable aversive event, relevant cues for examining the various processes of encoding/decoding information can be identified and examined.

From this author's perspective, the cognitive theories are rich and only now bearing fruit. As the victim processes unbidden trauma intrusions, extant schemas are violated, and the information encoding/decoding domains are subverted. Two constructs, schema and personality, are the most salient features of this process. While not addressed by many information processing theorists, the speculation is reasonable that these structures are learned early and activated by representative elements in the environment. If one is concerned about issues of competence, for example, the belief is that this was not only learned early; but any situation reflective of performance makes this schema prepotent. Horowitz and other information processing therapists have provided a schematic and clinical understanding of the information flow of the trauma victim in a deliberative way.

Constructionism

Borrowing from self psychology, McCann and Pearlman (1990) provided the area of trauma care with a major work. Their thesis was that individuals develop core beliefs, assumptions, or expectations in fundamental need areas called schemas, and these are maximally influenced by trauma. The care of these core cognitive structures is required for the meaningful integration of trauma. Their position is constructionist; schemas are core cognitions that dictate or construct the expression of trauma. In fact, these authors are most concerned about the trauma victim's individuality. They stated:

> We believe that a current challenge in the field of traumatic stress studies is to avoid the danger of depriving trauma survivors of their individuality and uniqueness by focusing exclusively on the commonalities in response patterns among survivors. We must remember that trauma is experienced by persons, not dehumanized "victims," and that their differences, as well as their commonalities, must be respected and understood. (p. 4)

The expression of the person's individuality starts with the experience of the trauma. Trauma, according to these authors, exceeds the individual's ability to meet its demands, disrupting the basic psychological needs of the person (schemas). From a constructionist position, individual differences "determine" whether trauma is really trauma, and if so, how reality is consequently formed and apperceived. To understand this, McCann and Pearlman (1990) believed that the clinician must evaluate and know two psychological systems of the person, schemas and the self and ego resources, that allow for their regulation as the schema interacts with trauma. Regarding the former, schema work is processed through a clinical psychohistorical inquiry, in which schemas are evaluated and prioritized. Treatment consists of a self-paced exploration of each adaptive and maladaptive core cognitive structure for the purpose of retrieving a balance within the person. Through the therapeutic and curative features of education, exposure, reframing, and reordering of the value of each schema, balance can be returned. In this way, the therapeutic process attempts to normalize or balance core cognitions.

If schemas represent the person side of the treatment, then the trauma memory represents the stressor side. Trauma work involves a careful evaluation of self and ego resources and a dose response via exposure of the trauma memory. The therapist assesses these features to know how far to probe the trauma memory. This work precedes trauma work. The self-capacity includes the individual's ability to maintain a cohesive sense of identity or self and to regulate self-esteem; ego resources entail the individual's ability to negotiate with the world outside for growth or change. In addition, an evaluation of what the victim is experiencing, feeling, thinking, and reacting to when the memory is accessed, is conducted. Important issues of how the client avoids, what is required for safety—both externally and internally, and pacing are considered. Based on the client's abilities in these areas, as well as the working relationship, the therapist dose relates treatment with the trauma memory while presenting a positive model or image.

Schema. The centerpiece of this formulation is the schema. Trauma disrupts schemas and the person's ability to use these in efficient ways. The processing of information is compromised. Under this formulation the emphasis is placed on the response to trauma, not on the trauma itself: "Individuals possess an inherent capacity to construct their own personal realities as they interact with their environment" (McCann & Pearlman, 1990, p. 6). Each person then has already organized central beliefs on how he/she is to act and how the world is. The heart of the constructionist position is that the person uses his/her skills (ego skills) to support or reinforce the self; that is, the person constructs a reality and regulates self-esteem through self-serving person agendas (schema). Trauma disturbs the balance of these beliefs, necessitating rigidity and eventual turmoil. As a consequence, victims redouble efforts to keep consistency or reasonable levels of adaptation. Since assimilation or accommodation does not occur, these now hardened schemas refurbish current reality into reenactments that protect the person. Schemas most central to self are especially affected.

In an earlier work, McCann, Sakheim, and Abrahamson (1988) identified a set of schemas representative of various developmental stages on positive and negative views of life. These included safety, esteem, intimacy, power, and trust. To these, the authors (McCann & Pearlman, 1990) have added one other schema: independence—as well as a generalized superordinate schema, frame of reference. These are given in Table 3.4. What is important is that each schema is evaluated and prioritized within the context of the person's self-structure. Also in recent years, several other authors, most notably Epstein (in press), Janoff-Bulman (1985), and Ulman and Brothers (1988), have described an identical process to McCann and Pearlman, but emphasized to a greater extent the existential and central organizing features of the self and the meaning of the traumatic event (by the person) rather than distinct schemas. However, trauma symptoms, like nightmares, are thought to symbolically represent the fragmentation of the self due to trauma.

The strength of this model is its conceptual appeal, the schema taxonomy, and the self and ego assessment of the trauma memory. Trauma is destructive because it disrupts the person's core elements of being. The response is a cognitive one. Schemas become maladjusted and order information

TABLE 3.4
Schemas and Their Trauma Expressions

Frame of Reference	—	Why did this happen to me?
Safety	—	I am fearful for myself.
Trust	—	I cannot depend comfortably on anyone.
Self-trust	—	I cannot make self protective judgements.
Independence	—	I am not in control of my own behavior or destiny.
Power	—	I feel powerless from the influence of others (or life).
Esteem	—	I no longer have value in myself (no self-esteem).
Intimacy	—	I feel alienated or apart from others (can't get close).

Extrapolated from McCann and Pearlman (1990).

and affective responses. Once this is set in motion, schemas "unbalance" the person. The antidote involves two curative processes: (1) the schema must be listened for, explored, and challenged; and (2) the trauma memory requires a careful evaluation (self and ego assessment) and tending. McCann and Pearlman have identified victim problems and therapist's tasks with an important conceptual formulation and exacting method.

Biological

In the decade of the 90s, an explosion of information on the biological properties of PTSD will occur. In this brief section, we only highlight what general areas have been considered and studied. Already mentioned was the now somber fact that trauma at extreme levels alters the body's normal physiology and health. What now appears, is that PTSD is associated with a number of biological alterations that are physically disturbing. Chronic victims exhibit distinctive physiological, neuropharmacological, and endocrinological alterations.

In Table 3.5 is presented a brief outline of abnormalities according to physiological alterations and neurohumoral/ neuroendocrinological abnormalities (Friedman, 1991). Unlike most other psychiatric disorders, several animal models are directly applicable to PTSD. Furthermore, a good possibility exists that eventually psychophysiological laboratory techniques, designed to understand the pathophysiology of PTSD, will also lead to reliable diagnostic tools of these biological alterations (Keane & Kolb, 1988). More will be presented on this in future chapters.

The phenomenon PTSD is so intense and so disruptive of normal body functions that it is "easily" associated with a complex set of biogenic markers. This has led to noradrenergic models of PTSD, all positing hyperarousal of the central noradrenergic system. The most popular of these have been Kolb's (1987) conditional fear response model, van der Kolk's (1987) kindling hypothesis, and to a lesser extent De la Penna's (1984) brain modulated, compensatory information processing formulation. These theories involve an admixture of disturbances of neural tissue (leading to permanent changes in cognitive or affective responses) or of regions subserving higher order or "executive" functions (affective responses noted in personality). Prigatano (1992), for example, identified 22 active or passive "personality" changes as a result of trauma to the brain. Many of these are directly related to PTSD symptoms.

While these models speak directly to the pathophysiology of the fear response, maybe something more exists. On the

TABLE 3.5
Biological Changes Associated with PTSD*

A. Physiological Alterations Associated with PTSD

1. Sympathetic nervous system arousal
   a. Elevated baseline sympathetic indices
   b. Excessive response to neutral stimuli
   c. Excessive response to traumamimetic stimuli

2. Excessive startle reflex
   a. Lowered threshold
   b. Increased amplitude

3. A reducer pattern of cortical evoked potentials in response to neutral stimuli

4. Abnormalities in sleep physiology
   a. Increased sleep latency; increased movements; increased awakenings
   b. Decreased sleep time
   c. Possible disturbances in sleep architecture
   d. Traumatic nightmares differ from other types of nightmares.

B. Neurohumoral/Neuroendocrinological abnormalities associated with PTSD

1. Increased noradrenergic activity
   a. Increased urinary catecholamine levels
   b. Down-regulation of alpha-2 and beta receptors
   c. Reduced platelet MAO activity
   d. Yohimbine-induced panic and PTSD flashbacks

2. HPA Axis abnormalities
   a. Decreased urinary cortisol levels
   b. Elevated urinary catecholamine/cortisol ratio
   c. Increased sensitivity to dexamethasone suppression
   d. Blunted ACTH response of CRH

3. Opioid system dysregulation
   a. Decreased pain threshold at rest
   b. Stress-induced analgesia
   c. Decreased endorphin levels

*From Friedman (1991). Used with permission.

one hand, there may be a paradoxical drive for more trauma. Addiction to trauma implies that trauma victims reexpose themselves to severe stress because this results in a positive reinforcement (endogenous opiods), resulting in a high and then a relief of pain and discomfort. We have alluded to this in the previous chapters. On the other hand, Wilson and Walker (1989) nicely highlighted another "something more" in their discussion of the psychobiology of trauma. At its core, these authors noted that a "central given" of trauma responses is the integrated mind and body reaction.

Rossi's (1986) position is worth considering here. His formulation is an attempt conceptually to bridge the mind/body gap in PTSD (Rossi, 1990). Rossi (1986) believed that different levels of the same thing are happening; information is being transduced in various forms. According to Rossi, the conceptual challenge is to explore the dynamics of information transduction: How is information transformed from one modality to another? How do thoughts, feelings, images, reactions, etc. transform themselves into neural networks of the physical brain and ultimately every cell in the body? How, also do these body modalities communicate back to the brain and mind? At present, an important point is to identify some information substance as the common denominator allowing for the bridging of mind and matter. For Rossi, it is state-dependent learning. He hypothesized that state-dependent memory, learning, and behavior (SDMLB) are the common dominators that bridge mind and body. The SDMLB *is* the person at that time, *is* the template for the information transduction, and *is* the psychobiological basis for learning. He wrote:

> Dissociation, repression, emotional complexes, and partially reversible amnesia are all state-dependent psychological processes. The classical phenomena of hypnosis, multiple personality, neurosis, the post-traumatic stress disorders, psychosomatic symptoms, and mood disorders can all be understood as manifestations of state-dependent behavioral symptoms. Under stress, certain patterns of memory, learning, and behavioral symptomatology are learned and encoded by the release of stress hormones and information substances throughout the entire mind-body. When the

stress is removed, these information substances disappear and the person apparently recovers and seems symptom free. Reintroduce stress to varying degrees and the mind-body responds by releasing the information substances that re-evoke the corresponding degree of SDMLB symptomatology. (pp. 450-451)

If this is true, the person has biological/psychological behavioral templates that exist between the brain cells of the body and the mind that signal expression, completing a cybernetic flow of information. Symptoms and the psychopathology of everyday life (e.g., traumatic memories) correspond to the SDMLB of an earlier time. These "schemas" are self-contained, rigid, and intricate effector loops or complexes that provide the person with a rigid posture in life, a hyperarousal "set," and self-reinforcing/self-defeating patterns. They are deeply altering biologically. They are chronic PTSD.

Currently, the biological model is on the threshold of scientific "explanation." The biogenic paradigms of PTSD possess their own unique form, interacting with the psychological, social and cultural componets. These models provide several assists in the thinking of PTSD, offering insights into behavior patterns, especially the various paradoxical reactions of hyper- and hypo-arousal. In addition, these models have allowed for a psychopharmacologic understanding providing largely symptom specific prescriptions for PTSD victims.

Cognitive Behavioral Therapy (CBT)

This healthy hybrid represents the dialectic of the last two decades emphasizing both the cognitive and behavioral features of a person. Meichenbaum (1975) defined what would become the major components of CBT: behavior, cognitive structures, and the "inner dialogue." In recent years behaviorists have become more "inner oriented," focusing on coping behaviors, as well as cognitions. In fact, CBT attempts to alter the inner dialogue or the cognitive structures. Even behavior is viewed as governed by tacit schemas and automatic ways of thinking. The central component of the CBT position is the person's constructs or beliefs. The principled process used to unearth these, especially cognitions of "high salience" value to the person, represented the central focus of treatment.

One other new trend has emerged in CBT, a focus on schemas. No longer is identifying only automatic or surface cognitions (or behaviors) appropriate, and no longer appropriate is proceeding from a symptom-by-symptom approach for change. Rather, an ordering of beliefs and an integration of these beliefs deserve clinical consideration and care. The closer the clinician can attack the core cognitions, the greater the chance for lasting change. This cognition continuum ranges from more functional, at a level of conscious awareness, to deeper, more intrinsic schema reconstructing. In CBT terms, this gradient of change has been labeled *schema reinterpretation* (slight modification or reinterpretation of schema), *schema modification* (moderate level of change, akin to renovating a home), or *schema restructuring* (building a new structure, akin to urban renewal) (Freeman & Leaf, 1989). Again, the greater the ability of the CBT therapist to access and alter this unaware knowing, the greater the chance for a positive outcome.

Beck. Spurred on largely by Beck (Beck & Freeman, 1990; Beck & Emery 1985; Beck, 1991; Freeman, Pretzer, Fleming, & Simon, 1990), the attributional process unique to CBT deepened and widened. No longer was the interest in peripheral cognitions only. Cognitions are organized in hierarchical networks of beliefs, assumptions, formulas, and rules. Thereby, some cognitions are more "core" than others and more important; these are schemas. These central or core cognitions activate other mechanisms in the person (affective, motivational, and behavior) as would an effector loop setting in motion automatic processes. Different types of schemas have different functions, each taking care of its own domain (cognitive with thinking, affective with feelings, etc.), and each being triggered by various types of stimuli, all serving more "master" schemas in an organized fashion. Regarding their basic functions, Beck and Freeman (1990) wrote:

> Schemas have additional structural qualities, such as breadth (whether they are narrow, discrete, or broad), flexibility or rigidity (their capacity for modification), and density

(their relative prominence in the cognitive organization). They also may be described in terms of their valence— the degree to which they are energized at a particular point in time. The level of activation (or valence) may vary from latent to "hyper-valent." When schemas are latent, they are not participating in information processing; when activated, they channel cognitive processing from the earliest to the final stages. The concept of schemas is similar to the formulation by George Kelly (1955) of personal constructs. (p. 32)

In addition, the influence of personality disorders, or *Axis II* problems, was vigorously studied by this group. The point at which the schema activates the personality style is not totally clear, nor need it be. Conceptually sufficient is that schemas are more central to the person, giving way to modal styles and self reinforcing patterns of personality activity, descriptively punctuated as Axis II disorders. When an extreme stressor is present, the schema/personality mix hardens and becomes inflexible and nonadaptive. A sequence is initiated culminating in overt strategies or behaviors that are attributed to personality traits. Often the strategies are maladaptive and the beliefs become dysfunctional. Eventually these may be associated with a personality disorder and remain operative on a consistent basis. If so, an Axis II disorder results.

The Beck group provided one more conceptual assist. Recall that their overall paradigm is dependent most centrally upon the schema and less centrally upon the automaticity of surface cognitions. Within this cognitive realm, personality styles operate—sometimes at deeper levels and sometimes at more surface levels. The deeper structures are "hard wired" and always asserting an influence. If these structures are ever affected by internal and external stress to extreme levels, an Axis I disorder can result. This is caused by a *cognitive shift,* which involves an alteration from typical Axis II rules to a total preoccupation with the new Axis I condition. We expand on this idea later. At this point, what is important is the emphasis on the schema/Axis II dimension and the conceptual distinction to symptom dominated states.

Finally, in CBT the emphasis is on a *case formulation* approach. Basically, this provides for an individualization of treatment in which each case depends on two clinical factors: case specific information (and formulation) and a theory driven program for change. Persons (1991) labeled this an assessment-plus-treatment approach. She wrote:

> The choice of assessment and treatment procedures and measures is idiographic and theory-driven, determined by the nature of the patient's problems and the therapist's model of psychotherapy. The therapist uses the information obtained by the assessment procedures to develop a working hypothesis about the nature of the mechanisms underlying the patient's symptoms and problems; this working hypothesis is the case formulation. (p. 102)

At this point, the professional is most involved in the treatment process, in which information of the client (idiographic and nomothetic) meets the clinician's theory. To the extent that the treatment outcome is related to the accuracy of the case formulation and the underlying core mechanisms outlined by the treatment model, a positive correlation will occur. The CBT practitioner, who has an understanding of this process, the formulation of the client's schemas and their connection to theory driven interventions that are sensitive to change, can work more effectively with the victim and produce change. The CBT practitioner then assists the client in the management of information, in formulating the process and content of information, and in altering "deep habits" (of information processing). This is a "true" eclectic approach—an integration of technique based on the total person's needs. This applies both to schemas as well as to symptoms.

TRAUMA: SELF SHATTERING AND DESTRUCTURING PROCESS

These theories have a common feature: the person's identity or growing self cannot incorporate or assimilate/accommodate "something different" and seeks to adapt, doing so poorly. Whether the maladaptation process is due to the vagaries of excessively zealous stimulus generalization (learning theory), broken stimulus barriers and poorly repressive defenses (psychodynamic), poorly functioning cognitive processes (information processing or CBT), neurological overcharges (biological), or poorly adapted meaning structures (constructionism), among others, remains to be tested. Only one issue is clear: the person is altered at various levels of own understanding.

For many, no words are adequate to reflect a self shattering process after trauma. It is a "death imprint" (Lifton, 1979). At the least, an individual can expect from life a sense of identity, continuity, and internal consistency in the face of both internal and external events. Above all else, the self must have a sufficient degree of adaptability. This implies a continuous assimilation to life, or if necessary, an accommodation of new material. This has been described as a balanced state resulting either in an open state—the ability to merge with something else, or a closed state—the ability to shut down or disconnect from the external environment. Under normal conditions, an easy shift occurs from one state to another, as this capacity is self regulated. In fact, one can argue that this is so natural as to be the essence of normalcy.

What happens in the trauma experience? Several descriptions of this inner self-shattering process due to trauma have been advanced (e.g., Janoff-Bulman, 1985; Epstein, in press). The individual's appraisal of trauma is perhaps the central factor in adjustment. How does the trauma victim relate to self? At the least, an illusion of order would satisfy some of the turmoil around the trauma experience: "This event makes some sense to me." Unfortunately, standard measures or queries of one's attributions are not sensitive to a trauma victim's terror. Some monitoring of the victim's inner belief system, then, is reasonably important, as this inner experience may be the one person component that never receives full attention. Also noted is the **real impact** of the event. Ulman and Brothers (1988) specified how trauma affects unconscious meaning of the person. The person is shattered because of this root-level interpretation of a real stressor. Tait and Silver (1989) also noted that negative stressful events impoverish the realization of dreams, opportunities or aspirations in which the person is invested. Last, Shay (1991) noted a betrayal of "what's right"—the normative expectations or the moral order and shared values of a society. This creates a state of cognitive dissonance in the person (me/ideal me, moral me/combatant, etc.), necessitating a healing that must include elements of society.

Roth and Newman (1991) identified four inner representations of self whose parameters are shattered—belief in a benign world, meaningful world, trustworthy people, and self worth. Janoff-Bulman (1989) posited a similar approach. When trauma occurs, one or more of the four inner beliefs are invalidated and a compensatory search for meaning ensues. Based on one's belief, compensation, and how close this permits a realistic coping in life, adaptation will occur or not. Using a *Schema Dimensions Scale,* these authors attempted to pinpoint where this inner struggle is at any point in time (Table 3.6). The scale addresses two person dimensions—conscious awareness of the schema and efforts at resolution. Although not validated, this scale is noteworthy for its representation of the trauma struggle and the process of change. The goal is integration, as avoidance and cyclic turmoil are too costly.

Benyakar et al. (1989) described this shattering process differently. The human state has a drive for balance and coherence. From an analytic perspective, these authors isolated two referential planes and dimensions as "tools": **structural—**defining the relationship between elements in the psychological structures, and **functional—**defining the actions that occur between elements of the structure. Examples of structural referential planes include the intrapsychic forces, defenses, and ego strength. These are "hard wired" dispositional factors. Examples of functional referential planes include the relationship between members of a given social unit (e.g., a couple, or a family) or types of prevailing moods or behaviors that express the interactions of a social frame (e.g., power or morale). These are "expressions" of acts in the person. Psychic trauma is the collapse of the structure of self along referential planes resulting from an encounter of stressor and response. This occurs at a discrete point in time and results in the loss of the person's identity, continuity, and internal consistency. The "me-ness" of the person is threatened.

A traumatic experience occurs when a threat infringes on the self structure (usually because the stress involves loss, unpredictability, proximity, or suddenness) and results

TABLE 3.6
Schema Dimensions Scale*

---

1. No conscious awareness that there has been any disruption or invalidation of schema, but evidence for same.

2. Movement toward consciously acknowledging that there is uncertainty about some reliefs, or that there is a maladaptive schema, but movement that is tentative in some way.

3. Acknowledgment that some basic beliefs feel threatened, or acknowledgement of a maladaptive schema, but not directly associated with trauma.

4. Awareness that basic beliefs have been challenged by the trauma, or awareness that one has, as a result of the trauma, adopted a schema that is maladaptive.

5. Attempt to resolve discrepancy trauma presents, or to change maladaptive schema.

---

*From Roth and Newman (1991). Reproduced by permission.

in a chaotic response (a destructuralization or inability to organize previous working structural and/or functional abilities). Initially, the victim experiences the trauma as a feeling of being flooded. The "protective shield" or "boundary" is shattered and forced into an open state. This means that the usually self-regulated boundaries are forced open. The normal closing of the boundary that follows assimilation fails. This inability to shift back and forth at will from relatively closed to open states captures the essence of the trauma experience. In effect, the forced open state is inundated with uncontrolled cognition/ affect. To the extent that something new and terrible is unstoppable, the horror that the world will never be the same again reigns. The open state continues, unacceptable emotions mount, and functions are chaotic. Poignantly, these authors stated:

> The central feature of the traumatic experience is the final horrible "realization" that the rules that define the individual's identity and reality are not operational any more. In structural terms, this means that wholeness, transformation, and self-regulation are no longer feasible, and hence, the very existence of the structure itself is questionable, incomprehensible, or nonexistent. At its very core, the traumatic experience is the sudden perturbation of relationship that produces helplessness, manifested in the sense of loss of mastery, identity, and existence. Traumatic experience is an unstructured experience. (Benyakar et al., 1989, p. 442).

However, this chaotic state—the loss of relationships and function—cannot last long. The post-traumatic state (PTSD) is the reorganizing attempt to restore autonomy after the destructuralization has occurred. The result is a new steady state of two incompatible configurations, chaos and structure. What is novel is that the trauma victim "adjusts" by the absence of any integration of the trauma itself, often reorganizing with subclinical problems. Benyakar et al. (1989) stated:

> Reorganization occurs by isolating and representing this unstructured experience, without ever having the experience become an integral part of the rest of the system. The combined effect of isolation and repression is what we refer to as "encapsulation" of the traumatic experience. The reorganization process that eventually culminates in the encapsulation can appear as a full-blown clinical disorder with a host of dramatic symptoms, or may proceed unrecognized, manifested by subtle, attenuated, or hidden symptoms. Thus, presence or absence or the nature and severity of symptoms cannot be a sole indicator of the past occurrence of a trauma. (p.443)

A representation of a destructuring process is given in Figure 3.3. Based on a transition process involving issues like death, illness, stages of life structure, and moral behavior, Cytrynbaum, Blum, Patrick, Stein, Wadner, and Wilk (1980) provided a two-stage process of destructuring and restructuring. This model represents a whole organism description of change from unboundedness to integrity. This representation is how

Stage:	Destructuring	Reassessing	Restructuring	Adaptation
Process:	-Oh, God! ⟶	-I can't change this ⟶	-this is I ⟶	-self-confidence
	-intrusion ⟶	-balance of oscillation of intrusion/avoidance ⟶	-less frequent and intense oscillation ⟶	-insight and balanced defenses
		-death anxiety ⟶ -realization of death anxiety ⟶	-change identity ⟶	-self-questioning and insight
		-poor coping ⟶ -realization of some changes or limits and mourning ⟶	-positive coping ⟶	-positive coping and appraisal
Functioning:		-consumed in turmoil ⟶ -disrupted by trying ⟶	-integrated authentic ⟶	-growing

Figure 3.3. A two-stage process of destructuring and restructuring. Extrapolated from Cytrynbaum, Blum, Patrick, Stein, Wadner, & Wilk (1980).

a trauma experience "should" proceed. The destructuring process starts with the uncontrolled reaction that something is wrong and scary, and will not go away. At this point, the task is to tolerate the emergency changes in self-perception and loss of old ways, while maintaining sufficient functioning capacity to cope with everyday matters. At some point the transition from destructuring to reassessment occurs: "I cannot change this process." Usually, the person feels "at sea," lost and alienated, and can't believe that this way can exist for anyone. Restructuring occurs when an appearance coincides into consciousness of other imaginary aspects of the personality, of a new identity, of new roles, and of newer defenses and coping. These begin to feel rooted in the self with a new sense of authenticity. Usually self-confidence, self-knowledge, and a firmer purpose of conviction develop. Positive adaptation results.

We remain grossly ignorant regarding the basic shattering experience of the person. When educated in this process, trauma victims will feel a sense of relief. An awareness of a journey and of where "I am" in this struggle is present. Epstein (in press) also observed that recovery is contingent upon building a "new assumptive world" that can assimilate the victim experience adaptively. Epstein has even proposed that this process of adaptation to trauma (PTSD) has a "positive" value. The victim is constantly seeking a resolution or meaning in this turmoil. In this sense, the problem is not the intrusion but the lack of meaning. What is striking is that this may be trauma's most noxious feature—the existential reaction of the person. The self-referenced view of personhood is shattered. The stuck victim has stopped the meaning research. The person comes up short on the question, "Do I have sufficient control to go on or to search for meaning?" This level of concern is so basic, that without it, no meaningful inner journey can occur. One's relationship with self is unfriendly and disruptive, a negative inner dialogue. Even simple reflection on human issues results in alienation or dispiritedness. In later chapters, we will discuss how the narrative of the self is stuck; it is trauma saturated. This shattering experience and its impact on the human change process demands recognition and validation by the professional.

CONCLUSION

Theories are not necessary for exactitude, but because they provide something in place of chaos or randomness. Most importantly, they provide order which establishes reasonable patterns of organization and consistency. The theories addressed provide us with a sufficient knowledge of the boundaries of the workings of the trauma response. Based on the existing literature, the initial reaction of the person to trauma quite probably is "explained" by the learning model (an unconditioned response to trauma and the development of a conditional response). However, over time other person, biological, and psychosocial factors become engaged. These include the many person variables we shall address, as well as family history, social support and the like. The person of the victim is deeply involved in form and management of this adaptation.

REFERENCES

American Psychiatric Association (1987). *Diagnostic and statistical manual of mental disorders* (3rd ed.-revised). Washington, DC: Author.

Andreasen, N. C., & Noyes, R. (1972). Factors influencing adjustment of burn patients during hospitalization. *Psychosomatic Medicine, 34,* 517-525.

Andrews, G., Christensen, H. & Hadzi-Pavolovic, D. (1985). Royal Commission on the use and effects of chemical agents on Australian Personal in Vietnam. Canberra, Australia: Australian Government Printing Service.

Barlow, D. H. (1988). *Anxiety and Its Disorders.* New York: Guilford Press.

Baum, A., O'Keefe, M., & Davidson, L. (1990). Acute stressors and chronic response: The care of traumatic stress. *Journal of Applied Social Psychology, 20,* 1643-1654.

Beck, A. (1991). Cognitive therapy: A 30 year retrospective. *American Psychologist, 46*(4), 368-375.

Beck, A., & Emery, G. (1985). *Anxiety disorders and phobias: A cognitive perspective.* New York: Guilford Press.

Beck, A., & Freeman, A. (1990). *Cognitive Therapy of Personality Disorders*. Guilford Press: New York.

Benyakar, M., Kutz, I., Dasberg, H., & Stern, M. (1989). The collapse of structure: A structural approach to trauma. *Journal of Traumatic Stress*, 2(4), 431-450.

Blanchard, E. B., Kolb, L. C. Pallmeyer, T. P., & Gerardi, R. J. (1982). A psychophysiological study of Post Traumatic Stress Disorder in Vietnam veterans. *Psychiatric Quarterly, 54*, 220-229.

Bolin, R. (1985). Disaster characteristics and psychosocial impacts. In B. Sowder (Ed.), *Disasters and mental health: Selected contemporary perspectives* (pp. 3-28). Rockville, MD: NIMH.

Boudewyns, P. A., & Hyer, L. (1990). Physiological response to combat memories and preliminary treatment outcome in Vietnam veteran PTSD patients treated with direct therapeutic exposure. *Behavior Therapy, 21*, 63-87.

Boulanger, G., & Kadushin, C. (1986). *The Vietnam veteran redefined: Fact and fiction.* Hillsdale, NJ: Lawrence Erlbaum Associates.

Boyle, C. A., Decoufle, P., & O'Brien, T. R. (1989). Long-term health consequences of military service in Vietnam. *Epidemiologic Reviews, 11*, 1-27.

Brende, J. O. (1983). A psychodynamic view of character pathology in Vietnam combat veterans. *Bulletin of the Menninger Clinic, 47*, 193-216.

Brende, J. O., & McCann, I. L. (1984). Regressive experiences in Vietnam veterans: Their relationship to war, post-traumatic symptoms and recovery. *Journal of Contemporary Psychotherapy, 14*, 57-75.

Chemtob, C., Roitblat, H. L., Hamada, R. S., Carlson, J. G., & Twentyman, C. T. (1988). A cognitive action theory of posttraumatic stress disorder. *Journal of Anxiety Disorders, 2*, 253-275.

Cytrynbaum, S., Blum, L., Patrick, R., Stein, J., Wadner, D., & Wilk, C. (1980). Midlife development: A personality and social system perspective. In L. Poon (Ed.), *Aging in the 1980's* (pp. 463-474). Washington, DC: American Psychological Press.

Davidson, J., & Foa, E. B. (1991). Diagnostic issues in posttraumatic stress disorder: Considerations for the DSM-IV. *Journal of Abnormal Psychology (Special Issue)*.

De la Penna, A. (1984). PTSD in the Vietnam vet: A brainmodulated, compensator, information-augmenting response to information underload in the CNS. In B. A. van der Kolk (Ed.), *PTSD: Psychological and biological sequelae.* Washington, DC: American Psychiatric Press.

Dohrenwend, B. P., & Shrout, P. E. (1985). "Hassles" in the conceptualization and measurement of life stress variables. *American Psychologist, 40,* 780-785.

Elliott, G. R., & Eisdorfer, C. (1982). *Stress and human health.* New York: Springer-Verlag.

Emery, V., Emery, P., Shama, D., Quiana, N., & Jassani, A. (1991). Predisposing variables in PTSD patients. *Journal of Traumatic Stress, 4*(3), 325-344.

Epstein, S. (in press). The self-concept, the traumatic neurosis, and the structure of personality. In D. Ozer, J. M. Healy, Jr., & A. J. Stewart (Eds.), *Perspectives on Personality* (Vol.3). Greenwich, CT: JAI Press.

Epstein, S. (1985). The implications of cognitive-experiential self-theory for research in social psychology and personality. *Journal for the Theory of Social Behavior, 15,* 283-310.

Epstein, S. C. (1990). Beliefs and symptoms in maladaptive resolutions of the traumatic neurosis. In D. Ozer, J. Healy & A. Stewart (Eds.), *Perspectives on personality,* Vol. 3. London: Jessica Kingsley, Pub.

Ettedgui, E., & Bridges, M. (1985). Post-traumatic stress disorder. *Psychiatric Clinics of North America, 8,* 89-103.

Fairbank, J. A., & Keane, T. M. (1982). Flooding for combat related stress disorders: Assessment of anxiety reduction across traumatic memories. *Behavior Therapy, 13,* 499-510.

Fairbank, J. A., & Nicholson, R. A. (1987). Theoretical and empirical issues in the treatment of Posttraumatic Stress Disorder in Vietnam veterans. *Journal of Clinical Psychology, 43,* 44-55.

Figley, C. (1978). *Stress disorders among Vietnam veterans: Theory, research and treatment.* New York: Brunner/Mazel.

Foa, E., & Kozak, M. (1991). Emotional processing: Theory, research, and clinical implications for anxiety disorders. In J. Safran & L. Greenberg (Eds.) *Emotions, Psychology and Change* (pp. 31-49). New York: Guilford Press.

Foa, E., Steketee, G., & Rothbaum, B. (1989). Behavioral/cognitive conceptualization of post-traumatic stress disorder. *Behavior Therapy, 20,* 155-176.

Foy, D. W., Carroll, E. M., & Donahoe, C. P., Jr. (1987). Etiological factors in the development of PTSD in clinical samples of Vietnam combat veterans. *Journal of Clinical Psychology, 43,* 17-27.

Freeman, A., & Leaf, R. (1989). Cognitive therapy applied to personality disorders. In A. Freeman, K. Simon, L. Beuther & H. Arkowitz (Eds.) *Handbook of cognitive therapy,* (pp,403-434). New York: Plenum.

Freeman, A., Pretzer, J., Fleming, B., & Simon K. (1990). *Clinical application of cognitive therapy.* New York: Plenum.

Freud, S. (1964). In J. Strachey (Ed. & Trans.), *An outline of psycho-analysis.* Standard edition, vol. 23. London: Hogarth Press.

Friedman, M. (1991). Neurobiological alterations associated with post traumatic stress disorder. VA teleconference from National Center for PTSD, White River Junction, VT.

Gerardi, R. J., Blanchard, E. B., & Kolb, L. C. (1989). Ability of Vietnam veterans to dissimulate a psychophysiological assessment for Post-traumatic Stress Disorder. *Behavior Therapy, 20,* 229-243.

Green, B. (1990). Defining trauma: Terminology and generic stressor dimensions. *Journal of Applied Social Psychology, 20,* 1632-1642.

Green, B., Grace, M., Lindy, J., Gleser, G., & Leonard, A. (1990). Risk factors for PTSD and other diagnoses in a general sample of Vietnam veterans. *American Journal of Psychiatry, 147,* 729-733.

Green, B. L., Wilson, J. P., & Lindy, J. D. (1985). Conceptualizing posttraumatic stress disorder: A psychosocial framework. In C. R. Figley (Ed.), *Trauma and its wake: The study and treatment of posttraumatic stress disorder.* New York: Brunner/Mazel.

Helzer, J. E. (1981). Methodological issues in the interpretation of the consequences of extreme situations. In B. S. Dohrenwend & D. P. Dohrenwend (Eds.), *Stressful life events and their contexts* (pp. 108-129). New York: Prodist.

Hendin, H., Pollinger-Haas, A., Singer, P., Gold, F., Trigos, G., & Ulman, R. (1983). Evaluation of posttraumatic stress in Vietnam veterans. *Journal of Psychiatric Treatment and Evaluation, 5,* 303-307.

Hocking, F. (1970). Extreme environmental stress and its significance for psychopathology. *American Journal of Psychotherapy, 24,* 4-26.

Horowitz, M. (1979). *States of mind.* New York: Plenum.

Horowitz, M. (1986a). Stress response syndromes: A review of posttraumatic and adjustment disorders. *Hospital and Community Psychiatry, 37,* 241-249.

Horowitz, M. (1986b). Stress response syndromes: Post-traumatic and adjustment disorders. In A. Cooper, A. Francis, & M. Sacks (Eds.), *The personality disorders and neuroses,* (pp. 409-424). New York: Lippincott.

Horowitz, M. (1990). Post-traumatic stress disorders: Psychosocial aspects of the diagnosis. *International Journal of Mental Health, 19,* 21-36.

Horowitz, M., Marmar, C., Krupnick, J., Wilner, N., Kaltreider, N., & Wallerstein, R. (1984). *Personality styles and brief psychotherapy.* New York: Basic Books.

Janoff-Bulman, R. (1985). The aftermath of victimization: Rebuilding shattered assumptions. In C. R. Figley (Ed.), *Trauma and its wake: The study and treatment of post-traumatic stress disorder.* New York: Brunner/Mazel.

Janoff-Bulman, R. (1989). Assumptive worlds and the stress of traumatic events: Applications of the schema construct. *Social Cognitions, 7(2)* 113-136.

Jay, J. (1991 Nov/Dec). Terrible knowledge. *The Family Therapy Networker,* pp. 19-29.

Kahana, E., Kahana, B., Harel, Z., & Rosner, T. (1988). Coping with extreme trauma. In J. Wilson, Z. Harel, & B. Kahana (Eds.), *Human adaptation to extreme stress: From Holocaust to Vietnam* (pp. 55-81). New York: Plenum Press.

Kasl, S. (1990). Some considerations in the study of traumatic stress. *Journal of Applied Social Psychology, 20(2),* 1655-1665.

Kaylor, J. A., King, D. W., & King, L. A. (1987). Psychological effects of military service in Vietnam: A meta-analysis. *Psychological Bulletin, 102,* 257-271.

Keane, T. M. (1989). Post-traumatic stress disorder: Current status and future directions. *Behavioral Therapy, 20,* 149-153.

Keane, T. M., Fairbank, J. A., Caddell, J. M., Zimering, R. T., & Bender, M. E. (1985). A behavioral approach to assessing and treating post-traumatic stress disorder in Vietnam veterans. In C. R. Figley (Ed.), *Trauma and its wake: The study and treatment of post-traumatic stress disorder* (pp. 257-294). New York: Brunner/Mazel.

Keane, T. M., Fairbank, J. A., Caddell, J. M., & Zimering, R. T. (1989). Implosive (flooding) therapy reduces symptoms of PTSD in Vietnam combat veterans. *Behavior Therapy, 20,* 245-260.

Keane, T. M., & Kolb, L. (1988). The importance of psychophysiological measures in the determination of PTSD among combat related victims. VA Cooperative Study.

Keane, T. M., Wolfe, J., & Taylor, K. L. (1987). Post-traumatic stress disorder: Evidence for diagnostic validity and methods of psychological assessment. *Journal of Clinical Psychology, 43,* 32-43.

Keane, T. M., Zimering, R., & Caddell, J. (1985). A behavioral formulation of Posttraumatic Stress Disorder in Vietnam veterans. *The Behavior Therapist, 8,* 9-12.

Kilpatrick, D. G., Veronen, L. J., & Resick, P. A. (1979). The aftermath of rape: Recent empirical findings. *American Journal of Orthopsychiatry, 49(4),* 658-669.

King, D., & King, L. (1991). Validity issues in research on Vietnam veterans adjustment. *Psychological Bulletin, 109(1),* 107124.

Kohut, H. (1977). *The restoration of the self.* New York: International Universities Press.

Kolb, L. C. (1983). Return of the repressed: Delayed stress reaction to war. *Journal of The American Academy of Psychoanalysis, 11,* 531-545.

Kolb, L. C. (1984). The post-traumatic stress disorders of combat: A subgroup with a conditioned emotional response. *Military Medicine, 149,* 237-243.

Kolb, L. C. (1986). Treatment of chronic post-traumatic stress disorder. *Current Psychiatric Therapies, 23,* 119-127.

Kolb, L. C. (1987). A neuropsychological hypothesis explaining post traumatic stress disorders. *The American Journal of Psychiatry, 144,* 989-995.

Kolb, L. C. (1988). A critical survey of hypotheses regarding post-traumatic stress disorder in light of recent research findings. *Journal of Traumatic Stress, 1,* 292-304.

Krystal, H. (1978). Trauma and affects. *Psychoanalytic Study of the Child, 33,* 81-117.

Kulka, R., Schlenger, W., Fairbank, J., Hough, R., Jordan, K., Marmar, C., & Weiss, D. (1990). *Trauma and the Vietnam war generation.* New York: Brunner/Mazel.

Lang, P. (1979). A bio-informational theory of emotional imagery. *Psychophysiology, 16,* 495-512.

Lifton, R. J. (1976). *The life of the self.* New York: Simon & Schuster.

Lifton, R. J. (1979). *The broken connection.* New York: Simon & Schuster.

Linn, M. W. (1986). Modifiers and perceived stress scale. *Journal of Consulting and Clinical Psychology, 54,* 507-513.

Litz, B., Penk, W., Gerardi, R., & Keane, T. (1991). The assessment of posttraumatic stress disorder. In P. Saigh (Ed.), *Posttraumatic stress disorder: A behavioral approach to assessment and treatment.* New York: Pergamon Press.

Litz, B. T., & Keane, T. M. (1989). Information processing in anxiety disorders: Application to the understanding of posttraumatic stress disorder. *Clinical Psychology Review, 9,* 243-257.

Lyons, J. A. (1991). Strategies for assessing the potential for positive adjusting following trauma. *Journal of Traumatic Stress, 4*(1), 113-122.

Mahoney, M. C. (1991). *Human change processes: The scientific foundations of psychotherapy.* Delran, NJ: Basic Books.

McCann, C., Sakheim, D., & Abrahamson, O. (1988). Trauma and victimization: A model of psychological adaptation. *Counseling Psychologist, 16,* 531-598.

McCann, L., & Pearlman, L. (1990) *Psychological trauma and the adult survivor: Theory, therapies, and transformation.* New York: Brunner/Mazel.

McCranie, E., Hyer, L., Boudewyns, P., & Woods, M. (1991). Negative parenting, combat exposure, and PTSD symptom severity: Test of a person/event interaction model. *Journal of Nervous and Mental Disease, 180,* 431-438

McFall, M. E., MacKay, P. W., Donovan, D. M. (1992). Combat related posttraumatic stress disorder and severity of substance abuse in Vietnam veterans. *Journal of Studies on Alcohol, 53,* 357-363.

McFarlane, A. (1990). Vulnerability to posttraumatic stress disorder. In M. Wolf and A. Mosnaim (Eds.), *Posttraumatic stress disorder: Etiology, phenomenology, and treatment* (pp. 2-21). Washington, DC: American Psychiatric Press.

McFarlane, A. C. (1988). The aetiology of post-traumatic stress disorders following a natural disaster. *British Journal of Psychiatry, 152,* 116-121.

Meek, C. (1990). *Post-traumatic stress disorder: Assessment and forensic evaluation.* Sarasota, FL: Professional Resource Exchange.

Meichenbaum, D. A. (1975). A self-instructional approach to stress management: A proposal for stress inoculation training. In C. Spielberger & I. Sarason (Eds.), *Stress and anxiety,* Vol. 2. New York: Wiley.

Millon, T. (1969). *Modern psychopathology.* Philadelphia: Saunders.

Millon, T. (1981). *Disorders of personality: DSM-III Axis II.* New York: Wiley.

Millon, T. (1983). *Millon clinical multiaxial inventory manual,* (3rd ed.). Minneapolis: National Computer Systems.

Mowrer, O. (1960). *Learning theory and behavior.* New York: Wiley.

Nolen-Holksema, S., & Morrow, J. (1991). A prospective study of depression and posttraumatic stress symptoms after a natural disaster: The 1989 Loma Prieta earthquake. *Journal of Personality and Social Psychology, 61,* 115-121.

Norris, F. (1990). Screening for traumatic stress: A scale for use in the general population. *Journal of Applied Social Psychology, 20,* 1704-1718.

Othmer, E., & Othmer, S. (1989). *The clinical interview using using the DSM-III-R.* Washington, DC: American Psychiatric Press.

Peralme, L. (1991). *Empirical and theoretical analysis of reexperiencing of trauma in combat veterans. A critical review.* Florida State University, Department of Psychology.

Persons, J. (1991). Psychotherapy outcome studies do not accurately represent current models of psychotherapy: A proposed remedy. *American Psychologist, 46*(2), 99-106.

Peterson, K., Prout, M., & Schwartz, R. (1991). *Posttraumatic stress disorder: A clinician's guide.* New York: Plenum.

Pitman, R.K., Orr, S.P., Forgue, D.F., de Jong, J.B., & Claiborn, J.M. (1987). Psychophysiologic assessment of posttraumatic stress disorder imagery in Vietnam combat veterans. *Archives of General Psychiatry, 44(11),* 970-975.

Prigatano, G. P. (1992). Personality disturbances associated with traumatic brain injury. *Journal of Consulting and Clinical Psychology, 60,* 360-368.

Rabkin, J. G., & Struening, E. L. (1976). Life events, stress, and illness. *Science, 194,* 1013-1020.

Reich, J. (1990). Personality disorders and posttraumatic stress disorder. Etiology, phenomenology and treatment. In M. Wolfe & A. Mosnaim (Eds.), *Posttraumatic stress disorders* (pp. 64-79). Washington, DC: American Psychiatric Press.

Resnick, H., Veronen, L., & Saunders, B. (1988). Symptoms of posttraumatic stress disorder in rape victims and their partners. Paper presented at the annual meeting of the Society for Traumatic Stress Studies, Dallas, Texas.

Rossi, E. (1986). *The psychobiology of healing.* New York: Norton.

Rossi, E. (1990). From mind to molecule: More than a metaphor. In J. Zeig & S. Gilligan (Eds.), *Brief therapies: Myths, methods and metaphors* (pp. 445-472). New York: Brunner/Mazel.

Roth, S., & Newman, F. (1991). The process of coping with trauma. *Journal of Traumatic Stress, 4*(2), 279-298.

Safran, J., & Segal, Z. (1990). *Interpersonal processing in cognitive therapy.* New York: Basic Books.

Saigh, P. (1989). The development and validation of the Children's PTSD Inventory. *International Journal of Special Education, 4,* 75-84.

Scrignar, C. B. (1984). *Post-traumatic stress disorder.* New York: Praeger.

Seligman, M. (1975). *Helplessness: On depression, development, and death.* San Francisco: Freeman.

Shay, J. (1991). Learning about combat stress from Homer's *Iliad. Journal of Traumatic Stress, 4,* 561-580.

Snow, B. R., Stellman, J. M., Stellman, S. D., & Sommer, J. F. (1988). Post-traumatic stress disorder among American Legionnaires in relation to combat experience in Vietnam: Associated and contributing factors. *Environmental Research, 47,* 175-192.

Sowder, B. J. (1985). *Disasters and mental health: Selected contemporary perspectives.* Rockville, MD: NIMH.

Stegman, R. L., & Blanford, R. V. (1992, August). Combat experiences: Identification of false reports and judgments about trauma. Paper presented at the One Hundredth Annual Meeting of the American Psychological Association. Washington, DC.

Sudak, H. S., Martin, R. S., Corradi, R. B., & Gold, F. S. (1984). Antecedent personality factors and the post-Vietnam syndrome: Case reports. *Military Medicine, 149,* 550-554.

Sutker, P., Uddo-Crane, M., & Allain, A. (1991). Clinical and research assessment of posttraumatic stress disorder: A conceptual overview. *Psychological Assessment: A Journal of Consulting and Clinical Psychology, 3,* 520-530.

Tait, R., & Silver, R. (1989). Coming to terms with major negative life events. In J. S. Uleman & J. A. Bargh (Eds.), *Unintended thought.* New York: Guilford Press.

True, W., Goldberg, J., & Eisen, S. (1988). Stress symptomatology among Vietnam veterans. *American Journal of Epidemiology, 128,* 85-92.

Ulman, R. B., & Brothers, D. (1988). *The shattered self: A psychoanalytic study of trauma.* Hillsdale, NJ: The Analytic Press.

van der Kolk, B. A. (1987). *Psychological Trauma.* Washington, DC: American Psychiatric Press.

van der Kolk, B. A. (1988). The trauma spectrum: The interaction of biological and social events in the genesis of the trauma response. *Journal of Traumatic Stress, 1,* 273-290.

Wilson, J., & Krauss, G. (1982). Prehistory post-traumatic stress syndrome among Vietnam veterans. Paper presented at the 25th Neuropsychiatric Institute.

Wilson, J., & Prabucki, K. (1989). Stress sensitivity and psychopathology. In J. Wilson (Ed.) *Trauma transformation and healing: An integrative approach to theory, research, and posttraumatic therapy* (pp. 75-110). New York: Brunner/ Mazel.

Wilson, J., & Walker, A. (1989). The psychobiology of trauma. In J. Wilson (Ed.), *Trauma transformation and healing: An integrated approach to theory, research, and post-traumatic therapy* (pp. 159-199). New York: Brunner/ Mazel.

Wilson, J. P. (1989). *Trauma, transformation, and healing; An integrative approach to theory, research and post-traumatic therapy.* New York: Brunner/ Mazel.

Worthington, E. R. (1978). Demographic and preservice variables as predictors of post-military adjustments. In C. R. Figley (Ed.), *Stress disorders among Vietnam veterans: Theory, research, and treatment* (pp. 173-187). New York: Brunner/Mazel.

Young, J. (1990). *Cognitive therapy for personality disorders: A schema focused approach.* Sarasota, FL: Professional Resource Exchange.

Chapter **4**

LIFE-STYLE AND "PARTS" OF THE PERSON

"Be careful how you create the world: it is like that." (Heller)

Problems resulting from trauma can be so amorphous that dealing with them is living proof of the popular tale about the three blind men describing the elephant, each from a different perspective. The ability to distinguish conceptually and clinically among the various person and trauma components has several advantages—most notably to provide a working framework from which to understand victims. As discussed in the previous chapters, we have duly respected the objective reality of the trauma and its measurable features (nomothetic position) and, of course, emphasized how these events are filtered through the person of the victim (idiographic position). In fact, an idiographic orientation can serve well a nomothetic science (Nesselroade, 1990).

In this chapter we outline and describe the model. The most important task in the treatment of the trauma victim is to understand the person. This is captured most accurately by the life-style or LS, which in turn is represented most efficiently by the schema-personality style-beliefs-symptom model [Sc+P+(B)+Sy]. Schemas are the core cognitive structures that serve as the infrastructure of the person. Some schemas are more "core" to a person than others and as a consequence assert a greater influence over the person's affect, behavior, surface cognitions, and the controls for the monitoring of these. In addition, based on Adlerian theory, schemas organize needed protectors to perpetuate their existence. These "methods of operation" include the latter three components of the model. Young (1990) labeled these schema maintenance behaviors. The overall view is that trauma care is best constellated through an understanding of the LS, the schema and its safeguards, personality style, beliefs, and symptoms [Sc+P+(B)+Sy].

In this chapter, the case formulation of the person is considered. Its connection to psychotherapy is a given. With such information about the trauma victim, psychotherapy is the application of the curative elements in a considered way. The goal of care is the collaboration in the observation and evaluation of current experience of the victim in the treatment setting. The task of the therapist is to struggle so as to fully understand the client from his/her perspective and reality; a victim's trauma response becomes both logical and "inevitable." As noted in Chapter 1, this involves both **schema therapy** and **symptom therapy**. *The former addresses and evaluates directly the person's LS, or schema plus personality plus beliefs.* These core elements are responsible for the psychological exemplars that are the result of their unique brand of information processing. These exemplars are the symptoms. *The understanding and treatment of symptoms is,* of course, **symptom therapy.**

Both types of treatment are seen as important and will hold precedence at various times. Long term precedence, however, is given to schema therapy. Mahoney (1991) wrote:

> To reiterate, all experience—including the experience of change—is recursive or self-referential. This is the essence of the principle that all significant psychological change involves changes in personal meanings and, furthermore, that all such changes involve different relationships among the core ordering processes. These changing relationships are inevitable correlates of the structural reorganization

that is inherent to the dynamics of development in living systems. Our understanding of those dynamics is still rudimentary, however; and our efforts to learn more are hampered, in part, by the inadequacies of languages and the historical momentum of misguiding ideas. (pp. 338-339)

This model for change encourages self-caring and social responsibility. This is a total person act in any number of areas: relationship to self, to feelings, to boundaries in life, to ambiguities, and to own personal meaning. Just as the victim has a unique pathway to his/her recovery, each has his/her own fingerprint in the orchestration of the trauma response. Based on this profile, either schema or symptom therapy is required at any one time. As in other models, this treatment efficacy depends on the bonds, tasks, and goals of therapy (Bordin, 1979). From our perspective, these include an understanding of the "client's plan," commitment, a strong relationship, and the judicious pursuit of the goals of treatment, self change and reexperiencing. If commitment and arousal are optimal and if the "client's plan" is understood, the clinician can facilitate self repair of dysfunctional schemas, self-defeating personality styles, beliefs, and symptoms.

This treatment position implies one further piece of information. The objective of psychotherapy is not to eliminate developmental oscillations of clients. Characteristic of the CBT tradition, treatment serves to enlighten and empower the client and to foster choice. It encourages a healthy respect for the person's role in the dynamics of psychological change. Both schema and symptom therapy are conducted under the coattails of this therapeutic ideal, client empowerment and individuality (Ochberg, 1991).

This chapter is connected to the next one. The focus is case formulation, most notably according to the Adlerian concept of LS, and its components—goal orientation, private logic, and symptoms. This is the "conceptual base camp" of our model (Mahoney, 1991). It is intended to be uncomplicated in its formulation—usable, and parsimonious. The central focus is always a holistic one emphasizing normalcy and the individuality of the person. Also, this position has one additional advantage: it allows entry into the person at the person's level of commitment. The clinician then can respond to the "ready" person parts.

PARADIGM

Primarily, the intent in this part of the book is to provide briefly an overview of our model, based on the theory of Alfred Adler. This theory provided the friendly environment for our principles and their interrelationship. The driving question remains: what are the required assessment data and the required treatment-related theories for the understanding and care of the trauma victim?

Alfred Adler was one of the first theorists to articulate the individuality of the person. His approach was holistic, idiographic, and teleological, and placed central importance on the person. This formulation could be understood by the LS—an on-going, dynamic formulation of a person that is impossible to fully conceptualize. By using a formalized assessment procedure *(Life-Style Analysis)*, however, a reasonable knowledge of the person is attainable. Adler believed that a formulation, using only nomothetic criteria and operationalized types and dimensions of a person, fell short of true knowledge. The messy nuances of the person's uniqueness also required conceptualizing. The LS then is a goal; it is the best map of the territory available. It is also always beyond full understanding. As Bugental (1987) noted, "There is always something more."

Patterns and convictions take form continuously in the development of a person. Endowed with capabilities, strategies, energies, and temperaments, as well as experiences with others, the child establishes patterns that are both permissible and rewarding. These gradually become narrowed as distinct rewards further sharpen the person. Eventually, strategies become crystallized into preferred ways of relating to others. These patterns are "stamped," as they are repetitively reinforced by the interaction with the environment. These become observable redundancies—cognitive-interpersonal cycles of the person. They are "me-you patterns" (Sullivan, 1953), experiential invariants (Stern, 1985), or structured schemas (Leventhal, 1984) of the person.

Fuzzy Boundaries

Through these LS patterns, two structured constructs emerge that define and direct the person: schemas and personality. Millon (1984) labeled these structural attributes "images and inclinations that provide a template of imprinted residues which guide and transform the nature of ongoing life events" (p. 460). These are the cognitive and affective substrate that is quasipermanent, containing the residues of the past in the form of memories, intrapsychic constructs, and self-images. At the center are core schemas. These are invariant patterns of awareness through which psychological processes are organized. These schemas select and synthesize incoming data, direct actions, and organize patterns of the person. In turn, schemas unfold, giving rise to personality styles or traits. Beck and Freeman (1990) wrote:

> Attributes such as dependency and autonomy, which are conceptualized in motivational theories of personality as basic drives, may be viewed as a function of a conglomerate of basic schema. In behavioral or functional terms, the attributes may be labeled as "basic strategies." These specific functions may be observed in an exaggerated way in some of the overt behavioral patterns attributed, for example, to the dependent or schizoid personality disorders. (p. 7)

> Personality "traits" identified by adjectives such as "dependent," "withdrawn," "arrogant," or "extraverted" may be conceptualized as the overt expression of these underlying structures. By assigning meanings to events, the cognitive structures start a chain reaction culminating in the kinds of overt behavior (strategies) that are attributed to personality traits. Behavioral patterns that we commonly ascribe to personality traits or dispositions ("honest," "shy," "outgoing") consequently represent interpersonal strategies developed from the interaction between innate dispositions and environmental influences. (p. 7)

This is an unerring, designed growth process, but lines of demarcation between schema and personality and symptoms are not crystal clear. This should not be surprising since the present nosology (DSM-III-R or IV) also avoids any boundary clarification between normality and disorder. Core schemas are "person" positions or cognitions that are most central to the person. In the words of CBT, they are "compelling" to the person, even when latent. Somewhere in the developmental sequence, "security operations" (Sullivan, 1953) are required for protection. Adler (1932) labeled these safeguards or "methods of operation." They consist of modal styles and self-perpetuated patterns. These are the structural (hard-wired) and functional processes or attributes that transpire within the person and between him/her and others (expressive modes of regulatory action). These are the personality styles. They also involve cognitive styles (beliefs). These cognitions, however, are the more surface level construals. Adler described these as a *person's private logic.*

A representation of the model is given in Figure 4.1. The LS serves as a center construct; it represents the person. Schemas are "more core" and give rise to deeply etched personality styles, —some biogenic and some learned. In turn, these are subserved by less core beliefs or automatic thoughts. Beck (Beck & Freeman, 1990) described these less core beliefs as serving a necessary function in this schema process. They are devised from schemas and provide regular feedback or appraisal of the ongoing proceedings of the person. The last part of the model is symptoms. Symptoms are extensions or descriptions in the client's coping style. They are anchored to the client's schema and personality styles and take significance and meaning in that context. Symptoms tend to be phasic and reactive to external as well as internal perturbations. They also are largely transient. If a person does become symptomatic, depressed, anxious, or does show PTSD problems, he/she does so by undergoing a "shift." In this state, typical schema and personality styles are unduly influenced by the current disorder. In the case of depression, this would involve problems of hopelessness and negativity; in the case of anxiety, danger and uncertainty; and in the case of PTSD, trauma-specific intrusions, hyperarousal, and numbing. The Beck group (Beck & Freeman, 1990) wrote:

> The typical schema of the personality disorders resemble those that are activated in the symptom syndromes, but they are operative on a more continuous basis in information processing. In dependent personality disorder, the schema 'I need help' will be activated whenever a problematic situation arises, whereas in depressed persons it will be prominent only during the depression. In personality disorders, the schema are part of normal, everyday processing of information. (p. 32)

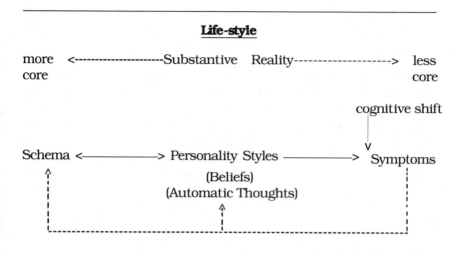

Figure 4.1. Paradigm of life-style; Sc + P + (B) + Sy sequence.

Figure 4.1 also presents the way in which schemas and personality styles (Axis II) give way to symptoms (Axis I). Schemas and personality styles are "hard wired," structuralized, and overdeveloped. Axis I symptoms are temporary and plastic. Under the force of a "cognitive shift," normal schema and personality style rules are less in evidence. The manner in which schemas provide the regulatory actions, resulting in a "logic" to person activity, can now be seen. They provide both the context and direction for resultant person actions. This model is "dynamic" with each construct influencing the others.

Anxiety plays the central role in the mobilization of the Axis I shift. During trauma, schemas become inflamed and trauma symptoms preoccupy the person. Beck stated that the orderly processing of data is "systematically bound in a dysfunctional way" (Beck & Freeman, 1990, p. 37). Not until this insult is rectified, either by means of a reordering of its own material or by an alternative schema, does tranquility return. However, schemas and personality styles always assert some influence, even in the decompensation pattern of the trauma response.

Various CBT proponents discuss four components of this process (Table 4.1). First, schemas represent both core **cognitive structures** and **content.** These are most central to the person. From this perspective, the treating clinician can choose schema reconstructing (deep core changes); schema modification; or reinterpretation of the schema, the most superficial schema alteration. Next, **cognitive processes** refer to tasks of encoding, storing, and retrieving of information. **Cognitive operations,** like selective attention, perceptual distortions, biased encoding and retrieval, are also included. Cognitive processes are most similar to personality styles. Third, the products (by-products) of these operations are the person's beliefs or thought content. The many scales of CBT (e.g., **Automatic Thoughts Questionnaire)** are used to measure the various formulations of beliefs. Finally, the "fruits" of these various cognitive labors are symptoms, the **Axis I problems,** that result.

TABLE 4.1

Reformulation of CBT Concepts

Our Model	CBT
Schema	Structure and content
Personality Style	Cognitive Processes and Operations
Belief	"By-products"
Symptoms	Axis I problems

This whole CBT procedure is then a total person, meaning-making operation to protect consistency and protect known boundaries. CBT is many things, but it is always phenomenological (Vallis, 1991). Many variants (perhaps as many as 20) can be placed on a gradient ranging from "less core" to "more core." The former has been labeled a rationalist position, in which the emphasis is on cognitive content and specific behavior or cognitive techniques. In that case, the emphasis is accessible thoughts, images, and, of course, behavior. The latter position has been labeled constructionist, and the focus is rather different. An effort is made to understand the client's phenomenology via core schemas. Interventions involve the ways in which clients assess/process themselves, how they experience their activities, and how they can become a participant observer (decentering) in this process. The emphasis is less on specific intervention techniques (Vallis, 1991). As we shall emphasize and see, the person of the victim demands both; "more equal" status is, however, accorded the constructionist position (where the person is).

The task of the therapist is to identify these processes and respond at the level appropriate to the client. Unfortunately, support for the idea that a focus on core cognitions is superior to one on peripheral cognitions is lacking (except clinically). Nonetheless, a self emphasis (examining cognitions with a high degree of centrality of self) represents an "interiority journey" (where the person is) and is a natural extension to "technique therapy."

Naturally, this task requires an awareness of the person (LS) or the Sc+P+(B)+Sy model. As previously noted, Millon (1988) likened the therapeutic task to that of an orchestra conductor. The maestro must know the score and its various parts and be able to respond when necessary, ignore when necessary, and provide overall direction and harmony. Jointly, the clinician and client strive to expose the inefficacy of negative core schemas and their protectors, personality styles, beliefs, and symptoms. At times, more surface level personality styles or beliefs must be isolated and given attention. At other times, symptoms are most in need of attention. The conductor can never stray too far from the client's core cognitions, however. Their derailing represents substantive change.

LIFE-STYLE

> Any attempt to assess the influences of Adler's work brings
> about a paradox. The impact of individual psychology stands
> beyond any doubt. . .(but) it would not be easy to find
> another author from which so much has been borrowed
> from all sides without acknowledgement than Alfred Adler
> (p. 645). Ellenberger (1970)

Adler reached beyond psychiatry and had a profound effect
on society as well as the social sciences. His professional
stance stressed the person's individuality, interpersonal behavior,
and personal responsibility, as well as a reduction of such
reified constructs as the unconscious. He promulgated a
psychiatric science based on practicality and humanity. His
interests stressed the social, emphasizing the equality of man,
prevention, community psychiatry, education, and the promotion
of human care. Between his scientific and social interests,
he was able to form a school of psychiatry that has been
infectious in the 20th century. His wisdom has been
continuously rediscovered.

Adler's position starts with the holistic unity of the person.
The person responds as an organized whole that can only
be understood from the person's internal frame of reference.
The person reacts to life in rather consistent ways that are
"softly determined" once the LS is formed. Alder viewed the
LS as the product of the person's early environmental choices
and the person's life goals (teleology). Accordingly, the person's
actions are not the result of drives or traditional causality
in psychiatry. To the extent that a person's goals are connected
to social interest, he/she is free, flexible, and open to change.
A feeling of belonging (social interest) is considered essential
for social and emotional well being. Not belonging is based
on reduced social interest, which can be measured by the
amount or area a person senses freedom. The smaller the
area, the more vulnerable the person. When the person feels
restricted (not belonging), "protectors" or safeguards become
necessary. Disorders or pathology come from human
imperfection, a discouraged person who has little social interest.
Adler (1932) was specific in his definition of social interest
as both an ability to transcend self-boundaries and to know/
accept others as oneself. Ansbacher (1968) operationalized

this as "the abilities of cooperating and contributing, as well as understanding others and empathizing with them" (p. 132). The goal of treatment is to cooperate humanly with the person, to provide insight into the LS, and to offer choice on behalf of social actualization.

Adler's crowning achievement was the LS. Its influence cannot be emphasized too strongly. The LS is responsible for the characteristic patterns of thinking, feeling, and acting on what is unique to the individual. It is the personal guiding image of a person. It has been labeled the **causa formalis,** the ordering or patterning of relationships that leads to specific results. In this sense, the LS becomes a governor that gives direction and sets limits, provides necessary feedback, and anticipates any disrupting conditions in life, such that self-perpetuating patterns persist. The LS is the "unique law of movement," "the rule of rules," and a "cognitive blueprint" for action (Shulman & Mosak, 1988).

As the superordinate organizing pattern directing behavior, the person develops a LS through trial and error, being influenced by physical, cultural, and familial factors. The LS is developmentally formed at early ages and serves to provide order. The growing child develops an image of what he/she wants to be in order to count, to be safe, to be superior, to belong, and so forth. That becomes the central goal of movement through life. This "movement" of the growing child, goals set for self, and the behavioral acts are the LS. The LS is further a unity, a cohesive force. Shulman and Mosak (1988) wrote:

> If we consider the life style a pattern, then perhaps we can recognize the recurrent themes in the life of each individual that can convey to us the essence of the individual pattern. Where, however, we examine a great many individual themes, we find that they cluster around a few main elements. (p. 5)

Despite simplicity and unity, the LS does possess specific features, and these components are given in Table 4.2. They include the **self and world images,** the **ideals or goals,** and the **methods** used for protection. Adlerians hold that the developing LS grows from its own internal environment (who and what am I), external environment (what others want), the person's goals (what should be), and the methods of operation or safeguards. This is a mixture of self views, social images (what others will or will not allow), and the most important motivator(s) or goals established. The sum, however, is a totally unique individual that protects self by a "schema of apperception" (Ansbacher, 1965).

TABLE 4.2
Elements of Life-style

What is	Key Issue	Measure
Self-image	Who am I? Location What am I? Evaluation	I am. . .
World Image	How does life work? What is my relationship to others?	The world is. . .
What should be		
Ideal	I want, I must have, "only if". . .	I want. . .
Moral Judgement	I should . . .	I should. . .
Methods		
Personality Style	Self perpetuating patterns Model styles	Behaviors/ cognition/ affects that are consistant

In the next section, goals are discussed. Any discussion of the LS without addressing goals is akin to attempting to calculate the area of the surface of an object with only the length. The person moves from a felt minus to a plus. Each person strives to be something and defines self goals and the methods to assure his/her attainment. No choice exists in this matter. Goals drive or give direction to the LS and are absolutely necessary for its formation. In this sense, behavior is construed as goal directed or teleological. The individual strives to be significant, to excel, to make a mark, or to define self teleologically. The person says, "**only if** I can be X, will I be okay"; "**only if** I can be X, can I feel like I belong." Typical goals include control, comfort, superiority, adequacy, perfection, assertiveness, flawlessness, and an infinite number of others tailored to the individual. They are fictitious in that they are "desired realities" below which the person feels uncomfortable. The operative question for each person in every situation is: "How does this behavior help me to achieve my goal? How do I seek to be known?" This has been labeled *teleocausality.* Common meanings are teased from each situation naturally.

This goal process is highly coordinated: the person is "pushed" by the goal. In turn, the LS creates conditions to pursue goals, even to distort the environment. Functions of the LS can be limitless—organizing and simplifying, problem solving, controlling, myth making, reinforcing, self-protecting, and ultimately self-defining. The structures of the LS act in unison, apperceiving information on behalf of the goal and doing so consistently, effortlessly, and unconsciously. The LS is the person, the dynamic organization of a growing being—its development, motivation, emotions, cognitions, and behaviors.

Life-style Analysis

Many methods exist for measuring the LS (Dinkmeyer, Pew, & Dinkmeyer, 1979; Sweeney, 1989; Shulman & Mosak, 1988). These have been labeled *Life-style Analysis* (LSA). Lombardi (1973) outlined a finite number of ways to know another's LS: case history, family constellation, early recollections

(ER), symptoms, behavior, testing, interaction, and interviews. Any are adequate, as each provides a method for an understanding of the victim across the life span.

Our interest is the efficient procurement of meaningful idiographic information on trauma victims—LS data. Accordingly, we have developed our own LSA given in Table 4.3. The components of the LSA include childhood questions, parental descriptors and perceptions, family life (values, atmosphere, and behavior), sibling ratings, early recollections (ER), and personal meaning questions. Also some questions on trauma are included. Based on these areas, a summary of the person's LS, their methods of operation and goals can be formed (and reformulated) to assist in an understanding of the person's cyclic patterns. We also encourage the use of personality measures which will be discussed in the next chapter. Finally, a special note is directed to the meaning questions as these represent a collection of "agency specific" self perceptions, the way the person sees/objectifies self and has developed a sense of meaning.

The LSA is a interviewer-rated questionnaire, designed to have the person discuss distinct areas of development. It is open ended to emphasize individuality. It is meant as a reference guide to stimulate thinking about early life issues usually rarely reflected upon. Remember that the intent is not to determine the LS of a trauma victim in any absolute sense, but to allow for a fuller understanding of the person— the pre-trauma person. Even a less "accurate" approximation of the person is helpful, as the LSA serves to highlight how the person has negotiated the press of history, attitudes toward life, and of course, the formation of core schema and self-perpetuating patterns (personality). Through an adequate representation of the family atmosphere, values, priorities, functioning, sibling positions, and ERs, the child's unique place in life takes form.

A helpful tool in the evaluation of the LS is the lifeline (Table 4.4). The victim is able to scan and compare events, pre- and post-trauma, to draw conclusions, assess obstacles, and provide predictions. It serves as a blueprint from which to react (or alter). Again, this is an approximation of the

(continued on page 174)

TABLE 4.3
Life-style Analysis

Childhood:

Meaning   What makes life worthwhile for you?
How would you describe yourself growing up?
How do you feel about your childhood?
How did you feel about religion?
What lessons did you learn?
Was anyone afraid at home?
Could you make a difference (be in control)?
What was your role in the family?
How did you feel about the family?

Sex   How did you feel about being a boy/girl?
Describe how sex played a part in growth?
Was anyone (you) in your family sexually abused?
How did you first learn about sex?

Social   Were you accepted by other kids or were you more
    to yourself?
What kinds of groups or gangs were you in?
How did you feel about your social life?
Were you different from others in your
    neighborhood?
Did you have any nicknames?

Physical   How did you feel about your body (advantages/
    disadvantages)?
How did you regard yourself?

School   What types of schools did you attend?
What were you like as a student?
Did you like school?
Did you ever get sent home/expelled/left back?
What were your favorite (worst) subjects?

Trauma   What was the worst thing you can recall happening
    to you while growing up?
Has this left an impact?
How did that experience change you?

(continued)

TABLE 4.3 (continued)

Discipline   How did you comply with rules?
What did you do when you were angry?
How did you get your way?

Parents:

	Father	Mother
Current age		
Age at subject's birth		
Description		
(If divorced or other family involved, establish when this occurred)		

Who was dominant?
Who was decision maker?
Who was responsible for discipline?
Occupation for each?
Who handled money?

Questions:
Was it a good marriage?
What did each demand?
What did each value?
What did each reject?
What did each permit?
How did your father act when he was angry?
How did your mother act when she was angry?
How did they handle conflict?
Describe their relationship—Put X on line
pleasant ....unpleasant
affectionate ....unloving
close ....distant
conflictual ....harmonious
cooperative ....selfish
playful ....serious

(continued)

TABLE 4.3 (continued)

┌─────────────┐
│ Family Life:│
└─────────────┘
Family Values
    What did parents want from you?
    What was ambition for you?
    What was success/failure?
    What was significant?
    Describe any cultural influences.
    How was religion important?
Family Atmosphere
    Mood. . .anxious - calm
           hostile - friendly
           discouraged - hopeful
           unhappy - cheerful
    Order. . .chaotic - orderly
           strict - permissive
           inconsistent - consistent
           arbitrary - logical
    Relationship. . .distant - intimate
           competitive - cooperative
           rejecting - accepting
           blaming - understanding
           hidden - open
           conflict - harmony
Parental Behavior
           accept - reject
           authoritarian - laissez-faire
           consistent - inconsistent
           overprotective - encouraging
           demand for achievement - rewarded achievement
           excessive morality - encouraging
           excessive criticism - accepting
           excessive strictness - encouraging
           warm - cold
           nurture - non-nurture
           neglected - cared for
           competing - cooperating
           encouraging - discouraging
           pampered - accepting

(continued)

TABLE 4.3 (continued)

Siblings:

Describe each sibling focusing on what each was like as a child growing up.

Name_____
Age Difference____ M___F___
Description

Name_____
Age Difference___ M___F___
Description

Name_____
Age Difference___ M___F___
Description

Name_____
Age Difference___ M___F___
Description

Sibling Ratings:

Please rate yourself and your brother(s) and sisters(s) on the following traits putting an M (most) for most or more of the trait and an L (least) for least or less of the trait.

Sibling Names

Traits	_____	_____	_____	_____
Academic	____	____	____	____
Intelligence	____	____	____	____
Helpfulness	____	____	____	____
Responsible	____	____	____	____
Ambitious	____	____	____	____
Actual				
Achievement	____	____	____	____
Idealistic	____	____	____	____

(continued)

TABLE 4.3 (continued)

Obedient	____	____	____	____
Mischievous	____	____	____	____
Sociable	____	____	____	____
Outgoing	____	____	____	____
Considerate	____	____	____	____
Dominant	____	____	____	____
Temper	____	____	____	____
Stubborn	____	____	____	____
Complained	____	____	____	____
Fights	____	____	____	____
Independent	____	____	____	____
Depended on others	____	____	____	____
Moral standards	____	____	____	____
Easy going	____	____	____	____
Control	____	____	____	____
Impulsive	____	____	____	____
Masculine	____	____	____	____

Sibling Questions:

> Who was most similar to you?
> In what way?
> Who was most different from you?
> In what way?
> With whom did you interact most?
> Who did you like the most?
> What is each doing today?

Early Recollections:

Go back as far in your memory as you can and tell me of your earliest recollection. Make this a one time event, almost like a snapshot in your mind.

What is most vivid about this?
What is your feeling?
What would you change?
How would you interpret this?

(continued)

TABLE 4.3 (continued)

| Clinician's Ratings of ER: |

Behavior toward environment

withdrawn	gracious
passive	active
competitive	cooperative
dependent	independent

Affective Response

hostile	friendly
feels rejected	feels accepted
discouraged	confident
depressed	cheerful
feels mistrusted	feels befriended

Themes

dethronement	excitement
surprises	sexuality
obstinacy	acceptance
affiliation	competence
security	gender
depending	nurturance
control	confusion
power	luck
status	sickness/health
morality	manipulations
problem solving	revenge
resolve	denial
avoidance	overconfident
criticism	social interest

Repeat ER procedure three more times.

(continued)

TABLE 4.3 (continued)

| Personal Meaning Questions: |

Pre-trauma Questions

Do these issues seem relevant to you in your life?
What were your expectations for yourself?
What was your goal in life?
How did you feel about right and wrong?
Do you feel that life is worthwhile?
What was fun for you?
How would you describe yourself as a person?
What are your strongest characteristics? Weakest?
What are your main values—beliefs you use to deal with life?
Looking back, what do you think was the most important
    influence on you outside your trauma?
What gives you the greatest satisfaction?
What are your expectations about treatment?
What are you doing that is helpful for you?
How do you ask for help?
Can you get a "broader sense" of your situation—your meaning
    in life?
Where are you vulnerable?
What one feature of yourself would you change?
Is this the way you want to be?
Was there ever a time when you didn't feel that way?
What do I need to know about you that really matters?
What is your "inner life" like?
Who is your role model, the one you want to be like?

Post-trauma Questions

Can you envision a positive (possible) self for you?
If you were not experiencing trauma symptoms, what would
    you be doing?
Where do you get stuck in your life?
What feeling gives you the most trouble?
What is the influence of your problems over you?
What is the influence of you over your problems?
How can you reclaim your life?
What is the most "fitting" thing to be done in your life now?
How can you help a therapist work well with you?

TABLE 4.4
Lifeline

Instructions

The line below represents the span of your life. The dot at the left represents your birth date. Write the actual date under it.

The dot at the other end represents the date of your death. Over this dot write the number—your best guess of years you think you will live. Under this dot write the estimated date of your death.

Place a dot that represents where you are now on the line between your birth and death. Then write today's date under this dot. To the left of today's date, write what you believe are your most significant accomplishments or experiences up to this point. To the right of today's date indicate in a few words some things you would like to do before your death.

Place a dot(s) on the approximate time of your trauma(s). Describe how you were before and after that (those) event(s).

Birth ....Death

(continued)

TABLE 4.4 (continued)

TASKS

1. Identify by the year all significant episodes/events in your life (take your time).

2. Attempt to group years together (e.g., early school years, divorce years, etc) and give those years a title.

3. What are the most important "learnings" from the group years?

4. How were you changed as a person because of these years?

5. How have you remained the same up to the present? How have you changed?

6. What events do you regret most? Why?

7. What are your strengths/weaknesses?

8. How did the trauma alter the "pre-trauma you"?

9. At a minimum what do you need to change to get on with your life?

10. Are you optimistic about the future?

Extrapolated from various sources, authors unknown.

person, of features that are totally individual, unknown to personality measures. Also, this method suggests to the victim that stressor preoccupation alone may be unwise. The tunnel vision opens.

The ER

A key element of the LSA yet to be discussed is the ER. This is viewed by Adlerians as a reflector of the LS. ERs constitute a projective test from which the individual reveals long term patterns and goals. Adler maintained that *people remember only those events from early childhood that are consistent with present views of themselves and the world.* The idea is that whatever causes their ER to remain in consciousness is reflective of the LS. Gushurst (1971) held that the ER "provides a picture of how an individual viewed himself, other people and life in general" (p. 33). Beck and Emery (1985) also considered the importance of ERs and developed a method of combining them with current fears to help identify negative cognitions.

ERs are really products of the interaction between an attitudinal set and external stimuli. They are an internalized repertoire of interpersonal relationship paradigms and are often related to current problems—they "softly determine" behavior. In this sense, they both influence the person and, as a result of life experiences (or psychotherapy), are influenced by the person. (The ER then is subject to shaping and reshaping due to experiences). This makes the ER directly reflective of the LS, asserting an influence on behavior. As we will see in Chapter 6, the ER is similar to the trauma memory ("stuck narrative") and requires a distinctive approach for alteration.

Whether the ER influences situations and subsequent behavior (relative to a trauma) or vice versa, has never been completely determined. Hyer, Woods, and Boudewyns (1989) studied ERs of 70 Vietnam veterans with PTSD. These were obtained as part of a LSA on each subject. Independent ratings of social interest, positive/negative features, and the presence/absence of early trauma were obtained. Results showed ERs with low social interest and negative and trauma features. The authors suggested that person factors be considered in the assessment and care of trauma victims. The ER, then, is considered a mini-narrative reflective of the person's own (self) narrative. This is not an arbitrary or ad hoc constructed embodiment of the person, but rather a carefully fashioned summary of personal meanings as represented in an event.

Our experience has been that clinicians *are* interested in the person of the victim. In addition to a trauma history and mental status, a developmental history is often obtained. We would encourage some developmental case formulation of the person. Discussion of earlier vestiges of the person is often stimulating, freeing, and clinically challenging. Related techniques like the time line or mirroring (Mahoney, 1991) are most useful. This process sends important messages. The person of the victim who becomes intellectually and psychologically curious about his/her own development is by these very acts pushing aside the crust of the trauma response. Any requirement of absolute accuracy is less important than the effort (and product) of conceptualizing patterns of experience as uniquely individual. The understanding of LS provides a developmental perspective for an understanding of the trauma response. PTSD then can be understood progressively through development, rather than regressively from present symptoms.

GOALS

Within the past decade, a growing shift has occurred toward the idea that human behavior is fundamentally goal-directed and that motivation, satisfaction, frustration, and psychological distress are intimately related to the pursuit of both conscious and unconscious goals. The thesis is that behavior is motivated by the desire to reach a particular objective or goal. Recently, the shift toward information processing, holding that future events could be represented cognitively and that these cognitions could precede in time the behaviors designed to actually bring about these desired objectives, meant that goals could logically serve as causes of behavior. Many current ideas about human functioning now treat the goal construct as a key explanatory variable.

Increasingly, the goal concept appears to be the best supported and least problematic of the possible sources of motivation.

The Adlerian idea is that the goal represents a guiding self ideal, a self-created notion that is the final goal of the behavioral program of the LS. In effect, all behavior is organized toward the goal. Ansbacher (1965) wrote:

> The striving for success or perfection derives its direction from the goal of success which is influenced by all kinds of objective conditions but which is ultimately of the individual's own creation. The individual is generally only dimly aware of his goal or may never have conceptualized a goal so that he does not understand his own actions. In this case the goal, like the unconscious, is the psychologist's heuristic fiction. The function of the fictional goal is to provide the psychologist with a working hypothesis toward understanding a case. "Causes, powers, instincts, impulses, and the like cannot serve as explanatory principles....Experiences, traumata, sexual development mechanisms cannot yield an explanation, but the perspective in which these are regarded...which subordinates all life to the final goal, can do so" (p. 92). With regard to any kind of behavior in a person, the Adlerian will always ask himself not "How did he get that way?" but "What is he accomplishing or trying to accomplish by this?" (p. 350)

Our position is a simple extension of this concept. *The goal, as we have developed it, is the direction setter and internal motive of the schema.* The goal is to schema what it is to the LS. Just as one cannot speak of the LS without the goal, so too the goal provides the reinforcement for the schema. The trick is to develop a method to integrate this concept into treatment.

Organization: Past and future

The key function of the goal is orientation, for directing the movement of the LS. The striving is ceaseless. The goal is the chosen way of fulfilling basic psychological motivations. In the previous section, goals were noted as giving direction to the LS. In effect, the LS grows out of the goal. Goals provide the orienting, prioritizing, coordinating, monitoring, evaluating, and rewarding to the LS. Unfortunately, few goals formulated by people are grounded in social interest or human betterment.

They fall short. As such, they are private creations "to be." They are fictions, being real only to the person. Since goals are mostly unconscious in their activity and the person is directed in the most persistent of ways toward this end, goals with low social interest are a problem in life.

Goals are feed-forward mechanisms. Borrowing from information processing, a goal in the future exists in the present and asserts an influence. In a sense two realities are created; the first is the "mental" reality of the cognitions and the second involves the "actual" reality of the experience. In this sense too, goals are the central reinforcers for the LS. Without goals the person feels lost; "If I give up my goal, then I will be lost." The intriguing aspect of this "only if" component is that the goal is really the essence of the LS. However distorted, this is the one feature of the person that must be attended to or respected for organized activity. Anything less than reasonable compliance results in internal problems, and "governors" are set in motion to alter the situation.

Markus and Nurius (1986) perhaps put their fingers on what may be one cutting-edge—"means-end" component of this goal process. These authors believed that all of us are motivated by possible selves. They are each person's repertoire of "what could be," a cognitive manufacturing of enduring goals, motives, fears, and aspirations. In effect, these constructs allow each of us to be multifaceted, to do all the hard work to insure that our LS possesses needed motivation and behavioral skills and to do this in infinitely varied ways depending on the context. Also of interest, these authors, along with Porter (Porter, Markus, & Nurius, 1984), examined the possible selves of 30 victims of a life crisis with 30 who had not experienced one. The crisis group was further divided depending on whether or not they had recovered from the trauma. All three groups were compared on various definitions of their now and current selves—how each perceived him or her self now in various life areas. No differences occurred between the two trauma groups, and predictable differences occurred between the non-trauma group and the two trauma groups (non-trauma group was "healthier" for current self).

Intriguing results occurred when the authors compared the groups on possible selves—"what is possible for you." Of special interest was how the two trauma groups differed from one another. The recovered trauma group was "better"—more motivated, creative, trusted, active, powerful, intelligent, independent and the like. These individuals who had negative now selves had more positive possible selves. The authors wrote:

> It may be that the presence of these possible selves, or the ability to construct them, may have actually facilitated recovery. That is, these possible selves may be the carriers or cognitive representations of feelings of mastery. The fact that the high recovery subjects endorsed many positive possible selves, and evaluated them to be quite likely, suggests that these selves were available in the working self-concepts of these respondents and were functioning as incentives. (p. 962)

The bottom line is that an organized system of future events (goals) best seems to account for the patterns of motivation, emotions, and of course behaviors. Even in future events (goals), the self organizes a vision of what can be and "seeds" its functions. Emotions, for example, provide evaluative feedback on actions taken at the direction of the goal. Positive possible self then focuses and organizes one's activities. By editing positive self-relevant possibilities, the clinician has already been therapeutic.

Another way of conceptualizing life goal is in terms of each person's life span. One does not have to be a hard-core Eriksonian to know that people respond to their life spans with different beginnings, endings, and transitions. While no clearcut demarcation of stages may be identified (Erikson, 1975), the person's identity is formed in a complicated interaction of personality, culture, and life span issues (what issue ascends for a person at different ages). Somewhere along this line of growth, probably at the age of five or six, an identity is born, made up of episodes of continuity and change. These are nuclear episodes resulting in a decision of how I will take charge of me and interact with others. As this style(s) becomes molded through a constant reconciliation of opportunities and frustrations, a vision or ending becomes more apparent and more defined. Sartre (1964) pointed out that the ending of the story shapes all that comes before it. Life in this way is actually formed by the **telos,** the end point that justifies the life striving. The future selects past events and current options to become the ingredients to form the present behavior. In this ongoing process one's direction in life is teleologically anchored. However, in most cases only at middle or later life does the person actively seek to integrate and better know the sense of unity and purpose in life.

Finally, an understanding of the goal and LS supports a theme of this book—the unity and emergence of the person's **comprehensible narrative.** Our belief is that the person develops his/her own life story across the life span, a continuous process that is probably sequential (based on previous developmental changes), but always reactive to the salient "person-life" dimensions of time, memory, and relationships. Therefore, growing older and being with others influences the content of this story. The course of one's development is really a series of transformations leading to a reordering of these three (and other) dimensions, an elaboration on the narrative or LS. At various life stages or for various situational reasons, the person is disrupted and a transformation of the narrative (LS) is required. These are the "teachable moments" in a person's life. When trauma occurs, the person's narrative also must be reconstructed. The person always seeks to keep narrative order and predictability (sense of coherency in LS). The importance of this life story (LS) or narrative is realized in the joint (re)construction of the person in the process of psychotherapy. What this means is that the person develops a working narrative (LS) and comprehends "facts" and stressors according to this story, with all those influences of the various life stages. Only psychotherapy can alter this. (We will pick up on this theme in the next section and address it again in Chapter 14, PTSD among the Elderly.)

To Goal or Not to Goal

Unfortunately, goal directedness is often confusing to trauma victims. The clinical appeal that is so evident with other clients is often muddied due to the influence of the trauma symptoms. Goal formulation also is confusing to victims because a dominant goal generally has one or more methods of attainment commonly found in association with it. The person who wants to be "first" can choose many methods of operation (personality styles) on behalf of that goal. The permutations can be confusing, especially to a chronic trauma victim seeking peace and simplicity. Finally, goal formulation may prove confusing because goals often appear at odds with actions. In fact, actions are usually in line with the goal, but the individual is not aware of the objectives he/she sets for self. Again, for chronic trauma victims the connection of goals to acts may be lost.

Despite this concern, many positive features exist for the clinical use of goals. Recall our thesis: The goal is the direction setting and internal motivating force of the schema. So, if the therapy process is attached to the unearthing of the schema, then the connection of the goal formulation has merit. Several other advantages exist also. First, assessment questions that are goal based have meaning beyond their purpose. Such questions as "What would it mean for you to give up your anger?", "Is this the kind of person you want to be?", or "How is this behavior serving your goal?", have information value regardless of one's position about teleology. In addition, many victims can appreciate that like all actions, people begin with the end in mind. The person's script for actions, thoughts, and feelings conform to end states. Also, goals may be future in focus but they are grounded in the past, the baseline of the person. In a sense they are "knowable" because of their elevated status in the past. Clients know this. From an intellectual perspective victims can understand that goal directed behaviors, as much as anything, are reasonable, consistent, and can represent a challenge in self-monitoring. Frankl (1969) wrote that people "detect" rather than invent their miseries in life. People have a radar system locked on one end state, even for self-defeating reasons.

Also, one added advantage of the clinical use of goals is "goal thinking" which should remain in the consciousness of the clinician. In therapy this has been labelled goal alignment; that is, the therapist is goal aligned in therapy when a match between his/her goal and the client's occurs. Any deviation leads to resistance. Ultimately, distorted goals need to be exposed, gently confronted, respectfully tagged, and alternatives provided. A useful rubric is that when treatment bogs down, plateaus become apparent, or resistance is evident, the therapist has strayed too far from the client's goal. This is a most common form of treatment failure with chronic trauma victims (Catherall, 1991).

Measurement

As with the LSA, several measures of goals are in the research literature (Suich, 1991). Since goals "direct" the person's LS and are central to all action, a simple and parsimonious clinical measure involves asking the client to complete the following sentence: "Only when I am _____, am I worthwhile." Remember, goals anchor the meaning-making activities of the person. Victims are surprisingly able to provide information. Psychometric scales also have been developed based on various goal typologies (e.g., Dreikurs, 1967). Kern (Kern, Matheny, & Patterson, 1978), for example, has developed a *Life Style Scale* measuring five goals: control, perfectionism, need to please, victim, and martyr. Using a **Redecision Therapy Model,** Goulding and Goulding (1972) identified five universal methods (be perfect, try hard, please me, hurry up, and be strong) that serve distorted goals. Based on early negative injunctions (e.g., don't grow up, don't feel), the child develops these distorted goals to feel adequate. Therapy in this model involves the client's recall of childhood scenes and subsequently "trying on" healthier responses. Not until the victim "redecides" against these learned injunctions and compensation responses does change occur. The work on Axis II disorders by Beck and Freeman (1990) also emphasized goals in treatment. From this CBT perspective, goals evolve from core schemas and serve to influence behavior.

Also, clinicians know that when behavior is ego-dystonic (symptoms), the client is inherently inclined to view this as "bad" or "out there." Under these circumstances, a helpful procedure is to suggest that this behavior is a solution (a bad one) to his/her conflict. A reasonable course of action, then, is to backtrack from this solution to an understanding of the problem. Resolution involves finding another solution. The PTSD victim, for example, is asked to identify what the anger outburst accomplished. Often the victim can identify a deviant goal and identify what this means in the context of his/her person. In this way, the person owns the behavior and now can ask self, "Is this the way I want to be?"

We favor one other method of measurement. In Table 4.5, Nichols (1991) outlines the central features of goals. He has labeled these core goals. In Part I is specified that the core goal is the single feature of the person that is best situated to account for behavior. These core goal features are very "schema-like" and encompass central person elements. Simply put, satisfaction or dissatisfaction results because the core goal is or is not met. Knowing what is wanted explains what is rewarding or dissatisfying.

In Part II of this table is specified a method for goal identification. Nichols (1991) has made goal seeking clinically useful, understandable, and fun. This procedure is a structured self-inquiry, looking a "best moments" or positive experiences. As the victim proceeds in this process, two to four core goals are isolated. These goals are developed from positive memories (possible selves), so they are "real" and appealing. Since they are emotional experiences, the goals often become "alive" and assume a life of their own.

At this center, in a current group with victims on the identification of positive goals, two conclusions applied: (1) due to the avoidant process of PTSD, many victims related "problems" regarding positive experiences—don't deserve these, incapable of these, positive and negative feelings are mixed, positive feelings "always" give way to bad feelings, etc.; and (2) the narrowing process itself (Table 4.5, Part II) was exciting, appealing, and engaging. Referring to this section of Table 4.5, clinical application of this procedure reduces concerns (#1) and whets the appetite for knowledge about the core goal (#2). In one example, a Vietnam combat victim described an auto race where he finished second. The veteran noted several features that were positive—being nosed out at the finish, racing three abreast for five laps, strapping his battery to the car after a close call, exhilaration at start of race, and feeling of car "purring." During this narrowing stage he described several micromoments of each of these events that were rewarding. One stuck out (#3). This cognitive/affective high was his reaction to the car purring perfectly—a team

TABLE 4.5
Core Goals*

I. Key Ideas of Core Goal

   1. Core goals are cognitive representations of desired consequences.
   2. Core goals represent desired internal emotional states.
   3. Core goals are individual constructions, not universal constructs.
   4. Core goals must be desired primarily as ends in themselves, not as means to achieving other more important or more basic goals.
   5. Core goals are highly stable yet continuously evolving entitles that organize many behaviors in many situations over many years.
   6. An individual has a limited set of core goals.
   7. Core goals have both positive and negative aspects.
   8. A core goal may trigger strong feelings of contentment when its positive side is satisfied and, conversely, strong feelings of frustration when its negative side is unintentionally attained.
   9. Core goals can function outside of conscious awareness.

II. Core Goal Identification Process

   1. Identify 15 to 25 satisfying experiences.
   2. Reduce to these to 15 and describe "the moment" of peak satisfaction of each one.
   3. Narrow this peak moment to the single best moment that provides the strongest feeling—describe in detail.
   4. Change focus from what happened to a feeling— describe in detail that feeling.
   5. Identify common emotional themes from each of the experiences. Construct a common verbal description of these clusters—perhaps 2-4 core clusters.
   6. Rewrite these 2-4 descriptions to accurately reflect your satisfaction. These are your core goals.

* Extrapolated from Nichols (1991). Printed with permission from Consulting Psychologists Press.

effort of precision ("I am a central part of a finely tuned operation")(#4). Several other independent positive episodes were reduced to this core goal of a perfectly running event in life that he was involved in (#5). This core goal was striking as this person was highly engaged, was surprised at his discovery, and had organized his life (its positive and negative moments) around needs of harmony and perfection. Strikingly too, his trauma was directly tied to this core goal (schema).

The pursuit of core goals also assists therapy in other ways. First, they provide meaning to schemas. Recall that goals are the "telos" part of the schema—the purpose of the action, the direction setting function, and the motivation behind behavior. Second, core goals can be used as clinically useful monitors for understanding emotions or frustrating events. Recall that when a core goal (or aspects of a core goal) is not represented in an action—dissatisfaction ensues. Listing core goals on one side of a page and negative (or positive) events on the other is one way to provide a reference for the monitoring of satisfaction. Next, core goals can lead to further brainstorming regarding the "reasons" for being the source of pleasure or distress (if deprived). Finally, victims can experience first hand the stuck quality of their trauma response and develop methods to challenge these.

No one method is best. Goal formulation should remain alive and well in the clinician's orienting concepts. The key idea is that the goal is developed through the schema. In fact, we "softly" suggest that core goals are the schemas, only described from the motivation perspective. Unfortunately, chronic victims are most often oblivious to goals in their behaviors. The task of the therapist is to translate a client's aspirations and ambitions into a goal and, if possible, attach these to the schema. Clients who are autonomy centered, for example, often have goals of being first, of winning, or of being on top. Clients who are dependent often desire to avoid humiliation or to be accepted. Many negative and self-defeating behaviors are "logical" knowing the teleological push of the goal. The pursuit of core schemas then "reveals" this interesting marker—the existence of a goal. Often the two are fused. Goals are really oversimplified words for purpose and consistency; as such, their clinical value can be high.

PRIVATE LOGIC

A supporting self-protective process of the LS, along with personality styles and symptoms, is private logic (or beliefs). These are biased perceptions/beliefs that justify behavior. They are one's private logic: that is, they are "hidden" self statements used to justify a behavior or a position. When a person behaves or reacts contrary to normative patterns or remains "stuck" in treatment, private logic is operating.

In regard to Adler, until the clinician understood the patient's private logic, nothing could be done to change the person. This is the essence of the phenomenological position: in reference to Adler, "everything also could be different" (Ansbacher, 1965). Horney (1937) described these positions as overdriven attitudes, identifying characteristics, or "neurotic claims." Driekurs (1953) described these as "basic mistakes," faulty social values related to standard norms, and social prescriptions for behavior. For Driekers these positions grew out of social values which were harmful to growth. Others have considered beliefs as universal in the sense that all people, to some extent, feel defective, exposed, disapproved of, and the like. More contemporary positions emphasize also the basic mistakes notion of faulty thinking, including Albert Ellis (1962), Beck (Beck & Emery, 1985), and several Adlerian theorists (e.g., Shulman & Mosak, 1988).

The notion of cognitive distortions is implied in much of the treatment of trauma injury. For many, however, the assumption is that cognitions are disrupted by trauma. However, the emphasis on integration of trauma memories often "overpowers" cognitive correction interests. The trauma focus drowns out the cognitive one. Horowitz (1986) emphasized the aberrant memory processing: Lifton and Olson (1976) discussed impaired symbolization; Krystal (1978) considered ineffective defenses; and Brett and Ostroff (1985) even described trauma integration as failed attempts at mastery. Recent treatment formulations (e.g., Dye & Roth, 1991) also followed suit.

Recently, some changes in emphasis have been made. McCann and Pearlman (1990) have noted that the adaptation

TABLE 4.6
Irrational Cognitive Patterns at Times of Trauma and Current Meaning*

Strategy	Vietnam	Current
1. Intolerance of Mistakes	-no mistakes or one dies -trust in men	-rigid intolerance thinking -no patience
2. Denial of Personal Difficulties	-psychic numbing -nonemotional responses -no personal problems	-affective constriction -numbing
3. Anger as a Problem Solving Strategy	-learned violence in military -cold combat feelings -anger rewarded as reason to kill	-impulsive violence -acting out as a conflict method
4. Hypervigilance	-self protection -reduce unpredictability	-startle response -world is dangerous -protective environment
5. Black and White Thinking	-"us versus the enemy" -military teachings	-absolutistic thinking -trust loss -few friends
6. Cognitive Rigidity & Resistance to Change	-absolute belief in military methods	-not enough non-fear extinction -overvalued ideation

*Extrapolated from Alford, Mahone, and Felstein (1988).

which occurs cognitively not only "suggests" much about the person but also drives the action of the trauma response. These authors argued that cognitions are tacit or explicit reflectors of the schema. Consequently, the emphasis should be on the deeper cognitions altered by the trauma experience. The representation of the cognitive need (schema) requires treatment. In addition, a handful of studies have been done that address the importance of cognitions in trauma victims. Alford, Mahone, and Felstein (1988) evaluated chronic combat victims with PTSD and identified cognitions that cause day-to-day problems. They were directly related to learning from the early trauma experience. They are given in Table 4.6. These are beliefs that are readily learned and relearned under stressor conditions and perpetuated at later times. What was a necessary learning in combat, however, does not apply now. Parson (1988) has identified similar surface beliefs that are overlearned during the trauma and assert a negative influence later.

Three decades have passed since Ellis (1962) popularized Rational Emotive Therapy, which holds that thinking causes problems in living. If irrational beliefs are held, symptoms or emotional problems will result. In the context of trauma, basic mistakes, whether stylistic, syntactical, paralogical, or based on content, are common fare of victims of trauma. The universal drive to avoid pain, to parry secondary trauma, or continually to make sense of trauma, necessitates an uneasy time for the processes of thinking and perceptions. Distorted thinking occurs. From the CBT perspective, these beliefs are the top level of thought distortions—the "by-products" of schema. They are automatic and on the surface. They have lower core cognition salience. Nonetheless, these thoughts start the process. Surface level distortions are what are presented by the client, what can be measured, and thereby, what is accessible. Their importance cannot be overstated. Several CBT proponents like Meichenbaum (1985) advocate for the use of "surface" techniques only, like self-coping or problem solving. Highlighting their importance and the dynamic between surface and core cognitions Safran and Segal (1990) wrote:

...the patient is able to have a concrete, meaningful experience of how deep structural rules (dysfunctional attitudes) and the surface level activities (automatic thoughts, discounting activity) are linked. Oscillating between the exploration of high-level constructs and the reality test of cognitive activities guided by these constructs keeps the patient's recognition of the impact of these constructs grounded in immediate experiences, thereby contributing to the loosening of her constructs.

Once both the negative self-evaluative activity and the guiding dysfunctional attitudes have been made explicit, and the patient becomes aware of the complex interconnection between deep structure and surface structure in the moment, cognitive interventions, such as reality testing or inspecting evidence, can then contribute to the modification of the underlying interpersonal schema. (p. 133)

Private logic is highlighted in this section because it is so central to personologic strategies. Private logic acts as an "organizer" in the same way that an RNA messenger performs in the cell: it is both director and worker for all needed activities. While Adler viewed private logic to be beyond consciousness (and thereby more core), the position here is that private logic is best represented as surface cognitions, day-to-day material of the person. The clinician slides up and down this cognitive dimension with varying degrees of "coreness." The point on the continuum at which a belief merges with or becomes a schema is unknown. What is known is that schemas are entrenched, far-reaching, and hierarchically arranged so as to borrow many surface beliefs for continuance. The clinician's focus, though, should always be downward.

SYMPTOMS

Adler viewed symptoms as important expressions of the LS. They were the safeguards for self-esteem. Unfortunately, this formulation is too simple for addressing the complexity of the psychological status of the trauma victim. Above all, symptoms alter the relationship the victim has with his/her inner self and own feelings and boundaries (Mahoney, 1991). In effect, the person does not feel comfortable with his/her core ordering processes. Something more is ordered—a sort of trophy room of problems always ready for viewing. In addition, symptoms also demand constant consideration. In treatment, leveling is the complex phenomenon reflecting the choice of how and where to focus energy. When symptoms are inflamed, the choice is easy. When they fade in and out of awareness, the therapeutic focus can be elsewhere. Their presence is always felt, however.

In this section, we address four issues related to symptoms: (1) the need to contextualize symptoms within the person, (2) the relationship of personality disorders to symptom formation and treatment, (3) the complexity of symptoms in trauma victims, and (4) a brief note on the need to assess trauma, given our model.

Contextualization

In regard to Adler, symptoms serve the same function as do personality styles and beliefs, only more dramatically. People choose symptoms and emotions based on the LS in order to justify actions. In fact, symptoms are construed as tools to convince others of noble purposes. In the eyes of the individual psychologist, the significance of the symptom lies in its service to the individual in maintaining the LS. Like private logic, symptoms have a "secret intent." Intents have a clear mission. This mission includes securing a triumph, retiring from danger, reproaching another person, providing an exemption from demands, forcing the environment into one's service, or compelling others to take notice, among others. Less subtle than cognitive distortions, the symptoms of the person are paraded on the social stage of life for purposes of fostering the LS, of keeping consistency, of stamping nobility, and of providing continued fuel for action. They are often action-prone, but always excuses or safeguards for LS. They are "necessary," natural, and encompassing. Symptoms are suboptimal solutions; better solutions, therefore, can be found.

Regarding the placement of symptoms in a classification system, Millon (1983) wrote:

> A classification system will go awry if its major categories encompass too diverse a range of clinical conditions; there is need to subdivide psychopathology in terms of certain

fundamental criteria. In this regard, particular attention must be paid to drawing distinctions among patients who appear overtly similar but differ in ways that have significant prognostic consequences. It is for this reason that an attempt is made here to differentiate among personality patterns, symptom disorders and behavior reactions.

The essential criterion for making these distinctions is the extent to which the observed pathology reflects ingrained personal traits versus transient situational difficulties. Thus, personality patterns are defined as clinical syndromes composed of intrinsic, deeply embedded, and pervasive ways of functioning. At the opposite end of a continuum are the behavior reactions, defined as highly specific pathological responses that are precipitated by and largely attributable to circumscribed external events. Between these two extremes lie the symptom disorders, categories of psychopathology that are anchored simultaneously to ingrained personal traits and transient stimulus events. Conceived as intensifications or disruptions in a patient's characteristic style of functioning, symptom disorders are viewed as a reaction to a situation for which the individual's personality is notably vulnerable. (p. 10)

From this description, different kinds of symptoms can be identified: one type related to the "inner stimuli" of the person and one type independent of this. The most typical symptoms are those reflective of ingrained personal traits. In this sense, symptoms are logical extensions of stress conditions; they fit the person. These are "protectors," distinctive of the person. In trauma, however, something else also occurs. Given excessive stress, the response of the person does *not necessarily* pass through a chain of complicated and circuitous transformations. Trauma has an immediate, direct, and often *practical* impact on the person. In this sense, the decompensation pattern of a trauma victim is non-specific— reflective of an uncontaminated person process. Given enough stress, *everybody* would act the same.

Previously, we have emphasized "specific" trauma symptoms, those organized and formed by schemas. These are present and strongly influence the person. Schemas then are "responsible" for the function of most symptoms. One might say that predisposing schemas and personality styles "more strongly argue" for their position. As intensity increases or the situation warrants, however, the symptom influence can reach levels that may be wholly Axis I driven. Pure trauma-driven rules come into being as a result only of excessive stress, and they impact generically on the person (Millon's behavior reactions). As these are less anchored to the person's core cognitions or schemas, less predictability of the type of symptom formation results. Perhaps this reflects the severe impact of the stressor, both on the core ordering processes and on the existential core.

Beck (Beck & Freeman, 1990) discussed both types of symptoms. Recall that a cognitive shift occurs passing the "power" in the activation of behavior from personality styles to symptoms. At some point then a shift or transition into Axis I symptoms occurs, most notably PTSD or other anxiety disorders. As the shift occurs, schema and personality styles, while still present, become less visible and less influential. Accordingly, "Axis I schemas" are activated and the phenomenological field is distorted in dysfunctional ways. They take over. As discussed in Chapter 1, if a person has sufficient vulnerabilities (biological and psychological) *and* anxiety-related concerns (action-readiness, unpredictable/ uncontrollable fears, or focused attention), anxiety (Axis I) schemas will pervade. If the person has vulnerabilities *and* depression-related concerns (helplessness or hopeless, negative views of self, others, or the future), depression (Axis I) schemas develop. And, if the person has some anxiety related vulnerabilities *and* trauma related issues (schema sufficiently disrupted preventing assimilation or accommodation of trauma), PTSD (Axis I) schemas develop. Often there is some combination of all three.

An argument may be that "real" clients can be complex mixtures of schemas, personality styles, and the current psychosocial and trauma symptoms. The final result is largely an unfolding of this interactive mix, which is organized by the person. In only the one instance just discussed, in which symptoms "burst forth" due to the excessive nature of the stressor, is the symptom reasonably "free" of the person's schema influence. At these times treatment should be highly symptom focused, often with supportive techniques— psychopharmacologic agents (Friedman, 1988) or crisis intervention. At other times care is directed by the schema, its content and rules. This means, of course, that symptom focus must constantly be titrated according to the availability of schema and personality styles. This, it will be argued , is the usual case with trauma victims.

Symptom-by-symptom Versus Personality

The second issue of this section involves the conceptual link between symptoms and personality styles (and schemas). Simply put, personality is the profile of the enduring dispositions of the person—as measured by psychometrically sound trait indices. We believe, as do McCrae and Costa (1990), that personality remains relatively stable, is measurable, and is reflected in traits. In its pathological form, personality is kept stable and consistent by self-initiating inflexibility—the fostering of vicious circles and repetitive patterns. In its normal form, the personality is stabilized by *cumulative* (choices that dictate behavior across time) and *interactional* (day-to-day interactions) continuity. These person consistencies are his/her traits (McCrae & Costa, 1990).

In recent years, debate has addressed the behavior and symptoms characteristic of personality disorders. On the one side is the view that the treatment of personality disorders is a matter of systematically responding to each of the symptoms or behaviors presented by the client. The person thereby is put aside, and clients are treated symptom by symptom. No theory-driven strategy and no broader conceptualization using the personality styles or other components of care are required. The assumption is that the use of symptom specific techniques to treat clients will proceed effectively. In fact, scant evidence exists for the therapeutic integration of character traits and psychotherapy techniques and outcomes. Turkat (1991) described a well-thought-out procedure for a symptom by symptom approach, in which the formulation and the care determines the nature of the evaluations and subsequent treatment.

A more integrated approach between symptoms and personality is generally accepted, however. It involves two issues: the manner in which personality influences symptoms and the problems inherent with such a personality disorder.

We have already addressed the first of these. Trauma symptoms are largely signatures of decompensation personality patterns (Millon, 1969). Now what do we do? Therapeutic interventions are widely accepted as less effective with clients who have personality disorders (e.g., Chambless & Renneberg, 1988; Giles, Young, & Young, 1985; Mays, 1985; Rush & Shaw, 1983; Turner, 1987). Problems are created as the very nature of rigid personality patterns greatly complicates treatment efforts. In recent years, CBT has raised hopes that specifically tailored treatments for the complex interactions of Axis I and Axis II disorders may be a productive pursuit and a fruitful area for research efforts. Skeptically, Beck and colleagues (Beck & Freeman, 1990) wrote:

> The evidence that cognitive-behavioral treatment can produce beneficial results with difficult problems such as avoidant personality disorder, antisocial personality disorder, and borderline personality disorder is quite encouraging. However, it is clear that a conclusion regarding the efficacy of cognitive-behavioral therapy with specific personality disorders would be premature. In particular, many of the more comprehensive treatment approaches that have been proposed in recent years have not yet been tested empirically, and it is clear that "standard" cognitive-behavioral interventions often prove ineffective with clients diagnosed as having personality disorders. (p. 20)

We have argued that clients have symptoms that are ego-dystonic. They desire to rid themselves of these. Chronic victimization means, however, that the person is altered. As we noted previously (person event model), the victim's schema and personality styles that are entrenched, less flexible, and influential upon the trauma process, apperceive, distort, and protect, but do not integrate the trauma stimuli. The "corrective emotional experience" in therapy for the trauma victim then involves the reexperiencing of the trauma through the schema and personality style, and their interaction with symptom formation, as well as the remembering and reintegration of the symptoms themselves. The experience is "corrective" because the trauma is alive now in therapy through the filters of the ever present schema and personality.

In the course of treatment, the clinician usually defines a hierarchy of problem areas that require a response and proceeds in a rough sequential fashion from symptoms to conflict. However, surveys on the usefulness of the current diagnostic formulation have shown that diagnosis and severity of symptoms can determine only short term treatment goals (Hadley & Autry, 1984). For treatment to be effective with personality disorders, something more is required. Longer term treatment outcome is related to person dimensions. These must be known and plans developed for their managed care. We shall discuss treatment issues later (Chapter 6), but for now, the managed care of the victim with personality problems requires "external" changes (longer term therapy, psychoeducation, etc.) and "internal" alterations. Regarding the former, the focus of the therapy is to set up conditions for personality traits to be less extreme or rigid. Regarding the latter, it is at the interface between client formulation, including both person and symptoms, *and* goals of treatment, that clinical person-centered decisions are made. This point is that the "internal," developmental, and symptoms-connected-to-personality case formulation and treatment unfold. More on this will be presented later (Chapters 5, 6, and 7).

We have argued that schema therapy, based on knowledge of the person of the victim, is more important and should be driving the clinical theories and the managed care. At the risk of simplification (and some distortion) of our formulation, "easy" problems can be labeled symptoms and the "hard" ones labeled schema and personality patterns. Here, level of difficulty is measured by the connection to the person and his/her resistance to change. Clinical decisions then are made at "easy" and "hard" levels. We now know that even "easy" problems involve the ("hard") person dimensions, at least to some extent.

Complexity of Symptoms

The third issue involves complexity of symptoms among chronic trauma victims. Chronic victimization is unrelenting. In Chapter 1, we discussed comorbidity and the existence of secondary symptoms. Chronicity not only means persistence, but also involves excessive "stuff," multiple diagnoses, and severity of problems (Beutler & Clarkin, 1990). Chronic trauma victims assume a new steady state, a default mode of lessened functioning. Hiley-Young (1992) exquisitely described this chronic PTSD status, labeling it "complicated." A transmutative process (acute to chronic) somehow occurs in which the victim holds fast to negative symptoms, is vulnerable to stimuli less related to the original trauma, and requires a "feeling understood," (long-term, psychodynamic) process of treatment for care. Other studies (e.g., Hyer, Gratton, & Melton, in press) not only have provided evidence for extreme levels of symptoms across an array of choices, but also unique profiles for veteran subtypes. Distinct but high level profiles of Vietnam veterans are commonly found, as for example, on the *Vietnam Era Stress Inventory,* a scale that provides an index of severity in seven orthogonal areas related to PTSD: depression, physical symptoms, somatization, sensation-seeking, rage/anger, intrusive imagery, and intimacy conflict (Wilson & Kraus, 1981). Other measures also have identified distinctive individual patterns among PTSD victims (Krupnick & Horowitz, 1981).

The heart of victimization is the trauma memory and its intrusions. For chronic trauma sufferers, the fear network caused by trauma is consistently aroused, avoided, and reconditioned. Even given opportunities for exposure, chronic victims show a failure of response prevention, as they continue to avoid. Extinction or habituation is difficult under such conditions. In the PTSD research literature, data now substantiate the postulate that distinct networks of trauma meanings exist and are involuntarily activated when definite internal or external cues occur (Wolfe & Charney, 1991). From this point on, information is "screwed up": orienting responses, habituation modes, psychophysiological reactivity, selective processing of threat perceived cues, recall abilities, and of course, the symptom-influenced process of data gathering. Information processing is not only compromised, but it also becomes "comfortable" with patterns of approach/avoidance that reinforce the status quo. Based on experimental research, for example, an attentional bias is shown toward trauma-related cues in the environment and memory deficits for similar cues during retrieval (Litz & Keane, 1989). As we discussed (Chapters 2 and 3), these patterns may become "hard wired" over time, producing conditioned emotional responses (CERs) and perhaps neurological damage (Kolb, 1987).

Memories As Exemplars

If this is the natural course of information processing of intense trauma, we take it one step further. A relationship exists between memory intrusions and existing schema or personality styles. Memories are products or exemplars of the abused schema. Kramer, Schoen, and Kinney (1984) noted that traumatic dreams reflect past and current life events of the individual. The combat events of the dream are symbolic of problematic life themes: Kardiner (1959) noted the theme of helplessness: Wilmer (1982) noted danger. In addition, Ulman and Brothers (1988), among others, have noted that "empathic influences" are appropriate in therapy regarding the match of the trauma experience and its unconscious expression of the person. This applies most especially to personality styles. Dependent trauma victims tend to cringe with ineffectual performance and guilt. Independent trauma victims develop anger and pain memories around helplessness, or in the case of combat veterans, recollections of atrocities.

At this treatment center, ratings of trauma memories were requested on nine dimensions (Figure 4.2). These ratings were done by two raters blind to the personality code of the victim. A high degree of compatibility between the trauma content and the particular personality code was obtained. Trauma memories were directly related to the personality of the victim. Victims who are influenced by a dependent style, for example, had trauma memories reflective of more withdrawal, passiveness, cooperation, dependence, and the like; antisocial styles reflected more active and acting out ratings; and schizoid styles tended to have memories characterized by withdrawal, passivity, and more negative features. Perhaps trauma memories are indeed exemplars of the personality. Safran and Segal (1990) wrote:

> We hypothesize, therefore, that memories that emerge spontaneously when an interpersonal issue is being explored in an emotionally immediate way, are often prototypical exemplars of the interpersonal experience that contributed to the development of the interpersonal schema being activated. It may also be that some memories accessible in therapy do not correspond to the events that actually took place, but may instead be prototypical constructions that capture the essential features of a class of relevant events. (p.113)

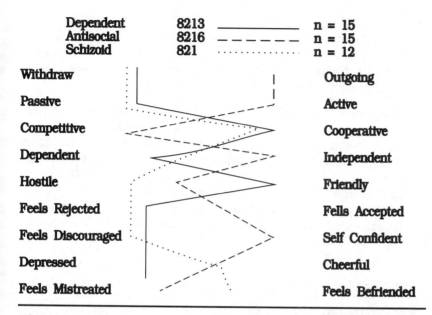

Dependent	8213	———————	n = 15
Antisocial	8216	– – – – – –	n = 15
Schizoid	821	··············	n = 12

Withdraw	Outgoing
Passive	Active
Competitive	Cooperative
Dependent	Independent
Hostile	Friendly
Feels Rejected	Fells Accepted
Feels Discouraged	Self Confident
Depressed	Cheerful
Feels Mistreated	Feels Befriended

Figure 4.2. Ratings of trauma memories for three subtypes of PTSD.

Also in this regard, Beck and Freeman (1990) considered the global distinction between sociotropy and autonomy. **Sociotropic styles** tend to be deprived, dependent, affiliative and fear loss of support. **Autonomous styles** are disappointed, defiant, protective/controlling, and fear powerlessness. The former tend to be dependent, narcissistic, histrionic and borderline; the latter, paranoid, antisocial, schizoid, schizotypal, passive aggressive and obsessive compulsive. In regard to their trauma, Beck and Freeman (1990) wrote:

> Patients who were heavily invested in autonomy (independent achievement, mobility, solitary pleasures) were prone to become depressed after an "autonomous stressor" such as failure, immobilization, or enforced conformity. Patients who deeply valued closeness, dependency, and sharing were hypersensitive to and prone to become depressed after "sociotropic traumas" such as social deprivation or rejection. (p. 370)

To some extent, Southwick, Yehuda and Giller (1991) validated these constructs. Using a measure of sociotropy and autonomy, this group showed that PTSD victims have higher scores on autonomy (self-criticism) than a depression group. In addition, scores of the PTSD victims on autonomy and sociotropy were negatively correlated. These authors concluded that at least two types of PTSD victims exist; autonomous being more angry and guilt prone, and sociotropic being more fearful and concerned with abandonment.

Symptoms are the loudest noise but should never be the last word. All symptoms require contextualization within the person. The therapeutic goal, then, is to reframe these problems within the confines of the "person." In Freudian terms trauma overwhelms the stimulus barrier, making integration and mastery of the traumatic experience impossible. A repetition-compulsion and denial pattern ensue. Initially, symptoms can be identified, addressed, and clinically validated. Eventually, however, psychotherapy should "get beyond" these to issues of LS.

Measurement

The final issue involves measurement. As we have discussed (Chapters 2 and 3), the stressor and resultant trauma symptoms show a low correlation. Nonetheless, both require independent evaluation to observe objectively the interaction (what symptoms covary with what stressors). In general clinical use, the assessment of trauma is directly related to the needs of the situation. As with the stressor, if the focus is for diagnosis, research, or forensic purposes, then the methods should be based on scales with discriminant and convergent validity that provide the best fit between clinical hits and misses, given prevalence rates for treatment-seeking clients. If the focus is treatment, then emphasis is placed on the conditions of treatment or intervention. The former seeks sanctuary in refinements and operationalization of the DSM-III-R; the latter seeks to meld person variables with known treatment approaches. In fact, in the behavioral sciences one feeds off the other.

We have argued that the person of the victim "stands" in the information paths of the stressor and the symptoms. The primary focus then is the understanding of the evolving person, and secondarily the information needed for trauma. This understanding provides vision and direction for treatment. We have placed as primary the unfolding narrative of the person, the LS. The therapist uses the information obtained by the assessment procedures to develop working hypotheses about the nature and impact of the stressor, about types of coping or patterns of PTSD. Above all, the inquiry should validate the person, even at the expense of historical "truth" or stressor accuracy. If done slowly and carefully, a picture of the person will emerge.

So, maladaptation to trauma involves symptoms and these deserve a careful and objective evaluation. A studied assessment of these, however, provides information on how the schema is abused, which personality styles are activated or hardened, and which coping methods become engaged to safeguard the damaged integrity. Objective measures of PTSD symptoms should be included. The latter's use should be more than "clinician curious," and be vigorously pursued for hypotheses about the person. The person of the victim is all of these; all demand understanding. Hopefully, a kind of "clinical reflective equilibrium" can be reached, this being the appropriate balance between person and symptom components.

CONCLUSION

Alfred Adler has several legacies. One was that a leopard never changes its spots. If we know the "leopard," we also are informed about the "spots." Unfortunately, the LS is impossible to fully know and is always dynamic in formulation. As we proceed into Chapter 5, our task then is to better operationalize the proxies of the LS [S+P+(B)+S]. Our emphasis changes then to operationalization and later care.

REFERENCES

Adler, A. (1932). *The practice and theory of individual psychology*. New York: Harcourt, Brace.

Alford, J., Mahone, C., & Felstein, E. (1988). Cognitive and behavioral sequelae of combat. *Journal of Traumatic Stress, 1*, 489-502.

Ansbacher, H. L. (1965). The structure of individual psychology. In B. Wolman (Ed.), *Scientific Psychology* (pp. 340-365). New York: Basic Books.

Ansbacher, H. L. (1968). The concept of social interest. *Journal of Individual Psychology, 24*, 131-149.

Beck, A., & Emery, G. (1985). *Anxiety disorders and phobias: A cognitive perspective.* New York: Guilford Press.

Beck, A., & Freeman, A. (1990). *Cognitive Therapy of Personality Disorders.* New York: Guilford Press.

Beutler, L., & Clarkin, J. (1990). *Systematic treatment selection: Toward targeted therapeutic interventions.* New York: Brunner/Mazel.

Bordin, E. (1979). The generalizability of the concept of working alliance. *Psychotherapy: Theory, Research, and Practice, 16*, 252-260.

Brett, E. A., & Ostroff, R. (1985). Imagery and posttraumatic stress disorder: An overview. *The American Journal of Psychiatry, 142*, 417-424.

Bugental, J. (1987). *The art of the psychotherapist.* New York: Norton Press.

Catherall, D. C. (1991, Spring). Aggression and projective identification in the treatment of victims. *Psychotherapy, 28*, 145-149.

Chambless, D. L., & Renneberg, B. (1988). *Personal disorders of agoraphobics.* Paper presented at the World Congress on Behaviour Therapy. Edinburgh, Scotland.

Dinkmeyer, D. C., Pew, L. L., & Dinkmeyer, D. C. (1979). *Adlerian counseling and psychotherapy.* Monterey, CA: Brooks Cole Publishing.

Dreikurs, R. (1953). *Fundamentals of Adlerian psychology.* Chicago: Alfred Adler Institute.

Dreikurs, R. (1967). *Psychodynamics, psychotherapy, and counseling.* Chicago: Alfred Adler Institute.

Dye, E., & Roth, S. (1991, Spring). Psychotherapy with Vietnam veterans and rape and incest survivors. *Psychotherapy, 28*, 103-120.

Ellenberger, H. (1970). *The discovery of the unconscious.* New York: Basic Books.

Ellis, A. (1962). *Reason and emotion in psychotherapy.* New York: Lyle Stuart.

Erikson, E. (1975). *Life history and the historical movement*. New York: Norton Press.

Frankl, V. (1969). *The will to meaning: Foundations and application of logotherapy*. New York: New America Library.

Friedman, M. (1988). Toward rational pharmacotherapy for posttraumatic stress disorder: An interim report. *The American Journal of Psychiatry, 145*(3), 281-185.

Giles, T. R., Young, R. R., & Young, D. E. (1985). Behavioral treatment of severe bulimia. *Behavior Therapy, 16*, 393-405.

Goulding, R., & Goulding, M. (1972). *Changing lives through redecision therapy*. New York: Brunner/Mazel.

Gushurst, R. S. (1971). The technique, utility, and validity of lifestyle analysis. *Counseling Psychologist, 3*(1), 30-39.

Hadley, S., & Autry, J. (1984). DSM-III and psychotherapy. In S. Turner & M. Hersen (Eds.), *Adult psychopathology and diagnosis* (pp. 465-484). New York: Wiley.

Hiley-Young, B. (1992). Trauma reactivation assessment and treatment. *Journal of Traumatic Stress, 5*(4), 545-555

Horney, K. (1937). *The neurotic personality of our time*. New York: Norton.

Horowitz, M. J. (1986). Stress-response syndromes: A review of posttraumatic and adjustment disorders. *Hospital and Community Psychiatry, 37*, 241-249.

Hyer, L., Woods, M., & Boudewyns, P. (1989). Early recollections of Vietnam veterans with PTSD. *Journal of Individual Psychology, 45*, 300-312.

Hyer, L., Gratton, C., & Melton, M. (in press). Assessment and treatment of PTSD: Understanding the person. In R. Craig (Ed.), *Readings of the MCMI and MCMI-II*. New York: Erlbaum.

Kern, R., Matheny, K., & Patterson, D. (1978). *A case for Adlerian counseling: Theory, techniques and research evidence*. Chicago: Alfred Adler Institute.

Kardiner, A. (1959). Traumatic neuroses of war. In S. Arieti (Ed.), *American Handbook of Psychiatry* (pp. 245-257). New York: Basic Books.

Kolb, L. (1987). A neuropsychological hypothesis explaining post-traumatic stress disorders. *American Journal of Psychiatry, 144,* 989-995.

Kramer, M., Schoen, L. S., & Kinney, L. (1984). Psychological and behavioral features of disturbed dreamers. *Psychiatric Journal of the University of Ottawa, 9*(3), 102-106.

Krupnick, J. L., & Horowitz, M. J. (1981). Stress response syndromes. *Archives of General Psychiatry, 38,* 428-435.

Krystal, H. (1978). Trauma and affects. *Psychoanalytic Study of the Child, 33,* 81-117.

Leventhal, H. (1984). A perceptual-motor theory of emotion. In L. Berkowitz (Ed.), *Advances in experimental social psychology.* New York: Academic Press.

Lifton, R. J., & Olson, E. (1976). The human meaning of total disaster: The buffalo creek experience. *Psychiatry, 39,*1-18.

Litz, B. T., & Keane, T. M. (1989). Information processing in anxiety disorders: Application to the understanding of posttraumatic stress disorder. *Clinical Psychology Review, 9,* 243-257.

Lombardi, D. N. (1973). Eight avenues of life style consistency. *Individual Psychologist, 10(2),* 5-9.

Mahoney, M. C. (1991). *Human change processes: The scientific foundations of psychotherapy.* Delran, NJ: Basic Books.

Markus, H., & Nurius, R. (1986). Possible selves. *American Psychologist, 41,* 954-969.

Mays, D. T. (1985). Behavior therapy with borderline personality disorder: One clinician's perspective. In D. T. Mays & C. M. Franks (Eds.), *Negative outcome in psychopathology and what to do about it.* New York: Springer.

Meichenbaum, D. (1985). *Stress innoculation training.* New York: Pergamon Press.

McCann, L., & Pearlman, L. (1990). *Psychological trauma and the adult survivor: Theory, therapies, and transformation.* New York: Brunner/Mazel.

McCrae, R. & Costa, P. (1990). *Personality in adulthood.* New York: Guilford Press.

Millon, T. (1969). *Modern psychopathology.* Philadelphia, PA: Saunders.

Millon, T. (1983). *Millon clinical multiaxial inventory manual*, (3rd ed.). Minneapolis: National Computer Systems.

Millon, T. (1984). On the Renaissance of personality assessment and personality theory. *Journal of Personality Assessment, 48*, 450-466.

Millon, T. (1988). Personologic psychotherapy: Ten commandments for a posteclectic approach to integrative treatment. *Psychotherapy, 25*(2), 209-219.

Nesselroade, J. (1990). Adult personality development: Issues in assessing constancy and change. In A. Rabin, R. Emmons, & S. Frank (Eds.), *Studying persons and lives* (pp. 41-85). New York: Springer.

Nichols, C. (1991). *Manual for the assessment of core goals*. Palo Alto: Consulting Psychologists Press.

Ochberg, F. (1991, Spring). Post-traumatic therapy. *Psychotherapy, 28*, 5-15.

Parson, E. (1988). Post-traumatic self disorders (PTsFD): Theoretical and practical consideration in psychotherapy of Vietnam War veterans. In J. Wilson, Z., Harel, & B. Kahana (Eds.), *Human adaptation to extreme stress: From Holocaust to Vietnam* (pp. 245-284). New York: Plenum.

Porter, C., Markus, H., & Nurius, P. (1984). Conception of possibility among people in crisis. Unpublished manuscript. University of Michigan.

Rush, A. J., & Shaw, B. F. (1983). Failure in treating depression by cognitive therapy. In E. B. Foa & P. G. M. Emmelkamp (Eds.), *Failures in behavior therapy*. New York: Wiley.

Safran, J., & Segal, Z. (1990). *Interpersonal processing in cognitive therapy*. New York: Basic Books.

Sartre, J. (1964). *The words*. New York: George Braziller.

Shulman, B. H., & Mosak, H. H. (1988). *Manual for life style assessment*. Muncie, IN: Accelerated Development, Publishers.

Southwick, S. M., Yehuda, R., Giller, E. L. (1991). Characterization of depression in war-related posttraumatic stress disorder. *American Journal of Psychiatry, 148*(2), 179183.

Stern, D. N. (1985). *The interpersonal world of the infant*. New York: Basic Books.

Suich, P. (1991). Social interest: Triangulating the construct with measures of national attitudes, commununal vales, and cooperative behavior. Ann Arbor, MI: Dissertation Abstracts.

Sullivan, H. S. (1953). *The interpersonal theory of psychiatry.* New York: W.W. Norton.

Sweeney, T. J. (1989). *Adlerian counseling: A practical approach for a new decade,* 3rd ed. Muncie, IN: Accelerated Development, Publishers.

Turkat, I. (1991). *The personality disorders; A psychological approach to clinical management.* New York: Pergamon Press.

Turner, S. M. (1987). The effects of personality disorder diagnosis on the outcome of social anxiety symptom reduction. *Journal of Personality Disorders, 1,* 136-143.

Ulman, R. B., & Brothers, D. (1988). *The shattered self: A psychoanalytic study of trauma.* Hillsdale, NJ: The Analytic Press.

Vallis, T. (1991). Theoretical and conceptual bases of cognitive therapy. In T. Vallis, J. Howes, P. Miller (Eds.), *The challenge of cognitive therapy: Application to nontraditional populations* (pp. 3-21). New York: Plenum Press.

Wilmer, H. A. (1982). Vietnam and madness: Dreams of schizophrenic veterans. *Journal of the American Academy of Psychoanalysis, 10(1),* 47-65.

Wilson, J., & Kraus, G. (1981). *The Vietnam Era Stress Inventory.* Cleveland: Cleveland State University.

Wolfe, J., & Charney, D. (1991). Use of neuropsychological assessment in posttraumatic stress disorder. *Psychological Assessment: A Journal of Consulting and Clinical Psychology, 3,* 573-580.

Young, J. (1990). *Cognitive therapy for personality disorders: A schema focused approach.* Saratoga, FL: Professional Resource Exchange.

Chapter **5**

Sc+P+(B)+Sy MODEL

"Science commits suicide when it adopts a creed." T. H. Huxley

We have argued that the person organizes life experiences by a sophisticated system of schema processing. These are templates of interaction patterns that are encoded at various levels within the person: expressive-motor, affective, and conceptual. In previous chapters we have noted that these patterns establish roots early, directing activities and experience and determining their own requirements for "security operations." The paradigm Sc+P+(B)+Sy represents these redundant styles; schema dictates personality styles, served and monitored by beliefs, which, if necessary, decompensate into symptoms. In the previous chapter we noted that this model is a reasonable approximation of the LS, which is individualistic and can never be fully known. The Sc+P+(B)+Sy model then allows for a measured understanding of the LS. Since relatively little understanding of the relationship between the specific structures and content of schema and its "safeguards" (personality, beliefs, and symptoms) is known, this pursuit is important.

The Zeitgeist of current professional interaction is rapprochement; periods of controversy are giving way to a spirited dialectic. This spirit bodes well for our paradigm, since it is both heuristic and evolving. Our constructs are anything but final and fixed and are often beyond full understanding. Good clinical thinking often requires a suspension of certainty. Regarding schemas, for example, Stern (1985) suggested that because these protypical representations are abstract and have many referents, possibly no single specific behavior will correspond exactly to the person's schema. No doubt a considerable amount of averaging, matching, censoring, checking, and inaccurate planning occurs before the "person correct" action is implemented. This is the essence of the constructionist position. The person is the source of his/her acts; cognitive-affective structures set in motion images, memories, motor actions, autonomic arousal, and a host of cognitive rules in a calculated fashion. If there is a $64 Question, it is: What is the relationship and what are the activating mechanisms between the core cognitions and redundant intra- and inter-personal patterns? The therapist has the task of unpacking these. This process also is far from exact.

In this chapter we acknowledge again the influence of two positions: information processing has provided us with a reasonable model to conceptualize interpersonal activity, and CBT has given us a defined way to move these structures/processes along so change can occur. The former is really the application of the methods of cognitive science to the complexity of the person. Variously defined processes of the person can be disaggregated into distinct structures and processes, thereby providing a blueprint. Hartman and Burgess (1988), for example, identified the phases of trauma using an information processing model: (1) pretrauma (history); (2) trauma encapsulation (mechanism used to regulate trauma) including input, throughput, output, and trauma replay (reenactment, repetition and displacement); (3) disclosure, the social ramifications or secondary trauma impact; and (4) posttrauma, the pattern that results. Using different constructs Mischel (1973) parses the person apart according to construction competencies (knowledge and problem solving), encoding strategies (appraisal process), expectancies (self-efficacy judgements), values (preference of reinforcing), and self-regulatory systems (self-management ability). Time, too, can be "played with"; the past (schemas) is held in active cognition, influencing behavior, and the future (goals) is stored cognitively to affect current behavior. Clinical knowledge of these "person markers" allows for a better understanding of the complexity of the holistic process. The latter, CBT, has provided both structure and conceptualization for understanding and fostering the human change process, while always focusing on cognition. Early cognitive therapies were considered "insight" therapies in that the therapy was assumed to change a client's "thinking personality." Ellis (1962) has consistently emphasized the therapeutic impact of his technique on cognitive schemas. As noted, the Beck group (Beck & Freeman, 1990) has also emphasized the clinical importance of schemas. The thesis is that CBT is more efficacious and efficient when it is focused on "core" problems. This group now endorses the centrality of personality styles, especially two general styles (sociotropy and autonomy) that account for a person's behavior. Colorfully, Foa and Kozak (1986) used the term "overvalued ideation" to portray the energy and importance of these "hot" cognitions.

Recently the CBT theorists Safran and Segal (1990) have broadened the conceptualization of schema in clinical theory, permitting both a marriage and extension of traditional ideas. In effect, the person as a "cognitive organizer" is emphasized. These authors endorse the pivotal role of the transaction between cognitive and interpersonal actions (schema). This combination serves as the structural supports of the schema, resulting in a readiness and expectation for action regarding self and others. In fact, these authors highlight the notion of interpersonal schema, a generic representation of self-other interactions. In this context therapeutic goals involve the movement of cognitions and interpersonal patterns to deeper levels (core schemas). The clinician oscillates among various patient markers, identifying, disconfirming, and integrating changes. Again, this therapeutic emphasis extends CBT, emphasizing a whole person integration of responses, especially at the interpersonal level.

Our task in this chapter is to respect these positions and further describe and operationalize the Sc+P+(B)+Sy model. By gaining access to this constellation of cognitive and affective structures and exploring their interactions, we will be better able to effect change at all levels of the person. We discuss each in turn.

SCHEMA

Schemas contain the whole story of the person's life. They have several natural functions, but two are especially important (Table 5.1). These are to organize and construct reality. Again, this is the essence of the constructionist position. Schemas represent the immune system of the person that "kicks in" various needed defenses preventing infection or change. They start the several modes of regulatory action in the person.

What happens when trauma occurs? The incoming stimuli are rudely treated and the normal learning processes of assimilation and accommodation cannot continue. Initially, the person attempts to assimilate new information into the existing schemas. In fact, the schema rearranges the environment so this will occur. Given severe trauma, attempted assimilation fails. Accommodation, the effort to rearrange existing schemas, then proceeds. With severe trauma, this too fails. Wachtel (1981) suggested that a neurotic "stuckness" occurs (because assimilation/accommodation does not occur). One might even say that at this point the stressor becomes trauma. Symptoms evolve. The most typical trauma response is one of reasonable coping, followed by shock, numbing, and persistent intrusions. These last two components recycle over time, never being fully worked through.

TABLE 5.1
Functions of Schemas

organize reality
construct reality (pro forma)
always operating
hierarchally arranged
dominant or latent ("hot" or "cold")

Susan Whitbourne (1986) developed Piaget's model of (adult) development that has applicability to trauma victims (especially as a result of Vietnam). Two processes were identified to keep one's identity, assimilation and accommodation. Assimilation refers to the processes a person uses to keep one's identity as right, as good, and as competent: "I did the right thing" can be assimilated by means of self-justification, defensive rigidity, lack of insight, and identity projection. Basically, the person "makes the environment a place that can be understood in terms that reinforce the individual's existing identity" (p. 18). Assimilation involves distortion, a "making nice" with the environment. As can be guessed, reliance on this mechanism too strongly leads to problems— an erosion of one's ability to withstand any disconfirmation from experiences.

In contrast, when events are very discordant or disruptive to the person's self-view as a worthwhile person, accommodation occurs. Now, the person uses different processes of appraisal to ensure a self-view as loving, competent and good. The individual realistically appraises identity and experiences, and the congruence between the two. Here, the person "searches" for external information to alter self (e.g., "my family says I am good, therefore I am") or looks for alternative ways to be ("I decided to change my life"). Accommodation then, goes beyond the appraisal process and actually tries to change identity. While the "correct" mixture of assimilation and accommodation is unknown (requiring a balance), for PTSD victims the process of accommodation is "more central" as the victim's assumptions of self require revision.

Trauma victims engage in both mechanisms. Victims distort, seek a safe haven, organize their environment, and otherwise avoid or reduce dissonant circumstances (assimilation). Some victims never alter this stance. Avoidance wins. Others develop a moral antinomy (see Chapter 15) and attempt to change self or look for other experiences (accommodation). Here, depending on the victim and the level of change needed, a different struggle between intrusion and avoidance takes form. With psychotherapy, the pain of change, of the healing process, and of the search for meaning can unfold. At least, there is a chance for change, for a new identity that is solid and safe.

Schema Development

McCann and colleagues (McCann, Sakheim, & Abrahamson, 1988) have proposed a model for this self-reinforcing process as a result of trauma (Figure 5.1). This model represents a natural developmental process. Schemas come into existence early and serve to organize and interact with the on-going events of life. In this way each schema forms a positive or negative belief about life and how the organism needs to interact for acceptable levels of adaptation. Its basic task is to set up redundant patterns that seek completion for interactive tasks, a comfort zone in any situation. Most often this task is one of finding a best fit between the stimulus, meaning, and responsive attributes of the schema, and incoming stimuli.

When trauma occurs, schemas do not stand idly by. They seek to do what is familiar, becoming rigid, hardened, hypersensitive, and influential. Each new situation that represents the trauma (internally or externally) is recapitulated as a "best fit" of the now "negative" schema and the current situation. So, what once served to protect the individual, now serves to isolate and reinforce rigidity. Incoming information is addressed as if the new situation is the same as the old. The schema is fixed. At a simple level Wilson (1988) maintained that trauma victims organize personality characteristics around either safety needs (e.g., security, dependence) and thereby constrict information, *or* self-enhancing or competency schemas (e.g., dominance, achievement) and thereby foster augmenting or exploring cognitive styles. Whatever the typology of schema, treatment must invalidate these maladaptive organizers through integration or alternatives.

Emery (Emery, Emery, Shama, Quiana, & Jassani, 1991) described the development of the schema around early stressors. The child develops a life theme—"hierarchically structured set of perceptions that direct the person's perceptions through life" (p. 331). This group elaborated on this interaction:

> A life theme develops during childhood as a coping response
> to some fundamental unresolved familial issue. The life
> theme has its origin in the stress variables experienced

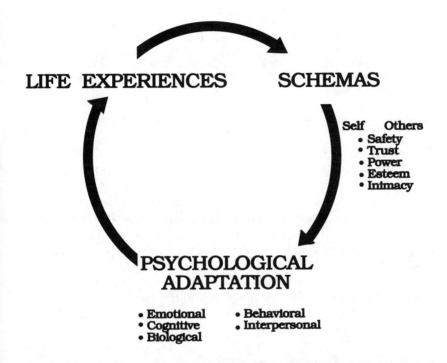

Figure 5.1. The relation among life experienes, schemas, and psychological adaptation. From McCann, Sakheim, & Abrahamson (1988). Reproduced by permission.

in family of origin during early years. The stressors that create the greatest anxiety in the child, i.e., stress variables which the child perceives as the 'chief problem' in his life, are the stress variables around which a life theme develops. The life theme involves a perceptual set that becomes structuralized and serves to filter, organize, and interpret reality. This perceptual set represents an attempt to facilitate the adaptation of the person in relation to experienced stress through the life course. Adult behaviors, including behaviors revolving around clinical symptoms and psychopathology, often incorporate, reflect, and show continuity with fundamental features of the life theme. (pp. 231-272)

Dysfunctional Schemas

We also know that schemas can turn "bad." This can occur early in life or as a result of trauma. As children mature, they no longer need to cry, to be fed, or act primitively to acquire needs: now they can use words or actions. The child retains the message and the style of action and with time elaborates on earlier forms of relating. But, just as growth can be arrested, schemas may not mature and may be maintained at an earlier level of development. They can become maladaptive. Borrowing from Stern (1985), a foreclosure occurs prior to the healthy formation of his four experiential invariants. This is the beginning of problems; what was once functional is no longer so. Unconditional, once helpful assumptions about life, become inflexible. Stress too can potentiate problems. Moretti, Feldman, and Shaw (1990) wrote:

> As psychopathology worsens, the processing of self-relevant information becomes increasingly dominated by dysfunctional schemata that have become 'hyperactive' (Kovacs & Beck, 1979). Consequently, dysfunctional schemata are evoked in response to more diverse and less logically related information and experiences— that is, 'the orderly matching of an appropriate schema to a particular stimulus is upset by the intrusion of these overly active idiosyncratic schemas' (Beck et al., 1979, p.13.). In extreme instances, the processing of information may become dominated by dysfunctional schemata to the extent that patients are insensitive to environmental cues (Beck et al., 1979). In such cases, dysfunctional schemata may be inappropriately used to interpret a wide range of events. Dysfunctional schemata can also be applied during early and inappropriate stages

of information processing, subsequently giving rise to idiosyncratic, dysfunctional, and inappropriate interpretations of events. (pp. 220-221)

Dysfunctional schemas run automatically, often without the individual's intent or awareness. They are the front lines and are the first to "know" what their actions portend. To act risky or needy, for example, will feel bad and may lead to other more risky responses. Like the thermostat, the schema reads its surroundings, organizes context, activates the processes necessary for encoding, storage, and retrieval, and calls up "by-products" or automatic construals for confirmation. When a clinician detects an inappropriate private logic, the cause is the schema activating automatic thoughts, cognitive distortions, and underlying assumptions (Young, 1990). Schemas simplify all levels of information processing both latent and manifest structures (Beck, 1976). They are the default mode of activity in the person. Not only does the schema particularize the category of response but it titrates its dimensional requirements. It determines quality and quantity in a measured, calculated way. The "activation" required for a particular connection varies; at times cognitive processing involves many changes in the strength of the constructs; at other times only a little. The schema arranges this organized response, titrating the needed effort. When trauma occurs, underlying faulty cognitions (schemas) become irresistible to even simple stimuli. A characteristic cognitive-interpersonal style is set in motion. Early on, it is not unusual for the person to pay little heed to the trauma itself. Later is when problems develop.

Deep Level Schema

What then is the best way to conceive the composition of the schema? Based on the evolving literature and the logic of everyday trauma, the belief is that schema may have three levels (Table 5.2). At the *deepest level,* core referential and existential structures exist. With trauma they become unsettled. "Person" meaning is disrupted. This turmoil further prevents a healthy integration of the trauma. In addition, this invalidation prevents any salubrious search for meaning, thereby disrupting both middle level and surface level schemas; these latter two

TABLE 5.2
Levels of Schema

Level	Type	Clinical Availability	Example
Innermost	Existential	Unknowable	Death, Meaninglessness, Isolation, Freedom, Identity
Medium	Core Schemas	Clinically Relevant Orienting Concepts	Automony, Safety
Outermost	Automatic Beliefs	Surface Beliefs	Need to be first

being more accessible to clinical intervention. Janoff-Bulman (1985), Epstein (1991), and Dye and Roth (1991) have variously outlined the inner shattering process. We described the work of Benyakar (Benyakar, Kutz, Dasberg, & Stern, 1989) in the previous chapter. A human destructuring process is set in motion, often becoming "stuck" in its own cognitive programming. War trauma certainly reaches this inner level. Laufer (1988) wrote:

> The war self develops under the aegis of the death principle and is never able to free itself from the premature encounter with death or its preoccupation with death and survival. The war self episodically attempts to dominate the adaptive self at moments of vulnerability in the life course and in so doing creates intrapsychic discontinuities and dualities that are inherently conflicted. (p. 49)

Similarly, Lifton (1982) described this as a death imprint, a radical intrusion on the self. Parson (1988), in addition, stated that the self of the combat sufferer becomes fragmented as "one in which adult ambitions, ideals, introspection, self caring skills, empathy, and affective tension management are diminished or virtually absent" (p. 240). McCann and Pearlman (1990) too pay tribute to a meta-schema, frame of reference. This superordinate cognitive structure includes the ability to feel comfortable with self, to strive for growth, to have an observing ego, and to trust others. Without a stable frame of reference, experiences cannot be trusted or meaningfully interpreted; causality has little meaning. Incoherence and inconsistency provide the only grounding of reality.

PTSD, the legacy of trauma, can be conceived as an attempt at providing some semblance of organization after abuse. In this sense a maladaptive reorganizing response occurs to a chaotic event (Benyakar et al., 1989). The reexperiencing symptoms can be viewed as symbolic representatives and the numbing symptoms as necessary outlets of this whole process of maladaptation. It is a way of providing a reconciliation to the horrible realization that one's identity will never be quite the same. It is the organism's attempt to bridge living with death. This inner level is "being," not just meaning or identity, but the person's own uniqueness and the ability to persevere.

Hermeneutics the science of interpretation, examines how a given text of beliefs and assumptions influence the "deeper structure" of a person. Through this method the person can both sense the deepness of being and choose other realities from the past. In a sense hermeneutics is the "archeological dig" into one's personhood. It provides a glimpse of the inner level and its individual shades of personhood. This method allows for adaptations other than the trauma reality. Each person has his/her own unique story, untouched, unknown, safe, the "me-ness" of life. Therapy involves questioning and gently challenging deep unacknowledged assumptions and beliefs. Its curative elements include not only the natural human process of self care, but hermeneutics also allows for the possibility of other selves. The mystery of the individuality of the person, the one that was "listened to", is now only one reality. In a sense new meanings arise from an encounter of this old area. The fixed notion of a trauma memory, for example, gradually takes on distinctions, ambiguities or dynamic alterations as the person re-reads the text of the whole experience. Meaning involves the content, its surround, the current relationship and the ever changing person (Winograd & Flores, 1986). Existential psychotherapists too describe the "dasein", acceptance of the reality of being, and, through this, the choice in being. But we are getting ahead of ourselves here (Chapter 6—psychotherapy).

Surface Level Schemas

If one's very personal (and collective) being is housed at the innermost level, the outermost serves the day-to-day particulars. Beck and Emery (1985) used the label "cognitive set" to identify *specific* concepts or assumptions of a person. These are relevant only in a given situation and at a given time. A person, for example, may have deep level concerns about competence, which are activated only in certain areas, such as mathematics. In a later work (Beck & Freeman, 1990) this group identified automatic thoughts as serving self-monitoring and self-evaluating functions, secondary appraisals after a choice. These are surface cognitions that are "active" and can be monitored. In the phraseology of Beck, they are automatic in everyday actions. From the perspective of CBT, they are the "by-products" of core cognitions, the daily thoughts or beliefs of the person as measured by various CBT scales, including the *Automatic Thoughts Questionnaire* and the *Idea Inventory* (Hyer, Woods, & Boudewyns, 1991). In CBT the therapist attempts first to identify automatic thoughts, then to identify the stylistic thinking (behind these), and last to present alternatives. The identification of schemas comes later. Janoff-Bulman (1985) believed that these surface schemas are easier to adapt to or change; higher order ones are not. We have described these as beliefs (Chapter 4).

Middle Level Schemas

Middle level schemas are grist for the clinician's mill. They are situated at the person's operative "command center," at a level sufficiently knowledgeable and representative of complex behaviors and patterns. They are "orienting concepts" in clinical work. In recent years various taxonomies have been offered. At this center we have developed one grouping based on an earlier version of McCann (McCann, Sakheim, & Abrahamson 1988) and Beck and Emery (1985) (Table 5.3). (We have used these schemas in several studies—see Chapter 14). This formulation identifies the polarities of each schema. All eight are rated by the client, discussed with the clinician, and then changed over time to more accurately fit the client. Often others will be added. They are intended to provoke working hypotheses regarding core beliefs, processes, and actions. This checklist, then, is dynamic, maintaining a certain integrity, but changing or intermixing with other schemas as the person becomes more known.

The middle level schemas are clinically useful cognitions. Initially, the therapist's task is to accept the trauma victim's schema presentation. Often this involves a surface level cognition. The task then becomes one of proceeding "downward" toward deeper levels and broader exemplars of the person. Remember that core schemas serve two basic functions: organization of the structure and processes of the person and construction of reality. Remember too, that core schemas often lie dormant; at other times they may be "hot." They are, however, always influential at some level. The goal of the therapist is to get as "core as possible" and to unearth schemas that are abused due to trauma. The more self-referent or emotionally laden

(continued on page 221)

TABLE 5.3
Schema Checklist

Instructions:

    Below are eight themes (I - VIII). Please look at each one, and circle the number that best represents how you feel about that theme. One (1) always represents the worst choice and ten (10) the best choice. The eight themes you are about to rate are

Safety	Intimacy
Trust	Acceptance
Power	Competence
Esteem	Control

I. SAFETY

    1   2   3   4   5   6   7   8   9   10

I cannot   midpoint   I don't feel
  protect myself.   vulnerable.
Others are   Others are okay.
  dangerous.   I do not avoid
I fear for myself.   life events.

II. TRUST

    1   2   3   4   5   6   7   8   9   10

I do not trust   midpoint   I make good
  others.   judgements.
Others are out   I feel comfortable
  to get me or make   with people.
  a fool of me.   I can trust others.
I don't trust myself.

(continued)

TABLE 5.3 (continued)

III. INDEPENDENCE

1	2	3	4	5	6	7	8	9	10

I often feel
  helpless and like
  I cannot control
  things.
Others are out to
  control me.
I fear being
  vulnerable.

midpoint

I am in control
  of my life.
People are not
  out to control
  or force me.
I don't feel
  vulnerable.

IV. ESTEEM

1	2	3	4	5	6	7	8	9	10

I have little
  value.
I mess things up.
People are out
  for themselves.

midpoint

I have value; I
  am okay.
People are not
  evil or
  uncaring.

V. INTIMACY

1	2	3	4	5	6	7	8	9	10

I cannot be alone
  with myself.
I am emotionally
  distant.
I cannot relate
  to others.

midpoint

I care about
  myself.
I can relate
  to others.

(continued)

TABLE 5.3 (continued)

VI. ACCEPTANCE

1	2	3	4	5	6	7	8	9	10

I need to be loved.
Criticism means rejection to me.
I need to be understood.

midpoint

I accept me.
I can take criticism.

VII. COMPETENCE

1	2	3	4	5	6	7	8	9	10

I have to be "somebody."
Success is everything.
Failure is the "end" for me.

midpoint

I can accept my status.
I am able to fail.

VIII. CONTROL

1	2	3	4	5	6	7	8	9	10

I must always be in control.
I always have to be my own boss.
Others expect to be dominated by me.

midpoint

I can accept help.
I can accept authority.
I can depend on others.

Extrapolated from McCann et. al (1988) & Beck & Emery (1985).

the schema, the more its influence on the person. Considerable evidence exists that a focus on or disconfirmation of core pathogenic beliefs result in anxiety reduction and better therapy outcomes (Safran & Segal, 1990).

Schemas insure that selected person components and environmental elements are provided to meet needs. Young (1990) described the process of "schema-driven behaviors" (Table 5.4). These are the self-initiating patterns, both protecting and reinforcing the status quo. They include schema maintenance, schema avoidance, and schema compensation. Schema maintenance entails both self-perpetuating behaviors and ongoing coping styles; schema avoidance includes emotional, cognitive, and behavioral attributes to defend or protect schemas; and schema compensation includes adaptive cognitive and behavior styles opposite of what one would predict for a schema (reaction formation or compensation). Together, they appear as an organized symphony on behalf of the person.

Young's formulation is appealing because of its ability to accommodate the organization and connections of the schema process. Each element rearranges itself to accomplish its goal, self-preservation. Our eight schemas and their "organization," interacting patterns and behaviors, as well as probable symptom patterns, are similarly conceived. Any model of information processing always starts with these "deep habits" (schemas). When abused by trauma, they are placed in overdrive. At this point in the flow diagram, possibilities become legion; no two people appear similar. When "orders are given" to personality, many styles can unfold. Currently, for example, a borderline personality requires five of the eight characteristics, allowing for 93 possible combinations. When schemas and symptoms are added, resulting possibilities are many and complex.

Homunculus Revisited (Chapter 1)

Goleman (1985) has articulated nicely this process. Schemas work backstage, in what Goleman labeled long-term memory. The schema then, is aware of events and of meanings before the significance of it reaches awareness. Since data is prepared prior to full awareness, the schema can organize experience

TABLE 5.4
Early Maladaptive Schemas*
(EMS)

I.	Schema Maintenance:	process by which EMS are reinforced
	Cognitive -	magnification, minimization, selective abstraction, etc.
	Behavioral -	dysfunctional or self-defeating behaviors
	Affect -	feelings associated with lack of change
II.	Schema Avoidance:	volitional or conditioned avoidance
	Cognitive -	blanking, denying
	Affective -	dulling emotional experience
	Behavioral -	avoidance behaviors (agoraphobia, social isolation)
III.	Schema Compensation:	cognitive or behavioral patterns opposite of what is predicted from schemas. These are reaction formations—a "flight" into acceptable patterns with little commitment or psychological adaptation.

*Source: Young (1990). Reproduced by permission from Professional Resource Exchange.

and filter data before it reaches awareness. In fact, Goleman devotes considerable space to prove that awareness is not a necessary stop for information as it flows through the system (witness hypnosis, subliminal perception, perceptual defense, etc.). The schema lets in what it desires. In this context, the person somehow "knows" what is important, unimportant, interesting, tedious, or, most importantly, threatening. Information, then, is never pristine, never unembellished, and never absolutely vertical. Through repetition and social reinforcement, a style develops early in life, one that will remain. The defensive structure of the person becomes overlearned and eventually forms the armor-plating (the outer layer) for interpersonal action. Goleman (1985) wrote:

> Defenses are, in the main, attentional ploys. But attention is just part of the process. As we have seen, every part of the sequence, from perception through cognition to response, is vulnerable to skews in the service of defense. The person's entire mental apparatus—his mode of being in the world—is shaped in part by his defensive strategy, by his armoring of character. (p. 132)

This armored style, then, is the "face" the child/person shows to the world.

The final insult here is that this is now played out in "world friendly" to self-perpetuation. All the elaborate hypersensitive and avoidant mechanisms are allowed, even nurtured in the family, and later within carefully designed relationships, groups, and culture. In this way communication is a self-defending process to keep the status quo and to organize "my" life. Again, Goleman wrote:

> What is being repaired is the schemas at hand. When we reach an understanding, I grasp your schemas, you grasp mine. The match may not be perfect, but it's closer than before. In a long-term relationship, schemas can become exquisitely calibrated, so that a single word, gesture, or emphasis can evoke in one's partner a fully understood statement. The more schemas we share, the less need be said. (p. 156)

The collective self of the person reads his/her needs and walks a clever path between vital lies and simple truths (Goleman, 1985). The cycle then is complete: The schema is the theory of the person, takes what it wants, and reinforces itself. In Chapter 1 we labeled this process as one under the direction of a homunculus. Indeed, it is. Given trauma, this well-managed gaze at life pays many prices before integration.

Fortunately, order does exist. Schemas initiate the expression of personality styles, which often allow the person to adapt. When problems are due to excessive trauma, poor learning patterns, or rigid styles, maladaptation or a decompensation into Axis I problems may result. When trauma occurs, the middle level schemas are most visibly affected, clinically influencing and influenced by constructs above and below. The result is a mosaic, the person.

PERSONALITY

If schemas are core constructs or learnings that establish the direction of the separation and individuation process of the person, *personality styles are the person's chief methods of action.* In Chapter 4 we briefly addressed how this process works. Here, we can elaborate. Adler held that as the person strives to be better and to find his/her place in life, personality styles or methods of operation develop in order to cope with deficiencies. Consistent patterns develop, therefore, as a way of handling felt deficiencies, of coping in life so as not to reexperience a negative state. Beck and Emery (1985) described this process as a "psychological double." The person possesses a dual image of self, one that is despising and involves inferiority, and one that represents a correction or overcompensation for the despising image. They wrote:

> The image of rejection is combined with one of superiority and the one of being dominated by one of being in control. The dual images are inversely related. The more despising the one image, the more grand the other has to be in order to compensate for it. (p. 295)

How does this process occur? The response to compensate for a flaw has been explained differently by psychodynamic, interpersonal, and personality theorists. We quickly develop personal theories about ourselves, and these core concepts (schemas) are at the center of all experiences. We become rather self-absorbed in our own definition. Implied is the fact that after a while in day-to-day workings, our behavior is inseparable from (and influenced by) the core concepts. A central process of the conceptual pyramid is the interface of schema and personality; a "core" becomes a "method." Bugental (1987) noted that Allport believed that "structure is the secretion of process"; one melds into the other. Freeman and Leaf (1989) wrote:

If we visualize the personality, we may liken it to a large wheel of Swiss cheese. Different cheeses may be of differing sizes, and the wheel would probably be solid enough to support a person's weight. However, when cut through the center, the cheese will be seen to have many holes. These holes may be many or few; they may be large or small. In terms of personality disorder, the larger the holes in what are basic areas, the greater the disorder. If the "hole" or area of deficit is affiliation, the avoidant or schizoid personality disorders will result—autonomy (dependent personality disorder), acceptance of social norms and strictures (antisocial), impulse control (borderline, histrionic), altruism (narcissistic), or flexibility (compulsive). If there are many areas of deficit, there will, of course, be several areas of disorder. Smaller "holes" may cause behavior labeled eccentric or may cause some minor psychic discomfort and life difficulty. (p. 407)

Any dividing line exists only conceptually, of course. Personality patterns are important because they are "closest" to the schema and represent hard core styles difficult to change. Personality is also "responsible" for the type of coping pattern used during and after trauma—denial\numbing and intrusive experiences, reinterpretive efforts to make the data "fit," and interactions with others (Janoff-Bulman, 1985). McCrae and Costa (1990) even contextualized personality as one part of the self; the former is stable and measurable, and the latter is "deeper" and more encompassing. In addition, Sullivan (1953), among many other interpersonal therapists, believed strongly that personality patterns or recurrent interpersonal distortions require understanding and eventual challenge for meaningful change to occur. For him, it was personality patterns (and not Axis I disorders) that require the emphasis in treatment. The multiaxial model of conflict and symptom development "understands" this. Although neglected, this model of the human change process divides therapeutic labor into personal variables and symptoms. All too often, as symptoms evolve from the personality structure, the Axis II perspective (and schema) is lost. This can be a problem with chronic trauma victims who utilize psychiatric facilities and tend to have at least one Axis II diagnosis.

Personality Traits: A Nosological Aside

We do not wish to over address the problems of personality styles; neither do we want it to appear as if all is well. The measurement and understanding of personality disorders are reasonably recent, having all the problems of Axis I disorders. Formidable concerns start with a very basic concept of conceptual formulation, construct validation. The question, "what is a personality disorder," influences everything. Knowing only that a personality disorder is pervasive, persistent, and (mildly) pathological is one thing and helpful (DSM-III-R), but what constitutes a particular disorder is quite another. Diagnostic items or exemplars are ultimately dependent on "something," that criteria are often cloudy. In addition to the multiple errors that can exist with measures, most of the effort on Axis II classification has been directed at the contents of the diagnosis, particularly inclusive criteria for a personality disorder. Less attention has been paid to domain sampling, the underlying principles used to organize such criteria, the definition of the diagnosis, and the rules governing the selection and evaluation of criteria. This is the real work of construct validation of a clinical entity (Livesley & Jackson, 1991).

Given imperfect criteria or at the least poor criteria rules, the work of validating a personality style on an assessment measure, any measure, becomes difficult, since no validity standards exist. Many questions are unanswered. What is the gold standard? Are personality disorders distinctive psychopathological states or normal styles exaggerated? Are dimensions of traits or categories of diagnostic criteria better representatives of personality states? Is personality truly invariant across time? Remember every clinical judgement made about a personality style is directly related to the validity of the criteria of that style and the method employed to assess it. In the DSMs, both are faulty. It appears that there has been "premature attention" directed at applied research, use of Axis I methods for Axis II issues, and an excessive dependence on clinicians' views of these (rather than the individuals themselves) (Grove & Tellegen, 1991). "Better" classification thinking is needed regarding whether different concepts of personality require different classification and measurement; whether conceptual or real distinctions among types (real, ideal, eidetic, and existential) (Kraus, 1991) exist; whether categorical approaches should be applied to severe disorders and dimensional approaches to less severe ones (Gunderson,

Links, & Reich, 1991); and whether a personality type's phenomenology (what is meant by the style) should be distinct from its criteria (Widiger, 1991).

It would be nice if the noise stopped here, but it doesn't. This unstructured thinking has allowed for excessive overlay and common baggage. Comorbidity, co-occurrence, and covariation among the personality disorders are rampant. Using semistructured interviews, the level of over-inclusive Axis II diagnoses can reach five in patient groups (Widiger, Frances, Harris, Jacobsberg, Fyer, & Manning, 1991). Comorbidity between Axis II disorders and Axis I disorders is also high. In addition, we know that the presence of an Axis II disorder worsens the course of care or makes for a poorer response to treatment than having an Axis I disorder alone. This raises questions about the actual presence of an Axis II disorder, perhaps being present only when there is an Axis I problem. Some personality disorders even may be considered characterological variants of known Axis I spectra (e.g., borderline along an impulsive/affectivity dimension). Alternatively, perhaps personality disorders are milder forms of Axis I problems.

In this context one might additionally ask what comorbidity itself means. It is the co-occurrence of independent disorders reflective of a common etiology or a unique causal relationship between disorders, or is it a definitional artifact resulting from shared diagnostic criteria? We know that comorbidity is increased by the presence of common or overlapping criteria, emphasis on multiple diagnosis, or the lowering thresholds for a diagnosis. We need more clarity, better definition, and more consistency. In fact, the whole idea of comorbidity may reflect an "Axis II bias"; the concerns of (trait) overlap do not apply with as much gusto to Axis I.

This brief section is intended to foster a skeptical attitude, one where a hefty dose of chaos and preconception is a staple. Unfortunately, the whole psychiatric nosology suffers from this status. Work is already under way to alter things. Cutting-edge criterion validation issues are forming the DSM-IV. Several theoretical classifications that were developed to be checked empirically and that permit an interplay between theory and empiricism (leading to increased validity) are beginning to take better form. Millon's system is one where the connection to the DSMs and other criteria is being checked. In many current studies on personality, for example, subjects are being chosen more carefully, rated on several instruments, and by several people. Often too, composite decision rules are used. Discrepant cases now present less noise. In future years it is a good bet that personality disorder status will depend upon multiple cutoff points for an individual in different contexts. This will depend upon severity of a dimension(s). For the present, a healthy and open direction has formed. Our choice is to recognize this condition as it is, develop a perspective, and proceed.

Personality Traits: Our Act of Faith

We take a stand on the definition of personality, an enduring profile of a person's traits. Given this definition, other aspects are implied. First, a personality type can be very healthy and adjusted, or more fixed in its patterns and thereby considered a personality disorder. Second, the theory of psychopathology ascribed to holds that stress can enervate the personality style (or disorder) and cause symptoms. PTSD is one result. Third, the person is both a type and amount of several traits related to personality. As such, the person can be categorized *and* have a varying amount of that category. The person in effect has a profile of traits. *In this sense, interest is less on the degree of pathology or threshold above which a person has a problem, and more on a type of person with a unique profile, whose reaction to stress can be predicted or logically understood.*

In a treatment situation the therapist experiences several shades of behavior and traits (Table 5.5). Particular attributes and variations of their frequency characterize personalities. The Axis II label "personality disorder not otherwise specified" (DSM-III-R) has become popular because of this. Everyone has a personality, reflected in traits. These may be less intense than a personality disorder, but are consistent and distinctive. Discussing PTSD, Hyer (Hyer, Davis, Woods, Albrecht, & Boudewyns, in press) wrote:

The clinician is not being asked to accept a conservative position, espousing the underlying coherency of personality or a premorbid personality problem. Rather, the linkage to PTSD should provide a more holistic perspective of the person. Clearly, there are problems or confounds with the PTSD and Axis II diagnoses. Many of the explicit criteria for personality disorders share a common variance with the diagnostic criteria and symptoms of PTSD.... What appears to be most logical is that the traumatic event such as combat exposure can impact on normal personality patterns and transform them in pathological directions which might be expressed as one of the personality patterns noted, depending on the nature of the pre-trauma personality structure and stage of ego development. The stressful event appears to alter personality processes and coping patterns in normally fixed ways but dependent too on the preexisting patterns. (pp. 19-20)

The argument is then, that whatever the cause of the perturbation, the profile reflects the relative dominance of person traits and provides information for treatment. Needleman (1982) noted this as "being in front of the question of oneself" (p. 13). This is information both about the human knower and the human knowing process (Mahoney, 1991). This is intrinsic to the multiaxial system and our schema-personality styles interaction. Knowledge of the personality pattern and of its relative strength are both important. Therapeutically, knowing patterns allows us to excise underlying cognitive mechanisms and observe self-defeating patterns, as well as predict decompensation routes. And, knowing the intensity of a trait provides the clinician with the "right" priority in care. In turn, a double focus (personality and symptoms), coequal in clinical merit, can develop. Here the therapeutic interest is the interactions among client traits, their strength, and the measure of care needed. If a victim is in turmoil (or for that matter if any person experiences psychiatric symptoms), the likelihood of an Axis II disorder being present, either as a "real" premorbid condition or an artifact of the current intense emotion, is high (Choca, Shanley, & van Denburg, (1992).

Increasingly this awareness of the importance of personality in the diagnosis and treatment of victims has influenced clinical thinking. In addition to the studies advocating the person

TABLE 5.5
Indicators of Personality Disorders

1. Self or collateral reports of trait consistencies since childhood.

2. Non-compliance

3. Treatment "stops" for little reason

4. Unaware of effect on others

5. Not motivated (e.g., court ordered)

6. Heavy resistance around change

7. Ego syntonic character problems

8. Axis I problems seen as "out there"

9. Secondary gain to behavior

10. Fear of change of character patterns ("I could never be that")

11. Fear others will not accept new me

12. Characterological rigidity or obvious self-defeating patterns that persist

13. Schemas that prevent therapeutic efforts at change (e.g., loss of autonomy)

14. Inability to see merits of collaborative process

15. "I have always been that way" is obvious

event model, this interest has evolved from the psychodynamic literature (Emery & Emery, 1989; Hendin, 1983; Horowitz, 1986; Wilson, 1988), and from a handful of studies at various trauma centers highlighting personality problems (Hyer & Boudewyns, 1985), especially anti-social traits (Jordan, Howe, & Lockhart, 1986; Lipkin, Scurfield, & Blank, 1983; Wilson & Zigelbaum, 1983) and borderline personality functioning (Berman, Price, & Gusman, 1982). Most notable among these studies is the work of Horowitz (Horowitz, Marmar, Krupnick, Wilner, Kaltreider, & Wallestein, 1984), whose method of treatment of PTSD dissects the connectional network of trauma and the information processing of the stressor, by highlighting the character structure of the individual.

The fact that much of the research on PTSD during the seventies and eighties has been directed at symptoms (Lyons, Gerardi, Wolfe, & Keane, 1988) and has lagged in success, additionally endorses this position. Research has duly noted that clients with a given diagnostic grouping (PTSD) experience varying amounts of assistance from different treatment packages. Maybe something exists in the dynamics of the person, the presence and degree of selected traits, that is more important than a stock package of care given by a manual which only addresses symptoms. There is something very different in the symptom-based clinical question, "What is the patient's conflict and problems?", to the personologic-based probe, "What intrapsychic or person variables interfere with the solution of these conflicts?". The idea that personality styles arm-twist trauma expression is increasingly persuasive. The question remains, however: How do we make this more manageable clinically?

Enter Millon Model

A model that is theory based, anchored to the DSM-III, and can be measured is that given by Millon (1969, 1981, 1983). During the last decade this model has served as a guide for the renewed interest in the importance of personality in the multiaxial system (Millon, 1969, 1981). The Axis II dimension of DSM-III was influenced by this paradigm. According to this model personality is the central focus around which symptoms and behaviors evolve. Initially, eight core types of personality were based on the nature of reinforcement (pain or pleasure), source of reward (self or others), and instrumental style (active/passive). Over time, two additional Axis II disorders, sadistic and self-defeating, have been added to this model (Table 5.6). The personality styles represent a typology where relative dominance of key traits is posited. This is a social or interactional model that exists on a continuum from normal autonomous functioning to psychopathological functioning depending on the level of adaptive inflexibility, the fostering of vicious circles, and tenuousness of stability. Three severe personality types also exist and represent extensions or exaggerations of the basic eight personalities. These are schizotypal, borderline, and paranoid. *The clinician's task is first to establish the basic personality pattern(s) of a person; second, to modify this information with any existing elevations in the severe personality styles; and, third, to integrate the unique personality profile with the current clinical symptoms.*

Traumatic Personality

In the current literature a small group of studies exist on the character adaptation of the Vietnam veteran using the Millon Clinical Multiaxial Inventory (MCMI and MCMI-II). At least six studies have reported the existence of the passive aggressive and avoidant profile (8/2 or 2/8) in this population (Choca, Peterson, & Shanley, 1986; Hyer & Boudewyns, 1985; Hyer, Woods, & Boudewyns, 1991; McDermott, 1986; Robert, Ryan, McEntyre, McFarland, Lipps, & Rosenburg, 1985; Sherwood, Funari, & Piekorski, 1990). The Sherwood study is especially interesting. One hundred and eighty-nine male Vietnam veterans who were categorized as having PTSD according to the MMPI-PTSD scale were evaluated on the MCMI. The character styles, passive-aggressive, schizoid, avoidant, and borderline, were significantly related to PTSD patients, but not to non-PTSD patients. Once again, the most common two-point profile was the 8/2 or 2/8. In this sample a hit rate of 80% would be obtained if the sample was classified as having PTSD on the basis of scales 8 and 2 on the MCMI (BR$\geq$84). The authors concluded that the surprisingly homogeneous character styles among this group represented

TABLE 5.6
Theory-Based Framework for Personality Pathology

Pathology Domain	Self - Other			Pain-Pleasure	
Reinforcement source	Other + Self -	Self + Other -	Self<—>Other	Pain<—>Pleasure	Pleasure-Pain ±
Instrumental coping style/ pattern	Dependent	Independent	Ambivalent	Discordant	Detached
Passive variant	Dependent	Narcissistic	Compulsive	Self-Defeating (masochistic)	Schizoid
Active variant	Histrionic	Antisocial	Passive-Aggressive	Aggressive (sadistic)	Avoidant
Dysfunctional variant	Borderline	Paranoid	Borderline or Paranoid		Schizotypal

From Millon Clinical Multiaxal Inventory Manual, 1983. Reproduced by permission from Dr. Theodore Millon and National Computer Systems, Inc.

adaptive patterns utilized to cope with the traumas of Vietnam. These styles were viewed, therefore, as defenses which better enable the veteran to manage high levels of anxiety.

The Hyer group at the Augusta War Trauma Project used the MCMI and MCMI-II on PTSD veterans and emphasized the role of personality in a different way. In one study, "A Three Tier Evaluation of PTSD Among Vietnam Combat Veterans," Hyer, Woods, & Boudewyns (1991) attempted to unpack the complex PTSD picture. The belief was that a molecular view of the clinical components of this chronic population would better serve both assessment and treatment. This formulation was a precursor to the model of this book. Tier 1 advocated for the development of the life-style according to the methods of Adler. Tier 2 involved the use of the MCMI. Resultant personality styles of the trauma victim were conceived as a direct "outgrowth" of the life-style. Tiers 1 and 2, therefore, reflect the idiographic character of the person. Table 5.7 presents the profile of the MCMI and MCMI-II for 100 Vietnam veterans in PTSD (Hyer, Davis, Woods, Albrecht, & Boudewyns, in press). Tier 3 involved symptoms, which will be addressed in the last section of this chapter.

The highlight of Tier 2 was a typology of the MCMI based on a sorting procedure outlined by Millon (1983). Only the eight basic personality codes were used. Initially, a code was arrived at by prominence of a style; that is, any of the eight mild personality styles at or beyond BR-84 was included. Next, each veteran was sorted into additional codes based on presence (BR$\geq$74), that is, person endorsed features of a style. As result of these two procedures, a parent code, the 8-2 *(Traumatic Personality),* was identified, as well as three additional codes. A later study (Hyer, Davis, Woods, Albrecht & Boudewyns, in press) added one other personality style: the self-defeating influence. Information on these is given in Table 5.8. They include a basic description of the Traumatic Personality, its core beliefs, strategies, and fears, as well as information on the four types. At the end of each personality influence is the projected percentage of the therapist's focus of care on the patient's key problem (character, trauma

(continued on page 240)

TABLE 5.7
Means and MCMI and MCMI-II
of Combat-Related PTSD

Personality Scales	MCMI MEAN	MCMI-II MEAN
1 Schizoid	81.65	89.547
2 Avoidant	89.80	92.267
3 Dependent	44.15	34.942
4 Histrionic	30.07	40.640
4 Nacrissistic	38.01	61.593
6A Antisocial	64.80	86.291
6B Sadistic		50.61
7 Compulsive	33.15	50.605
8A P. Aggressive	94.62	101.767
8B Self-Defeating		82.28
S Schizotypal	64.98	86.465
B Borderline	76.84	85.186
P Paranoid	60.00	68.570
Symptom Scales		
A Anxiety	97.88	88.733
H Somatoform	67.50	60.000
N Hyptmanic	37.29	44.709
O Dysthymic	93.70	91.535
B Alcohol Abuse	76.27	82.651
T Drug Abuse	64.23	79.477
SS Psychotic Thinking	68.75	80.523
CC Psychotic Depression	73.94	89.465
TT Psychotic Delusions	60.20	58.733
Response Set Scales		
Disclosure		35.12
Desirability		91.99
Debasement		89.54

n=100

Taken from Hyer, Davis, Woods, Albrecht, & Boudewyns, (in press).

TABLE 5.8
Traumatic Personality and Variants

Traumatic Personality
(8-2 Code)

Client's behavior is typified by a central conflict between avoidance and fears of being independent. Being close is important, but expectation of pain is pervasive. Behind these interpersonal tendencies is a deflated self-image. Any effort at independence, then, is filled with fantasies of failure. Reality being what it is demands interaction, but, as noted, failure results. In turn, others have disparaging reactions or have avoided him/her. Being resistant and on occasion even bellicose toward others for not understanding him/her are most usual. The security that is sought is severely compromised under these conditions. The result is a pervasive and stifling anger. An anxious withdrawal with feelings of depression is concomitant.

Over time every avenue of outlet appears to be replete with conflict. Acting alone feels bad; acting with others is filled with mistrust and failure. This only leads to stronger avoidant and passive aggressive interpersonal actions. The victim is now misunderstood, not appreciated, and demeaned. Also, he/she is most negative toward self. Depression and anxiety now become chronic. Eventually he/she turns against self given to the multiple avoidant strategies that disrupt self-patterns of affect and cognition. He/she feels no respect anywhere. During periods of relative calm, he/she may even come out of a brooding shell and feel good. This feeling is temporary and gives way to the slightest stress.

Often "borderline" components are added to this picture. Here instability both interpersonally and emotionally is pervasive. Every feature of the passive-aggressive/avoidant style is made more "noisy." Now what exist are no inner security, massive inner resentment, little self worth, much alienation, considerably

(continued)

TABLE 5.8 (continued)

cognitive disruption, and pervasive chronic agitation. Moodiness, erratic behavior, sulkiness and helplessness become the norm.

A reasonable therapeutic strategy involves patient awareness of personality patterns, fostering of control, reduction of vacillating and self-defeating patterns, and support for change.

Therapeutic Focus: Character 60%
Trauma 20%
Psychosocial 20%

Schizoid Influence
(8-2-1 Code)

The addition of the Schizoid style (1) provides an insidious component to a person's personality. These patients are interpersonally aloof, behaviorally lethargic, cognitively impoverished, affectively flat, and relatively devoid of intrapsychic mechanisms. These schizoid features mix with the hypersensitivity and avoidance, as well as the contrariness and moodiness of the passive-aggressive style. Vietnam combat veterans with this 8-2-1 profile appear cognitively and affectively confused. These veterans do not understand themselves and believe that no one else does either. They experience themselves as strange, lost, and despairing. In the parlance of combat veterans from Vietnam, at times they may need the "woods." This provides a needed and hopefully short-term sanctuary. The risk is that these patients may feel rebuked, may give in to the detached style, and consequently may drop out of treatment. A reasonable therapeutic stance for this profile is to respect the detachment pattern, not to allow for environmental overload, and to build trust over time. As with the 8-2 code, the addition of severe personality styles further complicates the treatment (paranoid or borderline or both).

(continued)

TABLE 5.8 (continued)

Therapeutic Focus: Character 60%
Trauma 40%
Psychosocial 0%

Dependent Influence
(8-2-1-3 Code)

The addition of the Submissive style (3) to the 8-2-1 profile can be viewed as positive. This profile occurred frequently, being present in 33% of the sample. Often this problem is modified, as the borderline or borderline plus schizotypal personality styles are added. The "benign but annoying" dependent traits are poor self-image, interpersonal submission, affective passivity, and cognitive naivete. Dependence serves to increase complaints and symptoms, but also to increase compliance. In a sense this influencing personality style, although it does not simplify a patient's personality, allows for an injection of likability. The 8-2 and 8-2-1 personality code is, however, present and remains debilitating. The addition of dependency provides some measure of hope, as it increases, however, potential therapeutic options, patient compliance and lessens the possibility of negative transference. The therapist, therefore, can become more assertive, provide structure and support, educate, and become a model for change.

Therapeutic Focus: Character 60%
Trauma 40%
Psychosocial 0%

Antisocial Influence
(8-2-1-6 Code)

This personality code is perhaps the biggest challenge in treatment. When the Antisocial style (6) is added to the 8-2-1 code, the "influence" is action-oriented and often negative.

(continued)

TABLE 5.8 (continued)

Hostile affectivity, assertive self-image, interpersonal vindictiveness, fearlessness, and projection are characteristic of these people. Victims high on this style are given to acting out, to stamp out fears counterphobically and to demean affection. A general "I'm-gonna-get-you-before-you-get-me" stance is practiced. These veterans need control and are highly reactant. Decompensation is in a paranoid direction and can be anticipated. Resistance can be expected when any loss of control is experienced. In addition, these veterans do not seek out psychotherapy. Treatment for them often is a by-product of multiple failures or of an external force such as a court order. Trust-building and empathy should be practiced. To the extent that the therapist is viewed as an advocate/friend, a "working alliance" can exist and a rechanneling of self-defeating strategies can be initiated. Eventually self-defeating behaviors can be addressed and basic characterological issues of independence and attachment fears can be discussed. Finally, the probability is high that the severe personality styles, paranoid or paranoid plus borderline, are added (60%).

> Therapeutic Focus: Character 50%
> Trauma 0%
> Psychosocial 50%

Self Defeating Influence
(8-2-1-8B* Code)

The addition of the code 8B floods the avoidant and ambivalent character traits with a repetitive series of misfortunes. These victims undermine any temporary successes by negatively assessing their affective/cognitive life or interpersonally eliciting failure or rebuff. Researchers have shown that this group tends to be both victimizers and overreporters of symptoms. They tend to increase problems and undermine progress in treatment. Most notable is the possibility of multiple symptoms, suicidal gestures, negative therapeutic reactions, noncompliance, and outright treatment failure. They also have a special brand

(continued)

TABLE 5.8 (continued)

of passivity, making themselves unlovable, submissive, and self-destructive. Nothing seems to have a lasting effect. Their automatic thoughts are often hidden or vague but always replete with negative or failure constructs. They truly live by the code that misery in life is better than happiness or being ignored. Strikingly, these victims, who often challenge their environment to take steps on their behalf, can never reach beyond themselves to suffer quietly and struggle with pain. Life is unfair, and they are out to prove it.

> Therapeutic Focus: Character 60%
> Trauma 0%
> Psychosocial 40%

*MCMI-II

memory, and psychosocial problem) at the *beginning* of treatment. As therapy progresses these percentages will change.

This is a "clinical" taxonomy and represents anything but perfect classification. It is also based on personality and not on PTSD symptoms. All codes possess the Traumatic Personality plus others. The importance, therefore, is in the incremental information provided by the other codes (3, 6A, 1, and 8B). A recent cluster analysis on PTSD veterans largely corroborated these influences, however (Hyer, Davis, Woods, Albrecht, Boudewyns, in press). In addition, severe personality styles (schizotypal, borderline, and paranoid) also were present and measurably influence the clinical expression of these milder styles. Finally, while the MCMI and MCMI-II protocols divide the personality codes according to strict decision rules (280 code types) (Millon, 1983) to describe the clinical status of the person, there are virtually no studies that have validated clinical types of patients. No definitive code types of persons exist.

As we end this section, we provide one further table (Table 5.9). As noted, the interface of the schema and personality is a natural birth process without a clear division: no fine cutting lines are based on time, pattern, or intensity that stand out. Personality styles evolve naturally from schemas. Table 5.9 then is a list of the most likely schemas implied by the personality pattern. The schemas evolve into cognitive, affective, and behavioral styles unique to each personality pattern. Most notably, the schema-related self-image and core strategy of each style are highlighted. According to the model of Millon (1969, 1981) schemas and self-images are relatively "uncomplicated" for the less severe personality styles. Although less is known about their effects, the two newer personality styles, self-defeating and sadistic, are also given. Some (Choca et al., 1992) believe these two newer personality styles should not be included among the basic personality styles (as these two styles are intrinsically pathological). Regardless, once more severe personality styles develop, more problems are in evidence. These styles are influenced by the original milder level personality styles. Victims with schizotypal personality, for example, may show one of two patterns, an "affectively lame" schizoid pattern or an alienated and anxious one (avoidant). Victims with a borderline pattern have decompensation trajectories in any one of four directions based on independent or ambivalent styles. Victims with paranoid styles develop these from independent or ambivalent patterns. (The discordant patterns, self-defeating and sadistic, also influence borderline and paranoid styles. Since less is known regarding these, they are not specified). Therefore, when a person has a schizotypal, borderline, or paranoid disorder, the clinician should investigate for a milder personality style, influencing the composition of the unique configuration (of the person). When these styles are included, however, any character simplicity is compromised. This is in keeping with current research suggesting that the number of schemas of the severe personality styles exceed milder levels (as high as nine with borderline styles) (Young, 1990).

Finally, it is emphasized that there is no one personality scale with a "psychometric lock" on a PTSD (or any)

TABLE 5.9
Personality Style and Schema

Basic Personality Styles	Probable Schema	Image	Strategy
1. Schizoid	Control/Autonomy Self Suffering/ Insensitive	Complacement	Detachment
2. Avoidant	Competence Trust Acceptance	Alienated	Sanctuary
3. Dependent	Esteem Acceptance	Inept	Attachment
4. Histrionic	Esteem Intimacy Acceptance	Sociable	Appealing
5. Narcissistic	Independence/ Insouciance Control Power	Admirable	Explosive
6. Antisocial	Responsible Trust Control	Autonomous	Independent
6B. Sadistic	Fearless Power-control	Competitive	Intimidating

(continued)

TABLE 5.9 (continued)

Basic Personality Styles	Probable Schema	Image	Strategy
7. Compulsive	Competent Control	Conscientious	Performance
8. Passive Aggressive	Control/Self-Sufficient Independence	Discontented	Guarded
8B. Self Defeating	Esteem (Self-effacing) Depreciated	Undeserving	Sacrificing

population. We endorse the use of other personality instruments, especially the NEO-PI (Costa & McCrae, 1989) and the 16-PF, both well-known scales we have evaluated. The NEO-PI especially was selected because it appears to account for much of the variance of the Axis II personality disorders, contributes additional information (to both Axis I and II disorders), and assists in treatment (Costa & McCrae, 1992). In addition, in keeping with the multimethod-multisource assessment, we highly endorse "checking out" cognitive/affective/behavioral styles via item checking on the personality scale or use of an interviewer-rated personality scale, like the SCID-II (Structured Clinical Interview for the DSM-III-R, Axis II) (Spitzer, Williams, Gibbon, & First, 1990) or both. Routinely, we give the SCID-II.

BELIEFS

Beliefs are the private logic used by the individual to validate schemas and to support modal, often self-defeating personality styles of the person. As was noted in Chapter 4 (and above), surface beliefs provide the "private logic" for schemas and personality. Relative to schemas, beliefs are less "salient" cognitions that sit at the top of the thought hierarchy. They are easily accessible to consciousness and are readily apparent. They are the "automatic" thoughts available to the person that can be challenged, parsed out, reframed, or altered. As noted, Beck and Freeman (1990) maintained that beliefs have an internal control function. They are concerned largely with self and external regulation, assuring that everything is "on course." Recall too, coping strategies are not random events (Wilson, 1988). Beliefs then are the icing on the cognitive cake, representing both automatic thoughts and "on course" appraisal functions.

Beliefs also can be considered as cognitive styles or products of personality styles. The avoidant style, for example, is easily distracted, that is, preoccupied and battered by disruptive and often perplexing inner thoughts. This cognitive style is so adept at avoiding pain that it automatically becomes hypervigilant, discounts data, disrupts painful emotions, and senses relief in avoidant acts. The narcissist has automatic thoughts reflective of unmet expectations, the shortcomings and inferiorities of others, as well as the uniqueness of his/her problems. The passive aggressive is often negative, distilling thoughts of felt injustice, victimization, or anger. These people are skeptical, cynical, untrusting, and ambivalent. Once these surface level cognitive styles have been identified, more central or "salient" cognitions (schemas) can be approached.

Measurement

Many existing tools are available to measure beliefs. In CBT the number has been called "staggering" (Goldberg & Shaw, 1990). Two types are typically measured. First, stylistic distortions are evaluated by the majority of the CBT measures. Examples include overgeneralization, magnification, black and white thinking, and selective abstraction. While there are several extant measures to assess "basic mistakes" in thinking, one scale, the *Self Control Schedule* (SCS) (Rosenbaum, 1980), is a measure of strategies for handling emotional responses. This measures the person's ability to implement problem-solving skills, to postpone instant gratification, to believe that one is able to self-regulate internal processes, and to use cognitions to contend with emotional and psychological reactions. In effect, the SCS assesses the person's ability to intervene cognitively with disruptive reactions. This scale is distinguished because it is sensitive to CBT changes (Goldberg & Shaw 1990).

Second, content distortions are present. Two scales are especially noteworthy. The first is *Dysfunctional Attitude Scale* (DAS) (Weissman, 1978), a self-report questionnaire developed to assess negative attitudes or schemata associated with depression. A second less used measure is the *Idea Inventory* (II). This is a simple and appealing measure anchored to Ellis' irrational beliefs (Ellis, 1962). It is easy to use and can be self scored. Also, this scale allows for the application of Ellis' ABC technique. The II serves as an entre into the schema. Table 5.10 presents results of a study by Hyer and colleagues (Hyer, Woods and Boudewyns, 1991) using the II on chronic trauma victims. Sufferers of chronic trauma endorse high levels of irrational beliefs. Such endorsements should serve as a springboard to identify fixed natural beliefs, faulty information processing, and eventually "deeper" cognitions. Persons (1991) has proposed a cognitive method to ferret out more enduring cognitions (Figure 5.2). In this procedure thoughts (C), situations (B), and moods (M) are accepted at "face value," and deeper distortions (schemas) are considered. Over time, more salient patterns emerge and become the new core cognitions identified for change. These patterns are, of course, related to (core) schemas or personality styles.

The method used to identify cognitions is less important than the therapeutic pursuit of cognitions that support schemas. Often the clinician can simply request the client to keep a record or identify thoughts in a given stressful situation. In therapy the victim is taught that thoughts influence the schema (and mediate emotions), that both realistic and unrealistic beliefs exist in any given situation, and that a person can evaluate his/her own beliefs. The victim knows ahead of time that these surface beliefs are reflective of more central underlying assumptions ("deep habits") that are affect laden and self-referent. This is the collaborative empiricism

TABLE 5.10
Percentage of Idea Inventory Beliefs Endorsed

Belief	Percentage above mean*
1. Love from everyone is necessary	65
2. Competence is necessary	45
3. Villains should be punished	71
4. Disaster happens if hopes are not satisfied	59
5. Unhappiness is externally caused	68
6. Dwell on negative possibilities	74
7. Difficulties should be avoided	72
8. Others are necessary for advice and strength	62
9. My past or old beliefs can't be changed	72
10. Problems of others upset me	71
11. Expect precise solutions to problems	51

*Range is 3-9, x=6 for each item

From Hyer, Davis, Boudewyns, Woods (1991). Reproduced with permission from the *Journal of Clinical Psychology.*

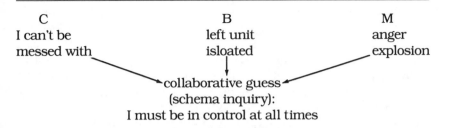

C	B	M
I can't be	left unit	anger
messed with	isloated	explosion

collaborative guess
(schema inquiry):
I must be in control at all times

A method that has been helpful in the process is that used in Rational Emotive Therapy. Persons (1989) used a CBM procedure: C standing for cognitive, B for behavior, and M for mood. Almost all problems or symptoms can be formulated in this way. At the base, a schema or irrational belief can be guessed at or agreed to for each situation. Through gentle challenges, guidance, and "collaborative empiricism," consistent schemas can be arrived at.

Figure 5.2. Rational emotive process for schema exposition. From *Persons* (1989). Reproduced with permission from Norton Publishing.

proposed by Beck and colleagues (Beck & Freeman, 1990). Perceptions are considered hypotheses to be evaluated as more or less true regarding a situation or interaction and more or less salient relative to the schema. Through education, the client learns that awareness is on a continuum, that thinking involves sequences of "events" (e.g., cognitions lead to emotions), that he/she has all the necessary information for change, and that consistency and practice are required. Surface cognitions start this process.

A few rules of thumb can be identified. First, the more central or core the cognition is to the schema, the more difficult it will be to change and the greater the amount of resistance can be expected. Second, the more the person is fully immersed in the cognition, unable to take distance or accept any dissonance, the more that belief reflects core schemas. Safran, Greenberg, and Rice (1988) noted that two factors are predictive of better outcome: the client's awareness of and ability to report his/her intrusive negative thoughts and the client's awareness of frustrations in his/her emotions. To the extent that these abilities are available and that the clinician can remain on task, typical CBT procedures *will* be successful. Third, as we will see later (Chapter 6), the task of the clinician is not to convince the sufferer of his/her "error," but to empower the client in a cooperative fashion with a will and a skill to challenge cognitions. Fourth, the more the person understands his/her Sc+P+(B)+Sy profile, the greater the chances of success. Finally, clients who understand the "rules of the game" (for treatment) and understand the maladaptive influences of their cognitions, can now ask self, "Is this the way I want to be?"

SYMPTOMS

"Woe is wondrously clinging: The clouds ride by" (Anonymous). This old saying describes the perseverance of symptoms especially in PTSD. If schemas and personality styles are concerned with "What power do I have over symptoms?"; symptoms are concerned with, "What power do symptoms have over me?". The symptom part of the Sc+P+(B)+Sy sequence is strewn with a commingling of problems, defenses, coping skills, intervening traumas, as well as the person factors just discussed. As a result, we have divided symptoms into two types—psychosocial and trauma. It is the symptom that receives clinical attention. *The task of the clinician is two-fold: (1) to establish a convenient method for assessment and (2) equally important, to contextualize symptoms within the person of the victim.* We address the overall issue of assessment of trauma, especially the measurement of psychosocial symptoms. We also consider a distinct aspect in the symptom expression of trauma victims, the response style known as overreporting.

Psychosocial Symptoms

Excellent reviews on the assessment of chronic PTSD (e.g., Litz, Penk, Gerardi, & Keane, 1991; Lyons et al., 1988) are available. These emphasize the need for a multimethod-multisource approach, including structured interviews, clinical ratings, psychometric scales, collateral reports, psychophysiological indices, and even biological markers, along with a complete record review. The central components of PTSD—intrusion, numbing/avoidance, and arousal—must be covered along with comorbid symptoms that form the unique expression of each person's disorder. For this to occur, assessment should be a continuous process. Also, for a disorder that so massively disrupts coping and balance, *treatment and assessment should complement one another.* In fact, PTSD may be the one disorder when treatment "assists" assessment.

Clinical Interview

Without question, no substitute has been identified for the clinical interview. This is so, despite obvious problems of measurement error and inconsistency among interviewers. The need for a careful interview is important, so much so that recommending other measures may lend them excessive validity. The clinical interview provides optimum flexibility in both depth and breadth of decisions. Structured interviews should be rigorously followed but should never be so rigid or limited as to provide only diagnosis or classification. *The trained clinician will be able: (1) to assess trauma-related issues, including the three DSM-III-R criteria; (2) to assess associated symptoms and disorders; (3) to formulate treatment issues; and (4) to make clinical judgements recommending psychological tests or further structured interviews or both.* These issues are implied in the measures that follow. In this process, too, the caring clinician knows that the anxiety generated by a clinical evaluation can be formidable, and this always is respected.

It should be noted that no gold standard exists. None of the instruments that follow fully possess criteria noted by Watson (1990); close correspondence to the DSM-III-R, robust reliability, empirical validity, both dichotomous and continuous outputs, and ease of administration (by a subprofessional).

The goal is a concurrently validating approach using both clinician and client rated measures with sound psychometric properties, validated by independent data. Validation of diagnostic instruments always has been a problem. Kulka, Schlenger, Fairbank, Hough, Jordan, Marmar, and Weiss (1991) noted that the question of validity is best "broadly" considered (i.e., in terms of relationships between the index measure and the broad array of biopsychosocial variables rather than between two instruments). In fact, these authors recommend several diagnostic decision rules, including composite diagnoses, "hits" on two or more scales, peer assisted decisions, or a combination of these. Spitzer's LEAD standard (Longitudinal, Expert, and All Data) (Spitzer, 1983) is certainly applicable here. Parrott and Howes (1991) emphasized four elements of assessment related to the trauma experience itself: appraisal of the trauma (the person's schemas); belief of vulnerability (how shattered or unsafe life is); quality of self questions ("why me" self statement); and self appraisal (idiosyncratic deeper self positions—"I am a stupid person"). Alterations in the victim's identity require these queries.

In Table 5.11 is specified the recommended protocol. To start with, the clinician can decide among these structured interviews. The first is the SCID (Spitzer & Williams, 1985). Since our interest is PTSD, often only this section need be used. Several PTSD centers have elected, however, to use other sections, especially Anxiety Disorders, Affective Disorders, and Substance Abuse. This is an interviewer-rated measure and provides diagnostic data on the Axis I categories including PTSD—Current Full PTSD, Current Partial PTSD, Full PTSD in Remission, Partial PTSD in Remission and No PTSD. Information is provided, therefore, on the various subclinical or past states of PTSD. Data are also available on "subthreshold" problems (ones almost a problem). The major advantages of the SCID are absolute anchoring to the DSM-III-R, its ability to distinguish types of Anxiety Disorders (and distinguish this family of disorders from mood and dissociative states), and its high inter-rater reliability. Unfortunately, the SCID provides only a dichotomous rating of PTSD and the relationship of this categorical typing to other PTSD measures or symptom patterns is sketchy at best (Green, 1991).

Recently a new measure, the CAPS-1 *(Clinician Administered PTSD Scale)* (Blake, Nagy, Kaloupek, Klauminzer, Charney, & Keane, 1990), fashioned after the SCID-PTSD section has been successfully used (Table 5.12). This measure assesses DSM-III-R PTSD criteria and highly related symptoms along dimensions of frequency and intensity (0-4), as well as provides a designation for current or lifetime PTSD. This scale remains true to the DSM-III-R criteria for PTSD, has behavioral referents, and has a compendium scale for follow-up. Table 5.12 presents data on this scale on 80 confirmed PTSD combat-related veterans at our medical center. Results suggest three findings: (1) intensity and frequency levels of most symptoms for the whole group are high; (2) recurrent thoughts (B-1), avoidant thoughts (C-1), and feelings of detachment (C-5), sleep difficulties (D-1), concentration problems (D-3), and hypervigilance (D-4), and depression (associated features) are rated especially high; and (3) flashbacks (B-3), memory of the trauma (C-3), physiologic reactivity (C-6), and homocidality (associated features) are rated lower. Noted, however, is that this scale, as with all existing scales, provides no "proof" that a specific rating on intensity or frequency results in a hit for a category of PTSD. The answer to this question awaits better scaling and validation research.

Finally, two other scales are also recognized. The *Anxiety Disorders Interview Schedule-Revised* (ADIS-R) (DiNardo, Barlow, Cerny, Vermilyea, Vermilyea, Himadi, & Waddell, 1985) and the *PTSD Interview* (PTSD-I) (Watson, Kucala, Juba, Manifold, Anderson, & Anderson, 1991). The former provides a careful measure of the Anxiety Disorders; the latter scale assesses presence or absence and severity/frequency of PTSD symptoms.

As noted, a major advantage of the CAPS-1 (and SCID) is that the victim can meet criteria for the current PTSD or have symptoms below the threshold (Partial PTSD). Subclinical or past designations are interesting and await exact clinical meaning. No one knows fully what they mean, only that they are prevalent in this group of trauma victims (Kulka, Schlenger, Fairbank, Hough, Jordan, Marmar, & Weiss, 1988). Perhaps, as we change criteria or levels of criteria in the DSM, partial categories will provide increasing clinical information. Furthermore, what is beginning to appear is that combat veterans with other problems may require distinctive treatment

(continued on page 254)

TABLE 5.11
Assessment of PTSD

1. Structured Interview
   SCID-NP-V- (PTSD)
   CAPS-1
   PTSD- Interview (PTSD-1)
   ADIS-R

2. Psychometric Measures
   Mississippi Scale for Combat Related PTSD
   MMPI-PTSD (Keane)
   MMPI-PTSD (Schlenger)
   Stress Response Rating Scale
   Penn Inventory of PTSD
   Impact of Events Scale
   Glover Numbing Scale
   Glover Vulnerability Scale

3. Combat Exposure
   Combat Exposure Scale
   Modifiers and Perceived Stress Scale (MAPS)

4. Psychophysiological Measures
   Elegant-   psychophysiological monitors to
                   baseline, personal stressor scripts,
                   and difference between the two.
   Inelegant-   blood pressure, heart rate, etc.

5. Psychohistory and Objective Factors
   Pre-trauma
   Trauma description
   Social support after trauma
   Collateral reports

6. Personality
   Schema Checklist
   MCMI or MCMI-II
   NEO-PI
   16 PF

TABLE 5.12
Clinical Assessment of Current PTSD Symptoms

CURRENT RATING		SYMPTOMS
FREQ	INTS	Category B. The traumatic event is persistently reexperienced:
3.21	2.96	1. recurrent and intrusive recollections
3.49	2.66	2. distress when exposed to events
1.23	2.01	3. acting or feeling as if event recurring
2.76	2.94	4. current distressing dreams of event
		Category C. Resistent avoidance of stimuli: Numbing of responsiveness
3.12	2.53	1. efforts to avoid thoughts or feelings
2.81	2.44	2. efforts to avoid activities or situations
1.81	1.81	3. inability to recall trauma aspects
2.69	2.78	4. markedly diminished interest in activities
3.32	2.49	5. feelings of detachment or estrangement
2.63	2.54	6. restricted range of affect
2.35	2.19	7. sense of a foreshortened future
		Category D. Persistent symptoms of increased arousal
3.51	3.32	1. difficulty falling or staying asleep
2.72	2.95	2. irritability or outbursts of anger
3.15	2.70	3. difficulty concentrating
3.46	2.85	4. hypervigilance
2.47	2.47	5. exaggerated startle response
1.96	2.05	6. physiologic reactivity

(continued)

TABLE 5.12 (continued)

CURRENT RATING

FREQ	INTS	Associate features
2.48	2.55	guilt over acts
2.20	2.22	survivor guilt
1.24	1.44	homicidality
2.85	2.59	disillusionment with authority
2.66	2.42	feelings of hopelessness
2.80	2.65	memory impairment, forgetfulness
3.06	2.94	sadness and depression
2.04	2.30	feelings of being overwhelmed

Extrapolated from Blake, Nagy, Kaloupek, Klauminizer, Charney, & Keane, 1990.

programs: combat veterans with depression may have more of a genetic loading (for example), those with dissociation experiences may have experienced more intense or distinct types of stressors, and those with panic attacks may have clear and comorbid disorders. The CAPS-1 is one procedure that provides a measure of stress-related symptom clusters that can be evaluated against the "broader domain" of the person, personality and other symptom disorders. This has yet to be done, however, empirically.

Paper and Pencil Scales

Diagnostic accuracy has progressed considerably since the early 1980s when only a few checklists were available. Currently several psychometric scales have been used. These measures lag behind clinical progress in diagnosing PTSD. It is less complicated to define a problem than to develop reliable and valid measures (Litz et al., 1991). Psychometric measures possess all the problems of structured interviews, but with time and concurrent validation (and reliability), provide essential and incremental information. A major advantage is that certain psychometric scales provide information on response styles; many trauma victims possess distinctive styles, notably overreporting of symptoms. Green (1991) has shown correlation coefficients between a SCID-PTSD diagnosis and several paper and pencil scales to be at or above .5. Paper and pencil measures nicely complement the structured interviews. In the words of Gerardi, Keane, and Penk (1989), "some combination of preferred tests" (p.700) will be decided upon as a way of obtaining accuracy of diagnostic results (in the absence of a gold standard).

The most used scale is the MMPI. The *MMPI-PTSD scale* of Keane, Malloy, and Fairbank (1984) has 49 items and has been applied to a number of clinical combat-related samples. This measure also has been cross-validated on various treatment seeking samples. Also, it reflects all 17 DSM-III symptoms of PTSD, each appearing to make an independent contribution to the diagnosis (Watson, Kucala, Juba, Manifold, Anderson, & Anderson, 1991). In addition, this MMPI scale has been factored on various treatment seeking samples of Vietnam veterans and seems to reflect anxiety and depression, intrusive imagery or dissociation, demoralization, as well as fear of loss of control (Hyer, Woods, Harrison, Boudewyns, & O'Leary, 1989). Also Koretzky and Peck (1990) found the MMPI-PTSD scale to adequately identify trauma of a non-combat type.

The *MMPI-2* retains this PTSD scale. Three less items are on this PTSD scale (46) than the *MMPI*. Adjustments should be made for cut-off point (e.g., 30 on *MMPI* should be reduced by 2 points on *MMPI-2*) (Lyons & Keane, 1992). While both scales are helpful, the false positive rate is high for the MMPI (and probably MMPI-2), especially among psychiatric patients with a depression diagnosis (Forfar, 1992).

A new scale, *Penn Inventory for PTSD*, shows potential. This measure has a non-specific stressor frame of reference. Hammarberg (1992) demonstrated that it functioned well as a screening tool with high prevalence rates. This is a 26-item self report measure of the severity of PTSD, meeting initial criteria of reliability, validity, and utility (Hammarberg,

1992). This scale may be specially easy to 6dminister, as it is given in the format of the *Beck Depression Inventory.* As with all these measures, the presence of a traumatic stressor must be confirmed.

One other MMPI scale has been used to assess trauma. Schlenger, Kulka, Fairbank, Hough, Jordan, Marmar, and Weiss (1989) developed a longer scale (60 items) on a non-treatment seeking group of combat veterans. This was done on a national randomization sample. Little research has been done on this scale, but it correlates highly with the original MMPI and MMPI-2 PTSD scales.

The "best" psychometric measure to date, however, is the *Mississippi Scale for Combat Related PTSD* (Keane, Caddell, & Taylor, 1988). This is a 35-item, five-choice Likert scale that was normed and later cross-validated on combat treatment seeking samples. Factor analysis revealed six factors: intrusive memories and depression, interpersonal adjustment, lability of affect and memory, ruminative features, interpersonal problems, and sleep problems. This measure was developed from an earlier combat scale, is subject rated and has item weighting. A shorter form of this measure *(Miss-10)* is given in Table 5.13 (Hyer, Davis, Boudewyns, & Woods, 1991). This is highly correlated with the parent scale, has adequate reliability, has two factors (numbing/anger and guilt), and can be used quickly by clinicians. It can also be considered as a monitor of change in treatment. Also note that a *Mississippi Scale for Combat-Related PTSD-Spouse/Partner* is available. It was initially developed for use in the National Vietnam Veterans Readjustment Study (NVVRS). Initial results of its psychometric properties appear promising (Fairbank, Schlenger, Caddell, & Woods, in press). Finally, one scale, the *Stress Response Rating Scale* (Weiss, Horowitz, & Wilner, 1984), is a sign and symptom, clinical observer rating on three categories of trauma: avoidance, intrusion, and general stress. The presence of signs and symptoms are rated on a 4-point scale according to behaviors during the past week. This measure may be especially helpful in designing or updating treatment interventions.

(continued on page 259)

TABLE 5.13
Miss-10

Circle the number that best describes how you feel about each statement.

1. The people who know me best are afraid of me.

1	2	3	4	5
Never True	Rarely True	Sometimes True	Frequently True	Very Frequently True

2. When I think of some of the things that I did in the military, I wish I were dead.

1	2	3	4	5
Never True	Rarely True	Sometimes True	Frequently True	Very Frequently True

3. I wonder why I am still alive when others died in the military.

1	2	3	4	5
Never True	Rarely True	Sometimes True	Frequently True	Very Frequently True

4. I feel like I cannot go on.

1	2	3	4	5
Never True	Rarely True	Sometimes True	Frequently True	Very Frequently True

5. I do not laugh or cry at the same things other people do.

1	2	3	4	5
Never True	Rarely True	Sometimes True	Frequently True	Very Frequently True

(continued)

TABLE 5.13 (continued)

6. I still enjoy doing many things that I used to enjoy.*

1	2	3	4	5
Never True	Rarely True	Sometimes True	Frequently True	Very Frequently True

7. I have trouble concentrating on tasks.

1	2	3	4	5
Never True	Rarely True	Sometimes True	Frequently True	Very Frequently True

8. I enjoy the company of others.*

1	2	3	4	5
Never True	Rarely True	Sometimes True	Frequently True	Very Frequently True

9. I am frightened by my urges.

1	2	3	4	5
Never True	Rarely True	Sometimes True	Frequently True	Very Frequently True

10. I lose my cool and explode over minor everyday things.

1	2	3	4	5
Never True	Rarely True	Sometimes True	Frequently True	Very Frequently True

* reverse direction

From Hyer, Davis, Boudewyns, & Woods (1991), reproduced with permission from the *Journal of Clinical Psychology.*

A recommendation is that the intensity of the two central symptoms of PTSD, numbing and intrusion, be separately evaluated. *The Impact of Event Scale* (IES), is helpful. This is a 15-item measure developed by Horowitz, Wilner, and Alvarez (1979). This scale has excellent sensitivity (identify potential true cases) but poor specificity (rule out false ones). Two new scales also are worth noting. The first is the *Glover Numbing Scale* (Glover, 1990a), a 38-item, self-report measure that evaluates a broad array of numbing symptoms—feeling paralyzed, in a fog, like a robot, heavy, slowed down, empty, unclear thinking, etc. Similarly, the *Glover Vulnerability Scale,* (Glover, 1990b) is a 30-item measure accessing the intrusive feelings of threat, lack of trust, being uncomfortable, easily hurt, unsafe, not understood, watchful, and encroached upon. These measures yield continuous scores reflective of the intensity which is then subject to change and can be monitored.

An increasing number of scales measure combat stressors. The *Combat Exposure Scale* (Keane, Fairbank, Caddell, Zimering, Taylor, & Mora, 1990) can be used as a simple but good measure of stressor intensity. It has been validated in clinical settings and is an improvement over previous scales (e.g., Gallers, Foy, Donahoe, & Goldfarb, 1988; Litz, 1991). The *War Zone Stressor Scale* (WZS) of Kulka and Schlenger (Kulka et al., 1988) is a 98-item measure assessing exposure to combat, exposure to abusive violence, related conflicts, deprivation, loss of meaning and control, and prisoner of war status. This scale is to be commended for its development and breakdown of trauma. In addition, a more generic measure of various stressors and their impact on the person is the *Modifiers and Perceived Stress Scale (MAPS)* (Linn, 1986). This scale (Table 5.11) evaluates perceived stress, unexpectedness of the event, perceived responsibility, and degree of support. Increasingly, it is important to assess the perceptual features of the stressor and social support related to this concern.

Psychophysiological Measurement

Finally, the importance of measuring psychophysiological reactivity is now established. This is a key symptom of PTSD and one that is hard to mask. In studies of trauma victims the basic paradigm involves the presentation of trauma related stimuli as well as neutral or control stimuli. This paradigm is the "gold standard" of psychophysiological procedures. Several psychophysiological response channels (especially heart rate), along with self-reports of arousal and possibly behavioral responses, are taken in a laboratory environment. These are based on the central idea that combat veterans are hyperaroused even to non-trauma cues. The clinician, therefore, can choose to employ standard trauma material, the client's individualized trauma script, or simply measure basic physical indices. At this center we used individualized trauma scripts according to the methodology of Pitman, Orr, Forgue, Altman, deJong, and Herz (1990). This is a formal laboratory procedure that uses four psychophysiological channels and assesses reactions at baseline to trauma stimuli and again to baseline conditions. Blanchard, Kolb, Pallmeyer, and Gerardi (1982), for example, used a zero cutoff score difference of the single largest heart rate response of combat sounds to mental arithmetic and correctly classified 73% of subjects with PTSD and 88% of subjects without PTSD. Unfortunately, the methodology is not available in most clinics. A more detailed description of the psychophysiologic method is given by Boudewyns and Hyer (1990).

Several less elegant procedures may be used to access the psychophysiologic responses. Such a procedure calls for an evaluation of basic physical monitors. These include heart rate or blood pressure (systolic and diastolic) via cuffs or from records. Heart rate reactivity as well as subjective distress appear to be especially good indicators of PTSD (despite discordance between these two measures). Such a measure even used crudely may rule out false negatives.

Recommendation Measurement

It should be said here that the best time for assessment is shortly after the stressor event. At this time objective measures (noted in Table 5.11) are easier to obtain and more vertical. Raphael, Lundin, and Weisaeth (1989) have developed a *complete acute disaster package,* parts of which can be used for a given disaster. The package includes pre-disaster variables, multiple dimensions of the disaster, behavior during and perception of the disaster, post-disaster adjustment and morbidity, desired help, and a group of psychological variables, including coping, depression, anxiety, bereavement, and symptoms. The intent of this package is to utilize various parts for a given disorder. With delayed or chronic victims, however, retrospective reporting and state dependent factors become distorting influences.

No battery of tests is perfect. Assessment at its best is a task focused, interactive process that optimally engages the person. With PTSD a multimodal package performed over time in a relationship based on trust is ideal. With a solid bonding the more objective requirements of the trauma evaluation, pre and post issues, as well as collateral reports can proceed reliably (Table 5.11, Item 5).

This is the nomothetic side of measurement, and results should never be so highly regarded as to override person variables (idiographic). As previously intimated, information regarding treatment and the passage of time may prove helpful in diagnostic formulation of chronic PTSD. If the victim is an underreporter of symptoms, perhaps as a result of numbing, only time and treatment will allow for appropriate symptom expression. If the individual is an overreporter, perhaps in need of validation, again time and treatment will allow a titration of symptoms downward for the "correct" human change process to continue. Finally, if a victim possesses a personality disorder, these two components will provide room for its expression.

In addition many symptoms (and disorders) are comorbid with PTSD and deserve measurement. Their awareness is important because it allows for a more complete understanding of the disorder, as well as a sense of how these secondary features interact with primary ones. Remember again, the composition of symptoms for any one person is individually orchestrated. Among these, Peterson, Prout, and Schwartz (1991) included depression, anxiety (including death anxiety), impulse behavior, substance abuse, somatization, alterations in time sense, changes in ego functioning, and various other problems, including sexual difficulties, mistrust, and problems with interpersonal relations (Chapter 2). The area of psychosocial symptoms, then, can be both intense and broad. The clinician must decide on measures that represent core and ancillary symptoms, as well as ones that monitor both type and frequency.

Overreporting

A special concern for chronic trauma victims is overreporting. Many exaggerate their experiences and suffer high levels of psychophysiological reactivity in various life situations, reinforcing the victim status. In several previous studies, profiles of the MMPI were filled with classic "fake bad" signs (e.g., high F-K, obvious-subtle, high dissimulation scales) (Hyer, Fallon, Harrison, & Boudewyns, 1987; Hyer et al., 1989). Many chronic victims of trauma overstate their experiences, despite already high levels of psychological symptoms in various life situations. We have labeled this overreporting and considered it a response style. This places an additional burden on the therapist to respect the integrity of accurate information but also to insure symptom validation by not opposing a self-image of victimization. Hyer et al. (1987) wrote:

> Symptom overreporting among Vietnam veterans may be retained as a pathogenic response style, employed to convince others of more severe pathology. This may very well become intrinsic to the PTSD symptom complex. Severe and extended trauma tends to produce changes in self assessment and self-understanding of one's problems in changing the way symptom modulation is processed. Symptom overreporting, therefore, whether because of a need to validate psychopathology, to dissimulate, or as a way to express confusion becomes a modal feature of Vietnam veterans, especially in-country veterans. (p. 82)

Overreporting can mean many things to this population. It can be so convincing as to alter vertical claims. As in other disorders where "narrative truth" creatively melds with historical truth, the PTSD victim of combat-related trauma appears to have an insatiable need for external validation. Hopefully the clinician can view overrepporting as little more than a clinically curious feature and contextualize it within the person. In effect, it is argued that this style of response is so characteristic of combat veterans with PTSD that it may be a diagnostic feature of PTSD itself or at least a variety of this disorder. While concerns regarding compensation, malingering, and the like require careful consideration, the overreporting concept should given first consideration. Interestingly, overreporting is not distinguished by psychophysiological reactivity to combat cues; overreporters and non-overreporters do not differ on this measure (Litz, Kaloupek, Wolfe, Blake, Penk, Marx, & Corey, 1990). This condition then may be considered as "real." Chronic victims are intensely involved and convinced of their problems and demand validation.

Overreporting is pervasive also on the MCMI-II. On response style indices, most chronic PTSD victims indorse high levels of both disclosure and debasement, two scales reflective of complaining and self-denigration. In addition, the Traumatic Personality, passive aggressive and avoidant (8-2), is stress sensitive and correlates with a need to exaggerate or fake bad. It is an overreporting code. Elevated profiles of chronic victims are shown on most other psychometric measures (relative to other groups). In one interesting study, Leaf, Alington, Mass, DiGuiseppe and Ellis (1991) evaluated the MCMI and its relation to stress. As was true of our data, these authors found that some scales are associated with less distress (histrionic, narcissistic, antisocial, and compulsive) and some with more (e.g., passive-aggressive, avoidant, schizoid, and dependent) among the milder personality types. It is unclear what this portends but these authors speculate that some personality scales (the former group) may be associated with hardiness (attitudinal toughness) and some scales (the latter group) are weakening factors. Once again, person factors dictate the stressor experience—amount and type.

Recommendation

One recommendation on the use of scales with this group is to query the victim on the critical items of the various measures, both type and intensity. We have alluded to this above in discussion on personality scales. We know that victims possess negative schemas and dysfunctional personality styles, as well as symptoms. For effective treatment the victim must eventually put experiences into words. This includes person rules (schema and personality styles), which highlight distinctive patterns like avoidance, as well as some symptoms like hyperarousal or sleep disturbances. In addition, the phenomenon of "cognitive shift" may become clear in the labor intensive process of item checking. When the clinician evaluates modal items on personality measures like the MCMI, or symptom scales like the MMPI, the person becomes "alive." Why does this victim endorse this item? What is the unique decompensation pattern of this victim? How does the person know/experience this? Item checking is a method of accepting and validating the person and his/her unique way of encoding problems. Finally, this type of perusal permits the clinician en passant to determine if traumatic exposure may be associated with central nervous system damage and thus if a neuropsychological evaluation may be in order. Wolfe and Charney (1991) strongly documented the need to determine whether symptoms are brain-based or PTSD based. Item checking (thinking out loud about one's problems) assists in this determination.

The therapeutic task then is to identify this irrational style, to appreciate the need for self-validation, and to contextualize these findings properly within the clinical interview. Once again, the phenomenon of overreporting, as with all other symptoms, is driven by the person. The person of the victim demands to be heard and to exaggerate symptoms. While this may muddy the waters diagnostically, it need not be a burden therapeutically.

Trauma Symptoms

The evaluation of the trauma memory is an important clinical deliberation, because without some ability to address and treat the trauma memories, no specialized PTSD treatment is needed. We know that trauma symptoms are the core problems of PTSD, the direct residuals of the intense stressor. Unfortunately, these symptoms are anything but unidimensional or simple. For some victims the total memory can be accessed; for others, only parts. Individuals adapt differently. To the extent that memories are accessible consciously and the individual is able to tolerate the trauma memory, the trauma can be understood and processed. Where the individual possesses sufficient self and ego capacities (McCann & Pearlman, 1990), the clinician can facilitate access to the memory more directly, using several approach techniques highlighting exposure. If, on the other hand, traumatic memories are largely fragmented, partially or completely unconscious, or with a weak ability to tolerate access, then memories will be only representations of the trauma. Where an excessive level of intrusions or a reduced capacity/willingness to retrieve trauma is present, a supportive procedure is appropriate. Unfortunately, evidence now appears to suggest that the trauma memory is the most resistant component to treatment of PTSD (of chronic victims), and the incessant searching for meaning is associated with less adaptive functioning (Silver, Boon, & Stones, 1983). At the least, the clinician should have a sensitivity that this symptom is often "hot and raw," and should proceed with respect and care. These raw feelings are linked closely to core schemas, however.

Procedural Questions

At our center, chronic sufferers of PTSD are interviewed and requested to transcribe their most traumatic memory (Hyer, Woods, & Boudewyns, 1991). This memory is later taped and used as the central stimulus for therapy. Over time we have developed boundary conditions both for memory assessment and for treatment. Four "procedural questions" were found helpful in the understanding of intrusive experiences and the subsequent use of the memory in treatment (Table 5.14). While every victim possesses intrusive experiences, most place the frequency (during a given day) of these events in the middle percentage range (m=46%) *(Question 1).* This is a most helpful query as the range is considerable on this issue. Some victims are intruded upon virtually the entire day. Most victims also have some control over these events (m=85%): Can the victim stop the intrusion with his/her usual method? *(Question 2).* An understanding of the person's control processes answers only one concern, the person's success or lack there of in closing the gate to trauma.

The *third question* is a logical extension of the previous one. It involves a description of methods used to avoid the trauma experience in daily life or in treatment. Avoidance is as central to trauma as the experience itself. The issue is how the victim breaks up or avoids his/her pain. Many combat veterans utilize some form of distractibility, often substance abuse or acting out. At this center, we applied a coping scale (Ways of Coping-Revised) to 88 combat veterans with PTSD to assess their *current coping style* regarding combat trauma. Results showed an overuse of escape-avoidance ("wished it away"), confrontation (fights), and (ineffective) self-control (keeps feelings to self), and an underuse of positive reappraisal ("grew as a person"). Interestingly, the way one coped with memories also was related to personality style.

Apropos, the personality style takes on life with this *third question*. The fact that the trauma response is a highly individualized process becomes apparent. No set or correct stage model of stress and coping exists. In fact, a good deal is known about more effective coping methods in trauma situations: breaking down problems into manageable parts, setting small goals, rewarding self for small wins, actively helping others, being active and consistent in requesting help, balancing both intimate and social support, and applying distinctive coping strategies where appropriate (e.g., emotion focused versus problem focused), among others. Similarly a good deal is known about poor coping in trauma situations: excessive self or other blame, avoidance strategies of all kinds, substance abuse, cynicism and excessive pessimism, and prolonged social isolation, among others (Hobfoll, Spielberger, Breznitz, Figley, Folkman, Lepper-Green, Meichenbaum, Milgram, Sandler, Sarason, & van der Kolk, 1991). Various mixtures are possible and do exist of these and other methods, resulting in individual paths to healthy and non-healthy adaptation. The third question allows for a glimpse at the various coping strategies "where the rubber meets the road," where the trauma victim meets the trauma memory.

The *fourth and last question* is a most important one; will the victim allow access to the memory? Surprisingly, even though every veteran possessed intrusive experiences, a subset of patients were reluctant to permit treatment access to trauma memories (36%), and a subset believed they could adjust in life by addressing other PTSD issues first (42%). Reluctance is reflective of many concerns. Among these are lower trust, fears of exposure or psychosis, or becoming defenseless. Litz, Blake, Gerardi, & Keane (1990) noted that even seasoned behavior therapists choose to use directive exposure methods with this population only 42% of the time. An assessment, however, of trauma accessibility may prove especially helpful, as this issue alone demands trust, respect, and appropriate expectations of the caregiver.

These preceding four questions are "preliminary" considerations for the assessment and treatment of the trauma memory. Recall that in Chapter 2 was discussed the complexity of reexperiencing symptoms. Little is known about intrusions of all kinds (waking and non-waking) and their characteristics (reality based or not, amnestic or not, level of intensity, degree of frequency, etc.). These confusions should only increase efforts at clinical inquiry into the unique features of each victim. Many methods are available to increase accessibility of the trauma memory, limited only by the creative sense of the clinician. Clear too is that for many the trauma identified will not be either the most severe, the only one, or in many cases will only be partially represented. Fortunately, it appears that treatment to one intrusive symptom has some positive generalizing influence on others. This symptom area, however, requires therapeutic sensitivity.

Other Questions

In Table 5.14 we provided a brief outline of client indicators for successful trauma work. They are adapted from our work, as well as from works of McCann and Pearlman (1990) and Safran and Segal (1990). Basically these questions provide information on the use of planned abreactive work by assessing the intrapsychic, interpersonal, and environmental context (largely for safety). In effect, the person must be able to maintain functioning in the world. Answers to these concerns assist in the therapeutic decisions of whether and how to focus on trauma. After procedural questions are answered, the client is queried on: (1) ability to collaborate and provide feedback on the tasks required; (2) the verbal and imagery skills necessary to access memories; (3) willingness to remain open on the task; (4) the nature of memories (whole or fragments); (5) self-relationship (inner dialogue) conditions needed for this process (e.g., able to tolerate frustrations, not be self-condemning, etc.); and (6) the capacity for change in this process. Clients at risk for memory work have special problems with the regulation of affect and self-loathing. Clinicians should assess any problems that block this process, develop a plan to intercede (coping mechanisms anchored in safety), and conjointly decide on whether to pursue memory work. Otherwise an alternative treatment should be considered (McCann & Pearlman, 1990).

These questions are not techniques for the management of trauma memory. This is addressed in the next chapter. Table 5.14 should be considered a method for understanding the victim's capacity for memory work—how aware is he/she, how open, how far along the path to integration. The clinician is most interested not in the facts regarding the memory but the *ability to reprocess* this "fear of memory" in the present—"What are you feeling now?", "Where in your body?", "What are you afraid may happen?", "Can you stand back from this experience and relate it to the whole you?", and "What power do you have over it (or it over you)?". As can be seen, the potential to identify and handle "triggers" is implied. As can also be seen from these questions, an understanding of the person is important in the contextualization of the processing of the trauma memory. The ultimate goal here is treatment, to "move" the trauma story and to facilitate any change possible.

All too often clinicians become scared off, avoiding a full exploration of events and fearing that the client will be adversely affected. Equally troubling is that the client has felt or experienced "bad" reactions to trauma, such as excitement at the events, at times behaviorally contributing to these events, as well as sadistic fantasies of revenge. Clients need to know up front that these events have happened but now are over. In this sense they are normal or acceptable as past events, as something that others also do and something that requires work now for integration. Each has lived through the worst part, and this "worst" has no negative value to the therapist. This value judgment is central to the therapeutic experience (Eth, 1992).

A sometimes useful exercise to assist in this process is one that requests the client to become active early in the trauma memory process. The clinician requests the client to:

> Close your eyes, focus on your trauma memory. After seeing and feeling this, take a view from a distance and think about what would stop you from discussing this with me? What fears do you have? What strengths do you need? What strengths do you have? What can I do

TABLE 5.14
Trauma Memory Assessment

Procedural Questions

1. What percentage of your day is disrupted due to intrusion of trauma?
2. Do you have control over these intrusions?
3. How do you usually avoid your memories?
4. Will you allow access to the trauma memory?

Client Indicators for Trauma Work

1. Task
   Knows/accepts client role
   Collaborates; provides on-going feedback to experience (e.g., SUDS levels);
   Adequate imagery and verbal skills

2. Psychologically Minded
   Ability to and willingness to stay on task and struggle non-defensively

3. Trauma Memory
   Determine if memories are whole or fragmented
   Assess Self Skills:
   > Tolerates frustration/pain
   > Not self-condemning
   > Able to use calming self talk
   > Ability to place symptoms in perspective
   > Ability to cope outside of therapy
   > Able to be alone
   > Able to establish boundries between self and others

4. Success Monitors
   Reduces avoidance mechanisms
   Less anxiety/pain within/across sessions
   Committed to procedure
   Future oriented/hope

---

to help with this? How do you prevent you from exploring the memory?

Again, similar techniques are restricted only by the creative limits of the therapist. In effect, the therapy hour is a laboratory, a balancing of many positive and negative processes related to the trauma that changes over time.

Really no better example exists of how the assessment and treatment process are co-occurring events than in the understanding of the trauma memory. Assessing the client's inner dialogue, his/her ability to tolerate pain and affect, ego skills, and general level of information processing constitutes a "parallel processing" with the actual uncovering of traumatic memories. For some, a more confrontative technique, such as direct therapeutic exposure (DTE) (Chapter 11), will be appropriate; for others, support and dose-related techniques are most effective. With chronic sufferers, one must recognize that for now no technique will provide instant cure. Treatment is long term and the use of various techniques will be necessary. The important points are to assess the conditions of the client's trauma, obtain permission for accessibility, provide a framework for treatment, and reevaluate across time. In the area of the trauma memory, more than any other one, the therapist can be both a true "container" of client turmoil and pain, as well as a facilitator/director.

Two Troubling Symptoms

Two problems are especially troubling—panic attacks and dissociative experiences. These two symptoms reoccur with unremitting frequency in PTSD victims as well as in a Panic Disorder or Dissociative Disorder. If the former symptom meets the conditions for a true Panic Disorder, it should be labeled such. Biological evidence has suggested a connection between these two disorders (Davidson & Foa, 1991). Panic Disorders are comorbid with PTSD at high levels. Treatment should focus on the panic, usually utilizing exposure, relaxation, and cognitive training (Gelder, 1991). In PTSD victims, often these attacks are intrusive symptoms and can be seen as exogenous or cued attacks. They are representations of the uncued or unexpected panic attacks in a Panic Disorder. More typically, panic reactions are part and parcel of PTSD and require their own care regimens (education, coping, desensitization, and perhaps core cognitive identification). Borrowing treatments from the Panic Disorder literature may prove helpful also (Michelson & Marchione, 1991).

The latter symptom, dissociation, is also upsetting. Dissociative experiences appear to be common in PTSD groups. Two symptoms, psychogenic amnesia and flashbacks, are part of the criteria of PTSD. Even when strictly defined, the presence of flashbacks (in this case unconscious flashbacks) and psychogenic amnesia occur in PTSD groups about one third of the time (Roszell, McFall, & Malas, 1991). In fact, the symptoms of amnesia, depersonalization, and derealization, symptoms common in PTSD, combine with identity confusion and identity alteration to constitute the SCID-D (Dissociative Disorders) (Steinberg, Rounsaville, & Cicchetti, 1990). Flashbacks are specially troubling as these events retraumatize the victim. The extent to which these symptoms "really subserve" the anxiety syndrome PTSD, are comorbid with PTSD (as a Dissociative Disorder), or are reflective of a distinct trauma subtype is at present unknown.

Currently, investigation of dissociation is undergoing a renaissance within psychiatry. Braun (1988) noted that PTSD symptoms have a direct or indirect relation to dissociative experiences. Some studies (Blank, 1985; Bliss, 1986; Kolb, 1985) have more directly implicated their presence in PTSD. The relationship in fact has run the gamut from the dissociative experience being reflective of combat related trauma solely, to a loose overlap where "the essential forms of the disorder have not been shown to be similar" (Brett, Spitzer, & Williams, 1988, p. 1235). Spiegel (1988), however, articulated overall the role of dissociation in PTSD. Discussing PTSD, he wrote:

> Many of these symptoms are dissociative in nature. DSM-III points out that the essential feature of a dissociative disorder is 'a sudden temporary alteration in the normally integrative functions of consciousness, identity, or motor behavior' (p. 253). Such dramatic alterations in mental state can be understood as well suited to reflect a sudden temporary and often severe alteration in physical state.

Indeed, dissociative disorders are characterized by a marked loss of control over mental state, either via psychogenic amnesia, fugue, or, in the extreme multiple personality disorder. These dissociative symptoms can be conceptualized as a reflection of the profound loss of physical control experienced during the trauma. The sudden reliving of traumatic experiences, sensitivity to stimuli which are reminders of the traumatic event, and the intensification of symptoms by exposure to such stimuli are often accompanied by alterations in self-perception. Indeed, the psychic numbing described by Lifton (1967, 1973) and characterized by the Diagnostic Manual as a sense of isolation from others is consistent with this dissociated self-image. The self which experienced the trauma is detached from the everyday self but continues to exert a demoralizing influence upon it. Thus, dissociation can be understood as a fundamental mechanism through which individuals experience and suffer from trauma. (pp. 21-22)

Whether this experience is a partial one (short term disconnection from present reality) or a total one (an amnestic dissociative experience), the dissociative experience becomes at once a help in the immediate pain experience (to foster survivability) and a problem (resulting in subsequent fragmentation of self).

Indeed Spiegel and Cardena (1991) argued for a new diagnosis reflecting the overlap of this state or symptom and PTSD, *Brief Reactive Dissociative Disorder.* Specifying the contribution of dissociative processes to PTSD, these authors noted:

A coherent characterization of PTSD can be made by using three central hypnotic dimensions. The PTSD features of intense, unreflective reliving of trauma, psychological numbing, and hypervigilance roughly correspond to the hypnotic dimensions of absorption, dissociation, and increased suggestibility. (p. 371)

Regardless of the need for a separate designation, the question of the mechanics of the relationship of a dissociative experience to PTSD is unknown: Do traumatic experiences increase the tendency to dissociate? Is the dissociative experience (trance capacity or hypnotic susceptibility) a stable trait that makes one susceptible to trauma? Does the type of defense influence the nature of the dissociative experience or are these phenomena manifested in similar ways regardless of defense?

Despite interest in dissociative experiences and PTSD, only a few studies have been made. Waid and Urbanczyk (1989) used a dissociative scale developed by Berstein and Putnam (1985), and evaluated 25 high and 25 low dissociative PTSD combat veterans. Based on their results veterans who were high in dissociative experiences responded in a more pathological direction on a variety of measures, including level of PTSD intrusions, flashbacks, sleep problems, and nightmares. High dissociative veterans also were rated as more severe on hyperalertness, survivor guilt, and memory problems. Finally, veterans high in dissociative experiences scored significantly higher on many basic MMPI scale scores, as well as on the Beck Depression Inventory.

At our center two studies were carried out. First, 57 consecutively admitted, chronic, combat-related PTSD sufferers were grouped according to the same dissociative scale used by Waid and Urbanczyk, the *Dissociative Experience Scale* (DES). Three groups (High, Medium and Low) were compared on personality measures (MMPI basic scales and subscales, and MCMI), PTSD measures, and the psychophysiological index of heart rate under baseline and trauma conditions. Results showed that PTSD victims with higher dissociative levels have more "specific" problems—excessive fearfulness, sensation of strange experiences, and high psychophysiological reactivity, as well as higher levels of PTSD (on the Mississippi Scale) (Hyer, Albrecht, Boudewyns. Woods, & Brandsma, in press).

Having established that PTSD sufferers score high on the DES, this group again studied a chronic PTSD population and factor analyzed the *DES* (Albrecht, Hyer, Touze, & Boudewyns, 1991). In Table 5.15 is provided a three-factor solution. This PTSD sample scored highest on Memory Complaints, Absorption, and lowest on Dissociation. These three factors accounted for just under 70% of the variance and seem representative of "typical" dissociative problems with this population. Independent correlations on external variables provided concurrent validation for these factors.

TABLE 5.15
Factors of Dissociative Experience Scale (DES) (items)

Factor 1:   Memory Complaints

1. driving in car, no memory for part of the trip
2. attentional lapse during conversation
3. finding self in a place, with no memory of how having gotten there
6. strangers insisting they know them
14. vivid memory of past event, as if being relived
20. sit staring into space
24. cannot remember whether something was done or thought
25. finding evidence of having done things, but no memory of having done them

Factor 2:   Absorption

10. being accused of lying, but doesn't think so
15. not sure if something really happened or was dreamed
17. being absorbed intensely in TV or movie
18. being intensely involved in daydreams or fantasies

Factor 3:   Dissociation

4. dressed in clothes, no memory of having put them on
7. watching self as if another person
11. not recognizing self in mirror
12. things not seeming real
13. body feeling as if it does not belong to self
22. acting so differently in different situations, feels like two people
26. finding writings, notes, drawings, no memory of having done them
27. hearing voices inside, that tell what to do or comment on actions
28. looking at the world through a fog

Dissociative experiences are probably best conceptualized as reflecting a generalized hyperarousal of PTSD, involving both cognitive and affective states. It appears to be anxiety driven and not a Dissociative Disorder. Another belief is that the phenomenon of dissociation may *lead* to the symptoms of PTSD; i.e., flashbacks, nightmares, and the like are really dissociative experiences, and denial, avoidance and the like are attempts to avoid these (Kingsbury, 1992). A flashback, therefore, may very well be a result of this poor processing of trauma, as it potentiates avoidance/numbing for purposes of sanctuary. When these symptoms occur, the victim requires special treatment—at least, anchors or bridges between the "now" and "then," some ability to use a safe place, ability to read prodromal signs (triggers), and a supportive environment that "permits" this symptom. The goal is to be able to access trauma memories so they are under the control of the victim. This is only done as planned interventions in therapy.

Dissociative phenomena are then annoyingly and pervasively a part of the chronic PTSD experience. Who gets these, with what other symptoms, and what they portend for treatment, are questions where only speculative answers exist. What is troubling is that this "borderline symptom complex" is amorphous and softly influences the whole symptom picture. This symptom is a grim reminder that PTSD may be something else. At the least, other learnings are stored; state-dependent knowledge remains unintegrated and unprocessed and, as a result, influences conscious events. As if to rub salt into the wound, over 25% of chronic combat related PTSD victims also scored as schizophrenic on the *Diagnostic Interview Schedule.* Most of these victims had high DES scores. Perhaps the dissociative experiences have other components of a more bizarre quality. At any rate the breakdown of the DES allows for a way to attack this symptom complex.

CONCLUSION

The Sc+P+(B)+Sy model fosters integration. Hopefully this model provides some short-term focused thinking for some long-term benefits. First, this is an evaluation process that gives a blueprint for action. It is a new beginning regardless of past treatment. Second, the thrust is for a case formulation. Hypotheses evolve from the person of the trauma victim on the psychological ways that PTSD and its symptoms are processed. In this way the person-event model is employed. The character of the person influences and is influenced by trauma. Third, since the processing of information is disaggregated according to known person components, treatment can occur on the "ready" parts of the person, while others are "prepared" for their time. In the next chapter we turn to this issue.

Before we do, however, an underlying issue of this chapter, the relative importance of personality versus symptoms, bears highlighting: Does the clinician integrate trauma symptoms or dampen troubling symptoms? The decision may be very important. In previous chapters we have implied that there may be a subgroup of victims who are more resilient or who have high levels of self-complexity that prevent influence or mood shifts due to stress (Morgan & Janoff-Bulman, 1992). Cohen (1992) nicely identified two "recovery styles" of victims of combat related problems, *integration* and *sealing over.* Integretation is a style that involves a curiosity about one's reactions, and the ability to accommodate these into a continuous sense of self. In inquiry regarding pre-trauma development, the integrator is intellectually curious about self, tries to attach struggles to an internal locus of control and sense of self, and sees choice in trauma as part of an ongoing struggle across one's own life. Sealing over victims, on the hand, will have "none of this." A lack of curiosity about self (in growth), feelings that life dealt them a hard hand, a belief that they are passive victims of circumstances, and a penchant to blame others or externalize problems, are common fare. In short, they are uninterested in understanding what they did; they do not want to work out a cure or will be reactively angry or self-defeating.

This dichotomy is more than fascinating. Each necessitates a different philosophy of care and will require distinct forms of treatment. To no one's surprise, the integrator is the victim who shows more favorable recovery rates. This sense of continuity between the pre-trauma self, the self experiencing the trauma, and the post-trauma self seems critical. The turbulence seems to "result in" a stronger sense of self which in time adjusts to life. However, this can be an intense treatment process. Sealing over seems to be an inherently negative strategy. A style devoted to the encapsulation of information processing seems one dimensional and virtually certain to eventuate in a numbing/avoidant stance with little self-reflection. "Cure" clearly means very different things for each strategy.

Our goal is integration through the person of the victim. What has been presented in this chapter is a series of scales to assist in the thinking process for *trauma integration* despite the penchant to "seal over." The assessment of PTSD is in its infancy. Various "other" measures are imminent—psycho-social, somatic, neuropsychological, information processing, etc.—and will soon take their place in the evaluation of distinctive components of this disorder. When these measures enter into the formulation of PTSD, many will provide deeper and broader understanding of the person of the trauma victim. It is these that will contribute the most to an understanding of the care of the trauma victim.

REFERENCES

Albrecht, J., Hyer, L., Touze, J., & Boudewyns, P. (1991). Principal components analysis of the Dissociative Experience Scale (DES) in PTSD. Poster presented at the Ninety-ninth Annual Meeting of the American Psychological Association, San Francisco, CA.

Beck, A., & Emery, G. (1985). *Anxiety disorders and phobias: A cognitive perspective.* New York: Guilford Press.

Beck, A., & Freeman, A. (1990). *Cognitive therapy of personality disorders.* New York: Guilford Press.

Beck, A. T. (1976). *Depression: Clinical, experimental and theoretical aspects.* New York: Harper and Row.

Benyakar, M., Kutz, I., Dasberg, H., & Stern, M. (1989). The collapse of structure: A structural approach to trauma. *Journal of Traumatic Stress, 2,* (4), 431-450.

Berman, S., Price, S., Gusman, F. (1982). An inpatient program for Vietnam combat veterans in a Veterans Administration Hospital. *Hospital and Community Psychiatry, 33,* 919-927.

Berstein, E., & Putnam, F. (1985). Development, reliability, and validity of a dissociation scale. *The Journal of Nervous and Mental Diseases, 12,* 63-70.

Blake, D., Nagy, L., Kaloupek, D., Klauminzer, G., Charney, D., & Keane, T. (1990). A clinical rating scale for assessing current and lifetime PTSD: CAPS-1. *The Behavior Therapist.* September, 1987-1988.

Blanchard, E. B., Kolb, L. C. Pallmeyer, T. P., & Gerardi, R. J. (1982). A psychophysiological study of Post Traumatic Stress Disorder in Vietnam veterans. *Psychiatric Quarterly, 54,* 220-229.

Blank, A. (1985). The unconscious flashback to the war in Vietnam veterans: Clinical mystery, legal defense, and community problem. In S. M. Sonneberg, A. Blank, & J. A. Talborr (Eds.), *The Trauma of War: Stress and Recovery in Vietnam Veterans* (pp. 211-226). Washington, DC: American Psychiatric Press.

Bliss, E. L. (1986). *Multiple personality, allied disorders, and hysteria.* New York: Oxford University Press.

Boudewyns, P., & Hyer, L. (1990). Physiological response to treatment outcome in Vietnam veteran PTSD patients treated with direct therapeutic exposure. *Behavior Therapy, 21,* 63-87.

Braun, B. G. (1988). The BASK (behavior, affect, sensation, knowledge) mode of dissociation. *Dissociation, 1,* 4-23.

Brett, E. A., Spitzer, R. L., & Williams, J. B. W. (1988). DSM-III-R criteria for posttraumatic stress disorder. *American Journal of Psychiatry, 145*(10), 1232-1236.

Bugental, J. (1987). *The art of the psychotherapist.* New York: Norton Press.

Choca, J., Peterson, S., & Shanley, L. (1986). Factor analysis of the MCMI. *Journal of Consulting and Clinical Psychology, 44,* (5),760-763.

Choca, J., Shanley, L., & van Denburg, E. (1992). *Interpretative guide to the Millon Clinical Multiaxial Inventory.* Washington, D.C.: American Psychological Press.

Cohen, R. (1992). Psychodynamic theories of recovery from adult trauma: An empirical study. Paper presented at the 100th Annual Convention of the American Psychological Association. Washington, D.C.

Costa, P., & McCrae, R. (1989). *The NEO-PI/NFO-FFI manual supplement.* Odessa, FL: Psychological Assessment Resources.

Costa, P., & McCrae, R. (1992). Normal Personality Assessment in Clinical Practice: The NEO Personality Inventory. *Psychological Assessment,* 4(1), 5-13.

Davidson, J., & Foa, E. (1991). Diagnostic issues to posttraumatic stress disorder: Consideration for the DSM-IV. *Journal of Abnormal Psychology,* 100(3), 346-355.

DiNardo, P. A., Barlow, D. H., Cerny, J., Vermilyea, B. B., Vermilyea, J. A., Himadi, W., & Waddell, M. (1985). *Anxiety Disorders Interview Schedule-Revised* (ADIS-R). Albany NY: Phobia and Anxiety Disorder Clinic, State University of New York at Albany.

Dye, E., & Roth, S. (1991, Spring). Psychotherapy with Vietnam veterans and rape and incest survivors. *Psychotherapy, 28,* 103-120.

Ellis, A. (1962). *Reason and emotion in psychotherapy.* New York: Lyle Stuart.

Emery, P., & Emery, V. (1989). Psychoanalytic considerations on post-traumatic stress disorders. *Journal of Contemporary Psychotherapy, 19,* 19-53.

Emery, V., Emery, P., Shama, D., Quiana, N., & Jassani, A. (1991). Predisposing variables in PTSD patients. *Journal of Traumatic Stress,* 4(3), 325-344.

Epstein, S. (1991). The self-concept, the traumatic neurosis, and the structure of personality. In D. Ozer, J. M. Healy, Jr., & A. J. Stewart (Eds.), *Perspectives on personality* (Vol. 3). Greenwich, CT: JAI Press.

Eth, S. (1992). Ethical challenges in the treatment of traumatized refugees. *Journal of Traumatic Stress, 5,* 103-110.

Fairbank, J., Schlenger, W., Caddell, J., & Woods, G. (in press). Post-traumatic stress disorder. In P. Sutker & H. Adams (Eds.) *Comprehensive handbook of psychopathology,* (2nd ed.). New York, NY: Plenum Press.

Foa, E., & Kozak, M. (1986). Emotional processing of fear: Exposure to corrective information. *Psychological Bulletin,* 99(1), 20-35.

Forfar, C. (1992). Keane's MMPI-PTSD Scale: A false positive analysis. Unpublished Dissertation. Ann Arbor, Michigan.

Freeman, A., & Leaf, R. (1989). Cognitive therapy applied to personality disorders. In A. Freeman, K. Simon, L. Beutles, & H. Arkowitz (Eds.) *Comprehensive handbook of cognitive therapy*, (pp. 403-434). New York: Plenum Press.

Gallers, J., Foy, D. W., Donahoe, C. P., Jr., & Goldfarb, J. (1988). Posttraumatic stress disorder in Vietnam combat veterans: Effect of traumatic violence exposure and military adjustment. *Journal of Traumatic Stress, 1,* 181-192.

Gelder, M. (1991). Psychological treatment for Anxiety Disorder: Adjustment Disorders with Anxious Mood, Generalized Anxiety Disorders, Panic Disorders, Agoraphobia, and Avoidant Personality. In W. Coryell and G. Winokur (Eds.), *The clinical management of anxiety disorders* (pp. 10-27). New York: Oxford University Press.

Gerardi, R.J., Keane, T.M., & Penk, W. (1989). Utility: Sensitivity and specificity in developing diagnostic tests of combat-related post-traumatic stress disorder (PTSD). *Journal of Clinical Psychology, 45,* 691-703.

Glover, H. (1990a). *Glover Numbing Scale.* East Orange, NJ: Veterans Administration Hospital.

Glover, H. (1990b). *Glover Vulnerability Scale.* East Orange, NJ: Veterans Administration Hospital.

Goldberg, J., & Shaw, B. (1990). The measurement of cognition in psychopathology with clinical and research applications. In A. Freeman, K. Simon, L. Beutler, & H. Arkowitz (Eds.), *Comprehensive handbook of cognitive therapy* (pp. 37-60). New York: Plenum Press.

Goleman, D. (1985). *Vital lies, simple truths: The psychology of self deception.* New York: Simon & Schuster.

Green, B. (1991). Evaluating the effects of disasters. *Psychological Assessment: A Journal of Consulting and Clinical Psychology, 3,* 538-546.

Grove, W.M., & Tellegen, A. (1991). Problems in the classification of personality disorders. *Journal of Personality Disorders, 5,* 31-41.

Gunderson, J.G., Links, P.S., & Reich, J.H. (1991). Competing Models of Personality Disorders. *Journal of Personality Disorders, 5,* 60-68.

Hammarberg, M. (1992). Penn Inventory for Posttraumatic Stress Disorder: Psychometric Properties. *Psychological Assessment, 4*(1), 67-76.

Hartman, C., & Burgess, A. (1988). Information processing of trauma: Care application of a model. *Journal of Interpersonal Violence, 3,* 443-457.

Hendin, H. (1983). Psychotherapy for Vietnam veterans with PTSD. *American Journal of Psychotherapy, 37,* 86-99.

Hobfoll, S., Spielberger, C., Breznitz, S., Figley, C., Folkman, S., Lepper-Green, B., Meichenbaum, D., Milgram, A., Sandler, I., Sarason, I., & van der Kolk, B. (1991). War related stress: Addressing the stress of war and other traumatic events. *American Psychologist, 46,* 848-855.

Horowitz, M. (1986). Stress response syndromes: A review of posttraumatic and adjustment disorders. *Hospital and Community Psychiatry, 37,* 241-249.

Horowitz, M.J., Marmar, C., Krupnick, J., Wilner, N., Kaltreider, M., & Wallestein, R. (1984). *Personality styles and brief psychotherapy.* New York: Blair Book.

Horowitz, M.J., Wilner, N., & Alvarez, W. (1979). Impact of events scale: A measure of subjective stress. *Psychosomatic Medicine, 41,* 209-218.

Hyer, L., Albrecht, J., Boudewyns, P., Woods, G., & Brandsma, J. (in press). Dissociation in Vietnam veterans with chronic PTSD. *Journal of Traumatic Stress.*

Hyer, L., & Boudewyns, P. (1985). The 8-2 code among Vietnam veterans. *PTSD Newsletter, 4,* 2.

Hyer, L., Davis, H., Boudewyns, P., & Woods, M. (1991). A short form of the Mississippi scale for combat-related PTSD. *Journal of Clinical Psychology, 47*(4), 510-518.

Hyer, L., Davis, H., Woods, G., Albrecht, W., & Boudewyns, P. (in press). Relationship between the MCMI and MCMI-II and value of aggressive and self-defeating personalities in Posttraumatic Stress Disorder. *Psychological Reports.*

Hyer, L., Fallon, J. H., Jr., Harrison, W. R., & Boudewyns, P. A. (1987). MMPI overreporting by Vietnam veterans. *Journal of Clinical Psychology, 43,* 79-83.

Hyer, L., Woods, G., & Boudewyns, P. (1991). A three tier evaluation of Posttraumatic Stress Disorder. *Journal of Traumatic Stress, 4,* 165-194.

Hyer, L., Woods, M., Harrison, W. R., Boudewyns, P., & O'Leary, W. C. (1989). MMPI F-K among hospitalized Vietnam veterans. *Journal of Clinical Psychology, 45,* 250-254.

Janoff-Bulman, R. (1985). The aftermath of victimization: Rebuilding shattered assumptions. In C. R. Figley (Ed.), *Trauma and its wake: The study and treatment of post-traumatic stress disorder* (p. 15). New York: Brunner/ Mazel.

Jordan, H. W., Howe, J. G., & Lockhart, E. W. (1986). Posttraumatic stress disorder: A psychiatric defense. *Journal of the National Medical Association, 78(2),* 119-126.

Keane, T. M., Caddell, J. M., & Taylor, K. L. (1988). Mississippi scale for combat-related posttraumatic stress disorder: Three studies in reliability and validity. *Journal of Consulting and Clinical Psychology, 56,* 85-90.

Keane, T. M., Malloy, P. F., & Fairbank, J. A. (1984). Empirical development of an MMPI subscale for the assessment of combat-related posttraumatic stress disorder. *Journal of Consulting Clinical Psychology, 52,* 888-891.

Keane, T., Fairbank, J., Caddell, J., Zimering, R., Taylor, K., Mora, C. (1990). Clinical evaluation of a measure to assess combat exposure. *Psychological Assessment: Journal of Consulting and Clinical Psychology, 1, 53-55.*

Kingsbury, S. (1992). Strategic psychotherapy for trauma: Hypnosis and trauma in context. *Journal of Traumatic Stress, 5,* 85-96.

Kolb, L. C. (1985). The place of narcosynthesis in the treatment of chronic and delayed stress reactions of war. In S. M. Sonneberg, A. Blank, & J. A. Talbott (Eds.), *The Trauma of War: Stress and Recovery in Vietnam Veterans* (pp. 211-226). Washington, DC: American Psychiatric Press.

Koretzky, M. B., & Peck, A. H. (1990). Validation and crossvalidation of the PTSD subscale of the MMPI with civilian trauma victims. *Journal of Clinical Psychology, 46,* 296-300.

Kraus, A. (1991). Methodological problems with the classification of personality disorders: The significance of existential types. *Journal of Personality Disorders, 5,* 82-91.

Kulka, R. A., Schlenger, W. E., Fairbank, J. A., Hough, R. L., Jordan, B. K., Marmar, C. R., & Weiss, D. S. (1988). *Contractual report of findings from the National Vietnam Veterans Readjustment Study.* Research Triangle Institute, NC: Research Triangle Institute.

Kulka, R. A., Schlenger, W. E., Fairbank, J. A., Hough, R. L., Jordan, B. K., Marmar, C. R., & Weiss, D. S. (1991). Assessment of posttraumatic stress disorder in the community: Prospects and pitfalls from recent studies of Vietnam veterans. *Psychological Assessment: A Journal of Consulting and Clinical Psychology, 3*, 547-560.

Laufer, R. (1988). The serial self: War trauma identity, and adult development. In J. Wilson, Z. Harel, & B. Kahana (Eds.), *Human adaptation to extreme stress: From holocaust to Vietnam*, (pp. 3354). New York. Plenum Press.

Leaf, R.C., Alington, E. E., Mass, R., DiGuiseppe, R. & Ellis, A. (1991). Family environment characteristics and dependent personality disorder. *Journal of Personality Disorders, 5*, 264-280.

Lifton, R.J. (1982). The psychology of the survivor and the death imprint. *Psychiatric Annals, 12*, 1011-1020.

Linn, M.W. (1986). Modifiers and perceived stress scale. *Journal of Consulting and Clinical Psychology, 54*, 507-513.

Lipkin, J.O., Scurfield, R. M., & Blank, A. S. (1983). Posttraumatic stress disorder in Vietnam veterans: Assessment in forensic setting. *Behavioral Sciences and the Law, 1*, 51-67.

Litz, B. (1991). The parameters of emotional processing in combat-related PTSD. Veterans Administration Merit Review Grant. Boston, MA: Boston, VAMC.

Litz, B., Blake, D., Gerardi, R., & Keane, T. (1990, April). Decision making guidelines for the use of direct therapeutic exposure in the treatment of post-traumatic stress disorders. *The Behavior Therapist*, 91-94.

Litz, B., Kaloupek, D., Wolfe, J., Blake, D., Penk, W., Marx, B., & Corey, T. (1990). The validity of self report in the assessment of combat-related post-traumatic stress disorder. Paper presented at the meeting of the Association for the Advancement of Behavior Therapy. San Francisco.

Litz, G., Penk, W., Gerardi, R., & Keane, T. (1991). The assessment of posttraumatic stress disorder. In P. Saigh (Ed.), *Posttraumatic stress disorder: A behavioral approach to assessment and treatment*. New York: Pergamon Press.

Livesley, W., & Jackson, D. (1991). Construct validity and classification of personality disorders. In J. Oldham (Ed.), *Personality disorders. New perspectives on diagnostic validity* (pp. 1-22). Washington, DC: American Psychiatric Association Press.

Lyons, J. A., Gerardi, R. J., Wolfe, J., & Keane, T. M. (1988). Multidimensional assessment of combat-related PTSD: Phenomenological, psychometric, and psychophysiological considerations. *Journal of Traumatic Stress, 1,* 373-394.

Lyons, J. A., & Keane, T. M., (1992). Keane PTSD Scale: MMPI and MMPI-2 update. *Journal of Traumatic Stress, 5,* 111-118.

Mahoney, M. C. (1991). *Human change processes: The scientific foundations of psychotherapy.* Delran, NJ: Basic Books.

McCann, C., Sakheim, D., & Abrahamson, O. (1988). Trauma and victimization: A model of psychological adaptation. *Counseling Psychologist, 16,* 531-598.

McCann, L., & Pearlman, L. (1990). *Psychological trauma and the adult survivor: Theory, therapies, and transformation.* New York: Brunner/Mazel.

McCrae, R. & Costa, P. (1990). *Personality in adulthood.* New York: Guilford Press.

McDermott, W. (1986, March). The influence of Vietnam combat on subsequent psychopathology. Paper presented at the Conference on the Millon Clinical Inventory, Miami, Florida.

Michelson, L. K., & Marchione, K. (1991). Behavioral, cognitive, and pharmacological treatments of Panic Disorder with Agoraphobia: Critique and synthesis. *Journal of Consulting and Clinical Psychology, 59(1),* 100-114.

Millon, T. (1969). *Modern psychopathology.* Philadelphia: Saunders.

Millon, T. (1981). *Disorders of personality: DSM-III Axis II.* New York: Wiley.

Millon, T. (1983). *Millon clinical multiaxial inventory manual,* (3rd ed.,). Minneapolis: National Computer Systems.

Mischel, W. (1973). Toward a cognitive social learning reconceptualization of personality. *Psychological Review, 80,* 252-253.

Moretti, M., Feldman, L., & Shaw, B. (1990). Cognitive therapy: Current issues in theory and practice. In R. Wells & V. Giometti (Eds.), *The handbook of brief psychotherapy.* New York: Plenum Press.

Morgan, H.J., & Janoff-Bulman, R. (1990). Positive self-complexity and reactions to traumatic events. Paper presented at the 100th Annual Convention of the American Psychological Association. Washington, D.C.

Needleman, J. (1982). *The heart of philosophy*. New York: Collier.

Parrott, C., & Howes, J. (1991). The application of cognitive therapy to posttraumatic stress disorder. In T. Vallis, J. Howes, P. Miller (Eds.), *The challenge of cognitive therapy: Application to nontraditional population* (pp. 85-110). New York: Plenum Press.

Parson, E. R. (1988). The unconscious history of Vietnam in the group: An innovative multiphasic model for working through authority transference in guilt-driven veterans. *International Journal of Group Psychotherapy, 38*, 275-301.

Persons, J. (1989). *Cognitive therapy in practice: A care formulation approach*. New York: Norton.

Persons, J. (1991). Psychotherapy outcome studies do not accurately represent current models of psychotherapy: A proposed remedy. *American Psychologist, 46*(2), 99-106.

Peterson, K., Prout, M., & Schwartz, R. (1991). *Posttraumatic stress disorder: A clinician's guide*. New York: Plenum.

Pitman, R. K., Orr, S. P., Forgue, D. F., Altman, B., deJong, J. B., & Herz, L. R. (1990). Psychophysiologic responses to combat imagery of Vietnam veterans with posttraumatic stress disorders versus other anxiety disorders. *Journal of Abnormal Psychology, 99*, 49-54.

Raphael, B., Lundin, T., & Weisaeth, L. (1989). A research method for the study of psychological and psychiatric aspects of disaster. *Acta Psychiatrical Scandinavia*. (Supplement) *353*, 1-75.

Robert, J., Ryan, J., McEntyre, W., McFarland, R., Lipps, O., & Rosenburg, S. (1985). MCMI characteristics of DSM-III posttraumatic stress disorders in Vietnam veterans. *Journal of Personality Assessment, 49*, 226-230.

Rosenbaum, M. (1980). A schedule for assessing self-control behavior: Preliminary findings. *Behavior Therapy, 11*, 109-121.

Roszell, D. K., McFall, M. E., Malas, K. L. (1991). Frequency of symptoms and concurrent psychiatric disorder in Vietnam veterans with chronic PTSD. *Hospital and Community Psychiatry, 42*, 293-296.

Safran, J. D., Greenberg, L. S., & Rice, L. N. (1988). Integrating psychotherapy research and practice: Modelling the change process. *Psychotherapy, 25*, 1-17.

Safran, J., & Segal, Z. (1990). *Interpersonal processing in cognitive therapy.* New York: Basic Books.

Schlenger, W., Kulka, R., Fairbank, J., Hough R., Jordan, B., Marmar, C., & Weiss, D. (1989). *The prevalence of post-traumatic stress disorder in the Vietnam generation: Findings from the National Vietnam Veterans Readjustment Study.* Report from Research Triangle Institute, Research Triangle Park, NC.

Sherwood, R., Funari, D., & Piekorski, A. (1990). Adapted character styles of Vietnam veterans with posttraumatic stress disorder. *Journal of Traumatic Stress, 2*(2), 199-223.

Silver, R. L., Boon, C., & Stones, M. H. (1983). Search for meaning in misfortune: Making sense of incest. *Journal of Social Issues, 39(2),* 81-102.

Spiegel, D., & Cardena, E. (1991). Disintegrated experience: The dissociative disorders revisited. *Journal of Abnormal Psychology, 100*(3), 366-378.

Spiegel, D. (1988). Dissociation of hypnosis in posttraumatic stress disorders. *Journal of Traumatic Stress, 1,* 17-34.

Spitzer, R. L. (1983). Psychiatric diagnosis: Are clinicians still necessary? *Comprehensive Psychiatry, 24,* 399-411.

Spitzer, R. L. & Williams, J. B. (1985). Structured clinical interview for DSM-III-Revised, SCID. Version prepared for the National Vietnam Veterans Readjustment Study. New York: State Psychiatric Institute, Biometrics Research Department.

Spitzer, R. L., Williams, J. B., Gibbon, M., First, M., (1990). *User's guide for the structured clinical interview for DSM-III-R.* Washington, DC: American Psychiatric Press.

Steinberg, M., Rounsaville, B., Cicchetti, D. (1990). The structured clinical interview for DSM-III-R dissociative disorders: Preliminary report on a new diagnostic instrument. *American Journal of Psychiatry, 147,* 76-82.

Stern, D. N. (1985). *The interpersonal world of the infant.* New York: Basic Books.

Sullivan, H. S. (1953). *The interpersonal theory of psychiatry.* New York: W. W. Norton.

Wachtel, P. L. (1981). Transference, schema and assimilation: The relevance of Piaget to the psychoanalytic theory of transference. *The Annual of Psychoanalysis, 8,* 59-76. New York: International Universities Press.

Waid, L., & Urbanczyk, S. (1989, August). A comparison of high versus low dissociative Vietnam veterans with PTSD. Paper presented at the annual meeting of the American Psychological Association, New Orleans, LA.

Watson, C. G. (1990). Psychometric posttraumatic stress disorder measurement techniques: A review. *Psychological Assessment: A Journal of Consulting and Clinical Psychology, 2,* 1-10.

Watson, C. Kucala, T., Juba, M., Manifold, V., Anderson, P., & Anderson, D. (1991). A factor analysis of the DSM-III posttraumatic stress disorder criteria. *Journal of Clinical Psychology, 47* 205-214.

Weiss, D., Horowitz, M., & Wilner, N. (1984). The stress response rating scale: A clinician's measure for rating the response to serious life-events. *British Journal of Clinical Psychology, 23,* 202-215.

Weissman, A. (1978). Development and validation of the Dysfunctional Attitudes Scale. Paper presented at the annual meeting of the Associates of Behavior Therapy. Chicago.

Whitbourne, S. K. (1986). *The me I know: A study of adult identity.* New York: Springer-Verlag.

Widiger, T. (1991). Definition, diagnosis, and differentiation. *Journal of Personality Disorders, 5,* 42-51.

Widiger, T., Frances, A., Harris, M., Jacobsberg, L., Fyer, M., & Manning, D. (1991). In J. Oldham (Ed.), *Personality disorders: New perspectives on diagnostic validity* (pp. 163-194). Washington, DC: American Psychiatric Association Press.

Wilson, J. P. (1988). Understanding the Vietnam veteran. In F. Ochberg (Ed.), *Posttraumatic therapy and victims of violence.* New York: Brunner/ Mazel.

Wilson, J. P., & Zigelbaum, S. D. (1983). The Vietnam veteran on trial: The relation of posttraumatic stress disorder to criminal behavior. *Behavioral Sciences and the Law Journal, 1,* 25-50.

Winograd, T., & Flores, F. (1986). *Understanding computers and cognitions: A new foundation for design.* Reading, MA: Addison Wesley.

Wolfe, J., & Charney, D. (1991). Use of neuropsychological assessment in posttraumatic stress disorder. *Psychological Assessment: A Journal of Consulting and Clinical Psychology, 3,* 573-580.

Young, J. (1990). *Cognitive therapy for personality disorders: A schema focused approach.* Saratoga, FL: Professional Resource Exchange.

Chapter **6**

TREATMENT OF THE TRAUMA VICTIM

"One's real life is often the life that one does not lead." Oscar Wilde.

Chronic victimization is phasic, consisting both of positive and negative symptoms that are filtered through the person. Therefore, assuming that only one type of victim or one type of treatment is curative for all is unrealistic. The only common feature is that victims feel trapped in the trauma (Wilson, 1989). In previous chapters, we have discussed the nature of trauma and how its meaning is encoded through the person. We have presented a framework for the conceptualization of this process [Sc+P+(B)+Sy]. We have argued that the person of the trauma victim organizes the trauma response, even in decompensation patterns. The same trauma is apperceived distinctly by the person in information processed, in emotions experienced, in defenses used, in symptoms manifested, and in the course of the disorder. This occurs primarily through the core ordering processes.

Knowing about someone is not the same as knowing how to change him/her. This involves psychotherapy—the human change process. This is an inherently formless process in which a neat and tidy conceptualization occurs only in writing. Nevertheless, a direction is to be taken, the boundaries of which are worth our examination. One boundary demands that the *case formulation* of the client is a "living document" describing the core cognitive processes of the person. This conceptualization is revised in an on-going fashion in response to emergent information. It is kept at a fairly informal level. The case formulation is subject both to experimentation and a modification methodology (Turkat, 1991), a dynamic checks and balances process tapping into the individualized expressions of core ordering processes or schemas. Good client information, therefore, is heuristically oriented—an "action" construction of the cognitive, emotional, and behavioral features of the trauma victim. Although fluid, the victim is ontologically fixed in the psychic reality of the trauma memory. This perturbation did not cause the "changes" in the person. It altered core structures of the person.

A second boundary has become a refrain of this book: psychotherapy demands an *integrated treatment approach* based on the individual case formulation of the trauma victim. Residual problems, such as reexperiencing, avoidance, hyperarousal, and comorbid problems, are sufficiently distinct and entrenched, often refractory to any one form of treatment. The clinician's task is to individualize treatment. Safran and Segal (1990) likened the psychotherapy process to an expert chess player who possesses a memory stored with a wealth of information about moves in previous games and operates largely from a holistic conceptual position rather than from a digital or explicit one. This implies "therapeutic artistry" (Bugental, 1987), knowing the person and selecting the "ready" parts of the person in the struggling process of care. Even when individuals possess common distorted automatic thoughts or core cognitions, *that* particular person's schema and automatic thoughts are addressed and not those that apply to other trauma victims.

Third, life-changing psychotherapy pursues the *inward journey* of the trauma victim. It is a disciplined compassion, a professional titrating of science and care. Bugental (1987) described this as interiority. This simple assumption is that salient cognitions nest in the person and must be validated, witnessed, explored, metaphored, and evaluated for change to occur. This interior tropism is a result of a friendly therapeutic tension between top-down and bottom-up approaches. The therapist's task is to keep the client committed to the inward struggle. The content and process of therapy with a trauma victim is not for the squeamish.

Finally, the therapist is challenged with fostering an **optimal environment** for dialogue. This requires much of the therapist, most importantly a professional and caring self used as a governor in the yin and yang of various care deliberations. This stance disciplines the "task environment" in the work of therapy. The judicious pursuit of the client's schemas, relevant construals, and interpersonal action rules are energized by the safe working alliance. In effect, the client becomes both a participant and an observer, and the therapist, a witness to the remembering and re-experiencing in therapy. Treatment is first a **top-down** approach where the goal (above all else) is the exploration and challenge of the open and tacit rules and beliefs that guide the processing of cognitive and emotional information. The clinician is ever watchful of the "tyranny of the technique" (Mahoney, 1991). Further, since the effort is to intensify these experiences in emotionally immediate ways, a **bottom-up** approach is required (Safran & Greenberg, 1991). (See note p. 382.) The bottom-up position addresses the infastructure of the victim, often through the relationship in therapy. Thus, the clinician builds from both ends, top and bottom, toward a balance in which the epiphanic moment of change occurs. This position is consonant with cognitive behavioral tenets (Howes & Parrott, 1991). Once again, the clinician starts with the top-down cognitive construals and interpersonal patterns and mixes these techniques with bottom-up issues—ones core to the person. In this regard too, the depth of the relived trauma experience is limited only by the ability of the clinician to be "free" in the experience with the client. The trauma client can progress no further than the level of openness, concern, and care of the therapist.

Hopefully, the reader will experience a tension in this chapter. Once again, we seek a balance between art and science. This tension exists regarding the therapy dimensions of help giving versus help experiencing and between becoming specific and concrete versus general and abstract. On the one hand, a pull for the refinement of psychotherapeutic techniques exists, requiring a careful delineation of treatment approaches for trauma victims with specific schema and personality pattern profiles. On the other hand, the realization is that psychotherapy is truly a life changing procedure, complete with all that is messy and undefined in the human experience. The final tightrope to be walked in meeting the needs of both of these and manualizing the deliberations on the care of the trauma victim has yet to be strung. Strikingly, the history of the research on efficacy factors in psychotherapy started with the "right stuff" (what works in the interaction of client, therapist, and treatments) (Dewey, 1934), but has evolved into "just stuff" (correlations and main effect models devoid of practical and clinical information). Such is the price paid by the blanketed use of prescriptions given by "science."

We have divided a chapter into several sections again. This is a long chapter with many tables and suggestions to act as a springboard for the reader's own experiences: You may want to examine it in chunks. First, we start with the overall treatment rubrics of Adler, Millon, and CBT—partializing psychotherapy to meet our needs. Second, a discussion of the treatment suggestions most applicable to the chronic trauma victim based on research and experience is given. This is an extension on the use of psychotherapy begun in Chapter 2. Third, the importance of cognition is espoused. Cognitive primacy is seen as the compass from which the clinician can plot a course in the care process of trauma. Next, we address our tripartite model of psychotherapy, client understanding, the relationship and schema, and symptom therapy. The "guts" of our model of psychotherapy involve the right mixture of schema and symptom therapy. The desire is for these musings to provide a flexible care program for the treating clinician and to shift the attention of the client from despair to hope. We conclude with a brief discussion regarding "the other side of the coin"—care of the therapist. A short case is provided at the end, addressing both assessment (Chapter 5) and treatment (Chapter 6).

DIMENSIONS OF PSYCHOTHERAPY

Ideal treatment for the trauma victim comes in two forms: before the trauma (prevention) or at the time of the trauma (or directly afterward). The more the trauma victim expects or is trained for trauma, the better the chances are for resolution. Also, the sooner the client is provided assistance, information, coping training, and support after the trauma, the less likely is an unhealthy resolution. *What seems to exist is only a short window of opportunity after a crisis within which a therapeutic response can occur.* This is the most appropriate time for a crisis intervention model to be applied—active therapy, support, replay events, expose pain, relabel feelings, validate experiences, and identify personal schemas in a flexible collaborative relationships. After this window, the person "adapts," covers over, and returns to friendly defenses or styles. As chronicity takes over, the goal can more appropriately be described as one to arrest the decompensation process and to provide an alternative to a maladaptive accommodation. Better management may even become a compromise solution. The final goal, of course, in the treatment of the person of the trauma victim is to return that person to the level of functioning prior to the trauma.

The "Big" Picture

Once trauma has become a problem, choice points in the therapeutic process can be complex. The levels of psychotherapeutic analyses can be imposing. They can range from the breadth of goals, depth of experience, mediating tasks (stages of therapeutic involvement), and the in-treatment structure, to cite one formulation of therapy tasks (Beutler & Clarkin, 1990). Beutler (1991) noted that at least 175 categories of patient characteristics can be explored as potentially relevant for predicting differential responses to treatment. The therapeutic task is to simplify these components and to fit existing psychotherapy techniques of trauma to the client's unique needs. By the selection of questions and interventions the therapist directs the action, gently determining the direction of solutions. In this effort the Adlerian tenets hold; treatment is solution focused, individually based, upbeat, and firmly entrenched in the belief that change is always occurring (despite problems). Psychotherapy remains the mainstay in the treatment of PTSD.

An understanding of the polarities involved in this social and interpersonal effort is in order. A listing of the major ones is provided in Table 6.1. This list is not intended to match Sundland (1977) or Prochaska, Velicur, DiClemente, and Fava (1988) in which psychotherapy is reduced to ten or so basic dimensions. Rather, these dimensions represent important choice points for clinical decisions where the therapist takes a stand. Hundreds of instances will occur during therapy in which a "mini-confrontation" will arise regarding a fundamental disjunctiveness between the client's commitment to change and ontology of fear. For example, in the first four or five sessions the client must develop one component above all others for continuance and compliance, hope. Later in therapy, other components ascend in importance. But, wherever the position in psychotherapy, moments exist either for the potentiation of life changes or, if ignored, more of the same (Bugental, 1987). This is the point and time that a hidden collusion with the client can occur, as the therapist becomes part of the "trauma membrane," or worse, the "second wound." *Alternatively,* the journey inward continues. If the choice is the latter, the therapist commits to core issues of the person. Every step inward is a destructuring one—an unsettling rummage into difficult areas. In Table 6.1 "better" choices (interiority) are represented by those on the right.

Micro decisions are made during the therapeutic hour about who will carry the responsibility for the work of therapy. This client/therapist selection process has been described nicely by short term psychodynamic and cognitive therapists. Writers such as Sifneos (1972), Mann (1973), and Davanloo (1980), as well as Beck (1976) and co-workers, have articulated criteria for the inclusion and involvement of patients in this more active treatment process. These criteria address the "presence" of the client in psychotherapy: his/her motivation for treatment, the degree of psychological mindedness, the capacity to perform in a struggling therapeutic relationship and the ability to comply with intra- and extra-therapy tasks. Clients can also be evaluated and challenged according to their current stage of change—their present "developmental" readiness for psychotherapy (Prochaska, et al., 1988). Mahrer and Nadler (1986), for example, complied a list of good moments in therapy in which clients tend to show therapeutic progress. These include an exploration of feelings and emergence of previously warded off material, expression of insight, presentation of strong feelings toward the therapist, and development of new behaviors. What these authors have in common are criteria that endorse client commitment, arousal, compliance, and the ability to keep therapeutic focus. The dimension of client openness versus defensiveness appears to be central. When all is said and done (about psychotherapy), only cooperative and open clients make progress.

Our Three Friends

In our formulation of assessment, we borrowed heavily from the work of Adler, Millon, and CBT. We do the same here. Adler emphasized the importance of revealing the epistemology of the client's "wants," empowering ownership and providing understanding. For Adler, the goal of therapy was to alter the person's life-style by encouraging caring and

TABLE 6.1
Tensions in Psychotherapy

Supportive	. . .	Insight
Client presence	. . .	Client arousal
Objectivity	. . .	Subjectivity
Task oriented	. . .	Interiority
Therapist ordered	. . .	Client ordered
Help seeking	. . .	Collaborative
Closed-end	. . .	Open-end
Planned	. . .	Spontaneous
Directive	. . .	Evocative

social interest in the client. Adler attempted to keep issues simple. He established four goals of therapy (Table 6.2); validate, understand, expose and empower. While the relationship (I) was the crown jewel (of his therapy), the real trick involves consistency and perseverance—an ongoing cooperative assault of life-style exposure (II), "facilitative confrontation" (III), and encouragement (IV). These last three components force the therapist to be simultaneously interpretive (II) and challenging (III and IV); "exerting a constant but not excessive pressure" (Alexander & French, 1946, p. 37). The emphasis is on practicality, utility, efficiency, and humanism. Although structured, these ideals are intended to respect the process of psychotherapy, not define it.

An updated version of Adlerian psychotherapy is given by Walter and Peller (1992). Although not represented as Adlerian, these authors have developed a *solution-focused* therapy reflecting Adlerian ideals. Their thesis is upbeat; clients are in possession of solutions to problems, are changing all the time, and need only be reminded of their goals in a solution-focused manner. In this form of therapy no failure exists, issues are kept simple, the emphasis is on what works, and the focus of care is on providing what the client defines as a goal. Using the client's language, the therapist establishes well-defined goals (what does the client want), taking pains to avoid demands or complaints. Goals are framed in the positive (what would you be doing instead?), in the process form (doing), in the here and now (if you were on track, what would you be doing differently now?), and in the domain of the client's control and language.

Perhaps the critical element here is that therapy is guided by solutions. Walter and Peller (1992) have identified several avenues to discover solutions; all involve an unfolding discovery process based on a commitment to what the client wants. Exceptions to problems or goals (how is/isn't this happening now?), current "good" behaviors (how did you get that to happen?), possible behaviors (what will you be doing differently?), miracle solutions (if magic could occur, what would you be

(continued on page 299)

TABLE 6.2
Adlerian Treatment

I. Relationship

Non-specific factor

tentativeness—"could it be that. . ."

mutual respect—"trust yourself in the process"

Participant-observer factor

cooperation—"help me here with. .."

"How am I doing?"

decentering—"What do you think about what you (I) just said?"

"Would you like my reaction?"

contract—"Let's work on. . ."

responsibility—"What were you thinking when?. . ."

"How is this already happening?"

guessing—"Let me see if I got this correct"

Theoretical factor-goal alignment

"Is this what you want?"

"How is this fostering your goal?"

"What would you be doing differently if. . .?"

"How would you know what your goal is?"

"How would others know what your goal is?"

"I am very sorry you are suffering this way but can you tell me what you want?"

"This may seem silly but how is X a problem for you?"

"Only do what is agreeable to you; don't do what is disagreeable"

II. Life-style identification

Evaluation—use Life-style Analysis (Chapter 4) (holistic synthesis based on patterns, goals, private logic, and symptoms)

Therapy—constant identification of life-style (schema and personality style):

"From what you know about you, how would you interpret. . .?"

"Sounds as if you were again in need of control."

(continued)

TABLE 6.2 (continued)

III. Insight (based on #II, an understanding and challenge of the life-style)

Education—understanding of a working model of self

'Is this the kind of person you are/want to be?"

"Knowing what you know, what will you being doing instead. . .?"

"So if you are on track, what would you be doing/doing differently?"

"How specifically will you be doing this?"

"When are you already doing some of what you want?"

"What kind of person are you that keeps this going?"

"What will happen if you continue X?"

Challenge ("facilitative confrontation" and "don't fight . . .don't give in")

"Act 'as if'. . ."

"What prevents you from. . ."

"As you leave this session, how will you stay on target?"

"What would you be doing differently?"

"How is this happening now?"

"How can you continue to do it?"

"What are you saying to yourself now that helps with the new you?"

"If you are feeling different, what would you be doing different?'"

"What would I see you doing different?"

"Tell me when you did this differently. . .how did you do that?"

"When doesn't the problem happen?"

"What is different about these times?"

"How do others act differently to you when you act differently?"

"How do you explain your change?"

"How will you keep this going?"

"Do as homework"

(continued)

TABLE 6.2 (continued)

IV. Reorientation-bridge goals with new behaviors
    Encouragement, empowerment and social interest
        "Do unto others, as you. . ."
        "Act as if you are not depressed"
        "How convinced are you that this change will
            stick?"
        "How will you keep this going?"
        "How will you know you no longer need to come?"
        "What percentage of the time will you succeed?"
        "What is the probablity that you can continue
            this process?"
        "How will you continue to make decisions to
            keep this going?"

doing differently?), and the perspective of others (when acting differently, how would your wife/I know this?) are the main injunctions to this "solution-focus" care. Once the exception becomes the rule, the emphasis switches to bridging this into current goals (how will you keep this going?). The emphasis is solutions, using a spirit of cooperation and encouragement. This is Adlerian psychology at its best.

Millon also endorsed these goals but emphasized a broader and integrated approach. For Millon, understanding the unique mosaic of the person's traits, defining a distinctive therapeutic formulation, and effecting change by a harmonizing balance in the client's life were important goals. Having the client less extreme on personality dimensions was critical for Millon. The therapist also could predict problems and prescribe interactions for change. Millon's theory-driven paradigm for understanding the person and the person's decompensation patterns dictated core strategies.

The work of CBT extended these positions by making these ideas operational. The central view is that the problem of change in psychotherapy is one of changing inadequate and distorting cognitions. Basically, CBT emphasized the practical utility in the access and exposition of cognitive processes in an immediate way. CBT made both the patient and the therapist active in this witnessing process. It also emphasized the maintenance of a therapeutic focus by attending carefully to cognitions and therapeutic goals. Perhaps, above all else, CBT emphasized an attitude of adaptation—awareness of being on a continuum, sharpening discriminations, addressing the "how" of interpretation, and importantly identifying sequences between cognitions and virtually every other expression of the person. This was all done in a collaborative relationship using the therapeutic hour as a laboratory for exploring cognitive/affective processes and challenging interpersonal patterns. Finally, CBT provides for a total person experience. Howes and Parrott (1991) noted that CBT starts with content (automatic thoughts), moves to a tripartite conceptual framework (focus on errors of content, structure, and process), then to core beliefs, eventually a developmental analysis, and finally the "here and now" relationship.

An interesting aside is that many popular therapies are similar in design and goal to CBT. Gestalt or experiential psychotherapy as well as client centered therapies essentially operate from the phenomenological perspective and increasingly have acquired an information processing and schema view of change. A schema focus has become important to the change techniques of these therapies. Their common goal is to alter, usually through experiential approaches, the distorted schemas involved in pathological processes. The focus is the discovery of the unacknowledged experience with the creation of new meanings by various methods of internal challenge on the inner experience. Like CBT, these other therapies emphasize active collaboration and participation in the alterations of how the client treats his/her inner life. These therapies also emphasize the importance of the bottom-up approach. Only the role of the therapist changes.

No adequate way exists to describe psychotherapy. To say that a psychotherapy is successful with depressives and not with phobics belies the nature of the process. Isolating its processes is a convenient fiction, though a necessary one, for our descriptive needs. Whatever one's stance is regarding psychotherapy, the goal is to seduce the client into being accessible, expressive, and open. Once again, Bugental (1987) provided a poignant label to catch this process, "presence," or real contact of the outer and inner processes of the person. The pursuit is an inner orientation (through the application of CBT methods), which becomes the compass course of care.

Psychotherapy Potential

Unfortunately, the trauma victim's excessive emphasis on avoidance and pain reduction prevents any easy access to the inner pursuit. In Table 6.3 is a listing of therapeutic indicators for trauma victims. Safran and Segal (1990) have provided these evaluative criteria. They represent a litany of monitors of the client's ability to struggle with and discover his/her pathogenic beliefs. At a practical level clients will not be able to perform well on all criteria. Two overall issues are specified: schema (1-6) and other therapy (7-10) factors. The former concerns the ability and willingness to struggle in a CBT format; the latter, interpersonal or history factors. (In the previous chapter, Table 5.14, our focus was the assessment of the trauma memory for therapy.) At a dynamic or therapeutic level this is important information, not just regarding the cognitive/interpersonal markers of the psychotherapeutic struggle, but also to assist in the tempo and pacing of the psychotherapeutic processes. These represent the "psychotherapy quotient" of the client—skills from which the encouragement process of psychotherapy is built.

PTSD AND PSYCHOTHERAPY

No comfort can be taken regarding the effects of psychotherapy on PTSD problems. In Chapter 2, we briefly addressed this issue concluding that the clinician's guide to the care of trauma victims would not be soon forthcoming with any confidence. In fact, no single treatment exists for PTSD, the results of the research being disappointing. Much of the research in the treatment of PTSD (usually on Vietnam veterans) also has been disappointing because it is directed at symptoms. The use of behavioral and milieu inpatient programs

(continued on page 303)

TABLE 6.3
Assessment of Therapy Potential

I. SCHEMA FACTORS

1. Accessiblity to automatic thoughts (self talk): "I" mental pictures.
   > Describe/relive the situation.
   > Can you put yourself in that situation now?
   > Goal—access feelings/thoughts.

2. Awareness of emotion:
   > What were you feeling? How strong?
   > Can you get in touch with feeling now?
   > Goal—access emotions.

3. Awareness of responsibility for change and compatibility:
   > What do you know about this therapy?
   > What is my/your role?
   > What causes problems?
   > Goal—accept the idea of CBT; to examine the relationship between thinking and feeling and active collaboration.

4. Alliance potential (In session evidence):
   > How are you feeling about what is going on right now?
   > Goal—able to deal with current concerns/frustrations.

5. Security operations:
   > Evidence of in-therapy defenses, such as controlling interview, changing topic, confusion, preoccupation with topics, being too rational, etc.
   > Goal—tolerate anxiety sufficient for therapy.

6. Focality:
   > Evidence of being able to stay on a topic and "work" in therapy.
   > Goal—problem oriented focus.

(continued)

TABLE 6.3   (continued)

II.   OTHER THERAPY FACTORS

7.   Alliance Potential (Out-of-session evidence):
How are your relationships with spouse (parents, children, etc.)
Tell me about previous psychotherapy.
<u>Goal</u>—ability to relate to others.

8.   Chronicity vs acuteness:
Tell me about your history.
<u>Goal</u>—recent onset of problems is ideal.

9.   Patient optimism/pessimism about the process of therapy:
<u>Goal</u>—client feels she/he can benefit from therapy.

Extrapolated from Safran & Segal, 1990, and reprinted with permission.

(e.g., Scurfield, Kenderdine, & Pollard, 1990), along with symptom specific medication (Friedman, 1991), has proven only partially helpful (Hyer, Woods, & Boudewyns, 1991). While various treatment modalities including group,desensitization, flooding, cognitive restructuring, hypnotherapy, family or couple therapy, among others, have been proferred as helpful (Ochberg, 1991; Peterson, Prout, & Schwartz, 1991), these are only holograms for the "real work" of therapy. In psychotherapy research in general, controlled studies are few in number.

Problems of outcomes

This shabby state of affairs in psychotherapy research has many causes, most related to methodology problems that rub against reality in clinical settings. At the risk of simplification regarding treatment efficacy research, two major problems can be identified. First, different clinicians do not share the same assumptions regarding treatment change with trauma victims. For example, therapists who advocate group psychotherapy often have quite different psychological tasks and goals for their patients than those who advocate therapies directed more toward symptom remission. To date, the information on the differences in these assumptions has been small but these differences may be more important than the actual techniques used. In one review on a survey of practicing clinicians who work with survivors of sexual assault, Dye and Roth (1991) showed little consensus on the use of therapeutic strategies with this population. These authors divided the cognitive and emotional activity of therapists during the process of treating stress into approach and avoidance strategies. Approach is psychological activity which is directed toward integration of the trauma, while avoidance is intended to reduce the dose of exposure. Both strategies have potential advantages and disadvantages and are to be intermingled in a considered and careful fashion. Treatments that differ in degrees of approach and avoidance affect the coping process and interpretation of trauma in different ways. Experiential psychotherapy versus stress reduction techniques, for example, lead to very different changes within trauma victims yet both may prove successful (or not). A "cure" then that proves to be equally effective in outcome measures may do so for different reasons.

Second, the many symptoms of PTSD are not equally reactive to any given treatment. Fairbank and Nicholson (1987) noted that a number of complimentary approaches are subsumed within a broadly conceived psychodynamic tradition, but that none of these is sufficient or persuasive enough to represent an appropriate model for the care of PTSD. The nature of the varied symptoms of PTSD make any simple formulation of treatment impossible. Reexperiencing symptoms may be treated with one type of treatment, perhaps exposure. Avoidance symptoms may need treatment with another type; coping skills and hyperarousal symptoms may need yet a third, perhaps stress management skills. In a similar way Horowitz (1986) has classified treatment techniques according to whether they are more appropriate for addressing intrusive thoughts or the denial patterns. During the state of intrusion, supportive interventions may be more useful to alleviate painful affects.

During the denial or numbing phase, however, uncovering or efforts to reduce controls may be more appropriate.

Other Treatment Models

Since treatment of PTSD is anything but clear or routine, five models of healing are sketched (Table 6.4). They represent care at various times after trauma and emphasize different aspects of the care equation. None of these applies to any particular person. Trauma victims differ in their baseline personal agendas, resources, and supports, and in the timing and nature of the trauma response. The first issue addresses acute care. Treatment rarely is available immediately or post-trauma. Acute treatment depends on immediacy, protection, information, exposition of the various aspects of the problem, and needed follow up. Wolfe (1991) also has discussed a model (Table 6.4, A) of immediate aftercare intended for health care professionals but applicable to all victims that included debriefing on critical incidents. This model has six basic stages ranging from introductory facts to teaching and wrap-up. An earlier edition of this model had been popularized by Mitchell (1988). This pardigm has been widely used in acute care situations with apparent success. Like the Wolfe model, this is a structured technique to be applied directly after a disaster. These models have appeal because they recognize the "best" in acute care, information (facts), support (part of a larger whole), and individualized coping features.

Directly related to this model of care, Brom and Kleber (1989) advocated an education model (6.4, B). The informed trauma victim, like the proverbial consumer, does better in therapy. Next, Ochberg (1988) reminded readers of the unique and deadly themes of trauma (6.4, C). Ochberg strongly endorsed the concept of post-traumatic therapy (PTT) which concentrates on recent events, coping skills and strengths of the victim, options, self-defeating patterns, and the whole notion of psychological health as a way to facilitate change.

The Horowitz group (Horowitz, 1986), however, has provided the care model that has become associated with the "guts" of treatment (6.4, D). As noted in Chapter 3, this group emphasized the key dynamic of PTSD, oscillation of intrusion

(continued on page 309)

TABLE 6.4
Treatment Variables of PTSD

A. ACUTE TREATMENT

1. Immediate recognition of the abnormal stressor and trauma situation.

2. Protection/Support to avoid being terrorized by conditions.

3. Expectation of recovery.

4. Psychoeductional material informing of effects of stressors (normalization).

5. Explication of the problem and return to problem area if possible (with support).

6. Follow-up care and monitoring.

B. NORMAL OR CHRONIC CARE
(extrapolated from Brom & Kleber, 1989)

1. Process characteristic of working through the experience of powerlessness and disruption.

2. Alternation between intrusion and denial.

3. Normal, functional character of the process.

4. Search for meaning as a motivation factor for the process.

5. Possibility of occurrence of PTSD as related syndrome.

6. Multiple determination of the content and intensity of the consequences and patterns of coping.

C. SPECIFIC THEMES
(extrapolated from Ochberg, 1988)

Bereavment	-loss
Victimization	-low self esteem, humiliation

TABLE 6.4 (continued)

Autonomic arousal	-internal/external trauma cues
Physical injury	-coping with handicap
Negative intimacy	-personal violation especially in relationship

D. HOROWITZ MODEL
(Horowitz, 1973)

1. Phases of Care

Priority I	-Evaluate stress: -protect victim -remove patient -terminate external event
Priority II	-Swings in numbing-intrusion: reduce swings of oscillation, provide emotional/ideational support,
Priority III	-Frozen in numbing or intrusion: dose the experience (divide into small bits)
Priority IV	-Tolerate episodes of intrusion: work through (emotional/cognitive)
Priority V	-Termination: work through ideas relative to event.

2. Therapeutic Strategies for Intrusion and Numbing

A. Intrusions: (1) Structure events and organize information; (2) reduce the number of external demands; (3) structure

(continued)

TABLE 6.4 (continued)

periods of rest and recuperation; (4) provide a model for identification and permit temporary dependency and idealization; (5) facilitate cognitive reappraisal and interpret in educative ways; (6) facilitate the differentiation between past and present self-schemata; (7) reduce exposure to stimuli or situations that trigger associations with the trauma; (8) teach "dosing" technique to deal with trauma memories; (9) provide support; (10) evoke positive emotions that are different from negative affect associated with the trauma; (11) employ desensitization and stress-reducing measures; and (12) use anxiolytic or other drugs when necessary to attenuate severe symtoms that interfere with psychotherapy.

B. Numbing/Avoidance: (1) Reduce excessive controls by interpreting defenses and behaviors that are maladaptive; (2) encourage abreaction and catharis; (3) facilitate a detailed description of the stressors through association, speech, visual images, role-playing, artwork, or reenactment; (4) reconstruct what happened in the trauma; (5) explore emotional dimensions of relationships to others during the event; and (6) encourage emotional relationships with others to counteract psychic numbing and isolation.

E. SOCIAL CONTEXT AND HEALING
(extrapolated from Figley, 1988)
(Phases developed in family/social context)

Phase 1: Build commitment to therapeutic objectives
Phase 2: Frame the problem (overcome "victim blame")
Phase 3: Reframe the problem on behalf of loving/struggling process
Phase 4: Develop a healing theory for growth
Phase 5: Closure and preparedness (review and relapse prevention).

and numbing, as excessive rather than unnatural. The goal is the gradual reduction in the intensity and frequency of this cycle. Until the traumatic life event can be successfully integrated into existing self structure, the psychological elements of the event will remain in memory as determinants of intrusive images or other stress symptoms. In this case the key is to reduce this oscillation process, to modify the need for controls gradually, and to reappraise the event and meanings associated with it. Table 6.4 provides a list of Horowitz's treatment principles for both phases. During the intrusion phase, the reduction of symptoms is paramount (working against the reconstruction of the trauma). During avoidance, the facilitation of the working through of the trauma is advocated. As noted earlier, this trauma process occurs through the character structure of the victim.

Last, Figley (1988) specified the social context of care and a central requirement for healing, the meaning making effort of the participants (a healing theory) (6.4, E). The trauma context meets the recovery context. After commitment and boundaries are established and conflict areas isolated, healing is addressed. Each victim must struggle with self and decide on a meaningful "why me" solution. The absence of this leads to incessant repetition of trauma saturated memories. Also, the importance of these healing phases is not their phase specific value, but the actual process of leading to a developed healing theory. Most unlearning occurs in the social setting of the family. Family goals include a consensus about what has occurred, optimism regarding the future, ongoing validation of all family members, and empowerment of the parties. This problem of secondary traumatization (Rosenheck & Nathan, 1985) is woefully underreported. Children of trauma victims have both immediate family and transgenerational effects (Davidson, Smith & Kudler, 1989). Verbosky and Ryan (1988), for example, found increased levels of stress among wives of PTSD combat veterans. Several other studies have found problems with intimacy, self-disclosure, physical aggression, and expressiveness (Fairbank, Schlenger, Caddell, & Woods, in press). Clearly a comprehensive treatment plan is in order, to include intervention with the victim, the victim's marriage, and the victim's family.

These treatment models were chosen carefully. All emphasize the vertical reality of trauma and paths to normalization. Prevention/education, the psychodynamic process of PTSD, the search for meaning, and the recovery context are highlighted. They verify that a general pattern of PTSD is both human and normal and that the therapeutic process is a collaborative struggle with the goal of personal empowerment. In fact, Wilson (1989) even maintained that "good" post-traumatic therapy assumes that the patient's current emotional problems are caused by the event, not preexisting psychopathology—a focus on the latter being counterproductive. This strategy is necessary for initial bonding and often for periodic validation during the course of therapy as primary and secondary trauma issues intermix and unfold. But also an individual factor exists. This position implies that every individual has a unique pathway to recovery in the traumatic stress process. The mechanisms of care include an analysis of the trauma event, teaching of techniques which permit emotions to be tolerated without avoidance, the discovery of acceptable meanings, and the realization that this is a process that is comprehensible and manageable. The position of Horowitz is most important in these regards. The person of the victim is respected.

Element 1: Exposure

We are at the threshold of our treatment model. Before explication, however, we address the three central curative elements of the change process of the trauma victim (considered in Chapter 2). They include exposure, search for meaning, and coping/social support. The reexperiencing of the trauma is a highly individual process that is involuntary and often intense. Some element of reexposure occurs in every type of psychotherapy with trauma victims. Unfortunately, most reexperiencing of trauma "breaks off" when it becomes excessive. In Chapter 2, we noted that due to the persistence of the person's avoidance response repertoire, the trauma is not "absorbed." The person tends to react in terms of who he/she is. In fact, a number of factors operate against change—victim's self-perception of weakness, the emotional struggle to lock out the pain, feelings of embarrassment, expectation that others will not understand—as well as a slew of vulnerable/helpless feelings specific to the person. Strangely, the effort of the person to reexperience and assimilate the trauma material constructively backfires and turns on itself. Catherall (1991) eloquently described this. He noted that the ego, which is a protector of the person, ends up in conflict with itself. The forces oriented toward integration try reexperiencing the trauma, while the forces oriented toward defending against disintegration try to suppress the same material. The result is conflict, an incomplete reexperiencing of the trauma. Exposure to trauma must be integrated into the care of trauma victims.

Element 2: Cognitive Meaning

The second element involves the person's search for meaning. The subjective experience of trauma involves both a neurophysiological response (biological and state dependent learning) and psychological response (shattered basic beliefs and existential crises). If the former demands exposure, the latter requires a meaning reformulation. Consensus arises in the therapeutic community that the trauma memory must be addressed (Lyons, 1991). A change in meaning results in a change in experience. Simply put, goals are formed by the victim's meaning— the belief one has regarding trauma determines the actions taken. Meichenbaum (1991) believed that poor trauma recovery was a result of negative self attributions, self beliefs that foster a "stuck' narration. Schrader and Steele (1992) noted that existential crises (I am going to die; I am alone; I can't take charge of me; I am not me; I want to die; I was let down) necessarily result and must be addressed. Janoff-Bulman (1989) believed that the essence of treatment involved the reconstruction of a new, acceptable assumptive meaning. Foa and Kozak (1986) described this state, noting that two components are essential for change— exposure of the trauma and the placement of a new learning. If not, an incessant, negative recounting of the same stuck story reoccurs. Any psychotherapy must at some level unearth the individual's core cognitions regarding the meaning of the trauma event or they will develop lacunae, other equally penetrating noxious core beliefs that influence behavior. We have argued that treatment must address the schemas of the person that are disrupted due to trauma and attempt to alter their distorting influences (McCann & Pearlman, 1990a).

The time of the trauma also is important. If trauma occurs in infancy, basic assumptions or schemas may never have developed and the young victim may never change. In combat-related PTSD this circumstance did not occur. In adolescence, (mostly) males were forced to address several identities or issues for which they were not prepared. Of the many conflict areas, one appears most frequently: the struggle to relinquish power and accept vulnerability. This schema (in this case the male trauma victim) becomes imbalanced and rigid, and it sets in motion defective personality styles, inadequate automatic beliefs, and eventually strong trauma symptoms (PTSD). In therapy, therefore, cognitive schemas can be thought of as windows into understanding the entire hierarchical symbolic process within the person. Rice (1984) described this as a reconstruction process of subjective construals, where a "systematic, evocative unfolding" occurs between aspects of the stimulus situation and the cognitive schema of the ongoing experience. This is the work of therapy.

Recall that PTSD is an Anxiety Disorder—an amorphous cognitive/affective structure composed of various levels and combinations of activation or arousal, perceptions of poor control over future events, and a shift in attention to self-evaluated concerns. PTSD grows out of an anxiety base, a person replete with psychological vulnerabilities and bruised meaning propositions that are easily triggered by the environment. As is the case in other Anxiety Disorders, collaborative work between client and therapist unfolds around four issues: belief in the understanding of anxiety, vulnerability to danger symbols, location (internal or external) of danger cues, and present versus future anxiety (anticipated anxiety) (Bowers, 1991). However, the anxiety of PTSD is an insult to both "gut" and "head." An exclusive focus on the universal psychophysiological processing of trauma alone may fail to modify maladaptive patterns that perpetuate problems. An exclusive focus on the cognitions involved may fail to attend appropriately to the arousal and anxiety patterns. In fact, trauma work involves a careful balance of the cognitive structures or propositions of the person and the arousal structures of the traumatic experiences.

Having noted this, our position espouses a cognitive primacy. Recall that behavior is governed by tacit schemas and the automatic ways of thinking that go off track leading the client to maladaptive patterns. These underlying faulty constructs must be unpacked if treatment is to succeed. Trauma takes its form from schema. So, while cognitive schema work must be balanced with exposure work (as both will occur naturally in therapy anyway), trauma is driven and organized by the schema. Therefore, judicious clinical pursuit of this unaware knowing is what is most central in the care calculus with the trauma victim.

As noted, Foa and Kozak (1986) believed that to cure trauma you must bring up the memory, obtain arousal, and put something new in the memory's place. The unique formulation of the trauma victim's numbing and avoidant response makes this very difficult. This symptom also disrupts meaning making. In effect, the victim can only access the trauma memory "so much." Also, if failure occurs at resolution, the denial/intrusion cycle develops and eventually becomes fixed. Lifton (1967) believed that ultimately the problem is psychic numbing because this mechanism prevents living. An out-of-bounds control develops and any thought of future (symbolic immortality) is crushed. Horowitz (1976) labeled this "frozen overcontrol," and Tichner (1985) saw it as post-traumatic decline, which is devastating, long lasting, and often irreversible. In sum, the individual senses a Kafkaesque dilemma. He/she must deaden the self to keep destructive impulses in check. A state of pervasive personality constriction, of overcontrol (of rage), and of inevitable decline, result. Meaning making turns "bad" or ceases. Emphasizing aggression in the process, Tichner (1985) wrote:

> In short, after serious trauma, the human becomes a reflection of the violence wrought upon him and remains so until there are dynamic changes in adaptive resources modifying and moderating the violent impulses via interactions with others. (p. 15)

Whether it is the first or second task of psychotherapy, meaning altering must occur: "Bad" meaning must give way to "good." Increasingly, the psychotherapies of trauma are articulating processes for this to occur. In fact, a loose continuum of these therapies can be made according to depth of processing—"deep," existential beliefs (altered assumptive worlds), constructionist schemas, reconstruction of trauma, story repair, cognitive restructuring, and surface cognitions. Each adds its own language to metamorphosis of current trauma; Each applies.

Element 3: Coping and Support

The last therapeutic component of treatment of the trauma victim entails coping and social support. Virtually axiomatic is that if the trauma is intense and if the social support and coping mechanisms are inadequate following the trauma, the risk of pathological adjustment is high. What has emerged in recent years is that the client's *perception* of the danger is critical, but so is his/her *perception* of the adequacy of social supports. Acute disorders may differ from chronic ones, largely due to the combination of vulnerability factors (pre-trauma variables) and ability to solicit coping or support after the stressor experience. Research data show that subjects with PTSD possess more avoidant mechanisms than similarly matched patients (Penk, Peck, Robinowitz, Bell, and Little, 1988). Coping and the collaboration in social support (in all its dimensions) must be an active, engaging, and broad-based endeavor. Evidence from recent Israeli engagements suggest this (Solomon, 1990). Solomon, Bleich, Shoham, Nardi, and Kotler (1992) designed a total treatment package that deemphasized chronicity. This model (labeled "Koach Project") attempted to attack the (negative) social reward system and generalization of negative or avoidant stimuli among Israeli combat victims. No focus was given to "sick" role beliefs or patterns, not even "why me?" concerns. Rather, the focus was on the present and the future; "massive pressure" being provided for the defeat of avoidance and for a supportive environment. The quality and quantity of coping and social support after the trauma are a priority in care.

TREATMENT MODEL

Somewhere in the processing of trauma the victim begins to experience annoying stress of the event, gets stuck, and "determines" what aspects of the experience will remain. This starts the pattern of malabsorption. The categorical structures (schemas) of the person fail to integrate the pain, becoming free radicals in the memory system. In effect, the trauma saga "continues" even in the absence of cues. How another human being who is designated as helper identifies person issues, joins the problem maker, and rectifies the problems, requires a reflective practitioner.

In Table 6.5 is presented our care model which has three parts: client self-understanding and role expectancies, the relationship, and the work of therapy (schema and symptom therapy). As we muddle through these components, the obvious applies. This abstractly principled process is highly individual, infinitely dynamic and interdependent, and always insufficiently described. This is the privilege of psychotherapy.

Interestingly, the treatment of Anxiety Disorders is often described by reviewers as management (e.g., Winokur & Coryell, 1991). This term is not serendipitous. Anxiety, as with much of depression, is a deviant response in one of three domains: physiological, cognitive, or coping. Management involves a comprehensive attack in all three areas. Accordingly, the typical CBT combination of Socratic questioning, monitoring and recording thoughts, generating alternatives or adaptive responses, reframing or retributing thoughts, and the attack on cognitive errors also applies. Various emphases are given to exposure (Panic Disorder, Simple Phobia, Obsessive Compulsive Disorder, and PTSD), response prevention (Obsessive Compulsive Disorder), anxiety management (Generalized Anxiety Disorder and Social Phobia), skills training (Social Phobia), modeling (Simple Phobia), relaxation (Panic Disorder), and behavioral interventions (Agoraphobia), among others. Consistently, researchers have found that two components are operative in the care of Anxiety Disorders (Bowers, 1991; Gelder, 1991). First, a psychoeducative procedure consolidates the method currently in use, and second, some form of cognitive intervention exists. Our model incorporates these and "more."

I. Understanding Self and Role Clarity

Treatment starts with an individual formulation of the person. This map in turn suggests the directions for the management of care. The trauma victim is usually "hungry" for classification of his/her turmoil, for any normalization

TABLE 6.5
PTSD Model of Treatment

I. Client understanding of self and role
    Tasks:
    1. Map of self (construals and personality patterns)
    2. Role of client (needed tasks to work in therapy)

II. Relationship
    Tasks:
    1. Bonding with client
    2. Undoing—disengage from expected therapeutic role
    3. Oscillation (between levels of cognition and between experience and observation of therapy)

III. Work of therapy
    Tasks:
    1. Schema—unearth cognitions via CBT (top-down) and experiential methods (involve the person—bottom-up)
    2. Symptom—reduce perturbations or problems by involving the person (bottom-up schema and personality) or using techniques (top-down).

---

of the struggle and for any road map to relief. The case formulation then is shared with the client, feedback elicited, and the goals established. Due to the range of variables, this process has no point-by-point method. Nevertheless, order does exist. Table 6.6 presents the needed material for creating the atmosphere and for gathering information on the construction of the case formulation. The necessary ingredients involve a collaborative attitude on the interactive struggle for a "healing theory," a workable (and changeable) map of the person, a choice on the drama of change, and a commitment to the process. Turkat (1991) has outlined a similar method ("Behavioral Interview"). Regarding its complexity, he wrote:

TABLE 6.6
Ingredients for Case Formulation

I. Atmosphere Building
   -collaborative enterprise
   -data are dynamic and changeable
   -all answers exist in the client
   -goal is the development of a "healing theory"

II. Map Development
   -obtain data (life-style, psychohistory, testing, etc.)
   -elicit client theory of self and problems
   -challenge with "person" questions (Chapter 4)
   -explain "person" centered approach and how schema influences behavior
   -provide provisional case formulation (to be tested by person directed hypotheses)
   -address client readiness
   -use client as consultant

III. Decisional Balance
   -discuss positive and negative aspects of treatment
   -predict problems
   -outline treatment alternative
   -discuss case at two levels, schema/personality and symptoms
   -emphasize requirement of client "therapy focus" (here and now focus, concrete and specific, process questions, inferiority, etc.)
   -provide time for decision on treatment (1-2 weeks)

IV. Obtain Commitment
   -outline all obstacles
   -reward/empower the pursuit of the struggle (not comfort or cure)
   -develop self inquiry and treatment adherence expectation
   -build in treatment monitors ("quality assurance")

Extrapolated from Turkat, 1991.

Given the tremendous range of variables that could be generated from the diverse nature of psychopathology presented by personality disorder cases as well as the infinite possibilities involved in formulations of those behavior problems, it is impossible at present to articulate very specific step-by-step guidelines for engaging in clinical experimentation. The notion is in its infancy and at the present time its success in everyday clinical practice depends on the ingenuity and skill of the particular clinician involved. (pp. 28-29)

This procedure is important because it places emphasis on client engagement, responsibility, and reality based treatment expectancies. De Shazer (1985) developed a standard intervention in therapy, a "formula first session task." The client was instructed first to observe what is happening in life that he/she would like to continue. This solution focus reorients the client to expect a therapy process that involves a unique frame—therapy work and experience are interactionally constructed. This position establishes a no nonsense understanding of therapy. In addition, our stance (and Turkat's) endorses the life-style formulation, developmental issues, client sharing, as well as the on-going drama of the "diagnostic" procedure. This position endorses too the pursuit of *convergent validation* in the struggle of care; what is working in treatment (emerging from and anchored to the person). Last, it specifies ideal goals (and obstacles), thereby establishing a blueprint for optimal care. This plan then provides a jump start, eliminating several barriers between assessment and managed care.

If this is the form for "understanding of self," the content represents the specifics of information on schemas and personality styles [Sc+P+(B)+Sy]. At base, the process of psychotherapy "means" a working understanding of the participating roles in the defined domains of therapy. The *Schema Checklist* (Chapter 5) provides a good starting point. This list is a thinking-out-loud task requested of the client. It begins the journey inward. As this proceeds, two key elements of personality, core cognitions and modal interactive styles, become discrete monitors. A listing of both is given in Table 6.7. Core beliefs are based on enduring and embedded learnings

(continued on page 322)

TABLE 6.7
Core Beliefs of Personality

Personality	Belief	Interpersonal Strategy
Schizoid	I am complacent. I do well alone.	Detachment
Avoidant	I am inept/ undesriable and may be exposed. I cannot tolerate unpleasant feelings.	Sanctuary
Dependent	I am needy and weak. I feel abandonment.	Attachment
Histrionic	I am okay if stroked (attention is like drug). I need to feel intense (and am "vague" about life).	Marketing
Narcissism	I am better than others; rules don't apply. I feel no empathy and fear weakness.	Explosive
Antisocial	I am autonomous and unfettered by rules. If I don't act, they will.	Independent
Compulsive	I must avoid mistakes to be worthwhile. I am vulnerable and must have order in my life.	Performance

(continued)

TABLE 6.7 (continued)

Passive Aggressive	I am misunderstood and unappreciated by others. I am self sufficient but vulnerable.	Guarded
Self Defeating	I have failed to be good; therefore I must sacrifice. Others accept me only if I degrade myself.	Sacrifice
Sadistic	I am tough, reckless, thin skinned and like it. Pride comes from independence.	Intimidating
Schizotypal	Schizoid: Being alone, insensitive to others, and estranged is my way. Inwardly I am self absorbed; outwardly I am joyless. Avoidant: Being alone is the only way since I am excessively guarded. Inwardly, I break up my thoughts/feelings; outwardly I am watchful.	
Borderline	I do not know who I am but I feel wanting and hate it. I am afraid of abandonment, being alone, and being rejected.	

(continued)

TABLE 6.7 (continued)

<u>Dependent</u> Preoccupation with security and abandonment.

<u>Histronic</u> Preoccupation with worthiness and self destruction.

<u>Compulsive</u> Preoccupation with resentment and self condemnation.

<u>Pass Aggr</u> Preoccupation with impulse control and extreme remorse.

Paranoid

I am special, but people will try to manipulate you. Others have hidden motives; they must be watched.

<u>Narcissist</u> Preoccupation with omnipotence and special identity.

<u>Antisocial</u> Preoccupation with projection and power.

<u>Compulsive</u> Preoccupation with anger, control and resentment.

<u>Pass Aggr</u> Preoccupation with feeling misunderstood and active misinterpretation

that are often assumed and must be explored, repeatedly tagged, challenged, and hopefully altered. Based on the Millon model (1969) core beliefs of the milder personality disorders follow developmental patterns, as well as self and socially reinforced learnings. These are reasonably anchored to DSM-III-R, Axis II. For the more severe personality styles—schizotypal, borderline, and paranoid—the content and experience of the core beliefs "start" with the milder personality styles and proceed in more rigid and at times aberrant directions. The severe personality styles are given expression through the milder personalities. Often these beliefs and styles become the focal point for "transference tests." They are repeated and cause therapy to become "stuck." Their presence in therapy is assured: Their care must be considered.

Interpersonal strategies and modal styles of the personality are markers of core cognitions that also need to be addressed. These are the "person" representations that foster and maintain the personality styles. They are the scripts that imply deeper issues. These also must be noted, tagged, and altered.

Ideally, the person has a completed *Person Analysis Form* (Table 6.8). This involves information from the *Schema Checklist* (Chapter 5)—a personality measure (MCMI) which is divided into core cognitions and modal styles, beliefs (from the *Idea Inventory*), and symptoms (from interview or psychometric scale) (Chapter 5). This is *the feedback* on the central schemas, personality patterns, irrational beliefs, and symptoms [Sc+P+(B)+Sy]. Again, this is an in-hand template that is altered with time and understanding. In the fashion of CBT, sufferers are asked to "work on" this and add or subtract patterns that occur during the course of therapy. This form has been used in a CBT outline study with the elderly (Hyer, Swanson, Lefkowitz, Hillesland, Davis, & Woods, 1990). Its in-hand assistance, built-in quality for updating, and ease of use were noteworthy. Collaboration is made easier. Any emerging cognition, interpersonal style, or psychosocial or traumatic symptom can be framed into this format. This *is* psychotherapy— the pursuit of the emotional, interpersonal, cognitive, and behavioral referents of the schemas.

TABLE 6.8
Person Analysis Form

Schemas	Personality Styles	(Beliefs)	Symptoms
_____	_____	_____	_____
_____	_____	_____	_____
_____	_____	_____	_____

Also in this effort, a helpful procedure is to have clients "know" the difference between schema and symptom therapy. This entire process should be explicated and outlined. With a clear understanding of the focus of treatment and under the umbrella of a collaborative and supportive relationship, schema restructuring, modification, or reframing ensues.

Commitment to the therapy process is more than compliance. Compliance involves adherence to treatment, specifying acts, behaviors, and reports. Commitment is the will to "experience" the treatment process. The person of the victim is "engaged." This is interiority—the inward journey. Following a similar model, Miller and Rollnick (1991) identified an exciting method of psychotherapy, labeled motivational interviewing. This method assists the client to free self from being stuck (ambivalence). It is more than a set of techniques, however; it is a way of being with the client. In an Adlerian sense the therapist "joins" with the client (expressing empathy, avoiding arguments, rolling with resistance, and supporting self-efficacy). The emphasis is on "building motivation for change at the level and pace of the client."

From a more objective view (CBT), commitment means that the participating role of the client is self observation, the unpacking of the "understanding." The client becomes his/her own care agent (personal scientist). The rules of the game are applied simply but persistently. Therapist and client use the "downward arrow," through modal patterns and into core cognitions. Access to the salient tacit and obvious construals is the "stuff" of therapy. Perceptions are person markers of schemas and hypotheses for clinical unearthing. As both therapist and client acknowledge the existence and power of schemas, functions of dictating and organizing personality styles and surface beliefs become evident. The greater the ability of the therapist to engage in this process, the more the person becomes immersed in the change process and the more change "really" happens.

Personality Problems

Unfortunately, self defeating patterns are omnipresent in chronic trauma victims. Victims remain fixed in fruitless "why me" patterns, as well use as poor attributional processes. For example, in one study McCormick, Taber, and Kruedelbrach (1989) found that many victims of trauma process on-going experiences poorly, using attributional styles consistent with learned helplessness (internal, stable, and global). Their view of life is that it is not "fixable." These authors found further that learned helplessness was most characteristic of victims of a previous trauma. Apparently, learning failure once leads to non-mastery later. From another perspective, Luborsky, Crits-Christoph, and Mellon (1986) described these repeated patterns of a person (as a result of conflict) as "core conflicts." Each person has identified repeated wishes that, when frustrated, become negative and fixed responses. These tend to occur and recur in interactions with others. The frustrated wish/ fixed patterns have been labeled "core conflictural relationship themes" and become the center grist for the therapist's mill. Fortunately, only a relatively small number of these recur and are problems. Unfortunately, trauma tends to activate these themes making them rigid.

We know also that chronic trauma victims often have personality disorders. This raises the ante in therapy, demanding extra effort. Victims with rigid patterns are stuck in their ways, having chosen this style carefully to get others to accommodate to them, even in their unhappiness. Trauma victims universally show various degrees of lack of self-observation, poor motivation, lack of skills, secondary gains, fears of vulnerability, a view of hopelessness, fears that others will not accept change, and characterological rigidity.

Rothstein and Vallis (1991) have eloquently discussed this problem. They believed that treatment of personality disorders requires alteration—both a **procedural adaptation** including longer term sessions, and **process adaptation** including detailed exploration of self-protective resistance. With these in place, the authors argued for two phases of treatment (with character disorders). The initial phase includes a careful understanding of the meaning of the symptoms— their functional value (secondary gain) for the person. Interestingly, Rothstein and Vallis (1991) noted that this process can only be performed with a careful developmental history (life-style), as well as a hierarchical conceptualization of the person's schemata.

The second phase of treatment involves the actual interventions. Not surprisingly, this entails an exploration through CBT procedures using vertical-to-self questions, the relationship of affect to cognition, and decentering (taking distance). Interventions involve a weaving of the developmental issues, the use of the relationship, and standard CBT techniques. In this instance, the important point is that the therapist's main interest remains the core schema of the trauma victim (what does this central driving force do to continue problems?), but uses developmental information and the relationship for assistance. For example, the therapist attacks the histrionic's need to receive praise (a core issue), rather than a current concern with situational stress (and does this using the relationship).

Labor Intensive

Psychotherapy is a labor intensive process that demands much of the therapist and client. Recall that the essence of psychotherapy is to have the client collaborate in a non-defensive manner in the observation and evaluation of the current experience—in the access of the past as it is currently lived. Weiss, Sampson, and Mount Zion Psychotherapy Research Group (1987) have described the essence of the struggle noting that the patient's plan (the goal to eliminate problems) should take center stage. Problems arise in the difficult work involved in the identification and challenge of the multiple inner obstructions that the client uses to test the therapist and his/her own plan.

To an Adlerian this effort is one of goal alignment, the task of not straying from the client's goals. As the initial desires of the client are often very different from the eventual goal formulation (and our goal is for the client to be an active participant in his or her own treatment), this task can be a concern. Goal formulation must respect the client's agenda, what is in the victim's power to change, and that the client is responsible for all change—what to change, how fast, and in what way. Anything done in psychotherapy must follow the flow of the patient's want (goal); everything is aligned toward that end. When a victim does not change, a goal is not aligned. As noted too, this participant process is made all the more troubling due to the high incidence of personality problems, high degree of belief in automatic thoughts, high level of Axis I problems, endogeneity, and often a negative or skeptical attitude regarding psychotherapy.

Fortunately, this process does not have to be a full court press for change. Concern with the science or technology of psychotherapy should not be a runaway preoccupation. The person and his/her strengths (nature of the problem, readiness, soundness of ego functioning, character issues, and current life situation), along with the therapy situation, should always dictate the intensity and focus of care. The internal structure of the therapy hour should be mixed, schema work and trauma work, as well as mixed with heavier and lighter periods. The across-sessions structure also should be represented by a mix, but with more emphasis on schema work. With trauma victims especially, some of the therapy hour should be on the lighter end of the interpersonal press towards interiority (Bugental, 1987). Accordingly, the therapist can back up, be supportive, reassure, teach, use humor, reveal or otherwise deflect intensity. Psychotherapy may be serious business, but the psychotherapist should not always be serious. This is necessary because few clients desire (or require) the intensity of a "no-holds-barred," one hour effort.

The result often is noncompliance or therapy dropout. A defocusing on stress then should be as routine a part of therapy with trauma victims as other components. Adler labeled this alternating process, "spitting and stroking." Finally, most therapists desire this respite.

II. Relationship

No other component of therapy is more accepted than the second treatment factor—the working alliance between patient and therapist. In fact, to find a description of psychotherapy with the trauma victim without the heavy endorsement of a positive relationship is virtually impossible. Basically, this therapy component creates an atmosphere for the management of care. It allows for the collaborative process to occur and for the work of therapy to proceed within safe bounds. Attention to the therapeutic relationship is, therefore, an absolute imperative with the trauma victim.

No book ever does justice to the differential change processes of the two parties interacting humanly. You might say two "trends" are involved. One involves the minimal conditions for the work of therapy. These are the non-specific care elements that keep the client open, cooperative, and non-defensive. This focus emphasizes the relationship as a necessary but insufficient condition that allows for the pursuit of the patient's plan—an "okay atmosphere" for the evolving, growing edge of the client's experience to remain engaged.

The second focus highlights relationship as the centerpiece in the work of therapy. How a person acts and then what is done to those actions constitute the main ingredients of care. The relationship is both of these. It is not an epiphenomenon. It is the phenomenon. The transference or the interpersonal happenings are therapy. Kahn (1991) wrote:

> The clinical relationship contains within it the whole story of the patient's problems, indeed the whole story of the patient's life. It is an astonishing microcosm. And it lays before the therapist a remarkable opportunity, not only for learning the secrets of the human mind, but for helping the patient as well. It was puzzling and painful to Freud that he had not found the way to extract the full potential from this opportunity. (p. 33)

Our formulation is somewhere between these positions. In the next chapter we will discuss it more fully. Emphasis is on the therapist's "working rules" in its use. The clinician is asked to be both himself/herself, sufficiently human and caring, and to be the operating part of the fiduciary contractor, the technician in this human change process. Since psychotherapy is an experience that inherently threatens the victim's sense of control, this balance is important.

A monitor of the relationship, at least in the beginning of therapy, is trust. This component of care is so important that, without a solid relationship, the victim may respond to the therapist as one who is revictimized. This phenomenon certainly occurs in other interpersonal contexts and can be as subtle as activating avoidance/numbing feelings. Catherall (1991) has developed a model of treatment related to it. Clients can only trust if they trust themselves. Catherall holds that the victim feels alienated from self due to a loss of basic trust: "It is the individual's experience of his or her own aggression and capacity to victimize which underlies basic trust in others" (p.146). In effect, the victim who can avow his/her own aggression will be able to trust others and grow. But, the way to self-trust in victims (according to Catherall) is to "connect" both with the victim's own aggression and with the *therapist's* aggression. This is only done by care, understanding, modeling by the therapist, and the realization that this person (the therapist) is *okay*. The victim now knows that he/she can live with these thoughts and feelings without losing control (since the therapist has similar feelings) (Catherall, 1991). In this model, trust (the relationship) is curative.

Interpersonal Circle: Unhooking and Oscillation

In our formulation the therapist is asked to calculate and carry out two relationship tasks, **unhooking** and **oscillation.** First, let's look at **unhooking.** Several interpersonal theorists (e.g., Carson, 1982; Cashdan, 1973; Kiesler, 1982) have specified a series of "interpersonal laws" in therapy. Based on various conceptualizations of the interpersonal behaviors (interpersonal circle) (Kiesler, 1982), the person interacts with others continuously by negotiating two major relationship dimensions—friendliness and hostility. Depending on the composite blend of these two factors (so many units of friendliness and so many units of hostilities), the individual's interactions unfold. The interpersonal circle represents distinct behaviors, punctuated on a continuum of normal to abnormal. Based on the information of this circle the therapist can make precise predictions regarding the behaviors of patients. Sullivan (1956) labeled this the "theorem of reciprocal emotion." Its key law is complementarity. The assumption is that a person's interpersonal actions tend to initiate, invite, or evoke from other people reactions that lead to a repetition of the person's original actions. If the interactant receives a **complementary response,** his/her behaviors continue; if the interactant does not receive a complementary response, an **anticomplementary response,** the door is open for other forms of behavior. The goal of therapy is to facilitate interpersonal reactions from segments on the circle opposite to typical patterns, anticomplementarity.

Each client attempts a series of "**transference tests**" designed to elicit from the therapist a continuance of the maladaptive pattern. For example, many times victims who require control in life elicit different degrees of governance from the therapist. If the therapist "takes the bait," he/she has failed the test and must now observe the response of a victim who has problems with control. Safran and Segal (1990) referred to these patterns as "either/or" or "if/then" impasses. The client who is the perpetrator of dichotomous styles (e.g., unduly accommodating or unreasonably angry) will eventually set up conditions for this choice point in therapy and demonstrate the rigidity of the style. One common pattern is to feel "put upon," become defensive, and entrenched in a hardened position. However, if the therapist responds with an unhooking response (anticomplementarity), the client is now open to other options. Often this is freeing by itself. Table 6.9 specifies the behaviors that "feed" these maladaptive styles (complementarity) and those that are formative in change (anticomplementarity). We further elaborate on this in Chapter 6.

In addition to metacommunication which is involved during this unhooking process, oscillation occurs. To unhook oneself from the client's dysfunctional cognitive-interpersonal cycles, the therapist is required to be a participant observer. Sullivan's (1956) stance of a participant observer was that the therapist

TABLE 6.9
Interpersonal Table of
Positive and Negative Behaviors
of Axis II Disorders

Personality	Therapist Goal or Anticomplementarity	Transference or Complementarity
Schizoid	Gregarious Outgoing	Warm Pardoning
Avoidant	Outgoing Spontaneous Confident	Cold Mistrusting
Dependent	Dominant Assured	Critical Dominant
Histrionic	Unresponsive Realistic	Trusting Respectful
Antisocial	Friendly Sociable	Hostile Argumentative
Sadistic	Devoted Absolving	Hostile Detached
Conforming	Spontaneous Revealing	Cold Mature
Passive Aggressive	Cooperative Helpful	Hostile Cold
Self Defeating	Objective Confused	Helpless Exhorting
Schizotypal	Trusting Sociable	Inhibited Cold

TABLE 6.9 (continued)

Borderline	Consistent Confident	Unassured- Assured Cold-friendly
Paranoid	Merciful Warm Helpful	Inhibited Guarded Hostile

Extrapolated from Kiesler (1982).

should allow himself/herself to feel the patient's interpersonal pull and then use this observation. He/she was to participate and observe in the interaction simultaneously. This is a kind of a parallel processing that involves the therapist distinguishing his/her feelings and thoughts from those that are taking place in the interaction with the client. **Oscillation** means that the therapist feels free to interact in a back and forth fashion between aspects of the stimulus situation that are reflective of the client and the client's personal reactions to these aspects. The client is asked to do the same. Safran and Segal (1990) labeled this process **decentering.** The therapist (and client) steps outside of his/her (and the client's) immediate experience, thereby changing the very nature of the experience. This task, as Safran and Segal noted, accounts nicely for interpersonal gaps between ongoing events and the client's reaction to the event. Through this process the client begins to distinguish between reality and the reality as he/she construes it.

This process of oscillation also facilitates other important events in therapy. The client learns that perceptions are to be viewed as hypotheses, and hypotheses are to be tested. In effect, the client is able to see "self" as a tool for growth. This is the observing ego. This process of oscillation also "enforces" a sense of emotional and cognitive immediacy regarding ongoing events. This maximizes the level of involvement of the client and presumably the process of change. When this is working, the oscillation process also provides access to more relevant construals. The client is able to bounce back and forth between surface and deeper cognitions. In effect, two oscillations are occurring: one between the therapy experience and the observation, and one between levels of cognitions. From this, one can see how this process fosters the "agency" of the client in the change process (Safran & Segal, 1990).

The labor intensive part of the relationship (in our formulation) is the unhooking and oscillation processes. The client is always more skilled at his/her position than is the therapist. These two tasks involve reading the client, as well as the therapist's own feelings (Table 6.9). Once these disengagement processes take hold, therapeutic tasks (both schema and symptom focused) can be better applied. More information on this will be found in Chapter 7.

Also remember too that psychotherapy is an alien environment for the client. The client is always "one-down." A bonding relationship, however, assures the client that a real person and partner recognizes the pain, bears witness to themes and accesses recovery resources. A sound relationship also involves a careful dance between bonding or therapeutic connection and work or task issues. The working alliance makes this process less painful. However, the working alliance is not only alliance; it too is work. Many family therapists view the psychotherapist as an architect of dialogue. This "effortless work" is intensive. The therapist has many requirements. He/she is required not only to join, but to read, back off, and then provide alternatives. Short of this, he/she may become part of the problem, a conspirator in the trauma membrane. When performed well, an individual healing theory starts with the relationship.

Corrective Emotional Experience

One last issue is discussed. Many therapists believe insight is necessary for change in psychotherapy. Its role, however, is unclear: It is enough; it is never enough; it is necessary but not sufficient; it is an epiphenomenon; and so on. Clients seem to resonate to the reasons for their actions, but only fully "appreciate" this when accompanied by re-experience, usually as a result of the relationship. Gill (1982) noted that understanding is necessary for clients but never as "explanation." This must emerge from the client's re-experiencing in his/her current life. Gill's position supports the information processing model: clients do not distort their world, rather they arrive at the most plausible conclusion, given their ambiguities and history. Validation of the client's perception and affirmation of the plausibility of the *client's* interpretation are imperative procedures. Obviously, some reconstructing of the story of the client's life must develop at some point. Yet, only in the re-experiencing of these patterns (supported by the therapist) is the client free to express them, in the presence of a therapist who meets them with interest and objectivity. Only then can these patterns, now expressed as attitudes toward the therapist, and not determined *entirely* by the situation, be isolated, exposed, and offered as hypotheses for change.

This is the corrective emotional experience—letting the client know that the therapist is doing the best he/she can to understand the way the situation looks to the client (empathy) and allowing this to occur in the present. An "optimal frustration" eventually develops. Clients hunger to know why they choose that one way and how they can alter that one way. It now oozes through the interpersonal actions—the relationship.

III. Schema and Symptom Therapy: Schemas

Assume that a client has information on his/her person (Component 1) and trusts the process (Component 2). The ecology is now set for Component 3. The essential features of Components 1 and 2 have already planted seeds necessary for the recalculation of schema and symptom issues. This is the essence of the case formulation approach to treatment, in which assessment and treatment are tightly linked and the formulation of the case dictates the specific aspects of the care plan. Given a careful person analysis, stemming largely from schemas and personality (MCMI or MCMI-II), working hypotheses about the mechanisms specific to the person's core cognitions (behavioral/affective/interpersonal styles, and symptoms) take form. Remember that perturbation brings out the worst in people and that personality traits, whether rigid and inflexible or not, will be inclined to become so, making treatment more difficult. Finally, recall that symptoms are differentiated. On the basis of this understanding, carefully identified treatment interventions are devised and tested.

Our model [Sc+P+(B)+Sy] specifies that schemas abused by trauma should be considered *first* in the curative process. The principal tenet in this pursuit is to identify the schema wherever and whenever it occurs. Implied is an evaluation of the degree to which the cognition is salient and the degree to which it disrupts and creates an imbalance in the person and the individual's awareness of this process. Through an understanding of the self, the first task of treatment, and the on-going relationship, the second task of treatment, schemas are then identified, reidentified, and hopefully modified in treatment. From the "action focus" of the treatment itself four central features occur in therapy: (1) the therapist uses self to discern reactions/feelings regarding the interaction (Component 2); (2) the therapist "translates" these reactions into real cognitions and interpersonal behaviors (e.g., grimacing, hesitations, anxious, shaking) (Components 1 and 3); (3) the therapist requests the client to be a participant observer in this process (Components 1 and 3); and now (4) the therapist acts—identifies surface and core construals as well as interpersonal patterns wherever they are present (Component 3). This is the human struggle—the collaborative approach. Schemas, core cognitions, and modal styles are exhumed. Again, Young (1990) described this as schema-focused therapy, in which maladaptive schemas are protected by an armamentarium of schema maintenance, schema avoidance, and schema compensation (Chapter 5). Therapy then is a debriding procedure, in which the inward orientation is pursued and cleansed of impurities.

CBT techniques

As a result of Component 1, the information required for schema therapy, identification of the schema and its key protectors (core cognitions and modal styles), is present. The undoing of these over-involved patterns requires multiple techniques (CBT) applied in a persistent fashion. In Table 6.10 is a listing of methods geared to identify and pursue maladaptive schemas and tacit cognitions to make these explicit. Four points need to be remembered. First, therapy is not so much a thing of beauty as it is a repetitive process, yet always "alive" in a new way. Second, the therapeutic focus is interiority—the downward arrow with person referents. Third, the benignly persistent but relentless unearthing process intended to expose core cognitions. On behalf of this, surface cognitions, the client markers of core cognitions, and modal styles are identified. Fourth, efficacy of this task is increased when performed concretely in cognitive and emotionally immediate ways. Cognitive processes experienced in the here and now enhance therapeutic communication and the change experience.

Butler and Strupp (1991) described this process using four interpersonal components. These authors labeled these maladaptive patterns, *clinical maladaptive patterns* (CMP). Using a time limited form of psychotherapy, the four components necessary for CMP are acts of self (I want or I did), expectations of others toward self (I expect of others), acts of others toward self (observed acts of others), and acts of self toward self (how one treats self—e.g., self-punishing, self-congratulating). As the therapy proceeds, these patterns are enacted. Chronic PTSD victims often ambivalently seek detachment (acts of self), but fear others will intrude or in some way invade or attack them (expectations). Eventually, this may occur (acts of others). The resultant self-attributions (self toward self) are negative and self-defeating. This cycle becomes standard fare in the behavior of these victims. The therapist's task is to identify these patterns (CMP), both in therapy and as they occur outside of therapy, and provide awareness. Hopefully, the client is able to take some distance (component) and identify construals attached to these. Again with chronic victims of PTSD, these often are character-based and rigid, but identifiable. By pattern identification, construals can be pursued and made clear.

Recall that in the previous chapter we discussed the rigid components of personality traits (Table 5.5) and assessment issues of trauma symptoms (Table 5.14). Table 6.10 (in this chapter) is intended to tease apart the schema-personality interaction and provide an understanding of both this process and, by means of this, their alteration. Remember that this is a labor intensive therapeutic task. This task is all-the-more troublesome because of intensity/chronicity of symptoms, or Axis II patterns, or both. However, the evidence is that if the client's pathological beliefs can be better or more reliably formulated, their undoing is easier (Weiss, Sampson, & the Mount Zion Psychotherapy Research Group, 1987) and anxiety is reduced (Silberschatz, 1987). The more immediate and realschemas become, the greater the chance for change. Also, the client presumably has an expectancy that he/she is to collaborate in this process. The therapist often can begin with cognitive probes that move slowly interior (downward arrow, explication, imagery) and proceed to other "unearthing" methods ("What does this mean to you?"). Throughout, the therapist uses a reasonable clinical sense: supporting the ego's highest level of development, improving defenses, encouraging positive affective connections, aiding in verbalization, differentiating various affects, supporting effort and trust, and in general empowering the client.

This is the reason why the relationship is so important. As we have been advocating, the therapist balances top-down and bottom-up strategies (in both schema and symptom therapy). When a solid relationship exists, these choices can be made easily as less need to fear a therapeutic error arises. Safran and Segal (1990) noted that the therapeutic relationship itself can be the mechanism for change. So, the clinician is able to bounce back and forth with comfort between techniques (e.g., "what is the evidence for the thought?") or interpersonally based injunctions in the service of the schema or personality (e.g., "Do you feel put off by me?"; "What does it mean to you to be ignored by others?").

TABLE 6.10
Schema Therapy Tasks

Key Tasks: Identification of schema and personality style components (core cognitions and modal styles) in a concrete and emotionally immediate way.

A. Downward Arrow (vertical-to-self):
      "And what does that mean?"
      "How does this apply to you?"

B. Explication:
      "Sounds like control again."

C. Cognitive or Emotional Immediacy:
      "You feel this right now."

D. Imagery:
      "Can you picture the time when you were independent?"

E. Childhood Experience:
      "Recreate that situation when you were a child."

F. Role-play:
      "You be the stern, angry you; I'll be the passive one."

G. Scaling/Continuum:
      "Specify total distrust for me."

H. Concreteness:
      "Describe the situation once again."

I. Repetitive Negative Experience:
      "Recall an event in your past when you were a child that represents this problem you consistently have. Recall a time when you were feeling bad and describe what was happening; who was there; what was the emotional climate; what made it unpleasant; what were you feeling/thinking/saying/doing/wanting; what responses did you get; what was your attitude/fears to self or others; how did this turn out; how does this episode influence you; how do you influence it?"

(continued)

TABLE 6.10 (continued)

J. Procedure for Automatic Thoughts
1. Identify thoughts
    Recall
    Imagery
    Role-play
    Record of daily thoughts

2. Specify Distortions
    All-or-none
    Over-generalization
    Selective abstractions
    Personalization
    Mind reading
    Labeling (and other stylistic errors)

3. Test automatic thoughts
    What is the evidence?
    Does it follow?
    Is there another way to think of this?
    So what if it happens?

4. Look for schemas
    Patterns of thoughts/behaviors
    Common distortions

Extrapolated from various sources.

As in all good psychotherapy, progress is cyclical—change followed by impasse, by change, by impasse. The interior press is pursued because it is where the action is. The person must know, experience, and redecide his/her core constructs. Symptom reduction is not therapy. The "dynamic focus" is inward and the methods consist of various techniques limited only by the caring boundaries of this objective. The work of therapy then progresses to the client's intrapsychic zone, having proceeded from the interpersonal patterns of the therapy interaction. This is the therapeutic commitment—the well being of the person and his/her authenticity. Along the way, the therapist will often elicit hopelessness, defenses, and aspects of despair. Even the "post-trauma sense-making" of chronic

PTSD victims involving secondary gains (social or system support for symptoms) is exposed and reframed according to core construals. "Is this the way you want to be?" becomes a ready refrain.

Schema Interventions

Table 6.11 presents interventions for each schema on the *Schema Checklist.* This non-exhaustive list is extrapolated primarily from the work of McCann and Pearlman (1990a). These schemas are face valid for clients. The client can understand the schema and its entrenched quality. The therapist's role involves the consistent identification of any person markers and the offering of choice. This is a gradual and evolving venture, in which constant connections are made between schemas and symptoms. Interventions often are direct challenges. At other times, more indirect or even paradoxical offerings are attempted. Throughout, the therapist acts as a gentle consultant helping the client explore his/her inner world—at times teaching, at times confronting, at times supporting, and at times demanding experiential responses. Through the progressive unfolding of these unacknowledged experiences and connections, a new meaning is created. Ultimately, the client reconstructs his/her own reality.

Personality Interventions

A compendium table to Table 6.11 is presented (Table 6.12). Interventions for personality styles (or disorders) are provided. Personality styles are core elements in schema maintenance—the chief processes by which maladaptive schemas are maintained and reinforced. In Table 6.12 is represented common interventions that have been helpful for a specific personality style. For example, with the avoidant personality style, reducing evaluation apprehension and slowly exposing victims to various sources of anxiety is helpful. Avoidant personalities are especially adept at disrupting their internal processes, going blank, or escaping even minimal stress. As such, avoidant people are never fully "aware" of their pain,

(continued on page 347)

TABLE 6.11
Maladaptive Patterns of the Schema

Schema	Interpersonal Style	Compensation	Psychopathological Pattern
Safety feels insecure others are dangerous feels vulnerable	Caution Reserved Protective	Reckless Carefree	Phobia Schizoid style Anxiety

Dependence
can't rely on own
  judgement
vulnerable to others
feels betrayed
	Avoidant
	Defensive
	Inferior
	Testing
		Overcommits in
		  relationship
		Opens self up
		Acts independent
			Panic
			Abandonment
			Dependent
			Depression

Independence
vulnerability
  is weakness
overdriven to
  control due to
fear of helplessness
	Overcontrolled
	Defensive
	Aloof
	Mistrusting
		Excessively
		  aggressive <u>or</u>
		  helpless
			Antisocial style
			Paranoid style

(continued)

Schema	Interpersonal Style	Compensation	Psychopathological Pattern
Esteem no self value worthless/flawed self	Constricted Needy Introspective	Numbing Solicitous	Depression Guilt Self Blame
Intimacy self alienation can't comfort self uncommitted to others	Detached Alone Careful	Outgoing Attacks others	Anxiety Addiction Loneliness Isolation
Acceptance flawed in some way others must like me plays to gallery	Pleasing Submissive Serving	Doesn't ask for help Excessive anger	Depression Anxiety Patient role

(continued)

TABLE 6.11 (continued)

Schema	Interpersonal Style	Compensation	Psychopathological Pattern
Competence feels inferior/ failure feels the need to be "somebody"	Controlled Responsible Integrated	Risky behavior Impulsive	Obsessive Compulsive Anxiety
Control fears ambiguity/ authority/rejection needs to control others or problems result	Assertive Demanding	Admits weakness Asks for help	Acts out Substance abuse

Extrapolated from McCann & Pearlman (1990).

TABLE 6.12
Intervention with Personality Styles

Personality Style	Short-term Interventions	Fear	Struggle
Schizoid	Feedback on responses Social skills building Automatic thoughts identified Reduce vagueness	Being overwhelmed	Remaining in contact and organize self
Avoidant	Reduce evaluation anxiety Reduce "going blank" or cognitive disruption Scaling/continuum of trust Slowly expose painful feelings	Pain Inadequacy	Maintaining contact and reducing fears of others (trust)
Dependent	Dichotomous thinking Imagery of change Assertiveness/decision making Means/end thinking	Loss of attachment (abandonment)	Function adequately and feeling of mastery

(continued)

TABLE 6.12 (continued)

Personality Style	Short-term Interventions	Fear	Struggle
Hysterical	Aloneness fears exposed Confront vagueness Teach problem solving (thinking) Explore relationship in detail	Loss of excitement	Connection between feelings and thoughts
Narcissistic	Entitlement needs exposed Fear of criticism Empathy teaching Explore thinking process (all or none)	Being average	Feel normal without exaggeration
Antisocial	Be explicit with rules Choice review Empathy training	Being vulnerable	Feel safe to make contact and tolerate anxiety
Compulsive	Origins of low self esteem Need for rules/fears Cognition rigidity (shoulds) Explore/expose feelings	Helplessness feelings	Connect thinking with feelings

(continued)

TABLE 6.12 (continued)

Personality Style	Short-term Interventions	Fear	Struggle
Passive Aggressive	Contributors to negative affect Automatic thoughts identified "Other" demands explicated Fears of vulnerability	Being controlled by others	Act and express (anger) directly and reduce liability
Sadistic	Automatic thoughts identified Fears of intimacy Anger management Empathy training Continuum techniques	Loss of competitiveness Feeling vulnerable	Cooperate and accept others
Self-defeating	Expose defeating strategies Repetitive negative experience Interpretation—suffering is pleasure Expose suffering as controlling	Success	Accept success

(continued)

TABLE 6.12 (continued)

Personality Style	Short-term Interventions	Fear	Struggle
Schizotypal	Anxiety reduction Social skills Fear in relationships Problem solving skills	Depersonalized Overwhelmed (Arise from milder personality)	Maintain contact
Borderline	Dichotomous thinking Focus on relationship Boundary needs explored Indentify basic assumptions Reduce "noise"/impulsivity	Unworthiness or abandonment (Arise from milder personality)	Differentiate self Feel okay/normal Problem
Paranoid	Reduce sensitivity to criticism Trust questioning exercises Empathy training	Being exposed (Arise from milder personality)	Feel safe Make contact Feel comfortable with vulnerabiltiy

either within themselves or within their environment. Use of scaling methods or the slow desensitization to painful feelings insures that any comfort in the future use of this style be "reconsidered." Adler considered this "spitting in the soup" of the patient. He/she can never quite perform the self-defeating activity without reconsideration. These interventions are largely CBT methods and are a first line attack on the protective belt of each style and eventually of schemas (Beck & Freeman, 1990). Often, they can be used as trial explorations to assess whether a victim has a sufficient "psychological quotient" to partake in schema therapy.

Bottom-up Therapy

Recall that Table 6.5 has outlined the PTSD model of treatment. The work of therapy is involved in two parts, schema and symptom therapy. Tables 6.10, 6.11 and 6.12 have presented methods to intervene in this unearthing venture focusing either on schema or personality. These interventions are modal top-down strategies. Hopefully, these tables communicate an emphasis on "how" the patient misinterprets reality, stay in the here and now, and emphasize a constant sharpening and correcting procedure that clarifies and alters the inner relationship of thought to feelings and to behavior. This is a slow but focused reshaping process in which the patient functions best when he/she is authenticated, cooperative, and decentered, and can experience the erroneous learnings of trauma (corrective emotional experience). In time, "deep habits" are owned and (hopefully) substituted.

Unfortunately, this CBT, top-down approach stumbles with chronic patients. *Trauma entrenches personality patterns for the worse.* The typical CBT methods of automatic thought identification, testing and challenging cognitions, and experimenting (Table 6.10), require clinical assistance. Several negative "predictors" of intransigence are present—fixed personality patterns, severe levels of PTSD (and other disorders), poor patient expectations, high levels of belief in negative construals, and often a reduced role in the development of a therapeutic alliance. Previously noted, Rothstein and Vallis (1991) emphasized the importance of process adaptation—

use of cognitive-developmental process, core schema influences, and especially the importance of the relationship. One of the process adaptations recommended (for treatment of personality disorders) was the exploration of the functional value of symptoms for a personality style(s), the meaning of the symptom vis-a-vis the self. The personality style, therefore, requires "checking out" ("Is this true of you?"), decentering ("What do you think of this behavior?"), connections of cognitions to affect ("see how your independence leads to anger"), and constant "how" processing. These interventions are more bottom-up or relationship based and compliment the injunctions in Table 6.12. Meichenbaum and Fitzpatrick (1991) also noted the special care required of psychotherapy with fixed personality problems (or chronicity), notably a slow and lumbering process of discovering "prescriptive behavioral interventions" specific to heretofore resistent attributions.

Table 6.13 is the "big picture," a procedure to use with chronic victims combining both top-down and bottom-up methods, with schema (A) and symptoms (B). Here the focus is on Part A, the schema process. The emphasis is to interweave the bottom-up, more relationship-based experiences and top-down approaches. Donovan (1987) noted that this is where the action should be for the entrenched patterns, a focal inquiry on the pathogenic convictions about the self (usually involving self esteem). In effect, he was saying that therapy is successful to the extent that the victim could tolerate confrontation of self.

Furthermore, an engaging "task environment" is required. Not only does the client (according to our system) have both schema *and* symptom problems, but the intricate artistry of a "schema ordering" of a whole sequence of actions—specific images, memories, motor behaviors, autonomic arousal and plans, or if-then contingencies—is unknown. No data or manuals exist which tell clinicians that a cognitive construal eventuates in *this* interpersonal action. Only guidelines are present to make the client committed, expressive, and a true believer in this self-directing endeavor. The victim must "confess" the processes. If this method is working (at the least), the patient's communication should become more expressive and accurate and his/her behavior less rigid. Remember that this is hard therapeutic work that sets the stage for later symptom therapy. (More discussion on this interweaving process follows).

One other added benefit is that the schema work assists in the ongoing relationship task of therapy (Table 6.5). Safety is both a persistent schema of victims as well as a concern of the relationship itself. Weiss (1971) has identified three processes of psychotherapy that influence safety: external circumstances, degree of control over defenses, and the therapeutic relationship. Interesting to note is that these three criteria are highly affected by the person's pathogenic beliefs (schemas). Therefore, according to our model, exposing and defusing construals have the additional benefits of fostering safety.

As this transactional dance of schema (Part A) into symptoms (Part B) proceeds, the therapist "should" empower self in several ways. First, there should be no requirement to establish a firm diagnosis (use provisional diagnoses). Second, the clinician should learn to think on two levels—the schema-personality axis *and* symptoms (trauma story). Success can be differentiated according to each one. Third, remember that the clinician becomes hooked by the schema-personality pull (Table 6.9) and should use this for unhooking and decentering strategies. This is beneficial anticomplementarity. The patient should be made as much a part of this process as possible—as consultant, to share schemas, and cognitions and styles, and to allow the patient to assist in this "unstuck" process. Once again this is labor intensive.

III. Schema and Symptom Therapy: Symptoms

Finally, symptoms are to be considered. Again, the distinction between schema and symptoms is important for both conceptualization and treatment purposes. The former involves the person, and the latter, the perturbation of the person that often is all consuming. The former necessitates the careful monitoring of the collaboration and understanding

(continued on page 354)

TABLE 6.13
Schema and Symptom Processes

A. Schema Process
  1. Identify underlying beliefs and core strategies (Table 6.7).
  2. Create an atmosphere for dialogue and safety for each style (e.g., antisocial requires control and awareness of "getting over" patterns).
  3. Schema therapy assessment (Table 6.3) and trial interventions—experiment with short-term interventions (Table 6.11 and 6.12).
  4. Reeducation, normalization, and reconceptualization fostering an adaptive attitude ("This is what you are going through.") and role clarification ("This is your task here.") (Table 5.6). Also apply Table 6.6.
  5. Balance top-down (self monitoring, coping self statements, situational analysis, manageable verses nonmanageable tasks, etc.—Table 6.10) and bottom-up (relationship) interventions, assessing what works. This involves a balance between "What is the evidence?" and "What does this mean to you?"
  6. Identify schemas and personality styles wherever and whenever they appear ("Sounds like you need control again."). "Deep habits" require a concious attack. Also, awareness is on a contimuum.
  7. Use the relationship often (tilting this process in the direction of bottom-up experiences) (Table 7.2). The relationship accesses the schema best.
     -"How does this patient react to my interventions?"
     -check out (and note) person markers
     -use downward arrow frequently ("What does this mean to you?")
     -identify "hot" areas—entrenched beliefs, feelings, puzzles, obvious discrepancies of belief and behavior and use relationship
     -go to self ("When you said this, I backed off.")
     -go to patient ("Do you feel pushed by me?"; "Tell me what you just experienced.")

(continued)

TABLE 6.13 (continued)

-decenter patient often

-connect cognition and affect

-identify sequence between cognitions and "everything" (emotions, behaviors, etc.)

8. Use any technique to stop the process and highlight the "how" of current behavior, especially emotional immediacy and imagery. Slow down the stuck schema/ personality style and let it "sit" there.

9. Use developmental data

-use LSA data (Chapter 4)

-"Where in the past did you. . ."

-use repetitive negative experiences (Table 6.10)

10. Use meaning questions from LSA (Chapter 4).

11. Reinforce trying and gains, and reframe successes in a broader/longer vision of success. Talking about person issues, crisper self dialogue and emotional differentiation are successes.

12. Recycle through these 11 guidelines.

B. Symptom Process

1. Psychoeducation

-effects of trauma (inner shattering)

-longer/more intense the trauma, the stronger the residual

-hyperalertness externally and hyperarrousal internally (victim naturally scans for cues, occupying time and energy)

-intense symptoms (e.g., flashbacks) retraumatize

-avoidance has short term benefits but keeps the process going

-arousal/numbing cycle occurs naturally

-negative self attributions (self-blame versus character blame) cause special problems

-"cure" comes in exposure—dose related or flooding (requirements include retelling story, affect atonement, catharsis [if needed], and meaning search)

(continued)

TABLE 6.13 (continued)

-state dependent learning explicated (a triggering device yielding many unwanted non-symptom contingent cues)

-completion tendency (trauma seeks outlet)

2. Normalization

-gamut of symptoms even "crazy" ones are part of process

-search for meaning is universal ("Why me?")

-intrusions are adaptive attempts to make sense of trauma and will stop when enough "sense" is provided; avoidance prevents this

-personal healing theory is underway

-"narrative truth" not "historical truth" is the goal

-generalization effect to other trauma

3. Tasks

-perform trauma memory assessment (Table 5.14)

-develop self coping or safety requirements

-obtain a clear rendition of story (see text)

-have client be a personal scientist in this effort (what prevents victim from accepting this memory)

-"logical" clinical tasks:

-provide structure

-support when necessary

-correct distortions, especially self attributions that are negative ("What is the evidence?"; "What prevents you from less emotionally?")

-work with memory using techniques (e.g., Gendlin-see text) and story destructuring probes (#4)

-facilitate a "now" experience of the past story (use present tense, and encourage arousal and hope)

-have client perform personal experiments to test and move the stuck story

-share aspects of narrative (e.g., journal writing) with others

(continued)

TABLE 6.13 (continued)

-meaning search starts an enriching process through life

-establish personal efficacy and empowerment

4. Liberally use "Story Destructuring Probes"

When did you decide to believe that?

How did you get that to happen?

How do you know *deadness, fear, anger*?

What is trust for you?

Have you had this kind of problem in the past?

What would you need to do to get this to occur again?

How is that different from the way you might have handled it?

I wonder if there is any way you can keep your memory but stop harassing yourself.

Bring back the memory, take two deep breaths and tell me if the feeling of the memory changed.

When was the "best" time you had this memory?

Are you more "rational" or "irrational" with this memory?

What would have to happen to make you symptom free?

What's going on with you that doesn't fit into what you've been telling me?

Does this understanding explain other parts of your life?

5. Establish a personal self-coping repertoire for safety, for negotiating stuck areas, and for experiments to continue process (outside therapy). Also assist in use of social supports.

6. Discuss phase out process and use of relapse prevention plan for future "slips" (Chapter 13).

(of self and role). The latter is more technique directed, with remission as its immediate goal. Should symptoms override the person ("cognitive shift"), then symptom therapy is required. At this time, symptoms "demand" attention from the therapist. In trauma work, typical symptom methods include exposure techniques like direct therapeutic exposure, eye movement desensitization/reprocessing, stress reduction, or grief/trauma therapy, among others. These are described in later chapters. Among the micro-skills addressed are relaxation training, various coping methods, behavioral skills, anger management, thought stopping, assertiveness, guided self statements, positive reframes, problem solving, relapse prevention techniques, and others. Several of these have been successfully employed in treatment studies of other trauma victims (e.g., Veronen & Kilpatrick, 1983; Resick, Jordan, Girelli, Hutter, & Marhoefer-Dvorak, 1988).

As we have described throughout the book, schema and personality issues are "more equal." Everly (1989) directly tackled this issue as it regards trauma victims. Overall, he posited a "principle of personalogic primacy." Personality style represents the undergirding of the stress response to such an extent that this person pattern has a role in the creation of psychosocial stressors, in the dictation of the phenomenological course of stress related disorders, and in the influence of psychotherapy and long term prognosis of the encoding of stress. Character vulnerabilities then interact with the stressor to form a signature-based stress disease. Everly did not stop here. All treatment of the stressor response is not personality (or schema) based. Everly (1989) wrote:

> ...personality traits play an important role in the nature and treatment of the human stress response. This is not to say, however, that formal psychotherapy needs to be an integral aspect of all stress treatment/stress management paradigms. Processes such as relaxation training, biofeedback, and even health education practices are clearly capable, in some instances, of altering dysfunctional practices. Yet, there are instances where chronic stress-related diseases are a direct function of personologic disturbances such as dysfunctional self-esteem, persistent cognitive distortions, irrational assumptions, inappropriate expectations of self and others, and so on. In such cases, some concerted psychotherapeutic effort would clearly be indicated. The

most effective "mix" of therapeutic technologies (e.g., relaxation training, psychotherapy, hypnosis) remains to be determined by the therapist on case-by-case basis. (pp. 117-118)

Arguing for this same personality-symptom distinction, L'Abate (1992) stated that symptom therapy is the province of the professional until symptom reduction occurs. This happens at the beginning stages of therapy and is short-lived. Next, a paraprofessional can enter the picture to use psychoeducation, for purpose of improving the knowledge and skills of the client. The emphasis is to spend time on basic person or coping issues (personality) in such a way as to ensure behavioral change. While this is a strange juxtaposition of professional use, the idea of person-symptom distinction melds with ours. Care of the stressor response is a multi-therapeutic enterprise.

Further recall that we have divided symptoms into two types, psychosocial and trauma. Both kinds of symptoms of the trauma victim require intervention. They include psychosocial symptoms, the litany of DSM-III-R symptoms specific to each person, and trauma symptoms. Each type of symptom should be addressed separately. The clinician should outline and treat these according to their intensity and/or frequency. Remember that both forms of symptoms are ego dystonic. Also, recall that both psychosocial symptoms and trauma memories represent exemplars of personality (Chapter 4).

Trauma Symptoms: Contextualization

Since PTSD is basically the poor processing of trauma, we direct our attention to the trauma memory. Relatively little is known about the manner in which clients with PTSD attend to and retrieve fear-relevant information from memory. This is unlike other Anxiety Disorders of which more is known. Interestingly, the conventional list of potential responses to victim status (e.g., shock, depression, numbing, helplessness, hyperarousal, etc.) involves the very reactions that are opposite to those necessary for retrieval (risk taking, disclosure, anxiety arousal, etc.). From an experiential perspective, clients with PTSD most often recall trauma-related information accurately when given the right set of retrieval cues, when in the appropriate mood state, or when given sufficient arousal. Failures in emotional processing of information in treatment often occur because information encoded during exposure fails to activate the fear structure sufficiently, or information may not be sufficiently compatible with elements of the fear structure. Clients who are depressed, who are hyperaroused, who have overvalued ideation, who persist in cognitive avoidance, and who show no short term habituation within the therapy hour are especially resistant (Foa & Kozak, 1986). Also, recall that in the study by Hyer et al. (1991), trauma victims did not permit access to the trauma memory and, even when this occurred, were reluctant to give up avoidance mechanisms. Each client has a discomfort index beyond which they will not comfortably go. At this point, the clinician must stop, reorganize, discover avoidant mechanisms, and offer choices. In such situations, the therapist must note the stuck position and explore the underlying intrusive appraisals rather than simply support the client's tendency to avoid. The *clients* should know what they are choosing—retention of old way versus processing stuck memories.

In Chapter 5, we discussed the assessment of person variables related to schema and symptom therapy (Table 5.14). McCann and Pearlman (1990a) believed this evaluation should include the characteristics of the trauma memory itself, as well as the verbal and imagery systems, and the readiness to explore memory. These involve ego and self skills. In this chapter, Table 6.13 (Part B) elucidates the trauma symptom process—psychoeducation, tasks, destructuring probes, coping, and phase down issues. Again, this represents a loose outline for treatment.

In previous chapters, we emphasized how the trauma memory emerges through the filters of the abused schema. Early (1990) noted that particularly with continued trauma, idiosyncratic meaning is attached to the whole trauma experience, including all the conditioned cues and their proxies (and their proxy's proxies). The products then are constructions that capture the essential features of the schemas and not necessarily the trauma event. Safran and Segal (1990) viewed memories as representations of the person's cognitive and interpersonal schemas. Further, they viewed memories retrieved as significant, rather than accurate, information about the patient's history, as a representation of the interpersonal experience significant only to the patient. Consequently, the important feature of the therapeutic test probe is to increase the possibility that the patient will understand the meaning of his/her trauma memory through attachment to the schema. The memory is understood and integrated through the understanding and integration with the schema.

Trauma Symptoms: The Narrative

The connection between schema and trauma memory is apparent in the narrative, the person's own story. McAdams (1990) noted that everyone develops an identity composed largely of nuclear episodes that represent continuity or change across time—continuity as a result of stable patterns (of the person) and change coming from transitions. The result is a historical unit that serves the purpose of bridging past and present. In this sense and in this way, something very important happens: past and present cocreate each other. Each person creates his/her own history to justify the present and in so doing "chooses" his/her own parents, heroes, and scenarios. Also, as a function of this, each person creates his/her own present to conform to the past. Each person then chooses the present reality to conform to the known past. McAdams (1990) wrote:

> In the making of history, there is no objective bedrock of the past from which to fashion the myth. The past is malleable, changing, ever synthesized and resynthesized by present life choices. Yet it is not infinitely malleable, and certain more-or-less validated facts must be woven into a story that attempts to be both coherent and true. History and identity are both "made" and "found out," in Sartre's view. Imagination and discovery work together and nourish each other. (p. 169)

In effect, the trauma victim is "compelled" to apperceive the past to conform to the ongoing identity and "compelled" to conform the present to the ongoing past. Past indeed is prologue, but created prologue.

Hermeneutics, the personal study of a person's narrative story, also describes this process. A memory is but one story that represents only a selection of events about a life. It is the person's own view or story of self. Through a hermeneutic process, the power of a particular story can be challenged. In time, the person's perceived story, taken for granted as truth in life, can now be seen differently. No single truth exists, only different perspectives, each one a perspective of the world from different vantage points. Through the gradual discovery process with other stories, the original story can have a new voice. After all, this is what is occurring in the reintegration of the trauma memory. The trauma victim has perceived "reality" in one way through damaged schemas. The existence of other stories now can emerge through the gentle message of the schema (Parry, 1991).

The search for meaning is not only necessary for change, but it probably must be done timely, in the presence of an empathic listener, and communicated with a sense of hope. Pennebaker (1989) demonstrated that survivors of trauma improved in their psychological and physical health if they discussed their trauma with someone. Presumably, people are able to work through and resolve incompletions, at least partially, and adapt when this occurs. Harvey, Orbuch, Chivalisz, and Garwood (1991) noted that account-making (story-like constructions) was positively related to successful coping and that this effect was most notable with a confidant. This group assessed victims of sexual assault and used traumas occurring greater than a year. Results showed that those who processed their trauma adjusted better than those who did not do this. The rationale is that this form of reconstruction builds trust in others, defuses the perception of personal culpability, restores a sense of self-worth, and facilitates coping. In addition, this effect was greatest on those with the most intense trauma (Harvey et al., 1991). One implication was that victims who can express (account) trauma early (post-trauma) actually activate the information processing necessary for self-care, the working through of trauma (Horowitz, 1973).

Other areas also are converging to assist in the rescripting process of story repair. One is the stress literature. The client possesses an implicit theory of self, the tool for establishing a consistency to his/her own confirmatory bias. In effect, the client selectively tells self and others "stories" to fit his/her own theories. Cognitions are the information in this confirmatory bias process; emotions are the supports. Baumeister, Stilwell and Wotman (1990) and McAdams (1985) have described the nexus between these stories and readjustment. If a victim sees self as a victim or a perpetrator, for example, the content of the narrative alters for the worse. If the victim blames self or assumes responsibility in the content of the story, the constructivist narrative so orders that felt experience. Meichenbaum and Fitzpatrick (1991) have identified positive and negative features of the narrative's expressions of coping. Issues related to the appraisal process, social comparison processes, attributional processes, personal control perceptions, and the like, have been implicated. Positive biases, positive illusions, the search for meaning, and a striving for coherence are components that inoculate against the negative effects of trauma. Unfavorable comparisons, seeing self as victim, blaming others, incessant meaning researches, a focusing on negative implications, and feeling vulnerable are examples of negative ones (Meichenbaum & Fitzpatrick, 1991). Kendall (in press) even noted that the presence of negative thinking does not necessarily result in a "negative narrative," but the frequency, timing, affect, meaning and significance attached to stress (ratio of positive to negative thinking) correlates with adaptive coping. *The bottom line is that those who construct positive narratives will, as a result of this, cope well with distress and vice versa. This is the victim's own "healing theory."*

Trauma: The Treatment Process

Story repair is based on a few basic assumptions. *These include the belief that social reality is co-created, that small changes are all that are necessary, that victims have the resources to solve problems, and that the therapist does not need to know all the story to solve its problems.* The therapist search is for a conversation that is friendly for rescripting. This is what occurs in many rituals of healing in our and other cultures—religious ceremonies, sweat lodge rituals, and ceremonial testimonials (by torture victims), among others (Meichenbaum, 1991). Under such conditions, the story is "forced" to entertain other feedback, feel pressure from another perspective, rehearse other coping methods, correct distortions, and consider personal attributions that reframe the stuck features (of the story). A new assumptive world about victimization is built. In a novel repositioning of Stress Inoculation training (SIT), Meichenbaum (1991) discussed the constructionist narrative. He noted:

SIT helps clients find a way of explaining, conceptualizing, reframing, minimizing and coping with stress. In short, SIT helps clients to experientially rescript, or to create a new narrative about their ability to cope. By carefully arranging proactive learning trials both in the clinic and in vivo, clients can collect "data" that they can take as "evidence" to "unfreeze" their beliefs about themselves and the world. In this fashion, clients can formulate new schemas and develop more differentiated assumptions, and thus, inoculate themselves to future stressors." (p. 9-10)

The trauma victim is a victim of a stuck story. To process the past, more than "reexperiencing past" must occur. A processing of the past in the present must occur. How does the present change the past? By the very act of making the past present, a new reexperience, a carrying forward, and a new texture evolves; a different surrounding, different therapist, different intensity of feelings, and so forth. Often more "differents" occur, as something very new unfolds: *the story is being processed and not avoided.*

Table 6.13 (Part B) outlines suggestions for treatment of the trauma memory. *Just as with schema therapy, symptom therapy demands a mixture of top-down and bottom-up interventions. At any particular point in therapy then, the "right mix" of these two methods provides for the needed titration of interiority; the right place at right time for the curative processes of therapy with trauma.* Procedurally, the sequence of tasks in the treatment of trauma is straightforward. The therapist first assesses for client skills, willingness, and needed safety issues. Next, he/she attempts to obtain facts, a "clean" rendition of the events. Concurrently, affect is attended to, but defused. Now is the time for information gathering. In addition, confusion, misattributions, fears, and gaps are highlighted and gently challenged. The objective is not cure, but an understanding of the event and any surface construals. Often new information is introduced. Often, the paralyzing affect which stopped the story telling dissipates (temporally). At this early juncture, when emotion is present, the therapist is advised to interpret upward or to focus on reality issues. When a reasonable accounting has been settled upon, a final run at objectification (facts, sequence), as well as a renewed and repeated education regarding the reasons for unearthing the memory are provided. This is the story that will be returned to. The time for stopping the process and teasing apart emotional accouterments is later—why this emotion, why these contruals, how does the victim see "self" in this process, etc. (see below). The curative process is now ready for activation; both habituation and completion tendencies are activated.

Table 6.13 (Part B) is only *our* map. Our recommendation also is that the therapist develop his/her own core strategy to "carve nature at its joints" (that artificial aspect of the person called trauma memory). The translation of the "bad" to a "good" internal dialogue requires some structure and some acceptance of chaos. Ultimately, the stuck story requires a new perspective. Through psychoeducation, normalization, application of the story tasks, use of destructuring probes, self coping, and a relapse prevention plan, the story can be reformed. *The reader is encouraged to add to these.* Note especially the influence of the story destructuring probes on the challenge to the fixated self regarding the story (how/ where did the victim learn this; is there another perspective). *The goal is movement of the fixed story.* Past trauma only exists in current meaning.

Gendlin (1991) also described this "meaning changing" process as a felt sense. An exercise that may be helpful in this process is to imagine a troubling scene and its emotion and "try on" the questions noted below. Usually, the "bad emotion" evolved from a more flexible, wider context to a narrow one. Trauma victims are stuck in that narrow emotion feeling. But, as these probes are considered and experienced, the context changes again. Gendlin labeled this a "shift."

Can you get a broader sense of that feeling?

Can you stop and sense the meaning of that feelng?

What is that feeling?

What is that "sore spot" up against?

Can you get in touch with the whole issue?

What say do you have over those feelings?

What word/image/metaphor goes with that?

What's in the way of this being okay?

What is the worst of this?

What are you all about?

How are you stuck?

Just sit quiet, clear a space and see what else is there?

Be friendly to yourself, create a space.

Let your body tell you what all that feeling is about.

What occurs is that the whole of the person (mind-body) alters in the present as "clean language" accesses past reality and bypasses resistance. The gentle acceptance of "what is" eventually feels "right" or fits, and, as it does, the victim changes.

The assumption in the excision and healing of the memory is in many ways like the examination of values: some are clear and influential, some are vague causing divergent responses, and some are not clear or articulated. Different interventions are required for each—at times examination and empowerment, at times clarification and working through, and at times a sensitive client centered process and later psychoeducation. Also, remember the requirement to assess and be sensitive to self and ego functions of the client victim—his/her self care operations when intrusions are present (Table 5.14).

Remember that the trauma memory can be accessed and exposed "full running" (e.g., direct therapeutic exposure; Chapter 11) or dose related. This choice *to process trauma and not avoid* is made mutually. Whatever technique chosen to heal the trauma, approach and avoidant components are present. The former pushes and presents probes encouraging anxiety arousal (integration). When blocked, probes address what this stoppage is about. The latter backs off, seeks perspective, looks for sanctuary, or finds a reward focus. Recall that exposure techniques are not successful with many patients (McCann & Pearlman, 1990a). Over time, data will provide information on the salient variables for successful treatment. For now, each of these trauma memory techniques (Chapters 10-13) can apply its wares, scanning for obstacles to the trauma processing—the grief model searches for obstacles to grieving, direct therapeutic exposure attacks avoidance mechanisms, eye movement desensitization and reprocessing emphasizes the information flow of trauma process (positive and negative), and so forth. Perhaps a common language of these strategies (and obstacles) will evolve.

This model can be applied to other intrusive phenomena including dreams (nightmares), flashbacks (conscious or unconscious), and even intrusive auditory perceptions or hallucinations (Mueser & Butler, 1987). Given these occurrences, the trauma experience is traumatic because it is reflective of a true event (aspects of the trauma) (Laufer, Brett, & Gallops, 1985), even if distorted. Based on our model these phenomena are intrusive expressions of the person (schema and personality style) and need to be integrated. In a related model, Mahrer (1989) described a system of psychotherapy based on the "very special place" of the dream. The "deeper potential" of the person is housed in the unconscious and gives rise to the dream. Mahrer holds that the conscious, day-to-day personality works hard to prevent this from occurring. For Mahrer, therapy involves entry into the dream, attaining and "being the dream experiencing" (here and now meaning moments of the dream), and change behaviors suggested by the dream. Applied to our model, the conditions of Table 6.13 (Part B) apply, the goal being the integration of the intrusive experience into the person. When the person becomes the dream, he/ she is integrated; by altering the dream, the person has also altered self.

One last point is made regarding the context and care environment in the process of acquisition of a new meaning. Ultimately, the trauma story needs to have a place, a context free of intense emotions. Rozynko and Dondershine (1991) believed that four factors are required for effective treatment of the trauma memory: (1) physical safety, (2) emotional safety, (3) honesty, and (4) control of distractions which are resistance based. These factors underline the importance with management of the trauma. The goal is to have the client reconstruct his/her experience as completely and accurately as possible. Emotions are vented, new self-images reclaimed, insights accepted, and the reexperiencing is no longer terrifying. The goal is both emotional and cognitive "meaning," as well as desensitization. The purpose of the reliving experience is not simply catharsis: it is integration—a self-exploration of the self-defeating patterns (schema and personality) and the interface with the symptoms. The clinician should be neither intimidated nor awed by the story, but always respectful and "there."

Remember, the internal landscape of the trauma victim is most likely a combination of historical and narrative truths. That's how (retrospective) trauma memories work. It is not that the person manufactures a pseudohistory; rather it is that a victim defends/distorts/reframes information to match internal (schema) and external (environment) requirements. These "necessary fabrications" have been found in many disorders related to trauma, like Multiple Personality Disorders (Ganaway, 1989). Given this state of affairs and given the patient's insatiable need for external validation, the therapist's best stance is one of concern, respect, and probing, allowing for other realities. However, the therapist should always remain firmly anchored to reality and assist in the "breaking apart" process (fact from fantasy), one that facilitates a final truth that is victim friendly.

Psychosocial Symptoms: Don't Ignore

We have intentionally ignored psychosocial symptoms. Just as concurrent stressors strongly influence the expression and intensity of the trauma response, so too presently experienced symptoms can alter everything for the person. (Both should be evaluated separately, however, to objectively assess their independent influences). The importance of symptoms, however, comes from the person. They should be treated as such. Strong psychosocial symptoms have a way of subverting the schema focus. Nevertheless, time in therapy should be devoted to their care, especially sleeplessness, substance abuse, acting out, and depression. *Just as with therapy directed at the person or the trauma memory, psychosocial symptoms require a deliberatively considered mix of top down and bottom up interventions.* Again, Part III of this book is in part directed at these. Chapter 11 on stress management especially addresses psychosocial symptoms directly. Again, the informed client can appreciate the "shifting" process that symptoms show and, by this very knowledge, become his/her own caretaker empowered to redecide his/her condition.

Schema and Symptom Therapy Integrated

We have presented an array of tables. *Table 6.5 is the treatment model,* and *Table 6.13 is one way to integrate the "most important" components of this model.* The other tables (especially 6.10, 6.11, and 6.12) subserve these two key tables. No one best way exists. Often the time ratio of schema to symptom therapy is 4:1 (or greater), as the latter work is emotionally draining. Regardless, the principle for care is to engage the person, his/her schemas and personality, and present the right mix of top-down and bottom-up interventions that press into the interiority of the victim.

CARE OF THE THERAPIST

An important element missing in this chapter is the distinctive psychotherapeutic undertaking with the trauma victim that can be unfair to the therapist. As with few other kinds of clients, progress can only be made at the level of emotional depth with which the clinician is able to feel comfortable. The upper limits of the level of success are dependent on the "emotional capacity" of the therapist. Differentiating one's own feelings from those of the client and dealing with one's own vicarious issues of traumatization are ongoing. Therapists who work with trauma victims tend to burn out or experience painful images and emotions associated with their client's trauma memories. From a psychodynamic perspective, therapists may respond with disgust, distance, anger, or feeling personally depressed and vulnerable. In a worse case scenario, the clinician may even experience PTSD symptoms. In the treatment of trauma victims, neutrality does not exist; a moral commitment enters where a technical neutrality otherwise applies. (The features of this committed moral position will be addressed in the next chapter.)

The care of the therapist is important and is to be devised individually. Otherwise "negative influences" will intrude in care. If the therapist is not involved with feelings (and biases), he/she is not truly present. If the therapist is too much involved, he/she is guilty of counter transference. The result for the client is a "complicated reactivation" of the trauma—excessive pathology, avoidance, being stuck emotionally, and in general increased vulnerablity. The result for the therapist is counter transference or burnout. Therapists who treat trauma victims can easily fall prey also to a confirmatory bias (focus on issues related to therapist's bias), an availability heuristic (focus on what therapist recalls), or an illusory correlation (false attribution of causality) (Rothstein & Vallis, 1991). Parson (1988) and Wilson (1989) noted difficulties in the confrontation of the counter transference, the cornerstone of psychotherapy. Wilson (1989) identified two sources of cognitive counter transference—*prosocial overcommitment* and *emotional distancing.* The former occurs when the therapist is highly mobilized and senses a strong identification with the victim. Advocacy is often a feature. The latter, on the other hand, involves the inability to manage negative affect and empathy. Traditional therapeutic principles like control and predictability often are relied upon as defenses for the therapist.

Of course, other subtle aspects of professional sensitivity to the care of PTSD victims needs to be considered. Blank (1985) outlined several problems in assessment that are related to professional "involvement." These include a bias against PTSD as a valid diagnosis, denial of diagnostic workability, resistance to one or more DSM criteria, need for absolute corroboration or proof to establish the diagnosis, an aversion to PTSD when other diagnoses are present, and complication of the clinical picture with too many or too few symptoms, among others. To these, Atkinson, Henderson, Sparr, and Deale (1982) added some safety mechanisms, notably peer supervision, seeing less intense cases, and strongly limiting case loads. Often such self-care tasks have an understated value by the clinician. They require, therefore, detection and commitment. Once again, all professionals step into traps. The issues can best be prevented with covenantal responsibility, personal self care, and professional sensitivity.

A commitment to the authenticity of the person of the victim, to oneself, and to one's professional mandate demands work. Fortunately, most psychotherapists are not burned out. They are content. However, the greatest satisfaction is not received from money or power, but from the intellectual and human curiosity necessitated to assist and facilitate growth in human nature. The admixture of healthy components for this task represents a self constructed blend of in-therapy and out-of-therapy commitments, selfish and selfless care, emotional presence and objective distance; in short, a caring for self and client. McCann and Pearlman (1990a) and Mahoney (1991) have outlined several coping strategies for therapeutic work, both with trauma victims and clients in general (Table 6.14). Self-care is up to each clinician.

ESP

Information on care of the caregiver has developed from one other area, caregivers in acute (sometimes on-going) trauma. At the risk of simplification, the data now strongly suggest two "conclusions" regarding the acute trauma care of the caregiver: coping should be highly varied and immediate structured help for caregivers is important. Regarding the former, Dyregrov and Mitchell (1992) have noted many common coping mechanisms used by emergency or disaster personnel to assist in the processing of their own trauma—activity to restrict reflection, contact with other workers, sense of unreality, avoidance of thinking about ramifications of the event, mental preparation, self-assuring statements, exposure regulation, avoidance of information, specific on-scene task focus, and distraction. This understudied area of protective coping (for both victim and caretaker) probably involves a highly individualized profile of mechanisms. Regarding the latter, Armstrong, O'Callahan and Marmar (1991) outlined a critical incident stress debriefing model that was used on Red Cross personnel after the San Francisco earthquake. Notable was its focus on structure and sequence: simple ground rules, facts, thoughts, feelings, symptoms, teaching, and referral, if necessary.

One program that has been successfully applied to caretakers of trauma victims is *Emotional Structural Preparedness* (ESP) (Abueg, Gusman, & Friedman, 1991). This is a model for managing caregivers who are confronted by high-risk clients

TABLE 6.14
Professional Self Care

1. Expectations of Self and Work
   Do I demand too much/little of me?
   Do I demand too much/little of client?
   Do I expect change?
   Do I have confidence in my profession?

2. Commitment to Therapy
   Do I pace well?
   Do I believe in my profession's technology?
   Do I have a theory I trust?
   Can I be open for a change in plans?
   Do I empower possibilities in clients?
   Am I commited to helping?

3. Boundaries in Therapy
   Do I respect personal boundaries?
   Am I aware of and accept my limits?
   Do I allow ownership of problem?
   Am I emotionally present?

4. Balance in Personal and Professional Life
   Is there variety in my life?
   Do I have different types of clients?
   Is my therapeutic armamentarium well stocked
      and growing?
   Do I mix feelings with thoughts?
   Am I balanced on the important issues of life?

5. Nurturance of Self
   Do I care for me?
   Do I prepare (and self reflect) for sessions?
   Do I handle stress well?
   Do I have faith in self?
   Am I burned out?
   Can I ask for help?

Extrapolated from Mahoney (1991) and McCann & Pearlman (1990b).

or situations. It also entails several steps involving the identification of personal and organizational vulnerabilities and "hands-on" practice in potential problem situations. *Techniques include the use of guided imagery of problem situations, awareness of personal limits, cognitive techniques to manage blaming, problem solving to get help or expand choices, and social support, as well as the importance of physical health.* In addition, Talbot, Manton, and Dunn (1992) have argued that the needs of therapists of crisis interveners (debriefing the debriefers) are also important and distinctive. These authors proposed that a combination of perspectives (victim, professional, and person of professional) and "elements" (the individual, individuals in the group, and group as a whole) are required for understanding and care. The debriefers have a formidable task dealing with an event, victim, and their own responses to the event and the victim. In effect, debriefing is both professional and personal.

The hope is that the therapist's use of self in the care of trauma victims becomes a regular part of research in upcoming decades. It is important in most models of psychotherapy and critical in ours. Regardless of the merits of the professional's own psychotherapy, with trauma victims the therapist's emotional experience is instrumental in facilitation of change. The ability of the therapist to resonate to the victim's experience has been labeled by Safran and Greenberg (1991) **affect atonement.** This beyond-empathy response should also be applied to the therapist's own relationship to self, an *in situ* sense of self-care.

CASE EXAMPLE

A case is presented, representing information from Chapters 5 and 6. This case is an example of one of our "influences" (Table 5.8). Initially a battery of tests are given, and during the first two to five sessions a Life-Style Analysis is performed. (This is not shown here). Remember that schemas are the central construals of the person and represent a key therapeutic goal, often not reached (as in this case). Also, remember that our focus is understanding, the therapy relationship, and schema or symptom therapy (trauma and psychosocial) (Table

6.5). Treatment always begins with the first two, attempts to keep schema therapy "alive," and defers to techniques periodically as symptoms become prepotent. When the symptom is less in evidence, the "more important" work of treatment ensues. In fact, both always occur.

Schizoid Influence:

Donald B. was the sixth of eight children born in rural West Virginia. He grew up in poverty with an alcoholic coal miner father and a passive mother. He recalls feeling inferior, because of poverty and his critical and violent father. At age 18, he enlisted in the Marines as an escape from West Virginia poverty. In contrast to his family, the Marines provided structure and consistency. Hard work was rewarded.

Donald recalls numerous fire fights and the deaths and danger which resulted from the mistakes of superiors. Mostly he is vague about the details of his trauma experiences, but he does experience nightmares and has daily intrusions. Donald remained in the service after his tour in Vietnam. He was quickly promoted to drill instructor. He found this immensely stressful and recalls constant conflict between the need to maintain image as a DI (drill instructor) and the need for an outlet for dealing with his Vietnam experiences. He was married for ten years after his return to the U.S., but since then has had no serious relationships. In recent years, he has struggled to remain employed as a welder and has abused alcohol until the past year.

Evaluation Results

Schema Checklist (Table 5.3):
　　　trust—others are out to get me
　　　esteem—I have little value
　　　intimacy—I am emotionally distant

Personality Styles (Table 5.8):
　　　MCMI-II Personalities:
　　　Avoidant
　　　Schizoid
　　　Passive Aggressive

Core Cognitions (Table 6.7):
I am better off doing things on my own.
I am unsure of myself; sometimes nervous, sometimes not.
I should avoid others in order to avoid hurt.
Other people fail to understand me.

Modal Styles (Table 6.7):
Interpersonal indifference
Behavioral contrariness and avoidance
Affective alienation

PTSD Symptoms (Table 6.8):
Psychosocial (from CAPS-1 and MMPI)
Isolation
Tumultuous relationships
Anger
Sleeplessness
Depression (fatigue, negative self statements, hopelessness, ineffectuality)

Assessment of Therapy Potential (Table 6.3):
Schema Factors
  -accesses surface cognitions only
  -unaware of feelings
  -aware of client role
  -poor alliance potential
  -avoidant and fear based security operations
  -avoids topic (multiple person markers to avoid)

Other Therapy Factors
  -poor extra-therapy relationship
  -chronic history
  -pessimistic

Trauma Issues (Table 5.14):
Procedural Questions:
  1. 60% intrusion
  2. Good control
  3. Avoidance mechanisms - isolation and substance abuse
  4. Access—yes

Trauma Indicators:
1. Marginally accepts role, reluctantly collaborates with low imagery skills.
2. Defensive; not psychologically minded.
3. Trauma memory is fragmented and his self skills are varied. Strengths include abilities to use calming talk and to be alone.
4. Success Monitors: poor on all categories

The detached component of this veteran's personality is predominant and supersedes other aspects (Schizoid Influence). He is both fearful of others and desires his detached ways. He feels awkward socially and uses typical avoidant mechanisms (both cognitive and affective) to reduce his level of arousal. Engaging him in use of the Person Analysis Form (Table 6.8) was difficult. His general style of living is to avoid others and remain isolated. Yet, on the occasions when he must deal with others, he can justify the use of force or lying because of his overwhelming sense of unfair treatment. His psychosocial and trauma symptoms complicate his life-style: isolation, numbing, and occasional outbursts of anger. Therefore, his trauma symptoms reinforce his life-style of isolation.

During the treatment of this man the schema process and symptom process components of Table 6.13 were loosely followed. Goals in treatment were to encourage this veteran to participate in group therapy since he tended to remain on the fringes. Early in therapy, massive clinical efforts were applied on behalf of client education (Table 6.13 and Table 6.6). Schemas were hard to confront, as were core cognitions and personality styles (Tables 6.11 and 6.12). His tendency toward being a loner was confronted. CBT techniques (Table 6.10) were utilized to assist the veteran in understanding the function of his detached style and to develop strategies for more satisfying interactions with others. He continued to demonstrate extreme avoidance of intense feelings as he terminated his inpatient treatment early. He was encouraged to seek long-term outpatient treatment. In therapy, exposure of his feelings required a slow titration process (Table 6.3). Clearly, he is a candidate to drop out of outpatient treatment, as avoidance is a persuasive self-defeating mechanism.

Accordingly, he was made aware of these tendencies, given control of his situation, and supported. The trauma memory itself was carefully and infrequently addressed over time. Intrusive symptoms were actually reduced (Table 5.14). Concrete behavioral techniques were used. Desensitization and relaxation were also employed (Chapter 13). This had the added benefit of reducing his typical hyperarousal feelings. So, while the therapist was unable to process the trauma memory (Table 6.13), he was able to utilize many schema-based interventions, including identification of beliefs, trial interventions, normalization and reeducation, use of the relationship, meaning questions, and reinforcement of success (Table 6.13).

CONCLUSION

The victim enters therapy with an existential query: In order to change will I become a person that I do not know well enough to be? The answer is usually a fearful and reluctant yes. Through the process of psychotherapy a healing revolution occurs.

The role of the therapist is often clumsy, working to facilitate but not to influence unduly. Parrott and Howes (1991) noted that, when all is said and done, therapeutic flexibility is the hallmark of good therapy. Trauma victims present symptoms unfairly and unseemly: one client is too anxious for trauma memories, one too resistant for imagery techniques, one too filled with catastrophic self statements, etc. But, wherever the client is at, it is our belief that psychotherapy that is lasting is ultimately one that provides a journey into subjectivity. Not only is it a press toward interiority mostly through cognitive constructs, but also through affect and behavior.

In this chapter we have attempted to provide some principles for treating this unaware process. Until clinicians develop a better vocabulary (science) to represent their own internal personal operations at key moments in therapy, we can only approach this real process *post hoc*. Our formulation and procedures only approximate the existential pain of trauma. As we said before, always something more is present (Bugental, 1987).

REFERENCES

Abueg, F., Gusman, F., & Friedman, M. (1991). Emotional structural preparedness (ESP): A comprehensive model for management of traumatic stress. In Operation Desert Storm Clinician Packet DDSCP. White River Junction, VT: National Center for PTSD.

Alexander, F., & French, T. (1946). *Psychoanalytic therapy: Principles and application.* Lincoln: University of Nebraska Press.

Armstrong, K., O'Callahan, W., Marmar (1991). Debriefing Red Cross disaster personnel: The Multiple Stressor Debriefing Model. *Journal of Traumatic Stress, 4,* 581-594.

Atkinson, R. M., Henderson, R. G., Sparr, L. F., & Deale, S. (1982). Assessment of Vietnam veterans for posttraumatic stress disorder in Veterans Administration disability claims. The *American Journal of Psychiatry, 139,* 1118-1121.

Baumeister, R. F., Stilwell, A., & Wotman, S. R. (1990). Victim and perpetrator accounts of interpersonal conflict: Autobiographical narratives about anger. *Journal of Personality and Social Psychology, 59,* 994-1005.

Beck, A. (1976). *Depression: Clinical, Experimental and Theoretical Aspects.* New York: Harper and Row.

Beck, A., & Freeman, A. (1990). *Cognitive therapy of personality disorders.* New York: Guilford Press.

Beutler, L. (1991). Have we all won and must all have prizes? Revising Luborsky's et al.'s verdict. *Journal of Consulting and Clinical Psychology, 52,* 226-232.

Beutler, L., & Clarkin, J. (1990). *Systematic treatment selection: Toward targeted therapeutic intervention.* New York: Brunner/Mazel.

Blank, A. (1985). Irrational reaction to post-traumatic stress disorder and Vietnam veterans. In S. Sonnenberg, A. Blank, J., & Talbott (Eds.) *The trauma of war: Stress and recovery in Vietnam veterans* (pp. 69-98). Washington: D.C.: American Psychiatric Press.

Bowers, W. (1991). Psychosocial treatment for simple phobic, obsessive-compulsive disorders, posttraumatic stress disorder, and social phobia. In W. Coryell & G. Winohun (Eds.), *The Clinical Management of Anxiety Disorders.* New York: Oxford University Press.

Brom, D., & Kleber, R. J. (1989). Prevention of posttraumatic stress disorder. *Journal of Traumatic Stress, 2,* 335-351.

Bugental, J. (1987). *The art of the psychotherapist.* New York: Norton Press.

Butler, S., & Strupp, H. (1991). The role of affect in time limited dynamic psychotherapy. In J. Safran and G. Grienberg (Eds.), *Psychotherapy and change* (pp. 83-112). New York: Guilford Press.

Carson, R. C. (1982). Self-fulfilling prophecy, maladaptive behavior, and psychotherapy. In J. C. Anchin & D. J. Kiesler (Eds.), *Handbook of interpersonal psychotherapy,* New York: Pergamon Press.

Cashdan, S. (1973). *Interactional psychotherapy: Stages and strategies in behavioral change* (pp. 3-4). New York: Grune & Stratton.

Catherall, D. C. (1991, Spring). Aggression and projective identification in the treatment of victims. *Psychotherapy, 28,* 145-149.

Davanloo, H. (1980). A method of short-term dynamic psychotherapy. In H. Davanloo (Ed.), *Short-term Dynamic Psychotherapy* (pp. 43-71). New York: Jason Aronson.

Davidson, J., Smith, R., & Kudler, H. (1989). Familial psychiatric illness in chronic posttraumatic stress disorder. *Comprehensive Psychiatry, 30,* 339-345.

de Shazer, S. (1985). *Keys to solution in brief therapy.* New York: Norton.

Dewey, J. (1934). The live creature. In J. J. McDermott (Ed.), *The philosophy of John Dewey* (2 Vol). Chicago: Universal-Chicago Press.

Donovan, J. (1987). Brief dynamic psychotherapy: Toward a more comprehensive model. *Psychiatry, 50,* 167-183.

Dye, E., & Roth, S. (1991, Spring). Psychotherapy with Vietnam veterans and rape and incest survivors. *Psychotherapy, 28,* 103-120.

Dyregrov, A., & Mitchell J. (1992). Work with traumatic children: Psychological effects and coping strategies. *Journal of Traumatic Stress, 5,* 5-19.

Early, E. (1990). Imagined, exaggerated and malingered posttraumatic stress disorder. In C. Meek (Ed.), *Post-traumatic stress disorder: Assessment, differential diagnosis and forensic evaluation* (pp. 137-156). Sarasota, FL: Professional Resource Exchange, Inc.

Everly, G. (1989). *A clinical guide to the treatment of the human stress response*. New York: Plenum.

Fairbank, J. A., & Nicholson, R. A. (1987). Theoretical and empirical issues in the treatment of posttraumatic stress disorder in Vietnam veterans. *Journal of Clinical Psychology, 43*, 44-55.

Fairbank, J., Schlenger, W., Caddell, J., & Woods, G. (in press). Post-traumatic stress disorder. In P. Sutker & H. Adams (Eds.), *Comprehensive handbook of psychopathology* (2nd ed.).

Figley, C. (1988). A five phase treatment of post-traumatic stress disorder in families. *Journal of Traumatic Stress, 1*, 127-141.

Foa, E., & Kozak, M. (1986). Emotional processing of fear: Exposure to corrective information. *Psychological Bulletin, 99*, 20-35.

Friedman, M. (1991). Biological approaches to the diagnosis and treatment of post-traumatic stress disorder. *Journal of Traumatic Stress, 4*(1), 67-93.

Ganaway, G. (1989). Historical versus narrative truth: Clarifying the role of exogenous trauma in the etiology of MPD and its variants. *Dissociation, II*, 205-220.

Gelder, M. (1991). Psychological treatment for anxiety disorders: Adjustment Disorders with Anxious Mood, Generalized Anxiety Disorders, Panic Disorders, Agoraphobia, and Avoidant Personality. In W. Goryell & G. Winohus (Eds.), *The clinical management of anxiety disorders* (pp. 10-27). New York: Oxford University Press.

Gendlin, E. (1991). On emotion in therapy. In J. Safran & L. Greenberg (Eds.), *Emotion, psychotherapy and change* (pp. 255-279). New York: Guilford Press.

Gill, M. (1982). *Analysis of transference*. New York: International Universities Press.

Harvey, J., Orbuch, T., Chivalisz, K., & Garwood, G. (1991). Coping with sexual assault: The roles of account making and confiding. *Journal of Traumatic Stress, 4*, 515-532.

Horowitz, M. J. (1973). Phase oriented treatment of stress response syndromes. *American Journal of Psychotherapy, 27*, 506-515.

Horowitz, M. J. (1976). Psychic trauma: Return of images after a stress response syndrome. In H. Parad, H. Resnick, & L. Parad (Eds.), *Emergency and disaster management: A mental health source book.* Bowie, MD: The Charles Press.

Horowitz, M. J. (1986). Stress-response syndromes: A review of posttraumatic and adjustment disorders. *Hospital and Community Psychiatry, 37,* 241-249.

Howes, J., & Parrott, C. (1991). Conceptualization and flexibility in cognitive therapy. In T. Vallis, J. Howes, & P. Miller (Eds), *The Challenge of cognitive therapy: Application to nontraditional populations.* New York: Plenum.

Hyer, L., Swanson, G., Lefkowitz, R., Hillesland, D., Davis, H., & Woods, G. (1990). The application of the cognitive behavioral model to two older stressor groups. In T. Brink (Ed.) *Mental health in the nursing home* (pp. 145-190). New York: Haworth Press.

Hyer, L., Woods, M., & Boudewyns, P. (1991). A three tier evaluation of posttraumatic stress disorder. *Journal of Traumatic Stress, 4*(2), 165-194.

Janoff-Bulman, R. (1989). Assumptive worlds and the stress of traumatic events: Applications of the schema construct. *Social Cognition, 7,* 113-136.

Kahn, M. (1991). *Between therapist and client: The new relationship.* New York: Freeman.

Kendall, P. (in press). Healthy thinking. *Behavior Therapy.*

Kiesler, D. J. (1982). Interpersonal theory for personality and psychotherapy. In J. C. Anchin & D. J. Kiesler (Eds.), *Handbook of interpersonal psychotherapy.* Elmsford, NY: Pergamon Press.

L'Abate, L. (1992). *Programmed writing: A self administered approach for interventions with individuals, couples, and families.* Pacific Grove, CA: Brooks/Cole.

Laufer, R. S., Brett, E., & Gallops, M. S. (1985). Symptom patterns asociated with posttraumatic stress disorder among Vietnam veterans exposed to war trauma. *The American Journal of Psychiatry, 142,* 1304-1311.

Lifton, R. (1967). *Death in life: Survivors of Hiroshima.* New York: Random House.

Luborsky, L., Crits-Christoph, P., & Mellon, J. (1986). Advent of objective measures of the transference concept. *Journal of Consulting and Clinical Psychology, 54,* 39-47.

Lyons, J. A. (1991). Strategies for assessing the potential for positive adjusting following trauma. *Journal of Traumatic Stress, 4*(1), 113-122.

McAdams, D. (1985). *Power, intimacy and life story: Personological inquiries into identity.* Homewood, IL: Dorsey.

McAdams, D. (1990). Unity and purpose in human lives: The emergence of identity as a life story. In A. Rabin, R. Zucker, R. Emmons, & S. Frank (Eds.) *Studying persons and lives (pp. 148-200).* New York: Springer.

McCann, L., & Pearlman, L. (1990a). *Psychological trauma and the adult survivor: Theory, therapies, and transformation.* New York: Brunner/Mazel.

McCann, L., & Pearlman, L. (1990b). Vicarious traumatization: A framework for understanding the psychological effects of working with victims. *Journal of Traumatic Stress, 3*(1), 131-150.

McCormick, R., Taber, J., & Kruedelbrach, D. (1989). The relationship between attibutional style and post-traumatic stress disorder in addicted patients. *Journal of Traumatic Stress, 2*(4), 477-488.

Mahoney, M. C. (1991). *Human change processes: The scientific foundations of psychotherapy.* Delran, NJ: Basic Books.

Mahrer, A. (1989). *Dream work in psychotherapy and self-change.* New York: Norton Press.

Mahrer, A., & Nadler, W. (1986). Good moments in psychotherapy: A preliminary review, a list, and some promising research avenues. *Journal of Consulting and Clinical Psychotherapy, 54,* 10-15.

Mann, J. (1973). *Time-limited psychotherapy.* Cambridge, MA: Harvard University Press.

Meichenbaum, D. (1991). Stress inoculation training: A twenty year update. In R. Woolfolk and P. Lehrer (Eds.), *Principles and practice of stress management.* New York: Guilford Press.

Meichenbaum, D., & Fitzpatrick, D. (1991). A narrative constructivist perspective of stress and coping: Stress inoculation applications. In L. Goldberger & S. Breznitz (Eds.), *Handbook of stress.* New York. Free Press.

Miller, W. R., & Rollnick, S. (1991). *Motivational Interviewing: Preparing people to change addictive behavior.* New York: Guilford Press.

Millon, T. (1969). *Modern psychopathology.* Philadelphia, PA: Saunders.

Mueser, K. T., & Butler, R. W. (1987). Auditory hallucinations in combat-related chronic Posttraumatic Stress Disorder. *The American Journal of Psychiatry, 144,* 299-300.

Ochberg, F. (1991, Spring). Post-traumatic therapy. *Psychotherapy, 28,* 5-15.

Ochberg, F. (1988). Post traumatic therapy and victims of violence. In F. Ochberg (Ed.) *Post-traumatic therapy and victims of violence* (pp. 870-875). New York: Brunner-Mazel.

Parrott, C. & Howes, J. (1991). The application of cognitive therapy to posttraumatic stress disorder. In T. Vallis, J. Howes, & P. Miller (Eds.) *The challenge of cognitive therapy: Application to nontraditional populations* (pp. 85-109). New York: Plenum.

Parry, A. (1991). A universe of stories. *Family Process, 30,* 37-54.

Parson, F. (1988). Post-traumatic self disorders (PTsFD): Theoretical and practical considerations in psychotherapy of Vietnam war veterans. In J. P. Wilson, Z. Harel & B. Kahana (Eds.), *Human adaptation to extreme stress: From the Holocaust to Vietnam.* New York: Plenum.

Penk, W., Peck, R., Robinowitz, R., Bell, W., & Little, D. (1988). Coping and defending styles among Vietnam combat veterans seeking treatment for posttraumatic stress disorder and substance abuse disorder. In M. Galanter (Ed.), *Recent developments in alcoholism: Vol. 6.* New York: Plenum.

Pennebaker, J. W . (1989). Confession, inhibition, and disease. In L. Berkowitz (Ed.), *Advances in experimental social psychology, Vol.22* (pp. 211-244). Orlando, FL: Academic Press.

Peterson, K., Prout, M., & Schwartz, R. (1991). *Post-traumatic stress disorder: A clinician's guide.* New York: Plenum.

Prochaska, J., Velicur, W., DiClemente, C., & Fava, J. (1988). Measuring processes of change: Application to the cessation of smoking. *Journal of Consulting and Clinical Psychology, 56,* 520-528.

Resick, P. A., Jordan, C. G., Girelli, S. A., Hutter, C. K., & Marhoefer-Dvorak, S. (1988). A comparative outcome study of behavioral group therapy for sexual assault victims. *Behavior Therapy, 19,* 385-401.

Rice, L. N. (1984). Client tasks in client-centered therapy. In R. F. Levant & J. M. Shlien (Eds.), *Client-centered therapy and the person-centered approach: New directions in theory, research, and practice.*

Rosenheck, R., & Nathan, P. (1985). Secondary traumatization in children of Vietnam veterans. *Hospital and Community Psychiatry, 36,* 538-539.

Rothstein, M., & Vallis M. (1991). The application of cognitive therapy to patients with personality disorders. In T. Vallis, J. Howes, & P. Miller (Eds.), *The Challenge of cognitive therapy: Application to nontraditional populations* (pp. 59-84). New York: Plenum.

Rozynko, V., & Dondershine, H. (1991, Spring). Trauma focus group therapy for Vietnam veterans with PTSD. *Psychotherapy, 28,* 157-161.

Safran, J., & Greenberg, J. (Eds.) (1991). *Emotion, psychotherapy and change.* New York: Guilford Press.

Safran, J., & Segal, Z. (1990). *Interpersonal processing in cognitive therapy.* New York: Basic Books.

Schrader, S., & Steele, K. (1992, May 29). Abreactive work with survivors of childhood abuse: Theory, process, and techniques. Workshop presented at the Georgia Psychological Association. Savannah, GA.

Scurfield, R., Kenderdine S., & Pollard, R. (1990). Inpatient treatment for war-related posttraumatic stress disorder: Initial findings on a longer term outcome study. *Journal of Traumatic Stress, 3,* 2, 185-202.

Sifneos, P. E. (1972). *Short-term psychotherapy and emotional crisis.* Cambridge, Mass.: Harvard University Press.

Silberschatz, G. (1987). Testing pathogenic beliefs. In J. Weiss, H. Sampson, & The Mount Zion Psychotherapy Research Group (Eds.), *The Psychoanalytic process: Theory, clinical observation, and empirical research.* New York: Guilford Press.

Solomon, Z. (1990). Back to the front: Recurrent exposure to combat stress and reactivation of posttraumatic stress disorders. In M. Wolfe & A. Mosnahn (Eds.), *Posttraumatic stress disorder: Etiology, Phenomenology, and treatment.* Washington, DC: American Psychiatric Press.

Solomon, Z., Bleich, A., Shoham, S., Nardi, C., & Kotler, M. (1992). The "Koach" Project for treatment of combat-related PTSD: rationale, aims, and methodology. *Journal of Traumatic Stress, 5*, 175-194.

Sullivan, H. S. (1956). *Clinical studies in psychiatry*. New York: W. W. Norton.

Sundland, D. (1977). Theoretical orientation: A multiprofessional American sample. Paper presented at the eighth annual meeting of the Society for Psychotherapy Research. Madison, WI.

Talbot, A., Manton, M., & Dunn, P. (1992). Debriefing the debriefers: An intervention strategy to assist psychologists after a crisis. *Journal of Traumatic Stress, 5*, 19-37.

Tichner, J. (1985). Post-traumatic decline: A consequence of unresolved destructive drives. In C. Figley (Ed.), *Trauma and its wake: Volume II: Traumatic stress, theory, research, and intervention* (pp. 5-19). New York: Brunner/Mazel.

Turkat, I. (1991). *The personality disorders: A psychological approach to clinical management*. New York: Pergamon Press.

Verbosky, S. J., & Ryan, D. A. (1988). Female partners of Vietnam veterans: Stress by proximity. *Issues in Mental Health Nursing, 9*, 95-104.

Veronen, L. J., & Kilpatrick, D. G. (1983). Stress management for rape victims. In D. Meichenbaum & M. E. Jaremko (Eds.), *Stress reduction and prevention*. New York: Plenum.

Walter, J. L., & Peller, J. E. (1992). *Becoming solution-focused in brief therapy*. New York: Brunner/Mazel, Inc.

Weiss, J. (1971). The emergence of new themes: A contribution to the psychoanalytic theory of therapy. *International Journal of Psycho-Analysis, 52*, 459-467.

Weiss, J., Sampson, H., & The Mount Zion Psychotherapy Research Group (Eds.) (1987). *The psychoanalytic process: Theory, clinical observation and empirical research*. New York: Guilford Press.

Wilson, J. (1989). *Traumatic transformation and healing: An integrative approach to theory, research and post-traumatic therapy*. New York: Brunner/Mazel.

Winokur, G., & Coryell, W. (1991). Anxiety disorders: The magnitude of the problem. In W. Coryell & G. Winokur (Eds.), *The clinical management of anxiety disorders*. New York: Oxford University Press.

Wolfe, J. (1991). Applying principles of critical incident debriefing to the therapeutic management of acute combat stress. In Operation Desert Storm Clinician Packet OPS-CP. White River Junction, VT: National Center for PTSD.

Young, J. (1990). *Cognitive therapy for personality disorders: A schema focused approach.* Saratoga, FL: Professional Resource Exchange.

NOTE: Other authors (e.g., Safran and Greenberg, 1991) define *top-down* as processing where the emphasis is exploring and challenging beliefs, and *bottom-up* as processing that emphasizes the access of emotions (emotional processing). In this book, top-down refers to therapeutic interventions that are largely cognitive and "external" to the process. Bottom-up, on the other hand, is a person-based intervention, accessing more core (often emotional) processes ("deeper," coming from the schema).

7

THE THERAPEUTIC RELATIONSHIP

Jeffrey M. Brandsma
and
Lee Hyer

Together
It's time spent together that matters
Together is never alone
Say what you feel and feel what is said
The wisdom in time will be shown. (James Martin, circa 1988)

Relationship and technique have long been the two touchstones for organizing the phenomenon of successful therapy. Neither is complete without the other. Clearly, however, without a context of relationship grounding them, even the best techniques will fall on infertile soil. In dealing with trauma victims, attention to the therapeutic relationship is an absolute imperative; it is an essential part of facilitating the healing process. In fact, to find any therapeutic writing on the treatment of PTSD without relationship issues being highlighted is virtually impossible.

The history of attempts to ameliorate human suffering is replete with false starts, marginally effective interventions, and even harmful practices. This is true in the area of treating trauma victims. We now know that the trauma itself and the immediate post-traumatic period are critical to determining how the victim will respond over time. A post-trauma period of distinct helplessness/vulnerability appears to exist which may crystallize, or conversely, if "succored," will diminish the trauma over time. But the "second wound" is waiting to metastasize if help is not forthcoming. If left untreated, victims are likely to continue seeking reassurance and be unable to move successfully beyond this stage. PTSD that becomes chronic is the most virulent form of the process and often shows a deteriorating pattern. Clearly the best treatment for trauma is on-the-scene support, short-term follow-up, and brief crisis counseling. Understandably, but unfortunately, mental health professionals are rarely the persons who interact with victims immediately after their victimization and during the critical period.

Psychotherapy always has been more of an art than a science. Its curative elements seem to stay just beyond scientific reach. Ultimately, the client needs to feel safe and motivated to work. A central element of this process is client openness in the pursuit of defined problems. Necessarily, this involves the working relationship (working alliance) and attendant nonspecific features: hope, care, unconditional acceptance, listening, genuineness, and the like. These are the elements that keep the patient open, cooperative, and not defensive; and they help the therapist remain thoughtful and reasonable in the face of challenges or even deprecation.

The pain of trauma is not something that can be fixed; it must be healed. The healing can occur in two ways—through the experience of identification between the therapist and client, and through the treatment factors of exposure and meaning shift. The first of these depends on relationship. The second depends on both exposure technique and the cognitive pursuit of meaning shift. Both are equal in their importance to the trauma victim's therapy. While exposure and the search for meaning are addressed in other chapters, separating these from the relationship is a quixotic venture.

They intermix to provide the needed healing in treatment. The importance of relationship mandates that techniques in the treatment of trauma are not isolated, but wholly integrated into the treatment experience. The treatment process then becomes "dynamic," involving positive mirroring, hopefulness, and commitment, as well as re-exposure and the understanding of self. One might even argue that only to the degree that the relationship is experienced as real are the techniques permitted to have input toward and impact on the healing process. Only in a relationship can a client reexperience pain therapeutically.

The purpose of this chapter is to highlight the elements of relationship that are facilitative in dealing with traumatized people. The nature of the generalized therapeutic alliance has been addressed in a much more sophisticated fashion by such pioneers in the field as Sigmund Freud, Carl Rogers, Hans Strupp, and James Bugental. We shall attempt to address four issues more specifically. First, the essential aspect of trauma, a shattered self, is considered. However, this time we emphasize two distinct therapeutic tasks—one related to the trauma and the other to the aftermath. Second, the therapeutic relationship is more directly discussed. The belief is that the successful therapeutic relationship involves two tasks—therapeutic concern by the therapist and the commitment to work by the client. Next, two working components involved and intrinsic to the relationship, education and disengagement, are elucidated. In this instance, a major pitfall is the presence of misalliance (and resistance). Finally, a seldom discussed aspect of treatment with trauma sufferers—therapeutic commitment—ends this chapter.

PRIMARY AND SECONDARY TRAUMA

Remember that the essence of trauma-related problems relate to the individual being unable to assimilate the stressor event at the time of the event. The psychic structure of the person struggles to protect itself from a paralyzing reaction to the trauma stimulus. The personality breaks down structurally as "death drips into life." Some part of a person's self is abused in trauma, a portion that has been protected and self-reinforced. The person's view of self is shattered— the self is no longer healthy, is no longer safe, and can no longer depend on the usual comings and goings of life. Janoff-Bulman (1985) described this inner shattering as an attack on basic world assumptions—self-worth, predictability, and benevolence in the world. In addition, the effort of the ego to contain the traumatic material is infected with a festering wound and maladaptive efforts at ongoing damage control. These have been labeled the "trauma membrane." Thus, a constellation of defense mechanisms and associated behaviors surround the trauma-related affects and cognitions, and prevent their being assimilated. This is all part of the primary trauma itself, which was originally a "free radical" in the psychic equation, but now has costly checks and balances.

Concomitantly symptoms develop, including an impaired relationship between the individual and the environment. This has been labeled the secondary trauma and is defined as the breakdown in the individual's relationship with his/her social world. Symptoms related to this conflict are seen in the individual's interpersonal world—social withdrawal, lack of pleasure, alienation, identity diffusion, lowered self-esteem, and acting out. The primary trauma involves problems of inner affective turmoil and ego control. The secondary trauma, problems of the self, is defined in terms of its interrelationship with others (Catherall, 1989) (Table 7.1).

Etiologically the model is straightforward. The healthy self is basically formed early by good parenting. Problems evolve when no validation of the child's unique needs for empathy and importance is forthcoming. When trauma occurs, the victim is the "child part" of the personality. The victim then seeks sanctuary to fulfill these needs and to prevent a state of fragmentation, weakness, or disharmony. Often this is not forthcoming, largely because cultural self-objects (e.g., family, doctors, national organizations) do not validate certain actions or experiences. For example, in the Vietnam experience the returning soldier often felt no sense of commitment from society or the government. In addition, the medical establishment was virtually unaware of PTSD. The rape victim whose spouse no longer sees her as sexually desirable suffers a similar self and self-object breakdown. At this point, this combination of trauma (primary) and lack of validation (secondary) dictates the best adaptation the victim can muster. The adaptation becomes PTSD.

TABLE 7.1
Primary and Secondary Trauma*

Primary Trauma	Signs	Therapeutic Response
-trauma memory	-issues of stressor	-understand trauma in context of person
-ego	-stimuli of trauma	-interpret trauma or classify confusion
	-central affect of trauma	-strengthen experiencing ego
	-symptoms of trauma: flashbacks, numbing, intrusions	
	-dynamics of trauma: helplessness, meaning, fears, loss, pain	

Secondary Trauma	Signs	Therapeutic Response
-interpersonal problems	-not being understood	-empathy/understanding
-self	-alienation	-interpret alliance
-"second wound"	-relationship with people	-foster social contact
	-impulse control	
	-rage/bitterness	
	-feeling alone	
	-unable to love or "connect"	

*Extrapolated from Catherall, 1989.

Treatment Application—Primary Trauma

This distinction may at first appear simple, but it is actually rather complex. Catherall (1989) specified how these two conflicts should be treated differently. Treatment of the primary trauma entails aiding the mechanisms of the ego in their effort to bring the trauma material into consciousness and assimilate it. The therapist must be allowed to penetrate the *trauma membrane* by presenting a "good-enough" holding environment with a strong therapeutic alliance and by encouraging exploration of the traumatic material. This is titrated with the victim's tolerance level for experiencing the discouraging affect. The therapist's task is to provide understanding and exposure to the trauma. In turn, this material requires processing for meaning. Figley (1988) identified five steps in this examination process: what happened, why it happened, why he/she behaved the way he/she did, how he/she changed because of what happened, and what he/she will do if it happens again. This is the "stuff" of the trauma: sometimes whole and sometimes apperceived. The therapeutic aims are exposure (titrated to the ego skills of the client) and shift of psychological meaning for the person. The goal is a more complete accommodation through the relationship. As Catherall (1989) stated, "as the therapeutic relationship grows and the trauma survivor's observing ego feels connected to and strengthened by the therapist's ego, then the experiencing ego becomes less subject to being disorganized by the trauma affects, and more able to examine and experience that trauma material" (p. 293). The absence of validation becomes a problem. When the expected sanctuary (be it a therapy session, hospital, family, or country) provides an unfriendly reception, secondary trauma results. Then, primary trauma defenses are used to handle the secondary trauma (Obenchain & Silver, 1992).

Treatment Application—Secondary Trauma

The secondary trauma is treated differently. The therapist must aid the natural growth mechanisms of the self in its efforts to reestablish memory and self-coherence. By engaging in a relationship that will allow the trauma survivor to establish self-esteem and reengage in the needed developmental processes, the therapist provides the victim with the experience of being understood, valued, and cared about. The goal of treatment here is to bring the person to his/her old "self" and sense of esteem maintained prior to the trauma. The goal is for the victim to feel accepted and understood. If the individual had premorbid defects in the self, then treatment of course may need to continue beyond the trauma event. Therapeutic tools include accurate empathy, understanding, bonding, therapeutic alliance, and the therapeutic element of caring.

The trauma sufferer will vacillate between problems related to either state. However, appreciating the distinction is important because this awareness is responsible for a therapeutic response and the titration of the work of therapy. In fact, no better underpinning can be obtained for trust than an appreciation of this key difference and differential response. When the primary trauma is at issue, probing and exposure are paramount. When secondary trauma is activated, emotional experiences must be heard and acknowledged with some degree of accurate empathy. When alienation is understood by another, a person is no longer alienated. When suffering is providing meaning, it ceases to be useless or needless.

Through this interplay of primary and secondary trauma, the therapist is an external toggle switch, placing the emphasis in the care equation where it belongs. At times he/she is a "container" for trauma pain, and at other times a holding environment for control and care. Recall that the client is being "educated" before and during this relationship process. He/she attempts to comply with his/her new collaborative role: to know self, to be his/her personal scientist or observer, and to remain open to the deliberative and therapeutic struggle. Ultimately, the client becomes his/her own therapist, as he/she rearranges his/her relationship to his/her own internal painful parts.

Naturally, other therapeutic processes coexist. From task identification to termination, hundreds of choices are possible. However, a respect for the trauma victim's primary and secondary trauma provides a structure for these other elements to fall into place. Through the internal structure of each session, tempered by pacing and trauma boundaries, a living process can unfold. This is dose-related care, a recognition of the patient's limits and helping maintain boundaries so that pain is not exacerbated by a frightening and painful decompensation or by avoidance. The curative elements of the human change process take form. Over time, like the chess master, the therapist begins to "know" the potential moves and the distinction becomes intuitive. This helps in cases which the client's need is not clear cut or something else is necessary.

THERAPIST CONCERN AND CLIENT COMMITMENT

This primary and secondary trauma model represents the intrapsychic and interpersonal landscape. Now the major task is that of commitment to the work by both therapist and client. The former's is labeled concern (Bugental, 1987), and the latter's, client commitment. The pursuit of these consonant goals represents a delicate balance and sometimes a risky therapeutic undertaking.

Clients who are victims of trauma seek reassurance, understanding, and fixing. An understanding of these alone, however, does not necessarily result in effective functioning. Victims of trauma are suffering and require assistance with symptoms. These must be addressed, but a bigger picture involves a collaboration of the person of the victim and his/ her role in the trauma and in life. In this process the central task of the therapist is to keep the client open, non-defensive, and in constant touch with his/her known agenda. This is the "holding environment" that allows for a flexible bandwidth between safety and struggle. This is more than listening or nondirective confirmation. It is a dynamic sense that the therapist and client are both taking issues very seriously. It is concern.

Therapeutic Concern

Bugental specified "parts" to concern, including pain, hope, and inwardness. The client knows more than anything that "this is me suffering." The priority of concern is to validate the pain, but not to allow this to become the ultimate outcome. Something must be done with the pain. As pain exploration occurs, the "parts" of the trauma become rearranged, and greater understanding and perspective ensues. This allows a vision of hope—a way out. Often the victim distracts himself/ herself from hope, denies hope, or inappropriately wallows in hopelessness. The clinician addresses hopelessness, draws it out, is patient with it, and allows ownership of it. With hope, the client can come to the problem again, this time bringing new resources.

If pain and hope are the seesaw of concern, then inwardness is the fulcrum. The "place" for therapy is the interior self. The avoidant mechanisms of PTSD have resulted in victims becoming expert at denial, withdrawal, escape, and defense. Consequently, some components of the experiences of trauma will never be deconditioned or cognitively integrated. But the inward orientation allows the client to know that inner mastery, voluntary control, and meaning can overcome doubt and pain. The victim is most ambivalent about this task and seeks relief. Dosing the inward pursuit with care and permission on one hand, and allowing pain and doubt on the other, the clinician reconstitutes a respect in personhood and teaches that cure is not certain, but this struggle can be curative and actualizing. This is a careful dance of attachment and emotional regulation. The victim, however, is the only valid compass in its pursuit.

Nevertheless, the clinician must be ever wary. To collude in the process of avoidance is easy. Stale moments, excessively painful moments, and long therapeutic plateaus are especially risky. If these moments can be tolerated, reflected, and understood, a renewal of trust in self hungers to wrest the intrusion and avoidance patterns from their traumatic moorings. The victim's core referential and resource frames (the person's boundaries for change) always must be validated.

Client Commitment

Commitment is the superordinate task of the client. It includes the direct and indirect requirements of treatment: money, time, energy, planning, introspection, etc. Through these efforts, treatment becomes more than just sessions. The relationship becomes "covenantal"—a commitment with the professional that exceeds and transcends contract(s). It becomes a donative investment in a task that is workable and doable only through collaboration. It becomes a guarantee that the two can somehow stumble through the horror of trauma and the failures of life and come out whole to a greater degree. It is acting on the assumption that one's organization of life can be reoriented.

This is a considered and calculated interpersonal process between clinician and client in which the level of involvement is matched on behalf of increased "interiority." Therapeutic concern and client commitment allow this to come into being. Ultimately, good therapy conforms to the needs (skills, desires, etc.) of the client. But, the application of therapeutic concern heightens the client's ability to allow the therapist to share control. As therapy proceeds the stakes become higher. It starts from "I am with you" messages, continues with an interiority focus, and ends with hope and mastery.

One significant pitfall in the process is the victim role of the sufferer. The victim tries to seek information, to depend on diagnosis, and to use concrete strategies to objectify self. How the victim treats his/her inner life becomes the prepotent issue. What bothers each about himself/herself, the form of his/her presentation, how he/she asks for help, defends, gestures, and requests, become major emphases. These are important for coping, but placing of the power of the problem in the problem itself is self-defeating. Intervention tending toward the interior experience is important. Ultimately, the success of interiority will depend on a number of considerations—the nature of the current problem, the client's level of sophistication and ego functions, the amount of change desired, inner fears, etc. But, the argument is that only the therapeutic press into this realm will yield an understanding and respect for self. All else becomes a reinforcement of chronicity.

TWO "META" RELATIONSHIP TASKS

The position throughout this book has been that psychotherapy is the mainstay for treatment of PTSD. Furthermore, repeatedly the statement has been that person dynamics are more salient to treatment ends than survivor dynamics. Keeping the client open, committed, psychologically minded, and tied to the relationship are the necessary ingredients for this task. In addition, two other relationship-related processes are deemed important. Both follow and intermix with relationship dynamics; that is, they depend on it and support it. In addition, both are basic to the process of treatment.

Disengagement

The first relationship task is the **treatment process of disengagement** ("unhooking"). We have already discussed important aspects of this component (Chapter 6). Often the assumption is that the victim of trauma demonstrates behavior that is totally foreign to his/her self-image and that this must somehow be fixed. In fact, a better assumption would be that the victim is behaving in therapy in ways very much like all other relationships. A fundamental observation of the interpersonal theorist is that a considerable redundancy occurs in interpersonal patterns, and that these reflect core cognitions. PTSD victims display a pattern that is familiar and seek effects that are expected. This has been labeled "reciprocal causality" (Bandura, 1977), meaning that behavior is simultaneously its own cause and effect. With trauma victims these patterns become rather maladaptive, being both self-fulfilling and self-perpetuating. In this interpersonal forum, clarity of the cognitive construals and requisite interpersonal actions are enacted. This is the cognitive-interpersonal cycle. Therefore, at some point an important procedure is to identify the evoking style of the client. The client is "director" of his/her own drama. These patterns, the goals and destructive ends, play out interpersonally and reinforce the pattern in repetitive fashion.

Of course this does occur in a sequence. In early therapy sessions the client will evoke or pull covert or overt responses from the therapist that are precisely characterized to be complementary to those that define the client's maladaptive interpersonal behavior. This has been called the **evoking message** (Kiesler, 1986). In this case, the therapist is "hooked," experiencing greater or lesser intensities of these impact messages. At some point, however, the therapist is to disengage and to provide anticomplementary responses (Chapter 6). This has been called the *impact message.* This develops from the internal state of the therapist—his/her inner decoding of what the client wants. Most therapists have developed methods to be sensitive to this process. The therapist needs and has an internal governor that is calibrated to the client's evoking messages. In this sense, the therapist is truly "bilingual," part of the patient's reality and apart from it.

These two aspects constitute the interpersonal frame from which the therapist responds: What does the client want from me, and what do I feel in this situation? This interaction forms the needed information for the shaping process that the therapist is "supposed" to fit into. Cashdan (1982) held that the therapist cannot be uncontrollably involved or "hooked" in the process. The more extreme the behavior of the client, the greater the pull. When the therapist realizes he/she has been invited to be entertained, he/she can choose not to enjoy the entertainment. When he/she has been enticed to provide answers and advice, he/she can withhold these. The aid is to present the client with disengaged or asocial responses, sufficient "beneficial uncertainty." The client's preferred style does not produce the expected and familiar interpersonal consequences; this is the anticomplementary response.

In previous chapters, we provided the skeleton to this process (Table 6.9). The emphasis of this table was on the first basic task, being aware of the impact messages and the therapist's own feeling. Both client reading (impact message) and self reading (own feelings) are required for unhooking to occur. Now we take this process deeper as the unhooking phase unfolds. In Table 7.2 is presented a procedure and interventions for this to occur.

Unhooking

At this moment the therapist acts on the client's evoking messages differently. The therapist disrupts normal patterns by calling attention to them or disconfirming them. Usually the therapist can start with client features that are redundant, doubtful, or negative. This is the simplest level of the unhooking process: anticomplementarity upsets the client's expectations.

TABLE 7.2
Therapeutic Relationship Actions*

Therapist's Procedures and Interventions

Stages

1. Therapist is hooked
   -Empathetic listening and validation
   -Reading client's feelings

2. Therapist becomes aware of own feelings
   -What does this client want from me?
   -Use interpersonal circle and Table 6.9

3. Therapist unhooks
   -Asocial response
   > Delay—"tell me more"
   > Reflect content, feeling, and accurate empathy
   > Label style of interaction—"I noticed you just---"
   > Use a paradigmatic response—use of humor

4. Therapist provides feedback to client
   -Metacommunication
   > Conveys own feelings to make client aware of impact
   > Conveys own feelings to probe for client's internal experience

   -Oscillation
   > Identifies client's interpersonal behavior versus content
   > Identifies surface versus constructs
   > Identifies client's reaction to constructs versus therapy process

5. Therapist Explores Deeper
   -Elicit emotional immediacy
   -Confront behaviors/constructs
   -Pursue emotional/cognitive blocking
   -Use imagery or concreteness
   -Tag repeatedly constructs or interpersonal markers

---

*Extrapolated from various sources.

At this basic level then, the disengaging task of the therapist is to provide a response opposite to that of complimentarity. At a deeper level the therapist not only provides the anticomplementary response, but also is now "doing therapy." Essentially, this is a process of unhooking from expected reciprocal behaviors, of labeling these interactions, of gentle confrontation with metacommunication, and of providing alternatives. In effect, the therapist is observing the client's interpersonal markers that reflect patterned interpersonal styles. He/she pulls back, labels, and reflects this transaction to the client. The ability of the client to become aware of these action tendencies represents a monitor of treatment. Disengagement then is designed to disrupt typical interpersonal patterns for purposes of maximizing the press for interiority. The tasks and probes in Table 7.2 are intended to represent a process that builds and becomes increasingly immediate, focused, specific, collaborative, and connected to the "person." As the therapist proceeds in Stages 3, 4, and 5, the tasks are often repetitive and intense. The client requires much in the way of support. But at some point this process is taken on by the client, and the goal of empowerment is within sight. Again, this process can only be done in the context of relationship. In turn, it strengthens the relationship.

The therapist disengagement also allows the client to appreciate differences and connections between self-perpetuating patterns and symptoms. Symptoms take on a more "ego syntonic" perspective, from being "out there" to being "something I can make a choice about." The therapist can disaggregate symptoms and provide distinctions so as to form the basis for a more differentiated "theory" for the client. The therapist thus provides a client with a renewed sense of development of his/her person and an altered view of his/her victim status. A big advantage is that the therapist can reframe symptoms as extensions of the client's person. In effect, the client "steps off" his/her own time line or life cycle and is able to resonate to his/her control or influence over the symptoms, not vice versa. With war trauma, a useful procedure often is to discuss the client's youth and naivete and to explain the symptoms as survival mechanisms or "excess meaning" yet to be integrated. This tends to strengthen cognitive controls and eventually desensitize intrusive memories. In this dynamic of disengagement, symptoms become objective in a good way, as the therapist challenges the client to expand self-understanding and over time, self-mastery.

Client Education

The second "meta" relationship task is client education. In the previous chapter we also argued for the importance of education. Here we show its interdependence with the relationship. The point now widely recognized is that a good understanding of the trauma process is a necessary component of treatment. As we had noted in Chapter 6, Brom and Kleber (1989) outlined six elements in adaptation to trauma: an understanding of the process of working through an experience of powerlessness and disruption; the dynamic of intrusion and denial; coping and its disruptions as "normal"; a needed search for meaning (why me?); the possibility of a specific type of disorder (PTSD) that is cyclic; and the fact that each symptom picture is unique and is the result of the person and his/her unique situation. These components represent a holistic, individual-in-charge representation of the problem. These components are discussed and "taught" over time to a level where the participants believe in the formulation offered.

This point cannot be overstated. In the role of the patient, enough education can never exist: what is expected, what are reasonable treatment rules, and what can I do to help with openness and collaboration. This is the instance in which information and basic principles of treatment merge. The therapeutic goal of client education is a commitment for collaboration in the observation and evaluation of the client's experiences. Frequently, clients need to be reminded of the context, the therapeutic "holding environment," in which the rules of the game are different. This realization allows disengagement to be right and fitting for this context. Also, if done well, it allows for the building of trust—a feature of universal concern among sufferers, but of surprising brittleness in actual practice.

In Chapter 6, we discussed the importance of the role of the client in therapy. Clients do best if they know their person parameters, know the rules of the game (commitment to observe their involvement and struggle for change), and allow the therapist to participate in this process. Also, in this chapter we specified the importance of the client's ability to evaluate his/her construals, emotions, security operations, and expectations; the only good client is an active and participating client. We also provide a list that is attached more to the relationship. In Table 7.3, many of the important dimensions in treatment are included A helpful procedure is to have the client rate and discuss these dimensions often. These dimensions conceptualize the client's role, his/her challenges, and his/her inter- and intrapersonal focus. Another helpful procedure is to have the client "appreciate" the stage of psychotherapy readiness he/she is acting on (Prochaska & DiClemente, 1986), as well as the degree of responsibility for cooperation and self-control (Rosenbaum, 1980).

Education also is helpful in many PTSD-specific respects; many symptoms demand understanding. Chronic sufferers have special problems with dissociative experiences or intense and persistent image intrusions. The loss of control, or "going crazy" feeling, is terrifying. An explanation of the nature of intrusion and how and why dissociation occurs and reoccurs presented in a manner that can be understood is of great benefit. (An explanation of the empirical factors of the *Dissociative Experiences Scale* in Chapter 5 may prove helpful.)

Also, physiological hyper reactivity is virtually universal. The nervous system seems to take on a new set point (often exhibited in the easy startle response), which has plagued victims since the war experience. Explaining the biology and learning involved in this process is comforting, often validating the person's struggle. One common result is that trauma sufferers are more open to various hyperarousal treatments (other than medication) such as direct therapeutic exposure, relaxation, or hypnotic techniques.

Ambivalence and Avoidance

Information on the traumatic personality is important to a PTSD formulation—particularly the concepts of ambivalence and avoidance. If presented well, these "words" become templates

TABLE 7.3
Client Self Rating of Therapeutic Dimensions

Directions: Circle the number for each area that you believe represents you on that topic.

1. **Ability to listen to others in an understanding way**
   Not at all   Completely
   able   1: 2: 3: 4: 5: 6: 7: 8: 9   able

2. **Willingness to discuss feelings with others**
   Completely   Completely
   unwilling   1: 2: 3: 4: 5: 6: 7: 8: 9   willing

3. **Awareness of the feelings of others**
   Completely   Completely
   unaware   1: 2: 3: 4: 5: 6: 7: 8: 9   aware

4. **Understanding why I do what I do**
   No under-   Complete
   standing   1: 2: 3: 4: 5: 6: 7: 8: 9   understanding

5. **Tolerance of conflict and antagonism**
   Not   Tolerant
   tolerant   1: 2: 3: 4: 5: 6: 7: 8: 9

6. **Acceptance of expressions of affection and warmth among others**
   Uncomfortable   Readily
                 1: 2: 3: 4: 5: 6: 7: 8: 9

7. **Acceptance of comments about my behavior from others**
   Rejecting   Welcoming
                 1: 2: 3: 4: 5: 6: 7: 8: 9

8. **Willingness to trust others**
   Completely   Completely
   suspicious   1: 2: 3: 4: 5: 6: 7: 8: 9   trusting

(continued)

TABLE 7.3 (continued)

---

9. **Ability to influence others**

| Completely unable | 1: | 2: | 3: | 4: | 5: | 6: | 7: | 8: | 9 | Completely able |

10. **Relations with peers**

| Wholly competitive | 1: | 2: | 3: | 4: | 5: | 6: | 7: | 8: | 9 | Wholly cooperative |

Source: Extrapolated from Johnson, 1972.

to identify self-defeating patterns. Each victim can flesh out his/her pattern and view how his/her character meets his/her symptoms, how person meets PTSD. Ambivalence can be addressed by emphasizing the approach/avoidance conflict in practically every action. Strategically, the therapist tries to emphasize one side as long as possible before shifting to the other. Avoidance can best be considered by focusing on the DSM-III-R central ideas: detachment, hyperalertness, suspicion, and low self-esteem. Avoidance also prevents the victim from any full experience of trauma memory. Now, good evidence exists that "avoiders" demonstrate increased stress in response to explicit directive coping interventions (Meichenbaum, 1991). Developing strategies to monitor this hyperavoidant quality and to inoculate against anticipated pain is helpful.

Thus, when disengagement steps back in the therapeutic process, education steps forward. The former says, "This is the way we need to work"; the latter says, "we begin with the end in mind; this is where we are going." Both establish the primacy of the person of the victim. Both support the goal of the sufferer in the process; that is, understanding/control over the symptom expression. Over time, the process changes from a focus on symptoms to a core conflict within the person. From a research perspective, the victim unlearns the trauma response less as a result of extinction or habituation and more as a result of "data" now available for choice. The clinician never really knows how this struggle against demoralization and pain will unfold. The process does unfold however.

We borrow again from Kahn (1991). He "specified" both the art of the therapist and the evolving process of clients: feeling validated, working on their own current and past patterns, and feeling free to grow beyond themselves. The relationship is all of these.

> So we will let our clients know we have understood, and then we will find ways to let them know that their feelings are more than just understandable: We will let them know that, given their individual histories, we consider those feelings inevitable. (p. 152)

> Then, after a time, having begun to gain some understanding of a client and of the themes of that client's life, the therapist will begin helping the client see that reactions to the therapist are inevitably determined in part by the attitudes and expectations the client carries everywhere. (p. 157)

> Becoming increasingly aware of the themes of the client's life, the therapist will be in a better and better position to help the client see that there is nothing 'bad' about carrying these attitudes and expectations everywhere. Given the events of the client's life, they are fully understandable, in fact, inevitable. (p. 158)

Misalliance

With trauma sufferers, the misalliance is a hard state to avoid. Not only are the many methods of traditional therapy found wanting with this group (thereby leading to dropout or forced compliance), but also the therapist is involved routinely in intense and often negative ways with clients. This occurs as a matter of course in psychotherapy as all injunctions take their toll: good ones lead to a painful focus, bad ones to disengagement. In trauma, sufferers develop features of a traumatic personality, and the ability to sustain a stable, coherent sense of self and others gives way to mistrust, irritability, fear of connection, and a fractured self. Consequently, victims are never fully able to collaborate with the therapist regarding their own experiences.

McCann and Pearlman (1990a) described the toll of schemas in the transference. They held that trauma victims respond with two types of transference: intense transference reactions as a function of normal therapeutic processes, and transference reactions as a result of disturbed schema. Normal transference results in a collusion of pathology due to the therapist's responses being seen as threats to the client's self-esteem, the expectation that the therapist will react poorly to intolerable affects, or the desire for the therapist to show unconditional positive regard. On the other hand, transference reactions to disturbed schemas are logical, predictable, and interpersonally based. The disturbed schema of safety, for example, lies in wait for information about a threatening therapist. The disturbed schema of esteem easily attaches the status of judge and jury to the therapist. These events are modal in treatment, and when modal, require challenge. (See Chapter 6.)

Another common form of misalliance with chronic victims develops due to an emphasis on crisis. This is part and parcel of a therapy that cannot get beyond overreporting and a symptoms oriented focus. With chronic sufferers of PTSD, two testing points frequently present themselves to clinicians. The first is trust. Chronic victims reenact projected distrust with caretakers. Rigidity of cognitive style and "black and white thinking" often prevents any loosening of the distrust. Fortunately trust is not an all-or-none phenomenon, and with time clients become more accepting of treatment. We have found that the best procedure is to accept whatever level of trust the patient can generate and begin work at that point. At times, the therapist may need to be explicit and confront the specific issues of trust through exploration. However, just to acknowledge the level of mistrust is often enough.

Another misalliance problem occurs when external validation for trauma takes precedence. As the person of the victim attaches idiosyncratic meaning to trauma, secondary gains ascend. This becomes more evident as the condition becomes chronic. Titchener and Kapp (1976) noted that something akin to secondary gains happens pervasively to trauma survivors. A "character change" occurs which is related to the sense of the loss of community. Various overreporting forms, such as factitious symptoms, malingering, "romantic identity," distorted guilt reactions, apperceived memories, and focus on compensation interests become evident (Early, 1990). Walking the tightrope between the work of therapy and respect for trauma, while not being "taken down a primrose path," is no easy task. Early (1990) noted "the issue of rewarding a malingerer (false positive) versus denying a trauma survivor (false negative) is not just one of justice, but also of good professional practice, since appropriate treatment often follows accurate recognition and diagnosis of the disorder" (p. 151). Also remember that after a short period of time, the victim's meaning search turns negative—a fruitless iteration of fixed narrative cycling without progress.

Ideally, the therapist should remain neutral in regarding whether the patient deserves to be judged disabled (and to what extent). This issue is important in the context of the patient's natural tendency to take on a trauma identity, i.e., tending to integrate all aspects of their personality into their conceptualization of a "crazy vet" for combat PTSD victims. This often involves an externalization of responsibility onto the society, the armed forces, the Veterans Administration, or other abstractions from the Vietnam drama (Blank, 1985). Above all, therapists must conceptually keep the person separate from the symptoms. The therapist values the person as primary and identifies symptoms in the context of the overall personality. Fortunately in treatment, time commingles with trust allowing for a more accurate portrayal of the person of the trauma victim.

Resistance

Finally, the misalliance often has been associated with *resistance.* Victims of PTSD are at the mercy of resistance because, having been abused, this component "naturally" surfaces. Resistance is the need to protect familiar territory from threat: it is natural, universal, and prevents the victim from being truly subjectively present. It is both specific to the therapy situation and is part of the larger life-style. Rollo May has described how people shrink the world to proportions that feel safe (Bugental, 1987). This process holds off any real immersion into the therapeutic work because the victim avoids expansion of issues or self, maintains a surface orientation, or at worse, objectifies the self. Increasingly noted is that resistance develops because of therapeutic blunders of one sort or other; i.e., the therapist simply did not read the situation correctly (Goldfried, 1983). This is only partly true. While bad therapy may bring on resistance, good therapy works with it. Interventions with resistance start with a view that resistance is natural to therapy and highly useful in understanding the person. A working rubric of resistance is that the clinician should recognize that he/she is not the opponent of the resistance and is definitely not seeking to defeat it. Instead, the focus is on an identification of the "parts" of this process, tagging these repetitively—especially ones that are self-defeating and negatively protective, teaching their effects, and demonstrating alternatives. In Table 7.4 is provided an outline of this process. The clinician teaches the purpose of resistance, its ubiquitous quality, the necessity to pursue and understand it, and the need for alternative patterns.

Resistance most often expresses itself through the character style of the person of the victim. Typical expressions that are repetitive and rigid include any entrenched character style that becomes defensive in the treatment setting: being excessively pleasant or dependent (dependence), argumentative (antisocial or sadistic), complaining of injustices (passive-aggressive), overly rational (compulsive), flooded with feelings (borderline), seductive (histrionic), and confused or passive (schizoid, avoidant, schizotypal). In CBT terms, resistance can occur for two reasons. It can be due to poor techniques or pacing, in which case the therapist simply changes one or both. Alternatively, resistance may be the result of core cognitions. In this case, the therapist is entasked with their unearthing. Generally, as Rothstein and Robinson (1991) noted, the latter condition is present when a high level of emotionality is felt by the client. When this occurs, the relationship can be relied upon. Statements related to the client (what was that anger like for you; what provoked it; how is it like other times) or to the therapist (when you become angry, I backed off) can be used. Also, as these gentle interpersonal confrontations unfold,

TABLE 7.4
Resistance Components

---

1. Teaching: "What we resist persists"
    -natural human quality to protect self from change; part of life-style
    -ubiquitous, entrenched, and unconscious
    -requirements to tag the parts repeatedly
    -probable frustration and anger as a result

2. Identification
    -clinician focuses on character and trauma-related resistance "parts"
    -character problems flow from personality style
    -trauma problems usually center on:
    -avoidance
    -acting out
    -substance abuse
    -confusion
    -anger
    -excessive symptom dependence
    -excessive frustrated motivation
    -intense fear
    -blocking
    -crisis orientation
    -objectifying self
    -stay simple and focus on one part at a time

3. Loosening/Replacement
    -reward alterations in process
    -give permission for victim to "stay" with resistance
    -alternative ways of self-identification
    -reward active behavior of the process
    -empower client to "search" further

---

resistances increasingly roll back, and schema issues become better defined and more open for change. The client also becomes more aware of the centrality of his/her person, choice, responsibility, power, subjectivity, interiority, and how the obvious and subtle parts of resistance are geared to protect these. Ultimately, the client becomes his/her guide in separating person issues from resistance.

Once a misalliance takes hold, the therapist becomes incorporated into the "trauma membrane." The therapist loses the ability to provide perspective or facilitate change to disengage. Mostly this occurs when the therapist either consciously or unconsciously finds himself/herself colluding in the denial of events or affects. While the necessity is not to push but to keep the responsibility on the patient, this can easily be distorted into subtle and obvious attempts at denial and numbing. The therapist only needs enough control to maintain the boundaries and the structure of therapy. Beyond this minimum, the necessity is to have only a modicum of entre into the person of the victim, especially with highly resistant clients. The client has become expert at self-protection. The therapist must read this, allow this, join this, and in so doing create appealing conditions for reconsideration and change. Also remember that the therapist who completely understands the client not only scares him/her but also has ceased being a participant.

Vicarious Victimization

The other side of the misalliance coin rests with the therapist. In Chapter 6, the issue from the perspective of the care of the therapist was addressed. In this case, the importance of the person of the therapist and the potential for therapeutic problems related to this are noted briefly. Unfortunately, the topic has been addressed succinctly with trauma victims (McCann & Pearlman, 1990a; McCann & Pearlman, 1990b; Talbot, 1990). This occurs when the therapist's experience loses boundaries with those of the client. Typically, failure of treatment is not due only to a mismatch of method, but often is a result of a mismatch of therapist and client. This is a counter transference issue—a failure of the therapist to accept or appreciate the client from more than one perspective. This often results in a series of therapist infringements *(narcissistic infringements)* on the client, however "rational." In effect, being unable to separate the person of the therapist from problems of the client, the therapist subtly extends personal issues into therapy.

A vicarious victimization also can result, due to the nature of the trauma and its relationship to the schema of the therapist. This is broader than countertransference, as it implies a disruption of the cognitive structures of the therapist. McCann and Pearlman (1990b) believed that "all" therapists working with trauma survivors will experience alterations in their own schemas, which will affect their lives. Whether this negatively influences the helper and therapy depends on how the therapist cares for self.

These authors wrote:

> Therapists may experience painful images and emotions associated with their clients' traumatic memories and may, over time, incorporate these memories into their own memory systems. As a result, therapists may find themselves experiencing PTSD symptoms, including intrusive thoughts or images and painful emotional reactions. The helper must be able to acknowledge, express, and work through these painful experiences in a supportive environment. This process is essential if therapists are to prevent or ameliorate some of the potentially damaging effects of their work. If these feelings are not openly acknowledged and resolved, there is the risk that the helper may begin to feel numb or emotionally distant, thus unable to maintain a warm, empathetic, and responsive stance with clients. (p. 144)

Vicarious victimization occurs in various forms and at various levels. In addition to the self-care recommendations in Chapter 5, note that health care professionals generally "know" how they are affected, but have developed such a strong "adapted child" that vulnerable or negative feelings are simply not allowed. A loose axiom in this case is that the therapist can only take the client to a level of therapeutic experience that parallels his/her own ability to remain open to this event. Following is a procedure for self accountability which is requisite in this work.

A helpful division of therapist misalliance used at this Veterans Medical Center involves three features. Clinicians have shown the tendency to react poorly to trauma victims at a "surface level" in three ways: **pride, shame, and doubt.** Pride involves a narcissistic involvement of will ("I am the savior"). Shame entails excessive responsibility ("I didn't do enough"). Doubt represents the inability of the therapist to differentiate the person of the therapist from the role of the therapist ("I should not reward this dependence, but I feel he/she won't like me if I don't"). A sensitivity to these three attitudes can provide access into more dynamic components of the therapist. The systematic use of the relationship is required.

Finally, Chu (1988) addressed 10 treatment traps which outlined problems in psychotherapy with trauma victims. They specify a combination of common client and therapist factors in which a choice point exists and therapists often fail. In Table 7.5 we present the majority of that list with some additions of our own. All are fertile ground for the misalliance, and for a deepening of the trauma membrane. To this list each therapist is challenged to add own special fare.

Post-script

The visibility and pain of the trauma victim, especially Vietnam victims, are so strong that imagining that the clinician could remain free from influences that affect client management and care is difficult. The "presses" are many. The cultural press is particularly troubling. By now, the fact that Vietnam veterans were engaged in what only can be described as an engagement without meaning and later experienced a homecoming without validation is universally accepted. Many believe that these two cultural features were as important as any personal reactions to trauma. This implies that both society and the system that fostered these conditions represent ongoing reminders of this conflict. The clinician needs to be reminded of these markers.

A diagnostic press also exists. Clinicians have been noted to work more effectively with combat related victims if they do not emphasize predisposing factors (Wilson, 1989). Eth and Pynoos (1985) even advised therapists to refrain from diagnosing personality disorders until PTSD symptoms have abated. Titchener and Kapp (1976) also have described a permanent character change in a trauma survivor in which the loss of community is involved. The "good" clinician knows that no benefit is achieved by rewarding a false positive (i.e., malingering) and certainly none for a false negative (denying a victim help). These issues demand clinical awareness and consistent vigilance in order to avoid becoming a detective or losing the role of human-caregiver. Also, always recall that good care requires good problem formulation and all that is attendant to this—validation, understanding, and fiduciary components of the helping process. "Better" treatment follows. This is sufficient reason to us for the whole evaluative process in chronic victimization.

Finally the press of systems exists. Since 1980, PTSD has found its niche in the official nomenclature. Just as enough cannot be written or described regarding the difficulties involved in the parsing out the pieces to various ancillary or comorbid disorders and character issues involved with PTSD, enough also has not been written about the complexities of the various systems involved with trauma, insurance, government, legal, etc. On the one hand, these are the troubled waters of clinical decisions. Early (1990) noted (as have we) that many forms of attitudes/clinical positions on diagnosis and care, based on systems ranging from those that would ignore PTSD victims that have character problems to those that hold trauma alone, is sufficient for the diagnosis. Biases also are "at-the-ready" regarding clinical issues of secondary gain, combat identities, potential distortions, or factitious responses, as well as the more mundane relevancy of various PTSD criteria. Clinicians also possess attitudes related to cultural and ethnic issues.

No solution is known. If a victim meets conditions for Criteria A of the DSM-III-R, dilemmas will exist until science improves on the latter three criteria: some justified, some less so. However, for clinicians to pause and reflect on the "big picture" from the client's perspective is helpful. Modlin (1990) wrote:

(continued on page 412)

TABLE 7.5
Treatment Traps with Trauma Victims*

Factor	Struggle	Antidote
Trust	Wish to let go vs fear of pain, rejection	Time Relationship Active listening Acceptance
Distance	Therapist withdrawl vs therapist participation Therapeutic enmeshment or distance vs revealment/genuineness	Acceptance Accurate empathy Therapist concern Education
Limits	Gratify client vs limit setting	Metacommunication Reality testing
Responsibility	Support vs empowerment	Empower client Foster reality Empathy
Control	Client's under- or overcontrol vs titration of control	Education Empower client Teach resistance

Factor	Struggle	Antidote
Denial	Denial and therapist's collusion *vs* confrontation/clarity	Accurate empathy Exploration
Projection	Distortion *vs* acceptance/clarity	Empathy Acceptance Exploration Interpretation
Idealization	Therapist narcissism or aggrandizing *vs* healthy self awareness	Humility Genuineness
Ambivalence	Splitting *vs* cognitive and affective struggle	Experiencing struggle Interpretation
Motivation	Defensive/drop out *vs* openness/commitment	Encouragement Reality testing

*Extrapolated in part from Chu, 1988.

Distressed Vietnam veterans frequently express resentment at the government that ordered them to serve in Vietnam. Perhaps they more frequently express anger toward the Veterans Administration (VA) for failing to aid them with their disabilities or to provide treatment. One veteran noted that one has to be so well put together to jump all the VA hurdles that anyone with the least amount of irrationality could never do it. Certainly, veterans with low frustration tolerance, many of whom are alienated from all social institutions, have strong beliefs that the VA does not wish to help them. They will not pursue claims for disability for a number of reasons. Some, they state, are as follows: The screening procedure is designed to frustrate you so you will drop your claim. The appointments are arbitrarily set, with no regard for travel costs, employment, or convenience. Further, once a PTSD claim has been approved, the pension will likely be cut or disallowed if adjustment success is shown, such as achievement in education or employment. In other words, the pension is difficult to obtain and the procedure entails great personal discomfort. Frequently, veterans regard the procedure as demeaning and classify it as another discriminatory act of the same government that sent them to fight an unjust war from a strategically untenable position. (p. 83)

CLINICIAN'S COMMITMENT

No topic discussed can be more important than the commitment of the therapist to the client. The Scylla and Charybdis of the therapy experience is always present. On the one side, the treating clinician can err for being too soft, providing only support, "rescue," or acting out due to excessive conflict ("He has [I have] suffered too much"). On the other, the problem prevails of too much distance, too blank a screen, or too much countertransference or therapeutic dislike, revulsion, anger, etc. The clinician walks among these alternatives, and hopefully the relationship transcends many problems.

In the treatment of trauma victims, commitment is an attitude, an emotional investment, and a determination to respond with one's values and virtue ethics. Commitment is not an abstraction—not simply genuineness, revealment, or the other Rogerian therapeutic components. It is a real covenant—a vow or declaration of faithfulness to the client. It is superordinate to any contract. It is the clinician's commitment to treatment.

Recently, many professionals have come to understand, as philosophers have for a long time, that our deep metaphors are what ground and guide our lives, control our attribution of meaning, and organize our experience. These metaphors operate implicitly in science and personal experience, as well as more explicitly in religion. They guide us as we encounter the unknown; but more importantly they drive our therapeutic efforts and ground our ethics. *Technique becomes secondary to the trust in the relationship which underlies and contextualizes interventions.* The concept of **covenant** has become much too implicit in the role expectations of the professions. It provides an assumptive and ethical basis for the work of therapy from whatever psychological viewpoint. At base, a covenant is a vow or declaration to be faithful to someone for some purpose. The covenant is a promissory event that constrains and judges the rest of the relationship. It shapes the future not in terms of specifics, but in terms of a commitment. It extends to all contingencies and comprehends unforeseeable exigencies. In the ideal, covenant is totally engaging, in a sense gratuitous, and without limit.

The process of covenanting ends with an internalization of a promise, but it begins when one receives a gift. Exodus preceded Sinai; courtship precedes marriage; and early support precedes and grounds therapeutic work. The gift that a therapist has received in terms of education, training, and identity (and even life itself), is responded to by a vow which involves a set of moral obligations and rituals (techniques) which define how they will live, and involves their intentions and the internal state of both parties.

In therapy, the concept of covenant admits that the therapist is always at least in a **duplex relationship.** The degrees of freedom within the role are wide: at times the clinician is an advocate, at times confrontive, and at times vulnerable. But always the therapist is reparenting—presenting a human mirror from which to grow and a relationship into which no harm will come and from which life can be replenished. The commitment supersedes any contract and conditions. It allows the professional to balance integrity, professionalism, and the needs of the client in a way that will work for the client's good. It balances something within the clinician too.

The covenant humanizes the point in therapy for the clinician in which the professional, who is the ethical provider, meets the real caregiver, who is using his/her humanity to balance his/her science.

In religious history, the Hebrews reciprocated a covenant proposed by Yahweh, their God. Whatever occurred, they were His chosen people and ultimately He would not let them down. Some Hebrews never completely lost their commitment no matter what the circumstances (the remnant). In the same way, the client comes to know both the roles and tasks of therapy through a committed relationship (Hyer & Wallace, 1990).

Bordin (1979) outlined the central components of psychotherapy: bonds, tasks, and goals. Based on our model of treatment (Chapter 6) and these components, Table 7.6 outlines the therapist and client commitments in this dynamic care process. The central conflict of trauma and psychotherapy involves the reexperiencing of one's conflict within the relationship of the therapy—a current "learning" of how and why this victim chose this pattern and experienced this pain now in therapy. These three components involve commitment as well as a careful pursuit of the whole infrastructure of the therapeutic experience.

Bugental (1987) has provided the therapist with help also. His suggestions are given in Table 7.7. Like values, these are hard to derive and harder to objectify. However, they involve four parts: (1) a commitment to self (clinician's self), (2) a commitment to the client's values, (3) a commitment to the context and the broader picture, and (4) a commitment to the sense of actualization of the client. In this effort, the clinician becomes the true holding environment, the container of horror, the provider of support, the purveyor of hard realities, the nurturer, and the problem solver. *This is therapy. It is a reading of at what stage the client is, of what is fitting action at a given time, of authentic dialogue, and of curative principles (what is efficacious).* This balance is never easy and never clear cut. Moral traces often are residual long after the struggle with the various issues and the clinical decisions. Therapy from this perspective is empowerment because cure is never fully achieved, and pain is never fully retrieved or assimilated (Hyer & Wallace, 1990).

SUMMARY

Thus, we have struggled to characterize salient aspects of the therapeutic relationship with trauma victims both technically and philosophically. We must end where we began: *No therapy will occur without the context of a relationship, and deep therapy requires a deep relationship.* The pitfalls are many, but the rewards are great.

TABLE 7.6
Commitment to Treatment Components

Bonds:	Relationship tendering covenant
	Therapist commitment—non-specific qualities, accurate empathy
	Client commitment—time, energy, money, will to change, and positive expectations
Tasks:	Collaboration in the observation and experience of the drama in therapy
	Therapist commitment—focus on cognitions and interpersonal patterns, press to interiority
	Client commitment—collaborative empiricism, active participation, personal scientist, homework
Goals:	Person defined schema or symptom care
	Therapist commitment—case formulation, schema therapy (always)
	Client commitment—Compliance and feedback on struggle and goals in life

TABLE 7.7
Commitment of Therapist*

I am committed in my values and being to the client
(open to the real me and the real client, committed beyond my profession and issues of treatment and competence; committed to me as a friend and client as a person).

I am committed to client's authenticity
(not stroking for support, for being "technical" in treatment; commitment to client's vision of self in real ways).

I am committed to the context of the client
(context means family and society, committed to extra-therapy behavior and involvement; open to confront client on unauthentic behavior in this area).

I am committed to client's positive picture of self
(committed to future of the person he/she can be; committed to translate the client's negative image with renewed respect of self).

---

*Extrapolated from Bugental, 1987.

REFERENCES

Bandura, A. (1977). Self-efficacy: Towards a unifying theory of behavior changes. *Psychological Review, 84,* 191-215.

Blank, A. S. (1985). Irrational reactions to post-traumatic stress disorder and Vietnam veterans. In S. M. Sonnenberg, A. S. Blank, & J. A. Talbott (Eds.), *The trauma of war: Stress and recovery in Vietnam veterans* (pp. 69-98). Washington, DC: American Psychiatric Press.

Bordin, E. S. (1979). The generalizability of the concept of working alliance. *Psychotherapy: Theory, Research, and Practice, 16,* 252-60.

Brom, D., & Kleber, R. J. (1989). Prevention of post-traumatic stress disorder. *Journal of Traumatic Stress, 2,* 335-351.

Bugental, J. (1987). *The art of the psychotherapist.* New York: Norton Press.

Cashdan, S. (1982). International psychotherapy: Using the relationship. In J. Anchin & D. Kiesler (Eds.), *Handbook of interpersonal psychotherapy.* New York: Pergamon Press.

Catherall, D. R. (1989). Differentiating intervention strategies for primary and secondary trauma in Post-traumatic Stress Disorder: The example of Vietnam veterans. *Journal of Traumatic Stress, 2,* 289-304.

Chu, J. (1988). Ten traps for therapists in the treatment of trauma survivors. *Dissociation, 4,* 24-32.

Early, E. (1990). Imagined, exaggerated and malingered traumatic stress disorder. In C. Meek (Ed.), *Post-traumatic stress disorder: Assessment differential diagnosis and forensic evaluation* (pp. 137-156). Sarasota, FL: Professional Research Exchange, Inc.

Eth, S., & Pynoos, R. S. (1985). *Post-traumatic stress disorder in children.* Washington, DC: American Psychiatric Press.

Figley, C. (1988). A five-phase treatment of post-traumatic stress disorder in families. *Journal of Traumatic Stress, 1,* 127-141.

Goldfried, M. R. (1983). Behavioral assessment. In I. B. Weiner (Ed.), *Clinical methods in psychology,* Vol. 2. New York: Wiley & Sons.

Hyer, L., & Wallace, E. (1990). Clinical ethics with geriatric exemplifications. Department of Psychiatry and Health Behavior, Medical College of Georgia, Augusta, GA.

Janoff-Bulman, R. (1985). The aftermath of victimization: Rebuilding shattered assumptions. In C. R. Figley (Ed.), *Trauma and its wake: The study and treatment of post-traumatic stress disorder* (p. 15). New York: Brunner/ Mazel.

Johnson, D. W. (1972). *Reaching out: Interpersonal effectiveness and self-actualization.* New York, NY: Prentice-Hall, Inc.

Kahn, M. (1991). *Between therapist and client: The new relationship.* New York: Freeman.

Kiesler, (1986). Interpersonal methods of diagnosis and treatment. In R. Michels and J. Coveman (Eds.), *The personality disorders and neuroses* (pp. 53-76). New York: Lippencott.

McCann, L., & Pearlman, L. (1990a). *Psychological trauma and the adult survivor: Theory, therapies, and transformation.* New York: Brunner/Mazel.

McCann, L., & Pearlman, L. (1990b). Vicarious victimization: A framework for understanding the psychological effects of working with victims. *Journal of Traumatic Stress, 3,* 131-150

Meichenbaum, D. (1991). Stress induction training: A twenty year update. In R. Woolfolk and P. Lehrer (Eds.), *Principles and practice of stress management.* New York: Guilford Press.

Modlin, C. (1990). Forensic issues in post-traumatic stress disorder. In C. Meek (Ed.), *Post traumatic stress disorder: Assessment, differential, diagnosis and forensic evaluation* (pp. 137-156). Sarasota, FL: Professional Resource Exchange.

Obenchain, J., & Silver, S. (1992). Symbolic recognitions: Ceremony in the treatment of posttraumatic stress disorder. *Journal of Traumatic Stress, 5,* 37-44.

Prochaska, J. O., & DiClemente, C. C. (1986). The transtheoretical approach. In J. Norcross (Ed.), *Handbook of selective psychotherapy* (pp. 63-200). New York: Brunner/Mazel.

Rosenbaum, M. (1980). A schedule for assessing self-control behavior: Preliminary findings. *Behavior Therapy, 11,* 109-121.

Rothstein, M., & Robinson, P. (1991). The cognitive relationship and resistance to change in cognitive therapy. In T. Vallis, J. Howes, & P. Miller (Eds.), *The challenge of cognitive therapy: Application to nontraditional populations* (pp. 35-58). New York: Plenum Press.

Talbot, A. (1990). The importance of parallel process in debriefing crisis counsellors. *Journal of Traumatic Stress, 3(2),* 265-278.

Titchener, J., & Kapp, F. (1976). Family and character change at Buffalo Creek. *American Journal of Psychiatry, 133,* 295-299.

Wilson, J. (1989). *Trauma, transformation and healing.* New York: Brunner/ Mazel.

PART II

Cognition and Emotion

Unique Issues of Trauma

Chapter 8

CLINICAL IMPLICATIONS AND APPLICATIONS OF INFORMATION PROCESSING

MODELS OF POST-TRAUMATIC STRESS DISORDER

Brett T. Litz
and
Diana Hearst

"Consciousness of our powers arguments them." Vauenargues

INTRODUCTION

The theoretical assumptions, principles, and experimental paradigms of human information processing (cognitive psychology) have greatly contributed to our understanding of the etiology and maintenance of PTSD (Chemtob, Roitblat, Hamada, Carlson, & Twentyman, 1989; Foa, Steketee, & Olasov-Rothbaum, 1989; Litz & Keane, 1989). PTSD is uniquely suitable to be studied from the perspective of experimental cognitive psychology in that the core symptoms of traumatized persons entail disturbances of memory, imagery, and thought; all symptoms that serve as targets of clinical interventions.

The purpose of the present chapter is to introduce the information processing theory of PTSD and set forth general clinical guidelines and heuristics that are implied from the theory that can be useful in the treatment of traumatized persons. To date, the majority of the conceptual work in information processing and PTSD has been used to provide explanatory mechanisms for the formation of PTSD broadly defined rather than to derive clinical interventions for specific problems (for exceptions, see Horowitz, 1986; McCann & Pearlman, 1990; Resick & Schnicke, 1990). Because of this, the proposed general clinical guidelines below are intended to be used to augment existing methods of psychological treatment of PTSD rather than exist as stand-alone interventions. In this context, three broad and related content areas are discussed: first, a series of treatment guidelines are derived from information processing theory (e.g., guidelines are proposed that will facilitate traumatic event[s] processing as in direct therapeutic exposure, etc.); second, the information processing consequences of multiple traumatization (an under-explored area) are explored; and third, information that can be provided to traumatized persons about the high probability information processing sequelae of experiencing an overwhelming life event are discussed.

BACKGROUND

Information processing refers to a set of empirically derived hypothetical constructs, derived from experimental cognitive psychology, that address how individuals perceive, selectively attend to, and retrieve personally relevant information from memory (see Ingram & Kendall, 1986). Information processing psychology normatively addresses how life experiences are organized in memory in a manner that facilitates the utilization of past experience. Past experience is organized in memory in functional units called networks or schemas. Schemas are constructed highly organized bits of knowledge that typically allow us to effectively utilize our past knowledge about how our world works in order to respond to the environment in an efficient manner. As will be shown below, information processing theories of PTSD posit that traumatic life experiences are organized in a manner that profoundly influences how new information that is relevant to the trauma is processed. Before describing the specific aspects of information processing in PTSD, the reader is provided with a brief overview of the conceptual underpinnings of such work that is borrowed from experimental cognitive and social-cognitive psychology (see Taylor & Crocker, 1981).

Schematic Processing

A key set of empirical findings from information processing research are that perception, the allocation of attention, comprehension, and beliefs about situations are all subject to the biasing effects of what has been called schematic processing (see Winfrey & Goldfried, 1986). Schematic processing facilitates the encoding and retrieval of information in that extra information processing (cognitive and affective) resources are used up for situations or cues that confirm expectations based on prior experience. A corollary to this is that the more *self-relevant* and *emotion-based* the prior knowledge is, the more pervasive, automatic (unconscious), tenacious, and powerful the schematic biasing becomes (e.g., Bargh, 1982; Bower, 1981). Whole volumes have been written on these and related issues and the reader is referred to these for a more thorough rendering (e.g., Clark & Fiske, 1982; Cantor & Kihlstrom, 1981). What follows are some general statements about the effects of schematic processing that will provide a backdrop for a discussion of information processing in PTSD.

A schema is a unique construct in that it refers to both a content (stored, organized knowledge) and a process. In terms of a process, a schema, once activated or cued, is said to quickly direct attention to schema-relevant information in the environment, provides default (fill-in) understanding or meaning for events, scripts or programs for responding emotionally and behaviorally, and influences what is remembered and recalled subsequently about the situation (see Williams, Watts, MacLeod, & Mathews, 1988). A schema is activated by both internally generated (e.g., feeling states reminiscent of past experience) and external stimuli (situational retrieval cues). Schematic activation also can proportionally lead us, often unconsciously, to disrespect schemainconsistent stimuli. If our schemas lead us to behave a certain way in a situation, we are later likely to be overconfident in the belief that we were correct in our behavior, and be quite resistant to arguments to the contrary (See also Chapter 4).

Modern information processing theory has posited that cognitions, behaviors, and emotional/physiological reactions as response systems flow from the same schematic organization (e.g., Bower, 1981). In this way, information processing is not strictly the study of cognitive events (e.g., memory) but the study of integrated repertoires of organized responses (cognitive, behavioral, and affective). As stated above, research has shown conclusively that these cognitive, behavioral, and physiological effects of information processing are more pronounced and have a greater impact upon experience when the schematic processing is in the context of personally meaningful and emotional material (see Greenberg & Safran, 1989). Traumatic life experiences are, by definition, powerfully self-referent and emotionally significant. The biases in information processing that flow from the schematic processing of trauma-related information are in part responsible for symptom formation in PTSD (Litz & Keane, 1989). These will be described subsequent to a description of the theory of information processing in anxiety disorders that provides the backdrop for work in this area.

Information Processing in Anxiety Disorders

Lang (1985) has proposed an information processing theory of fear and anxiety that maintains that fear-relevant stimuli are encoded in highly organized, semantic, "fear networks" in memory (see Chapter 3 also). These fear networks, or schemas contain three types of information: (1) information about stimulus cues that elicit fear; (2) information about cognitive, motor, and psychophysiological responses (e.g., heart rate increases, scripts for behavioral avoidance); and (3) information that defines the meaning of the stimulus cues and responses for the individual (e.g., "I will faint or go crazy unless I escape this situation"). When confronted by a fear-relevant stimulus, the whole network of memories, responses, attitudes, and beliefs become primed and made more accessible to experience. The network of memories acts like a program for action, emotion, and thought whose integrated function is to marshal resources to cope with expected harm.

Anxiety disordered patients are characterized in Lang's model as having an unusually coherent and stable fear network which requires few matching elements in the environment for the network to be activated. Lang also proposed that subtle and highly generalized (and often ambiguous) events can lead to fear network activation in anxiety disorders because of the increased likelihood that other elements in the network are concurrently active (e.g., being slightly anxious or vulnerable). Anxiety disordered patients are hyper-prepared, so-to-speak, to perceive threat in ambiguous situations and to attend to fear-relevant cues in their environment. Such behavior can obviously be antithetical to adaptive social functioning.

Foa and Kozak (1986) elaborated on Lang's information processing model in an effort to explain processes of fear (symptom) reduction in anxiety disorders which has great relevance to the treatment of PTSD patients. They discussed different ways in which memory structures can be accessed so as to enhance what they called "emotional processing" (see Litz, 1992). Foa and Kozak (1986) proposed that pathological anxiety can change only when the fear network is fully accessed (i.e., emotional processing occurs) and is subsequently altered by exposure to corrective information (see below). (For more thorough explanations of the information processing models of anxiety disorders, the reader is referred to Barlow, 1988; Beck & Emery, 1985; Foa & Kozak, 1986; Hamilton, 1983; Lang, 1985; Litz & Keane, 1989; Williams et al., 1988.) (See also Chapter 3.)

Information Processing Theories of PTSD

Horowitz (1986) has proposed a comprehensive model of PTSD that has distinct information processing components. In the model, trauma creates two opposing sets of internal processes called intrusion and denial (or numbing), that signify that the person is naturally trying to cope with and resolve extreme stressors. The intrusion phase of adjustment following trauma entails the hallmark cognitive and emotional symptoms of PTSD: painful reexperiencing and hyperactivity. Intrusive memory reactivations occur because the organism is motivated by a tendency to completion or closure so that trauma memories can be integrated into existing schemas about the self. Horowitz argued that until a trauma is integrated into a person's schemas it is, in part, present in short-term memory. This process drives the intrusive reexperiencing of traumatic material, a hallmark symptom of PTSD. Such intrusions, however, trigger an opponent process of ideational and affective denial that represents the defensive phase that functions to ward off painful trauma-related affects and memories. This opponent process is emotional numbing that can function to shut down the system and aide in the avoidance of painful memories of the trauma. A PTSD patient shifts from this numbing phase to an intrusion phase, until resolution of the trauma. Resolution, then, entails accommodation of the trauma with the person's schemas of the world and the self. PTSD, therefore, reflects an inability to integrate the trauma due to excessive denial that thwarts the necessary emotional processing. Several other theoretical models of PTSD have incorporated similar information processing factors within a cognitive-behavioral framework. (See also Chapter 3.)

Foa, Steketee, and Olasov-Rothbaum (1989) attempted to extend Lang's fear network model to explain PTSD. They proposed that PTSD develops because of the horrendous nature and powerful intensity of the traumatic conditioning events that occurs during trauma and the attributions used by the person to explain why it happened. They further argued that such experiences, over time, lead to quantitative and qualitative changes in the trauma network or schema that distinguishes its impact on information processing from other organized pieces of self-related knowledge. Foa et al. (1989) specifically posited that the fear network in PTSD is characterized by the intensity of the response elements which produce psychophysiological arousal, the size of the fear structure (its generality), and the ready accessibility of the trauma-related network in memory. These processes lead to faulty and exaggerated beliefs about the probability that dire consequences will once again occur as well as the fact that

PTSD patients have a tendency to process present-day stressors as more severe and "bad" than nontraumatized persons.

A theoretical model proposed by Chemtob et al. (1989) to explain cognition in combat-related PTSD, has drawn heavily from the concepts discussed above and represents a very thorough treatment of the area. They proposed a *"cognitive-action"* theory of PTSD which suggests that memory structures are organized in a manner that influences behavior, biases attention, and exacerbates emotional responding in a vicious feedback cycle.

Chemtob et al. (1989) proposed that patients with PTSD typically respond to perceived threat utilizing a survival mode of functioning. This formerly adaptive pattern of behavior (hypervigilance, hyper-reactivity, and a perceptual "readiness" to attend and react to threat or danger cues) is currently represented in memory in a well organized structure (or schema). Similar to Lang's model, the trauma structure includes information about emotions (e.g., anger, dread, panic), plans for action or sequences of behavior (e.g., fight, flee) and associated images and memories of past threatening experiences (e.g., being physical injured). Because information about danger or threat is stored in memory in such a rich multidimensional framework, a host of cues in the environment and in the person can activate memories of the trauma that in turn drive trauma-related behaviors.

Chemtob et al. (1989) posed that trauma schema is always partially activated because some low-level anxiety and arousal always are present in traumatized individuals. The arousal partially primes a PTSD patients to expect threatening events to occur. This occurs because physiological arousal (e.g., fear-related arousal) is part of the trauma-network or schema. For example, PTSD patients have difficulty in thinking they are safe in ambiguous social situations because they are likely to already be anxiously aroused or concurrently have some degree of trauma memory activation. The latter state would then make the PTSD patient feel that something potentially harmful, dangerous, or threatening might occur. When this expectation of threat does exist, the person is motivated to be defensive (e.g., aggressive) or avoidant (e.g., make an attempt to escape the situation). They also are more likely to focus their attention on threat-salient cues in the environment (e.g., a quick movement in a crowd). Weak or ambiguous evidence of threat both in the environment and internally are used by the information processing system to further potentiate, bias, and select threat-relevant stimuli (at the same time inhibiting alternative, more adaptive behaviors and feelings, from being activated).

The outcome of the processes described above are, in effect, the symptoms that make up PTSD. For example, exposure to a generalized cue in the environment (e.g., a man on a date for a rape-trauma victim) will automatically activate the relevant trauma network leading to increased anxiety, hypervigilance, likely misinterpretation of approach behaviors on the part of the date, an increase in the likelihood of accessing images of the rape scene with corresponding feelings, and a conscious effort to avoid. Some of these processes are unconscious, however. For example, a rape victim might be on the one hand engaging in a conversation and trying to smile at a man whom she is genuinely attracted to, and be unaware that she is averting her gaze, covering parts of her body, being very tense, etc. As time passes, more and more internal retrieval cues are present (e.g., feelings associated with the trauma), more aversive memories get primed, more environmental stimuli are interpreted as threatening, and other more adaptive schemas are less influential in determining behavior (e.g., networks about what to do on a date when you are attracted to someone). However, further active suppression of the recall of such painful cues (e.g., distracting one's thoughts) coupled with active behavioral avoidance (leaving the scene) serve to reduce arousal and thus reduce the presence of these retrieval cues. In this manner full and sustained exposure to the trauma network is thwarted which serves to maintain symptoms.

Most forms of PTSD treatment target some aspect of the processes described above. Retrieval cues that trigger symptoms can be made less effective by exposure therapies (Keane, Fairbank, Caddell, & Zimering, 1989; Keane & Kaloupek, 1982) and reactions to such triggers can be made more effective and functional by skills based approaches that foster better coping (e.g., Keane, Fairbank, Caddell, Zimering, & Bender, 1985). Pharmacological interventions are designed, in part, to reduce the feedback produced by arousal mechanisms that provide powerful priming information and serve to reinforce meaning/belief systems that safety is not possible (Friedman, 1991). What follows are more specific treatment suggestions that are borne from the information processing models.

INFORMATION PROCESSING IN THE TREATMENT OF PTSD

The essential ingredients of the successful treatment of PTSD, according to the information processing models, include accessing the trauma network (through some method of direct therapeutic exposure), allowing for changes in the organization of the stored information by introducing new and corrective response and meaning elements (see Foa & Kozak, 1986). A post-treatment goal would be to transform the trauma network in a way that makes the response elements greatly reduced in intensity and produces new programs or propositions that prompt more flexible, distanced, and controlled responding (rather than the speedy and automatic schematic processing). A variety of corrective experiences for PTSD patients serve to alter the trauma network, for example, gradual and repeated exposure to stimulus, response, and meaning elements of the trauma network with the intention of extinguishing the severity of the conditioned response (e.g., through direct therapeutic exposure in vivo or in imagery). Expectations and beliefs like "the pain will never go away" or "I will go crazy if I don't avoid these memories" are similarly challenged experientially by reductions in arousal through exposure treatments. Over time then, stimuli that are reminiscent of the trauma, more general life stressors and ambiguous social stimuli are coped with more effectively because the trauma network is less predominant in information processing.

The meaning of events need to be similarly transformed. Most treatments of PTSD make formerly tacit trauma-related beliefs *verbally explicit* thereby allowing for changes in those meaning elements. This is accomplished by first accessing the trauma network allowing for more thorough and experiential processes to unfold. Second, when patients are experiencing feelings associated with the trauma in therapy, or remembering certain aspects of what happened to them, the therapist can more readily elicit the belief system or meaning elements that have been induced from traumatization. Once verbalized, such beliefs can be subject to reality testing. Patients also should be actively engaged to monitor their own information processing in stressful situations and trained to test out the veracity of those beliefs. Rigid and automatic schematic expectations are acknowledged and over time evidence supporting them become less and less available. The more experience someone has at challenging their trauma-related beliefs in the absence of re- victimization, the more the trauma network can change to accommodate the new more adaptive information. McCann and Pearlman (1990) have outlined some of the changes that occur in such schematic processes during this process of accommodation. They argue for example, that after treatment trauma victims should have beliefs that reflect realistic attitudes about once being a victim and now being a survivor, etc.

Cognitive Processing Therapy

To date, Resick and Schnicke (1990) are two of only a handful of therapists who have specifically developed a treatment package for PTSD (in this case for rape victims) that focuses exclusively on information processing variables. Their package highlights some of the mechanisms that were just described. In their cognitive processing therapy (CPT) they specifically address faulty thinking patterns that are posited to be directly causing anxious arousal and avoidance in rape-related PTSD. In the first phase of CPT considerable time is devoted to educating rape victims about the characteristic ways rape trauma effects fundamental beliefs and attitudes about the self and the world (see Janoff-Bulman, 1989). These beliefs are central to the development of symptoms. For example, if you believe that the world is no longer safe-enough or that no one can be trusted, then you will be terrified in new social situations and feel like your only option is to escape (Foa et al., 1989).

The second phase of CPT is akin to the stress inoculation approach to the treatment of PTSD (Foa, Olasov-Rothbaum,

Riggs, & Murdock, 1991) in that an emphasis is on changing maladaptive selftalk (or verbal scripts). The assumption here is that the statements PTSD patients say to themselves keep them from taking risks in their environment and this thwarts opportunities for corrective learning experiences that would serve to change those faulty beliefs. Some examples of the characteristic modes of maladaptive and extreme thinking that serve as target in CPT are (1) I can never feel safe again, (2) the only way I can regain a sense of control is to stay away from men, (3) danger is always lurking, and (4) I was naive to trust and my judgments are no longer sound.

Treatment entails the forming of new, more adaptive schemas about the social world. Again, schemas are most effectively changed if the faulty schema is accessed, rigorously and systematically challenged over time, and new corrective responses and meaning elements introduced based on success experiences (See Chapter 6 for a description of these strategies). Faulty schemas are accessed in group therapies where members explore the meaning behind their trauma (meaning elements are accessed) and current- day reactions to events are linked back to the things learned from the trauma. Members of groups learn to systematically challenge faulty thinking patterns once they are exposed experientially. Cognitive processing therapy also uses homework assignments that get patients to actively explore and challenge the manner in which they think and to monitor their emotional and behavioral reactions to significant events. The CPT approach, along with the stress-inoculation approach used by Foa and her colleagues, has been shown to be particularly effective in the treatment of rape related PTSD (see Foa et al., 1991).

Thus far the theoretical mechanisms that have been proposed to explain the development and maintenance of PTSD have been addressed as well as how these mechanisms can be used to conceptualize the change process. A specific example of a treatment (CPT) that specifically targets cognitive processes in traumatized individuals also has been described. The interventions derived from the information processing models have been used typically to treat one discreet type of trauma that occurs in adulthood (e.g., rape or combat trauma). To date, no information processing model has addressed the effects of multiple traumatization across the life span and the unique treatment needs of those so afflicted. The next section is a brief exploration of these issues.

INFORMATION PROCESSING AND MULTIPLE TRAUMATIZATION

What happens to information processing mechanisms when a history of multiple traumas exist? Unfortunately, no theory has attempted to explain the effects of multiple traumatic events on information processing. Yet this task is essential due to the very high incidence of multiple traumatic events across the lifetime. Issues about how multiple traumas may interact in memory are next discussed by using an example of a Vietnam veteran who experienced physical and emotional abuse by his father before entering the military, where he was subsequently traumatized by his combat experiences.

As shown in Figure 8.1 traumas can have intersecting or overlapping stimulus (S), response (R) and meaning (M) elements. Thus unique and shared aspects of traumas are stored in memory. The patient described in Figure 8.1 had a history of severe physical abuse and subjugation in childhood by his father, before he entered the military. In Vietnam, among other things, he was caught in an ambush, was pinned down, observed the death of a close buddy, and was wounded himself. The overlapping features of the two sets of memories are shown in the intersection of the two circles; this intersection is labeled the *trauma complex.*

Multiple traumatization has several information processing implications. Having multiple traumas in memory makes internal and external cues or reminders a lot easier to activate or prime traumatic schemas. The more frequently and developmentally early traumatic events occurred, the greater the variety and intensity of the emotional reactions, defensive maneuvers, and intrusive memories become primed. Developmentally early traumas, however, are not easily (fully) accessed and consciously recognized because they entail extensive and highly automatic programs for defensive responding

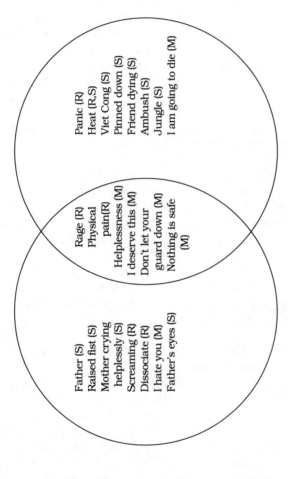

Early physical abuse
(left circle)

Combat trauma
(right circle)

Father (S)
Raised fist (S)
Mother crying
   helplessly (S)
Screaming (R)
Dissociate (R)
I hate you (M)
Father's eyes (S)

Rage (R)
Physical
   pain(R)
Helplessness (M)
I deserve this (M)
Don't let your
guard down (M)
Nothing is safe
   (M)

Panic (R)
Heat (R,S)
Viet Cong (S)
Pinned down (S)
Friend dying (S)
Ambush (S)
Jungle (S)
I am going to die (M)

The trauma complex is represented by the intersection of the two circles.
Code: M=Meaning; R=Response; S=Stimulus

Figure 8.1. An example of distinct and overlapping features of trauma memories (the trauma complex).

(dissociation, severe emotional withdrawal) that thwarts full access. In addition, sufficient retrieval cues may be lacking during therapy (Litz & Keane, 1989).

The more developmentally early the traumas are that contribute to the trauma complex, the more fundamental and far-reaching the meaning elements become. Gross distortions in fundamental beliefs and assumptions about such issues as safety and trust (e.g., "I can't protect myself from harm and people will betray me"), selfesteem (e.g., "I am bad"), intimacy ("I can't be soothed or comforted by anyone") or power (e.g., "I do not have any control over things that happen to me") have a profound effect on how a person takes care of self in response to current day demands and stress. Needless to say, these types of beliefs need to be accessed, verbally acknowledged, and modified in treatment.

In our treatment experience with Vietnam veterans, often the most recent traumas have pre-eminence in social information processing. This observation is consistent with current thinking about the accessibility of schemas (see Higgins & King, 1981). Moreover, axiomatically when the more frequent and vivid recent traumas are processed in therapy, then the more accessible the earlier traumas become. This is due to the more frequent retrieval of trauma-complex cues that over time more readily prime and access developmentally early memories of extreme stress and victimization.

In the treatment context, a therapist should assume a *direct link* between a more recent trauma and earlier traumas. When a patient is describing his/her most recent trauma in the context of strong primary affects (e.g., rage, terror) and meaningrelated themes (e.g., worthlessness, noncontrol, a lack of safety, or a sense of deserving bad things), they should (depending on the nature of the relationship, and depending on the current egostrength of the patient) look for linkages with early events that, by definition, would be traumatic and need to be explored in treatment.

A helpful procedure for a therapist may be to sketch out a *Venn diagram* like the one depicted in Figure 8.1, (or time line as in Chapter 4) and fill-in stimulus, response, and meaning elements derived from their work with patients on a recent trauma and begin to hypothesize response and meaning elements that make up the trauma complex. Assessment information derived from initial evaluations about childhood and developmental history can be used as a guide. (See also Chapter 4.) In the example depicted in Figure 8.1, a determination was made from the initial assessment and history taking that this patient had a very punitive father who was physically abusive. Meaning elements that were present when the patient described his Vietnam trauma provided ready cues for the therapist to explore the patients relationship to his dad which then facilitated the retrieval of formerly inaccessible and unconscious trauma memories of his father's brutal and humiliating treatment of him, that in turn would activate memories of his military experiences. Over time this patient was able to understand that his unique adaptation to combat was greatly colored by his schema about himself in relation to his dad. He also was able to make connections between some of his feelings during the combat trauma and his experiences with his dad (the trauma complex).

Whether the therapeutic intervention is general psychotherapy or direct therapeutic exposure, one can ask the following questions to patients that will serve to facilitate linking most recent (and most accessible) traumas to earlier ones (1) "When have you felt this way before?" (2) "As you are saying to yourself that you feel _____ when you think about what happened to you, can you go back in your memory to a time that you felt a similar way?" Similarly, therapists can take advantage of the priming that naturally occurs when a more recent traumatic memory is accessed in therapy by getting patients to focus on response and meaning elements that, based on assessment data, can be linked with earlier experiences (stimulus elements are more likely to be distinct and will be less effective at cuing the trauma complex). Finding such linkages and accessing early traumas (if they are present) in order to facilitate emotional processing and exposure to any number of types of corrective information is essential for effective treatment.

PROVIDING INFORMATION TO PATIENTS ABOUT TRAUMA RELATED INFORMATION PROCESSING

One of the things that brings traumatized persons to seek help is that they are naturally wanting to make sense out of their experience. If not explicitly stated, questions such as why is this happening to me, why can't I get this terrible thing out of my mind?, etc., should be implicitly assumed. As suggested in earlier chapters of this book, an essential task in working with PTSD patients, whether implementing symptom or problem-focused interventions or when targeting the changes that have occurred at the level of assumptions and beliefs about the world or the self, is to facilitate a collaborative enterprise. This working relationship is in part fostered by using a shared language system and a shared set of assumptions or a conceptual model about trauma and change. An important therapist function is to provide a conceptual model, geared toward the patients specific context, providing information about the universal effects of trauma and what recovery might look like over time.

The assumption is that providing a model to patients does two things; (1) assists the victim in making sense out of what happened to them, that is, their trauma(s); and (2) helps each one contextualize the trauma process from trauma to symptoms. Symptoms can be seen as natural adaptations to extreme stress and the mind's attempt, on the one hand, to protect the person from additional harm and, on the other, to heal and work-through the painful memories that are left of the incident(s). In addition, providing accurate information about treatment itself allows the recovery process to unfold in logical, sequential ways. In addition, this also will increase compliance and motivation for the arduous tasks ahead.

The following are brief descriptions derived from information processing theory that can serve as a guide to clinicians. To provide simple and concrete descriptions of these information processing mechanisms is extremely helpful. In keeping with the theme of this chapter, the intention is to provide information that will be helpful to any clinician working with traumatized populations regardless of the specific type of interventions used.

Storage of Traumatic Memories and Their Effects

Patients can be taught that trauma is an experience that unpredictably and uncontrollably shatters or violates assumptions about the fundamental aspects of human experience (e.g., that he/she has a reasonable sense of predictability and control over events, that the world is not inherently dangerous, etc., see Janoff-Bulman, 1989). Quite naturally, the event gets stored in memory along with any emotional reactions as well as what the event means to the person. The network of trauma memories is easily activated and once activated has a profound affect on behavior. Traumatic memories can be activated by several different methods: Physical reminders or cues, emotions or other physiological reactions related to original trauma, and through thinking or imagining trauma-related information. When the trauma network is activated, powerful emotions, similar to the ones that occurred during the trauma, are primed, making experiencing and expressing other types of emotions difficult (emotional numbing). Traumatic memories resurface when reminders are present; and the more a person (understandably) avoids and suppresses thoughts and feelings about what happened, the greater the likelihood that trauma-related images, thoughts, and feelings will resurface without intention in the form of intrusive thoughts and nightmares.

Selective Attention, Over-interpretation of Threat, and Misattribution of Anxious-arousal

PTSD patients can be taught how researchers have shown that traumatic events force individuals to see their environment as more threatening than it may be objectively, and how, when one has PTSD, the tendency is to interpret social situations as less safe than they need to be. When exposed to situations that are subtly reminiscent of their trauma, PTSD patients are likely to be anxious because the memories that are activated are frightening and the negative feelings are typically used by the person to confirm their beliefs that something is dangerous around them.

Completion Tendency

A helpful procedure is to explain to patients that a natural tendency for humans is to seek mastery, completion, or closure from traumatic experience. Two processes compete for their emotional resources: (1) the mind's natural attempts to recover from the terrible events via the resurfacing of memories that require resolution and (2) a tendency to avoid, stuff, or suppress these painful feelings and memories. This competition can use patients up and make them less able to concentrate or engage interpersonally.

Reexperiencing is directly proportional to the extent of avoidance and suppression that occurs. The greater the suppression and avoidance, the more frequent and intrusive the reexperiencing. In this way, suppression of traumatic memories never works in the long run. The suppressed memories will always come back in one form or another. Therapy entails the slow, careful, and deliberate disclosure and reactivation of painful memories so they can be accessed and then modified.

Exposure to Corrective Information

Patients can be instructed that trauma memories are very painful but inherently unharmful. What needs to happen in therapy is for the memories to be accessed and explored in order to provide opportunities for exposure to corrective experiences. Patients also should be taught that the longer the time since their trauma memories have been accessed, the more painful exposure will be. They also are likely to have more and more memories return to them as time passes. This too is natural and to-be-expected. Memories need to be accessed before they can be changed in a manner that facilitates closure and recovery from trauma. Once accessed, several curative features can occur; feelings associated with the trauma are less and less intense over time, the person can call up the memories voluntarily, reminders are less effective at cuing memories, among others. Finally, the changes in meaning and beliefs that occurred since the trauma can be altered and that in a way fosters more adaptive functioning.

SUMMARY

The conceptual model of human information processing has greatly aided our understanding of PTSD. To date, however, few information processing theories have posed specific treatment guidelines. The present chapter was intended to provide an overview of how information processing psychology has been used to conceptualize PTSD. The position taken in this chapter has been that an understanding of the various models and an attention to information processing in treatment can facilitate or augment most forms of clinical work with traumatized populations. General guidelines were described to help clinicians in their assessments (e.g., exploring with patients the stimulus, response, and meaning elements of their traumatic exposure during interviews) and in treatment (e.g., accessing trauma networks in exposure therapy and eliciting meaning elements experientially). A way of thinking about the effects of multiple traumatization on information processing was explored, something that previous work in this area has failed to address. And finally, specific areas of information processing were offered that can be shared with patients to facilitate accurate expectations about trauma, PTSD, and the recovery process.

REFERENCES

Bargh, J. A. (1982). Attention and automaticity in the processing of self-relevant information. *Journal of Personality and Social Psychology, 43,* 425-436.

Barlow, D. H. (1988). *Anxiety and its disorders.* New York: Guilford.

Beck, A. T., & Emery, G. (1985). *Anxiety disorders and phobias: A cognitive perspective.* New York: Basic Books.

Bower, G. H. (1981). Mood and memory. *American Psychologist, 36,* 129-148.

Cantor, N., & Kihlstrom, J. F. (1981). *Personality, cognition, and interaction.* Hillsdale, NJ: Erlbaum.

Chemtob, C., Roitblat, H., Hamada, R., Carlson, J., & Twentyman, C. (1989). A cognitive action theory of post-traumatic stress disorder. *Journal of Anxiety Disorders, 2,* 253-275.

Clark, M. S., & Fiske, S. T. (1982). *Affect and cognition*. Hillsdale, NJ: Erlbaum.

Foa, E. B., & Kozak, M. J. (1986). Emotional processing of fear: Exposure to corrective information. *Psychological Bulletin, 99,* 20-35.

Foa, E. B., Steketee, G., & Olasov-Rothbaum, B. O. (1989). Behavioral/ cognitive conceptualizations of post-traumatic stress disorder. *Behavior Therapy, 20,* 155-176.

Foa, E. B., Olasov-Rothbaum, B., Riggs, D. S., & Murdock, T. (1991). Treatment of traumatic stress disorder in rape victims: A comparison between cognitive procedures and counseling. *Journal of Consulting and Clinical Psychology, 59,* 715-723.

Friedman, M. J. (1991). Biological approaches to the diagnosis and treatment of post-traumatic stress disorder. *Journal of Traumatic Stress, 4,* 67-92.

Greenberg, L. S., & Safran, J. D. (1989). Emotion in psychotherapy. *American Psychologist, 44,* 19-29.

Hamilton, V. (1983). *The cognitive structures and processes of human motivation and personality.* New York: Erlbaum.

Higgins, E. T., & King, G. (1981). Accessibility of social constructs: Information processing consequences of individual and contextual variability. In N. Cantor and J. F. Kihlstrom (Eds.), *Personality, cognition, and social interaction.* Hillsdale, NJ: Erlbaum.

Horowitz, M. J. (1986). *Stress response syndromes.* New York: Aronson.

Ingram, R. E., & Kendall, P. C. (1986). Cognitive clinical psychology: Implications of an information processing perspective. In R. Ingram (Ed.), *Information Processing Approaches to Clinical Psychology.* New York: Academic Press.

Janoff-Bulman, R. (1989). Assumptive worlds and the stress of traumatic events: Applications of the schema construct. *Social Cognition, 7,* 113-136.

Keane, T. M., Fairbank, J. A., Caddell, J. M., Zimering, R. T., & Bender, M. E. (1985). A behavioral approach to assessing and treating post-traumatic stress disorder in Vietnam veterans. In C. R. Figley (Ed.), *Trauma and Its Wake,* (pp. 257-294). New York: Brunner & Mazel.

Keane, T. M., Fairbank, J. A., Caddell, J. M., & Zimering, R. T. (1989). Implosive (flooding) therapy reduces symptoms of posttraumatic stress disorder in Vietnam combat veterans. *Behavior Therapy, 20,* 245-260.

Keane, T. M., & Kaloupek, D. G. (1982). Imaginal flooding in the treatment of post-traumatic stress disorder. *Journal of Consulting and Clinical Psychology, 50*, 130-140.

Lang, P. J. (1985). The cognitive psychophysiology of emotion: Fear and anxiety. In A. H. Tuma & J. D. Maser (Eds.), *Anxiety and the Anxiety Disorders.* Hillsdale, NJ: Erlbaum.

Litz, B. T. (1992). Emotional numbing in combat-related posttraumatic stress disorder: A critical review and reformation. *Clinical Psychology Review, 12,*417-432.

Litz, B. T., & Keane, T. (1989). Information processing in anxiety disorders: Application to the understanding of post- traumatic stress disorder. *Clinical Psychology Review, 9*, 243- 257.

McCann, I. L., & Pearlman, L. A. (1990). *Psychological Trauma and the Adult Survivor: Theory, Therapy, and Transformation.* New York: Brunner & Mazel.

Resick, P. A., & Schnicke, M. K. (1990). Treating symptoms in adult victims of sexual assault. *Journal of Interpersonal Violence, 5*, 488-506.

Taylor, S. E., & Crocker, J. (1981). The schematic basis of social information processing. In E. T. Higgins, C. P. Herman, & M. P. Zanna (Eds.), *Social Cognition: The Ontario Symposium on Personality and Social Psychology* (vol. 1, pp. 87-134).

Williams, J. M., Watts, F. N., MacLeod, C., & Mathews, A. (1988). *Cognitive psychology and emotional disorders.* New York: Wiley.

Winfrey, L. P., & Goldfried, M. R. (1986). Information processing and the human change process. In R. E. Ingram (Ed.), *Information Processing Approaches to Clinical Psychology.* New York: Academic Press.

Chapter **9**

TREATMENT OF EMOTIONS: THE ROLE OF GUILT

Cynthia Gerrard
and
Lee Hyer

No Excuse
True knowledge is a precious possession
But it can be a trap
Once the truth is noted
The sanctuary of incapacity dies. (James Martin, circa 1990)

Emotion is an integrated response where each feeling seems to have its own specific pattern of psychophysiological reaction. These are presumably activated by distinct types of stimuli with cognitions serving as filters and monitors. Emotions even serve a survival value providing functional responses that allow for flexibility in human interaction. Several models of emotion have described this process. Leventhal (1979, 1984), for example, developed an integrative and comprehensive model that views emotion as a synthesis of three interactive levels of processing: expressive-motor, schematic, and conceptual. The first is innate, hard wired, and probably least affected by trauma; the second represents conditioned emotional responses and potentiates responses by increasing the probability of the experience of the feelings; and the last is strategic, controlled, and voluntary that augments or inhibits (emotional) responses by calling up memories, appraisals, etc. This model represents a total processing paradigm in which the experience of emotions, their development, their recall, and their intensity is integrated.

Emotions are also "sensitive" to context and allow for differential reactions including types of communication, motivation, distinct behavior, etc. In this sense emotion is the "best" fine tuner for one's core schemas: emotions (and behavior) validate one's construing. Emotions then provide the necessary feedback required to measure progress toward the completion of a schema's dictates. In Chapter 4 we further noted that emotions facilitate the cognitive representation of the desired outcomes (goals) by directing the attention process to stimuli that are perceived versus relevant. Feelings, behavior, and cognitions are all part of the process—not ends or final states.

Mahoney further has developed a "total" formulation for emotions. They: (1) cohabitate and are confluent with cognition on all person tasks—attention, retrieval, behavior, etc.; (2) are involved in perception, often at an unconscious level; (3) are integrally related to cognitive development; (4) are inherently related to individual's health and well-being; (5) are the experiential products of a number of information processing components that operate simultaneously at all levels; (6) are key elements in the individual's sense of self; (7) are highly related to psychological change; and (8) in a dysfunction (like PTSD), a deregulation of emotions occurs (stimuli with a positive valence are reduced and stimuli with a negative valence are increased in all processing operations). There is no "unemotional" psychotherapy.

In fact, as one skips through the key dimensions of psychotherapy—level of therapist directness, level of support/ exploration, balance of focus (behavioral, affective, cognitive), modality of treatment, and techniques— one finding is paramount; clients who are in touch with their emotions, able to express these emotions, and at a "reasonable" level of arousal, are better candidates for therapeutic change. Safran and Greenberg (1991) specified seven therapeutic features to this: (1) full awareness of emotions enhances adaptive functioning; (2) emotion provides information on target values and standards; (3) awareness of the communicative impact of one's emotions enhances interaction; (4) maladaptive emotions are learned (e.g., avoidance in PTSD leads to other problems); (5) emotional restructuring requires schema activation; (6) emotional experiences press for completion; and (7) the therapeutic relationship is an important medium for changing emotional schema. Emotional experiencing and immediacy are highly desirable states for change in psychotherapy.

This book has not always endorsed these notions. The not-so-subtle emphasis has propagated the role of cognition. But, although the central conflict of PTSD may be a cognitive one, whether to bear witness to the truth or to deny reality that is too painful, the healing process goes through the affective experiences of feeling safe, mourning, and reconnecting feeling with everything in the person's life. Explicit here is that emotions are far from the ugly step-child of two decades ago (according to cognitive behavioral therapy proponents). Experienced emotions provide information that guide and motivate the "needed" healing. Our task is to develop this position.

CBT Evolution of Emotion

The role that emotion plays in psychotherapy is also important, but has eluded characterization by any single therapeutic perspective. Traditional global theories have been less parsimonious or efficient under these new formulations. Psychoanalysis holds that emotions act as drives; cognitive/ behavioral approaches consider emotions to be post cognitive phenomenon; and experiential/humanistic approaches regard emotions as important motivators of change that require experiencing. In recent years traditional distinctions made regarding affect, cognition, and behavior have been bounced around in search of a comfortable place. Emotions in particular have been considered products of a synthesis of factors at the physiological, motor, semantic, and conceptual levels. Most recent trends in psychotherapy (e.g., Daldrup, Beutler, Engle, & Greenberg, 1988) show that the emotion does not play a single role in psychotherapeutic change. A more differentiated view of emotional change distinguishing various types of emotional processes is required.

Simplistically, researchers in CBT have progressed in the area of emotions and PTSD from two sources, one based on Lang (1983) and, more recently, the writings of Safran and Segal (Safran & Segal, 1990) and Greenberg (Greenberg & Safran, 1989; Safran & Greenberg, 1991). According to Lang (1983), an emotional network or prototype becomes activated and processed when an individual attends to information that matches a sufficient number of propositions of the schema. Once the right combination or "best fit" occurs, the emotion emerges and is consciously experienced. The emotion is then the "final common" experience of a total cognitive-affective network (schemas). Various other authors including Horowitz (1986), Litz and Keane (1989), Chemtob (Chemtob, Roitblat, Hamada, Carlson, & Twentyman, 1988), and Foa and Kozak (1986) have endorsed this bioinformational model of trauma networks. While largely cognitive these models also reflect the network of emotions involved in the trauma network. According to the Safran and Greenberg group, however, emotion is considered more of an integrated response with various levels of physiological, motor, and cognitive activation. The task of the therapist is to use reasonable psychotherapeutic processes of emotions—synthesizing, evoking, restructuring, and modifying emotions (Greenberg & Safran, 1989)—for purposes of exposure, understanding, and change.

In recent years an increasing agreement has occurred among these theorists: cognitions and emotions interact in such a way as to make any distinction quixotic. Izard (1991), for example, noted that cognition activates emotions and, once activated, emotions influence cognition (perception, thought, memory). Lazarus (1991) also discussed the detente in emotion-cognitive thinking, noting that emotions are organized motivational-cognitive-adaptational configurations and that, whatever component is piqued or altered, all others are influenced or changed as well. Affect is one type of action with meaning; cognitions may be at the center of affectaction themes but it is part of a complex involving other components. The "living connection" between thought and emotion constitute a centerpiece of therapeutic interest and focus (Lazarus, 1991).

The Person

In this book we have emphasized the integration of reactions, cognition, affect, and behavior, according to a whole person organization, life-style (schema and personality). In a sense meaning is assigned and given response probabilities as input. Each individual has his/her characteristic pattern of applying specific, selective, and elaborative rules to this process. When emotions are expressed, whether primary or secondary, the predisposition to any habitual pattern is the result of a whole person "meaning assignment" (Kreitler & Kreitler, 1988) or pro forma schema orchestration.

Trauma victims experience a plethora of intense primary and secondary emotions. Each has developed his/her own profile, based on "successful" approach and avoidance mechanisms. Assessment of the ongoing experience of the victim is often difficult and changing. Nonetheless, *the need for direct therapeutic attention to the internal processing of emotions appears to be a necessary way for change to occur.* Reasonable evidence (Greenberg & Safran, 1989) is available to conclude that the more differentiated this process is, the higher the level of client experiencing the process is (arousal). Also, the greater the level of client understanding in this process (meaning), the more the change of meaning structures (schemas) will result. Often this is a moment-by-moment process of experiences flushing out and deepening the amorphous mass of feelings. Eventually core schemas are accessed. The attention to internally valenced information, then, stimulates the cognitive-affective schemas, and over time new meaning structures are provided.

We have argued that cognitive and emotional experiences have a basic schema template. This consists of an elaboration of subtle and expressed blends of emotional expressions (anger, love, pride, envy, sadness) which are subject to continuous conceptual appraisal as they occur. All trauma sufferers are beset with a pervasive emotional apprehension that is attached to the cues of the trauma experience. It includes multiple person experiences of the event— dreams, associations, reactions, and the like. At the base of the trauma experience, however is a pervasive anxiety which mixes with inner or other directed valences (emotions) that are shaped by the trauma and by the person's original schema. The result is the current and dynamic phenomenology of the ongoing emotional experience. This expression is most pointedly a transaction between the person's central mechanisms, the trauma memory and the current situation.

Emotion and PTSD

A recognition is to be made that our formulation of emotion is far from complete (or even a representative accounting) in regards to PTSD. The nature and extent of emotional response deficits, both hypo- and hyper-emotionality, is at present largely unexamined. Safran and Greenberg (1991) specified that affect change takes many forms: emotional restructuring, catharsis, experiential symbolization, cognitive reorganization, motivation, corrective emotional experiences, and affect attunement. But, the position is that at some level affect alteration involves changes in schema restructuring. The "new self" formation takes place in a safe environment where the original memory or experience is explored and often a corrective emotional experience occurs—the therapeutic relationship itself facilitates change. Through this process cognitive appraisals serve a moderating role.

The emotional processes in a PTSD victim also reflect the person's trial and error efforts at coping. These are never easy to understand or differentiate but often are murky and subverting. Emotions are always influential. In PTSD if the challenges of life do not exceed the person's "capacity" to respond, life moves on; if they do, a crisis develops and some effort must be made to reorganize. Just as PTSD may be the victim's way to bring some level of adaptation to the situation, so too emotional disruption is the human system's way of bringing homeostasis (Mahoney, 1991). Victims react emotionally most of the time, some over- and some under-responding, in order to make sense of their own phenomenal world. Regarding under-responding, Mahoney (1991) wrote:

Researchers investigating emotional processes in psychotherapy have begun to acknowledge that individuals vary considerably in their capacities to experience different feelings. More often than not, those who are skilled at "not feeling" have survived traumas or training that somehow taught the adaptive value of emotional detachment. Indeed those skills appear to be related to personal identity and individual experiences of psychological change. (p. 209)

The clinician is the one who must assist in this differentiating and healing process.

We have chosen to address only one of these vehement complexes of trauma sufferers, **guilt.** This is perhaps the most complex, requiring a melding of several primary emotions. It is also pervasive, as most trauma victims experience it, and persistent, as it remains through time. We have chosen this also because less is written on this emotional complex regarding trauma victims. In addition, we have chosen guilt because it "demands" respect from therapists, a healing theory for its resolution. Finally, information on this most troubling of emotions is highly generalizable to others.

We address several issues. First, some background on guilt is provided followed by the purposes of guilt and then a contextualization of guilt in the person (schema). Second, a taxonomy of guilt is considered. Third, we also attempt to provide a treatment orientation, focusing on psychoeducation, dynamic issues, and techniques. Finally, we address an especially resistent problem among trauma victims—alexithymia.

GUILT: THE UNIVERSAL VEHEMENT EMOTION

Guilt can be defined as a painful affect, often accompanied by thoughts of self-blame, which occur after a violation in reality or fantasy of a schema regarding how one should behave (or think or feel). Despite the fact that guilt is not a part of the categories of the DSM-III-R, it has been found to be a frequent symptom among chronic combat related victims (Hyer, 1991). The role of guilt in the symptom picture of PTSD, however, is equivocal. On the one hand, the symptom picture of this disorder appears reasonably stable (Davidson & Foa, 1991). On the other hand, factor analytic studies of PTSD symptoms (Silver & Iacono, 1984;

Watson, Juba, Manifold, Kucala, & Anderson, 1991)) or scales of PTSD (Hyer, Davis, Boudewyns, & Woods, 1991; Keane, Caddell, & Taylor, 1988) have shown guilt to play an independent role. In addition, various symptom assessments of PTSD (e.g., Blake, Nagy, Kaloupek, Klauminzer, Charney, & Keane, 1990) consider guilt an important component of PTSD. While the current nosology has eliminated both survivor guilt and guilt over one's behavior, two separate studies (Kuhne, Baraga, & Czekala, 1988; Van Kampen, Watson, Tilleskjor, Kucala, & Vassar, 1986) showed the latter form of guilt (at least) to be correlated with PTSD.

Probably because guilt is viewed only as an occasional or minor symptom of PTSD, most diagnosticians would place these symptoms in the "ancillary" pile of symptoms for trauma. One cannot set up symptom structures on the basis of factor analysis alone, however. Watson et al. (1991), have suggested a two tiered process. First, a group of necessary symptoms should be established. Other symptoms (e.g., guilt) should be made to correspond to a list of necessary criteria which can be arranged into categories by factor analyses. Second, the approach advocated here builds on the "tier" formulation and the polythetic model, which posits that no condition is necessary or sufficient for a diagnosis but share various degrees of "centrality" of the disorder. Guilt in this sense applies to an individual or group of victims where appropriate. With combat veterans this would be quite substantial.

Psychoanalytic Positions

This symptom also has been well documented in the literature on the effects of various trauma. Regarding war veterans, Grinker and Spiegel (1945) noted that almost all returning combat veterans experience some guilt. Many related it to killing as well as to surviving while others did not. Classically, guilt related to combat was considered "neurotic" or not related to actual misdeeds. War related acts were assumed to be in the line of duty with guilt stemming from unconscious wishes and fantasies. The traditional approach to treatment was to "alleviate the guilt and thereby aid repression by taking the responsibility from the individual and placing it on a higher authority (one was following orders.)" (Haley, 1974, p. 192).

In the literature, references to splitting and fragmenting or the formation of new psychic structures as a result of intense and painful emotions, including guilt and its precursors, fear and helplessness, and the consequent denial of those emotions, are noted. The trauma related complexes or structures drain energy from the healthy part of the personality resulting in "mental exhaustion and disorganization" (van der Hart, Brown, & van der Kolk, 1989). In his *Introduction to Psychoanalysis and the War Neurosis*, Freud (1919/1955) spoke about a "war superego". . . which not only permits the expression of impulses otherwise forbidden, but even makes demands that are tempting to the ego because the superego never permitted such impulses to be brought into action. The war superego is a "parasitic double" (Freud, 1919/1955). PTSD has long been described as a state of disorganization, which is equivalent to a loss of memory. As the person tries to block out a memory, he/she creates disorganization. This blocking is like a convex obstacle on a billiard table which increases the randomness of the ball's movement (Bennett, 1988). This blocking is against distressing emotions, one of which is guilt.

One of the earliest formulations of PTSD came from Pierre Janet (van der Kolk, Brown, & van der Hart, 1989). The core issue of post-traumatic syndromes was the inability to integrate traumatic memory into the total personality. The traumatic experiences were frightening or novel and could not fit into already existing cognitive schemas. These memories were, therefore, split off from conscious awareness and control. Janet viewed the "vehement emotions" resulting from the trauma induced helplessness as interfering with memory storage. In Janet's analysis a subjective interpretation of an experience was essential to encoding it in existing cognitive schemes. Regarding guilt, Janet believed that this was best undertaken with a focus on verbal memories rather than traumatic imagery. This required a supportive and reassuring stance to the patient.

Holocaust and Vietnam

More recent writers also have documented the resistant and pernicious quality of guilt. Krystal (1981) studied holocaust survivors and found that even after nearly forty years guilt was still present. Chodoff (1980) considered guilt intractable to psychotherapy in holocaust survivors. Similarly, Goderez (1987) has described guilt as the most "implacable aspect" of therapy with combat veterans. Williams (1987) stated, that, as a result of his experience with over two thousand trauma victims, when someone does not improve in treatment, it is because survivor guilt has not been resolved. Auerhahn and Laub (1984) concluded about trauma survivors, "the survivor of war and genocide, at best, never achieves more than a perpetual oscillation and interpenetration between images of annihilation and those of mastery or nurturance" (p. 342). Lindy (1988) studied the efficacy of psychotherapy in treating Vietnam combat veterans and noted that, although treatment resulted in improvement in many areas, self-reports about guilt remained unchanged. He believed, however, that the treated veterans could be more tolerant of their guilt. In commenting on her clinical work with holocaust survivors Ornstein (1981) considered "one functioning sector" of the personality as a reasonable goal of therapy. This reduced goal was largely due to guilt. Finally, Catherall (1986) noted that Vietnam veterans who performed atrocities and were excited at the time are at greater risk for guilt.

Guilt in the Vietnam veteran is particularly difficult due to the multiple trauma events contributing to this feeling. Guilt has become a permanent condition more than a feeling associated with a particular episode. Events also may have become emotionally fused and confused. Since "real" psychological change requires a selforganizing process that touches personal meanings in life, guilt is very central to the human self. The assumption should not be that these emotions will be easy to alter or that guilt will go away with the passage of time. Untreated guilt in a patient with PTSD will probably be associated with no progress or a downward spiral. Patients often comment that the older they get, the worse the guilt is. Krystal (1981) stated:

> Old age, with its losses, imposes the inescapable necessity of facing one's past" (p.177). He notes further; " . . . Progressive loss of gratification, support, and distractions limits one's choices to integrating one's life or living in despair . . . In old age . . . we come to a point where our past lays unfolded before us, and the question is, What should be done with it? The answer is, it must be accepted or we must keep waging an internal war against the ghosts of our past. (pp. 167-168)

PURPOSES OF GUILT

Another parsimonious explanation of guilt is that it is a repetitive devaluation that serves some purpose for the person. In effect, what occurs is a reversal of the pain—pleasure polarity, resulting in an undoing of affect and intention and of transposing need qualifications with those leading to frustration. Many veterans pay the penalty for their self-perceived transgressions through self-condemning, self-punishing, and self-destructive life-styles. This behavior can be identified in acts of penance or self-punishment. In fact, clients can be offered the interpretation that their suffering is a self-induced way of punishing themselves. The sufferer can be challenged on how much more he/she needs to suffer until he/she has been punished enough. Often what prevails is an understanding of this self-defeating strategy but an unwillingness to change. Guilt is persistent.

Self-inflected Aggression

Psychodynamically, the theory is that the painful affect resulting from guilt is aggression directed against the self for having transgressed an inner standard of acceptable behavior. This was developed through interaction and identification with previous authority figures. Bergler (1952/1988) in his book *The Superego* noted that infantile megalomania is preserved when the child punishes the self: "It is not that the bad mother punishes me; I through my provocations make her punish me" (p. viii). In this unconscious version of logic, the child triumphs. By punishing self, the victim establishes that he/she is moral. The self-imposed punishment expiates some of the guilt and is a mechanism of atonement. The goal of such expiatory behavior is not self-punishment for its own sake, but the restoration of a feeling of parental love (Rado, 1956) or perhaps just homeostasis.

Given the undeserving repetition of guilt, one can understand why many victims act out or commit crimes to bring punishment to expiate the guilt. This dynamic was described in Freud's *Criminals From a Sense of Guilt* (1916/1957). In this brief but major paper, Freud noted that the very action of committing a crime can derive from an underlying sense of unconscious guilt for a deeper repressed "crime." The latent state of ill-defined distress can paradoxically be relieved by committing an actual (or repeat) crime for which the patient can then consciously feel guilt. In such cases the "sense of guilt was at least attached to something" (p. 332). In addition, the punisher becomes the state through real criminal activity instead of the omniscient and inescapable superego. This defensive activity is often interminable unless the patient becomes conscious of the earlier guilt that plagues him/her.

One patient felt guilt over having killed children in Vietnam. He pleaded guilty to an auto accident about one year after returning home from the service, even though he did not believe he was at fault.

> Patient: You have to understand the Marines. I went to the Marines when I was 17, I was a baby. They brainwashed us. We were taught to be patriotic and have pride. They tore us down and built us back up to be what they wanted. They wanted us to be killers.

> Therapist: Were you a killer?

> Patient: We did search and destroy. They would drop leaflets telling people to leave the area. If anyone was left, they were the enemy and we would shoot them.

> Therapist: What did you think about this?

> Patient: In the Marines you don't think. All you do is follow orders. It is almost like you are hypnotized. I thought only about doing my duty.

> Therapist: So you were really acting out of a sense of duty?

> Patient: I was involved in killing children. At first I did not feel anything. It did not bother me because I thought they would grow up to be the enemy.

But I started to visit the children's hospital. I saved the candy from my rations pack to give the children. At first I didn't want to visit the hospital, but I was ordered to. After a while, I wanted to go. I felt so badly about the children. I saw them in bed with limbs gone and tubes coming out. The injuries were terrible. I never saw so much pain and suffering in my life. They were all little bitsy children—five and six years old or babies. I started to realize that it was just luck whether a baby was born in the United States or in Vietnam. My dreams are about those children. And then I had a wreck about a year after the service. A child was killed and I spent a year in jail for vehicular death.

Therapist: Tell me what happened.

Patient: I had a date with a doctor's daughter. I was driving her father's car. We had a head on collision on a deep curvy part of the road in the mountains. There were controlled substance type prescription drugs in the trunk. I wasn't drinking or using drugs, but they wanted to charge me with something since they found the drugs in the trunk. They couldn't charge me with driving under the influence since my blood test came back negative, so they charged me with murder. It was reduced to vehicular death. I pleaded guilty since the family lost a child and deserved money from the insurance company. They could collect money if I pleaded guilty. No one really knows whose fault it was. There were no skid marks. It was a head on collision in a deep curvy road in the mountains. I wasn't speeding. They were in a small car, so they were hurt worse. We were in a large car. There was beer spilled all over the highway. We weren't drinking, so probably they were.

Therapist: So you pleaded guilty even though you weren't?

Patient: I thought that the family really deserved to get some money after losing the baby.

Therapist: Then you went to jail for a year.

Patient: At first I was put on probation, but I broke probation four times so I was sent to jail for two years. I was let out after one year for good behavior.

Self-devaluation becomes a powerful "drive." It iterates past injustices and sabotages possible positive events. It reminds one constantly of the worst features of self, asserting that one is worthy of shame and debasement. It is even more. Fenichel (1945) noted: "This fleeing from the conscious awareness of guilt becomes tragic when 'the mastery of guilt feelings becomes the all-consuming task of a person's whole life " p. 496). The now instinctively driven need to suffer infuses and misshapes the ego leading to syntonic "living out" atonement.

Other patients enjoy feeling high when they engage in a fight or good argument. This has been labeled **combat addiction** (Solursh, 1989), high sensation seeking, or given the biological notation of kindling (van der Kolk, 1985). Even psychosomatic symptoms in individuals with persecutory guilt function as a type of self-punishment (Grinberg, 1964). Freud (1923/1961, p. 50) described a guilt which is "dumb; it does not tell the victim he is guilty." The victim does not feel guilty; he/she feels ill. This sense of guilt expresses itself too as a resistance to recovery which is extremely difficult to overcome. Mowrer (1953) described guilty individuals as learning not to learn.

Clearly guilt is relentless in this population. Recent personality research (Hyer, Davis, Woods, Albrecht, & Boudewyns, in press) has documented the high incidence of the Self Defeating Personality, a disorder related to guilt. Victims of combat who have this personality disorder are distinctive; they show higher symptom levels, higher levels of psychological pain, greater problems in treatment, including earlier withdrawal, and greater amounts of suicidal behavior than comparable groups. The intrapunitive, intrapsychic structure of the guilty veteran of combat is a formidable foe in therapy.

Guilt As a Defense

Perhaps this is laboring on the obvious; guilt acts as a defense. The operative issues, however, are how does this emotion express itself and why is it so unforgiving in its actions.

To begin with, guilt is not subtle. Considerable evidence is available for deducting that guilt is a whole-body phenomenon. Physiologically, guilt is similar to fear in producing a rigidity of posture, staring, and feeling chilled (Gut, 1989, p. 77). Behaviorally, guilt may be expressed with a lowered head and lack of eye contact (Izard, 1977). The person may behave as if he/she were dead and vitality is reduced (Lifton, 1983). *Cognitively, the guilty person may be preoccupied with wrongdoing and invest significant psychological resources in an obsession* (Izard, 1977). The victim will condemn and criticize self. The self-concept is seen as a "bad person" who is responsible for death, destruction, or evil. The person is "responsible," the cause of terrible consequences. Intense guilt has been labeled "crippling" (Izard, 1977), and "tormenting" (Nunberg, 1934). Grinker and Spiegel (1945) have described the guilty combat veteran as "writhing under the strict and sadistic lashings of an irreconcilable superego" (p. 381). Thoughts of self-condemnation are accompanied by the belief that one deserves to die. Also, guilt can be associated emotionally with fears of punishment, loss of love, and loneliness (Nunberg, 1934).

Guilt frequently is combined with or preceded by shame. Shame is the emotion that results when a person becomes aware that he/she is deficient, a failure, worthless, and inadequate (Stone, 1992). It is characterized by downcast eyes, slumped posture, blushing, and cognitive blocking and confusion. Stone describes guilt as a coassembly of fear and shame. It is fear of punishment for a shameful transgression.

Because guilt is so tormenting, attempts are almost always made to defend against it. But, like the bad penny, guilt is always around. Out of conscious awareness or through numbing, guilt is easily projected and usually associated with belligerence or withdrawal. When this happens, a denial occurs and a separation of affect from cognition. In other cases (of numbing), somatization can occur. The guilt may be expressed on a visceral level. Grinker and Spiegel (1945) described guilty combat pilots who experienced digestive symptoms, but were not aware of their guilt. One pilot could keep nothing down. He explained, "this food is too rich for me—I've eaten C rations too long." Another experienced emesis or diarrhea following each meal. Rado (1956) hypothesized that a guilty person (as a self-defensive maneuver) may attack the very person he/she fears will punish him/her. He referred to this as "guilty rage" and construed this as different from projection—*Guilt demands action.*

Similarly, Cohen and Lohr (1992) have presented a description of the dynamics of trauma related guilt based on psychoanalytic theory. These authors discuss two types of guilt. The first involves unconscious guilt, people who are chronically and vehemently self-punitive. For them (unconscious) guilt is really fear that a paralyzing emotion will emerge if certain thoughts are allowed into awareness. These people go to great lengths to avoid acknowledging moral transgression. The second type entails conscious guilt and is characterized by those who constantly experience unremitting guilt. Most importantly, conscious guilt screens other more painful thoughts, feelings, or memories. It is also a product of complex affect and conflict. Often this guilt is a compromise affect defending against the emergency of less acceptable emotions, such as rage or shame. Conscious guilt can even represent an attempt to maintain a sense of control when faced with helplessness. In the case of severe ego weakness, guilt aids in preventing psychotic disintegration. So, both types of guilt serve other "deeper" functions, allowing for a more acceptable experience of this overdetermined emotion.

Developmental Level

While guilt is largely a defensive action, its expression is determined in part by its developmental level. Grinberg (1964) identified two types of guilt: persecutory and depressive. *Persecutory guilt* begins at a very early stage of development and is expressed clinically as resentment, paranoia, and hypochondriasis. *Depressive guilt* is developmentally more advanced and is characterized by sorrow, empathy, and concern for the victim. Individuals who experience depressive guilt are likely to have more control over impulses to act sadistically toward others. This type of guilt is then a better prognostic indicator (Grinker & Spiegel, 1945). Fox (1974) described a more primitive type of guilt. When a "buddy" dies in combat, the veteran may become aware of feelings of murderous rage and wishes for revenge. The primary feeling is revenge, rather than mourning. The buddy is a narcissistic extension of the self due to the close bonding inherent in the combat situation and in adolescence. The death of the buddy is, therefore, a narcissistic injury, and combat missions are opportunities for the expression of the revengeful wishes. If the individual actually acted on the murderous rage, he/she would suffer from primitive guilt in which the talion law of retribution operates. The wish for revenge is based on the stimulus of internal danger (the narcissistic injury) and does not end with removal from the battlefield. Rage and guilt persist with the passage of time, whether or not acts of revenge have been carried out against the enemy.

Developmentally, any delay in the application of reward or punishment by authority in the past caused the child to experience confusion about timing and the control of gratification. Guilty clients then develop a pattern in which immediate gratification was the primary interest (Stein, 1968). This behavior stimulates guilt and self-punishment long after the event. The "to-be" trauma victim is programmed for guilt. Reality testing is lacking. Recall too that guilt is a punishment system, as well as one of anticipatory anxiety. In this way a sense of future is lacking. Patients, especially those who learned to solve problems with physical aggression in Vietnam and did not experience censure from authorities, are particularly in need of help. The wary therapist should repeatedly call attention to cause and effect sequences.

The Proxy Emotion

If guilt is so obvious, what exactly is it defending? Several descriptions of this have been provided. Masters, Friedman, and Getzel (1988) assessed family members of survival victims of trauma. Several underlying reasons or behavior related to guilt were noted: (1) *defense from vulnerability;* (2) *reality based* as risky behaviors occurred before the trauma; (3) *rage and blaming* serves as a defensive displacement of guilt; and (4) a *defensive displacement* of anger against others. In special situations the reason for self-blame may even change. Roth & Lebowitz (1988) speculated that guilt among rape victims represents a sense of *control over fate* or over overwhelming affect. What seems clear is that the emotion guilt is used to establish a position, make a statement, or alter less acceptable feelings. It fails.

Several specific defenses have been noted. One of the most common involves *helplessness*. Individuals who survive massive trauma frequently experience profound feelings of guilt. A cognitive distortion is commonly experienced following a disaster, "paradox of guilt in disaster victim populations" (Rosenman, 1956). When an individual is placed in a helpless or dependent situation by an overwhelming force, primitive thought mechanisms are activated. The disaster is no longer an impersonal force; it becomes personified on an unconscious (if not conscious) level. The individual identifies with that force and feels that the disaster represents a hostile expression. *Identification with the disaster enables the individual to feel control over it.* Parson (1984) among others has described the ubiquitous *"victim self"* among Vietnam veterans.

Guilt serves the function of *self-protection both by inaction and feelings of superiority.* As noted, guilt protects against shame as well as being a result of trauma. Often guilt allows the victim to feel power or control over their situation. Guilt may enable the person, for example, to feel that he/she is moral. To be moral has many advantages including the chance to be forgiven. A related aspect of control with guilt involves dependency and passivity. If a victim has trouble controlling hostile impulses, he/she can assert control by assuming a powerless identity in which others are manipulated into making decisions and taking responsibility for him/her. Many guilty individuals develop psychosomatic symptoms, which further justify dependency. Guilt even allows the indirect expression of aggressive impulses. Guilt is contagious and the guilty person frequently causes those around him/her to experience the same painful affect he/she harbors. This indirect expression of hostility is not easily confronted by others.

Once the process of guilt "starts," it perpetuates itself.
The person, for example, begins to feel the need to continue
aggression in order to maintain a violent self-image (Glover,
1988). To remain "bad" is easier than to face the anxiety
of change. In these cases the guilt needs to be acknowledged.
Once the guilt in violent and self-destructive individuals is
acknowledged, victims can become verbal and self-reflective.
Grinker and Spiegel (1945) reported an "amazing change"
in patients when their unconscious guilt is made conscious.
These authors discussed the therapeutic benefits to intervention
on this guilt even as it effects the "traumatic dream."

As an interesting aside, soldiers are to some degree protected
from guilt by group dynamics (Grinker & Spiegel, 1945). Hostile
and aggressive activity is directed at the enemy for the purpose
of group goals. Identification with the group enables the combat
soldier to kill without guilt, since the expression of aggression
is controlled by shared group norms. If aggression is expressed
for the purpose of gratifying individual psychic needs, conflicts
will continue even after the war has ended (due to their
foundation in individual dynamics). Similarly, Hendin and
Haas (1984) noted that veterans without problematic guilt
after the war had killed strictly within the official military
context. Killing was not a source of excitement or an expression
of rage and was done with feelings of reluctance.

*A positive aspect of guilt is that it has a restraining function
and frequently controls rage.* This "good" control occurs because
the person anticipates the pain of a guilty conscience and
thus inhibits responses. Also externally directed aggression
is reduced. However, it can also lead to aggression. Some
combat veterans find guilt so painful that they ward it off
by projecting their own guilt and self-accusation onto others,
especially authority. This in turn justifies belligerent activity
toward them. Lifton (1983) also noted that "atrocity begets
atrocity." Many combat vets continue aggression to relieve
tension and avoid confronting guilt. In these cases the only
way to ward off guilt is to continue the aggressive acts in
order to justify them.

Somatic concerns, whether purely psychological or a
magnification of true problems, also help control rage. As

mentioned previously, this symptom justifies dependency and can act as a form of self-punishment. Some veterans will focus extensively on physical symptoms. Although a somatic preoccupation can be frustrating for the therapist, it should be dealt with gingerly. Frequently, it masks ferocious rage. As long as the patient feels he/she is a "cripple," then, he/she feels incapable of acting on his/her "murderous" impulses.

Guilt Is Expression of the Schema

Guilt is more than "just" a defense. Recall our model. *Once trauma has occurred, the individual's view of the world is selectively altered.* Victims perceive their environment in ways consistent with the schema. They fail, however, to assimilate discrepant information, which would enable the schema to be modified, since it arouses painful affect. In this way a bruised schema, which might have been an adaptive response to an extreme event, continues after a return to "normalcy." The individual is now defending a script and interpreting neutral stimuli in the context of a traumatic situation. A particular maladaptive resolution evolves on anyone of several emotional paths (Epstein, 1991).

The most common concerns that bring clients to psychotherapy involve intimacy, empowerment, openness to relationships, and guilt (Elliott & James, 1989). This last category, negative self-evaluation is an outgrowth of part of the person's process of acknowledging problems: "I did something wrong," can be a positive anodyne. Guilt becomes a problem when the person "internalizes" or "identifies with" his/her need for responsibility (through omission or commission). *Guilt, then, becomes attached to the person's schema, however, when the trauma cannot be truly integrated into the person and a key "guilt related" schema is affected.*

Learning how the client misinterprets is usually intimately related to the trauma and actions (Epstein, 1991), or to the schema (McCann & Pearlman, 1990), or both. In fact, reenactments of trauma that are guilt based are often rather transparent.

While this can involve any schema(s), it often involves the schemas, esteem or independence. The special meaning, therefore, that self-blame has for a victim in the context of the schema must be understood for repair work to be effective (McCann & Pearlman, 1990). The therapist can observe how the victim relates in therapy to others, to himself/herself and how he/she apperceives stimuli. Regarding esteem and guilt, McCann and Pearlman (1990) wrote:

> . . .resolving disturbed esteem schemas must take place in the context of a thorough understanding of the whole person, the strength of the self-capacities, the person's central needs, and the meanings of esteem for this individual. It is well known that traumatic experiences, as well as those that involve neglect, failures in empathy, or lack of validation, can result in varying degrees of disturbances in self-esteem. For some, the damage is circumscribed or balanced by positive esteem schemas. For others, the damage is pervasive, becoming a central issue for the individual, creating disturbances in his or her intrapersonal and interpersonal relations. (p. 197)

Victims frequently suffer a profound loss in self-esteem and in feelings of being worthy. So, in addition to abuse of selected schemas, a universal person disruption occurs also. McCann and Pearlman (1990) labeled this schema *frame of reference* (along with esteem and independence). "Authentic" human assumptions that the self is bad, evil, or destructive or that one is responsible for bad, evil, or destruction, develop. The belief that one deserves suffering infects clear thinking. Experiences which represent a violation of the self especially produce these reactions. In this way personal and universal schemas commingle and cause problem guilt. Male victims, for example, who find themselves in a powerless situation, due to high expectations for personal power (independence), may develop overcontrolling strategies, which include constricted affect, psychic numbing or avoidance in order to protect the schema from the experience of powerlessness. Conversely, this same person may decrease the discrepancy between input and schemas by revising his personal schemas to include a helpless or powerless self. The behavioral response may include passivity, depression, and hopelessness. Once a "guilty" schema has ascended as a result of a traumatic experience, giving up this "pain" is most difficult, both because of the anxiety aroused in modifying a particular schema and the universal human insult. Both appear "stuck."

In Table 9.1 is presented a list of common guilt expressions of various schemas. The idea is that any schema can express itself as guilt because the schema is centrally related to guilt (as in esteem) or to guilt-specific aspects of the person's schema (usually, as we noted, related to responsibility). Although everyone is predisposed to a breakdown of coping mechanisms under massive stress, the latent conflicts which will be activated depend on the individual's history. In addition, the emotion generated by some information will depend on the meaning of that information for the individual (Lazarus, 1989). The meaning goes back to previous experience and learning.

Other Authors. Various other authors also have described the phenomena of guilt through the filtration of the schema. Hendin, Pollinger, Singer, and Ulman (1981) described two different veterans responding differently to the same trauma, seeing a Vietnamese prisoner pushed from a helicopter. One veteran, who felt he had been deprived of adequate attention as a child, identified with the victim. After the war he continued to see himself in the victim role. A second veteran reacted to the trauma by identifying with the aggressor and felt he could have prevented the atrocity. This veteran had learned to be independent and self-sufficient at a young age. After the war he continued to find roles in which he could be a responsible protector.

Grinker and Spiegel (1945) also described how different personalities responded to war related trauma. The passive-dependent person becomes depressed when separated from the group or from supportive figures because he/she feels the loss of love. He/she feels disappointment. In contrast, the obsessive-compulsive personality reacts strongly to the "loss of a buddy, to poor living conditions and to deviations from smooth running performances." These men displace hostility from family to officers and comrades in their military group. Comrades will come to represent brothers and officers, fathers. When one dies, they will react with the same ambivalence that was felt toward the original family member symbolized. These authors wrote:

> Loss of these loved objects, toward whom quantities of unconscious hostility are harbored, disturbs the whole psychological equilibrium of the individual. In these cases the unconscious hostility evokes guilt and self punishment. The superego reacts against the unexpressed wishes, or interprets innocent deeds as the cause of the comrade's death. (p. 305)

Hendin and Haas (1984) noted the importance of prewar and postwar relationships; individuals with more significant interpersonal relationships before and after the war (than war related friendships) were less likely to suffer guilt over having survived comrades. They wrote: "Among many veterans we have seen with survivor guilt, friendships developed during the war appear to have superseded other attachments in their lives" (p. 214).

In a recent case a veteran had been overprotected prior to joining the Marines. He felt that he had been spoiled. Kids in his neighborhood called him a "big ole baby." He joined the marines to prove himself, since they are the "toughest." Prior to joining the Marines he had never had any responsibilities and had been shy. After serving six months in combat he was promoted to corporal and was proud. One of his first duties at this rank was to lead a squad on a patrol. While on this patrol several men were killed when a mine was hit. The patient continued to feel guilt about that incident. He stated that it was not unusual for men on patrol to fake visiting the various check points. According to his report they would hide about 25 feet from the bunker and radio the coordinates at appropriate time intervals. He felt that the officers were probably aware of the artifice but collaborated due to the highly risky nature of the patrol. Because he was just promoted, the patient followed the book and actually carried out the mission. He believes that if he only had "sense enough" to fake it, the deaths would not have occurred. As a result the patient refuses responsibility on a job. He devalues himself, having abused his long standing schema of esteem and competence; now he is a failure. He is unable to handle

TABLE 9.1
Schemas and Associated Guilt Expression*

Schema	Guilt Monitor
Safety	Survivor guilt Feeling cheated/abused Cowardly feeling Ineffectuality/devaluation
Trust	Alienation from self and society Abandoned by all Feeling inhuman Others are flawed. . .I am at risk
Power	One has superhuman qualities Avoid responsibility Feels like a monster Intellectualize/distances self
Esteem	I am flawed I can't be forgiven I am alone Survivor guilt
Intimacy	I am a monster/flawed Numbing I let others down/betrayal Abandoned
Acceptance	Numbing I am a monster I can't be forgiven
Competence	Survivor guilt Superman guilt Harsh superego I am useless
Control	Survival guilt Overcontrolling others Feels alientated from all Fears loss of control Ostracized from society

*Extrapolated in part from McCann & Pearlman, 1990.

anxiety associated with the possibility that he made a "mistake." Decision making is now beyond him. As he gained more seniority on jobs, he reacted by calling in sick and finally resigning.

Therapist: You feel sad about the guy who died?

Patient: I feel responsible. I was pretty close to him. He was white. He was a hillbilly. I look for them to be prejudiced, but we used to kid each other. I think about him a lot.

Therapist: How did this affect your work with the fire department.?

Patient: ". . . I had seniority. Sometimes a captain would take off. So, because of my seniority they made me in charge. That's a lot of responsibility in the fire department. I wouldn't take responsibility since people died when I was responsible in Vietnam. If a house is on fire sometimes you have to give an order to someone to cut a hole in the roof to let out gases and see what's happening and to attack the fire. That's a very dangerous job. As an acting captain you have to give an order and there was no way I was going to do that. I got written up. I got in trouble a lot because I wouldn't give orders. I felt a big load has been dropped off of me since I left the fire department two years ago. I went to the fire department straight from Vietnam. At the fire department I had a lot of problems with sick leave. I had made the one year probation, so that's why I lasted 15 years."

Exactly how this guilt process infects the schema, interacts with the schema and trauma, or "plays itself out" for long periods in a person's life has as many expressions as there are people. Also, how guilt interacts with other symptoms is not well understood. Numbing, for example, probably both masks and prolongs guilt. What does seem clear is that this emotion is pernicious and infects the schema at multiple levels. While we have argued that guilt is a whole person response, the cognitive element, responsibility, accompanies intrusions and alters the experience to one of guilt. Salkovski (1986) labeled this expression "magical thinking." Responsibility is more likely to occur if the individual has certain already learned schemas (e.g., esteem) or "deviant" acts occur (omission or commission). This combination especially appears to be a problem leading to guilt.

Some victims are guilty, some are not. With combat victims the latter group is small. The filters of universal meaning and particular schemas combined with trauma or guilt-specific issues make this emotion appealing. Perhaps, more than anything the particular sense of self that is violated (schema) along with having survived combat are just too overwhelming a combination to hold back the guilt. Catherall (1986) wrote:

> Their style of coping with guilt will be consistent with their lifelong psychologies and will be understood best in terms of their whole life histories. But the stimulus for the current conflict is best understood and interpreted in terms of the very real life experience of surviving in a traumatic situation when others did not survive. (p. 474)

TYPOLOGY

Classification systems often fail due to their own weight. This appears to be the case with guilt. A working conceptualization of this emotion would provide a clinically relevant basis with irresistible suggestions that are ecologically based. Unfortunately, those provided pale according to such criteria. The reason quite simply is that the emotion comes directly from the self (schema) and, as such, as many shades of self-condemnation exist as filters to a person's schema. No one has written the manual for the care of guilt.

Nonetheless, certain universal features exist about this feeling state and so do some helpful formulations. At best, guilt involves definite components: a transgression (even in fantasy), self-attribution or personal responsibility, and, in the case of chronic victims, repetition. Opp and Samson (1989) described guilt as a sense of regret over loss (experienced in the context of relative helplessness), accompanied by a theory of attribution that establishes personal responsibility and generates self-condemning thoughts. At the overt level, guilt commands the guilty party to conform or act; at the dynamic level, it mandates self-condemnation. Also, the form guilt takes is influenced by one's moral system. Price (1990) believed this is a function of four basic aspects: (1) the acentric (God), (2) forensic (laws), (3) ethical (society's press), and (4) personal (person's value system). So, we have a self-imposed emotion that "stops" or "unfrees" the person and takes form from the person's schema, the situation, and the culture.

Data from our archives (Hyer, 1991) indicate that virtually all chronic combat related PTSD victims expressed concerns about guilt. The belief is that of a ubiquitous phenomena because the trauma situation involved actions (omissions or commission) over which dire consequences occurred in a relatively "less mature" individual and has been reinforced for more than two decades. As noted, guilt is maintained because construals of war trauma center on some form of personal responsibility, leading to feelings of self-condemnation or regret. Always, combat victims relate that personal and social standards were violated. Much of these ruminations also involved reality based actions, behaviors for which guilt was intended to be a governor. Finally (as we noted), guilt is maintained because it serves multiple latent functions, such as defending against helplessness, continuing self punishment, inhibiting impulses (ones own self-rage), and preventing the trauma event from being meaningless (Opp & Samson, 1989).

Several efforts have been made at classifying guilt using this population. Opp and Samson (1989) divided guilt into five types (Table 9.2). These guilt expressions are helpful not because they are accurate, but they provide a way to disassemble the "vehement emotion", to muster a dialogue, to challenge positions, and to rearrange ideas. Of course, other forms of guilt do exist. Lindy (1988) described survivor guilt according to its "multi" richness—an organizer against helplessness, existential, neurotic, and real. Smith (1982) emphasized the importance of examining the role of commission and omission

(continued on page 474)

TABLE 9.2
Taxonomy of Guilt*

Type	Meaning/Symptoms	Treatment
Survivor	Believes own survival has cheated someone else	-obtain a dialogue with person who died
	Believes someone died so "I can live"	-identify self-destructive behavior as paranoid
	Is preoccupied with dead comrades	-ritualize "good bye" (mourning)
	Fears success	
Demonic	Is aware of a participation in atrocities	-work toward acceptance of human imperfection
	Often feels like a devil/animal	-obtain self-disclosure of other "monsters"
	Shows symptoms of	-foster control over action
	1. Excessive anger as uncontrollable "monster"	-integrate human and "monster" selves
	2. Personal isolation	
	3. Substance abuse	
	4. Fear of loss of control	
	5. Paranoid feelings	

Type	Meaning/Symptoms	Treatment
Moral/Spiritual	Violates moral/recited rules ("Thou shalt not kill")	-explore client's beliefs/values
	Has sense of moral condemnation ("I am going to hell")	-explore one incident (think out loud regarding transgressions and its moral context)
	Needs to be punished over an erroneous debt	-work toward confession
	Feels abandoned by society/God	-reframe value system to human forgiving one
	Finds fault with institution	
	Has feeling, "I am going to hell"	
Betrayal/ Abandonment	Believes "I had it easy; others suffered"	-expose reaction formation
	Fears abandonment/capture/being wounded	-identify real and ideal self
	Feels ostracized by society and responsible	-help overcome fear of being rejected by therapist,
	Feels selfish/inadequate/cowardly	-expose shame
Superman/woman	Fears helplessness in combat, (therefore I can do all)	-expose need for perfection
	Does magical thinking that fails	-expose control/intellectualization magical thinking
		-obtain cognitive exposition of narcissism schema

*Extrapolated from Opp & Samson, 1989

of action. Guilt causes acts of commission that are usually related to having committed violence which caused death or maiming, or to atrocities. This type of guilt is extremely painful. Guilt over omission is related to self-blaming for passivity or indecision which resulted in death or injury. Finally, Janoff-Bulman (1985) identified self-blame as a common reaction to trauma. Two types of self-blame are noted: behavioral, which is adaptive focusing on behaviors that are modifiable, or characterological, which is maladaptive and identifies some enduring character trait as the problem.

Also another form of guilt is evident among this population, existential. We previously alluded to this. **Existential guilt** is reinforced by years of self-reproach, responsibility, beliefs, and feelings of self-pity intermixed with self-rage. Existential guilt addresses issues such as: "What kind of person am I?" "Is this really my only life?" "What is my purpose in life?" "Who am I?" Existent guilt occurs when "predigested" data mixes with person issues. A self focus on unsolvable issues in life represents the concern. "Other voices in other rooms" cannot be shut out and become vexations on past self, current self, and even future self. This form of guilt cannot be "cured," as it is referenced in the human struggle (McCann & Pearlman, 1990).

While helpful, a taxonomy of guilt is limited. Opp and Samson's (Table 9.3) taxonomy, while helpful, eludes the pervasive overlap of this emotion and (except for demonic guilt) has few behavior referents. These authors (Opp & Samson, 1989) wrote:

> The central type of guilt experienced by a veteran is determined by an interplay among his or her personality as it was developed at the time of entering combat, the particular set of circumstances that the veteran encountered, and the impact of subsequent experiences influencing his or her interpretation of the events. (p. 164)

TREATMENT

Setting the Table

As we have iterated throughout this book, the approach considered maximally effective in therapy is extracting the most meaningful resource frames (person issues) of the person and parlaying these into the treatment model given in Chapter 6. This paradigm is most efficiently entered by the top-down approach (Safran & Greenberg, 1991). Over time, core schemas (bottom-up) can be unearthed and these person issues wrestled with. This same order applies here. Since guilt is the result of a transgression of a moral system, guilt has both "deep" and "surface" aspects. The former are human and existential and are the issues of identity or authenticity of a person. These may never be "healed", but can be exposed, understood, and better struggled with. Even if not cured, psychotherapy is helpful in their undoing. The surface aspects, on the other hand, involve both the day-to-day reminders of this condition (inner transgressions) as well as a "psycho-philosophy" on a larger perspective in self-care. A strange truism is that chronic trauma victims often believe that guilt is noble and the appropriate emotion for the "moral man": "After what I did who would not feel guilty!" A shift in contextualization is required: "My beliefs are contributing to my problems." This confrontation represents a relearning (psycho-philosophy) about guilt and about what to do at self-repair. Let us proceed from the outside-in.

Education and Skill Building

At the beginning the treatment of guilt is largely a process of information acquisition. The external aspect of self-knowing includes education and skill building. In a sense the client is given the primer course to understand and organize guilt related experiences. New information also can help to differentiate between situations where the victim was responsible and situations where no control was possible. Also data are involved about the whole experience; that is, the trauma experience, pretrauma experiences which are cognitively linked to the trauma, and current experience which are reminders of the trauma. This "unpacked" information objectifies the pain and facilitates the curative process. A secondary factor is that information facilitates in the control of distressing emotions (including guilt) which distract from the acquisition of "needed" new data. Remember, guilt need not reflect a disablement but simply the recognition that actions have consequences. People can "do good" in the future even if guilty. What "was" and what "is" are separate realities. *Guilt then is a moral truthfulness about the self.* To avow guilt is to make available for scrutiny the evaluation of acts.

Information starts with validation of the person, especially in the understanding of guilt. The therapist allies self with the patient in exploring the personal meaning of guilt related material. Accurate empathy is the goal; these feelings are real and *inevitable* given the victim's unique experience. With this sense consolidated, the therapist assists the client with the broader context: philosophical, emotional, and religious views about guilt in an effort to find meaning. The therapist also helps stabilize emotions by supporting impulse control during the examination of traumatic events. This feeling state then can be explored, understood, and challenged just like any set of cognitions. As the client sees "his/her condition" more clearly, he/she can achieve distance and perhaps a new understanding about his/her actions.

In Table 9.3 are presented important elements in the education of the guilty victim. Many features are involved in the education of guilt, but two are paramount. First is the issue of forgiveness. Obviously, maximal psychological health is a guilt free state, "I am forgiven." This sense of forgiveness is related to an acknowledgment of humanity, an understanding that the victim doesn't have to be perfect and that good people sometimes do bad things. At this point the victim can ask self, "Now that this has happened to me, what am I going to do about it?" (Clewell, 1987). The guilt is no longer avoided, numbed, or projected, but accepted. Innocence is not restored; integrity is. Perhaps the individual will choose to live with what he/she has done. The past cannot be erased or undone, no matter how much the patient would like it to be so. But, this "guilty past" can be reframed and smoothed. The victim can at least know that his/her bad feelings are "wrong," not a healthy position, or in some cases not reality based. At this moment, the victim's feelings— "why am I still this way?" —are now an entree into personal meanings and schemas.

Second, clients universally desire to forget. This victim must be reminded that he/she has tried unsuccessfully to forget for a long time and yet symptoms continued. The therapist might even tell the patient that: "Forgetting is only possible by first remembering, because you then know what you really have to forget or what problem you have to solve. You can't fight an unseen enemy" (Grinker & Spiegel, 1945, p. 378).

Skill acquisition can be viewed as teaching the person to behave as though he/she is not guilty. The person behaves as if dead in some ways. Activity, animation, and usual thought patterns are interrupted. Skill building counteracts self-defeating patterns as a result of guilt. These actions may lead to more guilt. Clients need to learn and practice coping skills before they can deal with trauma memories. The person may need "strength" to manage troublesome events including anger and painful thoughts. This prevents the continuous presence of secondary guilt—guilt as a result of day-to-day operations with self and others. Skill building helps control substance abuse and aggressive behavior, both of which interfere with the processing of traumatic material. Also, the underlying goal of unearthing self-punishing behavior is to achieve recognition and acceptance by society. The acquisition of skills can help the individual achieve this goal more directly.

Skill development means many things. Guilt is reduced as the person finds new interests in life which distract from mentally rehearsing a guilt related episode. Structure and balance in life help. As one's daily experience establishes new boundaries and limits, the client is able to set boundaries and limits on guilty feelings and memories. Victims report feeling less guilty as a result of a predictable environment. For some, a program of skill building therapy groups is a part of the structure. In sleep management, for example, patients are taught to follow a balanced daily routine with regular hours for rising, moderate exercise, controlled intake of caffeine and alcohol, and bedtime rituals. The self-discipline and challenge of guilt become fused in their struggle. Hygienic practice enables a new unconscious "doing"; guilt starts to be dislodged.

If Table 9.3 provides a "set table," then in Table 9.4 are specified coping techniques for the completion of the contextualization of guilt. It specifies the "stuff" of the attack

TABLE 9.3
Psycho-education: Elements in the Education of the Guilty Victim

---

Points:

1. Guilt is a <u>wrong</u> emotion/belief that is not moral.
2. Guilt is <u>human</u> and prevents further transgression and <u>abnormal</u> if it prevents growth or leads to destructive acts.
3. Guilt requires challenge as any negative cognition does. This means self-observation, self-talk, and self-reward.
4. A philosophy that challenges guilt is: "I was the only me I could have been; now I can choose to care for me."
5. By self-talk, actions, and commitment, a difference can be made.

Objectives:

1. To build observing ego (e.g., intent versus consequences of act, what is normal).
2. To separate emotional components from feeling of responsibility.
3. To emphasize military pride/achievement of good coping.
4. To encourage self-talk (rewards, tasks, etc.).
5. To balance and structure life.
6. To encourage self-mastery tasks.
7. To press for completion tendency of emtional experiences.
8. To use this therapeutic relationship as the arena for changing emotional schema.

---

process. Naturally this table is only a start in a therapist's armamentarium of tools. Increasing ego strength and self-esteem through skill building and the training of social competencies enable the victim to feel satisfaction through successful mastery and interaction with the environment. Self-esteem and self-worth increase. As the perception of being a worthwhile person increases, the capacity to examine weaknesses and deficits is greater. One technique involves the facilitation of positive images of the role of a soldier. This is not to whitewash or minimize responsibility for actions which occurred in a war zone, but to strengthen the ego by highlighting realistic strengths, so the person can recall and process information without "only" self blame. To confront "darker" aspects of one's life in a structured and balanced fashion rearranges the "governors" of guilt, an important start in treating guilt. The plainsong of "dark" and "light," of justice and care, begins.

Skill building is particularly important for chronic victims who have had inadequate and maladaptive life-styles. Almost always an atrophy has developed of competencies previously held. Again, failures in present-day life act as a stimuli triggering combat related guilt. For many victims current problems stimulate guilt in the same way combat events do. A merging occurs of reactions with stressful civilian events, such as loss of employment, legal difficulties, or loss of marriage (Hendin & Haas, 1984). Memory and concentration deficits, insomnia, outbursts of rage, passivity, self-sabotage (that success isn't deserved), and a disruptive lifestyle are just some of the complications of PTSD which contribute to ongoing stress.

In Table 9.5 is a brief listing of techniques for guilt reduction. They include visual, memory, and cognitive methods to elucidate and highlight guilt or its proxies. These procedures have the advantage of providing emotional immediacy and realness, as well as a new purview to "see" a contextualized pain. In addition, these techniques address the omnipresent cognitions that infect this process. We have discussed these in previous chapters (Chapters 6 and 7). Once again, a cooperative "battle free" zone is created to rearrange one's moral self.

Going Deeper

No cure or quick fix exists for the management of guilt. It must be experienced. Guilt is a soul sickness that extends beyond the psychological reality of the person. Borysenko (1990) outlined spheres of guilt: psychological, spiritual, and relationship. Guilt forces the person into a mask state, which "will not let go of an illness whose existence ensures it of the caring so vital to survival" (p. 55). Borysenko (1990) wrote:

> Unhealthy guilt is an autoimmune disease of the soul that causes us to literally reject our own worth as human beings. It is an affliction that robs life of joy. Instead of acting out of love and enthusiasm, we are led to act out of self-protection. Unhealthy guilt causes life to become organized around the need to avoid fear rather than the desire to share love. Guilt creates a psychic optical illusion that causes faults and fears to stand out while pleasure and happiness recede into the background. The result is a loss of joy and gratitude that creates fatigue, negativity, and depression. In guilt, we say no to life. (p. 20)

Guilt requires a **lysis,** the gradual dissolution of the person parts stuck in some evil. Ultimately, the victim meanders in the direction of a cosmic or spiritual view of self along with the human or psychological one. Regarding the former, the victim feels attached to a larger whole; that whatever evil was done (or not) has both good and bad sequelae in life. People are neither helpless nor in control but struggling somewhere on a road to becoming. No absolutes exist, only shades of gray. Bly (1988) said that we carry a long bag (behind us) of all our negative learnings and deeds. Bradshaw (1988) labeled this toxic shame; all people feel guilt, some more than others. *Trauma victims, however, are programmed for the experience of guilt, being forced to make sense of this tragedy.* All too often this legacy breeds either by denial (and reminded of its subtle levels across time) or by counterphobic stances that serve only to provide a temporary "rush," there being no anchoring of self.

The center of the dissolution of guilt is to free the self from guilt's narcissism, the recognition that a person is no better or worse than anyone else. This is the sphere of compassion,

(continued on page 484)

TABLE 9.4
Skills for Control and Guilt: Coping Techniques

Area	Skill
Anger Management	1. Engage in self talk. 2. Think before acting. 3. Practice relaxation. 4. Develop a sense of humor. 5. Anticipate (anger) trigger situations before they occur.
Self-condemnation	1. Think more rationally, e.g., learn that intention and consequence are not the same. The future can't be predicted; some events can't be controlled. 2. Think in gray rather than black/white adolescent categories. 3. Accept positive achievements and qualities as well as negative.
Intrusive Thoughts	1. Have an imaginary conversation with the person whose death you feel responsible for. 2. Recall comforting images from the past. 3. Connect traumatic memories to pre-trauma values and experiences.
Life-style	1. Balance life skills. 2. Develop structure and routines. 3. Set realistic goals. 4. Find a purpose in life which is congruent with lifetime values.

TABLE 9.5
Techniques for Guilt Alteration

Mode	Technique
1. Imagery	a. Have a client imagine how another soldier would have acted under the same circumstances.
	b. Have the client hold an imaginary conversation with a person whose death he/she feels responsible for.
	c. Ask the client to imagine he/she is in heaven looking down on his/her surviving buddy.
	d. Have the client imagine how his/her life would be different if he/she had not gone to Vietnam.
2. Memory Retrieval	a. Of early family relationship.
	b. Of the "Golden Age" before Vietnam.
	c. Of healing images before the trauma.
	d. Of early religions and cultural training.
	e. Of specific technical details of guilt (e.g., how much time was available for decision making).
3. Cognitive (Common distorted self construals)	a. My intentions and the consequences of my actions were the same.
	b. I was supposed to be able to predict the future (e.g., I should have known the enemy was there).
	c. I alone was responsible for death and suffering.
	d. I have nothing to be proud of.
	e. Other people can read my mind and know what I did.

(continued)

TABLE 9.5 (continued)

		f.	I am unclean because I killed. Furthermore, my uncleanliness is contagious; therefore, other people are uncomfortable around me.
		g.	I'm bad luck. Therefore, something disastrous will happen to another person who gets close to me.
		h.	I deserve to die because I enjoyed killing (milder form: I don't deserve a good job or good family because of the things I did).
		i.	I felt afraid, and, therefore acted like a coward.
		j.	I should have died in place of my combat buddy. He was a much better man than I.
4.	Structured Techniques	a.	Organize a hierarchy of values.
		b.	Discuss feelings of being unclean or guilty.
		c.	Help differentiate adult versus adolescence.
		d.	Build a relationship of responsibility to inner child (forgiveness, gratitude, or healing exercises).

to leave one's own sphere and to enter into the life of another. It is done through forgiveness, a commitment to one's self knowledge (non-judgmental), hope and recovery. Again, Borysenko (1990) wrote:

> Forgiveness is the exercise of compassion and is both a process and an attitude. In the process of forgiveness, we convert the suffering created by our own mistakes or as a result of being hurt by others into psychological and spiritual growth. Through the attitude of forgiveness, we attain happiness and serenity by letting go of the ego's incessant need to judge ourselves and others. (p. 174)

Only a few specifics are identifiable with this process. In Chapter 6 we specified a model of care, involving understanding, relationship, and trauma or symptom therapy. Understanding and relationship specify that the person is a willing and knowing witness and observer to his/her own workings. It is like being in the eye of a storm. The witness is above the fray regardless of circumstances. This allows the victim to establish a new ecology for the self, one more user friendly.

Like the Prodigal Son the victim can now return home to a new reality of self, one where amends can be made with self and others. This is the true essence of Adler's social interest (Chapter 4). Several features appear important in this effort. The first is the most transformational: All roads lead here. In treating combat related guilt the therapist eventually goes beyond the focus of irrational components and is confronted with the development of genuine guilt, the result of human choice. Again, the waxing and waning between "top-down" and "bottom-up" occurs. Mowrer (1976) viewed some guilt as reality based. Humans make choices, for which they are responsible. "Responsibility is always of primary concern in the resolution of guilt" (Clewell, 1987). Smith (1982) has emphasized the importance of examining the role of personal action or omission of action in catastrophic situations, which may have led to deadly consequences. The victim needs to confront impulses, values, and choices. Personal meanings need to be uncovered. When the victim understands his/her rage and the reasons for participation in certain acts, he/she can develop a new perspective. He/she can begin to forgive self. Further, as he/she experiences the therapist's understanding, he/she can believe that other people can also. The Adlerian reframe—"Is this the kind of person I want to be"—reaches new depths in the context of guilt.

Second, in this human struggle for the "right response" to diverted responsibility and noxious self-evaluation, is the presence (commission) or absence (omission) of human action. Guilt over acts of commission is usually related to having committed violence which caused death or maiming or to atrocities. This type of guilt is extremely painful. Guilt over omission is related to self-blaming for passivity or indecision which resulted in death or injury. A victim may believe he/she should have stepped in to prevent an atrocity he/she was observing. For some victims atrocities occurred which did not directly relate to the achievement of military objectives and for which some degree of guilt would be expected. One patient said,

> To make a long story short, I took a life that didn't have to be taken. We were in the wrong place at the right time. The older I get, the worse this is. I did things that were wrong. I know that people aren't responsible for things they have no control over. But, I was so pissed off I took it out on someone. I felt like I had complete control. I knew exactly what I was doing.

Third, is the *curative feature of the role of the therapist.* Clewell (1987) saw "guilt" therapy as having parallels with the rite of confession and the therapist as playing a priestly function. Lindy (1988) used this same metaphor in describing a patient's first therapy hour as having the appearance of a "frightened confession" (p. 62); the patient has an expectation of condemnation or punishment for his/her guilt and hopes of absolution. The therapist is like a priest. As the patient presents self in existential distress, the personal qualities of care and concern are critical, but so is the role of the listener. Pruyser (1987) said, "the religious essence does not lie in the answer but in taking the question seriously and with compassion" (cited in Clewell, 1987, p. 215). At these moments the therapist may be both listener and confessor.

Fourth is the issue of masked guilt. This has been labeled "guilt about guilt" (Parson, 1984). To thoroughly explore guilt related events over time is important. The initial reporting can serve as a cover for deeper guilt. Shapiro (1978) described a combat veteran who was guilty over having killed a dog. In his therapy group, the other vets could not understand the reason for significant guilt about killing a dog. Months later, the vet reported that he had killed the dog in a mad frenzy after three men he had sent on patrol were killed in an ambush. His guilt was sending subordinates on a mission which was of questionable usefulness. As already noted, *often guilt masks ferocious rage.* As long as the patient views self as a "cripple," he/she feels incapable of acting on his/her "murderous" impulses (Lifton, 1983). He expresses "numbed guilt." Numbed guilt includes maneuvers designed to avoid the feeling of guilt. The person anesthetizes or "freezes" the self from experience so as to not feel. In numbing, denial and "the will not to know" are prevalent (Lifton, 1986, p. 161).

Fifth, the issue of pacing is important. Timing is considered a crucial element in both the etiology of guilt (Stein, 1968) as well as the treatment of guilt. Lindy (1988) studied the efficacy of psychotherapy with Vietnam veterans and identified pacing as an essential element of effective treatment. If therapy proceeds too quickly, the patient may become avoidant and prematurely terminate treatment. The patient needs the support of the relationship to recall traumatic material. Premature interpretation of guilt can also lead to severe depression, anxiety, depersonalization, and suicidal preoccupation.

The symptom numbing also requires the therapeutic deliberation of timing. This problem is the "psychic clearing" of the pain (guilt) below. It may never be addressed. Victims after all are masters of avoidance. But, if confronted too early, this defense can result in the surfacing of uncontrollable anger. Some bolstering of healthy parts of the personality may be needed so that the patient has the emotional control and cognitive resources to face painful emotions and control aggression.

One last point is in order (relative to timing and pacing). *Guilt care requires tagging and repetition.* The first presentation of guilty episodes often is not fully accurate. The individual may be a much "worse monster" as later discussion reveals. Frequently, guilt over a pleasurable rush while in combat is disclosed subsequent to the initial presentation. Alternatively, the individual may experience a version that is much less incriminating when later uncovered. With each repetition the potential exists for further expression of emotional and factual nuances, which creates new "editions" of the same guilt associated trauma. Repetition is needed finally so it can be firmly established in long term memory and so it can have the potential to be only one story, not the only story.

ALEXITHYMIA

The one feature a trauma victim in emotional turmoil does not need is the inability to read or understand emotions, especially where guilt is concerned. Alexithymia is the name given to such a state. It is a clinically derived concept that refers to a cognitive-affective disturbance characterized by impaired ability of an individual to experience, label, and express emotions (Taylor, 1984). The term, literally meaning "no words for mood," was originally developed by Sifneos (1973) to describe certain patients with psychosomatic illness who responded poorly to traditional psychotherapy. Clinical criteria for alexithymia, as reviewed by Apfel and Sifneos (1979), include a diminished capacity for dreaming, an absence of fantasy production, and verbal output which is concrete, detailed, and repetitious. In addition, the alexithymic individual tends to focus conversation on endless physical symptoms and has difficulty finding appropriate words to express feelings (Lesser, 1981). Furthermore, interpersonal relationships appear stereotyped and mechanical, as alexithymics fail to express feelings and wishes as other people (McDougall, 1974). Other problems believed characteristic of alexithymia are low socio-economic status, age, lowered motivation, acting out, lowered frustration tolerance, a generalized resistance to psychotherapy (Lesser, Ford, & Friedman, 1979) and somatic problems (Martin, Pihl, Young, & Ervin, 1986). Recent evidence (Hyer, Woods, Summers, Boudewyns, & Harrison, 1990) has shown that this problem is common in chronic PTSD victims.

Guilt: A Primary Emotion

From our formulation, problems arise when a gap occurs between the schema and the stimuli or contents of the event. If the schema and "reality" cannot reach accord, many levels of emotional processing can lead to problems. Greenberg and Safran (1989) have identified four broad categories of emotional expression: (1) adaptive primary emotion—genuine or "real, biological" responses to situations; (2) secondary emotions—problematic and indirect responses to the environment; (3) instrumental emotions—learned emotions to influence reactions; and (4) maladaptive primary emotions—learned emotional responses (e.g., fear) to conditional or unconditional stimuli like trauma. *The belief is that alexithymics have no ability to access the primary emotion.* Therefore, since the adaptive primary emotions cannot be accessed, only "shadows" of the emotional states (2,3,4) exist. The inner primary emotional schemas or prototypes are left incomplete, unknown, or unclear. In practical terms clinicians are forced to treat only these indirect or secondary emotions. They convert defensive or reactive responses like crying in frustration when angry or expressing anger when afraid (2). Emotions, such as fear (in response to anticipated dangers) or hopelessness (in response to negative expectations), are really secondary emotional responses to underlying cognitive processes. Similarly, the clinician is often forced to handle emotions that are expressed to achieve some intended effect, such as crying to evoke sympathy or expressing anger to dominate (3). And, of course, avoidance responses to trauma (4) are most common among PTSD victims with or without alexithymia. All these emotions are "false fronts" and are best bypassed, confronted or interpreted, but not explored or differentiated.

What is required is a judicious assault on the client's current or primary mode of emotional processing (1). In the case of the alexithymic, this entails an attack on the primary affects so that eventually the person can use signals to access the emotional schema. Again, Greenberg and Safran (1989) have provided general principles of intervention: (1) direct attention to the inner experience, (2) refocusing on the inner experience, (3) encouraging present centeredness, (4) analyzing expressions, (5) intensifying experiences, (6) symbolizing experiences, and (7) establishing intents. These principles are based on a distillation of the essential therapist operations involved in the practice of emotionally focused interventions. Working with these principles the therapist directs the client's information processing in particular ways, and this deepens experiences and promotes the generation of new meaning.

The alexithymic is thus in a constant state of impasse. The therapeutic task is one of allowing the patient to acknowledge the experience, to commit this impasse to change, and to increase and magnify the patient's emotional state. The therapist assists the patient to address on inner experiences, to center on the present, to intensify feelings, and perhaps to symbolize intentions based on needs or strategies. This is a non-confrontive, moment-by-moment experience that, if done properly, provides clarification through a maze of inner experiences. Whether the tasks are done through intense focusing (Gendlin, 1981), emotional staging (Daldrup et al., 1988), or use of gestalt technique (e.g., Polster & Polster, 1973), the goal is to teach clients to attend to their own inner experience and to work through them.

Victims probably do not extinguish psychic pain because of active avoidance or because idiosyncrasies of the fear structure prevent access. In addition, impression in the mechanism of change exists—defenses, excessive arousal, depression, no state-dependent learning match, etc. Curative elements take hold when a tearing apart or dissociation of fear elements (stimulating meaning, and response elements) occurs and the past is reexperienced as the past within and as part of a wider present. The past changes in the current sensations/ functions/cognitions/feelings of the person. *The person is now the person who he/she was plus this new experience.*

To be an emotional dyslexic and in pain due to guilt is trouble. The victim feels forced to do something. As we can see, this often involves unintegrated responses that feel like guilt but are fed by other emotions. The clinician's task is to access, accept, unpack, and redo these affective states. In this process the "real" emotions become visible and guilt feelings less imponderable. Exposure and meaning are the big therapeutic guns in this effort. A new action intent is the victory.

SUMMARY

Guilt is a whole person phenomenon with emotional, cognitive, and somatic components. It is ubiquitous among trauma victims, although not a part of formal diagnostic criteria. The presentation will be chaotic due to the trauma having caused disorganization in the personality as well as a possible regression to a more primitive and a less integrated level of functioning. Memories of the events which cause the most torment will often be incomplete, and details will either have been forgotten or magnified out of proportion in their significance. Primary affects will have been totally warded off or transformed beyond recognition in the individual's attempt to defend against them. Nonetheless, the victim will wear guilt like a bad coat through life.

Just as guilt is a whole person phenomenon, so must treatment take a whole person approach. Guilt's expression in a given individual will depend not only on the trauma that triggered the guilt, but also on the pre-trauma personality, and on post-trauma interactions. Treatment becomes a process of sorting out memories, cognitions (self-attributions) and affects, and repacking them in a manner that allows for an understanding of the meaning of the trauma in the person's total life experience (i.e., pre- and post-trauma experience) and which enables the person to continue living with a sense of purpose. Psychoeducation and training in coping skills are the external aspects of treatment which enable the person to understand and organize his/her guilt related experience and to manage the painful emotions which can surface as traumatic memories are exposed. A deeper and internal aspect of treatment is the clarification of existential meanings. Finally, the phenomenon of guilt demonstrates that trauma can't be treated as an isolated phenomenon, but must be treated as an event in a continuous life process. Unfortunately, for some victims of trauma, the best that can be attained is manageability of guilt. The application of these ideas (in treatment) makes even this a more acceptable goal and process.

REFERENCES

Apfel, D. J., & Sifneos, P. E. (1979). Alexithymia: Concept and measurement. *Psychotherapy and Psychosomatics, 32,* 180-190.

Auerhahn, N. C., & Laub, D. (1984). Annihilation and restoration Post-traumatic memory a pathway and obstacle to recovery. *International Review of Psychoanalysis, 11,* 327-344.

Bennett, C. H. (1988). Notes on the history of reversible computation. *IBM Research and Development, 32,* 16-23.

Bergler, E. (1952/1988). *The superego: Unconscious conscience—the key to the theory and therapy of neurosis.* Madison, CT: International Universities Press, Inc. Reprint, with new foreword (originally published 1952). New York: Grune and Stratton.

Blake, D., Nagy, L., Kaloupek, D., Klauminzer, G., Charney, D., & Keane, T. (1990). A clinical rating scale for assessing current and lifetime PTSD: CAPS-1. *The Behavior Therapist.* September, 1987-1988.

Bly, R. (1988). *A little book on the human shadow.* San Francisco: Harper and Rowe.

Borysenko, J. (1990). *Guilt in the teacher, love in the lesson.* New York: Warner Books.

Bradshaw, J. (1988). *Healing the shame that bonds you.* Dearfield Beach, FL: Health Communication, Inc.

Catherall, D. (1986). The support system and amelioration of PTSD in Vietnam veterans. *Psychotherapy, 23,* 472-482.

Chemtob, C., Roitblat, H. L., Hamada, R. S., Carlson, J. G., & Twentyman, C. T. (1988). A cognitive action theory of posttraumatic stress disorder. *Journal of Anxiety Disorders, 2,* 253-275.

Chodoff, P. (1980). Psychotherapy of the survivor. In J. Dimsdale (Ed.), *Survivors, victims, and perpetrators* (pp. 205-218). Washington, DC: Hemisphere.

Clewell, R. D. (1987). Moral dimensions in treating combat veterans with post-traumatic stress disorder. *Bulletin of the Menninger Clinic, 51,* 114-130.

Cohen, M & Lohr, N. (1992). A typology of guilt in post- traumatic states. Paper presented at the 100th Annual Convention of the American Psychological Association, Washington, D, C.

Daldrup, R. J., Beutler, L. E., Engle, D., & Greenberg, L. S. (1988). *Focused expressive psychotherapy*. New York: Guilford Press.

Davidson, J., & Foa, E. (1991). Diagnostic issues to posttraumatic stress disorder: Consideration for the DSM-IV. *Journal of Abnormal Psychology, 100*, (3), 346-355.

Elliott, R., & James, E. (1989). Varieties of client experience in psychotherapy: An analysis of the literature. *Clinical Psychology Review, 9*, 43-67.

Epstein, S. (1991). The self-concept, the traumatic neurosis, and the structure of personality. In D. Ozer, J. M. Healy, Jr., & A. J. Stewart (Eds.), *Perspectives on personality* (Vol. 3). Greenwich, CT: JAI Press.

Fenichel, O. (1945). *The psychoanalytic theory of neurosis*, New York: W. W. Norton.

Foa, E., & Kozak, M. (1986). Emotional processing of fear: Exposure to corrective information. *Psychological Bulletin, 99*, 1, 20-35.

Fox, R. (1974). Narcissistic rage and the problem of combat aggression. *Archives of General Psychiatry, 31*, 807-811.

Freud, S. (1916/1957). Criminals From a Sense of Guilt. In James Strachy (Ed.), and trans. 1957, (original work published 1916). *The Standard Edition of the Complete Works of Sigmund Freud*. Vol 14, (pp. 332-333). London: Hogarth Press.

Freud, S. (1923/1961). The Ego and the Id. In James Strachey (Ed.), 1961. *The Standard Edition of the Complete Psychological Works of Sigmund Freud*. Vol 19 (pp. 48-59). London: Hogarth Press.

Freud, S. (1919/1955). Introduction to Psycho-analysis and the War Neurosis. In James Strachey (Ed.), 1955 (original work published 1919). *The Standard Edition of the Complete Works of Sigmund Freud*. Vol. 17 (pp. 205-210). London: Hogarth Press.

Gendlin, E. (1981). *Focusing*. New York: Bantam.

Glover, H. (1988). Four syndromes of post-traumatic stress disorder: Stressors and conflicts of the traumatized with special focus on the Vietnam combat veteran. *Journal of Traumatic Stress, 1,* 59-78.

Goderez, B. I. (1987). The survivor syndrome. *Bulletin of the Menninger Clinic, 51,* 96-113.

Greenberg, L., & Safran, J. (1989). Emotions in psychotherapy. *American Psychologist, 44,* 19-29.

Grinberg, L. (1964). Two kinds of guilt-their relations with normal and pathological aspects of mourning. *International Journal of Psychoanalysis, 45,* 366-372.

Grinker, R. R., & Spiegel, J. P. (1945). Men under stress. Philadelphia: Blakiston.

Gut, E. (1989). *Productive and unproductive depression.* New York: Basic Books.

Haley, S. A. (1974). When the patient reports atrocities: Specific treatment considerations of the Vietnam veteran. *Archives of General Psychiatry, 30,* 191-196.

Hendin, H., & Haas, A. (1984). *Wounds of war.* New York: Basic Books.

Hendin, H. Pollinger, A., Singer, P., & Ulman, R. B. (1981). Meaning of combat and the development of posttraumatic stress disorder. *American Journal of Psychiatry, 138,* 1490-1493.

Horowitz, M. J. (1986). Stress-response syndromes: A review of posttraumatic and adjustment disorders. *Hospital and Community Psychiatry, 37,* 241-249.

Hyer, L. (1991). The role of emotions in PTSD. Presentation at Operation Desert Storm conference. Dwight David Eisenhower General Army Medical Center: Ft. Gordon, GA.

Hyer, L., Davis, H., Woods, G., Albrecht, B., & Boudewyns, P. (in press). Relationship between MCMI and MCMI-II and value of aggressive and self-defeating personality in PTSD. *Psychological Reports.*

Hyer, L., Davis, H., Boudewyns, P., & Woods, M. (1991). A short form of the Mississippi scale for combat-related PTSD. *Journal of Clinical Psychology, 47,* (4), 510-518.

Hyer, L., Woods, M. G., Summers, M. N., Boudewyns, P. A., & Harrison, W. R. (1990). Alexithymia among PTSD Vietnam veterans. *Journal of Clinical Psychiatry, 52,* 317-319.

Izard, C. (1977). *Human emotions.* New York: Plenum Press.

Izard, C. (1991). Perspectives on emotions in psychotherapy. In J. Safran & L. Greenberg (Eds.), *Emotions, psychotherapy and change* (pp. 280-289). New York: Guilford Press.

Janoff-Bulman, R. (1985). The aftermath of victimization: Rebuilding shattered assumptions. In C. R. Figley (Ed.), *Trauma and its wake: The study and treatment of post-traumatic stress disorder* (p. 15). New York: Brunner/Mazel.

Keane, T. M., Caddell, J. M., & Taylor, K. L. (1988). Mississippi scale for combat-related posttraumatic stress disorder: Three studies in reliability and validity. *Journal of Consulting and Clinical Psychology, 56,* 348-350.

Kreitler, S., & Kreitler, H. (1988). Trauma and anxiety: The cognitive approach. *Journal of Traumatic Stress, 1,* 35-56.

Krystal, H. (1981). The aging survivor of the holocaust. Integration and self-healing in posttraumatic states. *Journal of Geriatric Psychiatry, 14,* 165-189.

Kuhne, A., Baraga, E., & Czekala, J. (1988). Completeness and internal consistency of DSM-III criteria for post-traumatic stress disorder. *Journal of Clinical Psychology, 44,* 717-722.

Lang, P. J. (1983). Cognition in emotion: Concept and action. In C. Izard, J. Kagan, & R. Zaponc (Eds.), *Emotion, cognition and behavior.* New York: Cambridge University Bridge.

Lazarus, R. (1989). Constructs of the mind in mental health and psychotherapy. In A. Freeman, K. M. Simon, L. E. Beutler, & H. Arkowitz (Eds.), *Comprehensive Handbook of Cognitive Therapy* (pp. 99-121). New York and London: Plenum Press.

Lazarus, R. (1991). Emotion therapy and psychotherapy. In J. Safran & L. Greenberg (Eds.), Emotion, psychotherapy, and change, (pp. 290-301). New York: Guilford Press.

Lesser, I. M. (1981). A review of alexithymia concept. *Psychosomatic Medicine, 43,* 531-543.

Lesser, I. M., Ford, C. V., & Friedman, C. T. H. (1979). Alexithymia in somatizing patients. *General Hospital Psychiatry, 1,* 256-261.

Leventhal, H. (1979). A perceptual motor processing model of emotion. In P. Pliner, K. Blankestein, & I. Spigel (Eds.), *Advances in the study of communication and affect.* New York: Plenum Press.

Leventhal, H. (1984). A perceptual-motor theory of emotion. In L. Berkowitz (Ed.), *Advance in experimental social psychology.* New York: Academic Press.

Lifton, R. J. (1983). *The broken connection: On death and the continuity of life.* New York: Basic Books.

Lifton, R. J. (1986). *The Nazi doctors.* New York: Basic Books.

Lindy, J. (1988). *Vietnam: A casebook.* New York: Brunner\Mazel.

Litz, B. T., & Keane, T. M. (1989). Information processing in anxiety disorders: Application to the understanding of posttraumatic stress disorder. *Clinical Psychology Review, 9,* 243-257.

McCann, L., & Pearlman, L. (1990). *Psychological trauma and the adult survivor: Theory, therapies, and transformation.* New York: Brunner/Mazel.

McDougall, J. (1974). The psychosoma and the psychoanalytic process. *Int. Rev. Psychoanal., 1,* 437-459.

Mahoney, M. C. (1991). *Human change processes: The scientific foundations of psychotherapy.* Delran, NJ: Basic Books.

Martin, J. B., Pihl, R. O., Young, S., & Ervin, F. R. (1986). *The association between alexithymia and stress-related disorders.* Paper presented at the American Psychological Association Convention, Washington, DC.

Masters, R., Friedman, L., & Getzel, G. (1988). Helping families of homicide victims: A multidimensional approach. *Journal of Traumatic Stress, 1,* 109-126.

Mowrer, O. H. (1976). From the dynamics of conscience to contract psychology. In G. Serban (ed.), *Psychopathology of Human Adaptation* (pp. 211-230). New York and London: Plenum Press.

Mowrer, O. H. (1953). Neurosis, psychotherapy, and two-factor learning theory. In O. H. Mowrer (Ed.), *Psychotherapy Theory and Research,* (pp. 140-149). New York: The Ronald Press.

Nunberg, H. (1934). The feeling of guilt. *Psychoanalytic Quarterly, 3,* 589-604.

Opp, R., & Samson, A. (1989). Taxonomy of guilt for combat veterans. *Professional Psychology: Research and Practice, 20,* (3), 159-165.

Ornstein, A. (1981). The aging survivor of the Holocaust. The effects of the Holocaust on life-cycle experiences: The creation and recreation of families. *Journal of Geriatric Psychiatry, 14,* 135-163.

Parson, E. R. (1984). The reparation of the self: Clinical and theoretical dimensions in the treatment of Vietnam combat veterans. *Journal of Contemporary Psychotherapy, 14 (1),* 4-56.

Polster, E. A., & Polster, M. (1973). *Gestalt therapy integrated.* New York: Brunner/Mazel.

Price, G. (1990). *Non-rational guilt in victims of trauma dissociation, 3*(3), 160-164.

Pruyser, P.W. (1987). A dynamic psychology of religion. New York: Harper & Row, 1968. A partial reprint in R.D. Clewell, Moral dimensions in treating combat veterans with posttraumatic stress disorder. *Bulletin of the Menninger Clinic, 1987, 51,* 114-130.

Rado, S. (1956). *Psychoanalysis of behavior.* New York: Grune & Stratton.

Rosenman, S. (1956). The paradox of guilt in disaster victim populations. *Psychiatry Quarterly Supplement, 30,* 181-221.

Roth, S., & Lebowitz, L. (1988). The experience of sexual trauma. *Journal of Traumatic Stress, 1,* 29-107.

Safran, J., & Greenberg, L. (1991). *Emotion, psychotherapy and change.* New York: Guilford Press.

Safran, J., & Segal, Z. (1990). *Interpersonal processing in cognitive therapy.* New York: Basic Books.

Salkovski, P. (1986). The cognitive revolution: New way forward, backward somersault or full circle? *Behavioral Psychotherapy, 14,* 278-282.

Shapiro, R. (1978). Working through the war with Vietnam Vets. *Group, 2,* 156-183.

Sifneos, P. E. (1973). The prevalence of "alexithymic" characteristics in psychosomatic patients. *Psychotherapy and Psychosomatics, 22,* 255-262.

Silver, S., & Iacono, C. (1984). Factor-analytic support for DSMIII's post-traumatic stress disorder for Vietnam veterans. *Journal of Clinical Psychology, 40,* 5-14.

Smith, J. R. (1982). Personal responsibility in traumatic stress reactions. *Psychiatric Annals, 12,* 1021-1030.

Solursh, L. (1989). Combat addiction: Overview of implications in symptom maintenance and treatment planning. *Journal of Traumatic Stress, 2(4),* 451-462.

Stein, E. V. (1968). *Guilt: Theory and therapy.* Philadelphia: The Westminster Press.

Stone, Andrew (1992). The role of shame in post-traumatic stress disorder. *American Journal of Orthopsychiatry, 61(1),* 131-136.

Taylor, G. J. (1984). Alexithymia: Concept, measurement, and implications for treatment. *American Journal of Psychiatry, 141,* 725-732.

van der Hart, O., Brown, P., & van der Kolk, B. A. (1989). Pierre Janet's treatment of post-traumatic stress. *Journal of Traumatic Stress, 2,* 379-395.

van der Kolk, B. A. (1985). Adolescent vulnerability to posttraumatic stress disorder. *Psychiatry, 48,* 365-370.

van der Kolk, B. A., Brown, P., van der Hart, O. (1989). Pierre Janet on Post-Traumatic Stress. *Journal of Traumatic Stress, 2,* 365-379.

Van Kampen, M., Watson, C. G., Tilleskjor, C., Kucala, T., & Vassar, P. (1986). The definition of posttraumatic stress disorder in alcoholic Vietnam veterans: Are the DSM-III criteria necessary and sufficient? *The Journal of Nervous and Mental Disease, 174,* 137-144.

Watson, C., Juba, M., Manifold, V., Kucala, T., & Anderson, P. (1991). The PTSD interview: Rationale, description, reliability and concurrent validity of a DSM-III based technique. *Journal of Clinical Psychology, 47,* (2), 179-188.

Williams, T. (1987). Diagnosis and treatment of survivor guilt: The bad penny. In T. W. Williams (Ed.), *Post-traumatic stress disorders: A handbook for clinicians* (pp. 75-91). Cincinnati, OH: Disabled American Veterans.

PART III

Symptom Therapies

EYE MOVEMENT DESENSITIZATION AND REPROCESSING: A NEW TREATMENT FOR ANXIETY AND RELATED TRAUMA

Francine Shapiro, Ph.D.

"To want to forget something is to think of it." French Proverb

In order to achieve a full therapeutic resolution of a traumatic event, both the client's obvious symptoms and self-attributions must be addressed. PTSD symptomatology includes nightmares, intrusive thoughts, flashbacks, psychological numbing, startle response, intimacy issues, as well as dysfunctional attributions that the client is making about self and/or the participation in the event. These cognitions must be addressed directly before a resolution can be assumed.

The very existence of the negative cognitions is an indication that the traumatic event is a powerfully defining factor in the person's life and has not yet been adequately assimilated into the individual's schema. Unresolved traumas are typified by negative perspectives on issues of self-control and empowerment which manifest in many forms throughout a person's life. Fully processed information is typified by access to a memory which incorporates an adaptive perspective, complete with positive cognition and appropriate affect. *The Eye Movement Desensitization and Reprocessing* (EMDR) modality defines the successful treatment of PTSD as a clinician assisted "self-healing" process, by which the individual reprocesses the dysfunctional information stored in nervous system as a result of the traumatic event.

Clinical experience has demonstrated that one to four sessions with EMDR can be sufficient to produce cessation of trauma-related anxiety, pronounced symptomatology and negative self-assessments suffered by many victims. While EMDR is not a panacea, it seems to catalyze an accelerated processing which allows the individual to assimilate the trauma into previously established positive frameworks, or shift cognitive perspectives to accommodate the presenting material. However, issues of secondary gains, previously existing pathologies, Axis II presentations, education and life-style deficits must all be directly explored and addressed before a full resolution can be expected. As noted in earlier chapters (4 and 5), these "person" features are often a problem with chronic trauma victims.

The EMDR method originated in 1987 when the author observed that some disturbing thoughts she was experiencing at the time were suddenly disappearing and not returning. Careful self-examination suggested that the cause of this phenomenon was the repeated saccadic eye movements she found herself making reflexively whenever the disturbing thoughts arose. Conscious use of these eye movements caused the thoughts to disappear completely and, if deliberately retrieved, they were no longer experienced as upsetting. The therapeutic possibilities of these eye movements were then systematically explored with the assistance of a variety of volunteers in order to substantiate and develop the procedure for a variety of different applications. What soon became apparent, however, was that a controlled experiment on this promising procedure would be necessary in order to rule out the confounding factors inherent in clinical observation.

EMDR Evidence

The study (Shapiro, 1989a) examined rape/molestation victims and Vietnam veterans. Twenty-two subjects (ages 11 to 53 years; m = 37 years) reported suffering from traumatic memories that had persisted for 1 to 47 years (X = 23 years). They had received previous therapeutic treatment for 2 months to 25 years (m = 6 years) and their presenting complaints included intrusive thoughts, flashbacks, sleep disturbances, low self-esteem, and relationship problems. The design of the experiment entailed an EMDR treatment group and a non-treatment (placebo) group. (After the initial comparison was made, the latter group also was administered the EMDR treatment, on the assumption that they too should be provided its presumed benefits).

The salient aspect of the subjects' psychopathologies was the memory of one or more traumatic events. The dependent variables in the study were measured at the initial session and one and three months later. The first of these dependent variables was a measure of anxiety as assessed by the *Subjective Units of Distress Scale* (SUDS) (Wolpe, 1982). The second measure was the perceived validity of subjects' positive self-statement/assessment of the traumatic incident. This was measured by means of a semantic scale (termed *Validity of Cognition;* VOC) from 1 (completely false) to 7 (completely true) for statements, such as "It was a learning experience," or "I did the best I could," as opposed to an initial assessment of "I should have done something." The third and final measure were the subjects' presenting complaints.

The results of the experiment, which are depicted in Figures 10.1 and 10.2, demonstrated that a single session of the EMDR procedure was sufficient to desensitize completely subjects' specific traumatic memories, as well as to alter dramatically their cognitive assessments. Thus, whereas subjects in the Placebo Group revealed little or no change in their

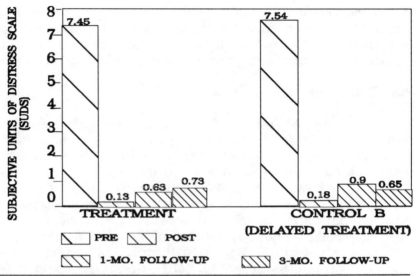

Figure 10.1. Mean SUDS for treatment and control B.
Session 1 and one month and three month follow-up.

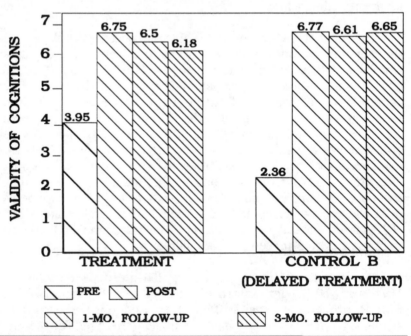

Figure 10.2. Mean validity of cognitions.
Session 1 and one month and three month follow-up.

high anxiety level and low perceived validity of desired cognitions (not shown in the figures), the EMDR Treatment Group underwent a marked reduction in anxiety, as seen in a pre-post shift on a 0 (neutral) to 10 (worst possible) SUDS (Figure 10.1) and a concomitant increase in rated validity of desired cognitions (Figure 10.2). As noted, the latter effect (VOC change) applied to the Placebo Group after they received the EMDR treatment. This dramatic treatment effect remained virtually unchanged at tests administered one and three months later and was accompanied by an alleviation of most or all primary presenting complaints.

Positive clinical reports of successful EMDR treatments have begun to emerge in the literature (Lipke, 1992; Marquis, 1991; Puk, 1991; Wolpe & Abrams, 1991). In addition, Boudewyns, Stwertka, Hyer, Albrecht, and Sperr (1993) evaluated EMDR, a yoked control exposure group, and a milieu therapy group on 30 Vietnam combat veterans with PTSD. The first two groups were given two sessions (EMDR or exposure for an equal amount of time) by an experienced and trained (in EMDR) psychotherapist. Psychological and psychophysiological measures were used to detect changes in response to the patients' self-defined "most traumatic memory." On the major psychological dependent measures (Mississippi Scale and Impact of Event Scale) and standard physiological dependent variables, there were no noted significant changes.

Two findings were of interest, however. First, the EMDR subjects self-reported a greater reduction in negative emotionality than control subjects. This finding is in keeping with other outcome data on changes; poor concordance among psychological and psychophysiological measures is not unusual. Also, the therapists reacted favorably to the EMDR effects and rated their sessions in a more positive direction than with the controls. In effect, each believed strongly that something positive occurred in the EMDR condition. Inconsistency of positive measures was attributed to too few sessions, a highly resistant population, and inadequate methods used to reflect changes.

On the basis of the initial experimental results, then, EMDR appears to afford a rapid and effective treatment of PTSD-related symptoms and traumatic memories. Over time, however, this procedure has continued to be refined by the author on the basis of observations garnered during thousands of treatment sessions. In general, the traumatic memory is treated by requiring the client to concentrate on one or more of the following: (1) an image of the memory, (2) a negative self-statement or assessment of the trauma, and (3) the physical anxiety response. Simultaneously, the therapist induces the presumably critical side-to-side eye movements by asking the client to follow his/her finger as it moves rapidly back and forth. While uncomplicated in theory and design, then, EMDR has evolved to a procedure with a variety of patterns and responses that demand specific choices and manipulations on the part of the therapist (Shapiro, 1989a, 1989b, 1991a, 1991b).

Theory

Given the dramatic and rapid effects that EMDR appears capable of achieving, it is useful to consider how such a seemingly innocuous procedure could prove so powerful. In the absence of any real evidence at this time, only speculation is possible (Shapiro, 1991a). One explanation may be an extrapolation of an admittedly oversimplified view proposed by Pavlov (1927) for the effects of psychotherapy and the basis of neurosis. Pavlov's hypothesis was that an excitatory-inhibitory balance of the brain is necessary for optimal information processing to take place. However, a trauma causes an over-excitation of a cortical locus and a resulting pathological change of neural elements. Placing Pavlov's notion in the present context, the proposal might be that "traumatic overload" results in a blockage of information processing, thereby causing the incident to remain in its anxiety-producing form, along with the originally perceived picture and negative cognitions. Presumably, this blockage prevents the information from being processed and integrated over time. Instead, intrusive thoughts, flashbacks, nightmares, and related PTSD-symptomatology are triggered. (The virulent effects of trauma and the "normal" information processing of the victim has been addressed in Chapters 3, 5 and 8.) The essence of a treatment, according to Pavlov (1927), is a restoration of the balance, and possibly EMDR restores this equilibrium.

Relating EMDR to Pavlov's notion, the proposal would be that the rhythmic, multi-saccadic movement used in this procedure represents the body's natural processing mechanism, similar or identical to "rapid eye movement" (REM) dream state of sleep, during which unconscious material surfaces and may be reprocessed, desensitized, and integrated. Thus, the rhythmic, bilateral saccadic movement of the EMDR procedure, along with an alignment of cognitive assessment and traumatic image associated with the physiological representation of the traumatic memory, may (1) restore the balance, (2) reverse the pathology, and (3) allow information processing to proceed to resolution with a consequent cessation of intrusive symptomatology (Shapiro, 1989a). In essence, the saccades provide a mechanism that naturally catalyzes appropriate information processing.

Curative Process

Congruent with this theory is the fact that EMDR treatment clients frequently report *progressive changes* of pictures and insights as concomitants to the decrease in anxiety. A previously vivid picture may become gray, blurred, smaller, or impossible to retrieve. The content also may change. For instance, a towering, terrifying figure may change in appearance to a tiny ineffectual one, as the client reports increased feelings of self-efficacy. Likewise, when asked to "think of the incident" post-treatment, clients report seeing the resolution of the incident and experiencing a feeling of safety, rather than the horrifying event itself with which they had been haunted.

One indicator of the progress throughout the EMDR procedure is to ask the client to think of the incident in order to check how the target information is being encoded and spontaneously generated by the brain. Those patterns that have emerged (Shapiro, 1989a, 1989b) indicate that the traumatic material is actually being processed and *ultimately integrated into the client's schemata in an accelerated fashion.* Also observed is an immediate generalization effect such that other memories with a sufficient number of similarities are equally desensitized along with the treated one. For example, when a multiple molest or rape victim is treated, one memory that represents an entire cluster of material is processed and it is generally reported that other incidents appear to be less anxiety-provoking and similarly cognitively restructured.

The clinical model utilized by EMDR practitioners, as well as the model developed in this volume, includes the notion of *information processing through the associative memory network*. A target event is isolated, and this, it is posited, is connected to a variety of other events that are naturally connected because of their shared cues. For instance, a Vietnam veteran was being treated for a dysfunctional reaction to an incompetent coworker. His intense rage and anxiety was ultimately found to be connected not only to the need for acceptance and approval by his boss, but to experiences in Vietnam where incompetence meant that people could die. During the EMDR session, he spontaneously remarked: "It's just a bunch of computers. Regardless of what happens we can turn it around. The point is the people aren't dying. That you can't reverse." Thereafter, he was able to think of his coworker without anxiety and anger. In the EMDR model, a variety of associative links to the target must be reprocessed before the event can be successfully integrated and desensitized.

By isolating a single traumatic memory, or **node**, the client may shift into recollections of similar incidents, or other memories involving the same participants, incidents that include a similar negative belief or self-statement, events that involved a similar emotion (e.g., despair or panic) or the same physical sensations. In many instances, the client will actually reexperience all or part of the physical sensations inherent in the incident. For instance, a rape victim who had her hands bound by the rapist, felt the sensations around her wrists, and, during the sets of eye movements, flashed on other memories where her hands were restrained, including being forced around her father's penis, being tied while her mother beat her with a broomstick, and awakening from an operation with her hands tied to the bed.

EMDR Benefits

Clients vary as to the degree of abreactive responses or revivification of the physical sensations inherent in the traumatic event being reprocessed with EMDR. As with the entire treatment model, EMDR is not a *"cookie-cutter."* The reaction of clients will vary and the reactions of the clinician are responsive rather than programmed. One client may not fully relive these memories during EMDR, while another will moan and writhe in pain, and yet they both will consistently report that an emotional and subsequent behavioral shift has occurred.

Another result of EMDR treatment is the *reversal of memory blockages* caused by dysfunctional information processing. Subsequent to treatment, the victim is better able to remember positive, rather than solely negative images. Typically, this occurs in clinical complaints of excessive/prolonged grieving. A little boy, for example, whose father had committed suicide, could only recall the ambulance on the day he died, and seeing him in a "ratty bathrobe surrounded by beer cans." After using EMDR with these two images, he was similarly cued to "Think of your father" and spontaneously imaged a memory of the two of them on a fishing trip. Similar cuing generated equally positive pictures, where previously they had resulted in only the two negative pictures.

Similar reports have been spontaneously and consistently reported by molest victims, who after an EMDR treatment are able to recall many more positive details and memories of the years during which the molestations occurred. The hypothesis is that the excitatory state of the traumatic memory blocks the access of other images associated in the memory network. Once the treated memory is processed, the network returns to a balanced more accessible state. Now, neutral or positive memories are "free" to occur.

Likewise, dysfunctionally held information results in a variety of numbing or even dissociative states. For instance, a Vietnam veteran related a horrific story of having been falsely accused of killing some men while actually performing a heroic task. While this memory was most representative of the feelings of failure that he had continued to hold through the past 20 years, he told the story with "0 suds." Although he reported no anxiety and no physical sensations when he imaged this target memory, after one set of eye movements, he reported a "7 suds." Based on information processing the belief is that the defense mechanisms that cause numbing, denial, or dissociation due to excessive anxiety, also were effected by EMDR. Once enough of the disturbance has been processed, such as after the set of eye movements, the defense mechanisms are deactivated and the individual emotionally can reconnect with the event and consciously can cope with the previously warded off anxiety.

This hypothesis is congruent with reports of clinicians who have used the EMDR procedure with Multiple Personality Disorder victims. Once the traumatic memory has been reprocessed, the amnesiac barriers are broken through and various alters share memories and become "co-conscious" (i.e., mutually aware) at an accelerated rate.

Procedure

To give a comprehensive description of the procedure its manifold applications and choice points, within the current space limitations, is impossible. However a brief overview of the procedural steps are provided. The most important emphases is that *training is ethically mandated for therapeutic use.* Reports nationwide have underscored that clients can be at risk if EMDR is used by untrained clinicians (Shapiro, 1991b).

While also focusing on highly-charged material at the "top of the hierarchy" (e.g., above 8 suds on the 0 to 10 scale), the EMDR procedure is different from flooding. With EMDR no attempt is made to exacerbate the level of anxiety for prolonged periods of time and the client need not give a description of the event. In essence, both the dose of the traumatic memory and the amount of detail disclosed is directed by the client. This particularly is helpful for clients who are guilt-ridden or embarrassed by their participation in the event, and for ritual abuse or incest victims that have been instructed "not to tell." It is also helpful to clinicians who have certainly been victims of vicarious traumatization (Chapter 6 and 7) through the vivid traumatic imagery they have been forced to sort through during the standard clinical practice.

In EMDR, only the individual is required to focus on the traumatic image. The client is well-aware of what occurred. *The clinician does not need any of the details.* The image chosen, however, should be one that best represents the entire traumatic event. If possible, it should also be representative of an entire cluster of such events, since that will allow for a generalization effect to other events with similar cues.

Since irrational beliefs are part of the PTSD symptomatology (DeFazio, Rustin, & Diamond, 1975; Keane, Fairbank, Caddell, Zimering, & Bender, 1985), the client is asked to verbalize what dysfunctional belief best goes with the picture (e.g., "I am worthless"). Care must be taken to elicit a self-assessment statement of **belief** rather than simple description (e.g., "I was used"). Likewise, a positive statement is elicited by asking "What words would you like to have go with the picture" (e.g., "I did the best I could"). This positive statement will be used to round out the session by connecting it distinctly with the previous traumatic imagery.

This cognitive restructuring aspect of EMDR has proved quite successful due to the discovery by the author that, while the eye-movements serve to diffuse and weaken negative imagery and self-statements, the eye-movements also vivify and make positive imagery and beliefs more valid. This can best be understood by remembering that the conceptual underpinning of EMDR is information processing. As the information is reprocessed to adaptive completion, the negative valence and associations are weakened and the positive is strengthened. Recall that the preponderance of negative cognitions and emotions occur in both the encoding of information and retrieval of experience with victims (Litz & Keane, 1989).

Once the positive self-statement is established, the client is asked to evaluate the validity on the basis of a 7-point VOC scale (1=completely false; 7=completely true). This VOC level is to be based on "gut level" response, not intellectualization. This provides a baseline for the positive cognition and is used for comparison purposes at the end of the session.

The client is then given very specific instructions regarding the procedure. The instructions reduce demand characteristics, give the client permission to observe the processing as it unfolds and to report the experience without judging its validity. These kinds of instructions are particularly important because these changes of picture and affect that occur during EMDR can be so rapid that often the client attributes the change to their inability to perform correctly, e.g., "I must be doing something wrong, I cannot see the picture clearly." The clients must be reassured that everything is fine and they should "just let it happen, without judging." This is particularly important for PTSD clients where problems of self-efficacy, performance anxiety, and self-assessments of themselves as "failures" are extremely problematic.

While therapy has already begun with these procedures, we are now ready for the intensive reprocessing. Clients are asked to imagine the target picture and the negative self-statement and to (1) assign a SUDs level and (2) identify the location of the physical sensations that are generated. A particular kind of eye-movement is then generated by having the client follow the clinician's finger. After each set of eye-movements, the client reports the predominate experience, and the clinician assesses the appropriate direction of client focus for the next set.

The clinician is basically assessing the client's responses for indicators of unblocked information processing. This is revealed by the degree of change evinced by pictorial, cognitive, or sensory shifts. In 50% of the cases, once the EMDR is initiated on a target event, a consistent desensitization and shift of cognitive processing are evident. With little input from the therapist, the client will spontaneously reveal psychodynamic material, new insights, hitherto repressed memories, and positive self-assessments that show the information has been integrated into the pervading schemata.

As information shifts therapeutically, clients reposition and reintegrate their experiences. During this time is when the curative elements of the eye movements, which may be the body's own mechanism for catalyzing information processing, occurs. The processing appears to accelerate which results in a clinically observable adaptive resolution with subsequent shifts in symptoms, behavior, and self-assessment.

The process often proceeds "unaided," with consistent and rapid effects. At other times, the clinician must assist in the refocusing of attention and employ a number of variations of the EMDR to assist the processing. These variations are extremely important during the client's abreactive responses, feelings of dissociation, or when cycling through pronounced negative cognitions that are indicative of the client's dominate schema.

According to the EMDR model, the information processing involves the accessing and stimulation of the neural network which contains the traumatic material. It has remained traumatic, locked in the cognitive and sensory perceptions that occurred at the time of the event. These have remained fused in the nervous system, and as hypothesized, are easily stimulated as the positive symptoms of PTSD.

This reaccessing and stimulation of the material can cause a vivid reexperiencing of the thoughts and sensations embedded at the time of the trauma. The eye movements appear to catalyze the requisite schemata and information processing, allowing for generative movement towards an adaptive resolution. However, until this resolution occurs, the client can reexperience the full extent of the fear, vulnerability, lack of control, and powerlessness that were inherent in the traumatic event. Care must be taken with clients during the EMDR session and subsequent processing. If EMDR variations are not appropriately used to complete the reprocessing, and if proper briefing and debriefing are not done, then retraumatization and suicidal ideation can occur.

The successful resolution of the trauma with EMDR includes the restructuring of the self-attributions in a more positive light. This cognitive restructuring, in turn, generalizes throughout the associated memory network which causes changes in behavior, along with the reduction of pronounced symptomatology.

EMDR is an important procedure used on the person who was victimized. The person is the one who now becomes free to accept a view of self and his/her experiences. In deference to this, a vital step is that the client be approached with a view towards the overall life-style and social system. Essentially, reprocessing a trauma is like removing a quilt from the bed; only then can you really see the lumps in the mattress. Subsequent to a trauma reprocessing, clients may have to confront a number of dysfunctional relationships, behaviors, and attitudes that have been obscured by the rape/ molest/accident/war experience. In addition, the reprocessing of dysfunctional information allows the client to adopt new behaviors that may stimulate other dysfunctional beliefs. For instance, when a client is finally able to be assertive and is finally achieving professional success, the neural network that contains the belief "If I am successful, I will be abandoned" may be stimulated for the first time. Another vital step is for the client to be debriefed by keeping a journal of new anxieties. These data "reveal" themselves, in vivo, for subsequent reprocessing. One double session may be enough to reprocess a trauma, but follow-up is necessary for the "reverberations."

The person of the victim also may require skills training. EMDR is not a substitute for assertiveness training, communication skills, dating skills, etc. Treatment of a molestation victim, who has kissed only her father is not complete by simply reprocessing the earlier trauma. Regardless of how relaxed the client may be in the clinician's office, this will not tell her how to act out on a date. An important procedure is to interweave skills training and life-style information with the EMDR for full therapeutic success. EMDR can be used to facilitate the understanding of new ideas and to desensitize the reactions to present anxiety-producing situations.

CASE STUDY

One 18-year-old molestation victim was seen on an emergency basis. She was evincing suicidal ideation and pushing for hospitalization. At the time she was brought in by her parents, she had been in therapy for over two years for anxiety stemming from a molestation by her grandfather during the ages of 3 to 9 years old. A depression had been precipitated upon the death of her grandfather, three years previously, when she finally felt free to reveal the molest to her parents.

Her schoolwork had suffered greatly, and school problems precipitated suicidal ideation which had resulted in hospitalization. At the point she was seen by this clinician, she had not attended school for a month because of feeling "tired, depressed, and anxious."

During the first session an *Impact of Event Scale* was taken (Table 10.1). Based on information from the scale and from statements by the client and her parents, clearly the young woman was in a great deal of distress. A history was taken and the client was asked to provide a few of the memories and pictures that were causing her the most difficulties. She reported five pictures that were profoundly upsetting (i.e., 10 on a 0 to 10 suds scale). During a 90-minute session, the most representational memories were reprocessed. The positive cognition, "He did not mean to hurt me, he was just ignorant," was interwoven using EMDR. The suds levels dropped to "0" and the client spontaneously remarked on new memories of her having locked herself into the bathroom and telling the grandfather to leave. She stated, "He actually left. I guess I really was powerful after all." The client reported a sense of relief and memories of times that her grandfather was loving and non-threatening, stating "He really did love me. He just didn't know what he was doing." The client was given a stress reduction tape, instructed in its use, and told to keep a journal of any upsetting memories or events.

The second week of treatment the *Impact of Event Scale* revealed no reports of intrusions from any of the treated memories. (Table 10.1). However, a new picture had emerged of "the last time it had happened—lying on a couch with him." This was reported at an "8 suds" level. The client reported only occasional feelings of depression, much reduced in intensity and frequency compared to the previous week. The reported memory was reprocessed and the positive cognition included that "Something good came of it" (e.g., the ability to be compassionate and understanding to others in the same condition). The client was instructed in a thought control technique (changing any internal critical voices to make them sound like "Donald Duck") and once again told to keep a journal.

During the third visit, the *Impact of Event Scale* was uneventful. The client reported the memories of the grandfather to be non-problematic. The sense of self-power in relation to the grandfather had maintained. The picture reported in the scale was one of her grandmother with an attendant feeling of sadness. This stemmed from her grandmother not having believed the client when told of the molestation.

The client was asked to concentrate on the memory of her grandmother calling her a liar and the feeling of helplessness/sadness was reported as a "4 suds." The reprocessing of the memory resulted in the client spontaneously remembering that her grandmother did love her and subsequently tried to protect her, offering money for treatment. She reported feeling "released" and relieved by the thought that "Grandfather did not go to hell." The client reported an overriding feeling of forgiveness. She was instructed again regarding the journal, and an appointment was made for two weeks following.

Two weeks later, the client's mother arrived at the office, stating that the client had had a reaction to a sulfa drug and was unable to attend. She reported the client was "doing well." She had "calmed down" and was "no longer flying off the handle." An appointment was scheduled for one month following.

At the next appointment, the client arrived reporting difficult school problems. The Impact of Event Scale revealed feelings of being hurt precipitated by her teachers, who were not "compassionate enough" regarding her efforts to make up the school work missed during her previous time of crisis. The thoughts of the molest occurred when upset by her teachers. She thought that she would not have been so behind in her schoolwork and under such pressure if the molest had not occurred. She also had gone to a hypnotist as a "birthday present" and had "fantasized a 'new' molest scene" which she reported, "did not feel like a real memory." Although she reported no particular memories surfacing, an EMDR treatment was done on this fantasized scene as a preventative step. The problems in school were addressed using both EMDR and educational suggestions.

TABLE 10.1
Results of Successive Impact of Event Scale of Molest Victim

1 = not at all   2 = rarely   3 = sometimes   4 = often

Item		Pre	Post	Time 3	Time 4	Time 5	Time 6
1. thought about it not wanting to		4	2	1	2	1	1
2. avoid getting upset when reminded		3	2	2	1	1	1
3. tried to remove it from memory		4	2	1	1	1	1
4. can't fall/stay asleep		3	1	1	1	1	1
5. waves of strong feelings		4	2	2	2	1	1
6. dreams about trauma		2	1	1	1	1	1
7. avoided reminders of trauma		2	1	1	1	1	1
8. felt as if it hadn't happened		1	1	1	1	1	1
9. tried not to talk about it		3	2	2	2	1	1
10. pictures popped in my mind		4	3	1	1	1	1
11. things kept me thinking about it		4	2	1	1	1	1
12. aware I didn't deal with feelings		4	2	1	3	1	1
13. tried not to think about it		4	2	1	1	1	1
14. reminders brought feelings		3	1	1	1	1	1
15. feelings were numbed		3	1	1	1	1	1
	Total	48	25	18	20	15	15

During subsequent sessions at one and two months the *Impact of Event Scales* reported her "feeling good," that "the molestation is behind (her) and the anger is all gone." Both mother and daughter reported that she was "handling stress beautifully" and appeared like a "new person."

Seven months after treatment, both reported "a straight progression since treatment with no relapses." Thoughts of the molest no longer surfaced, and she was actively coping, using information gleaned from the molest for a friend who was undergoing a similar experience. The client said she became aware of the lack of reactivity and avoidance when she noticed that she was going through some books on molest to assist her friend's court case, and was not upset or "self-applying." She also reported using the eye movements, as well as the stress reduction techniques and cognitive reminders on herself for minor anxieties.

CONCLUSION

Results with EMDR have been encouraging. Currently replication studies are underway. Meanwhile, the primary support for its efficacy is found in the case reports of the trained clinicians and in the reports of the clients. Follow-up interviews as long as six years post-treatment indicate that positive effects are maintained. During that time, EMDR has proven to be a teachable approach and procedure, since the author has trained researchers and therapists who are presently achieving comparable results. However, after replication, much research needs to be done to determine the pertinent boundaries, mechanisms, applications, interactions with personality traits, degree of efficiency and longevity of treatment effects.

Remember, EMDR is not a "cookie-cutter." As iterated through this book, the victim is foremost a person. Each client must be approached interactively. The needs of the client dictate the initial framing, focus, specific target, type of eye-movement, length of set, cognitive interweave, final debriefing, journal assignment, etc. No two clients are exactly alike—and no two sessions are exactly alike.

EMDR interfaces with other clinical skills and is not a substitute for them. As the research assists in the feedback process of this new method, modifications will be made for maximal efficacy. Already, however, EMDR has assisted clients, providing them with an opportunity for accelerated reprocessing of traumatic material and adoption of appropriate, life enhancing schemata.

Perhaps the final words should be those of a client. The following is a summary of a clinician, who sought treatment as a patient because of being tortured over a 48-hour period by an ex-lover who was in the midst of a psychotic break. The resultant wounds caused months of severe debilitation. Her pre-treatment Impact of Event Scale was only five points shy of the maximum possible score. Her intrusion and numbing experiences were excessive. She was treated during two 90-minute sessions with EMDR. Her summary statement illustrates the effects of treatment on the client's pronounced symptoms, and natural information processing:

> After the trauma, my whole being was contracted and frozen. As I was trying to heal, I spent most of my time in bed—in a fetal position—because I felt safe there. I had difficulty being around more than a few people at one time and I felt vulnerable in public places. I also suffered from intense flashbacks and severe anxiety.

> As a result of the EMDR, I experienced a great deal of relief in a brief period of time. My entire body became softer and began to open to the world around me. My flashbacks stopped completely, my anxiety lessened, and I was able to think about the trauma in a detached manner. In addition, I began to experience deep levels of insight about the experience itself, and about myself in general.

> Once the healing process started, it seemed to connect with deeper and deeper levels of my being. I found myself dreaming "healing dreams" about unresolved grief issues— a past divorce and the death of someone dear to me. Now almost a year after the trauma and about six months after the EMDR, I feel stronger and more whole then ever.

REFERENCES

Boudewyns, P. A., Stwertka, S. A., Hyer, L. A., Albrecht, J. W., & Sperr, E. V. (1993). Eye movement desensitization and reprocessing: A pilot study. *Behavior Therapy, 16,* 30-33.

DeFazio, V., Rustin, S., & Diamond, A. (1975). Symptom development in Vietnam veterans. *American Journal of Orthopsychiatry, 45,* 640-653.

Keane, T. M., Fairbank, J. A., Caddell, J. M., Zimering, R. T., & Bender, M. A. (1985). A behavioral approach to assessing and treating post-traumatic stress disorder in Vietnam veterans. In C. R. Figley (Ed.), *Trauma and its wake,* New York: Brunner/Mazel.

Lipke, H. (1992). Brief case studies of eye movement desensitization and reprocessing with chronic post-traumatic stress disorder. *Psychotherapy* 4, 591-595.

Litz, B. T., & Keane, T. M. (1989). Information processing in anxiety disorders: Application to the understanding of posttraumatic stress disorder. *Clinical psychology Review, 9,* 243-257.

Marquis, J. (1991). A report on seventy-eight cases treated by eye movement desensitization. *Journal of Behavior Therapy and Experimental Psychiatry, 22,* 187-192.

Pavlov, I. P. (1927). *Conditioned reflexes* (G. V. Anrep, Trans.). New York: Liveright.

Puk, G. (1991). Treating traumatic memories: A case report on the eye movement desensitization procedure. *Journal of Behavior Therapy and Experimental Psychiatry, 22,*149-151.

Shapiro, F. (1989a). Efficacy of the eye movement desensitization procedure in the treatment of traumatic memories. *Journal of Traumatic Stress Studies, 2,* 199-223.

Shapiro, F. (1989b). Eye movement desensitization: A new treatment for post-traumatic stress disorder. *Journal of Behavior Therapy and Experimental Psychiatry, 20,* 211-217.

Shapiro, F. (1991a). Eye movement desensitization & reprocessing procedure: From EMD to EMDR—a new treatment model for anxiety and related traumata. *Behavior Therapist, 14,* 133-135.

Shapiro, F. (1991b). Eye movement desensitization and reprocessing: A cautionary note. *Behavior Therapist, 14,* 188.

Wolpe, J. (1982). *The practice of behavior therapy.* New York: Pergamon Press.

Wolpe, J., & Abrams, J. (1991). Post-traumatic stress disorder overcome by eye movement desensitization: A case report. *Journal of Behavior Therapy and Experimental Psychiatry, 22,* 39-43.

11

DIRECT THERAPEUTIC EXPOSURE: A LEARNING-THEORY-BASED APPROACH TO THE TREATMENT OF PTSD

Patrick A. Boudewyns

Life must be lived forwards,
but can only be understood
backwards.
(Kierkegaard)

The goal of this chapter is to give experienced therapists an understanding of how to use **direct therapeutic exposure** (DTE) to treat PTSD sufferers. DTE, which for years has been used for the treatment of several other anxiety disorders (Boudewyns and Shipley, 1983), has been shown more recently to be effective with PTSD, especially combat-related PTSD (Cooper & Clum 1989; Keane, Fairbank, Caddell, & Zimering, 1989; Boudewyns, Hyer, Woods, Harrison & McCranie, 1990; Boudewyns & Hyer, 1990). *DTE is defined as repeated or extended exposure, either in reality or fantasy, to objectively harmless, but feared, stimuli for the purpose of reducing negative affect* (Boudewyns & Shipley, 1983, p. 3). The term *direct* indicates that the exposure is not necessarily offered to the patient in a graded fashion, such that efforts are made to "break up" the feared stimuli into a hierarchy of intensity; as would be the case, for example, in systematic desensitization therapy. Nor is it always carried out in a non-graded fashion, as is normally the case with flooding or implosive therapy. In DTE the "gradedness" of the therapeutic exposure in actual clinical practice is determined by practical or clinical considerations, such as the patient's willingness or ability to withstand the temporary anxiety engendered by the non-graded approach. The term *therapeutic* implies that the patient benefits from the exposure by an eventual reduction in the negative emotion being experienced [in learning theory terms, a reduction in the conditioned emotional response (CER)], even though a temporary increase may occur in negative emotionality during the early part of therapy.

DTE has its roots in the two-factor learning theory of Mowrer (1960) and the non-graded, applied approach of Thomas Stampfl's Implosive Therapy (Stampfl & Levis, 1967). All exposure therapies are based on the notion that if people suffer from negative emotional responses to objectively harmless stimuli, then repeated and extended exposure to those stimuli will eventually reduce those emotions. Accomplishing effective therapeutic exposure, often in the face of the patient's lifetime habits of resistance and avoidance, requires considerable clinical skill. Therefore, I would not recommend this therapy to any professional who has not at least acquired basic training in the science of psychotherapy. For veterans of the science this technique can be of enormous potential. It should be part of any skilled clinician's therapeutic formulary.

Does DTE Harm Patients?

As early as 1981 a conference of researchers and leading behavior therapists concluded that exposure therapy was the treatment of choice for fears and phobias, including agoraphobia and also may benefit patients who suffer from obsessive-compulsive disorder (Barlow & Wolfe, 1981). In spite of this, many therapists are still reluctant to use forms of direct or non-graded exposure such as *imaginal* and *in vivo flooding, implosive therapy,* and *response prevention* because of an historically acquired "bad reputation." Early on, several authors from varying theoretical orientations seemed to agree that *non-graded exposure* would be harmful to patients even though no clear evidence was available to support these concerns (see Boudewyns & Shipley, 1983, pp. 11-14 for a detailed review of these early concerns). Over the past two decades, however, research has shown that this is not the case. When used properly, non-graded exposure and/or DTE has no more lasting negative side-effects than any other psychotherapy technique (Boudewyns & Levis, 1975; Levis & Hare, 1977; Shipley & Boudewyns, 1980; Boudewyns & Shipley, 1983; Shipley & Boudewyns, 1988).

Research into the Effectiveness of DTE

As already noted, controlled studies also have shown that the technique is helpful for patients who suffer from combat-related PTSD. However, in one of these same trials, Boudewyns and Hyer (1990) found only a trend for psychophysiological responding to be reduced immediately following therapy when DTE was compared to a more traditionally treated control group. A long-term follow-up of this same sample found a continuance of this trend (Boudewyns, Albrecht, & Hyer, 1992). In sum, these data indicate that DTE derives psychological benefit for PTSD sufferers. However, little evidence exists that exposure is effective in reducing psychophysiological reactivity to imaginal scenes of the traumatic memories, at least for combat-related PTSD. Nevertheless, to date more positive controlled treatment outcome studies are supporting the effectiveness of DTE for PTSD, especially combat-related PTSD, than for any other single psychotherapy technique or pharmacotherapy treatment.

Given these results a curious note is that DTE is little used in VA special treatment programs for PTSD, even though the VA has made an effort to train therapists in the technique through teleconference workshops and other educational programs. A national VA in-house research report by Fontana, Rosenheck, and Spencer (1990), for example, found that of the 18 types of therapy being used by professionals in the 24 specially funded PTSD clinical treatment teams (PCT teams) at various VA medical centers around the country, "exposure therapy" was rated to be the most effective. Yet exposure was among those treatment modalities that were "least frequently delivered" (p. 51). The authors of the report speculated that the reason that exposure therapy was so infrequently used was because it was among "a class of treatment approaches that were considered to be 'specialized interventions' that focused on delimited problems" (p. 51). This would seem an unlikely explanation however, since intrusive thoughts and dreams and hyperactivity—the "hallmark" symptoms of PTSD—are the very symptoms directly addressed by DTE. My own inquiries have found that this "under usage" is because therapists find the process contrary to their training, and they are uncomfortable using it. As therapists, we are trained to help the patient reduce anxiety. While DTE is ultimately very effective in doing this, it can and does result in an initial increase in anxiety. But this temporary increase in emotional responding should not be interpreted as undesirable. One aim of this chapter is to help the reader to properly interpret the patient's emotional response to the treatment. Strong negative emotional responses in the context of exposure therapy are not necessarily undesirable and are quite often a necessary and desirable response to effective therapy.

A BRIEF OVERVIEW: THEORY AND TECHNIQUE OF DTE

This brief overview is offered here as a way of helping the reader to gain a summary conceptualization of this rather complex treatment approach and its theoretical underpinnings before presenting the specifics of the process in the remainder of the chapter. A more thorough account of this approach can be found in Boudewyns and Shipley (1983, pp. 68-98).

Thomas Stampfl originally developed **Implosive Therapy** based in part on O. H. Mowrer's two-factor theory of learning. DTE has been developed based on Stampfl's original approach. Two-factor theory hypothesizes that an event that has been paired with pain or deprivation or other negative affect, can produce a **conditioned emotional response** (CER). According to the theory these CERs motivate defensive maneuvers or, more specifically, avoidance responses which are only partly effective in reducing the effect of the CERs on the individual. However, continued successful but symptomatic avoidance of those stimuli (both internal and external) that elicit CER, prevents extinction or habituation that would permanently reduce the effects of the CER. In DTE if the patient is repeatedly exposed to those objectively harmless stimuli that he/she has learned to avoid because they were once paired with an aversive event which no longer exists, then a reduction of the CER will occur. In other words, the repetition of these avoided stimuli in the absence of real physical pain or deprivation leads to a progressive reduction in the emotional response that drives the symptomatic behavior. Reduction in this drive state leads to an elimination of the patient's avoidance symptoms. The probability that these CERs will be diminished effectively is directly related to the frequency and duration of the exposure; much in the same manner as combat-related PTSD is *increased* in its intensity in proportion to the intensity and duration of the combat experience. Thus, CERs are stronger in a victim with PTSD, when the intensity and frequency of the original event was strong. Likewise, the greater the intensity of the original traumatic experience, the more intense the exposure must be in order to reduce the CER and the symptomatic avoidance behavior.

Therapists using DTE with PTSD patients must make every effort to help the patient to invoke images of the original traumatic scenes until the patient evidences a reduction in the CER. Using imaginal experience to vividly recreate the memories that the patient is trying to suppress or avoid will bring about the full emotional impact associated with those memories. These memory cues should be repeatedly experienced rather than avoided, in order to bring about extinction or permanent reduction in the CER.

Still debated is whether or not the patient must express significant anxiety during exposure in order to derive benefit from the procedure. However, after repeated and lengthy exposure to the **traumatic memory** of the experience, the emotional effect of the memory is reduced. In DTE the therapist's goal is to present repeatedly the scenes that represent the stressor. The patient's emotional response should be viewed by the therapist as a way of monitoring treatment. As progress is made, the intensity of these CERs should diminish. This is a sign to the therapist and patient alike that treatment is working and that other relevant material should now be introduced.

Patients who suffer from PTSD have put considerable energy into *not* thinking about the traumatic event; often for years or even decades. The patient's strategy has been to find effective ways to escape from these intrusive thoughts once they begin, or to avoid them altogether. *In using DTE, the first task of the therapist is to convince the patient to change this strategy, which has been at best only partly effective, and to adopt an exposure strategy that will initially, at least, require that the patient to experience strong negative emotions. Eventually this will have a positive effect.*

Because DTE may cause some initial negative emotionality, therapists should expect some resistance to this notion at first. In order to deal with this resistance, an important procedure in the initial sessions is to continue presenting the scenes or memories until at least some reduction in the CER takes place so that the patient will realize that the technique will eventually work if one sticks with it long enough. The speed with which patients begin to realize benefit from DTE varies from patient to patient, and will depend on the cooperation of the patient and the skill, effort and commitment of the therapist.

In the early sessions of DTE, another important task of the therapist is to do what Boudewyns and Shipley (1983) called **detective work.** This involves exploring with the patient in a question and answer interview salient aspects of the traumatic memory so that when the scene is presented as many specific emotional cues as possible may be presented.

Then, as these scenes are presented and negative emotionality is reduced, the patient often will recall many otherwise forgotten but emotionally incubative memories. The therapist must organize this new material as it becomes available to the patient's consciousness and investigate it so that it can be presented in later sessions. This detective work is vital to the success of the therapy. The hypothesis is that these forgotten (repressed) but related memories also may help drive the CER through a process of higher order conditioning. Stampfl and Levis (1967) originally called this the "avoidance serial cue hierarchy." If these related cues or memories are not discovered and presented for extinction, then, according to the theory, full reduction in the CER is not likely to be realized. This may in part explain why the patient has not reduced the CER over the years even in the face of what would appear to be repeated exposure to the symptom contingent cues. In other words, victims may have been successful *enough* at avoiding these memories to the point where significant portions of these repressed, forgotten, or avoided memories have not become available to consciousness and therefore to the usual extinction process. It is as if certain portions of the forgotten, but related memories continue to energize those aspects of the traumatic memories that *are* available to awareness.

Levis and Stampfl (1972) have developed and researched an interesting animal analogue model to demonstrate how this **higher order conditioning** can occur. In this model originally neutral stimuli that have been conditioned to elicit negative emotions can themselves be used as stimuli that produce conditioning and subsequent emotional responding. When extinguishing these higher order CERs in animals, through exposure to the conditioned stimuli, one must reduce the response to the initial conditioned stimulus. Otherwise, CERs to stimuli conditioned later in the **avoidance cue hierarchy** will not be reduced. For example, if a laboratory rat is first conditioned to respond with fear at the sound of a horn by pairing the horn with electric shock, then the horn can be paired with another neutral stimulus (e.g., a light) to produce also a CER (e.g., increased physiological responding) and escape/avoidance behavior to the light stimulus. Yet, in order to produce the most effective extinction, the organism must experience both the horn and light without primary shock. Exposure to the light without having reduced the CER to the horn first will not be as effective as the horn-light order. Similarly, in humans suffering from PTSD, many aspects of a traumatic event (stimuli) are not well recalled, and thus, are not available to extinction. The job of the DTE therapist is to uncover these cues closer to the unconditioned stimulus and subject them to the exposure process.

Therapist-patient Relationship

During DTE scenes, the therapist might appear to the outside observer as lacking in empathy. Of course, this is because the therapist often must have the patient visualize scenes that cause emotional discomfort. This part of the therapy represents only one level of communication, however. When a scene is not being presented, the therapist must be particularly supportive by recognizing the patient's suffering and courage in recalling and reliving the memories that are so difficult. A strong empathic attitude by the therapist is a necessary condition for effective DTE therapy, just as it is for any treatment approach. Showing empathy and regard for the patient is especially important for therapists using DTE however, because the treatment can be aversive at times. Conveying a supportive, empathic attitude when scenes are not being presented will reduce the patient's resistance to engaging fully in the scene material.

Also making a clear distinction between DTE scenes and the interactive process that goes on between therapist and patient before and after scene presentation is important in order to facilitate the patient's discrimination between the fantasy aspect of the scenes and the here-and-now reality of other therapeutic interactions. Helping the patient to make this discrimination will reduce the likelihood that the patient will develop a negative conditioned response to the therapist.

In DTE the imagined attitude and behaviors are to be accepted as true while the fantasy part of the treatment is in progress. However, no inferences should be made by the therapist that the attitudes and attributions from the imagined scene constitute an accurate reflection of the patient's real attitudes or behaviors at the present time. Once the patient completes a scene and opens his/her eyes then the therapist should always convey congratulations and support for the patient's courage and determination. In sum, nothing should prevent the application of the necessary curative components involved in the relationship as described in Chapters 6 and 7. A sound relationship is a necessary condition for any form of psychotherapy to be effective.

The DTE Rationale

Prior to beginning therapy the patient should be given an explanation of the theoretical basis for DTE and for the procedure that will be followed. While this may not be necessary in order for therapy to be effective, it will facilitate the patient's cooperation in the process. For example, early in the therapeutic process the therapist might say something like this to the patient:

> You have learned to be anxious in certain situations because you have experienced traumatic events in similar situations in the past. Regardless of how you learned to be fearful, many of your other symptoms, such as avoidance and numbing, are primarily ways of controlling those anxious feelings. Unfortunately this avoidance strategy does not always work and you find that memories or thoughts intrude in your thinking and that these memories cause strong negative feelings. If we could remove the anxiety or fear associated with these memories, then your other symptoms would drop out. You would not feel the need to avoid situations that bring on the intrusive thoughts and memories. And even if the intrusive thoughts did occur, no negative emotions would be associated with them.

> Let me give you another example: If at one time your child (or some other child if the patient has no children) had almost drowned, then he/she might learn to fear water, and would learn to avoid water in order to control his/her anxiety. The child might, through association, learn to fear the beach and anything else associated with the traumatic experience. If your child is successful in avoiding all contact with water, then he/she is likely to maintain his/her fear over the years. What would you do to help your child overcome this fear of water?

At this point the patient may or may not suggest that a repetitious exposure to situations involving water and beaches would be desirable until the fear was reduced. The therapist might then explore just how one would go about exposing the child in a therapeutic way that makes sense to the patient at his/her intellectual level. Once the therapist establishes the credibility of the exposure method, then the patient might be asked:

> Should you do this gradually or all at once? To introduce the child gradually to the water, you might first simply convince the child to sit on the beach, and after a while instruct the child to move nearer and nearer to the sea, until he/she is able to slip part of one foot into the water—always making certain that the fear was not overwhelming at each point in the process. An alternative approach might be to support the child and to encourage going directly into the water, while at the same time assuring your child that while he/she might be anxious at first, that he/she will soon overcome the anxiety by staying in the water for a while.

The therapist should note that the gradual exposure has the advantage of exposing the child to less fear. But it would probably require a great deal more time than the more direct approach. The more complicated and pervasive the fear stimuli, the more time will be necessary to complete repeated exposure sessions to each aspect of the fear stimuli. Those who have complicated and long lasting fears may need more DTE in order to overcome the fears in a reasonable amount of time.

The therapist might then explain that a treatment is available for the patient's own avoidance behaviors and fears, which is similar to the water fear "treatment" used with a child. Since most people's fears are more complicated than the fear of water, often imaginal exposure is necessary rather than participating in vivo or "real life" exposure. This can be done by having the person close his/her eyes and imagine the feared scene.

The therapist then can help direct a practice scene and make it seem quite real to the patient. This can be done gradually or all at once, similar to the methods one might use with the child afraid of water. The patient should be told that research has shown that the best strategy is to move along as rapidly as possible. This produces faster results. But that going over the most feared memories all at once can make one uncomfortable. Regardless of the ultimate strategy, the therapist should assure the patient that the memories will become less anxiety provoking after repeated exposures in imagination.

ASSESSMENT OF THE PATIENT FOR DTE

If the patient agrees to try the therapy, the therapist should then begin to investigate the specific elements of the memory that elicit the negative emotion and to determine the defensive maneuvers that the patient uses to avoid these negative feelings. First the therapist should ask: what are the stimuli or cues that this patient is attempting to avoid (either in memory or in vivo) because they are considered to be too aversive? The assumption can be made that these cues are multiple and not always available to the patient's conscious awareness. They usually involve many stimuli. The goal of the pre-treatment interview is to learn as many of the environmental or situational cues as possible, so that these can be presented in the exposure therapy scene later. Those events or stimulus cues that are readily available to the patient in memory are considered either *"symptom-contingent cues"* or *"reportable, internally elicited cues."* As noted in the overview, those cues that are remembered and known by the patient to be aversive are not all of the cues or stimuli associated with the traumatic memory that have the potential to cause aversive reactions. Therapists must assume that many other stimulus cues that may have been forgotten or repressed over time also are associated with the traumatic memory and, if "uncovered" through the DTE process, also may produce aversive consequences. In fact, those cues which are not readily available to the patient could be even more significant than the symptom contingent or other reportable cues.

As discussed above, ***non-symptom-contingent cues*** are associated to the symptom-contingent cues through conditioning and are ordered in a sequential fashion and become available to awareness as the symptom-contingent and other reportable cues are exposed and extinguished. Thus as the therapist exposes the cues available to the awareness of the patient, other stimuli or "memory bits" also will become available to the patient. Helping the patient to identify and uncover these cues and then exposing the patient to the newly discovered memory cues is also "detective work" of DTE and is an extremely important part of the process. As already noted, *symptom-contingent cues will not extinguish or habituate readily, unless the non-contingent but associated cues are discovered and exposed;* and this may account for the fact that traumatic memories continue to resist extinction even after apparent exposure to those memories through dreams and flashbacks for years. What occurs is the non-symptom-contingent but associated memory cues lend potency to the remembered contingent cues. For a more detailed discussion of these concepts see Boudewyns and Shipley (1983, pp. 71-78).

A common example of a symptom-contingent cue in combat-related PTSD patients for example, would be large crowds at a shopping mall or a restaurant. Avoidance or escape tendencies are increased by proximity to the feared object or situation. Combat PTSD patients become more fearful and their desire to avoid increases as they enter the situation. Forced exposure of the patient to such situations will increase affect and possibly set off flashbacks, intrusive thoughts of traumatic memories (e.g., large numbers of people in the shopping center are perceived as surrounding enemy soldiers). Therefore, just as the in vivo symptom-contingent cue (shopping mall) can spark other more threatening cues of past events, so can clear memories help set off less clearly remembered events that are associated with the traumatic event(s). In this regard the therapist should instruct the patient to be alert to any unusual or seemingly unrelated events or stimuli experienced during the scene presentation.

In DTE combat-related PTSD victims are encouraged to clearly imagine and embellish vague memories or flashbacks— going through the event slowly in imagination without effort to "control" or escape the memory. Under these circumstances useful detective work will bring out bits and pieces of the traumatic event not previously recalled. Therapists should take care to use the patient's own metaphors when communicating about their experiences. At first these avoided cues may not appear to be significant, but as they unfold the emotional impact is realized. With repeated intense exposure to both cues, the impact of both the symptom contingent cues and the previously unreported cues are less than they were before. *Once previously unreported cues become available to the exposure process, the impact of the associated symptom-contingent cues will be significantly diminished.* Thus, the exposure therapy process itself is an excellent way to discover stimuli associated through conditioning that are higher up on the stimulus-cue hierarchy which in turn also may be subjected to therapeutic exposure.

Stampfl offered a clear example of this process in a classic video of a female patient who was overwhelmed with fears of rejection by the man she wanted to marry even though he showed no objective evidence of wanting to reject her. She was also phobic of "bugs." After several sessions of implosive therapy, it became clear how the two were related. The woman remembered her early experiences in a German displaced persons camp, where she had been threatened with being segregated into a vermin-infested jail if she was not cooperative with authority.

Discovering such forgotten associations is an important part of many types of psychotherapy, especially analytically oriented therapy. With DTE however, the process is considerably accelerated, so that the therapist needs to be vigilant for any evidence of related but forgotten material that becomes available during the session. Additionally, in PTSD, where the patient has had so much practice and investment in avoiding and/or actively covering up horrible experiences, it is often the only way to accomplish this task effectively. Cognitive uncovering efforts usually go unrewarded because of resistance. Laborious nondirective and/or analytic methods are even slower and often unproductive because the patient becomes impatient with the pace of the treatment and lack of results, not to mention the cost involved.

Sometimes the associations discovered in this way appear on the surface at least to be illogical. In a case reported elsewhere (Boudewyns & Shipley, 1983) a man being treated for psychological impotence was asked to imagine an early traumatic incident of erection failure. Following the DTE scene the client remembered an experience that occurred in first grade. The teacher had asked him to write the numbers 1 through 10 on the blackboard and although he felt at the time that he could do this, he was unable to write the number 6. His inability to write this number resulted in experiencing extreme ridicule before his classmates. This memory provided material for a subsequent exposure scene of rejection that was effective in relieving his psychogenic impotency.

Other Detective Work

Of course using the exposure therapy process to discover unreported cues is not the only method. Certainly logical and clinical inferences can be used. The therapist may devise a scene that is based on a clinical hunch. A female patient feared sexual intercourse, was self-effacing, and lacked assertiveness, especially with men. The usual in vivo sex therapy emphasizing practice, sensate focus, etc. under relaxed conditions had not been effective. It was hypothesized that she may have been the victim of abuse as a child, and had repressed these memories. A session where the patient was asked to try to experience or imagine being abused was effective in bringing back early memories of an uncle who had sexually molested her. The affect associated with these now distant memories was easily reduced through several sessions of DTE. Also, in conjunction with DTE, cognitive therapy aimed at giving the woman a rational perspective on the trauma was helpful in this case. At that point her sexual fears were then more easily extinguished through the in vivo sexual exposure therapy methods that were previously ineffective.

A third way of discovering previously unreported cues is through a *debriefing process.* After a DTE session when the patient opens his/her eyes, the therapist should ask if the patient experienced any unusual or unfamiliar memories or imaginings. The patient often will report these cues without seeing their significance. More detective work and debriefing may be required at this point.

One patient suffering from severe obsessive compulsive symptoms had an obsessional fear that her daughter would be harmed by her in the kitchen. She was especially concerned the she might accidentally lose control and pour scalding water from the kettle on her daughter while she was cooking. She would "check" this fear by compulsively holding a kettle with boiling water in it over her daughter's head to "prove" to herself that she would not or could not do it on purpose. A scene in which she imagined "the worst thing that could happen to her daughter in the kitchen" produced a previously forgotten memory of going to the funeral of a cousin when she was a young child. The young cousin had died of burns from a kitchen accident. This memory, however, was only regained after much debriefing regarding a brief "flash" of her aunt's face (the young cousin's mother) during the DTE scene.

This detective work continues throughout therapy, but is initiated by conducting two or three diagnostic and assessment interviews prior to therapy. These initial interviews cover the material generally gathered in taking a clinical psycho-social history and mental status. When interviewing for DTE however, the therapist should pay particular attention to the stimulus content of the patient's report of past traumatic events rather than to the meaning of the content or theoretically based notions about what "really" went on the patient's "psyche", for example.

The memories of the specific stimuli that surround (precede and follow) the traumatic event are explored in detail (e.g., time of day, weather, color of walls, layout of the building, odors, etc.). If a combat-related PTSD patient has flashbacks, one should explore the situation of the patient just prior to flashbacks to see if common stimulus elements are in the environment or the inter- or intra-personal situation of which the patient is not aware that could be setting off the flashbacks.

The therapist should be careful not to lead the patient during the interview. Logical conclusions do not always hold. This can be demonstrated with public speaking phobia. One might assume that for people with this problem, that larger audiences would be more troublesome than small ones. Often however, the nature of the audience is the problem. Many public speaking phobics are not aware themselves of the stimuli involved. Small audiences full of authorities on the topic the patient is discussing are often much more troublesome than large audiences with no experts. Therapists should explore these details thoroughly and never assume anything unless the patient cannot report specific stimulus components that are troublesome. At that point, then, the therapist should present logical or theoretically plausible cues, and observe the patient's response to the cues as a clue to determining future scene content.

Also, the response that the patient might make in a feared situation can become a stimulus cue for DTE purposes. In the public speaking situation, for example, what is the feared response? It could be that the patient might say something that would be challenged later, or it may be that the patient is afraid that he/she will lose control and pass out from anxiety driven hyperventilation. Unlike the usual clinical interview, specifics (names, dates, times, and specific environmental stimuli) are very important in DTE. Again the therapist should continually ask what is or might the patient be avoiding or escaping from.

During these initial sessions the therapist should not only inquire about stimuli that surround the event in time, place and space, but also should ask about possible events similar to the traumatic experience that may have happened previous to or after the event. Thus, a rape victim also must be asked about earlier abuse experiences, as these could be associated with the rape experience and could block therapy if not also brought out for exposure. Likewise, therapists will make significant diagnostic and assessment errors if they do not insist on a good history prior to the trauma. This is especially true for combat-related PTSD, where the assessment should be aimed at uncovering any violent or traumatic events experienced prior to combat. Bringing such early experiences out in the open for exploration and exposure can mean the difference between treatment success and failure no matter how effectively you address the combat experience. Also when violence and aggression are involved in any way, the therapist should always investigate the parental punishment practices. If strong corporal punishment was used, then these scenes should be incorporated into the therapy, even if the patient does not consider them traumatic. They may well have been very traumatic at the time and can contribute to the effect of later violent traumatic events. Evidence is accumulating that early trauma exacerbates or increases the effects of later traumatic experiences (Lyons, 1991). Thus, investigation into childhood fears often reveals unusual or protracted fears that appear to be directly related to the current symptoms, and both may be related to the traumatic event.

Repetitive aversive dreams are also important for determining cues for therapy. For example, a man with combat-related PTSD who had been trapped in a firefight for a long period of time did not have dreams of the firefight but did dream of being hit by lightening and being killed. He asked for help only for his fear of thunderstorms. He did not, however, see any relationship between his combat experience and the thunderstorm fear. Yet, this relationship was clearly evident after one DTE session in which a combat experience with incoming mortar was reviewed, suggesting the possibility of this relationship.

Another patient who experienced repetitive nightmares of being chased by police, was clearly more disturbed by his guilt from childhood behaviors as depicted in the first DTE session. The client had very little, if any, conscious realization that the two may have been related. Regardless, the nightmares disappeared after only three sessions of DTE.

SCENES

Level of Emotion During DTE

The patient's level of emotionality during a particular DTE scene is indicative of the importance or salience of the material being presented. The clarity of imagery during the scene may also be used as an indicator of the relevance of the particular material being presented. If a portion of an exposure scene is pictured clearly and without any evidence of anxiety, it may or may not be relevant to the client's problem.

Some patients show little evidence of anxiety to even the trained observer, even when the material is quite disturbing. On the other hand, lack of emotionality during a scene is usually an indicator that the therapist is on the wrong track. Conversely, *high emotionality is almost always a good indicator that the material is relevant.* Also, high anxiety can interfere with imagery. When this happens, repeated scenes, or a more graded approach discussed earlier may be useful until the image is clearer. On the other hand, as any student of learning theory knows, very low levels of arousal may also reduce image clarity, but this is rare and easily discernable as caused by lack of motivation rather than anxiety.

A psychotic woman treated for PTSD related to childhood abuse by her stepfather was unable to visualize high anxiety scenes at first. After much encouragement and many repetitions of one scene she was able to involve herself adequately in the scene. Emotionality then became so high that she began to respond to me and my office through association with a CER even before beginning the therapy. I then re-exposed her to the office for several visits without other scene content and also taught her to use progressive muscle relaxation prior to treatment sessions. Also, I graded the scene making certain that she was completely extinguished to the anxiety of each phase of the scene or theme before continuing. Early rejection scenes by her stepfather would begin slowly with only mild verbal abuse recalled, and then after she was relaxed to these images, scenes of more physical abuse began. This was an exceptional case that required very graded exposure.

Also, DTE should not be used routinely for patients with psychotic disorders. Some psychotics can benefit from DTE, but it should only be used for those who also suffer from anxiety from past traumatic events separate from the psychosis; and should be carried out by a therapist with much experience with the procedure. Even here results are not particularly positive for this difficult population. Although one early study did find Implosive Therapy to be effective with psychotics (Hogan, 1966).

Finally, if a patient who otherwise has good imagery reports that he/she cannot imagine a particular memory clearly, but the traumatic memory is still reported by the patient to be anxiety provoking, then the material is assumed to be highly relevant. In that case, the therapist should work to help the patient to experience the memory or event in question as clearly as possible. This may be particularly important for clients who have had past abusive experiences and are not aware of the importance of these memories in their present life. For example, a woman whose husband frequently worked nights presented with extreme fear of staying alone at night. When asked what was the worst thing that could happen in that situation, she answered that someone might break into the house and beat her up. Other interview material suggested that the patient might desire forceful sexual contacts and that she feared that she would act on this desire, given the opportunity. An exposure scene was gleaned from this material with some hypothesized, non-symptom-contingent cues that depicted her home alone at night—and she hears a noise. A man breaks into the house, beats her, drags her to the bedroom, and rapes her and she responds lustily. During the first part of this scene the patient was able to visualize well. However, the latter part of the scene including the sexual material was a "complete blank." Her inability to imagine this part of the DTE scene was supportive of the hypothesis that sexual stimuli were important elicitors of anxiety and in need of repeated exposure. With repetition and encouragement the patient was gradually able to visualize and respond appropriately with negative conditioned emotionality— first with the rape scene and then to her imagined positive reaction to such a situation.

Neutral Scenes for Comparison to Exposure Scenes

Following the initial interviews, and prior to the presentation of the DTE scenes, one or more "neutral" scenes are presented to the client to test for the ability to imagine and become involved in the scene. In a neutral scene the patient is instructed to close his/her eyes and imagine a therapist directed scene. This neutral scene should begin with familiar environment scenes that have little or no movement in them. For example, I usually ask the patient to imagine the exterior of the building or the house that they live in—or remember living in, in the past. Then the patient is instructed to move slowly into the environment, through the front door, always emphasizing that the patient is an active participant; and not merely a viewer in this fantasy. The therapist directs the fantasy and then asks the patient to provide a description of the environment as he/she moves through the scene. The therapist may simply direct the patient to imagine opening the front door and *"feel the cold door knob in your hand. Now feel it turn and feel the change of air currents as you open the door—now tell me what you see as you enter the house or apartment."* After the patient describes the room the therapist asks him/her to imagine moving through the room—*"see the furniture and describe it."* The therapist can evaluate the clarity and completeness of the imagery by the amount of detail used by the patient in describing this familiar scene. An important aspect is to have the patient respond with all senses, not just visual.

The therapist should question the subject about sounds, smells, and textures as well as color and form. If this familiar scene can be visualized (less than 3% of patients are resistant to imagining such familiar scenes), then he/she is asked to imagine less familiar but still common scenes. He/she might be asked to imagine going to an airport and getting on an airplane (obviously not to be used with patients who have strong fears of flying) and experience flying.

A common neutral scene would go like this:

Imagine that you are now in the airport—handing your ticket to the gate-keeper—walking down the ramp to the plane—entering the plane—smiling and saying hello to the attendant—notice the change in air temperature as you enter—finding your seat—lifting your heavy carry-on luggage to the compartment above—sitting down, the pressure on your bottom as you sit. The plane is now beginning to move—feel this. Soon you are on the runway, about to take off. Feel the pressure build up slowly on your back as the plane increases speed, and the bumps on the runway as you move along faster and faster until you feel lift-off, and the change in air pressure in your ears, the G-force pushing you back into your seat becomes greater.

If this scene *is* familiar (e.g., the patient is an airplane pilot) then another scene with a similar but less familiar environment would be used. If the patient is able to fantasize the relatively less familiar scene, then the next step is to present a fantasy that could not possibly happen and could never be fully experienced except in fantasy. One often used follows easily from the airplane scene and goes like this:

> Imagine now that you get up out of your seat and begin walking toward the front of the plane to the door that you came in. Then, even though you are flying through the air, you open the door and step out, close the door behind you and begin to fly on your own. Feel the wind rushing through your hair and the pressure of the wind on your face. Look down and see the ground below as you fly along. See how small the houses look.

This fantasy continues until the patient flies back to the house in the original scene and lands at the front door.

After this scene, the patient is debriefed by asking him/her to compare the three levels of fantasy he/she has just experienced: (1) very familiar, (2) not so familiar, and (3) complete fantasy. If the patient has significant difficulty with either of the first two, then it would be helpful to have some practice sessions in which the therapist uses other neutral scenes.

At this point the therapist must determine if the lack of imaginal clarity is due to an inability to imagine or the result of resistance. If it is the latter then perhaps a more traditional therapeutic method should be used to explore this. If it is not resistance, and is simply a lack of skill in visual imagination, then the therapist should determine what techniques the patient uses to remember and/or "daydream." Some patients can maintain a better imaginal focus on a scene by using a dimly lit room, while staring at a blank wall with eyes open during scene presentation. Also the ability to imagine, like any skill, appears to improve with practice.

An important step is to find a method of scene presentation with which the patient feels comfortable before beginning

DTE. Therapists should continue to monitor the patient's limits and skills (i.e., strength of imagery, attention span, resistance, etc.) during therapy. Again, the emphasis needs to be made that DTE demands much of both the patient and the therapist. If a patient is willing to reexperience a traumatic memory, the therapist must be sure to reinforce that behavior with much praise and empathy. Communicating empathy and unconditional positive regard is an essential part of DTE.

In summary, using neutral imagery prior to beginning "real" DTE accomplishes four important aims: (1) It provides the therapist with at least a crude baseline of the patient's ability to use imagery so that later sessions can be paced and presented accordingly; (2) the therapist is established as the director of the scenes; (3) it demonstrates to the client the possibility of imaging something that has never happened— something many patients may never have consciously attempted before—and thus sets expectation for hypothesized scenes with non-symptom-contingent cues; and (4) it can be used to help demonstrate to the patient that he/she does not have to accept events occurring in fantasy as "real." The patient has now learned that he/she can experience and accept unusual therapist-directed fantasy, and that DTE may require experiencing incredible fantasies that will help to reduce negative affect associated with traumatic memories.

Content in DTE Scenes

After establishing an empathetic patient-therapist relationship and investigating the cues thought to be responsible for the symptoms, as well as practicing imagery with neutral scenes, the actual treatment sessions can begin. The patient is encouraged to be involved as an "actor" in the scene. They are asked to try to recreate or "re-live" the scene or the memory and to experience the emotion as if it were actually happening at the time. The patient is to try to picture the scene, not as an onlooker, but rather as if he/she is directly involved. The therapist should present the scene in the present tense. The patient need not accept the imagined memory as if it is existing now in the real world, but rather should try to accept the memory as if it is a fantasy—just as a good actor would accept a role in a play.

The therapist must make a decision as to which stimuli or cues to present first and which to present later so as to give some logical and acceptable order to the theme of the scene. Usually this order is straightforward and consistent with the way the patient remembers the incident. Concrete symptom-contingent cues that are clearly remembered by the patient, elicit anxiety, are associated with reportable internal cues, and are available to consciousness are usually presented first. Thus, if a patient who has combat-related PTSD recalls some specific events of a firefight (i.e., symptom-contingent cues), and this includes fear of being burned, even though he/she was not hurt (internal reportable cues), then a scene that includes a firefight with fear of burning, including perhaps a fantasy scene where he/she is actually burned, would be presented first. Other reportable fears might be associated, such as fears associated with going to movies that depict violence. These then also might be presented at the same time.

Hypothesized cues that are not as available to the client's awareness may have greater aversive "loadings" than those in awareness. These may be difficult to extinguish. The patient with intrusive and aversive firefight memories noted above, also may have had a strong fear of death, and/or the aversive consequences associated with an afterlife. These consequences (punishment) may elicit anxiety associated with guilt. Guilt cues may not be easily brought into the scenes until the patient has had some exposure to the reportable, symptom-contingent cues, and finds that he/she is reminded of his/her guilt by these scenes.

Other associated hypothesized cues might include a fear that others will attract or injure the patient while walking in a mall or crowded street. This could increase the patient's potential to lose control and attack strangers, wrongly thought to be enemies bent on destruction. Fear of loss of control is a very important cue for many PTSD sufferers. Vague fears of crowded places may be an indication that the patient has such underlying fears. In that case, the fear of crowds would be presented first and then the internal hypothesized cues which may be beyond the patient's awareness during the initial stages of therapy would be presented last.

Frequently an exposure scene for PTSD sufferers begins with some past traumatic incident or as a recurring dream. The therapist involves the client in the scene by describing the setting of the story or memory and by presenting relatively nonarousing material at first. This "warm-up" process is particularly helpful for patients who have problems imagining scenes or are otherwise difficult to get involved in the scene. For example, a warm-up scene could be introduced to a patient who feared crowds while attending a football game. The scene begins with the patient preparing to leave home for the game; driving to the stadium and then finally pictures him/her in the crowd. This relatively gradual approach allows the patient to become involved in the scene slowly and provides for the extinction of anticipatory fear—an important but often overlooked aspect of fear.

Likewise, a rape victim who may have only partial memory for the feared scene may have to begin with less threatening memories "surrounding" the incident in time and space that stimulate the memory of the actual attack. For example, the therapist might ask the patient to imagine the approximate place of the attack, including any tangible surroundings (buildings, houses, streets, or other environmental cues) prior to presenting the attack itself. Sometimes presenting other non-aversive memories of incidents that occurred at about the time of the attack is helpful in this uncovering process. These initial stimuli should be considered as "primers" (as priming a pump) that stimulate more relevant memories through association. The therapist must be attuned to the patient's response to these priming stimuli. Cues that stimulate even mild anxiety might be important leads to hypothesized cues that are relevant.

In presenting scenes the therapist should approximate as closely as possible the hypothesized traumatic events and reproduce the cues as realistically as possible. The more detailed and dramatic the description, the easier the patient is able to visualize the scene and thus experience the emotion. At the same time the therapist must "pace" the scene to the needs of the patient. Tone and volume should be monitored and should not overwhelm the patient and interfere with the imaginal process.

The therapist needs to be sure of finding out specific names and places and other similar identifying information in order to make the descriptions more detailed. One can increase the realism of the scene by providing details such as sound effects, or play the verbal roles of others in the scene. The patient is asked to become involved in the scene as much as possible. The therapist should **have the client verbalize responses to the scene in the present tense**— to respond to the scene in the way he/she would have, had the scene been "real" and use the patients own language and metaphors in the process.

The patient should be encouraged to move arms and legs in acting out the scene if this helps to enhance the reality of the imagined scene, but not if it interferes with the emotional process. A patient who fears being overly aggressive may be helped to imagine hitting someone by making a fist and stomping the floor while imagining hatred toward the ambivalently regarded person. Care must be taken here that no harm comes to a patient. Patients should be instructed to pound a couch, pillow, or something soft, as any pain experience during the scene could lead to conditioning and to a stronger CER.

The therapist should not avoid provoking maximum levels of emotion during a given scene. If high levels of emotion occur in the patient, this is to be maintained until a diminution of the emotion occurs. This is a critical point in the treatment process. A scene which engenders high emotion should be presented repeatedly until it ceases to elicit much response. Variations in the scene should be introduced in order to maximize the process of generalization of the emotional response to the traumatic stimuli. In this way, other related stimuli or cues are presented to the patient. If this increases anxiety, then these related cues or stimuli also are repeated until a reduction in emotionality is obtained. The process is clearly to confront and work through the anxiety and never to avoid.

Resistance

Presenting a highly aversive memory will motivate avoidance or resistance. The most frequent avoidance maneuvers observed during the presentation of scenes are (1) reduced image clarity and (2) blocking or suppressing of negative emotion. Some patients will claim that they cannot feel any emotion (numbing). This effect is more common among PTSD sufferers. If a patient cannot experience the emotion involved in an obviously relevant scene which at other times may even be intrusive, then the therapist must attempt to overcome this obvious resistance through any means possible.

The first and most straightforward approach is to direct the patient to focus more on the scene and then increase the intensity of the scene description, slowing down and focusing on particularly impactful elements of the scene. For instance, one patient complained that he could not recall the face of a particularly hateful commanding officer. His buddies had been killed presumably by the commanding officer's blundering leadership. This interfered with his response to the scene. By asking him to focus on the "blank" face and then try to "make out" some element such as his hair, eyes or nose, the patient was finally able to remember with some clarity. This, in turn, allowed him to experience the fear that the face held for him (as well as the anger). Theoretically the forgotten fear stimuli (facial characteristics) are high on the avoidance serial cue hierarchy, and once the associated fear response to this stimulus is extinguished the anger would also diminish through higher order extinction of the CER.

Another method for overcoming resistance to exposure therapy is to increase the demand to continue in a supportive manner. The therapist might say to the patient: "—sure you can see it—it doesn't have to be an exact image, just something close—try again. Visualize it now." Or it may be helpful to encourage the patient to reduce the responsibility for the scene with this theme: "something snaps in your mind, it's like you are not yourself anymore. Now go ahead see yourself as this crazed person hitting the assailant who attempted to rape you." The therapist may also re-emphasize that the scene is just fantasy: "Anything can happen in fantasy, Joan, now I want you to see your husband's face, notice his hateful smile, see your hand rising to strike him." Notice here how the therapist removes the patient from the active mode by requesting that she see "herself" doing something rather than seeing the other person as would normally be the case. This is a distancing ploy that helps reduce the anxiety associated with the aggressive behavior. Another method for accomplishing the same goal is to ask the patient to imagine that they are seeing a movie screen with actors that only resembles them.

Faced with strong resistance, the therapist also can present stimuli of lesser intensity, for a short time and in a graded fashion until the patient feels more comfortable in attempting to fantasize the resisted material. Resisted material also can be presented on a more symbolic level. A person having trouble imagining responding aggressively toward a male rapist might focus in on some other associated stimuli that represents the assault: *"see his (the rapist) car now, imagine that you pick up a sledge hammer and start to bash the windows in."*

An excellent method for facilitating the imaginal process is to offer more descriptive detail. The scene can be developed slowly with more than usual description of internal and external stimuli. The therapist should use as many of the imaginable sense modalities as possible, such as color, movement, temperature, olfaction, shading, audio stimuli, tactile stimulation, form, vision, and time.

With highly resistant and concrete patients the therapist can break through defenses by focusing on the present reality: *"see yourself sitting in my office as you are now"*. The therapist might ask the patient to close his/her eyes and to actually feel the texture of the chair he/she is sitting in: the cold wood, warm material, or smooth metal.

As with any therapy, occasionally resistance to exposure therapy becomes extremely stubborn. The patient frequently may miss appointments and/or arrive late; or repeatedly fail to accomplish homework assignments, etc. At this point more traditional cognitive means should be used to help explore this resistance through discussion, interpretation, and labeling, before continuing with DTE.

Once the reason for the resistance is discovered then exposure also can be used to reduce this directly. Suppose, for example, that the therapist discovers that the resistance is rooted in the patient's nonverbalized anger at the therapist for pushing the patient to expose himself/herself to emotionally laden memories. A scene can be developed whereby the patient is allowed, in fantasy, to act out the anger and aggression the patient feels toward the therapist—even imagine physically beating the therapist. Such scenes may result in the patient laughing or using other anxiety-motivated defenses. Surprisingly, this type of scene has been beneficial in reducing resistance toward the therapist, and can even lead to insight about the therapeutic relationship that can take much more time when using more conventional approaches. In my experience, angry feelings toward the therapy and the therapist are considerably diminished by this therapeutic ploy.

Many patients, particularly those who have obsessive-compulsive features, fear losing control or "going crazy" or "losing their minds." For these types of patients, scenes that include loss of control themes are useful. These patients will resist the exposure therapy because they fear that such imaginings will lead to loss of control and that they will be inclined to act out the scenes in reality. This resistance can be directed back into the scene. A typical scene that involves fear of going crazy includes having the patient imagine losing his/her mind by acting out and becoming too aggressive, too hostile, or too angry, or sexually acting out. The scene would then continue with the fears that underlie this, such as rejection by parents or by lovers, and finally punishment. With sufficient repetition such exposure generally lessens this form of resistance.

Homework

After each session patients should be asked to practice that session's scenes by themselves prior to the next session. Sometimes a helpful procedure is to tape-record the scene for the resisting patient. Recordings are also helpful for patients with low ego-strength. The patient is asked to find a quiet place where he/she will not be disturbed and to work through the scene at about the same pace as it was presented in the therapy session, at least twice daily. Patients should be counseled specifically to set this time aside only for this homework and that just thinking about the session for a few minutes here and there during the day is not effective, and may even interfere with their daily functioning. The patient should be told that he/she may not be able to elicit the same amount of anxiety that was felt in the therapist's office. Nevertheless he/she is asked to keep track of image clarity and amount of emotion produced during each homework session.

After completion of the homework the patient should be asked to rate their homework on a 0 to 10 anxiety scale like Wolpe's subjective units of distress scale (SUDs scale) where 0 is no anxiety and 10 is "as anxious as I have ever been." Homework can be very important to the therapy, as it provides the necessary repetitiveness to the exposure process. Therapy time can be reduced greatly if the patient is motivated to practice at home. This may be especially important for response prevention strategies where the patient is practicing not carrying out compulsive anxiety reducing rituals. Homework is vital to the success of in vivo exposure.

To demonstrate, if a combat veteran fears crowded places such as malls, he/she should be strongly encouraged to go to the mall and remain for at least two hours, practicing exposure for as long as possible. Again such homework sessions should be planned for extended periods of up to two or more hours. Brief, "passes" through the mall to buy something will not have a significant effect, especially if the patient leaves the mall in an excitatory condition. A particularly good step-by-step guide for in vivo exposure can be found in Craske and Barlow (1990) and Barlow and Craske (1990). The former is a therapist's guide and the latter is for use by the patient.

The homework scene also helps to teach the patient a technique for dealing with other fears. The patient is taught to analyze when they feel anxious about something, determine the cues, and then conduct a scene to expose themselves, either in vivo or in imagination (or preferably both if possible).

In vivo exposure should always be used where possible, as evidence is clear that this form of exposure is highly effective

(Barlow & Wolfe, 1981). In vivo exposure has long been the behavioral treatment of choice for all forms of phobia, including agoraphobia and panic disorder with agoraphobia. I also have found it very helpful with PTSD patients who have developed phobic symptoms. Formal in vivo therapy should always be used in conjunction with imaginal exposure for combat-related PTSD, where the veteran avoids crowds and interpersonal contact. Also as noted above, response prevention is a particularly effective form of therapy for those who suffer from severe compulsion symptoms.

Using DTE in the Context of Other Therapies

Rarely are patients treated only with exposure therapy outside of any other therapeutic context. Most patients who suffer from PTSD, as well as other anxiety disorders, will likely need other interventions as well. For example, the rape victim who can usually benefit by repeated exposure to the traumatic memory also may suffer from performance anxiety during desired sexual contact or fear of leaving the house alone. Here, a behavioral treatment program using in vivo exposure would be helpful. For all PTSD sufferers, but especially for combat-related PTSD, a group treatment approach is very helpful. Probably for combat-related PTSD, exposure therapy should always be used conjointly with group therapy. Also, patients who suffer PTSD for an extended period of time also may suffer from many related bio-psycho-social problems and disorders. Many will have interpersonal problems and may need family therapy or other individual cognitive-based therapies aimed at helping the patient explore and deal with interpersonal inadequacies. While DTE may be central to the process, it is often only one part of an overall treatment program for PTSD.

PTSD patients who also suffer from substance abuse brought on by early stressful experiences, should be provided a treatment program aimed directly at the substance abuse. My own experience with combat veterans is that dual diagnoses (PTSD and substance abuse) are more effectively treated together in a coordinated treatment effort, rather than having the patient attend a substance abuse treatment program prior to treating his/her PTSD.

Aides to Developing Scene Content

In their original publication on the Implosive Therapy process Stampfl and Levis (1967) defined 10 areas, for didactic purposes, that were descriptive of common cues that could be used by the exposure therapists to help develop relevant hypothesized scene content. These include Aggression, Punishment, Rejection, Bodily Injury, Loss of Control, Acceptance of Conscience, Autonomic Nervous System (ANS) and Central Nervous System (CNS) Reactivity, Oral Material, Anal Material and Sexual Material. Levis (Levis & Hare, 1977) later added an eleventh: Inferiority Feelings. A description of these areas is provided in Table 11.1.

While these areas are not an exhaustive classification of scene content, DTE therapists can benefit greatly by reviewing the history of the patient's trauma within the context of these areas. They represent common content areas for many patients. In my own experience, a routine review or "check off" of these stimulus areas can be extremely helpful in developing the relevant and effective scene content, and especially in developing effective hypothesized cues.

Session Termination

As reviewed in Boudewyns and Shipley (1983, pp. 30-34) based on research results, in general, *the longer the exposure session the better.* In practice, the length of the sessions will vary and practical considerations usually require that sessions last no more than an hour. The actual length of each scene presentation within sessions also will be dictated by practical considerations as most patients have problems with imaginal scenes that continue longer than 35 or 40 minutes.

A given scene can be terminated after some decrease in anxiety is observed. A DTE scene should never be terminated while a patient is still highly emotional however. The session should, if at all possible, never end in the middle of a scene or theme. Also after that part of the session involving imagery has ended, the therapist should allow at least 10 to 15 minutes

(continued on page 556)

TABLE 11.1
Didactic Content Areas for Developing Scene Content for DTE

Aggression: Many patients are afraid to be aggressive and hostile and find such activities anxiety producing even when carried out in fantasy (remember that the anxiety is diminished by DTE, not the aggression or hostility). Scenes in this area would center around describing various aggressive acts, experienced or observed by the patient.

Punishment: Patients can reduce their fear of punishment by visualizing themselves as the recipient of the anger, hostility and aggression of the various significant others in their lives. The punishment inflicted in the scene is frequently a result of the patient's engaging in some forbidden act. Many patients carry over fears of physical punishment by parents, and never realize the potency of these totally unrealistic fears. DTE can be used to extinguish these immature fears in adults quite rapidly.

Rejection: Scenes where the patient is rejected, deprived, abandoned, shamed, or left helpless are often at the root of fear, but are denied or avoided. Scenes depicting these often unrealistic fears can help the patient to overcome these common anxieties.

Bodily Injury: Scenes involving mutilation and death of the patient are introduced where fear of injury appears dominant. (In combat-related PTSD for example, even for memories where the patient may only have seen others suffer, a hypothesized scene of his/her own feared bodily injury may still be relevant.) Again, the goal is not to reduce a healthy concern for one's body, but to reduce the fear of imagining it or thinking about death and destruction.

Loss of Control: Scenes are presented in which the patient is encouraged to imagine losing impulse control to such an extent that he/she acts out avoided sexual or aggressive impulses. These scenes usually are followed by scenes where the patient is directed to visualize his/her own hospitalization

(continued)

TABLE 11.1 (continued)

or other incarceration for extended periods of time. Many patients fear becoming insane as a result of their symptoms. Imagining the worse is often helpful in diminishing these unrealistic fears, especially if it explained to the patient that, in reality, this will never happen. Therapists who use paradoxical techniques will see similarities here.

Acceptance of Conscience (e.g., fear of being guilty): Here scenes are often portrayed in which the patient confesses, admits, and believes that he or she is responsible and guilty for wrongdoing. Courtroom scenes, early confessions to parents or to superiors can be effective. This is a particularly important and powerful area and therapists should routinely include these cues in scene content. For PTSD of combat and early abuse, such scenes are very often effective in helping the patient to have insight into the fact that early transgressions do not have to be guilt producing in the present. Guilt is reduced to "embarrassment" over ethical and moral transgressions of childhood after repeated scenes in this area.

ANS and CNS Reactivity: The sensory consequences of ANS and CNS reactivity may themselves function as cues for anxiety—in a spiralling effect. Here scenes are introduced in which patients are asked to visualize the sensory consequences of their own nervous system reactions (e.g., heart pounding, perspiration increase, increase in muscle tension, blushing, involuntary discharge of the bladder). Imaginal role-play scenes emphasizing these reactions happening to the patient in public can be helpful in reducing anxiety about the possibility of a panic attack. Having the patient produce these feelings under controlled circumstances, by over-breathing for example, and then "extinguishing" them by slowed breathing (as demonstrated in Barlow & Craske, 1990) can be helpful for both symptoms of panic and PTSD. A combination of imagining the consequences of ANS and CNS arousal under relatively low arousal, as in imaginal flooding, and also experiencing ANS and CNS reactivity under relatively high arousal conditions such as in planned over-breathing, can give the patient a sense of

(continued)

TABLE 11.1 (continued)

control over these frightful experiences. However, it is not clear what the underlying mechanism is here. Is it extinction, or learning, or mastery? It is probably some combination of all of these.

Oral, Anal, and Sexual Material: These are all related to Stampfl's consideration of psychodynamic theory in developing the Implosive Therapy process. Scenes using this content are less useful for PTSD. Of course sexual material may appear in other contexts, especially in scenes of aggression or acceptance of conscience.

Inferiority Feelings: An additional area was described by Levis and Hare (1977) as feelings of inadequacy, cowardice, being a failure, and fearing lack of physical beauty or physical strength and abilities. Scenes that emphasize and exaggerate these fears can be helpful, although the underlying mechanism here is more likely a phenomenon originally described by Victor Frankl (1960) as paradoxical intention (rather than extinction or habituation), especially if the concerns are borne out, at least to some extent, in reality.

Extrapolated from Stampfl & Levis, 1967, and Levis & Hare, 1977.

for the patient to relax and/or be debriefed about the scene before leaving the therapist's office. My experience has been that after an exposure scene, the patient's anxiety recovers to an even lower level than was the case prior to the scene within about five minutes of scene termination. In fact, based on psychophysiological data emotional levels 15 minutes after scene presentation are significantly below presession levels (anticipation anxiety) (Boudewyns & Hyer 1990).

Following each scene the therapist should debrief the patient by asking about vividness of imagery and the strength of the emotion during various portions of the scene. This debriefing will allow the therapist to develop new hypothesized cues for future sessions.

After the session many patients will use phrases like "wrung out" or "tired" or "relieved" to describe their present feeling state. This is a positive indication that the patient has been working hard. If he/she still feels tense ten minutes after scene termination, it is a likely indicator that the scene may have been terminated prematurely or that non-symptom-contingent cues are still driving the anxiety. If this happens, what might be necessary is to go back and rehearse the scene later, either in that present session or in the next. Although no evidence has been obtained that premature scene termination will harm the patient (a concept known as sensitization), it does reduce the patient's satisfaction with the treatment. The patient should be warned that this can happen at times, and that all this means is that it will be necessary to continue to work on that scene later. During the early sessions an especially important point is for the patient's anxiety to be reduced at session termination in order to ensure the cooperation of the patient with the therapy.

If the patient's anxiety level does not subside after repeated and lengthy presentation of a particular scene during a single session, then the therapist should focus in on some small, specific part of the scene, and repeat it several times until anxiety to that particular aspect of the scene is completely diminished. For example, a patient who had problems with an abusing mother was asked to focus in only on her mother's hand as it held a "switch" (not in motion). This was continued until the anxiety engendered by the image was completely reduced. Here the important point was to instruct the patient to focus closely on the image and not to continue with any other aspect of the memory.

Regardless of the resistance shown by the patient, the therapist must always keep in mind that continued frequent exposure is the key to anxiety reduction. The more repetition and the longer one is exposed to the anxiety eliciting scenes, the greater likelihood that complete reduction in anxiety will occur.

SCENE TRANSCRIPTS

In this final section I will describe very briefly several edited transcripts of portions of DTE scenes. Therapists should not use these in a "cookbook" application for their own patients. DTE must be tailored to the patient. These transcripts are offered here only as brief examples of the process.

Rape Scene

This scene was used with a female patient, age 28, who had been raped in a mall parking lot eight months prior to consultation. She qualified under DSM-III-R for a diagnosis of PTSD. Her disorder made it difficult for her to leave the house at night alone. She also avoided malls and other public areas because of her fear of attack. Both in vivo and imaginal exposure were used in her treatment. She had considerable difficulty recalling the details of the rape experience, so to begin with, many hypothesized cues were used. The scene below included some of my own hypothesized cues. Close observation of her nonverbal behavior during the scenes and careful debriefing were used to help her recall many particulars that were then used in treatment scenes. The scene reported below was repeated over 20 times during her therapy and the content changed somewhat as her recall improved over the first six to eight repetitions. Initial resistance was strong, and a great deal of time and encouragement was necessary at first.

Therapist: Close your eyes—what do you see?

Patient: I can see the parking lot.

T. *Okay, now look around, see the cars, it is dark. Feel the hot summer night. You are looking for your car, but can't remember where you have parked. See what you remember as you walk down a parking lane (pause). Smell the air, recall the odor. Concentrate on your bodily sensation right now, feel the anticipation, check your heart-rate, the tension in your neck and shoulders. Now as you walk through a dark area, you look to your right and see someone coming toward you. The form is of a man, and you watch him. As he gets closer you hear him speak —"oh mam, can you tell me what time it is." You look at your watch, but it is too dark to see clearly. As you look up, you see him close to you. Feel the tension now as his hand grabs your wrist and the watch. (pause) Concentrate on the tight feeling of his hand on your wrist—You say: "what do you want", as he pulls you in between two cars "leave me alone" "stop." He pushes you against one of the cars and says: "I have a knife—do as I say"— Concentrate now on your body sensations (pause). Hear it again "I have a knife—do as I say" and you know you are about to be raped. As the thought crosses your mind you feel the dread, and fear wells up in your chest and stomach—concentrate on that feeling, as strong as you can.*

(At this point the therapist should spend some time working directly on the anticipatory anxiety until some diminution is observed before continuing with the actual rape scene. Often the anticipation of harm is more anxiety provoking than the act itself being relived.)

Now feel yourself resigned to your fate. You think of screaming, but are too afraid, so you resist little. He pushes you on to the pavement, and quickly pushes up your skirt, and pulls your underclothing off. Feel his hands as they pull on your legs, and quickly pushes into you— the pressure—the pain, and you black out or lose track of your consciousness—and all you can remember is the hope he'll leave. Try now to remember the feelings—your eyes are closed but recall the pressure as he enters you —feel it as clearly as you can.

(The goal here is to bring back to consciousness as much of the stimuli as possible. The patient claims to have blacked out at this point, but this is unlikely, since she remembers clearly the moment the rapist moved away from her and ran away. It is important to recall the details, as it brings the incident into perspective, is not overwhelming, and allows the memory of the stimulus complex of the rape itself not to be avoided and dreaded. What is important is the reduction of the fear of remembering. Learning to remember details without anxiety—since it is not really happening now—takes time but gives the victim a strong sense of control over her present state and this is most important in dealing with traumatic memories. By continuing to avoid remembering, the patient increases the fear that the memory holds. Thus with DTE we are often dealing with the "fear" of fear, or "secondary fear" as it is called in the phobia literature).

Feel the heaviness of his body on you, smell his alcoholic breath.

(The alcohol breath was originally a hypothesized cue that paid off. Olfactory cues are particularly effective in helping patients reintegrate other associated stimuli.)

Concentrate on the pressure, weight, heat, and alcohol smell—stay with this now.

(The therapist should continue repeating this portion of the scene with the cues available until diminution occurs.)

After he leaves, you feel continued fear, and don't move as he has warned. Finally you begin to open your eyes and slowly get up, put your clothes back on, thinking what you should do. You feel a strong urge to vomit as a wave of nausea overtakes you, and then you begin to cry. Be aware now of all your body sensations.

This scene lasted about 25 minutes, working slowly to reduce the CERs throughout each aspect of the scene, and repeating many aspects of it. Note that much effort went into having the patient be aware of her physical response (ANS and CNS activity). This is especially important for DTE scenes where the memories involve physical responding.

This was a critical scene and it required much work. However the patient was able to work through the scene to the point where it engendered little fear, only anger. The anger, which was appropriate, was then used to help her imagine scenes where she counter-attacked the rapist and later took part in in vivo training in rape defense classes. Fear of anger and hostility toward the rapist is common in less assertive women. DTE is an effective way of overcoming the fear of expressing anger and counter-aggression.

This particular patient evidenced little guilt over the event. Some women do—feeling "dirty," "guilty," and/or "alone." These emotions can be dealt with by exploring the stimuli that are associated with these feelings. They are usually based on beliefs many women have about the effect of allowing strangers to have sexual contact with them. They may feel like a prostitute, or defiled forever, even though they were forced. These issues can be worked through using a cognitive-behavioral (rational-emotive) methodology. But DTE scenes of rejection and even punishment by significant others that end in appropriately assertive behavior on the part of the patient can be helpful.

Sometimes rape will reintegrate memories of early sexual behavior for which the patient feels guilty. Giving permission to relive these scenes (often scenes of abuse, but even more often normal "left over" guilty memories of adolescent sexual behavior) until mastery or extinction takes place, is very effective and useful.

Fear of guilt based on religious beliefs also can be addressed with DTE, but if strongly ingrained, these beliefs are very difficult to change. Women patients who appear guilty or appear to need "forgiveness" for being abused or raped may have had sexual fantasies in the past that depicted strong aggressive men, and through magical thinking may have come to believe that these fantasies caused the rape. Strong religious beliefs that promote the notion that women should control and suppress their sexual fantasies can result in resistance to DTE.

For most rape victims, use of DTE to overcome the anticipatory anxiety about even remembering the event is helpful. If other early abuse scenes are relevant (and they very often are), then reliving these avoided memories to extinction also can be helpful. Imaginal scenes of aggressiveness and in vivo work on assertiveness and defense are also effective. Early childhood fears of parental punishment for sexual behavior with parental rejection may be relevant. For rape and abuse victims repeated verbal reinforcement, support, and congratulatory remarks are extremely important to success.

Combat-related PTSD

Perhaps the three most common themes in combat-related PTSD are (1) fear of death and injury (2) fear and conflict that centers on guilt, and (3) anger. In reality these themes are often intertwined and interrelated in a single event or in many traumatic events or memories. Fear of death and bodily injury are almost always part of a victim's theme, regardless of other factors. Guilt is often the result of the patient's unacceptable personal aggression toward innocent victims in combat. Guilt also may contribute to the problem even though the violence against innocent victims is accidental. Guilt scenes also may depict acting out by buddies against innocent victims which was observed by the patient, and for which the patient feels some responsibility. Guilt and acceptance of conscience are the most difficult to treat when the victim is a child. Another common type of guilt scene has to do with fear of guilt that is associated with having survived when a buddy did not (survivor guilt). Anger is usually directed at a specific individual, such as a superior that required the patient to carry out unacceptable maneuvers resulting in injury to the patient or a friend. Anger also can be directed at "the system", the government, or any bureaucracy, especially the VA, that is perceived as being responsible for the patient's present condition.

The following transcripts offer brief examples of symptom-contingent scenes in each of the first two areas: fear of bodily injury and acceptance of conscience.

(1) Fear of Bodily Injury.

T: *Close your eyes. What do you see?*

P: *Its dark, hot, hard to see anything in the jungle, but I am with my outfit, and we know there are enemy ahead near the village.*

T: *OK now see best as you can as you walk along. Feel the jungle around you—hot, moist, dark. You step along following to a small clearing where you begin to dig in. Your best friend Jerry and you stay low and wait. Its real quiet—too quiet. Then all of a sudden the whole sky lights up ahead of you and you know that all hell is going to break loose. You set up as fast as you can and can hear AK-47s in the front—looks like a real fire-fight. The Lt. calls for reinforcement and air (cover). Rounds are coming in everywhere—some tracers. You fire your M-16s and move ahead to catch up with the column that is camped ahead. Then, finally, choppers coming in at three o'clock, firing. It looks like they are going to land and get you out, but rounds are coming in everywhere. You think, I'm a short timer, I don't need this and the only thing you can think of is getting the hell out of there, and you don't want to fight this one any more.*

At this point you move away from Jerry and turn and yell at him to come on to get over to the pad (landing area) so you can vac out, since it looks like you are badly outnumbered. Then all of a sudden you look over and Jerry is slumped over, and his head is nothing but blood and the tree behind him has his brains all over it. See that scene now—see it clearly—try to remember what you do next. You want to help Jerry, but you know he's a goner and you're scared shitless, knowing it could happen to you. Concentrate now on your body sensation. (pause) Feel the pounding in your chest, and the tightness in your neck and head. Concentrate on Jerry's face, and the fear you have that it could be me—that it could be me—it is almost as if you can imagine yourself there, just like Jerry, dead, with your brains spilled out. What do you do now—that's right you turn and leave. When you are finally back at base camp you begin to go over the events.

(Here the therapist could start back through the same scene as many times as necessary, concentrating on different stimuli that may stimulate bodily injury fears. Bodily injury fears usually center on blood and wound images. Patients may need to imagine such stimuli many times if they are to be successful in reducing anxiety associated with bodily injury fears. Many associated memories and stimuli and even earlier bodily injury events will often be uncovered with such a scene.)

(2) Fear of Guilt or Acceptance of Conscience. This same theme may have resulted in survivor guilt. If so, repeated presentations of the following scene might be helpful.

T: *Now you are at the base camp, and it is several days later. You have not heard if anyone even found Jerry's body. You know that they (another outfit) went in the next day to find what they could, but none could account for Jerry. You feel like a real asshole for not staying with Jerry to see if you could have gotten his body out of there. You know you should write Jerry's parents, and tell them what happened, since you both had agreed to do that. Now you feel so bad about yourself, you feel too guilty to even write them. You try to avoid thinking about it and talking about it, but the thought that you were a real coward keeps intruding on your mind, and you think that Jerry wouldn't have done what you did if things were reversed. It is very hard to accept the fact that you were a coward, but you were.*

Concentrate on your body sensations as you realize that you did not act as strong as you should have. You really are guilty of not taking care of your buddy's body, because you were so afraid that you too might die. Concentrate on your body sensations as you recall this incident. Stay with that feeling as long as you can. Does anything else come to mind as you recall this?

(The goal here is to get the patient to accept his/her fear and cowardice, since he/she cannot find a way to excuse self. DTE is a very effective way of demonstrating to the patient that he/she can live with self, even if he/she betrays a friend. *Cognitive efforts at trying to excuse the patient's survivor guilt, are usually fruitless.* Often survivor guilt is based on magical thinking that the dead friend has not forgiven him/her. Sometimes a fantasy scene where the patient talks to his/her friend and is not forgiven can be helpful here. Such scenes can result in expressions of true anger for the friend that also drives the guilt.)

T: *Imagine now that you see a vision of Jerry's face, what does he say?*

P: *He is angry—he asks me, "Why?" "Why?"*

T: *You tell him that you are sorry, but he still somehow seems angry. Concentrate on that angry face* (faces are important stimuli when dealing with guilt cues) *and feel your guilt. Tell him you are sorry, but the face stays angry, and he says, "I wouldn't have done that to you." How does that make you feel? Concentrate on your feelings as Jerry says it again "I wouldn't have done that to you, coward." And you say: "Yes I was a coward then, I accept that." He still looks angry.*

(Here the goal is often to get the patient past the fear of his own guilt through extinction of the fear of facing his angry friend. Often feelings of anger at the dead friend are present. After these are exposed, more guilt for being angry at the dead friend for making the patient feel guilty is often seen. These feelings vacillate back and forth. But eventually, a long DTE session can simply "wear out" the conflict. After such a session, patients are more willing to deal with the anger at the dead friend for having "caused" so much guilt over the years.)

(3) **Anger at the System.** Scenes involving anger toward the system, or toward some figurehead of authority, often relate to the patient's feeling of being lied to; a feeling that so much life was wasted. And this in turn engenders anger and frustration at the system that won't help them now even though it is owed to them. Usually a cognitive-rational approach is most effective here. Noting, for example, that railing against the system is OK if he/she wants to put out the energy, but it may not solve many of the real personal problems, even if success in changing the system is achieved.

When treating combat-related PTSD, especially with Vietnam veterans, much of what is normally done in therapy may simply be conceived of as therapeutic exposure. Most of these veterans have been using avoidance strategies for years. Many of these strategies too are anger based. Any effort to deal directly with their fears, whether it be in a "rap" group, or practice at going to a shopping center or simply practicing going out to dinner to a strange restaurant with family and friends, should be encouraged and can be therapeutic.

SUMMARY

DTE can be an effective and efficient treatment approach for Specific Phobias, Agoraphobia, Panic and Obsessive-compulsive Disorder. More recently it also has been shown to be helpful for PTSD sufferers. Early concerns that DTE may have harmful side effects and may even sensitize patients has not been borne out by the research. Conditioned emotional responses associated with past traumatic events, especially fear and acceptance of conscience (fear of guilt) can be relieved with this procedure. Therapists who work with these disorders should use this technique in both its in vivo and imaginal forms as appropriate. DTE can be very effective for individual cases of PTSD either as one aspect of an overall therapy program or as the main treatment approach.

REFERENCES

Barlow, D. H., & Craske, M. G. (1990). *Mastery of your anxiety and panic.* Albany, NY: Graywind Publishing.

Barlow, D. H., & Wolfe, B. E. (1981). Behavioral approaches to anxiety disorders: A report on the NIMH-SUNY Albany Research Conference. *Journal of Consulting and Clinical Psychology, 49,* 448-455.

Boudewyns, P. A., Albrecht, J. W., & Hyer, L. (1992). *Long term effect of direct therapeutic exposure in combat-related PTSD.* Paper presented at the one hundreth annual convention of the American Psychological Association. Washington, D.C.

Boudewyns, P. A., & Hyer, L. (1990). Physiological response to combat memories and preliminary treatment outcome in Vietnam veteran PTSD patients treated with direct therapeutic exposure. *Behavior Therapy, 21,* 63-87.

Boudewyns, P. A., Hyer, L., Woods, M. G., Harrison, W. R., & McCranie, E. (1990). PTSD among Vietnam veterans: An early look at treatment outcome using direct therapeutic exposure. *Journal of Traumatic Stress, 3*, 359-368.

Boudewyns, P. A., & Levis, D. J. (1975). Autonomic reactivity of high and low ego-strength subjects to repeated anxiety eliciting scenes. *Journal of Abnormal Psychology, 84*, 682-692.

Boudewyns, P. A., & Shipley, R. H. (1983). *Flooding and implosive therapy: Direct therapeutic exposure in clinical practice.* New York: Plenum.

Cooper, N. A., & Clum, G. A. (1989). Imaginal flooding as a supplementary treatment for PTSD in combat veterans: A controlled study. *Behavior Therapy, 20*, 381-391.

Craske, M. G., & Barlow, D. H. (1990). *Therapist's guide for the mastery of your anxiety and panic.* Albany, NY: Graywind Publishing.

Fontana, A., Rosenheck, R., & Spencer, H. (1990). *The long journey home: The first progress report on the department of Veterans Affairs PTSD clinical treatment teams program.* West Haven, CT: Veterans Administration Medical Center.

Frankl, V. E. (1960). Paradoxical intention: A logotherapeutic technique. *American Journal of Psychotherapy, 14*, 520-535.

Hogan, R. A. (1966). Implosive therapy in the short term treatment of psychotics. *Psychotherapy: Theory, Research and Practice, 3*, 25-31.

Keane, T. M., Fairbank, J. A., Caddell, J. M., & Zimering, R. T. (1989). Implosive (flooding) therapy reduces symptoms of PTSD in Vietnam combat veterans. *Behavior Therapy, 20*, 245-260.

Levis, D. J., & Hare, N. A. (1977). A review of the theoretical rationale and empirical support for the extinction approach of implosive (flooding) therapy. In M. Hersen, R. Eisler, & P. Miller (Eds.), *Progress in Behavior Modification* (Vol. 4). New York: Academic Press.

Levis, D. J., & Stampfl, T. G. (1972). Effects of serial CS presentation on shuttlebox avoidance responding. *Learning and Motivation, 3*, 73-90.

Lyons, J. (1991). Strategies for assessing the potential for positive adjustment following trauma. *Journal of Traumatic Stress, 4*, 93-112.

Mowrer, O. H. (1960). *Learning theory and behavior*. New York:Wiley.

Shipley, R. H., & Boudewyns, P. A. (1980). Flooding and implosive therapy: Are they harmful? *Behavior Therapy, 11*, 503-508.

Shipley, R. H., & Boudewyns, P. A. (1988). The mythical dangers of exposure therapy. *The Behavior Therapist, 11*, 8.

Stampfl, T. G., & Levis, D. J. (1967). Essentials of implosive therapy: A learning-theory-based psychodynamic behavioral therapy. *Journal of Abnormal Psychology, 72*, 496-503.

Chapter 12

PTSD AND BEREAVEMENT: TRAUMATIC GRIEF

Richard W. Bagge
and
Jeffrey M. Brandsma

"To want to forget something is to think of it." French Proverb

Bereavement follows a major psychologically defined loss as a natural consequence in our species. Bereavement literally defined is the psychological processes surrounding one who has been robbed, deprived, or dispossessed, and is left in a sad and lonely state. Although understood as part of the human condition since ancient times, modern psychiatry (with the exception of Freud) did not contribute greatly to its understanding until 1944. Lindemann's article in that year evaluating the Coconut Grove disaster became a stimulus for many to consider this critical area of psychological functioning. More recent nosological classifications have recognized the association of trauma to specific psychiatric symptomatology, i.e., PTSD (DSM-III, DSM-III-R). Interesting to note, however, is that little attention has been paid to the association of traumatic events with loss and the bereavement process. This is especially true in the arena of combat related losses (Garb, Bleich, & Lerer, 1987). PTSD and grief, especially pathological bereavement, have significant areas of overlap in their symptomatic expression. This being granted, it would, therefore, be a natural extension of inquiry to consider what potential overlap may occur in therapeutic strategies.

Interest in the area of grief treatment dates back to the late 1800s with reports of the use of hypnosis for the treatment of traumatic grief (van der Hart, Brown, & Turco, 1990). Pierre Janet developed techniques using hypnosis to treat what today we call PTSD (van der Hart & Friedman, 1989). Only recently has this treatment entered into clinical use. In this chapter we propose a model which has helped to conceptualize this pathology and propose treatment rubrics for trauma induced bereavement.

LINKAGE: PTSD AND BEREAVEMENT

Conceptually an appealing overlap exists between PTSD and grief. Lindemann regarded the following as pathognomonic of grief: "somatic distress, preoccupation with the image of the decreased, guilt, hostile reactions, and loss of habitual patterns of conduct" (Lindemann, 1944). All these symptoms are reflected in PTSD (Table 12.1). In addition, both PTSD and an acute grief reaction involve an overwhelmingly traumatic event and loss. But remember, "loss is simultaneously a real event and a perception by which the individual endows the event with personal or symbolic meaning" (Garb et al., 1987, p. 424). The association between PTSD, loss, and subsequent grief is always implied and often persuasive.

The characteristics of PTSD are the reexperiencing of the event through intrusive recollections, distressing dreams, or "flashbacks"; avoidance of reminders, or a general numbing of emotional responsiveness; and persistent symptoms of increased arousal and dysphoria (American Psychiatric Association, 1987, p. 249). PTSD is differentiated from simple bereavement and other more common traumatic experiences

TABLE 12.1
Symptoms Found in PTSD and Acute Grief

Somatic symptoms
Sleep disturbances
Social withdrawl
Loss of capacity to love
Loss of habitual patterns of conduct
Seeking out or avoiding places or objects that remind
Sighing
Guilt
Anger (hostility)
Numbness
Image based memory of the deceased
    Visual hallucinations
    Intense, vivid recollections
    Day dreams
    Nightmares
    Reexperiencing, flashbacks
    Dreams
Substance abuse

---

by confining it to responses from events that are extremely psychologically distressing (trauma) and are "outside of the range of usual human experience." In Table 12.2 is a listing of losses common to combat-related trauma. Does the presence or nature of an intense stressor make these experiences different from bereavement?

Pathological grief is a state in which the mourning process is stuck. Parks and Weiss (1983) divided this category into three groups: (1) the ambivalent grief syndrome which follows the loss of a relationship characterized by ambivalence and anger; (2) chronic grief which is characterized by a prolonged,

TABLE 12.2
Losses Encountered in Combat and Its Aftermath

Exciting life-style
Human lives
Intense friendships
Sense of potency
Time of life
Intense vitality
Single mindedness
Innocence
An integrated self
Ability to hold a job
Capacity to love
Losses since combat experience because of PTSD
Patriotism
Body parts or function
Control over self
Sense of humanity
Sense of group cohesion, community

full blown grief reaction following a long term dependent relationship; and (3) the unexpected grief syndrome which follows "unexpected and untimely" losses, and is characterized by a persistent sense of the presence of the individual, self-reproach, and feelings of continued obligation. (See also Parks, 1985.)

Traumatic grief is a term used by van der Hart et al. (1990) to straddle the two diagnostic concepts of pathological grief and PTSD. He stated that "both exhibit the same biphasic symptom-swings from symptoms of arousal, intrusive traumatic imagery, and anxiety to defensive numbing and avoidance"

(p. 264). Neither pathological grief nor PTSD adequately describes the full range of the symptomatology and practically may leave out important elements for successful treatment. In fact, traumatic grief is considered a subset of both pathological grief and PTSD, an overlapping area where both models apply. A case may not present with the classic symptoms of PTSD (or grief) and yet require treatment for both aspects. Indeed the DSM-IV has considered a more appropriate melding of these two problem states (Davidson & Foa, 1991).

Imagery

A pathological extension of a grief reaction has significant overlap in symptomatology with PTSD. This is particularly so in the patient's use of imagery. The recollection of a particular event in the form of intense imagery is a hallmark of both disorders. Some have used this phenomenon to the patient's therapeutic advantage. Melges (1982) developed a *grief resolution therapy* in which he borrows the victim's own imagery and accompanying affects to allow for a completion of "unfinished business" with the decreased. This process is accomplished through both the expression of emotions, and the giving and receiving of forgiveness. His proposed three stage process of reliving, revising, and revisiting (discussed below) is remarkably similar to Janet's approach of uncovering traumatic memories, neutralization, and therapeutic revision (van der Hart et al., 1990).

The intense visual imagery found is these disorders is accompanied by a relived experiential sense of time and place which is so vivid that the individual has difficulty in completely testing current reality. It has the quality of being "here and now" rather than "there and then." A pale manifestation of this same phenomenon in ordinary experience includes recollections that we all experience when remembering a unique affectively significant event in our lives. Large segments of a population may share this type of experience for common events. For example, in the American culture the Challenger Space Shuttle disaster and John Kennedy's assassination are two such events. Most people who were old enough to remember these events can access a memory with affective, sensory, and cognitive components. They also have a sense of where they were and time of day the event occurred. For most, that sense of time and place (in a phenomenological sense) will be "then and there." It will have a sense of time ("pastiness"), as well as a place ("thereness"). Often in the normal state a person will have an ability to "enter" that recollection phenomenologically and "look around," as if the experiencing person is there, but without losing the time and place reference in the here and now.

In the pathological state the past becomes present and at times is experientially overwhelming. *The more traumatic the memory, the more it seems to remain in the "here and now."* If the person has used the defense of dissociation, the memories often become fragmented and the visual and affective parts may become separated. Extreme use of this dissociative defense causes fragmentation of the memory. This causes the individual to develop different lines of history isolating various aspects of an experience in an attempt to lessen its impact. This can be seen in PTSD and particularly in Multiple Personality Disorder (MPD). The result of this defense often is a fragmented memory, emotional disorganization, and cognitive slippage, the legacies of intrusions and avoidance.

PTSD GRIEF MODEL

A helpful theoretical framework for considering the use of imagery in the therapy of pathological grief and PTSD is found in Tulving's (1985) tripartite theory of memory. He hypothesized a three part memory system to conceptualize the full range of what we call memory. The three parts with modification are outlined in Table 12.3. The two sections most useful to this model are the historical (semantic) and the experiential (episodic) memories.

Tulving's description of experiential memory comes closest to the experiences of the patient with traumatic grief. He described the "phenomenal flavor of recollective experience characterized by 'pastiness' and subjective veridicality" (Tulving, 1985, p. 388). Of note is that this memory is seen as autonoetic, i.e., contributing to self-knowing. "It allows an individual to become aware of his or her own identity and existence in subjective time that extends from the past through the

TABLE 12.3
Memory Systems

Conditioned memory (procedural) enables the individual to learn connections between stimuli and responses. Repetitive stimulus patterns lead eventually to complex response chains which allow the individual to respond and adapt to the environment.

Historical memory (semantic) is characterized by the capability of internally representing states and chains of events. The individual develops a relatively affect free data base some of which is organized in a linear fashion to represent their historical time line. This memory is accessed and manipulated through language.

Experiential memory (episodic) affords the ability to acquire and retain memories of personally experienced events so that on recollection they are reexperienced in a spatiotemproal and affective context. The individual can travel back in time.

Extrapolated from Tulving, 1985.

present to the future" (Tulving, 1985, p. 388). The belief is that the disruption of this memory system is central to PTSD. The shock to the trauma victim's identity processed in the experiential memory is what results in the experience of trauma for any one person. Remember, identity depends on linkages of the person's memory where past, present, and future interchanges of cognitive and affective data exist.

The person's identity is inordinately tied to the experiential memory, possessing many "connectors" to the authentic person. The hypothesis is that in the pathological state the event (in the person's mind) never becomes assimilated and thus does not acquire a pastiness or become part of one's identity. Instead, it remains in memory as a present tense reliving of the past experience. In effect, unassimilated information infects the semipermeable memory system, where past, present, and future linkages form continuous identity. Now, flashbacks, intrusive imagery, and intense daydreams seen in PTSD, pathological bereavement, and also in Multiple Personality Disorder (MPD) form and influence behavior.

Normal Processing

Information/affective processing of the experiential memories becomes the substratum for one's identity. The person normally processes experiences largely by comparing them to previous similar events or categories. Experience is received through the perceptual apparatus and then interpreted in light of past history, current circumstances, future expectations, and life goals. Affect and meaning are added in the processes of perception and interpretation. *Experiences with little or no affect or survival value are likely discarded (not remembered). Experiences with a low or moderate level of affect are retained, processed, and inserted into the individual's historical memory or the experiential memory (past, then and there).* For the historical memory this becomes data, an important subset of which comes to be organized on a historical time line for the person. This time line is sequential, linear, conscious, and relatively affect free. It does not have an associated spatiotemporal/sensory context. Other data are "stored" as facts that are context free. For example, the formula for the area of a circle can be retrieved without conscious mental reference to a particular time and place setting.

Also retained are memories that have a complex of sensory, affective, and cognitive aspects. This recollection has a sense of time and place. Normally this "experiential" memory acquires a sense of being "then and there" and, as time passes, recedes subjectively further into the past. This seems to occur as the associated affect is detached and meaning applied. Theoretically, if all the affective and sensory components of the memory were assimilated, it would become a historical memory and no longer have the experiential quality to it. Normal grief may be seen in this fashion. As time passes, the intensity of the memory's affect decreases, and the memory fades further and further into the subjective past. The experiential nature of the memory will only remain as long as affect is attached.

Abnormal Processing

Experiences with overwhelming affect and unexpected meanings are much more difficult to process. The traumatized individual has no historical precedent to form a context within which to understand the experience and make comparisons or an interpretation. The experience does not fit; it has been "swallowed whole." Assimilation of the experience which involves the process of fitting together, comparing, understanding, and making sense of events does not occur. The more foreign the new experience is to the individual's previous experiences in content and intensity, the greater the difficulty in the information acquiring a sense of "then and there" or being processed and stored in the relatively affect free data base (historical memory). Previously unresolved experiences also may form a template on which new material may be placed, as probably happens in a traumatized child who develops MPD. Highly charged material never acquires a sense of "pastiness," but remains in an intense affective form that intrudes on the individual's consciousness in the "here and now," distorting their ability to interact appropriately with current reality. The stuck and bruised experiential memory underlines and "causes" the trauma response.

PTSD CARE USING GRIEF STAGES

Since many PTSD symptoms are coterminous with pathological grief reactions, we will consider the stages of normal grieving and point out how each can go astray, particularly in combat (Table 12.4). The first stage of a traumatic loss is shock. The homeostatic defensive mechanisms take over and produce a state of numbness (which in combat is very adaptive). Not only does the mechanism shelter the soldier from loss, but it provides an excellent defense for one's very salient fear of dying. The second stage, disbelief, is a form of denial (numbing), along with the often reported experiences of unreality that accompany combat.

With combat victims the protest found in the second stage of grief is acted out rather than expressed. Often it is turned into the common channel of most combat-contexted emotional expression, anger. One can see how a soldier would not be

TABLE 12.4
Comparison of Normal Stages of Grief
and PTSD Grief Equivalents

Normal Grief	PTSD Grief Equivalents
1. Shock and numbness	1. Shock and numbness
2. Expression of disbelief/ denial/emotion A "protest"	2. Acting out/repression of affect
3. Disorganization	3. Acute disorganization is not adaptive in a combat setting and is repressed letting a chronic disorganization develop.
4. Mourning/Restitution	4. This stage is never entered.

Extrapolated from Melges, 1982.

able to express and experience a range of feelings. The combat soldier must either deny affect or more likely isolate it. As the process of multiple traumas continues, disorganization becomes more likely. This is a natural process of psychological survival. Many theorists believe and therapists confirm that an acceptance of this process of disorganization is crucial to the initiation and continuation of the grief process (Bowlby, 1961). In a combat context for a young male this reaction is anathema. Many combat veterans report that by the end of their tour(s) they were "walking zombies." In effect, a chronic disorganization developed due to repeated trauma, despite their best efforts to "hold together." No doubt many experienced depression, despair, and yearning for their losses while in private moments. But in camp these are "fought off" or covered over with drugs. Thus, the last stage of mourning and restitution was never entered. Rather, a pathogenic mixture exists of conscious suppression, psychogenic amnesia (if the person was capable of dissociation), substance abuse, and acting out.

In this four stage conceptualization one can see that, since the healing process of disorganization cannot be tolerated in stage three, the person reverts to the first stage (numbness) to try again. This and continuing trauma cause one to become "stuck" in the process. Usually this involves a reliance on the phase of protest by acting out anger when in Vietnam, and utilizing numbness and depression in the post-trauma culture. Only with difficulty is the trauma victim able to shift from the past to the present in his/her current lives. The traumatic memories are unassimilated and experienced with vividness and freshness. They are never transferred into the narrative memory (historical). No opportunity was available to talk about feelings and reconsider their overwhelming content or intensity in better reframes of or perspectives on the situation.

This natural history of pathological grief was exacerbated by a number of factors among Vietnam veterans: (1) age— (a) veterans were 18 to 19 years old and personality structure, identity, and philosophy of life were not well developed, (b) the average soldier would have very little experience with death or grieving (or models of these), and (c) the coming transition to early adulthood (early twenties) requires considerable energy and adaptive capacity; (2) transitions, on return the veteran experienced a rapid transition from a war zone to a stable society (This occurred during a time a rapid cultural changes in the 60s and 70s); (3) augmentation of denial, combat rewards a limited, focused mind set and a suppression of all irrelevant affects; (4) type of attachments, bonding in combat is powerful, survival-oriented, and intense with little ambivalence permitted because of the narrow focused organization toward survival; (5) type of experience, the mode of death of buddies, civilians, and even the enemy was often grisly with no time allowed for grief; and (6) grief context— (a) grief had very little support in the macho, combat soldier network, (b) social supportiveness was glaringly lacking when military personnel returned to the United States, and (c) funeral rites were attenuated, if any. If one were to devise a scenario to produce the worst possible conditions for grief reactions, this one would be hard to beat.

TREATMENT

The goal of therapy in the patient with traumatic grief is to remove the barriers to the grief process and to facilitate its resolution. Normal bereavement generally does not require external assistance. Freud noted that, "Although mourning involves grave departures from the normal attitude of life, it never occurs to us to regard it as a pathological condition and to refer it to medical treatment. We rely on its being overcome after a certain lapse of time, and we look upon any interference with it as useless or even harmful" (Freud, 1917). In PTSD the element of traumatic grief requires active treatment. Normal grief is facilitated by the recognition of the reality of the loss and by the identification and processing of the positive and negative affects. This takes place naturally. These are often prescribed within a culture with certain rites of passage. In Table 12.5 are actions that have been found to be helpful in facilitating normal grief.

When the normal processes of grief have been blocked, special techniques can be helpful. (For a review of cognitive-behavioral approaches, see Fleming and Robinson, 1990). Melges (1982) argued for the use of imagery in this process. He (1982) employed present time guided imagery which optimizes the imagery skills already present in these individuals, and applies this directly to the situation of unresolved grief reactions. When multiple losses, have occurred, techniques of grief resolution are applied with care and precision in response to the multiple aspects of pathology, as the person's identity may have been successively traumatized.

In pathological bereavement feelings of loss and grief are components of the psychopathology of PTSD. Therefore, techniques useful in pathological grief could be helpful in PTSD. The first step is to identify the losses that the individual has experienced and the blocks that have become obstacles to resolution. In Table 12.6 is a list of obstacles found frequently in grief work. For example, an individual who gives evidence

TABLE 12.5
Facilitation of the Normal Grief Process

1. Facilitation of recognition of the loss
2. Recognition of both positive and negative feelings
3. Helping the family understand what is normal in the grief process
4. Assistance in decision making as necessary
5. Clinical observation for pathological developments

Extrapolated from Worden, 1982.

TABLE 12.6
Obstacles in Grief Resolution

1. Having persistent yearning for recovery of the lost object.
2. Over-identifying with the deceased.
3. Wishing to cry or rage at the loss coupled with an inability to do so.
4. Harboring misdirected anger and/or possessing ambivalence toward the deceased.
5. Interlocking grief reactions.
6. Having unspoken but powerful contracts with the deceased.
7. Holding unrevealed secrets and unfinished business.
8. Lacking a support group or alternative options.
9. Obtaining secondary gain or reinforcement from others to remain grief stricken.

Extrapolated from Melges, 1982.

of persistent yearning for the deceased may keep the clothing of the deceased in closets long after the loss. This can be a cardinal sign of unresolved grief. The next step is to help the individual to remove the obstacles by revising scenes through the use of present tense imagery. This helps to reactivate the grieving process in a controlled manner.

Guided Imagery

Guided imagery is the key to this work (Table 12.7). It begins with a decision to "regrieve" the losses. The patient is asked to relive the scene(s) of the loss in their imagination as it was happening at that time. The more traumatic and foreign the experience, the greater the difficulty with this stage. This reliving often helps to identify blocks to the grieving process, e.g., things done or not done and regretted. For an individual with traumatic grief, this process is easily initiated as the patient is already having intrusive images usually related to the loss. Revision of the scene is then planned with the patient to allow opportunity for completion of unfinished business. One woman was unable to express goodbyes toward her deceased son because of the presence at the funeral of her husband's former wife. In the revision, the scene could be reconstructed without the offending individual, this facilitating the expression of unfinished business. This is then effected in a controlled environment by revisiting the scene and allowing opportunities for "dialogues with the dead." Affective exchanges (both love and anger), confrontation of conflicts, expressions of guilt,and finally the giving and receiving of forgiveness, are important elements. When carefully done, this allows for a controlled detachment from the decreased. These sessions are often intensely emotional, which supports Bowlby's (1980) contention that weeping and anger appear to be necessary components in helping the patient recognize that the loss is final.

Future Oriented Identity Reconstruction

The last step that Melges suggests is future-oriented identity reconstruction. Again, imagery is used to help the individual construct his/her future in terms that recognize the finality

TABLE 12.7
Grief-Resolution Therapy

Techniques for Removing Obstacles	Process
1. Decision to regrieve	1. Decrease defensive avoidance
2. Guided imagery 　　Relive, revise, 　　　revisit scenes of 　　　the loss 　　Last positive exchange 　　News of the loss 　　The viewing 　　Funeral ceremony 　　Burial	2. Controlled detachment
3. Future-oriented 　　identity 　　reconstruction	3. Building new images and plans

Extrapolated from Melges, 1982.

of the loss and the need to continue in life. Giving up the past allows the renewal of a present-future focus. Using guided imagery, the individual can look to the future as well as to the past. This can be used to "create some time distancing between the present and the future. This can be done shortly after the completion of the guided imagery phase of grief-resolution therapy. The patient is asked to imagine that he is visiting a place once cherished by himself and the decreased together" (Melges, 1982, p. 207). From the future the individual can look back on the present. This ability to distance is a good test of the efficacy of the grief work.

Many other cognitive and behavioral techniques are available (Fleming & Robinson, 1990) depending on the client. We chose to emphasize the affective side because it is often the most difficult to address.

SUMMARY

Grief is a major element of PTSD but is often not adequately recognized. States of grief and PTSD are conceptually close and share many common features. We have argued that when trauma occurs, this information is not assimilated into the historical memory, being stuck in the "here and now" state. This is important in the treatment of the individual. The imagery that the trauma induces provides a helpful access to working with the victim's blocked grief. Completion of the mourning process is facilitated by discovering the blocks through reliving the traumatic experience via the experiential imagery. Guided imagery can be used to revise and then revisit the trauma memory. This dialogue of grief allows for completion of unfinished business, expression of affect and affection, forgiveness to be exchanged, and finally the saying of goodbye. The last step of mourning involves the opening up to a new future. Giving up the past allows for a renewal of a present-future focus.

REFERENCES

American Psychiatric Association (1987). *Diagnostic and Statistical Manual of Mental Disorders* (3rd ed. rev.). Washington, DC: American Psychiatric Press.

Bowlby, J. (1980). *Attachment and loss volume III, Loss.* New York: Basic Books.

Bowlby, J. (1961). Process of mourning. *The International Journal of Psycho-Analysis, 42,* 317-340.

Davidson, J., & Foa, E. (1991). Diagnostic issues in posttraumatic stress disorders: Considerations for the DSM-IV. *Journal of Abnormal Psychology, 100,* 346-355.

Fleming, S., & Robinson, P. (1990). The application of cognitive therapy to the bereaved. In T. Vallis (Ed.), *The challenge of cognitive therapy: Application to nontraditional populations* (pp. 135-157). New York: Plenum.

Freud, S. (1917). Mourning and melancholia. In E. Jones (Ed.), *Sigmund Freud: Collected papers.* New York: Basic Books.

Garb, R., Bleich, A., & Lerer, B. (1987). Bereavement in combat. *The Psychiatric Clinics of North America, 10,* 3.

Lindemann, E. (1944). Symptomatology and management of acute grief. *American Journal of Psychiatry.*

Melges, F. T. (1982). *Time and the inner future: A temporal approach to psychiatric disorders.* John Wiley and Sons.

Parks, C. M. (1985). *Recovery from bereavement.* New York: Basic Books.

Parks, C. M., & Weiss, R. S. (1983). *Recovery from bereavement.* New York: Basic Books.

Tulving, E. (1985). How many memory systems are there. *American Psychologist, 40,* 385-398.

van der Hart, O., & Friedman, B. (1989). A reader's guide to Pierre Janet on dissociation: A neglected intellectual heritage. *Dissociation, 2,* 3-16.

van der Hart, O., Brown, P., & Turco, R. N. (1990). Hypnotherapy for traumatic grief: Janetian and modern approaches integrated. *American Journal of Clinical Hypnosis, 32,* 263-271.

Worden, J. W. (1982). *Grief counseling and grief therapy: A handbook for the mental health practitioner.* New York: Springer Publishing.

Chapter 13

STRESS MANAGEMENT IN THE CARE OF PTSD

Ed Sperr
and
Lee Hyer

"Madness is to think of too many things in succession too fast, or of one thing too exclusively." Voltaire

INTRODUCTION

Stress Management Models

The relationship between stress and coping is complex. Stress management programs are wise, therefore, to be broad based and fluid in conceptualization and practice. Such programs also must consider the total health of their clients (Meichenbaum, 1985). In fact, the inherent strength in a carefully defined stress management program is the emphasis on the empowerment of the person—teaching skills, collaborating in problem solving, training/building coping patterns, rehearsing direct action, emotion-regulated or self control skills, and providing practice and feedback on tasks. Carefully performed, a stress management program can be all things to all people because it breaks down problems, demands success in its procedures, and matches problems with solutions until some change occurs. In Table 13.1 is provided a listing of guidelines used in typical programs.

Traditionally, stress management techniques have been utilized in response to anxiety. In other chapters (Chapters 2 and 3) we have described anxiety as a diffuse cognitive-affective response. It has stimulus, response and meaning propositions that give rise to arousal-driven apprehension (Barlow, 1988). We have noted that the key parts are action tendencies, uncontrollability, unpredictability, self focused attention, "hot" cognitions, and psychophysiological overarousal. We have noted also that PTSD is a most insidious form of anxiety disorder. It differs due to the intensity of response, size of fear structure and ready accessibility of fear structure. The fear structure (of PTSD) is based on a realistic event that remains and generalizes. Finally, we have noted the resistant quality of the trauma response and its almost "natural tendency" towards chronicity. Over time, psychophysiological hyperarousal appears to "drive" the chronic PTSD picture periodically fed by combat related (and other) stimuli. And, some believe (Kolb, 1987; van der Kolk, 1988) that changes occur in the biogenic makeup of the PTSD victim.

If stress exists largely in the eye of the beholder (aided by intensity and accumulation of affects), then its cognitive-affective management can be a very individual (person) response. In general, normal patterns of living blend with the avoidance/intrusion cycle to become negative life-styles. We have argued that avoidant symptoms are the client's attempt at adaptation or control of this pathological condition (intrusions). When trauma has been prolonged or intense, stressor symptoms can become "ego syntonic." Character defenses or coping patterns designed to protect the individual from future trauma become maladaptive. These patterns (coping) can be considered largely the result of the physiological stress response (Everly, 1989). They are directed by the person. Often acting out defenses are used to protect the self against further encounters with pain. Typical defensive scripts include rage, contempt, striving for perfection or power, withdrawal, and denial. In this way new scripts are difficult to establish, as the chronic sufferer is preoccupied with self protection and the status quo. A new identity is organized around the trauma script. These have been labeled maladaptive resolutions of stress (Epstein, 1990). Operative therapeutic issues concern the components that are reinforcing chronicity; patterns such as substance abuse, destructive family strategies, and disability focus (even if legitimate) become as important as the trauma itself. Issues involving who is to blame or who is going to pay for what happened become paramount.

Behind this picture of the chronic victim of PTSD is a distinctive and painful network of trauma-related memories. This network primes the cognitive processing of environmental information and biases it towards threat, which, as we have argued, contributes to the symptom picture in PTSD. Finding confirming evidence of threat continually reinforces this distorted pattern of thinking. Furthermore, this affects a person's ability to cope with future stressors.

How is a stress reduction program to fit into this chronic picture? The humorous answer to this concern is carefully, very carefully. As we noted, Meichenbaum (1985) has devised a model of care that includes conceptualization, skill acquisition and rehearsal, and application and follow-through. These stages are flexible and "portable" depending on the nature of the problem. Everly (1989) also has described a general treatment protocol for the human stress response. It is a multidimensional care program punctuated by three concerns: helping the client avoid/minimize/modify stressors (education and cognitive equilibrium); helping the client develop skills to reduce stress arousal (relaxation, meditation, hypnosis, etc.); and helping the client ventilate the stress response (psychotherapy or physical exercise). In this book we have prosecuted for a another formulation, the disaggregation of the Sc+P+(B)+Sy model.

The importance of these previously mentioned models is that they provide a conceptual structure from which to

(continued on page 592)

TABLE 13.1
Clinical Guidelines of Stress Management

1. Careful Analysis:

   think before acting;
   individualize care based on needs and research;
   be cautious in use of coping techniques;
   identify problems, response enumeration, and develop
   a management program.

2. Diversity:

   coping is a flexible constellation of problem solving methods;
   many acts involving type and intensity of problem;
   use both problem focused and emotion focused coping.

3. Sensitivity:

   individualize care;
   respect individual variability to stressful events and the
   context of the person's life.

4. Foster Flexibility:

   avoid cookbook formulation of stress reduction

5. Cognitions Influence Affective Responses:

   analysis of cognitive coping
   responses and appraisals is most effective.

6. Gradual Exposure:

   encourage stress innoculation and gradual exposure;
   engenders hope and responsibility.

(continued)

TABLE 13.1 (continued)

7. Direct Instruction:

   provide informal training including rationale, skills, and evaluation of procedures.

8. Anticipate Future:

   build in relapse prevention (RP) procedures that include an outline of potential setbacks, feelings of mastery, and general reaction to future setbacks.

9. Enlist Client:

   develop a "collaborative empiricism" and a sense of participation.

10. Client Feedback:

    relate duration of program to client performance, not time based;
    build in follow-up assessements and booster sessions.

11. Multilevel Interventions:

    assure multifaceted training at various levels beyond the teaching of specific skills.

From Meichenbaum, 1985. Reproduced with permission.

formulate stress management techniques. Stress reduction techniques are tailor-made to attack disaggregated components of the person's psychosocial and trauma symptoms. In turn, the person becomes empowered to respond to day-to-day stressors. Stress reduction methods go directly to solutions, bypassing explanations. If the stressor victim receives "informed training," collaborates empirically, practices the techniques and retains an open, problem solving set during the stress management procedure, chances of efficacy are high.

Stress Reduction and Alleviation of Trauma Symptoms

Stress reduction techniques are particularly useful as an aid with the trauma memory, and the numbing and hyperarousal symptoms found in PTSD. Victims react with a fight, flight, or freeze response that was appropriate with past traumas but not for their present environment. Individuals who experience PTSD should acquire a broad range of responses; both palliative and active coping which will enable them to react to the many varieties of stress. And, as noted, stress management assists in the amelioration or control of symptoms aiding the patient in the control of ongoing stressors. Control of daily stress is important for victims. Often daily hassles contribute to higher states of arousal. This state of emotional overload, then, can serve as a stimulus to initiate or intensify trauma memories or may push an individual into further numbing.

The use of stress management techniques on trauma victims has not been widely studied. Veronen, Kilpatrick, and Resnick (1979) applied a cognitive-behavioral program modified after Meichenbaum's approach to rape victims and found it to be helpful in fear diminishment. In one well controlled study Resick, Jordan, Girelli, Hutter, and Marhoefer-Dvorak (1988) found the stress inoculation (SIT), assertion training, and supportive psychotherapy were all effective in reducing rape-related symptoms. A wait-list control group did not evidence change. Frank, Anderson, Stewart, Dancu, Hughes, and West (1988) also used systematic desensitization and anxiety management in rape victims with success (reduction in both anxiety and depression). Finally, Foa, Olasov-Rothbaum, Riggs, and Murdock (1991) compared prolonged exposure, supportive counseling, and a wait-list control on rape victims. While all conditions produced pre-post treatment changes (post-treatment and its follow-up), the SIT procedure was better at post-treatment and the exposure method better at follow-up. The SIT employed a combination of coping skills, relaxation, thought stopping, cognitive restructuring, guided self-dialogue, covert modeling, and role playing. These authors concluded that both SIT and exposure should be employed on this population. In previous Chapters (2 and 3) we also have argued for this position.

We believe that some form of a stress management program is necessary for an efficacious treatment response. The purpose of the present chapter is to describe techniques that are found helpful in treating PTSD, especially among inpatients. We emphasize psychoeducation, focusing on the control of one's physiology (relaxation response), and a restructuring of one's cognitions. We then turn our attention to the central technique in stress management for chronic victims' coping, especially cognitive strategies. We also strongly advocate the use of non-directive hypnotic techniques. This hypnotic method deflects resistance and "absorbs" the person in psychologically healthy ways. Important components are knowing not only how to intervene, but at what point in the process to intervene; whether to intervene at the core of the trauma or to focus on the symptoms associated with PTSD. Always, however, the point of intervention depends upon the patient's desires, motivation, and resources. The victim should never be pushed beyond his/her resources, as the client decides how deep to explore the trauma. Finally, we address the aftercare method of Relapse Prevention (RP) in a more benign but absolutely necessary form.

PSYCHOEDUCATION

Normalization

Stress management always starts with education. For the trauma victim this is an absolute necessity and requires continued application. Meichenbaum (1985) has emphasized the importance of education in stress management. Similarly,

Scurfield (1985) has discussed the importance of utilizing an educational component in the treatment of PTSD. He emphasized seven points (Table 13.2). The central message is that the treatment of trauma is a process that extends over a certain time period, has phases that can be distinguished, and has features that can be understood. A particularly important point to emphasize is the normalization of trauma, especially the intrusion/denial process, as this constitutes a central dynamic of PTSD. At the time of trauma the person attempts to defend, often through natural measures and often succeeds. Depersonalization, dissociation, and various numbing defenses often occur also. The natural process of the trauma response involves a recoiling (disbelief shock and bewilderment). Shortly after trauma, "normal" trauma dynamics of avoidance and intrusion ensue, followed by adaptation of some form. *These responses to trauma are normal.*

Normalization of trauma can take many forms. Residual problems of grief and other stressors tend to persist in about 15% to 25% of society who experience extreme stressors. At some point stressor reactions probably occur in people who experience constant or extreme stressors (or both). As a general rule, people who experience daily hassles or minor stresses express stress differently than those who are victims of extreme stress. Categories B, C, and D, (intrusions, avoidance, and hyperarousal) are prevalent (by definition) and pernicious in PTSD. However, steps need to be taken to assure that PTSD victims reorganize the normalcy of their responses to trauma. As trivial as this seems, victims must have a perspective on their responses—dissociation, displacement, stressor related perceptual anomalies, confusion, rage, etc. Their "usual" responses require understanding and better coping. Intrusion and denial are then the body's way to protect against the intensity of the process. Grief is also a normal part of this procedure. In time, avoiding grief increases problems. The pain of loss is always integrated into the defensive structure of the individual (van der Hart, Brown, & Turco, 1990).

The victim must know that this process has logical "parts." Three determinants are key in behavior formation as a result of trauma: characteristics of the event and context in which it took place, characteristics of the person and his/her history, and characteristics of the social situation and social support.

TABLE 13.2
Educational Content of PTSD Program

---

1. At some point after catastrophic trauma, many people will produce symptoms;

2. To have PTSD symptoms for a period after trauma is normal;

3. Trauma symptoms can vary and may involve "crazy" symptoms like hallucinations and dissociative experiences in total;

4. Symptoms tend to wax and wane, getting worse and getting better;

5. Trauma memories, as well as other symptoms may never be eliminated, but experiences of them will change;

6. The client may receive positive benefits to victim symptoms; and

7. PTSD is responsive to treatment, at least controlled or reduced in severity.

Extrapolated from Scurfield, 1985.

As we outlined in Chapters 4 and 5, the victim is assisted with a blueprint of these features and a working set of rubrics for personal empowerment. You might say that education addresses two components of the model we have espoused (Chapters 4 and 5), *information processing specific* and *schema specific*. Regarding the former, clinical information involves the processing of trauma (easily activated to cues), biased apperception due to trauma (selective attention to stimuli), the intrusion and numbing sequence, resistance to extinction the need for exposure (of some sort), meaning, as well as coping and social support. Regarding the latter, victims are alerted that it is "their person" that is directing this whole process. Therefore, the therapeutic task is to establish the tie between their person (life-style or schemas and personality via early learning), the trauma, and current behavior. Much that is intrinsic to this molecular process also is intrinsic to a stress reduction thesis and to the personal awareness and application of psychophysiological, psychological and behavioral tools in the face of stress. The phenomenon of chronic victimization does nothing to assist the hope or commitment for change. The experience is debilitating and the outlook becomes bleak. For many, the PTSD presentation is chronic and phasic; in many it is subclinical, especially if an extreme stressor like combat has persisted. The proverbial question asked is "Will this ever go away?". This is never far from the client's thoughts. The clinician acknowledges the "typical pattern" of chronicity of the disorder. He can suggest that, even if symptom expression does not change, the experience of his/her person towards these symptoms will. This message respects resistance therapeutically and ushers in other treatment possibilities. The person of the victim becomes engaged and begins a path of learning the various internal and external stressor cues. The "story" of trauma can change, as the person of the victim "knows" his/ her victim-self in more flexible ways. From a hermeneutic perspective, we can never fully know ourselves because we are historical, living beings. The good news, however, is that we can alter our meanings by an active encounter of our narrative in new, dynamic, and reframed ways. We can reread our text (Suleiman & Crossman, 1980).

Effects of Trauma on the Victim

Education also involves the effects of stress or PTSD on the victim. We are didactic from the outset, tracking the response components of stress. The discussion of how stress affects one physically, cognitively, emotionally, and behaviorally is repeated. A presentation of Lazarus' phenomenological model of stress and his two stage appraisal system is provided (Lazarus & Folkman, 1984). We offer a list of the many ways in which stress can affect people, as well as ways in which victims most frequently respond to stress (Table 13.3). Clients also are requested to keep a diary, observing their responses— what they are doing and thinking at the time of stress symptoms. This represents a compilation of their own personal stress profile. Stress symptoms then change into stress signals telling and directing the victim that it's time to cope. These signals help victims recognize that one is in a potentially stressful situation.

Each victim is required to develop a personal *tool box* of coping skills. The chronic victim "directs" his/her life; going from a safety zone, to an intermediate zone, to a danger zone in stress settings. At some point problems develop, and the person shifts to a helpless/angry victim. A well developed tool box can change this. Now, the victim can apply stress management techniques: each victim "has" the necessary tools in the box. The victim, therefore, must be committed to their use. Ignoring these will likely result in excessive levels of stress and greater symptoms. This strategy not only "explains" how stress accumulates, but requires the use of existing tools and the importance of adding new ones. Through the use of diaries, education metaphors, and practice, the pool of coping resources grows. PTSD clients often feel out of control and victims of their environment just as they felt victims of their trauma. Thus, a conceptual shift occurs in the person, one committed to look for tools, to take responsibility to control stress, and to foster a greater internal locus of control.

Nothing succeeds more than learning from a life incident of stress. A patient in a group related that he felt anxious and had to run from a grocery store. When he first described the incident he related that it "just happened." He had no

TABLE 13.3
Relationship of Coping Strategies to
Combat Intensity, Symptoms, and Treatment

Coping Strategy	Combat Intensity	Current Symptoms	Treatment Success
Event Processing	X	X	
Focus on Living	X		
Time Out	X	X	
Sublimation/ Comparison			X
Emotional Expression			X
Denial	X	X	
Religion/Philosophy	X	X	

1. EVENT PROCESSING

   Tried to figure out why the events of the war made you have certain feelings?

   Tried to figure out when your responses to things were rational or irrational?

2. FOCUS ON LIVING

   Tried to concentrate on other things in your life?

   Tried to devote yourself to your work?

3. TIME OUT

   Spent more time listening to music, writing, etc.?

   Did you seek increased emotional support from others?

4. SUBLIMATION/COMPARISON

   Tried to be more helpful to others?

   Tried to weigh good things against bad things that happened?

5. EMOTIONAL EXPRESSION

   Found other veterans who had similar experiences and saw how they dealt with them?

   Tried to let yourself experience and deal with all your feelings about the war?

6. DENIAL

   Tried to put whole thing out of your mind—best just to go on living?

   Tried not to be bothered by mixed up and conflicting feelings?

7. RELIGION/PHILOSOPHY

   Turned to religion or philosophy for help?

Extrapolated from Green, Lindy, & Grace, 1988.

control over his behavior. Upon further exploration, he was able to see that he had warning of stress, his muscles tensing in his arms and his respiration increasing. He further could see that he had engaged in distorted thinking and felt that everyone was looking at him. Next, he engaged in negative self-talk and told himself that he was vulnerable, that he was in danger of experiencing a panic attack, and people would laugh at or hurt him. At this point he was requested to explore how he might have handled the situation if he had a better pool of coping resources (tool box). He explored the situation as if he were relaxed and had available a positive self-talk system which reduced stress rather than increased it. By reliving this incident and drawing it out, he was able to verbalize that his running just didn't happen. It was potentially under his control.

Chronic combat victims often seem to have a "parallel process" reinforcing system. Many chronic trauma victims verbalize that they think about Vietnam at times to obtain a "pumped up" feeling. Often, they act out to bring about this feeling. Victims seem to know that this reaction initially makes them feel good, but eventually leads to an intensification of their PTSD symptoms. van der Kolk (1988) described the probable role of physiological reinforcement in sustaining PTSD symptoms, the release of opiates following a depletion in catecholamines. At this center we have successfully reframed this as "combat addiction" (Solursh, 1989), emphasizing the importance of cue monitors.

In addition, the concept of positive stress or eustress has been helpful. Positive stress is the spice of life, feeling good to be alive. Activities, such as skydiving and skiing are highly challenging, but also safer activities, such as fishing, bring pleasure and involve excitement. These result in "pumped up" feelings also. We encourage a life-inventory to identify eustress activities in the past. These might be "relocated" into their lives. Activity scheduling, mastery planning, and self reinforcement toward a balanced life are stressed. The experience of Outward Bound, returning to nature to challenge self and facilitate bonding, has also been helpful. As chronic trauma victims have lost the ability to enjoy life and resist efforts to the contrary, the application of these ideas requires persistence and commitment.

Stripped to the bone, psychotherapy involves a relationship between the client and his/her surroundings, people, and situations. This is why the ability to cope is critical. (This also is why the therapeutic relationship is so important—Chapter 7). Stress management is the person's ability and commitment to develop a better relationship with self and others. If the victim knows his/her problems, the maladaptive interpersonal styles and patterns, then recurrent self-defeating and interpersonal dilemmas can be altered; a choice can be made. Stress management keeps "choice alive."

COPING AND COGNITION

Models of Coping and Response to Stress

Coping is a broad area that includes how individuals voluntarily control responses to stressful events. Various conceptualizations of coping strategies have been developed. Billings and Moos (1981) described active behavioral, active cognitive, and avoidance-oriented strategies; Pearlin and Schooler (1978) advocated coping strategies that change the meaning of the situation or control the stress of the situation; Lazarus and Folkman (1984) distinguished between problem solving versus emotion focused coping; Kahana, Kahana, and Young (1985) proposed a three part coping model including instrumental, affective, and avoidance strategies.

Lazarus' model (Lazarus & Folkman, 1984) is especially noteworthy. He suggested that coping falls into two categories, direct action and emotional management. Direct action occurs when one can affect some change on the environment to reduce stress; emotional management refers to those circumstances in which one can't change the environment directly. The primary task of the person is to perform damage control both at the time of the event and after. The Lazarus model, however, requires the victim to pick the correct management tool, check performance, and reapply needed alterations. Through secondary appraisal the stress victim has feedback on performance, an ongoing monitor of performance. At the time of stress, therefore, the victim assesses the coping tools he/she has in his/her pool of resources (tool box) and what other tools are needed in order to experience a lower level of stress. Through this process he/she continues to acquire new tools or bolster existing tools. The victim also does something else: each adds to self-empowerment, growing in the ability to alter stress.

Everly (1989) presented an integration phenomenological model of the stress response (Figure 13.1). Environmental events "cause" or "set the stage" for the mobilization of the stress response. The cognitive-affective domain "interprets" this. This is our person response. The actual stress response is a combination of three factors—neurological, neuroendocrine, and endocrine. As a result of these permutations, the stress response is extraordinarily mobilized and a target organ activation occurs. The final step in this process is coping. Here the victim can act to reduce the level of activation. From our perspective the whole person response is largely fostered by the cognitive-affective and coping responses. Therefore, an understanding of this process and an active pursuit of the coping needs should be undertaken.

In many psychodynamic models of care, success involves the understanding, processing and altering the trauma event. One might say that the trauma experience becomes integrated into the person and becomes "routinely" traumatic. Coping challenges this. Coping gives the victim methods to better function and in so doing methods to change. The victim learns to trust his/her condition and self better and to problem solve situations. In this context "real adaptation" occurs, such as an ability to simulate health "doing," ask for help, reality test, and solicit support. This package involves "learning to learn," the best of goals in treatment. Lazarus (1984), for example, maintained that coping occurs when an individual recognizes a signal of stress and responds to the stressor after assessing and picking a coping resource. This is a very individual process. This is repair work that represents healing generated by the person. This is also most appealing to victims since it involves methods to manage stress now. Eventually some form of adaptation is arrived at. Regarding the possibilities, Everly (1989) stated:

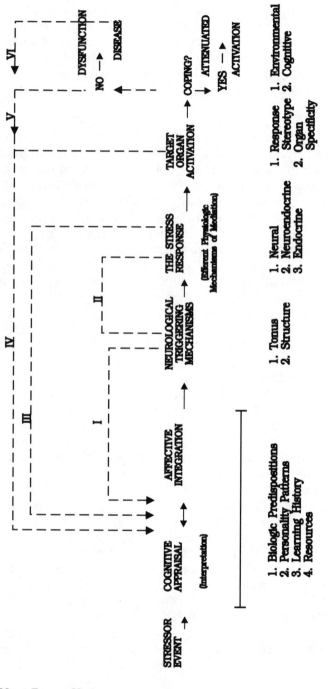

Figure 13.1. A systems model of the human stress response. From Everly (1989). Reproduced with permission.

Adaptive coping strategies reduce stress while at the same time promoting long-term health (for example, exercise, relaxation, proper nutrition). Maladaptive coping strategies, on the other hand, do indeed reduce stress in the short term, but serve to erode health in the long term (alcohol/drug abuse, cigarette smoking, interpersonal withdrawal). (p. 44)

Very few studies have assessed coping and the stressor response (Fairbank, Hansen, & Fitterberg, 1991). One study is, however, instructive. Horowitz and Wilmer (1980) developed the **Coping Inventory** to assess strategies associated with particular traumatic events. Thirty-three strategies cover areas of (1) turning to other attitudes and activities, (2) working through the event, and (3) socialization. Green, Lindy, and Grace (1988) factor analyzed this scale and applied it to trauma victims, arriving at a seven factor solution. These strategies are related to stressor intensity, current symptoms, and treatment success (Table 13.3). Event processing, time out for reflection, denial, and religion/philosophy were unsuccessful strategies both at the time of the trauma and for being associated with current symptoms. The most useful strategies at the end of treatment, however, were emotional expression and sublimation/comparison, as well as time out. These are factors that are reasonably characteristic of the curative components of the psychotherapy process and perhaps aspects of natural healing over time. Only one strategy, however, focus and living, was associated with heavy conflict but not with current symptoms. This is a practical strategy of living in the present, similar to helpful strategies in combat.

The importance of this study lies less in its results than in its implications. Coping starts at the time of the stressor and continues. Coping strategies can be both positive and negative. This study highlights the thinking process important for clinicians; how did the victim cope during and after the stressor and what strategies are helpful then and now. These questions, along with issues related to focal symptoms, such as depersonalization and dissociation, allow for an understanding of the positive and negative processes used for self care. Similar information can be obtained in studies of resilience or positive coping after a stressor event (e.g., Hendin & Haas, 1984; Lyons, 1991; & McFarlane, 1990).

Cognitions and Coping Strategies

The most important coping strategies, however, are cognitions. The role cognitions play in stress and PTSD now appears unimpeachable. Our paradigm (Chapters 4 and 5) is largely cognitive. Intrusive thought processes rumble through the victim's memories, causing increases in emotional stress and interfering with attention and concentration. Chemtob, Roitblat, Hamada, Carlson, and Twentyman (1988) described a cognitive action model where intrusions and other PTSD symptoms result from the activation of cognitive nodes associated with the trauma (Chapters 3 and 8). These nodes in turn activate cognitive and physiological systems (schemas) which result in thoughts and actions. Adaptive behaviors are inhibited because they don't fit the schema associated with the trauma. Avoidance behavior serves this purpose. Internal messages too (e.g., Beck's internal voices and automatic thoughts, or Ellis's irrational thoughts) directly influence the individual's assessment of the trauma and how he/she then evaluates self.

Cognitions play a major role in how the individual handles emotions and appraises daily stressors (Lazarus & Folkman, 1984). As we have come to know (e.g., Beck & Emery, 1985; Ellis, 1962), negative cognitions elicit emotional responses and influence how the individual mislabels emotions of the trauma memory. Meichenbaum (1985) wrote:

> When dealing with past traumas it is not just the discharge of emotions which is beneficial. The client must reexperience not only the trauma but must also achieve a more adaptive appraisal of what happened to them in order to aid them gain a sense of self efficacy and enhance their self esteem. (p. 92)

Therefore, the key stress management message emphasized from the beginning of treatment requires the victim to tune into internal voices, to observe these, and to derive better "meaning."

Patient as Participant Observer and Use of Internal Voices

Various methods are used to encourage the objectification or "personal scientist" focus on trauma. One useful intervention has been to inform clients that people were considered crazy in the past if they talked to themselves. We know now that people engage in internal dialogue constantly. This is especially true of PTSD victims who deal with intrusive thoughts and images. This message requires people to look at themselves and their past differently. Using standard cognitive procedures (Ellis, 1962; Beck & Emery 1985; Persons, 1989), we isolate and elaborate a recent event. Every effort is made to highlight the victim's self-talk, exploring irrational and distorted thinking and the resulting responses. Considerable time is devoted to the internal voices of patients. Voices are often humanized providing names or places in "their head." Often figures who force issues in only one way are identified. One voice, the "drill sergeant," has been especially helpful. Clients learn this quickly. Many indicate they have never really listened to this voice before. This is a significant step for most patients as up to this time thoughts had free reign; now they have the ability to question the validity of their statements. The victim becomes a participant observer.

As this process evolves we invite victims to discuss traumas, not just stories about the trauma, but how trauma allows them to feel and appraise themselves today. The victim is asked to describe what the little voice tells him/her about the trauma and what it tells him/her about self. Just bringing traumas from within and objectifying results is a change. By addressing trauma in this way victims not only rearrange the trauma, but also are provided feedback. As the victim "studies" the event, he/she becomes an observer in this process and the way they look at the event itself changes. Other input enters, influencing the appraisal of past trauma. In effect, the content and process of the negative inner voice are exposed and its power is weakened. One patient related, "You know once you get it out here, you just can't put it back exactly the same way. You know the pieces just don't seem to go together the same way."

Often victims relate that they have heard rational voices telling them to look at trauma. Unfortunately, the avoidant pattern is so strong that these voices were quickly dismissed by negative ones. At this point an internal debate is prescribed emphasizing the necessity to give other voices a forum. One technique is to set up a "trial." This time, however, a jury and defense attorney is available, not just a judge or a prosecutor. The victim acts as his/her defense attorney. Other group members serve as a prosecutor, judge, and jury. The patient can sort through issues: what are rational versus irrational appraisals concerning a trauma; do they deserve to experience feelings such as guilt; and what sentence or penance (if any) must they give themselves. This exercise allows for a better appraisal of the trauma, an increased awareness of irrational beliefs and more insight into behaviors often resulting from the trauma. It also allows clients to appraise events ecologically, namely the reality of past actions and rationality of guilt. Again, something curative is in this act of self mastering, studying, and parsing out hardened trauma and feelings.

One victim designated the therapist as the prosecutor, himself as the defense attorney and the rest of the group as the jury. The incident involved trading places with his friend who walked point. His friend was killed. As a result he gave the men under him permission to rape Vietnamese woman, receiving vicarious pleasure by listening. He charged himself both for his friend's death and for the woman being raped. The therapist acted as the prosecutor and brought both charges against him. The therapist and the patient (as the defense attorney) argued the facts before the rest of the group. The results were convincing. The client was able to objectify guilt feelings concerning his friend's death. He also could identify irrational thoughts. He was able to restructure his thoughts about this event and to start a grieving process. He could also see that the rape incidents involved a more rational guilt. However, he gave himself a different sentence. It was recommended that he channel guilt into constructive activity, as in volunteer work at a crisis rape center or shelter for battered women. He followed through on this sentence and reported that he was dealing with memories of this past trauma without feeling the intense guilt. He also noticed a marked improvement in his self concept. Furthermore, he reported that he used this exercise on other traumatic memories, as well as negative messages concerning more present stressors. He finally noted that intrusions from past traumas decreased and that his attention and concentration improved.

Labeling Emotions

This and similar techniques allow for a more accurate labeling of emotions. Another victim experienced guilt from an incident involving a buddy who was killed while taking his place in a convoy. He said that the man replaced him because he received orders to see his commanding officer. He could not understand why he felt guilty. In the reexperience of this trauma he remembered that a message from an officer (upon the return of the convoy) initially made him feel guilty. The officer ordered him to clean up the seat where the man was shot and inquired how it made him feel that this man died instead of him. After surfacing this incident, he was aware that the primary emotion was anger (at the officer). As his style was one of overcontrol, fearing loss of control of his anger, he felt it was safer to experience this event with guilt. The group was then able to assist him in focusing on his anger with strategies allowing him to tolerate this emotion, and with ways to express his anger in a more appropriate manner. This initial overcontrolled response eventuated in a "freer" view of his self image.

Cognitive Beliefs and Styles of Thinking

Another helpful technique is "data feedback." A list of irrational and distorted thinking patterns "typical" of veterans with combat related problems is given. Alford, Mahone, and Frelstein (1988) identified six thought styles characteristic of this population. (See Chapter 4, Table 4.5). Parson (1988) developed a similar list. These cognitive distortions are "known" to combat related victims because they are methods universally learned and applied in a combat setting. They do not apply to current life situations.

Other common irrationalities or distortions include personalization, generalization, catastrophizing, dichotomous thinking, and the idea that the world must be fair. Given these as stimuli, we are able to identify and explain how irrational and distorted thoughts once true now cause members to overreact to daily stressors and potential stressors. We explore how victims overreact to stressors that are potentially upsetting to anyone with a flight, fight, or freeze pattern, a response not appropriate in their present environment.

In a similar way data are generated by exploring intrusive thoughts; how they are not "intrusive by nature." Again, the victim is challenged. Symptom expression "might" rest upon a cognitive belief that each holds about the reason for thinking about Vietnam. Often combat veterans have fixed ideas about the "why" of combat focus. At this point we explore reasons about the thinking of other Vietnam combat vets regarding Vietnam (Table 13.4). Once exposed, the "why" belief can be considered, challenged, and alternatives provided. As with similar techniques, the victim is provided a larger context, as deeper self probes or alternative frames are considered from which to process the trauma (latter part of Table 13.4). This thinking-out-loud or hypothesis generating procedure provides clients the opportunity to rearrange their stories and to review their inner relationship and self care.

Avoidance a State or Trait Phenomena

A special focus concerns the avoidant component of PTSD. Whether this pattern exists as a trait (personality) or a state (symptom), clearly the disruptive features of avoidance are pathological, persistent, and pervasive in PTSD victims (thereby meeting DSM-III-R, Axis II criteria for a personality disorder) (Spitzer, Williams, Gibbon, & First, 1990). Avoidance consists of several noxious features that are disruptive (Table 13.5). The person is primed to engage in hypervigilence, a constant readiness to criticism or pain, a negativization of the self image, and an anxious mood. Turkat (1991) believed that avoidance is pushed by evaluation anxiety, depression, and pain. Fortunately, at some level the person desires to be involved and to succeed. This keeps the victim active in both the pursuit of some success or change and also active in the complex and ongoing titration process of measuring current pain level for entry into any situation. Although not specific to avoidance, Everly (1989) highlighted the issue of control, the ability to change an environmental transaction, as a powerful monitor of the stress response. Clearly, control is related to avoidance, the recovery process, as well as psychotherapy itself.

(continued on page 610)

TABLE 13.4
Reasons for Intrusive Thoughts and Antidotes

I.   THE "WHY" OF INTRUSIVE THOUGHTS

1.   A memorial for brothers who didn't make it
2.   Penance or punishment for perceived guilt
3.   Not to forget the injustice
4.   A spiritual moral battle within myself
5.   It's part of my identity as a soldier
6.   Attempts to complete unfinished business
7.   It makes me feel momentarily good about myself
8.   It might give me a chance to mourn
9.   It gives me a chance to experience feelings of brotherhood
10.   A way to hold on to hate and anger
11.   It gives me momentary feelings of power and control
12.   A means of dealing with self pity
13.   What goes around comes around (likely to happen again; be prepared)
14.   You can't get away from it (society and the media)
15.   A means of dealing with the uncertainty of whether some of my brothers survived
16.   A means of trying to regain my identity
17.   Find a meaningful reason (58,000 own people died)
18.   Prevent it from happening again
19.   As a means of dealing with feelings about myself and others
20.   A means of correcting mistakes in judgment: If I had only done it this way
21.   I think these things to test myslf to see if I can really control it (seeing if I can control my addiction).
22.   Find a reason why twice as many Vietnam vets have died since the war.

II.   ANTIDOTES

1.   I know I can't go back to Nam.
2.   I can't redo it; leave it be.

(continued)

TABLE 13.4 (continued)

3. Mistakes were made in Nam and people got killed but my brothers wouldn't want me to punish myself and feel guilty the rest of my life.
4. I can't let my mistakes in Nam haunt me the rest of my life.
5. I have to stop punishing myself; it doesn't change anything.
6. I'm a survivor; I can make it.
7. I wonder if I did my best. I know thinking about it won't change things.
8. A lot of things took place in Nam which were beyond my control and responsibility.

The most troubling avoidant feature, however, involves cognitive disruptions, labeled vexatious internalization (Millon, 1983). A constant cognitive interference exists as a result of trauma memories, limited avenues of gratification, and little openings available to channel needs or impulses. These need to be exposed and worked on. Sometimes the core cognitions (Chapters 5 and 6) are sufficient. Often more aggressive interventions are required. Victims who choose to go blank, fear going crazy, run from pain/hurt, sense rejection, think in a disrupted fashion, crush emotions, avoid impulsivity or tolerate poorly ambiguity among others need to fully understand the role of avoidance in their lives. *This is best done through information (education) about the avoidant process and "living" the experience.* Via the downward arrow (increasing interiority), scaling procedures (on issues like trust or rejection), exposure of automatic disruptive thoughts, point/counterpoint technique, and at times problem solving training (Beck & Freeman, 1990), the avoidant processes are exposed and altered. We also have used cognitive interference scales (Yee & Pierce, 1989) to assist in unearthing this process and convincing the victim of the level and type of disruption.

TABLE 13.5
Features of Avoidance

Component	Intervention
Active Detachment	Behavioral—emphasis on acting and experiencing acts
Hypervigilance	Psychophysiological—emphasis on activation or relaxation and their "blocks"
Alienated Self	Experiential—emphasis on self-view and experience of self-pain
Anguished Mood	Affect—emphasis on the feelings and identification of emotions
Control	Cognitive/Affective—emphasis on feelings of perceived abilities, mastery, and perseverance
Cognitive Disruption	Cognitive—emphasis on several CBT techniques to expose avoidant process

Thought Stopping

Finally, we have found some "basic techniques" helpful. Routinely, we have used thought stopping to control intrusions. This technique involves first identifying thoughts, and stopping them by imagining a stop sign in one's mind's eye, or by snapping a rubber band on one's wrist and saying "Stop!" Victims are then instructed to use a relaxation cue and engage in some positive self-talk, such as "I talked about this in group and know that it doesn't help just rethinking it." Victims are then instructed to insert another statement, again from a list of statements generated by other Vietnam veterans or themselves and then to reinforce themselves for having been successful for stopping the thought or at least trying to do so. If the thought returns, they are to repeat the same procedure. They are instructed that to stop a thought is not enough; they also need to replace it. The suggestion is that if they use a rubber band around the wrist to stop thoughts that at the end of the day they might have a red welt on their wrist. However, they will also likely notice that they have started to gain some control over thoughts. Once again, the victim is empowered to care for self.

HYPNOSIS

Hypnotherapy can be an effective therapeutic intervention in the treatment of PTSD. It has been found to be an effective technique dealing both with the symptoms of PTSD (Kingsbury, 1988) and more core issues such as the integration of self (Spiegel, 1988). The fact that Vietnam combat veterans who experience PTSD have been found to have high trance capacity (Spiegel, Hunt, & Dondershine, 1988) and that both PTSD and hypnosis involve dissociative phenomena support the use of this technique. In fact, Peterson, Prout, and Schwartz (1991) noted that hypnotizability scores of patients with PTSD is twice that of other Anxiety Disorders. Hypnotherapy can not only reduce the amount of time needed in treatment but also can aid in obtaining information relating to traumas which might not be accessible via other approaches. Hypnosis with this population, however, involves more than a revivification of the trauma and cathartic abreaction. Also the person is required to process the trauma, the "dance" of integrating the meaning within one's self percept.

Brende (1985) outlined four ways in which hypnosis is used: supportive, uncovering, abreaction, and integration. To this Peterson, Prout, and Schwartz (1991) added restructuring. These methods provide the clinician with an armamentarium of nondirective methods for uncovering trauma material, either exclusively or as an adjunct in a care plan. At our center we have emphasized non-directive techniques because they alter rigid positions, present different perspectives and are user friendly. Issues of control with trauma victims also suggest this approach. Hypnosis or non-directive methods emphasize the idea that PTSD symptoms are questions that the victim is seeking to answer. The person "knows" the solutions.

In this section we attempt to describe various techniques. We also emphasize differences between trance and normal states of consciousness. In addition, we address common problems of trauma victims related to fragmentation, psychogenic amnesia, coping, and describe the hypnotherapy methods of anchoring, desensitization, and reframing.

Trance and Induction

Trance is different from the normal waking state. This is apparent when the victim discusses a trauma in normal waking state and later describes it in trance. Images are clearer and memory more focused. One client pictured a memory where he led a group of men into a hot combat zone. After the firefight he said that he had placed the dead into body bags and loaded them on helicopters. In trance this same scene was described differently. There were no body bags. In fact, he was not picking up bodies but pieces of bodies which were sliding out of his hands due to wet, bloody, and muddy conditions. His affect was noticeably different. He was crying and more in tune with his feelings. Hypnosis not only highlights split off parts of the self, but vivifies the experience and provides "value" to various memory parts.

As stated previously, the use of non-directive induction procedures facilitates the inward focus of care (interiority) in this population. Victims feel helpless and out of control due to trauma. Control is highly related to the encoding of trauma and to recovery. Lack of control is helplessness, "giving in—given-up" (Engel, 1968) and a host of other negative features suggestive of failure. Victims search for any cheap imitation of control. As a consequence, resistance to more directive techniques occurs. One safe, non-directive procedure, an Erickson approach, involves the use of safe imagery, the subjunctive mood, and language of confusion. Clients are requested to become comfortable in a chair and are told that they are in a safe place and that it is okay for them to shut their eyes (Table 13.6). Even on the first session a moderate state of trance results. Victims don't feel they are giving up control and often verbalize that they feel in a relaxed and peaceful state. They are more open to suggestion, and their imagery skills become heightened. At this point the therapist has many choices. The mind can be likened to a computer and, like a computer, it can focus an image on their mind's screen. Now, the victim can travel to a safe place for relaxation. They can even travel to the time of trauma, before trauma, or after trauma. Victims are requested to explore images, thoughts, feelings and behaviors associated with the trauma events. Thoughts or feelings, can be traced to their origins. Often a helpful procedure is for the patient to describe where he/she is, what is being experiencing and then build upon the scene at that point. In addition, the therapist can request the victim to look at how he/she might think, feel, or behave to some event in the future. This procedure also allows the patient to develop one's own relaxation image rather than have one forced upon him/her.

Fragmentation and Integration

Hypnosis is the principal method for integration of the fragmented self that may result from dissociation of a traumatic experience. Various authors (e.g., Brende, 1985, 1987) have identified distinct identities, victim, killer, or protective self. In Vietnam veterans these split selves are associated with rage, guilt, or themes specific to the schema. Spiegel, Hunt, and Dondershine (1988) addressed dissociation and fragmentation. These experiences are common among chronic victims. Victims discuss the monster, the coward, the demon, or garbage man (that they have become). When a victim tries to recover an old self, the experience can become frightening.

(continued on page 617)

TABLE 13.6
Nondirective Inductions

Induction 1

"At this point there is no need to do anything but just focus on my voice. I want you to focus all of your attention on both your feet with complete attention and distraction. As you focus on your feet you may notice that one foot may feel like it's putting more pressure on the floor than the other foot. And it may seem that the foot that is placing the most pressure feels warmer and heavier and more relaxed. And now focus your attention on your legs and buttocks and notice the pressure that they are placing on the chair in which you are sitting. And now focus your attention on your back and neck and head and notice the pressure they are placing on the back of the chair as you may even sense your self sinking deeper and deeper into the chair. And now focusing all of your attention on both your arms and hands and it may seem that one arm or hand feels as if it is placing more pressure on the chair or on your body than the other arm or hand. And that the arm or hand which feels as if it is placing more pressure may feel warmer, heavier, and more relaxed. I would now like you to focus all of your attention with complete attention and distraction on your whole body. You may notice that some parts of your body have started to feel different. You may have noticed that your heart rate or pulse rate has started to change. You may have noticed that some parts of your body have started to feel warmer and heavier and more relaxed. (With therapist's voice slowing, continue.) You may have noticed that your breathing has started to change and that with each breath you exhale you can feel yourself going deeper and deeper. And you know it may seem confusing to wonder how you may continue to learn by looking inside. Just remember how confusing it was when you first went to school and when you first started to learn to read and what was the difference between an A and B. And how confusing it was when you first started to learn to count and what was the difference between a 6 and a 9.

(continued)

TABLE 13.6 (continued)

And was a 6 an upside down 9 or was a 9 an upside down 6? And now, just as then, you can learn new and different things about yourself each and every day. You can learn to control your mind and your body just as easily as you read and as you count. And you know that if you would like to go deeper, just imagine yourself on a set of 10 steps. With each step you descend, you can feel yourself going deeper and deeper. Now on step nine and eight and seven and six and five and four and three and two and one, you are in a very deep relaxed state."

Induction 2

"Your mind is like a computer and like a computer, it can focus an image on your own mind's screen or your own mind's eye. I would like you to see yourself back at a special place and time in the past where you felt secure and relaxed within yourself. Just notice the clothes you are wearing, the color of the clothes, and all the color around you there. Notice any sounds that might be present, any feelings of coolness, warmth, texture or touch that you might be experiencing there. Notice any smells or fragrances that might be there. And, just see yourself there now, at a place where you feel relaxed and at peace within yourself. Just see yourself there, hear yourself there, feel yourself there, and even smell and taste yourself there. I now want you to continue to experience any pleasant images or feelings that you may be experiencing for a few moments more. I'm now going to count to ten, and as I do that your eyes will open and you will be alert but will feel very relaxed."

The patient then opens his/her eyes and the experiences are discussed. This information is used to build on the image and to use stimuli within the image to further heighten the relaxation response.

As the "good" and the "bad" selves meet, usually the bad self can more easily block progress and remain in power. Spiegel et al. (1988) have described this as the unauthentic self. The goal is for the victim to know the fragmented parts, to appreciate their negative influence, and eventually to own or integrate these.

Unfortunately, since fragmentation takes many forms, the trauma victim splits the self or fragments a memory in an infinite number of ways. Trauma victims often have a sense of being lost or fragmented from an earlier self. Victims sense being unable to remember what they were like or what feelings they experienced when they were younger. Even if they can remember this, often they cannot "get in touch" with that person. Hypnosis facilitates the ability to retrieve this part of themselves. *The one constant value of hypnosis is its ability to find a perspective on some dimension to better evaluate/experience the trauma.* This may involve the development of inner resources, the reframing of dissociation or other symptoms, seeding a future enabling self along the time dimension or highlighting the reexperience of the problem state in such a way as to lead to the extinction of the trauma. Something new "connects" with something old and a change ensues.

In one case a combat trauma victim experienced trance on a number of occasions. He reported at the end of one therapy session that he had been having visions of a house and tree Upon further questioning he related that this scene was one that he saw frequently in the small town where he grew up. At the next session he was placed in trance and requested to travel back to that time and place where he saw the house and tree. While in trance he said that he was 2 years of age. He not only saw the house and tree, but viewed the colors, sensed the feelings and smells of that place. The victim was then given a suggestion that he could see a figure walking toward him and that, as "he" got closer, he could see that the figure was him (today). It was suggested that the boy and man might talk together; the boy might have something to tell the man and that the man might have something to tell the boy. He signaled that they were talking and a smile came over his face. After they talked it was suggested that the boy and man might now embrace and as they embraced might feel themselves merging together. After trance he related that he could see himself clearly at both ages in the image. He related that the boy and man wanted to know each other. He noted that the boy was smiling before he saw the man in the image. He could now feel a sense of being one with the boy and man as they embraced and merged together. He smiled when this happened and felt it to be a real smile. This was different from his usual forced smile, where he didn't feel anything. A week later he reported that he found himself smiling and that it felt real.

Psychogenic Amnesia

Hypnosis also facilitates the repositioning of psychogenic amnesia associated with a trauma. By definition, psychological trauma complicates recall and mourning, often resulting in dissociation, amnesia or some partial split off experience. We have already alluded this phenomena and the prices paid at later times. A combat veteran related that he felt guilty because he was convinced that he had killed his best friend. When discussing this incident in a waking state, he said that he and his friend were running for a helicopter in a hot zone. He said that they were both running when he felt his friend getting close to him. He then pushed him out of the way so he could get to the helicopter. When he reached the helicopter he hung onto the floor, feeling good that he had made it. It was only when he got back to the base that he had realized what he had done. Since this event he has lived with guilt.

In trance something else occurred. He could see himself and his friend running for the helicopter. He then saw his friend falling as he was shot in the back of the head. He said that he reached and touched him as he was falling but could not save him. He realized at that point that he was not responsible for his friend's death. He could now grieve for this loss and experience the anxiety and vulnerability associated with his inability to save his friend. Interestingly, this victim had primary schemas of esteem and acceptance, perhaps predisposing him to feel guilt and loss (Chapters 5 and 6).

Uncovering Coping Resources

Hypnosis also can aid patients in discovering new coping resources and develop the skills and desire for their implementation. Nondirective techniques are used in this fashion in pain management. Clients are instructed to foster an internal locus of control and develop self mastery. Chronic trauma victims feel that they have lost control. Hypnosis, therefore, allows victims to recall control experiences in other problem areas or in the therapy session. At times, too, a client who is out of control can find ways to soften emotions or behavior while in trance.

One combat veteran was hypnotized and instructed to find a special place and time (that he could travel to and relax). He returned to his grandfather's farm as an adolescent where he used to enjoy riding a horse. He saw himself in the fall of the year riding a black horse and experiencing the colors, sounds, feelings, and smells. He said that he felt as if he was floating and that he appeared quite relaxed for a few moments. Then, he became noticeably upset. When questioned, he said that a "black force" had entered the picture and was blocking his path. At this point he was brought out of trance and was queried about the black force. It was suggested that "maybe there was some way" that such an obstacle could be overcome. The client was then placed into trance and suggested that he return to the field and ride the horse. He could see the black force moving towards him. He appeared nervous. At this point the suggestion was given that he see himself floating over the black force on his horse, as if it were a black cloud. This seemed to calm him. After trance we discussed his experience and he related that he did not float over a black cloud. Rather his horse turned into a white horse and acted as wedge going through the black force. He was then returned to trance and it was suggested that he was on his white horse going through the black force.

At this point an **anchoring** procedure was used. Anchoring involves embedding feelings, thoughts, images, or behavior in a part of the patient's body. The material that is anchored can be accessed at appropriate times during the therapeutic process to experience feelings of relaxation or control; thoughts or emotions associated with a trauma and imagined behaviors which might aid in the resolution of trauma can become available. This technique can then be used to elicit relaxation or control. At times of stress this can become a routine action. Anchoring also could be used to store information about trauma which can then be accessed at appropriate times during the therapeutic process.

Trauma blocks the processing of grief. Anchoring allows for feelings of grief to be embedded from one period and then displaced in time forward or backward. This unblocks feelings surrounding the trauma event with which the patient has been unable to make contact. Anchoring also can foster self efficacy. Behaviors, particularly those involving competency can be anchored and later accessed to aid the client in performing adequately and in experiencing less anxiety. Anchoring techniques are described in detail by Grinder and Bandler (1981).

In the case above the client was anchored with an image associated with relaxation by touching his right hand. Then the suggestion was given that any time he wanted, this image and feeling would return. He simply had to touch his right hand. Also the suggestion was given that now he had the resources to deal with black forces, storms, and stressors that might come upon him in his everyday environment and that, when they appeared, he could use this anchor as a means of strength. "His" metaphor of the black force was used to generalize it to other stressors he might face in the future. As has been noted (Peterson et al., 1991), the development of themes of mastery, control, or competence provides a background for performance in various stress situations. Again, when possible the use of a patient's own metaphor is recommended. This is a personal container of significant information possessing meaning beyond its linguistic one.

This case is interesting because the client transformed a negative image into one that results in strength. He reported several weeks later that he had been using the anchor and the image of the white horse to deal with stressors that had overwhelmed him previously. The black force symbolized his inability to deal with many types of stressful situations. Whether or not the black force was present in Vietnam was never determined. If so, the anchor of the white horse might have been utilized in an age regression procedure. Suggestions could then be made that a white horse also might help him wedge through events that occurred "back there," which are still black forces in his life.

A companion anchoring method is a technique we call the **smart window.** Bandler in an unreferenced videotape discussed this approach. In trance the client is instructed to find a safe and secure place where he/she can relax. This image is then anchored in one of his hands (to aid in its retrieval). Next, the victim is again placed in trance and returned to the age when trauma was experienced. Victims are requested to experience themselves in all their senses at that time. The victim indicates readiness by raising a finger. At this point the suggestion is made that a scene is emerging in the upper left hand corner of their screen. This is a calm scene which was previously described. To aid in retrieval the anchor point is touched. The suggestion is given that he/she can see the scene appearing larger and larger until it finally engulfs the whole screen. As relaxation pervades the scene, the patient typically displays a decrease in signs of autonomic arousal and verbalizes calming feelings. Patients often verbalize greater control associated with the event and a decrease in frequency of intrusions.

Anxiety Reduction (or Desensitization)

Hypnosis is also helpful in the desensitization of anxiety. Desensitization techniques are not only used as a means of reducing anxiety associated with a past trauma, but also can foster a sense of control over intrusions associated with that trauma. Trance states enhance imagery to aid with relaxation. Trance also enhances images of anxiety provoking situations or trauma scenes via age regression. As noted, hypnosis also can place a victim into a trauma situation at the age in which they experienced this. This occurs "as they were then." The patient accesses isomorphic emotional, cognitive, or behavioral reactions which were associated with the trauma.

Hypnosis

Finally, hypnosis has been used to reframe aspects of the trauma. A Korean war veteran felt extreme guilt about friends who were killed by the enemy. He recounted this episode while in trance and described situation in which his position was overrun. Two of his friends were wounded and captured by the enemy. They were shot because they were not physically able to move. He himself was taken off by the enemy but later escaped. He felt guilt that he was not able to save his friends and that he never saw their recovered bodies. He said that he was obsessed with an image of the hill where they were captured and felt extreme guilt which would cause him to cry and prevented him from carrying on necessary work and social activities.

The image was reframed. He was instructed to return to the incident. However, this time the suggestion was given that he was able to escape sooner and returned to find the bodies of his friends. He was instructed to dig a grave on that same hill and bury his two friends. He relaxed while working through this scene. At one point he placed the cross and he smiled. At previous times in trance he had become upset and tearful. Now his friends could rest in peace as could he. Further the suggestion was given that the hill was now a peaceful place and would only be remembered as such.

RELAPSE PREVENTION (RP)

No inpatient (or outpatient) program of PTSD can be effective without rigorously addressing relapse. Relapse is defined as a step back in treatment, either a recurrence of symptoms after some improvement, a worsening, or back sliding. The Relapse Prevention (RP) treatment model developed by Marlatt (Marlatt & Gordon, 1980, 1985) has been a mainstay of many addiction programs. This treatment model focuses on new assumptions about treatment and behavior change, including the "development" of problem behaviors and the process of change itself (commitment, implementation of change behavior, and long term maintenance). In addition, the RP model is undertaken in a structured, didactic, and task-oriented manner (Marlatt & Gordon, 1985).

Due to the very nature of chronicity, some form of RP is integral to treatment of PTSD. This would appear to be particularly true when dealing with chronic PTSD or PTSD involving multiple traumas. Burstein (1986) noted the treatment dropout rate for such PTSD patients at 81%. While recent clinical data does not validate this high figure, clearly treatment adherence is critical towards self-care. Data from our (Specialized PTSD Unit) work have shown that 26% exit Specialized PTSD Unit before completion of treatment. Also, 56% return to the hospital status within one year. Despite a few isolated studies (e.g., Perconte, 1989), past treatment variables responsible for failure are unknown.

Brownell, Marlatt, Lichtenstein, and Wilson (1986) identified four determinants or predictors of relapse: individual, physiological, environmental, and social. The belief is that the "better" treatment models of PTSD address these determinants. The various treatment techniques used with this population, including behavioral therapy, stress management, and milieu imply aspects of the RP model.

RP and Treatment Strategies

Specifically, RP strategies fall into three main categories: skill training, cognitive reframing, and life-style intervention (Marlatt & Gordon, 1985). Skill training strategies include both the behavioral and cognitive responses to cope with high risk situations. Cognitive reframing procedures are designed to provide the client with alternative cognitions concerning the nature of habit change, to introduce coping imagery to deal with urges and early warning signals, and to reframe reactions. Finally, lifestyle strategies are designed to strengthen the client's overall coping capacity and to reduce frequency and intensity of urges that are the product of an unbalanced life-style (Marlatt & Gordon, 1985).

An early emphasis on the RP procedure is time well spent. *A central RP tenet is that a victim is using irrational thinking if a belief is that coping will result in success only.* Rather, people will slip. Better coping involves the ability to fall gracefully. When one makes a mistake or does not cope well with a stressor, this is the exact time that a negative voice (self-talk) has argued persuasively. This belief is now made objective; the whole experience (automatic thoughts, environmental cues, patterns, affects) is the enemy. To counter these, patients are requested to identify high frequency negative behaviors and presented with "facts" about RP, the typical relapse chain, as well as a listing of previously researched relapse situations (Table 13.7). This then becomes the acid test—can the victim cope with the short lived crisis and apply RP learning?

One patient was depressed. He had lost control of his anger and became verbally abusive. This occurred after he had undergone assertiveness and anger management training. He believed he made progress in this area. Using the RP model, staff indicated that if they could have wished for him to go through the program with no problems of anger versus one experiencing a loss of control, the wish was for the latter. This surprised him. His loss of control was now potentially a positive experience. Staff also were able to explore his negative self-talk, his negative voices requesting him to give up and accept his inability to control anger. They again stressed "his" option to replace such thoughts with more positive coping statements: "Just because I lost control this time doesn't mean that I can't continue to express anger more appropriately." At the same time staff explored the coping devices he could use more effectively in controlling his physiology, cognitions, and behavior in that situation. When exploring such relapse occurrences with patients, the *metaphor of a business entrepreneur is often used*. A true entrepreneur does not view a setback as a failure but rather as a learning experience which will enable him/her to achieve greater success. We emphasize that, like the entrepreneur, the victim needs to view a relapse occurrence as a learning situation which can teach improvement in coping skills.

Although we do not prescribe failure or program setbacks, as suggested by the RP model, we do recommend the role-play of potential failures. Also, as just portrayed, setbacks which occur while the patient is in the program are reframed in a positive manner. Finally, Meichenbaum (1985) discussed

(continued on page 627)

I. Facts:*

1. Relapse is not a failure or a sign that one is flawed.
2. A slip is a "small relapse," an isolated event interrupted immediately.
3. Relapse is a full blown return to poor trauma respnses. It occurs if a slip is not interrupted but can itself be stopped at some point.
4. Relapse does not occur when the slip occurs. It has a cycle, starting when feelings are "stuffed," coping slips and poor thinking returns.
5. Relapse is predictable with many warning signs.
6. Relapse does not necessarily apply only to one problem area. There can be many "false" choices or many false mood changes.
7. Relapse does not mean all is lost. It does not cancel out progress.
8. Relapse need not be dangerous; it is a step toward further healing.

II. Relapse Chain:*

1. Build-up of stress
2. Emotional overreaction
3. Denial/numbing sets in
4. Coping falters
5. No support is solicited
6. "Little" lies/excuses start
7. Isolation/avoidance builds
8. Problems grow
9. Hopelessness/failure begins
10. Self-sabotage/self-pity infects issues
11. Slip occurs
12. Relapse

(continued)

TABLE 13.7 (continued)

III. Post-treatment Problems:**

1. Return to (or incomplete treatment of) substance abuse or addiction.
2. Subsequent stressful life event resulting in increase or reoccurrence of PTSD symptoms and prompting self-medication or withdrawal.
3. Failure to address or eliminate stereotypic or phobic behavior related to the original trauma, i.e., maintaining behaviors or habits which remind of, or are adaptive to, combat.
4. Failure to establish or maintain open communication with family or friends, resulting in social isolation.
5. Failure to establish new activities and interests to replace intrusive thought and behavioral patterns.
6. Failure to recognize self-sabotage, e.g., testing oneself unnecessrily or prematurely, or undertaking too much change/responsibility without adequate time to adjust.
7. Failure to establish career and life goals appropriate to skills and abilities, and failure to establish proper groundwork to accomplish these.
8. Failure to recognize and address peer and family pressures that reinforce and maintain dysfunctional status.
9. Loss, or threat of loss, of disability compensation and resultant financial problems, i.e., failure to address financial reinforcement for disability.

*Extrapolated from Washton & Boundy, 1989.
**Extrapolated from Perconte, 1989.

the careful balance between need for RP and the concern for developing reduced self efficacy. He noted:

> The discussion of relapse, however, must be done in a delicate fashion. On the one hand, the trainer does not wish to convey an expectancy that training will inevitably lead to failure, but on the other hand, the trainer wishes to anticipate and subsume into training clients' possible reactions to the likely recurrence of stress. One possible way of dealing with such relapse is for the trainer to reanalyze with the client previous reactions that have followed relapses. The trainer can also use imaginary other clients, noting their reactions to failure and how they coped with such outcomes. The trainer can then ask clients if they are likely to have such feelings and thoughts.

> Because stress is a normal part of life, clients should continue to experience it even after successful training. The goal of SIT is not to eliminate stress but to learn to respond adaptively in stressful situations and to be resilient in the face of failure. (p. 83)

The RP model has no secret. It is appealing because of its simplicity, believability, and self empowerment. Once committed, the victim has entered a new dimension of care, self-initiated and self-controlled. One might say it is the structure or backdrop to positive coping.

CONCLUSION

While a considerable amount of information exists on how people cope with stress, the empirical basis is limited. Then comfort in any one formula is questionable. We have provided information on several stress management elements that "feel right." Since stress management is the loose term for generic care of stressed clients, we emphasize features appealing to us. Most especially, *we endorse an integration approach,* a carefully devised plan for each victim occurring in a total treatment unit. Inpatient care starts with an individualized approach, psychoeducation, and the central mechanics of the care equation, most especially cognitive coping. We have found the non-directive method of hypnosis to be specially helpful and engaging to the chronic population of victims, as it obviates resistance, empowers victims, and provides a sense of success. Finally, a judicious application of RP is necessary for aftercare. Without aftercare, care doesn't exist.

By necessity we have not discussed techniques more suited to psychophysiological arousal (relaxation and desensitization) or behavior, especially those that confront avoidance. Obviously these are important and part of any holistic program. These are considered, however, in other chapters and sources. For more information, the reader is encouraged to consult Everly (1989).

REFERENCES

Alford, J., Mahone, C., & Frelstein, E. (1988). *The practice and theory of individual psychology.* New York: Harcourt, Brace.

Barlow, O. (1988). Anxiety and its disorders: The nature and treatment of anxiety and panic. New York: Guilford Press.

Beck, A., & Emery, G. (1985). *Anxiety disorders and phobias: A cognitive perspective.* New York: Guilford Press.

Beck, A., & Freeman, A. (1990). *Cognitive therapy of personality disorders.* New York: Guilford Press.

Billings, A., & Moos, R. (1981). The role of coping responses and social resources in attenuating the stress of life events. *Journal of Behavioral Medicine, 4,* 2.

Brende, J. O. (1985). The use of hypnosis in post-traumatic conditions. In W. E. Kelly (Ed.), *Post-traumatic stress disorder and the war veteran patient* (pp. 193-210). New York: Brunner/Mazel.

Brende, J. (1987). Dissociative disorders in Vietnam Combat Veterans. *Journal of Contemporary Psychotherapy, 17*(2), 77-86.

Brownell, K., Marlatt, G., Lichtenstein, E., & Wilson, G. (1986). Understanding and preventing relapse. *American Psychologist, 4,* 765-782.

Burstein, A. (1986). Treatment noncompliance in patients with post-traumatic stress disorder. *Psychosomatics, 27,* 37-41.

Chemtob, C., Roitblat, H. L., Hamada, R. S., Carlson, J. G., & Twentyman, C. T. (1988). A cognitive action theory of posttraumatic stress disorder. *Journal of Anxiety Disorders, 2*, 253-275.

Ellis, A. (1962). *Reason and emotion in psychotherapy.* New York: Lyle Stuart.

Engel, G. L. (1968). A life setting conducive to illness. *Annals of Internal Medicine, 69*, 293-300.

Epstein, S. (1990). Beliefs and symptoms in maladaptive resolutions of the traumatic neurosis. In D. Ozer, J. M. Healy, & A. J. Stewart (Eds.), *Perspectives on personality, Vol. 3.* London: Jessica Kingsley, Publishers.

Everly, G. (1989). *A clinical guide to the treatment of the human stress response.* New York: Plenum.

Fairbank, J., Hansen, D., & Fitterberg, J. (1991). Patterns of appraisal and coping across different stressor conditions among former prisoners of war with and without posttraumatic stress disorder. *Journal of Consulting and Clinical Psychology, 59*, 274-281.

Foa, E., Olasov-Rothbaum, B., Riggs, D., & Murdock, T. (1991). Treatment of posttraumatic stress disorder in rape victims: A comparison between cognitive-behavioral procedures and counseling. *Journal of Consulting and Clinical Psychology, 59*, 715-723.

Frank, E., Anderson, B., Stewart, B. D., Dancu, C., Hughes, C., & West, D. (1988). Efficacy of cognitive behavior therapy and systematic desensitization in the treatment of rape trauma. *Behavior Therapy, 19*, 403-420.

Green, B., Lindy, J. & Grace, M. (1988). Long-term coping with combat stress. *Journal of Traumatic Stress, 1*, 399-412.

Grinder, J., & Bandler, R. (1981). *Trans-formations.* Moab, Utah: Real People Press.

Hendin, H., & Haas, A. P. (1984). Combat adaptations of Vietnam veterans without posttraumatic stress disorders. *American Journal of Psychiatry, 141*, 956-959.

Horowitz, M., & Wilmer, N. C. (1980). Life events stress and coping. In L. Poon (Ed.), *Aging in the 1980's* (pp. 363-374). Washington, DC: American Psychological Association.

Kahana, B., Kahana, E., & Young, R. (1985). Social factors in institutional living. In W. Peterson & J. Quadagno (Eds.), *Social bonds in later life: Aging and interdependence* (pp. 389-418). Beverly Hills, CA: Sage.

Kingsbury, S. (1988). Hypnosis in the treatment of posttraumatic stress disorder: An Isomorphic intervention. *American Journal of Clinical Hypnosis, 31*(2), 81-90.

Kolb, L. C. (1987). A neuropsychological hypothesis explaining post traumatic stress disorders. *American Journal of Psychiatry, 144*, 989-995.

Lazarus, R. S. (1984). On the primacy of cognition. *American Psychologist, 39*, 124-129.

Lazarus, R. S., & Folkman, S. (1984). *Stress, appraisal, and coping.* New York: Springer.

Lyons, J. A. (1991). Strategies for assessing the potential for positive adjusting following trauma. *Journal of Traumatic Stress, 4*(1), 113-122.

Marlatt, G., & Gordon, J. (1980). Determinants of relapse: Implications for the maintenance of behavior change. In P.O. Davidson & S.M. Davidson (Eds.), *Behavioral Medicine: Changing health styles.* New York: Brunner/ Mazel.

Marlatt, G., & Gordon, J. (Eds.) (1985). *Relapse prevention: Management strategies in the treatment of addiction behavior.* New York: Guilford Press.

McFarlane, A. (1990). Vulnerability to posttraumatic stress disorder. In M. Wolf & A. Mosnaim (Eds.), *Posttraumatic stress disorder: Etiology, phenomenology, and treatment* (pp. 2-21). Washington, DC: American Psychiatric Press.

Meichenbaum, D. (1985). *Stress inoculation training.* New York: Pergamon Press.

Millon, T. (1983). *Millon clinical multiaxial inventory manual,* (3rd ed.). Minneapolis: National Computer Systems.

Parson, E. (1988). Post-traumatic self disorders (PTsFD): Theoretical and practical considerations in psychotherapy of Vietnam war veterans. In J. Wilson, Z. Harel, & B. Kahana (Eds.), *Human adaptation to extreme stress: From Holocaust to Vietnam* (pp. 245-284). New York: Plenum.

Pearlin, L., & Schooler, C. (1978). The structure of coping. In H. McCubbin, A. Cauble, & J. Patterson (Eds.) *Family stress, coping, and social support* (pp. 109-135). Springfield, IL: Thomas.

Perconte, S. (1989). Stability of positive treatment outcome and symptom relapse in post-traumatic stress disorder. *Journal of Traumatic Stress, 2*(2), 127-136.

Persons, J. B. (1989). *Cognitive therapy in practice: A case formulation approach.* New York: Norton.

Peterson, K., Prout, M., & Schwartz, R. (1991). *Post-traumatic stress disorder: A clinician's guide.* New York: Plenum.

Resick, P., Jordan, C., Girelli, S., Hutter, C., & Marhoefer-Dvorak, S. (1988). A comparative outcome study of behavioral group therapy for sexual assault victims. *Behavior therapy, 19,* 385-401.

Scurfield, R. (1985). Post-trauma stress assessment and treatment: Overview and formulations. In C. Figley (Ed.), *Trauma and its wake: The study and treatment of post-traumatic stress disorder* (pp. 219-256), Vol. 1. New York: Brunner/Mazel.

Solursh, L. (1989). Combat addiction: Overview of implications in symptom maintenance and treatment planning. *Journal of Traumatic Stress, 3*(4), 451-462.

Spiegel, D. (1988). Dissociation and hypnosis in post-traumatic stress disorders. *Journal of Traumatic Stress, 1*(1), 17-33.

Spiegel, D., Hunt, T., & Dondershine, E. (1988). Dissociation and hypnotability in posttraumatic stress disorder: *American Journal of Psychiatry, 145*(3), 301-305.

Spitzer, R., Williams, J., Gibbon, M., & First, M. (1990). *SCID user's guide for the clinical interview for DSM-III-R.* Washington, DC: American Psychiatric Press.

Suleiman, S., & Crossman, I. (1980). *The reader in the text.* Princeton, NJ: Princeton University Press.

Turkat, I. (1991). *The personality disorders: A psychological approach to clinical management.* New York: Pergamon Press.

van der Hart, O., Brown, P., & Turco, R. (1990). Hypnotherapy for traumatic grief: Janetion and modern approaches integrated. *American Journal of Clinical Hypnosis, 32,* 263-271.

van der Kolk, B. (1988). The trauma spectrum: The interaction of biological and social events in the genesis of the trauma response. *Journal of Traumatic Stress, 1*(3), 273-290.

Veronen, L., Kilpatrick, D., & Resnick, P. (1979). Treating fear and anxiety in rape victims: Impications for the criminal justice system. In W. Parsonage (Ed.), *Perspectives on victimology* (pp. 148-159). Beverly Hills, CA: Sage.

Washton, A., & Boundy, D. (1989). *Willpower's not enough: Recovering from addictions of every kind.* New York: Harper Perennial.

Yee, P., & Pierce, G. (1989). Cognitive interference as a personality characteristic. Paper presented as the 1989 Annual Meeting of the American Psychological Association. New Orleans, LA.

Chapter 14

PTSD AMONG THE ELDERLY

Mary N. Summers
and
Lee Hyer

"No wise man ever wished to be younger." Swift

Despite the proliferation of research on PTSD among Vietnam veterans, very few studies have focused on PTSD among the elderly. Yet, if anything, the older cohort has experienced as much or more trauma, both in combat and otherwise, to warrant concern about the residual effects of PTSD. Many veterans were originally diagnosed with traumatic war neurosis, neurocirculatory asthenia, battle fatigue, and shell shock (Brill & Beebe, 1955; Futterman & Pumpian-Mindlin, 1951; Kardiner 1941). These various designations reflect significant and chronic emotional problems that date back to combat experiences, especially those in which the veteran felt overwhelmed and helpless to change his/her situation.

The needs and problems of older people are massive. Nationally, almost one-half of the acute-care hospital beds and 86% of the beds of long-term care institutions are occupied by Americans 65 years or older. By the year 2030, it is estimated that over 51 million Americans will be at least 65 years old (Carter, 1988). The mental health needs of this population will remain high (Pfeiffer, 1971). Yet to date, health care providers, have been found to be less than responsive to needs of older people compared to other age groups (Chafetz, Ochs, Tate, & Niederhe, 1982; Dye, 1978; VandenBos, Stapp, & Kilburg, 1985).

The old saying, "Old age is not for sissies," has a challenging but apt ring. Brody, Brock, and Williams (1987) speculated that for each good (healthy) year added to life, an additional 3.5 compromised years are added. Katzman (1988) projected that if the entire US population were to live to the age of 90, we could expect that one-third would remain intact intellectually, one-third would develop Alzheimer's Disease or its equivalent, and one-third would have benign senescent forgetfulness or other disorders that compromise cognitive functioning. Birren (1989) has indicated that although a death before age 80 may be considered "premature", after this age, life will be hard on many. At our medical center, the average number of medical problems is 5.8 for older medical patients (65), the average number of medical problems is 3.3 for older psychiatric patients, the average number of medicines per older patient is 6.1, and the average length of hospital stay for older groups well exceeds that for younger age groups. These data are not unique, are well beyond those of other age groups who are medically ill, and indicate problems that are pervasive and require care over the long run.

With age an eventual "adaptation to lessened resources" (Dibner, 1978) occurs that helps to compensate for the intrinsic mutagenesis that leads to senescence. This also has been labeled selective optimization with compensation (Baltes, 1987). *Older people utilize energy more efficiently and become more field dependent, externally controlled, and homeostatic seeking.* If stress is intense, or if internal changes are major, the adaptive process goes awry and becomes increasingly maladaptive. This has been labeled a "social breakdown syndrome," a vicious cycle of increasing incompetence (Bengston, 1973). This is the negative side. Kuypers & Bengston, (1973) described another aspect of aging, "social reconstruction syndrome." This construct from social psychology emphasizes a benign cycle of increasing competence through internal and external social system inputs, such as positive self-labeling, development of coping skills, positive self image, and environmental support. Through these ultimately the aging person can reduce his/her dependence on the environment or at least reach a better acceptance of his/her limitations. This represents the positive side.

The life-span developmental model addresses the relationship between stress, on the one hand, and growth or development, on the other. In normal situations, the experience of stress or crisis may be a prerequisite to continued growth. In fact, good evidence is available to show that older people respond well to loss or less severe stressors given some degree of anticipation, control, and support (Ryff & Dunn, 1983). Unfortunately, the area of stress and functioning at later life is messy (Aldwin, Levenson, Spiro, & Bosse, 1989). Further evidence is available to show that adjustments to stressors, especially physical illness, are more directly related to personality factors of the older person and less to objective physical criteria (Michaelson, Michaelson, & Swensen, 1985). Thus, people who were less complex in ego differentiation responded better to interventions in which they were passive recipients, whereas those with more complex ego differentiation benefitted more from active roles.

Aging is a highly individualized process. More variability is found at later life on almost every dimension than at other age periods. Along the way, people struggle to make sense out of what happens to them, to provide themselves with a sense of continuity and order. Therefore, to assess a person at later life without background data is not productive. Furthermore, people age at different rates and in various ways. Through the course of a long life, older people have evolved individual baseline agendas, resources, and environmental conditions that affect them over the duration of their lives (Lazarus & DeLongis, 1983). Older people, too, alter commitment to people, values, and causes over time. This change process is anything but simple and reflects previous crises, personality styles, support, etc. People, therefore, are engaged in a continuous story that can only be grasped across a life-span perspective, not with a single snapshot in time.

This theory also suggests that each person develops his/her own "life-span construct," a unique conception of his/her own life course from age parameters. This is a critical element of this chapter. This construct represents a unified sense of past, present, and future events. It is both cognitive and affective and is impacted upon by personality factors, beliefs, and values. The life-span construct develops transactionally with identity, changing the self-identity as it changes. In addition, two basic structural components, are present: one for the future and one for the past. In a sense, the life-span construct does everything: it alters the identity, it forms expectations about the future, and it builds a life story. When incoming stimuli are traumatic to the life-span construct, it must either distort the event, reconstruct itself, or change the relationship between the person and the environment. An event is assumed not to be difficult apart from the interpretation the individual places upon it. At later life, the life-span construct is well-formed and requires considerable understanding by the clinician (Whitbourne, 1985).

In addition to developing this theme, this chapter will address acute, delayed, and chronic PTSD among the elderly, including a brief review of studies that have focused on later-life veterans with PTSD. Particular attention will be paid to the interaction of relevant aging variables with trauma variables in an attempt to elucidate the phenomenology of later-life PTSD. These include variables from normative aging, geriatric psychopathology, and psychotherapeutic techniques, as all contribute to the manifestation of later-life PTSD. We shall spend time on the contextualization of PTSD as an anxiety disorder. Finally, we direct our focus to the most important part of this chapter, unique features at later life that impact upon the expression and treatment of PTSD.

PTSD AT LATER LIFE

Acute, Chronic, and Delayed Later-life PTSD

The elderly are at heightened risk for a number of non-war related traumas that may precipitate the onset of PTSD. Although this book has focused on combat-related PTSD, an important point to reemphasize is that other traumas exist that can be extremely dehabilitating. Because of compromised physical and mental resources, isolated living conditions, and fewer social supports, the elderly are at risk for crimes, such as muggings, thefts, rape, and assault. They are more likely to witness the unexpected death or sudden debilitating illness of a spouse than are other age groups. Whether these "on-time" events are more or less debilitating for this age group is, however, unknown. Furthermore, compromised visual-motor skills and slowed mental processing may impair driving skills, increasing the likelihood that the elderly may be victims of serious accidental injuries. Disorientation and problems with coordination may impair gait and predispose them to serious falls, and they may be unable to get assistance promptly, compounding the severity of their injuries. In fact, to tease apart the effects of disease on aging (or vice versa) on the basis of most research data is virtually impossible. Apparently the cumulative effect of a long life must include disease (Fozard, Metter, & Brant, 1990). Older age is indeed not for "sissies."

Thus, just as other ages, the importance of these stressors is understood only in the context of the person, other stressors, and the mitigating factors of support, experience, and the like. At later life an accumulation occurs of "more," more of everything. This multiple causation—the accumulation of stressors and the concurrent weakening of the person due to age—is considered a basic rule in trying to understand the life course (Fisk & Chiriboga, 1990). Levinson (1986) in his classic study of the "seasons of life" became most impressed with the increasing richness of the life structure (his central construct) and the problems of adequately measuring such a concept. Regarding the assessment of this whole process, Fisk and Chiriboga (1990) wrote:

One conclusion we come to after reviewing such findings is that the study of adult development requires a substantial commitment of time by investigators. The trajectory of the individual life course is frequently masked by false starts and detours and becomes visible only to those willing to grow old along with their subjects. Even with a commitment of time, the clarity of focus depends on the adequacy and breadth of measures, as well as on the social context. (p. 292-293)

In sum, the manner in which older adults live out their lives depends on the interplay between internal processes and external conditions (even the evaluation). Fortunately, an increasing rule of later life is one of continuity, especially in regard to personality (Costa & McCrae, 1988), and while stressors disrupt this pattern, they do so in an "organized" way.

Numerous cases have been documented in which some combat veterans appeared to have made a good adjustment upon their return to the United States, failing to display any major symptoms of PTSD for many years, and decades later experience full-blown PTSD (Richmond & Beck, 1986; Van Dyke, Zilberg, & McKinnon, 1985). We know from two decades of research on Vietnam veterans that Delayed PTSD does occur. In some cases, events common to later life may precipitate or trigger PTSD symptoms. These may be situations that are strongly reminiscent of the veteran's combat experience. For example, when Operation Desert Storm was under way, many older veterans presented to our facility with flashbacks and nightmares dating back to their own combat experiences. Less obvious are later-life events that may be extremely disruptive, although not reminiscent of combat, such as retirement or the loss of a loved one. At these times, the earlier trauma may be superimposed on the intrusive thoughts and dreams of the veteran. Finally, some veterans may have no identifiable triggers. Maybe the processes of life review and reminiscence that frequently occur during later life have arrested at the point of the original trauma, with development of PTSD symptoms. Interestingly, patients with progressive dementias are occasionally observed to fixate at some earlier year. Unfortunately, for many, the perceived "current" year is actually one in which a trauma occurred, with resulting agitation, insomnia, and perseverative verbalizations that suggest that in the patient's mind, the original traumatic events are happening over and over again.

Chronic PTSD is diagnosed when symptoms persist over a period of six months or more. The study of PTSD among World War II and Korean Conflict veterans has to date permitted the examination of the course of PTSD over four and one-half decades. For most of these veterans, periods of exacerbation alternate between periods of remission, making precise diagnosis difficult. In addition, as with Vietnam veterans, comorbid psychiatric illness is not uncommon (Summers & Hyer, 1991). Accurate diagnosis must take into account not only the patient's present symptoms, but also symptoms they may have experienced across their lifetime, some of which may be common to several psychiatric diagnoses (e.g., marked inability to concentrate, loss of interest in pleasurable activities, avoidance of other people, sleep disturbance). As in Delayed PTSD, patients with Chronic PTSD may be able to identify triggering incidents, or alternatively, no triggers may be recognizable. In sum, a careful evaluation of the client's condition is in order, including current and lifetime problems, existence and influence of disease, and a whole host of social and moderating factors.

Prevalence of Later-life PTSD

Unfortunately, no published studies on the prevalence of Acute and Delayed PTSD among later life combat veterans exist. The majority of studies have focused on patients with Chronic PTSD. For older POWs, estimates of the prevalence for Chronic PTSD have ranged from 50% to 67%, with symptoms enduring as much as 40 years (Goldstein, van Kammen, Shelly, Miller, & van Kammen, 1987; Kluznik, Speed, Van Valkenburg, & Magraw, 1986; Zeiss & Dickman, 1989). For non-POW World War II veterans, Rosen, Fields, Falsettie, and van Kammen (1989) found that 54% of their sample met criteria for Chronic PTSD; however, this sample was extremely small and excluded veterans without comorbid psychiatric illness. Historically, the World War II and Korean Conflict cohorts have been reluctant to admit to psychiatric problems, tending to deal with stress through somatization (Blake, Keane, Wine, Mora, Taylor, & Lyons, 1990). Thus, older people with PTSD may present to medical clinics, where PTSD is rarely evaluated and diagnosed. A prevalence rate based entirely on psychiatric visits or admissions is likely to be an underestimation of the true prevalence rate. In addition, prevalence surveys that take into account only current PTSD symptoms may miss many cases of Chronic PTSD, as patients frequently function relatively well for long periods of time. In addition, some veterans fail to meet the criteria for PTSD as given in DSM-III-R (American Psychiatric Association, 1987), but do experience some of the key symptoms, thus meeting the criteria for Partial PTSD. Partial PTSD has been defined variously but represents a subclinical variant of this disorder, usually with criteria A met and one or more of the phenomenological criteria (B, C, D) (Kulka, Schlenger, Fairbank, Jordan, Hough, Marmar, & Weiss, 1991) (Chapter 5). In our research, we have found that approximately 60% of our psychiatric and 40% of our medical treatment-seeking sample met the criteria for Current Full PTSD, based on the Clinician-Administered PTSD Scale (CAPS-1) (Blake et al., 1990), with approximately 20% of our psychiatric and 30% of our medical sample fulfilling requirements for a diagnosis of Current Partial PTSD. A recognition needs to be made that these prevalence rates were based on veterans who sought treatment for either psychiatric or medical conditions and do not include older veterans who experience PTSD symptoms but fail to report them to health professionals.

Diagnosis of PTSD

Age has been reported both as a risk and a protective factor in the development of symptoms (Lyons, 1991; Realmuto, Wagner, & Bartholow, 1991). In a series of natural disasters, older people proved more refractory to the effects of trauma (Cleary & Houts, 1984; Dohrenwend, Dohrenwend, Warheit, Bartlett, Goldstein, Goldstein, & Martin, 1981). Price (1978), however, reported few differences as a result of age but did show that veterans over 30 had greater problems with amnesia, thought avoidance, diminished interest, detachment, restricted affect, and sense of a foreshortened future. The standard position, however, regarding aging and stress is that older people are more vulnerable and susceptible to its effects, especially regarding spousal death (males especially). Compared to other ages, the elderly face more daily hassles, with different stressors potentiating problems. Other variables are equally or more influential (e.g., gender) than at other ages. Once again, an idiographic course of unique stressors occurs for each person across the life span.(Lazarus & DeLongis, 1983).

Accurate diagnosis of later-life PTSD must take into consideration different types of PTSD symptoms that vary in intensity. For example, Zeiss and Dickman (1989) assessed PTSD among POWs using a three-part rating scale composed of eight key trauma items. Symptoms common to both PTSD and aging, such as sleep disturbance and memory impairment, that could have confounded diagnosis were excluded. Further, the questionnaire was kept brief and worded simply, a strong asset for a population in which some early signs of dementia may be developing. For their sample, excessive startle reactions and persistence of painful memories were the most frequently reported PTSD symptoms, followed by survival guilt and flashbacks. The degree to which these symptoms were troublesome varied considerably among subjects; further, the cyclical waxing and waning of the symptoms was quite evident over the four decades that subjects had experienced PTSD. POWs from both the European and Pacific theaters were included so that the relationship of PTSD symptoms and severity of captivity could be investigated, as Pacific POWs generally received longer internment, and more extreme and inhumane treatment than their European counterparts. However, in this study, current PTSD symptomatology was unrelated to either duration of captivity or location of internment.

In our work (Summers & Hyer, 1991), we are using the CAPS-1, a interviewer-administered measure derived from the *Structured Interview for Diagnosis and Classification* (See Chapter 5). This scale contains questions about seventeen symptoms and permits determination of the frequency and intensity of each PTSD symptom, along with a determination of whether the patient meets the criteria for PTSD specified in DSM-III-R. A list of these symptoms is provided in Table 14.1, along with indications of whether the symptoms seem to be less distressing with age, more distressing, or about the same as for younger combat veterans with PTSD. Further, symptoms that are confounded by the effects of normal aging are indicated. Naturally, many confounds are found, especially for Criteria C (avoidance).

(continued on page 644)

TABLE 14.1
Relative Presence—PTSD Symptoms in Older Victim Group

Symptoms	Symptom Presence: Older Relative to Younger Group			
	Low	Same	High	Confound
Criteria B				
1. Recurrent intrusive recollections			X	X
2. Psychological distress that symbolizes or resembles trauma			X	X
3. Acting or feeling as if event were occuring	X			
4. Recurrent distressing dreams			X	
Criteria C				
5. Efforts to avoid thoughts/feelings of trauma	X			
6. Effort to avoid activities/situations of trauma	X			
7. Inability to recall aspects of trauma			X	X
8. Markedly diminished interest in activities			X	X
9. Feelings of detachment from others			X	X
10. Restricted range of affect			X	X
11. Sense of foreshortened future			X	X

Symptom Presence: Older Relative to Younger Group

Symptoms	Low	Same	High	Confound
Criteria D				
12. Difficulty falling or staying asleep	X		X	X
13. Irritability or outbursts of anger			X	X
14. Difficulty concentrating		X		
15. Hypervigilance			X	X
16. Exaggerated startle response			X	
17. Hyperarousal psychophysiologically to trauma events			X	X
			Present in Older Victim Group	
Other Symptoms				
18. Guilt over acts of commission or omission	X			
19. Survivor guilt			X	X
20. Homicidality	X			
21. Disillusionment with authority	X			
22. Feelings of hopelessness			X	X
23. Memory impairment			X	X
24. Sadness or depression			X	X
25. Feelings of being overwhelmed		X		

Misdiagnoses also can result from the inappropriate use of tests normed solely on Vietnam veterans with older populations. Therefore, studies that compare Vietnam veterans with older veterans must be interpreted with caution. A number of such comparative studies exist. For example, Rosenheck and Fontana (1990) surveyed treatment-seeking veterans from World War II, Korea, and Vietnam on demographics, PTSD symptoms, combat experience, and other social and clinical factors. They found that levels of combat experience had a similar effect on all groups but that some symptoms, especially emotional numbing, appeared to attenuate over time. The study demonstrated significant differences in types of combat experiences between different cohorts, especially in terms of participation in atrocities. To a large extent these results may reflect differences in the military strategy for each cohort. However, other factors such as selective recall, cohort differences in reporting psychological symptoms, integration of experiences across the lifetime, and even cohort differences in the interpretation of test items may have confounded these conclusions.

Related to this, symptoms cluster patterns differ among trauma victims. In certain populations, numbing is uncommon (e.g., many natural disasters); in others, it is very common (e.g., incest) (Green, 1991). Terr (1989) proposed that PTSD has two forms (regarding children): Type I results from a single incident of trauma and is noted for its reexperiencing symptoms; Type II results from a series of trauma events or from exposure to a prolonged stressor and is characterized by denial, dissociation, and numbing. Type II PTSD may lead to personality disorders. Clearly any veteran who has been struggling with trauma over four or five decades has had to "perfect" these latter mechanisms and has experienced alterations in his/her personality (Type II PTSD). In another study, nineteen World War II veterans were compared with twenty-five Vietnam veterans (Davidson, Kudler, Saunders, & Smith, 1990). All were diagnosed with PTSD, based on a 13-item structured interview developed from DSM-III criteria. The Vietnam veterans appeared to manifest significantly more severe symptoms than the older veterans, along with higher depression, hostility, and psychotic quality scores. Further, younger veterans demonstrated more survivor guilt, impairment of work and other interests, avoidance of reminders of the trauma, detachment and estrangement from others, higher startle responses, and greater suicidal tendencies than older veterans.

These conclusions must be regarded with caution. First, older veterans with strong suicidal, hostile, or psychotic tendencies may not have been included in the sample due to selective attrition. Such veterans may have been institutionalized through the mental health or legal systems, or may have committed suicide or died from illness due in large part to self-destructive lifestyles. Second, impairment of work and interests means rather different things, depending on one's stage of life. A retired veteran, whose interests are primarily watching television, gardening, and fishing, may report less disturbance on this item than a younger veteran, who interprets it to mean inability to hold down a job and to deal with the demands of young children. Third, decreased hearing among older veterans may cut down on the number of noises experienced that may trigger startle responses. Older veterans may experience few reminders of their combat experience in their daily lives, compared to Vietnam veterans. Selective recall, as well as coping strategies and support networks developed over the years, also may have reduced the amount of distress associated with PTSD for the older veterans. Finally, research on various types of psychopathology, such as depression, has shown that the cutoff points for scales normed on young and middle-aged adults may incorrectly diagnose the elderly (Zarit, Eiler, & Hassinger, 1985). Studies using older veteran populations find not only depression symptoms (relative to other ages), but many symptoms related to PTSD (Hyer, 1991). Frequently older veterans attributed symptoms such as impaired libido, feelings of depression and guilt, and loss of work and other interests to the aging process, rather than to their PTSD. The use of norms specific to the older population could reduce the confounding influence of other variables. In addition, validation of a typical PTSD assessment battery for use with older veterans would be helpful. Finally, preliminary work suggests that psychophysiological markers, such as heart rate, muscle tension, and skin temperature, that have been found characteristic of PTSD among Vietnam veterans also may have some utility in the diagnosis of later-life PTSD (Orr, Pitman, Herz, & Lasko, 1991).

Moderator Variables

A number of variables have emerged from the Vietnam veteran literature, with some replication on older samples, that appear to account to some degree for the severity and manifestation of PTSD over time. Health status, cognitive functioning, and social support have been found to be particularly relevant, along with combat trauma and other intervening trauma.

Health status includes both mental and physical illness, health promotion behaviors, compliance, and functional impairment resulting from illness (Summers, Haley, Reveille, & Alarcon, 1988). Many elderly veterans have comorbid mental and physical illness, and multiple diagnoses are common (Zarit, 1980). For many, alcoholism is a chronic problem, and with age its effects on the mind and body are more evident. Health status, which has been linked with exacerbations of PTSD, tends to be especially poor for the elderly (Summers & Hyer, 1991). During the next decade, the intersection of developmental issues and health psychology (or the three-way interaction of health, behavior, and aging) will become clearer. For now, note that age is a risk factor for most diseases, with PTSD likely one of these, but its full meaning is unclear.

Closely related to health status is cognitive decline. Increasing problems of the neuropsychological status of trauma victims have been outlined (Wolfe & Charney, 1991). The interaction between age and trauma regarding cognitive deficits is, however, unknown. Many of the elderly complain of memory problems and distracted concentration. Some are perhaps overreacting to some slowing that occurs normally with the aging process. For others, depression contributes to impairment in attention, concentration, memory, and judgment, creating a clinical picture that is similar to dementia, giving rise to the diagnosis of pseudodementia. With advancing age, the prevalence of numerous dementias, most notably Alzheimer's disease and multi-infarct dementia, increases sharply (Zarit, 1980).

Social support has received much attention throughout the PTSD literature, with both helpful and harmful social influences having been identified. The elderly often find that many of their previously rewarding networks are fading, as relatives and friends die, move away, or become compromised by illness. Just as psychosocial isolation upon homecoming was an important predictor of PTSD for Vietnam veterans (Keane, Scott, Chavoya, Lamparski, & Fairbank, 1985; Wilson & Krauss, 1985), the types of psychosocial isolation that can occur as a natural part of aging can lead to an exacerbation of symptomatology for the older veteran. At later life the density, intensity, and reciprocity of social networks have a consistent and strong impact on quality of life (Bear, 1990). Further, the more debilitated the individual (as is the case with older PTSD veterans), the more the environment must be activated to compensate for reduced activity.

Combat trauma, the severity of exposure to combat, accounts for more than one-quarter of the variance of PTSD and postmilitary adjustment for Vietnam veterans, with slightly less robust findings likely for World War II and Korean War veterans (Summers & Hyer, 1991). *Yet, over the course of the life span, combat trauma may not always be the worst stressor.* Of course, from a life span developmental perspective, the mere act of military service is clearly an influential milestone (for better or worse). Usually by later life, numerous subsequent traumas have intervened, and in many cases previous traumas have exacerbated current or intervening ones. The elderly are likely to have significant current traumas and problems and are more vulnerable than their younger counterparts, with the potential for loss and decline increasing exponentially with advancing age. These co-occurring traumas are a major problem for the elderly, and when asked, most elders can identify some trauma that bothers them (Tait & Silver, 1984).

The Relationship of PTSD to Anxiety Disorders at Later Life

Comorbidity with other mental illness is no less important an issue for the older veteran as for the younger one. Anxiety is a strong component of PTSD, and in fact, a veteran later found to have PTSD may earlier have been diagnosed with an anxiety disorder. The clinical presentation of anxiety in the elderly is as varied as the number of older people who experience it. Lifetime prevalence for the elderly tends to approximate that for middle-aged adults (Blazer, George, & Hughes, 1991). Attempts to compile a list of drugs, physical disorders, or types/lengths of hospital stays that either coexist with or cause anxiety at later life are truly formidable. Different variants of anxiety have been described, including death anxiety, masked anxiety, agitation, etc. In addition, many points of view have been offered—that anxiety is underreported, that it is common as a symptom, but considerably less so as a syndrome, that it is most often somaticized, that it is most commonly associated with physical disorders or medication side effects, and that it is so closely tied to depression that to unfurl them is to create separate but unknown entities in later life (Salzman, 1991).

As might be expected, opinions vary regarding anxiety and older people. Many believe that clinical criteria used to determine when an older person is anxious are outmoded or unhelpful (Gurian & Miner, 1991). For others, the expression of anxiety at later life is reasonably direct, expressing itself without the intricate conversion mechanisms frequently seen among the young (Pfeiffer, 1971). As noted earlier, for still others, anxiety is often masked or somaticized. Most anxiety disorders, however, are *a continuation of lifelong problems*, rather than a sudden, later life development of a new disorder. Anxiety tends to remain with people across time. At later life, it tends to mix with other problems as well. Comorbid depression, dementia, or other illness mandates that the clinician must have a thorough knowledge of all these conditions. Gurian and Miner (1991) wrote

> Being 85 is clearly different from being 35 because of 50 years of biological change; but the same 50 years can be described in terms of the life events experienced by the person in the aging body. (p. 33)

Anxiety, then, is by no means a "pure" disorder. Most cases are combinations of various symptoms. Johnson (1991), for example, noted that he found "not one case of uncomplicated acute or chronic anxiety syndrome" (p. 213) in the past 21 years of practice, as all cases were contaminated by many other symptoms. Moreover, virtually all of his patients revealed some form of anxiety.

Patients with a lifelong history of depression or anxiety problems present special challenges. Some older patients present with combinations that mix anxiety with other components (e.g., mixed anxiety with depressive or paranoid features, mixed anxiety, and confusion), but other subtypes are less easily described. A more logical and useful approach may be to isolate clinical criteria on the basis of response to different treatments. For example, Gurian and Miner (1991) found that older patients who ask for anxiolytic drugs tend to respond better than those who do not.

PTSD at later life is usually dragged from earlier ages kicking and screaming. As an isolated disorder (except for the phenomenon of grief, which does not qualify as a stressor for PTSD), PTSD at later life is rare (<1%). As with other anxiety disorders, however, it is rarely isolated. There are no preliminary prevalence ratings of later life comorbid anxiety disorders and PTSD, although clinical experience attests that anxiety is a primary component of PTSD at this age as at others. McCarthy, Katz, and Foa (1991) suggested that significant anxiety disorders among the elderly are likely to be phobias, with components that represent exaggerations of rational concerns, as well as generalized anxiety and mixed anxious-depressive states. Similarly, older people who have PTSD or PTSD symptoms are likely to be of two types based on onset. *Early onset is characterized by a PTSD pattern of both intrusions and avoidance, that is similar to that of younger groups ("chronicity is chronicity"); whereas late onset probably is more characterized by fewer avoidant symptoms* (Summers & Hyer, 1991).

Many reasons exist for the lack of information on the relationship between anxiety and PTSD. Some of these reasons reflect the underlying concepts. For example, Jarvik and Russell (1979) suggested that in addition to fight-flight responses, older people respond with a "freeze" reaction, probably producing somatic problems. Evidence is scant that older people have an increased likelihood of hyperarousal of the autonomic nervous system.

However, the major reasons for the information gap reflect measurement issues. No measures show discriminant validity between anxiety and other related disorders like depression, or for that matter, types or intensity of anxiety at later life (Skeikh, 1991). In addition, no measures are optimally sensitive or specific to the elderly who are medically ill. Existing scales tend to form "state" ratings at the expense of "trait" measures. As described earlier, research on other types of psychopathology has shown that cutoff points on scales normed solely on the young and middle-aged may incorrectly diagnose the elderly. Most of the standard tests now used for the diagnosis of PTSD were normed solely on Vietnam veterans, and must be validated against older veterans to assure that psychopathology is not confounded by aging variables. For these reasons, comparisons with Vietnam veterans must be carefully designed and interpreted. Hyer, Walker, Swanson, Sperr, Sperr, & Blount (in press) compared older patients with PTSD, older POWs without PTSD, older psychiatric patients without PTSD, and young patients with PTSD on the MMPI clinical scales, the MMPI-PTSD scale, the MMPI-Decision Rule, and the Mississippi Scale for Combat Related PTSD. Profiles of the older veterans with PTSD were found to be more similar to the younger PTSD group than to the non-PTSD groups of older veterans. These authors concluded by lamenting on the state of affairs regarding the assessment of older PTSD veterans. With combat-related veterans, older PTSD patients are more similar to younger ones (than other older groups) but are still substantially different both in degree (PTSD scales) and type. In conclusion, much is unknown, and designs for closing the information gap are just beginning.

Skeikh (1991) outlined some of the ideal characteristics of observer-rated and self-rated geriatric anxiety scales. Both should address multiple dimensions of anxiety, including its cognitive, affective, behavioral, and physiological components. Items should show discriminant validity between anxiety and depression and should measure panic attacks and phobic symptoms. They should be psychometrically sound, with norm and specific cutoff points for the elderly and should be sensitive to changes resulting from therapeutic intervention. Observer-rated scales should have some flexibility for open-ended questions, especially to discriminate between symptoms of medical comorbidity. Self-rated scales should have a maximum of 30 items, with large print and clear instructions that can be understood by the elderly. They should be written in simple language to minimize the biases of education, social status, and ethnicity and should require no more than 10 minutes to complete. Unfortunately, current measures of later-life anxiety fall far short of the ideal. For now, we need a good descriptive screening scale, to be followed by reasonably clear-cut paper and pencil and observer-rated measures of anxiety. More sensitive measures of change in the elderly also need to be developed. At these become available, the phenomenon of PTSD at advanced ages can be typed, quantified, and treated.

TRAUMA

The existence of trauma at later life is a "bad news-good news" situation. The "bad news" is that trauma may impact doubly on older people. Christenson, Walker, Ross, and Maltbie (1981) noted that the aging process is susceptible to trauma and once traumatized, susceptible to the cues of trauma. It appears that this process is particularly salient in the case of loss or physical disability. Beardslee (1986) noted further that even among resilient people, an increase occurs between developmental stage and adjustment. Individuals rework the original trauma at each developmental stage, as new cues become salient. Therefore, relapses over the course of the lifetime can and should be expected. Trauma survivors may become increasingly likely to experience severe symptoms of PTSD, and even formerly asymptomatic individuals may develop problems. Finally, as we have noted, much of the literature suggests that older veterans with PTSD continue to experience these insidious menaces forty years after the fact. This applies also to "everyday" trauma. Tait and Silver (1984), for example, interviewed community-dwelling elders regarding how long unwanted and intrusive cognitions about some relatively normal stressors persisted. Seventy-one percent experienced intrusive thoughts on an average of 22.8 years after the event at levels that were intense and uncontrollable.

The "good news" is that older people may in fact respond better to trauma than young people do. The evidence is good for this (Lyons, 1991). In fact, we shall argue below for this point: most older people have a unique capacity to adapt to stressors and older PTSD veterans, especially chronic ones, can apply this skill (now and in later life) to trauma memories in easier ways than earlier in life. As previously noted, many older people develop an adaptive coping style that overcomes impending problems. Kastenbaum (1985) noted further that older people essentially adapt to stress as well as novel stimuli. He labeled this "hyperhabituation, the well entrenched tendency to assimilate the novel to the familiar, to devour the stimulus" (p. 111). Cath and Cath (1984) also eloquently identified a key struggle at later life: growth versus depletion. The older person establishes a balance between factors that promotes self-esteem and sense of self (e.g., past accomplishments, wisdom from experiences, past philosophical world view) versus factors related to depletion (e.g., failing health, cognitive impairment). Through the balance between these two sets of forces, the person adapts in one of two forms, well-being or depletion/depression. In sum, the older person habituates to life, both the good and the troubled areas. Below we shall see how this capacity, along with the nature of the life review process, assists in the integration of trauma.

PSYCHOTHERAPY WITH THE ELDERLY

For more than two decades, much has been written about psychotherapy with older people. Reviews on the area (e.g., Gatz, Popkin, Pino, & VandenBos, 1985; Johnson, 1991; Knight, 1986) are of one mind. It works. In general, reviews and studies are also in agreement that most of the techniques of psychotherapy used for all ages are applicable to the elderly with a certain "plan compatibility" (Silberschatz & Curtis, 1989). These "special psychologic needs of the elderly" (Pfeiffer, 1971) involve distinctive themes (e.g., loss, increased dependency, existential approach of death), age-specific reactions (e.g., survivor guilt at having outlasted others), therapy needs (e.g., symbolic giving, more limited goals, greater amount of positive benefit), and general aging issues (e.g., slower pace, lack of termination). In addition, usually distinctive barriers exist: patient-related, family-related, professional-related, and societal-related (Gatz et al., 1985). Entry into therapy can be formidable as a result. Further, note that older people are not all alike, and that the form of psychotherapy changes with the type of problem. In Table 14.2 a listing of these is presented.

The operative concern with the treatment of the elderly involves a melding of the differences that are specific to later life and those most relevant to issues of treatment in general. When intrinsic compromises are related to organic issues, treatment change almost always involves alterations due to cognitive decline and personality changes. Otherwise, changes are psychological and can be used adaptively. Sherman (1981) noted that these changes included increased individuality, increased slowing, a greater correlation between psychological and physical processes, a drive toward interiority, and a decline in the "working" memory. Therefore, the therapist may wish to make some adjustments to traditional therapeutic techniques, such as being more active and task focused, and utilizing a group format and/or the CBT model, among others (Wellerman & McCormick, 1984). He/she also may need to be more sensitive to the patient's environment and to issues of decline (Knight, 1986). Finally, age-specific concerns of therapy also prove especially relevant in the treatment of later life PTSD. These include the life-review process, enjoyment, quality of life, cognitive mastery, and locus of control. We discuss some of these below in the following paragraphs.

Regarding treatment of the trauma memory at later life, we also have information. *Although the exact mix of core elements is unknown, treatment of the older adult involves relaxation (or its equivalent), perceptual change, and life review.* With younger victims, we noted the emphasis on exposure, search for meaning, and the combination of coping and social support. With older people who are victims of trauma, less emphasis should be given to exposure. Intensive exposure methods tend to increase the level of autonomic arousal and have adverse effects on cognitive performance, whereas relaxation-based techniques have the opposite effect. Based on case reports, McCarthy, Katz, and Foa (1991) noted that, while behavioral techniques and CBT appear to be effective for the treatment of anxiety problems, confrontational exposures may not be. However, in combination with CBT and progressive muscle relaxation (PMR), graded exposure in the form of systematic desensitization is likely to be helpful. Anxiety management

TABLE 14.2
Four Kinds of Patients and Applicable Therapies

1. Cognitive Decline

   Moderate to Severe
   - Reality Orientation
   - Environmental Intervention
   - Skills Training
   - Remotivation
   - Exercise (PT/OT)
   - Behavior Modification
   - General Support (clear up confusion)
   - Family Involvement

   Mild to Moderate
   - Memory/Social Retraining
   - Reeducation
   - Support
   - Environmental Intervention
   - Family Involvement

2. Premorbid Psychological Problems
   - CBT
   - Psychotherapy
   - Family Therapy

3. Crises (Acute or Chronic)
   - Supportive Therapy
   - Groups: Self-help or Therapy
   - Family Therapy
   - Grief Counseling
   - Life Review

4. Existential Issues
   - Life Review
   - Psychotherapy (existential)

training (AMT) includes all of these components. Foa, Rothbaum, and Kozak (1989) used PMR, controlled breathing, thought-stopping, cognitive restructuring, positive self-talk, and imagery with rape victims over eight sessions and successfully reduced anxiety and depression.

Schema Model

Recall that our model specified the psychotherapy concepts of **understanding of self and role, relationship,** and the **schema/symptom therapy** (Chapter 6). With certain modifications, these operations apply also at later life. In light of this, three issues will be addressed. First, the concerns of getting started and the therapeutic relationship will be briefly considered. Second, the similarity of older people to younger ones in regard to entrenched problematic beliefs and the trauma memory will be emphasized. Several aspects of these will be considered, with a heavy emphasis on the CBT model and the life-review process. Last, these therapeutic issues will be contextualized with later life themes.

For all age groups, only a fraction of veterans who have significant problems seek treatment. This is true for elderly patients with PTSD, as well. Many present first to medical clinics and are later referred for treatment of PTSD symptoms. In some instances, the veteran may hear about treatment now being offered to Vietnam veterans but may fail to realize that similar treatment could benefit him/her. Some older veterans are resistant to entering therapy, based on ideas that to admit to psychological problems or misguided fears over the therapeutic process is wrong. These factors can be addressed during initial screening, and once in therapy, the elderly tend to commit well, with a dropout rate less than (or equal to) younger patients. In Table 14.3 is presented a sample rationale that may be helpful with the older patient with PTSD.

Older clients have a hard time getting started. Identification of barriers is, therefore, helpful. What is it that stops an older person from describing problems to another person? Perhaps they no longer feel worthy, believe they may become an excessive burden, or do not understand what help is.

TABLE 14.3
Introducing the Veteran to Treatment

You are not senile, crazy, or suffering from a severe mental illness, but you are not happy and things could be much better for you. In some respects, the war is not over for you, and many veterans your age feel the same way. They often are able to be helped by therapy. We can work together to try to accomplish some things to help with your problems. Your memories of the war will never go away completely, but in therapy you can learn some new skills for coping with problems. You also may be able to get back in touch with old skills that helped you deal with bad things in the past. This therapy had helped other veterans your age have a better life, and I am confident that it can help you as well.

Building trust and rapport is of great importance. Kottler and Brown (1985) noted that a critical step is to find out what the older client knows about treatment, expects from it, and how he/she defines it. Based on this information, a plan can be made, commitment established, and a way of working identified.

Older clients resonate strongly to therapy issues that arise from the relationship. These include not just the positive transference so important with old age, but the "extra mile" issues of house calls, telephone contact, being an advocate, and providing concrete help. Other people need to feel a sense of **moratorium and hope,** so that the process of self-repair, so natural to this age group, can unfold. Hyer, Jacobs, and Pattison (1987) wrote:

> The role of the care-giver is to offer a 'moratorium' for the aging in their adjustment to self and life. This process is both simple and profound. It is a non-specific, accepting

therapeutic response that allows for the naturalness of the later-life struggle. It is similar to the grace period given to the young adult in determining his or her adult role. A moratorium allows for the older person to adjust at a natural pace of changes and losses. It allows for time to grieve. . .(p. 145)

. . .moratorium and hope are, then, key therapeutic elements of later-life struggle. Moratorium allows for healthy grief. It looks past the symptoms of later-life struggle and to the person. The person is accepted. Moratorium encourages a recentering of self, a new integration within the changes and losses of later-life. This recentering is spring-fed with hope. Hope gives affirmation to the person within the harshness of later-life struggle and offers an expectation of purpose for the future. Hope, then, builds from the moratorium in later-life. (p. 146)

Once accepting of the client role and committed to the relationship, the heart of our model involves a focus on constructs, schemas. During the past decade the use of the CBT model has proven effective with later life depression and anxiety (Beutler, Scogin, Kirkish, Schretten, Corbishley, Hamblin, Meredith, Potter, Bamford, & Levenson, 1987; Gallagher & Thompson, 1981, 1982; Thompson, Davies, Gallagher, & Krantz, 1986; Yost, Beutler, Corbishley, & Allender, 1986). Gallagher and Thompson followed more than ninety older adults diagnosed with a major depressive episode. After receiving a course of cognitive, behavioral, or psychodynamic psychotherapy, 70% of the sample had improved considerably or were no longer clinically depressed. At a one year follow-up, no evidence of depression was found in 52% of the whole sample. Although no differences among the treatment groups were found at treatment time, the cognitive or behavioral group had less attrition and greater compliance (Thompson et al, 1986). This study was important, because treatments were carefully noted, procedures given in a manual, patients randomized, measures specified, and patients followed for a year. As recent evidence suggests that antidepressant medications produce high levels of toxicity and are equal or less effective than CBT (Greenberg & Fisher, 1989), this therapeutic approach becomes especially important.

Hyer and colleagues (Hyer, Swanson, Lefkowitz, Hillesland, Davis, & Woods, 1990) followed up on these studies. They evaluated two groups of older clients, chronic PTSD or recent stress reactions due to loss, as well as a no treatment control group. Two CBT components were identified and practiced— cognitive schemas/irrational beliefs and relaxation/anxiety management training (AMT). Each group received a 12-session CBT program and was evaluated on several psychological and behavioral outcome measures. Although objective repeated measures showed no differences among the groups, subjective measures of outcome and individual change supported the treatment package. All subjects believed they benefitted from the schema discussions and the relaxation training along with the AMT. A subsequent study involving anxiety and depression with older groups corroborated the importance of these two core factors with both objective and subjective measures (Hyer, Wright, Swanson, Bauman, Wheale, Hillesland & Moore, in press).

Several features of these two studies are important. First, they used the *Schema Checklist* and highlighted cognitions in the alteration process. Each participant received a personal *Schema Profile* and *Schema Checklist* and was assigned homework to explore and dispute these. Second, PMR was taught and eventually gave way to cued relaxation using AMT. Past and expected stressor problems were noted, practiced, and eventually handled, initially in imagination and later in vivo. This was most beneficial. Third, no objective pre-post results were obtained due to the relatively short period of treatment (12 sessions), the group format, and most importantly, the resulting inability to establish total commitment among all participants. Commitment is extremely important at later life. In this study commitment was met if the client agreed to comply, whether or not each subsequently carried through with the labor intensive tasks of understanding role, homework, and practice on schemas and symptoms. Recall that these are the operative components of our model (Chapter 6). Knowledge, commitment, and practice of the cognitive model require the older client to attend to negative construals, practice alternative beliefs and relaxation, and apply these in their lives. These studies suggest, then, that a cognitive and relaxation focus are important for older people, especially those with a history of trauma or chronic PTSD. This can be a natural process at later life.

Life Review

Although facts of the past cannot be changed, perceptions can. As Sherman's (1981) integrative approach stated, the principles of increased interiority at later life, locus of control, passive mastery, reminiscence, self-concept, values, and the universal need to set the past right (life review) optimize later-life strengths (Table 14.4). In this way, the interaction of personality and environment are improved, and a retrospective focus melds with a present (future) focus to allow for self and interactive changes.

Throughout the aging literature, there is a tension: does one regress with age, or instead, is there an inherent developmental process of reintegration of one's life? Whereas there is evidence for both, one thing is certain: Aging does bring on a retrospective focus (Table 14.5). A "balance sheet of life" is drawn up, and an inevitable life-review process progresses (Butler, 1963). The last tasks of life—love, care, and wisdom (Erikson, 1963)—present themselves with the hope that a sense of integrity can be achieved. As described by Butler and Lewis (1977), the first component of the life review is the recall of life events. This recall is purposeful, presents the elder with a connection to life, and permits a perspective that leads either to integrity or despair. In effect, the act of making normal (and trauma) memories more conscious and deliberative fosters total integration and self-growth. The person picks out incomplete areas and completes the "homework of life," going back to adolescence or even earlier if necessary.

What is unique here is that older people seek this out; to look backward is natural. People at all ages generally seek change either by the push of pain (and its avoidance) or being pulled by purpose. Older people seek change due to both of these. Most importantly, they confront themselves with issues of self-evaluation—am I spending (did I spend) myself where it counts? They do this reflexively and naturally. While people at other ages must use techniques for self-care (e.g., set limited goals, self-imagery, etc.), the older person naturally stops, reflects, and self-cares. In other words, at

TABLE 14.4
Treatment Continuum

---

1. Reduce Stress
   - -identify stressors
   - normalize stressors
   - remove obstacles to change
   - assess life satisfaction
   - reduce dependence
   - provide support

2. Encourage Internal Locus of Control
   - stabilize self-esteem
   - sustain morale
   - sustain coping efforts
   - increase cognitive mastery

3. Foster Integrity
   - encourage life review/interiority
   - offer alternative self-evaluation
   - isolate/confront "narcissistic injuries" and offer perspective
   - self-actualization

Extrapolated from Sherman, 1981.

TABLE 14.5
Functions of Life Review

1. Coping mechanism for management of grief, loss, and stress
2. Consistency of self-concept
3. Linkage of present to past/past to present
4. Reminder to past mastery
5. Reinforce sense of identity/roots
6. Meaning to one's existence
7. Reconcile what might have been
8. Perspective for survivor guilt
9. Access repressed material
10. Address fear of death
11. Identify past strengths
12. Written family legacy
13. Opportunity for socialization (in groups)
14. Enhance long term memory
15. Recreational functions
16. Identify accomplishments
17. Intergenerational benefit to others
18. Fosters ease of other forms of psychotherapy

other ages extrinsic rewards are needed; at later life rewards are intrinsic. Interestingly, this intrinsic component is often "beyond self"—sometimes spiritual, philosophical, or importantly self-referent and considered.

In Table 14.6 a litany of clinical considerations to life review with trauma memories is presented. The point to be made here is that this process is easier at advanced ages. In essence, *the elder is given permission to meld positive and negative features of the trauma, empowering the struggle*

TABLE 14.6
"Letting Go"
Process in Reminiscence Therapy

1. Exposure of positive past
   - use of music, imagery, memorabilia, picture, autobiography, journals, etc.
   - "what was positive"; "what was learned"; "wh; values were represented"
   - positive self-identity highlighted

2. Exposure of negative past (trauma)
   - written script(s) of trauma
   - guide review—titrate affect, identify problems, b a historian and obtain information
   - reframe task as a "learning from past" or as single event in many experiences

3. "Work of therapy" on negative past
   a. Identify emotions
      - facilitate affective expression
      - allow feelings to amplify
      - identify guilt/worthlessness/anger/confusion

   b. Dispute negative generalizations
      - point out negative distortions
      - negative self-esteem altered
      - complete unfinished business
      - rational disputation

4. Apply coping skills
   - self-talk
   - alternative psychophilosophy
   - identify tasks (e.g., grief work, pilgrimage; autobiographies, etc.)
   - values clarification

5. Identify and apply new standards of self-evaluations
   - support and practice skills
   - consolidate "learnings from past"
   - become involved in environment

within, and renewing the "aging trophic" response toward ego transcendence (Peck, 1968). This is a distanced position of self that accepts life as a process, reduces the need to "hold on," and embraces a "being/becoming" mode of life. Ultimately, the person feels a sense of oneness of self and nature, a sense of universal togetherness that turns away from having or doing. This is the end part of acceptance. It is also the one feature that is distinctive at later life.

Dissenters also exist. Lazarus and DeLongis (1983) noted that life review should not be used with older people if guilt is a primary issue. Sparacino (1978-1979) noted further that older people should not be forced to examine in detail all their past traumas, failures, losses, or misdirected efforts. For many elders, denial and repression have been effective coping mechanisms that have helped them function relatively well for years after the original trauma. Opening up these extremely negative past events can run counter to one of the major purposes of life review, to blend trauma with good memories, shifting the balance sheet of life to the positive. However, some older people are not reluctant to bring up negative past events, including their trauma memories. In this instance, when done well, life review can facilitate the integration of trauma, and life can be made authentic.

Meaning at Later Life: The Special Ingredient

Before the refinement of the process at later life is further embellished, the life review developmental concept must be briefly addressed. Throughout this chapter, we alluded to "glue" provided by this construct to the person across time. From the more scientific perspective, explanations of the life course and its change have been discussed from a mix of cultural, demographic, and economic factors—how the individual transits life in a given culture. Elder and Caspi (1990), however, provided a method of studying lives in a changing society by identifying five mechanisms to account for the connection between a life and its changing patterns. By evaluating the control *cycles* (a cultured transition), *situational imperatives* (properties of the situation), *accentuation process* (personality), the *lifestage principle* (person's age), and *interdependent lives* (social relationships), the linkages between a life and social change can be known. We can know scientifically the variations in the life course for any given life with this mixture of components.

From a less scientific, more personal perspective, the constancy and change of a person also can be assessed. McAdams (1990) viewed the process as an interaction between several forces: developmental, cognitive, psychological, psychosocial, and cultural. Human beings, he noted, are basically tellers of stories—their own (McAdams, 1990). Through the life-span developmental process, the emergence of identity as a life story unfolds. Identity "binds our days together anew" (Langbaum, 1982). A person, in effect, is a history; the history of the organism is the organism. The process is natural, the emergence of a historical perspective: "How am I the same person? How am I a whole and unitary being?" This story, however, changes over time, as one develops.

McAdams (1990) has described this life review process of identity according to the context of the life cycle. This story begins in infancy with the caregiver-attachment bond, develops through early and late childhood with an admixture of agency ("I am in control") and communion ("I care for others"), as well as a "for-the-first-time," historical perspective with **nuclear episodes** (scenes or events that mark self-continuity and change). Interestingly, the nuclear episode is what is "picked out" as one journeys across life—to be representative of self (continuity) or representative of non-self (change). Once again, our past memories represent our current selves and are also formed and reformed by them.

As the individual matures, each one's narrative character is refined by self ideals as well as the offerings of the culture. In middle adulthood, a **generativity script** for the life story, a plan or outline for the future, is specified. This period of life is critical; a person must know self in order to commit to life and other people. This is but a logical extension of the nuclear episode. Mature generativity blends agency and communion with a creation and an offering to the environment. Finally, as we have noted, the process of life review begins— an iteration of one's own life story.

Now (at later life) the action begins. The story is either accepted as in "had to be" or rejected as a despairing episode in time. Either way, the person is drawn to this and steps away from story making, transcending personal history. Sartre (1964) noted that the ending of a story shapes all that has come before. The telos, or end point, provides the meaning, justifies all before, and allows transcendence (growth beyond the present). What is at later life influences and is influenced by all that has come before. Older people (as do younger ones) rework earlier stories, but now as a meta-historian. At later life there is a natural (life span developmental) tendency to integrate, to review, to be interior, and to create meaning. Even in a troubled person, this is good news. McAdams (1990) wrote:

> Up until old age, the adult operates both as historian and history, the agent and the object of his or her own story making. In the later years of adulthood, however, he or she may step away from the history and the process of becoming a historian. The history that has been made and the process that has made it become the objects of conscious reflection and review. (p. 189)

Once a historian of self, the mind is unyielding in its process and expands beyond itself as much as possible. Beginning in adolescence, the person's life in the present is chosen so as to resemble the past in distinctive ways. *The past then is a malleable, changing, and resynthesized series of previous life choices* (McAdams, 1990). *History and identity are both made and discovered.* At later life, however, life review enables something more to occur, a push for authenticity that is "beyond history." At later life, then, an incipient push is made to adopt a new world view, one that accepts assumptions of self and world that can provide meaning and coherence. This is both easier at later life (Hyer, Barry, Tamkin, & McConatha, 1984) and, when trauma arises, permissible.

It is not a stretch for any of us to know that the accumulation of living results in an accumulation of stories— our stories. We live in and through our stories; facts make sense only as comprehensible stories. Howard (1991) labels this *homo fabulans*—man the storyteller. In fact reminiscence in this sense becomes not regressive but an adaptive way to rework problems (bad stories). If people strive for narrative continuity or integrity, the idea that PTSD is a stuck story, one that is ontologically locked into fixed time and space, is appealing here. The therapeutic task then is to repair the story and rewrite the biography of the person. The therapist must identify the most meaningful resource frames of the person, bypass the elements of constraint, and facilitate the slow movement of the meanings. The narrative mode of the therapy also is not seeking truth or engaged in argumentation; it privileges the particulars of the experience. Further, as Howard (1991) noted that this is done better by therapists who can enter/join the core issues of clients' stories and provide the appropriate word repair for change. At later life this process is already at work.

Finally, in pursuit of this goal at later life, three issues, especially, have been identified as critical: **control, compassion,** and **personal development.** These are especially relevant where trauma memories are involved. In a previous discussion of Vietnam veterans, we noted that, when a loss occurs, if it is not dealt with quickly, it will persist over time. This also occurs at older ages. However, when given the opportunity in therapy for life review and reminiscence, the patient can readily achieve something more. These three issues are deeply implied in this struggle.

The issue of control is most relevant to trauma and aging. Control related experiences involving losses of all sorts increase with age. Also, the evidence is good that an association exists between lack of control and poorer health in the elderly (Everly, 1989; Rodin, 1986). Most systems expect older people to conform, to be dependent, and to be obedient. This was certainly the expectancy of the residents in many of the experiments conducted in nursing homes by Rodin and Langer (Langer & Rodin, 1976; Rodin & Langer, 1977). However, when these residents were afforded the perception of control, the mortality rate decreased, quality of life was enhanced, and functioning improved.

At later life, control is directly relevant to trauma. Loss of control in a trauma situation results in increased PTSD problems, a phenomenon Frankl (1978) described as "demoralization." Seligman and Bandura (see Langer & Rodin, 1976) also have described this issue, noting that control is a powerful mediator in stimulus response paradigms of behavior. Loss of control represents the "giving in/giving-up" complex pursuant to illness (Engel, 1968). Not having just the right amount of control can be a problem as well. Individuals who are still struggling for control may be more anxious and involved, whereas those who feel a loss of control are depressed or have given up.

When older people are stuck because of trauma, control is a focal issue. When addressed lovingly and therapeutically, its importance dissipates, as the patient realizes that life can be viewed at a greater distance and with enhanced meaning. At older age, the self, often with spiritual coping and/or imagery, is permitted to know a grander design.

Second, trauma victims are stuck at least in part because of a lack of compassion (self-hate). Chronic levels of PTSD at later life are as debilitating then as at other ages, with, as we are arguing, one additional component, the internal press of the person that life has "no future." If the person does not resolve at this point, this self-hate will never be assuaged. Rubin (1975) noted how insidious life guilt or self-hate can be and offered an antidote, compassion and acceptance of self. Sherman (1981) wrote:

> What this means in practice is that the clients have to take a more realistic and compassionate view of themselves. They have to accept their limitations as human beings, accept the fact that they were and are fallible. This is quite different from the defense mechanism of denial. One would not, of course, attempt to expose the use of denial by an older person if it serves a purpose. But in instances where the individual is aware of his or her involvement in some transgression, the mechanism of denial is not working. In those cases, one works on exposing the futility and debilitating effects of guilt, showing how it creates self-hate, and also on helping the client to be more compassionate toward himself or herself by recognizing human fallibility. (p. 195)

In this way, the older person is given permission to evaluate the self differently. The client sees the self compassionately and more realistically. Self-forgiveness is an exercise of compassion and a suspension of critical judgement; *"life is,"* not *"life ought to,"* is accepted. The acceptance of limits, the futility of narcissism, the debilitating effect of survivor guilt, and the limits of humankind, are viewed fairly. The older person comes to the realization that he/she did the best he/she could. Retrospective negativity and life regrets pale as soon as they occur.

Third, agreement on the central growth components at later life is rough. Ryff and Dunn (1983) identified six factors indicative of personal development regarding older people. These criteria were formulated from the research literature and are presented in Table 14.7. In effect, these criteria represent positive mental health, a total view of well being at later life. Each can be related to others as well as correlated among themselves. Naturally, where frail elders are concerned, the needs hierarchy is lowered. Elderly trauma victims who are cognitively or physically compromised must first struggle with biologic integrity before reaching for the higher levels of safety, belonging, self-esteem, and self-actualization (Ebersole & Hess, 1990). However, movement to grow is in that direction. Remember that debilitated states are not modal at later life, freeing most elders with the universal human need to place life in some perspective/meaning.

CONCLUSION

Care of the older trauma victim, whether acute or chronic, immediate or delayed, is dependent on what we know about psychotherapy in general, plus modifications due to aging-specific problems or issues. We believe that our model, through its focus on the understanding of self and role, a solid relationship, and the careful excision of cognitive constructs, relaxation procedures, and life review, are highly efficacious at later life. Modifications are due largely to cognitive decline (thereby mandating a slower pace, more overlearning, commitment

TABLE 14.7
Dimensions of Well-being

Dimension	Definition
Self-acceptance	Develops positive feelings about present and past life, and accepts both positive and negative aspects of self.
Positive Relations	Relates to other people with warmth, empathy, affection, trust, and intimacy.
Autonomy	Determines own behavior and resists social pressures to think or act in certain ways, and acts independently.
Environmental Mastery	Manages environment completely and efficiently with a good sense of mastery and control over external activities.
Purpose in Life	Feels present and past life have meaning, sets goals and objectives, and acts in a goal-directed fashion.
Personal Growth	Pursues activities that lead to continued growth and personal development, is open to new experiences, and seeks activities to increase self-knowledge.

Extrapolated from Ryff, 1986.

techniques, etc.) and aging issues (control, wisdom, integrity, and life review).

There has been a central issue in this chapter: does aging facilitate or hamper the unearthing process of the trauma memory? *Is the victim worse due to the accumulation of the stress residual or better due to the gifts of chronological maturity? Our bet is "better."* This better trauma processing is not due to resilience or inoculation. Older victims of trauma are almost always chronic and often have retained trauma baggage for many years. *Now they have the advantage of the emergent feature of later life—the natural tendency for life review, increased interiority, passive mastery skills, selective optimization by compensation and the very focus of the late life struggle (integrity).* As we have implied, it is at later life that the press for order is maximal. "What has to be" now must be: There is no future. The importance and press, therefore, of setting things in order reach its zenith.

We do not know conclusively how PTSD at later life is different—does PTSD influence age or vice versa? This information will evolve from longitudinal studies. We need information on distinctive symptoms and symptom clusters at later life, as well as correlates of later-life PTSD. Comorbidity and discriminant validity will be critical in the extension of such knowledge. Also, the value of specific stressors and the influence of modal events, such as loss, in later life on PTSD is largely unknown. Subclinical subtypes need to be identified and described.

One thing appears clear: older people resonate to intense issues or meaning better than other age groups. Without doubt other differences also exist. *The elderly are probably better at a meaning focus, but with a more external locus of control; more adaptive at avoidance strategies, but entrenched and more likely to use emotion-focused coping; more depressed, but perhaps less anxious; more concerned with primary trauma issues and less with secondary trauma; and less friendly toward treatment with lower expectations, but more compliant when engaged.* The belief is that these conditions allow for the refurbishing of one's life story, a task done easily at later life. Hopefully, this cohort of older people is not too unique. Most of us are likely to struggle with the same issues.

REFERENCES

Aldwin, C., Levenson, M., Spiro, A., & Bosse, R. (1989). Does emotionality predict stress? Findings from the normative aging study. *Journal of Personality and Social Psychology, 56,* 618-624.

American Psychiatric Association (1987). *Diagnostic and statistical manual of mental disorders* (3rd ed., revised). Washington, DC: Author.

Baltes, P. (1987). Theoretical propositions of life-span developmental psychology: On the dynamics between growth and decline. *Developmental Psychology, 23,* 611-626.

Bear, M. (1990). Social network characteristics and the deviation of primary relationships after entry into long term care. *Journal of Gerontology, 45*(5), 156-163.

Beardslee, W. R. (1986). The role of self understanding in resilient individuals: The development of a perspective. *American Journal of Orthopsychiatry. 59,* 266-278.

Bengston, V. L. (1973). *The social psychology of aging.* Indianapolis: Bobbs-Merrill.

Beutler, L., Scogin, F., Kirkish, P., Schretten, D., Corbishley, A., Hamblin, D., Meredith, K., Potter, R., Bamford, C., & Levenson, A. (1987). Group cognitive therapy and alprozolam in the treatment of depression in older adults. *Journal of Consulting and Clinical Psychology, 55,* 550-557.

Birren, J. E. (1989). Aging in the 90's. Paper presented at the annual meeting of the Southern Gerontological Society. Charleston, S.C.

Blake, D. D., Keane, T. M., Wine, P. R., Mora, C., Taylor, K. L., & Lyons, J. A. (1990). Prevalence of PTSD symptoms in combat veterans seeking medical treatment. *Journal of Traumatic Stress, 3,* 15-27.

Blazer, D., George, L., & Hughes, D. (1991). The epidemiology of anxiety disorders. In C. Salzman & B. Lebowitz (Eds.) *Anxiety in the elderly: Treatment and research* (pp. 17-27). New York: Springer.

Brill, N. Q., & Beebe, G. W. (1955). *A follow up study of war neuroses.* Washington, D.C.: Veterans Administration.

Brody, J., Brock, D., & Williams, T. (1987). Trends in the health of the elderly population. In L. Breslow, J. Fielding, & L. Love (Eds.), *Annual review of public health, 8,* 211-224.

Butler, R. N. (1963). The life review: An interpretation of reminiscence in the aged. *Psychiatry, 26,* 65-75.

Butler, R. N., & Lewis, M. I. (1977). *Aging and mental health.* St. Louis: C. V. Mosby Co.

Carter, J. (1988). Policy implications of the impact of continuing mortality declines and support systems for the elderly in the United States. *Journal of Applied Gerontology, 7,* 427-447.

Cath, S., & Cath, C. (1984). "The race against time." In R. Neimoff and C. Colarusso (Eds.), *Psychotherapy and psychoanalysis in the second half of life* (pp. 241-262). New York: Plenum.

Chafetz, P., Ochs, C., Tate, L., & Niederhe, G. (1982). Employment opportunities for geropsychologists. *American Psychologist, 37,* 1221-1227.

Christenson, R. M., Walker, J. I., Ross, M.R., & Maltbie, A. A. (1981). Reactivation of traumatic conflicts. *American Journal of Psychiatry, 142,* 1070-1073.

Cleary, P. D., & Houts, P. S. (1984). The psychological impact of the Three Mile Island incident. *Journal of Human Stress, 10,* 28-34.

Costa, P., & McCrae, R. (1988). Personality in adulthood. A six year longitudinal study of self reports and spouse ratings on the NEO Personality Inventory. *Journal of Personality and Social Psychology, 54,* 853-863.

Davidson, J. R. T., Kudler, H. S., Saunders, E. P., & Smith, R. D. (1990). Symptom and comorbidity patterns in World War II and Vietnam veterans with posttraumatic stress disorder. *Comparative Psychiatry, 31,* 162-170.

Dibner, S. C. (1978). The psychology of normal aging. In M. Spencer & C. Dorr (Eds.), *Understanding aging: A multidisciplinary approach.* New York: Appleton-Century-Croft.

Dohrenwend, B. P., Dohrenwend, B. S., Warheit, G. T., Bartlett, G. S., Goldstein, R. L., Goldstein, K., & Martin, J. L. (1981). Stress in the community: A report to the President's Commission on the accident at Three Mile Island. *Annals NY Academy Science, 365,* 159-174.

Dye, C. (1978). Psychologists' role in the provision of mental health care for the elderly. *Professional Psychology, 9,* 38-49.

Ebersole, P., & Hess, P. (1990). *Toward healthy aging.* St. Louis: Mosby.

Elder, L., & Caspi, A. (1990). Studying lives in a changing society: Sociological and personological explanations. In A. Rabin, R. Zucker, R. Emmons, & S. Frank (Eds.), *Studying persons and lives* (pp. 201-247). New York: Springer.

Engel, G. L. (1968). A life setting conducive to illness. *Annals of Internal Medicine, 69,* 293-300.

Erikson, E. (1963). *Childhood and society* (2nd ed.). New York: Norton.

Everly, G. (1989). *A clinical guide to the treatment of the human stress response.* New York: Plenum.

Fisk, M., & Chiriboga, D. (1990). *Change and continuity in adult life.* San Francisco: Jossey-Bass.

Foa, E. B., Rothbaum, B. O., & Kozak, M. J. (1989). Behavioral treatments of anxiety and depression. In P. Kendall & D. Watson (Eds.), *Anxiety and depression: Distinctive and overlapping features.* New York: Academic Press.

Fozard, J., Metter, J., & Brant, L. (1990). Next steps in describing aging and disease in longitudinal studies. *Journal of Gerontology, 45,* 116-127.

Frankl, V. (1978). *The unheard cry for meaning: Psychotherapy and humanism.* New York: Schuster.

Futterman, S., & Pumpian-Mindlin, E. (1951). Traumatic war neuroses five years later. *American Journal of Psychiatry, 108,* 401-408.

Gallagher, D., & Thompson, L. W. (1981). *Depression in the elderly: A behavioral treatment manual.* Los Angeles: USC Press.

Gallagher, D., & Thompson, L. W. (1982). *Elders maintenance of treatment benefits following individual psychotherapy for depression.* Results of a pilot study and preliminary data from an ongoing replication study. Paper presented at the annual meeting of the American Psychological Association, Washington, DC.

Gatz, M., Popkin, S., Pino, C., & VandenBos, G. (1985). Psychological interventions with older adults. In J. E. Birren & K. W. Schaie (Eds.), *Handbook of the psychology of aging* (2nd ed.) (pp. 755-788). New York: Van Nostrand Reinhold.

Goldstein, G., van Kammen, W., Shelly, C., Miller, D. J., & van Kammen, D. P. (1987). Survivors of imprisonment in the Pacific Theater during World War II. *American Journal of Psychiatry, 144,* 1210-1213.

Green, B. (1991). Evaluating the effects of disasters. *Psychological Assessment: A Journal of Consulting and Clinical Psychiatry, 3,* 538-546.

Greenberg, R. & Fisher, S. (1989). Examining antidepressant effectiveness: Findings, ambiguities, and some vexing puzzles. In S. Fisher & R. Greenberg (Eds.), *The limits of biological treatments for psychological distress* (pp. 1-37). Hillsdale, NJ: Erlbaum.

Gurian, B., & Miner, J. (1991). Clinical presentation of consulting in the elderly. In C. Salzman & B. Lebowitz (Eds.), *Anxiety in the elderly; Treatment and research* (pp. 31-40). New York: Springer.

Howard, G. (1991). Culture tales: A narative approach to thinking, cross-cultural psychology, and psychotherapy. *American Psychologist, 46,* 187-197.

Hyer, L. (1991). *Problems with cognitive behavioral therapy with older people.* Presentation at the Consortium on the Psychology of Aging, Augusta, GA.

Hyer, L., Barry, J., Tamkin, A., & McConatha, D. (1984). Coping in later-life: An optimistic assessment. *Journal of Applied Gerontology, 3,* 82-96.

Hyer, L., Jacobs, M., & Pattison, M. (1987). Later-life struggle: Psychological/spiritual convergence. *Journal of Pastoral Care, 2,* 141-149.

Hyer, L., Swanson, G., Lefkowitz, R., Hillesland, D., Davis, H., & Woods, M. (1990). The application of the cognitive behavioral model in two older groups. In T. Brink (Ed.), *Group therapy in nursing homes* (pp. 145-190). New York: Haworth Press.

Hyer, L., Walker, C., Swanson, G., Sperr, S., Sperr, E., & Blount, J. (in press). Validation of PTSD measures for older combat veterans. *Journal of Clinical Psychology.*

Hyer, L., Wright, L., Swanson, G., Bauman, M., Wheale, C., Hillesland, D., & Moore, L. (in press). Cognitive behavioral therapies: Another attempt at change. *Clinical Gerontologist.*

Jarvik, L. F. & Russell, D. (1979). Anxiety, aging and the third emergency reaction. *Journal of Gerontology, 34,* 197-200.

Johnson, F. (1991). Psychotherapy of the elderly anxious patient. In C. Saltzman & B. Lebowitz (Eds.), *Anxiety in the elderly: Treatment and research* (pp. 215-248). New York: Springer.

Kardiner, A. (1941). The traumatic neurosis of war. *Psychosomatic Medicine, 11*, 111.

Kastenbaum, R. (1985). Dying and death: A life-span approach. In J. Birren & K. W. Schale (Eds.), *Handbook of the psychology of aging* (pp. 619-646). New York: Van Nostrand Reinhold.

Katzman, R. A. (1988). Alzheimer's disease as an age-dependent disorder. In D. Everett & J. Whelan (Eds.), *Research and the aging population* (pp. 69-81). Chichester, U.K.: John Wiley & Sons Ltd.

Keane, T. M., Scott, O. N., Chavoya, G. A., Lamparski, D. M., & Fairbank, J. A. (1985). Social support in Vietnam veterans with posttraumatic stress disorder. *Journal of Consulting and Clinical Psychology, 52*, 888-891.

Kluznik, H., Speed, N., Van Valkenburg, C., & Magraw, R. (1986). Forty-year follow-up of United States prisoners of war. *American Journal of Psychiatry, 143*, 1443-1445.

Knight, B. (1986). *Psychotherapy with older adults.* Beverly Hills, CA: Sage Publication.

Kottler, J., & Brown, R. (1985). *Introduction to therapeutic counseling.* Monterey, CA: Brooks/Cole.

Kulka, R. A., Schlenger, W. E., Fairbank, J. A. Jordan, B. K., Hough, R. L., Marmar, C. R. & Weiss, D. S. (1991). Assessment of posttraumatic stress disorder in the community: Prospects and pitfalls from recent studies of Vietnam veterans. *Psychological Assessment, 3*, 547-560.

Kuypers, J. A., & Bengston, V. L. (1973). Competence and social breakdown: A social-psychological view of aging. *Human Development, 16*, 37-49.

Langbaum, R. (1982). *The mysteries of identity: A theme in modern literature.* Chicago: University of Chicago Press.

Langer, E. J., & Rodin, J. (1976). The effects of choice and enhanced personal responsibility for the aged: A field experiment in an institutional setting. *Journey of Personality and Social Psychology, 34*(2), 191-198.

Lazarus, R., & DeLongis, A. (1983). Psychological stress and coping in aging. *American Psychologist, 38*, 245-254.

Levinson, D. (1986). A conception of adult development. *American Psychologist*, *41*, 3-14.

Lyons, J. A. (1991). Strategies for assessing the potential for positive adjusting following trauma. *Journal of Traumatic Stress*, *4*(1), 113-122.

McAdams, D. (1990). Unity and purpose in human lives: The emergency of identity as a life story. In I. Rabin, R. Zucker, R. Emmons, & S. Frank (Eds.), *Studying person and lives* (pp. 148-200). New York: Springer.

McCarthy, P., Katz, I., & Foa, E. (1991). Cognitive-behavioral treatment of anxiety in the elderly: A proposal model. In C. Saltzman & B. Lebowitz (Eds.), Anxiety in the elderly: *Treatment and research* (pp. 197-214). New York: Springer.

Michaelson, R., Michaelson, C., & Swensen, C. (1985). *Personality factors influencing adjustment to chronic physical illness in the elderly*. Paper presented at the ninety-third annual meeting of the American Psychological Association.

Orr, S. P., Pitman, R. K., Herz, L. R., & Lasko, N. B. (1991). *Psychophysiologic assessment of posttraumatic stress disorder imagery in Korean and World War II combat veterans*. Paper presented at the American Psychiatric Association meetings, New Orleans, LA.

Peck, R. C. (1968). Psychological developments in the second half of life. In B . L. Neugarten (Ed.), *Middle age and aging: A reader in social psychology*. Chicago: University of Chicago Press.

Pfeiffer, E. (1971). Psychotherapy with elderly patients. *Postgraduate Medicine*, *50*, 254-258.

Price, J. (1978). Some age-related effects of the 1974 Brisbane floods. *Australian and New Zealand Journal of Psychiatry*, *12*, 55-58.

Realmuto, G., Wagner, N., & Bartholow, J. (1991). The Williams pipeline disaster: A controlled study of a technological accident. *Journal of Traumatic Stress*, *4*, 469-481.

Richmond, J. S., & Beck, J. C. (1986). Posttraumatic stress disorder in a World War II veteran. *American Journal of Psychiatry.*, *143*, 1485-1486.

Rodin, J. (1986). Aging and health: Effects of the sense of control. *Science*, *233*, 1271-1276.

Rodin, J., & Langer, E. J. (1977). Long-term effects of a control relevant intervention with the institutionalized aged. *Journal of Personality and Social Psychology, 35,* 897-902.

Rosen, J., Fields, R., Falsettie, G., & van Kammen, D. (1989). Concurrent posttraumatic stress disorder in psychogeriatric patients. *Journal of Geriatric Psychiatry and Neurology, 3,* 65-69.

Rosenheck, R. & Fontana, A. (1990). Long term sequelae of combat in World War II, Korea, and Vietnam: A comparative study. In R. Ursano, B. McCaughey, & C. Fullerton (Eds.). *Individual and Community Responses to Trauma and Disaster.* Boston, MA: Cambridge University Press.

Rubin, T. I. (1975). *Compassion and self-hate.* New York: McKay.

Ryff, C., & Dunn, D. (1983). *Life stresses and personality: A life-span developmental inquiry.* Paper presented at the Gerontological Society Meeting, San Francisco, CA.

Ryff, C. (1986). *The failure of successful aging research.* Paper presented at the Gerontological Society Meeting, Chicago, Illinois.

Salzman, C. (1991). Pharmalogic treatment of the anxious elderly patient. In C. Salzman & B. Lebowitz (Eds.), *Anxiety in the elderly: Treatment and research.* New York: Springer.

Sartre, J. P. (1964). Personality and the unification of psychology and modern physics: A systems approach. In J. Aronoff, A. I. Rabin, & R. A. Zucker (Eds.), *The emergence of personality* (pp. 217-254). New York: Springer.

Sherman, E. (1981). *Counseling the aging: An integrative approach.* New York: The Free Press.

Silberschatz, G., & Curtis, J. (1989). Research on the psychodynamic process in the treatment of older persons. In N. E. Miller (Ed.), *Psychodynamic research perspectives on development, psychopathology and treatment in later life.* New York: International Universities Press.

Skeikh, J. (1991). Anxiety rating scales for the elderly. In C. Salzman & B. Lebowitz (Eds.), *Anxiety in the elderly: Treatment and research* (pp. 251-266). New York: Springer.

Sparacino, J. (1978-1979). Individual psychotherapy with the aged: A selected review. *International Journal of Aging and Human Development, 9,* 197-220.

Summers, M., & Hyer, L. (1991). *Measurement of PTSD among older combat veterans.* VA Merit Review Grant. Augusta, GA.

Summers, M. N., Haley, W. E., Reveille, J. D., & Alarcon, G. S. (1988). Radiographic assessment and psychologic variables as predictors of pain and functional impairment in osteoarthritis of knee and hip. *Arthritis and Rheumatism, 31,* 204-209.

Tait, R., & Silver, R. (1984). *Recovery: The long term impact of stressful life experience.* Paper presented at the 92nd Annual Convention of the American Psychological Association, Torento, Ontario.

Terr, L. (1989). *A proposal for an overall DSM-IV category, post-traumatic stress.* Paper presented for the DSM-IV Workgroup on Post-traumatic stress disorder.

Thompson, L., Davies, R., Gallagher D., & Krantz, S. (1986). Cognitive therapy with older adults. *Clinical Gerontologist, 5,* 245-279.

VandenBos, G. R ., Stapp, J., & Kilburg, R. R. (1985). Health service providers in psychology: Results of the 1978 APA human resources survey. *American Psychologist, 36,* 1395-1418.

Van Dyke, C., Zilberg, N. J., & McKinnon, J. A. (1985). Post-traumatic stress disorder: a thirty-year delay in World War II veterans. *American Journal of Psychiatry, 142,* 1070-1073.

Wellerman, F., & McCormick, J. (1984). Counseling with older persons: A review of outcome research. *The Counseling Psychologist, 12,* 81-96.

Whitbourne, S. (1985). The psychological construction of the life span. In J. Birren & K. W. Schaie (Eds.), *Handbook of the psychology of aging* (pp. 594-618). New York: Van Nostrand Reinhold.

Wilson, J. P., & Krauss, G. E. (1985). Predicting PTSD among Vietnam veterans. In W. E. Kelly (ed.), *Post-traumatic stress disorder and war veteran patient.* New York: Brunner/Mazel.

Wolfe, J., & Charney, D. (1991). Use of neuropsychological assessment in posttraumatic stress disorder. *Psychological Assessment: A Journal of the Consulting and Clinical Psychology, 3,* 573-580.

Yost, E. B., Beutler, L. E., Corbishley, M. A., & Allender, J. R. (1986). *Psychology practitioner guidebooks: Group cognitive therapy.* New York: Pergamon Press.

Zarit, S. (1980). *Aging and Mental Disorders*. New York: The Free Press.

Zarit, S., Eiler, J., & Hassinger, M. (1985). Clinical assessment. In J. Burren & K. Schaie (Eds.), *Handbook of the psychology of aging* (pp. 725-754). New York: Van Nostrand Reinhold.

Zeiss, R. A., & Dickman, H. R. (1989). PTSD 40 years later: Incidence and person-situation correlates in former POWs. *Journal of Clinical Psychology*, *45*, 80-87.

PART IV

Person in Culture

Dissonance Reduction

Chapter 15

COGNITIVE DISSONANCE AND EXISTENTIAL PERSPECTIVES ON COMBAT REEXPERIENCING

Lynne Peralme, M.A.

"In a war of ideas it is people who get killed." Lec

"The face of horror" (Tick, 1987)—this is what survivors of trauma have experienced, be it trauma related to combat, disaster, or holocaust. According to Tick, the horror cannot be escaped from, forgotten, or denied, for it becomes a part of those who witness it. "The images of what men and women saw and did in Vietnam were so shocking, so beyond anything they had been prepared to encounter, so hair-raising, that they imprinted on the mind as if it were soft clay" (Tick, 1987, p. 104). For many, these images are as vivid and painful today as they were 25 years ago and they continue to haunt those with post-traumatic stress disorder (PTSD). Reexperiencing of trauma—reexperiencing of horror—has been considered the hallmark of PTSD.

The horror of war is unique. The responsibility for witnessing and/or engaging in immoral actions during war cannot be displaced. Ultimately, war leaves the individual combatant with no external source of blame. While we often succumb to the destructive forces of nature, or the evil desires of deranged villains, the discovery of the beast within ourselves requires us to question and struggle with our own human nature.

In investigations of PTSD and the effects of combat trauma, the essence and significance of the phenomenon of reexperiencing has often been overlooked. The purpose of this chapter is to expand upon existing theoretical conceptualizations of reexperiencing of trauma in combat veterans. A social psychological perspective is put forth and integrated with an existential viewpoint.

SOCIAL PSYCHOLOGICAL PERSPECTIVE

Cognitive dissonance is the most well-known and researched theory in the field of social psychology. However, according to Berkowitz and Devine (1989), over the past 10 to 15 years a marked decline has occurred in interest in and attention to this theory. They noted, for example, that in the *Journal of Personality & Social Psychology*, the number of articles related to dissonance theory in 1967 was 7, in 1977 was 2, and in 1987 was none.

Interestingly, unlike many other theories, the decline of interest in dissonance theory was not the result of the theory being disconfirmed or declared invalid. Berkowitz and Devine (1989) proposed three factors they believed account for the decline: (1) the theory's incompatibility with the current dominance of a cognitive orientation in which nonmotivational principles play a more important role, (2) an emphasis on an analytic as opposed to a synthetic approach to research, and (3) the priority among researchers to be up-to-date and make unique and innovative contributions to science.

Fortunately, a revival of interest in dissonance theory appears to be on the horizon (Aronson, 1989; Axsom, 1989; Berkowitz & Devine, 1989; Scher & Cooper, 1989). In an effort to develop a synthetic conceptualization of PTSD which can account for all aspects of the disorder, including reexperiencing symptomatology, the question arises as to what contribution a well-established theory of behavior, such as cognitive dissonance, can make. *Could the dissonance paradigm offer a new insight into the understanding, study, and treatment of PTSD reexperiencing symptomatology?*

An important point to note is that although dissonance theory has been valued because of its wide applicability, it has not heretofore been proposed as a basis for explaining PTSD in general, or reexperiencing in particular. This section will describe the theory of cognitive dissonance, draw parallels between the transformation from civilian to soldier and the principles of dissonance arousal and reduction operating during combat, draw parallels between the transformation from soldier to civilian and the principles of dissonance arousal and reduction operating post-combat, and discuss PTSD reexperiencing symptomatology from a dissonance perspective.

COGNITIVE DISSONANCE THEORY

Cognitive dissonance is a "motivational" or "negative drive" state which is aroused when a person simultaneously holds two cognitions that are inconsistent with each other (Aronson, 1978; Festinger, 1957; West & Wicklund, 1980; Wicklund & Brehm, 1976). For example, in the forced compliance paradigm frequently used to examine dissonance in the laboratory, subjects are induced to voluntarily engage in a behavior that conflicts with their personal attitudes, such as writing a counter-attitudinal essay. Internal conflict (dissonance) is subsequently aroused between awareness of having performed the behavior (writing the essay) and the person's pre-existing attitude. The more important the two cognitions are, or the greater the ratio of dissonant to consonant cognitions on a specific topic, the greater the amount of dissonance. As in other drive theories, dissonance is an uncomfortable state of arousal or tension which individuals are motivated to reduce. Although some researchers have focused on dissonance arousal and reduction as a consequence of making a decision, its occurrence is not restricted to post-decision situations and instead can be observed "every time a person says something he doesn't believe, or does something stupid or immoral" (Aronson, 1972, p. 109).

Aronson (1968, 1969) contributed one of the most useful and important "reformulations" or "theoretical refinements" to the field of cognitive dissonance. In essence, Aronson believed dissonance is produced, not by the existence of two or more inconsistent cognitions, but rather by inconsistency between an individual's behavior and self-concept. Aronson (1972) wrote, "dissonance theory makes its clearest and strongest predictions in those situations in which the dissonance is a function of a person's behavior that violates his own self-concept" (p. 138).

TRANSFORMATION FROM CIVILIAN TO SOLDIER SELF-CONCEPT AND JUSTIFICATION

Discourse regarding the development and alteration of self-concept in the context of combat that would be indicative of cognitive dissonance is limited and must be extrapolated from descriptive and theoretical statements. For example, Hendin and Hass (1984, p. 171), noted that combat veterans with PTSD "have often been so transformed by their combat experiences that they have difficulty in reconciling who they were with what they become" (p. 171). Tick (1987) agreed with the idea that self-concept is equivalent to one's behavior and for combat veterans the horror of war becomes the self. He eloquently stated, "the self during Vietnam was overwhelmed with horror, now it is horror. . . . not merely seeing horror in the outside world, not merely witnessing its occurrence, but embodying it as the essential quality of self" (Tick, 1987, p. 105). Statements such as these raise questions about the processes involved in the development of such disharmony in the combat veteran's concept of self. As early as 1974, Shatan spoke of a "perceptual dissonance" between the reality of civilization and the reality of the soldier's environment, filled with death and destruction. Although he did not speak of cognitive dissonance, he clearly identified a corresponding change in character or self-concept associated with passage "through the membrane of reality." He wrote:

> When the "induction phase" of counterguerilla training succeeds, the soldier patterns himself after his persecutors (his officers) and undergoes a psychological regression during which his character is restructured into a combat personality. . . . The trainee surrenders his personal identity to the corporate identity of his military legion. He adopts the paranoid stance of combat as his mode of being-in-the-world, as his new "reality principle." The world of military reality eclipses the world of civilian reality. His perception of events—his styles of cognition, affect, and action—are utterly changed. (Shatan, 1974, p. 10)

Williams (1983) briefly considered Aronson's extension of dissonance theory in her discussion of the self-concept of Vietnam veterans. She questioned how a pre-war concept of self as "decent, good, reasonable and fair" could be integrated with a post-war concept of self involving the killing of other human beings. Traditionally, the killing of other human beings, particularly during war, has been justified. Consequently, such actions are not contradictory to a self-concept of "decent, good, reasonable, and fair", at least not while the war is being prosecuted. For example, Kelman (1973) wrote that the occurrence of violence as self-defense against attack or the threat of attack is the most widely accepted justification. Furthermore, this justification can be extended to an international level when individual nations are attacked or their interests are threatened. On a national level, World Wars I and II were justified. While individual combatants may have questioned the justification for individual acts committed, the country did not. The easiest way for them to resolve the conflict was by saying, "If my country believes I did the right thing, then I must be a good person because I did what my country wanted."

What was different about the war in Vietnam is that the country decided a mistake had been made, our involvement did not meet the criteria for war, and therefore everything that took place in the context of that war was unjustified. This change in perception, which essentially eliminates all justification for killing, except perhaps to preserve one's life, is what makes reconciling the conflict between a positive self-concept and the killing of other human beings difficult, if not impossible. In essence, *during the Vietnam war the stage was set for the development, rather than the amelioration, of a discrepancy in self-concept within combatants lacking justification for their actions on a national level.*

Arousal of Dissonance During Combat

According to dissonance theory, the necessary elements or critical ingredients for inducing dissonance and influencing attitude change are choice, foreseeability, and responsibility (See Table 15.1). In other words, "dissonance is aroused only when the person is responsible for the decision. Dissonance-arousing consequences of the decision must have been chosen freely and either have been foreseen or be attributable to a central aspect of oneself" (West & Wicklund, 1980, p. 79). If the combat situation is examined with respect to these critical ingredients, what is discovered is that the design of warfare is actually antithetical to the arousal of cognitive dissonance.

Kelman (1973) identified three processes characteristic of the military combat environment that absolve individuals from the dissonance producing ingredients of choice, foreseeability, and responsibility. These processes are *authorization, routinization,* and *dehumanization.* According to Kelman, the moral principles that govern human behavior do not apply in authority situations. "When acts of violence are explicitly ordered, implicitly encouraged, tacitly approved, or at least permitted by legitimate authorities, people's readiness to commit or condone them is considerably enhanced" (p. 38). The authorization for such acts precludes the need for making judgements or choices. As a result the individual does not feel personally responsible for the consequences. Kelman further stated that via authorization, "the person becomes involved in an action without considering the implications of that action" (Kelman, 1973, p. 46). Thus, authorization reduces or eliminates all three ingredients of choice, foreseeability, and responsibility.

The second process of routinization is the execution of behaviors in a routine, mechanical, highly programmed fashion.

TABLE 15.1
Dissonance Arousal or Reduction According to Military Status

Military Status	Dissonance Arousal	Dissonance Reduction
Soldier	Choice	Authorization
	Foreseeability	Routinization Dehumanization of self or victim
	Responsibility	Positive attitude toward killing Denial
Civilian	Unavailability of authorization, routinization, dehumanization	Decreasing dissonant cognitions
	Reevaluation of choice, foreseeability, and responsibility	Increasing consonant cognitions
	Societal rejection	
	Failure to attain goal	

According to Kelman, routinization reinforces authorization because the individual maintains complete focused concentration on the task and avoids consideration of the moral implications of the actions being carried out. Secondly, because the task is performed in an automatic and stereotyped manner the decision making and questioning process is bypassed (Kelman, 1973).

Because strong inhibitions exist against killing other human beings, Kelman suggested that authorization and routinization are insufficient by themselves and the third process of dehumanization is necessary. He explained that moral principles do not apply to non-humans. Therefore, if killing is to proceed in a smooth and orderly fashion, victims must be deprived of their human status (Kelman, 1973).

Thus, the arousal of dissonance requires choice, foreseeability, and responsibility. The likelihood of dissonance arousal during active combat duty is significantly reduced via the processes of authorization, routinization, and dehumanization. If dissonance is aroused, however, the findings of studies in the dissonance literature indicate dissonance can be reduced via derogation of the victim.

Reduction of Dissonance During Combat

Early studies (Davis & Jones, 1960; Glass, 1964) in the field of dissonance that examined the relationship between engaging in cruel, immoral, or aggressive behavior and subsequent dissonance reduction, found that in situations in which an individual is induced to inflict harm upon another, dissonance reduction was accomplished via derogation of the victim. In other words, to justify their behavior perpetrators alter their view of the victim and the victim is seen as evil, dirty, and bad; someone deserving of punishment. Aronson (1972, p. 129) further speculated that less is needed to derogate the victim "if the victim is able and willing to retaliate." However, the results of one study by Michael Kahn (cited in Aronson, 1972) suggested that when combatants become victims and subsequently retaliate, they are likely to engage in overkill. After retaliation they justify the overkill by derogating the victim. Thus derogation can occur following aggression if the aggression extended to overkill. Derogation occurs prior to aggression in order to justify the upcoming aggression. According to Eisenhart (1975), derogation or dehumanization was an integral part of boot camp. "The terms 'gook' and 'slope' were continually used by training personnel as well as in written material and movies" (p. 18).

An important relationship exists between self-concept or self-esteem and derogation or dehumanization. According to Aronson (1972), individuals with high self-esteem are more likely to engage in derogation than individuals with low self-esteem. For individuals with low self-esteem, their behavior is not as incompatible with their self-concept so they have less need to derogate their victims. Wicklund and Brehm (1976) also have addressed this issue. In the case of high self-esteem, they pointed out that aggressive behavior would be highly discrepant with a positive self-concept and would result in dissonance arousal. Derogation of the victim would reduce dissonance arousal by bringing their perception of the other person in line with their behavior. In situations where barriers to derogation exist, for example the killing of innocent civilians, women and children, dissonance would be reduced by increasing feelings of dislike and hostility toward the self thereby bringing their self-concept in line with behavior. Thus, Wicklund and Brehm (1976), predicted that "the greater the person's self-esteem or the more favorable his self-evaluation, the more he will show aggression against the self when he commits a discrepant act of aggression" (p. 210).

Other Methods of Dissonance Reduction During Combat

Despite the effectiveness of the processes of authorization, routinization, and dehumanization, for most Vietnam combat veterans moments occurred during their tour when they questioned what they were doing and this questioning aroused dissonance. To continue functioning, this dissonance had to be reduced. The traditional mode of dissonance reduction involves changing the original attitude into one favoring the new behavior. A positive attitude toward engaging in immoral acts may develop for example, by adopting the belief that killing is enjoyable. In general, one's attitude toward aggression or immoral action becomes more lenient in order to justify the behavior (Aronson, 1972). Maybe the individuals described above, who have low self-esteem and are less likely to engage in derogation, are the ones who most easily adopt a positive view toward killing to reduce dissonance. Several anecdotal reports of this phenomenon have been described such as the following case reported by Langner (1971).

> The most startling aspect of Bob's case, however, was not simply that he had been capable of involving himself in a massacre but that he had enjoyed doing so. For mixed with his feelings of guilt and sorrow, which were real and deep, were unmistakable indications of the fascination and even pleasure he had derived from the mayhem he had witnessed and participated in. This was the deepest source of his guilt—that he had derived pleasure from his crimes. (p. 951)

In this situation, dehumanization is of the combatant rather than dehumanization of the victim. This is a process that develops gradually over time as the result of victimization. The dehumanization of the victimizer negates moral actions and conversely allows the experience of pleasure in the act of killing to occur (Kelman, 1973).

The following case reported by Brende and Benedict (1980) demonstrates the corresponding negative change in self-concept that occurs with dehumanization of the victimizer, the development of the two irreconcilable identities which Hendin and Haas (1984) spoke of, and Brende and Benedict refer to as an "identity split." Additionally, this case also presents a clear description of the subsequent reexperiencing symptomatology that develops as a result of the "identity split."

> The process of identification with the aggressors led to further alienation from the part of himself that experienced pain and helplessness, without which he could become dehumanized and could more easily dehumanize the Vietnamese. He suppressed his prior value system and slipped into the role of a "killer." He described with considerable guilt the fact that he had come to get pleasure out of killing so that following his discharge from military service, he had come close to accepting a job as a "hit man" for organized crime. The evolving change in his identity

had led him into an identity "split" between the "killer" and the healthy, protective "leader," both of which had been idealized by his peers. Ultimately, the "killer" part came into direct conflict with the protective part at the time when he found that he had accidently killed 34 school children. It was after that killing that he developed serious problems, including at least one dissociative episode when it was reported by a friend who had observed him that he was killing Viet Cong soldiers and laughing hysterically, although having complete amnesia for that episode at a later time. The presence of the "split" within him seemed related to his beginning and excessive reliance on alcohol and drugs as an attempt to suppress the conflict; he withdrew emotionally as he developed amnesia for the last five months of Vietnam. The subliminal awareness of the apparent dissociated "killer" part led to his statement during therapy: "I feel like there's a demon inside of me and I'm afraid it will break loose." (Brende & Benedict, 1980, p. 38).

The development of amnesia described in the above case, may be an extreme example of another method of dissonance reduction, that of denial. Amnesia is also a central symptom of the Dissociative Disorders, elements of which are common in combat trauma victims (see Chapter 5). Brehm (1967) stated that "this should be rare since it involves a distortion of reality, but it might occur in clinical settings" (p. 72). In the guerrilla warfare of Vietnam, often the enemy was invisible and combatants had no way of confirming an actual kill. This may have contributed to an individual's belief that another life had not been taken. The processes of authorization, routinization, dehumanization, adoption of a positive view toward killing, and denial, all serve to inhibit the induction of dissonance or eliminate it if it does arise during combat.

In summary, the discrepancy between the pre- and post-war self-concept of Vietnam veterans with PTSD has gained agreement with anecdotal support. The roots of this discrepancy are born in the transformation from civilian to soldier. From a social psychological perspective, the suggestion is that the withdrawal of justification for killing and other immoral actions that occurred in the context of the Vietnam war was the primary source of the pre- and post-war split in self-concept. During combat, the arousal of dissonance is lessened due to the processes of authorization, routinization and dehumanization. If dissonance does arise, it can be reduced via derogation of the victim or self-dehumanization. Denial is another possible method of dissonance reduction. The self-esteem of the combatant is an important variable in determining which mode of dissonance reduction occurs. Self-dehumanization may be reflected in the adoption of a positive attitude toward killing. Thus, dissonance reduction involving derogation of one's self may explain in part how the change in pre- and post-war self-concept evolved. Factors associated with the transformation from soldier to civilian will be explored next.

TRANSFORMATION FROM SOLDIER TO CIVILIAN

At what point do the processes of authorization, routinization and dehumanization become ineffective in blocking an individual's moral sensibilities? Theoretically, this could have occurred at different times for different individuals, depending on their individual experience. For some it may not have occurred at all, for others it may have occurred in boot camp, or upon first contact with the enemy, or after a buddy was killed, or months or years after return to "the world", or all of the above. Maybe the further removed one becomes from military acting, thinking, and feeling (i.e., after discharge and return to civilian status), the more dissonant one's actions during combat are perceived to be. Certainly these three processes are no longer available to the same extent after discharge from military service. Bourne (1970) speculated that the incidence of psychiatric breakdown in Vietnam returnees would peak after separation from service. Stretch (1986) hypothesized that "veterans who maintained a military affiliation most likely received more positive social support from friends and peers for their role in the war than did veterans who returned directly to the civilian community" (p. 158). He compared the prevalence of PTSD among Vietnam veteran civilians, reservists and active duty Army personnel and found the rates to be 18 to 54%, 10.9%, and 5.1%, respectively. Amen (1985) reported the case of a military veteran whose symptoms increased when he was discharged from the service, and then decreased when he reenlisted, and subsequently increased when he retired. Finally, Deeken and Bridenbaugh (1987) found no difference in the report of depression and nightmares between Vietnam veterans who had a history of extended active service (i.e., active duty or retired) and nonveteran outpatients.

Logically one can conclude then, that for veterans with PTSD, dissonance was aroused when the three processes of authorization, routinization, and dehumanization became *ineffective*. With the removal of these "military blinders" veterans gradually became aware that their actions during their military service were morally wrong and in opposition to their pre-war self-concept of "decent, good, reasonable, and fair." The suggestion is that this process is more likely to occur the further removed one is from the military. In other words, the transformation of the Vietnam combat veteran from soldier to civilian brings to light discrepancies between self-concept and behavior resulting in dissonance arousal.

Arousal of Dissonance Post-combat

In the minds of many of the young men who left their homes and families to serve their country in Vietnam—it was the only "right" thing to do. For some it was a family tradition, their fathers and grandfathers had served before them; for others, it was male role models such as John Wayne who reinforced the belief that a sign of manhood was bravery and courage in the face of battle; and then the infamous words of John F. Kennedy "Ask not what your country can do for you. Ask what you can do for your country."

According to Aronson (1972), being right is a basic underlying motivation of human behavior. Questions and controversy over U.S. presence in Vietnam began long before the war was ended and continue to this day. The consensus has been that the war was wrong. Perceptions of the war have been confused with the perceptions of the combat veteran. This has led veterans to be unwelcome in their own homes, communities, and country. Dissonance has inevitably been aroused when veterans grapple with their belief that they were doing the "right thing" and the fact that they engaged in actions which were subsequently considered immoral and unjustified. Are they noble warriors or murderers?

Five, ten, fifteen years after the war, as veterans view their experience from a different, perhaps wiser and less innocent perspective; the issues of choice, foreseeability, and responsibility are reevaluated and the potential for the arousal of cognitive dissonance increases. While at the time no choice seemed to be available, in retrospect their participation was voluntary (the majority enlisted), alternatives existed such as seeking refuge in Canada. Regardless of whether they were drafted or enlisted, a choice existed and ultimately they are responsible for their actions as a result of their choice.

Besides the realization that occurred for many combat veterans—that a choice existed and they are responsible for their actions—another major source of dissonance is the fact that the war was lost and many officials in high places knew the war would not be won and allowed it to continue unnecessarily. In looking back at the history of Vietnam one has difficulty imagining how victory could have been expected. The primary goal of war is to defeat the enemy. The North Vietnamese have never been defeated, so in retrospect, the conclusion by some was that the outcome of the war was foreseeable. An undisputed finding in the area of cognitive dissonance has been the observation that the more effort expended in attaining a goal the more valued and attractive that goal will be (Aronson, 1961). Failed efforts to attain the goal is another source of dissonance according to Aronson (1961); "his cognition that he exerted effort to attain the goal is dissonant with his cognition that he did not reach it" (p. 378).

In the post-Vietnam war period (and perhaps earlier) many sources of dissonance arousal occurred such as questioning the rightness of one's actions, retrospectively creating choice, foreseeability and responsibility, as well as failing to achieve a highly valued goal. Can the conflict between one's self-perception, of being a "good, decent, reasonable and fair person," and one's behavior of engagement in the taking of other human lives or other immoral actions be resolved? Can the conflict between risking one's own life and witnessing the lives of others being sacrificed for a valued goal, and the realization that the goal was never realistic or attainable, be resolved?

Reduction of Dissonance Post-combat

The process by which dissonance is reduced or resolved has been a major focus of researchers and a variety of modes of dissonance reduction have been explored in reviews of this subject (Aronson, 1978; Brehm, 1967; West & Wicklund, 1980; Wicklund & Brehm, 1976). In general, reducing dissonant cognitions or adding consonant cognitions will decrease dissonance (Aronson, 1978; West & Wicklund, 1980; Wicklund & Brehm, 1976). Predictions regarding the mode of dissonance reduction that will be utilized are based on the proposition that "some cognitions are more resistant to change than others, and the method used to reduce dissonance will use the least resistant cognitions" (West & Wicklund, 1980, p. 77). Interestingly, no evidence has been obtained to suggest the existence of situations in which dissonance cannot be reduced. However, the majority of published reports do not address serious/moral decisions and behaviors (e.g., abortion, extramarital affair, participation in war) that could result in lasting conflicts for individuals.

The statement "I did the right thing, I am proud to have served my country in Vietnam, I didn't run away like those draft dodgers" is an example of adding consonant cognitions to reduce dissonance. Difficulty may be encountered in the future in maintaining this cognition unwaveringly in the face of general opinion that the war was wrong and by association the veteran was wrong. An example of reducing dissonant cognitions is the statement "I was a naive kid, I didn't know any better, I was a pawn of the government, I was used." While this may have been true at the time, it may be difficult to maintain this cognition now that the individual is no longer innocent and naive.

Aronson (1978) stated that another way an individual reduces dissonance is by "convincing himself that the goal was not worth it anyway" (p. 197). This seems plausible if the goal is winning a football game and all that is lost is the game. In Vietnam, not only was the war lost, but so were 58,000 lives. By devaluing the purpose of the war, the sacrifices of those individuals who lost their lives are devalued (i.e., they died for nothing), and one's individual participation is devalued. Maintaining a belief that one is right and is a "good, decent, reasonable and fair person" becomes impossible if such devaluation occurs.

In summary, one can imagine repeated attempts at dissonance reduction and their subsequent failure. However, this is pure speculation as no empirical studies have been conducted examining dissonance reduction among veterans post-combat. The question arises as to whether or not dissonance can be temporarily or permanently reduced in these ways.

REEXPERIENCING FROM A DISSONANCE PERSPECTIVE

The parallels between cognitive dissonance and PTSD are striking. Both are associated with a state of discomfort, referred to as arousal in dissonance terminology and anxiety in PTSD. When comparing psychoanalytic conceptualizations of PTSD, which discuss splits within the self or identity, with the proposed discrepancy between self-concept and behavior described in dissonance theory, the parallels are obvious. Moreover, dissonance theory rests on the fact that a strong motivation is present to reduce dissonance, to reduce the discrepancy in self-concept. A similar intrinsic motivation is implied by psychoanalytic theorists who propose that reexperiencing symptomatology is the manifestation of this attempt, albeit unsuccessful, at integration. Horowitz' schema updating and completion principle bares a strong resemblance as well. And in fact, he compared the tendency to completion to Festinger's motivation to reduce dissonance (Horowitz, 1986).

The soldier at nineteen is very different from the veteran at thirty or forty. The process of maturation seems to play an important role; as one becomes less egocentric, the ability to critically reexamine one's past actions becomes important in guiding future actions. The desire is to not repeat the mistakes of the past. The process of self-actualization in human beings requires that one accept responsibility for one's self and actions, and that one aligns behavior according to moral values. Perhaps this task cannot be carried out until post-combat dissonance is reduced.

The proposition is that the motivation to resolve trauma related conflicts acts as a catalyst for the expression of reexperiencing symptomatology which mirrors the unresolved dissonance. Intrusive images, thoughts, memories, nightmares, and dissociative episodes represent the attempt to reconcile the conflicting sides of the self. Since the original justifications for participation in the war in Vietnam are no longer available, a new means of dissonance reduction must be found. Aronson (1978, p. 197) suggested that another way an individual may reduce dissonance is by finding "something else in the situation to which he can attach value in order to justify his expenditure of effort without achieving his avowed goal." What Aronson's statement seems to suggest if applied to the context of the Vietnam experience, is that *finding personal meaning in the experience of war, meaning that allows one to believe that what one did served some purpose and had some value, and most importantly, meaning that allows one to regain and maintain a positive self-image, would reduce dissonance and would reduce the reexperiencing symptoms that symbolize the conflict.* How such meaning can be found is discussed in the next section.

EXISTENTIAL PERSPECTIVE

Bleich, Garb, and Kottler (1986) have commented on the fact that theoretical approaches to combat-related PTSD "miss the existential aspect" (p. 495). Current theories of PTSD also appear to miss the reexperiencing aspect (Peralme, 1991) despite its designation as the hallmark of the disorder. A clearer picture of reexperiencing may emerge upon examination of PTSD within an existential framework. This section will discuss existential psychology and its relationship to traumatic events, the relationship between adaptation, meaning and values in combat-related PTSD, and the relationship between meaning and reexperiencing.

Existential Psychology and Traumatic Events

Existential psychology views the establishment of meaning as the primary endeavor of human beings. Meaning may be the very essence of human existence. The need for meaning has been found at all levels of human functioning from the neurological level to the social level. As an example of the creation of meaning at the level of perceptual organization, the existential theorists May and Yalom (1984) cited the well-established findings that when presented with a pattern of random stimuli, humans automatically organize it into figure and ground, and when presented with a broken circle, it is automatically perceived as complete. Thus, the need for meaning and its creation may explain a wide range of behaviors, from the very simple to the complex.

At a more complex level of human behavior, Taylor (1989) addressed the need for meaning in the face of traumatic life experiences. She explained that following a victimizing experience a search for meaning occurs which may involve answering the question of why the event happened, finding something positive in the experience, and/or reevaluating the purpose of one's life. She emphasized that this process not only helps individuals readjust and heal, but it may facilitate their growth beyond the limits they may have attained in the absence of the traumatic experience and motivate them to restructure their lives in a more meaningful way. She pointed out that for some individuals, the search for meaning is not successful, "some who struggle with the question of finding meaning never find any. Exactly who these people are and which events are less likely to yield a successful search for meaning remain questions to be answered" (Taylor, 1989, p. 197). Perhaps war is such an event, and combat veterans with PTSD may be a group for whom meaning remains painfully elusive.

Of the primary factors thought to be instrumental in the etiology of PTSD (Rundell, Ursano, Holloway, & Silberman, 1989), individual subjective perception and meaning is the only one that is both modifiable and potentially under the control of the individual. For this reason, exploring the role and significance of meaning in the lives of Vietnam veterans is imperative, particularly with respect to their combat experience, and the relationship of meaning to trauma and reexperiencing symptomatology.

Adaptation and Meaning

Yalom (1981) identified meaninglessness as one of the four ultimate concerns resulting in conflict for individuals in their existence. The process of discovering or creating meaning from experiences in Vietnam appears to have been impeded for many combat veterans. What happens when meaning is difficult to establish or cannot be found? According to May and Yalom (1984), "when any situation or set of stimuli defies patterning we experience dysphoria which persists until we fit the situation into a recognizable pattern" (p. 370). The chronicity of the state of chaos and dysphoria that has existed for many Vietnam combat veterans has had a detrimental effect upon their adaptation and adjustment.

According to Fairbank and Brown (1987), adjustment to catastrophic events can be conceptualized as a continuum along which the individual psychological reactions of trauma victims fall (See Figure 15.1). At one extreme of the continuum is psychological growth, in other words a positive adjustment has been made to the traumatic event and the individual is psychologically healthier as a result of the experience. This is similar to Taylor's findings mentioned earlier. At the opposite end of the continuum, psychological reactions representing a poor adaptation are found. As Fairbank and Brown noted, "some survivors never seem to recover to their pretrauma level of functioning" (1987, p. 57). At the furthest extreme, lie those who fail to adapt and do not survive.

If meaning is a critical variable in the adjustment process, it too may vary along this continuum (See Figure 15.1). Parson (1986) added that those who exhibit poor adaptation have "a perpetual sense that nothing matters" (p. 19). Parson (1986) added that "basically, this sense of self and world derives from a 'devitalized' meaning system stemming from war and postwar experiences and conflicts yet unsolved" (p. 19). Those who have adapted well, and have experienced psychological growth as a result of their experience, exhibit a vital meaning system. This viewpoint suggests that until meaning can be established, engagement in life will not occur and deterioration in functioning will ensue (May, 1974).

In Lifton's (1973) psychoformative theory, he distinguished between the formative process of mental function and the desensitizing process of psychic numbing. The centralizing point of this theory is that humans "can never simply receive a bit of information nakedly. The process of perception is vitally bound up with the process of inner recreation, in which one utilizes whatever forms are available in individual psychic

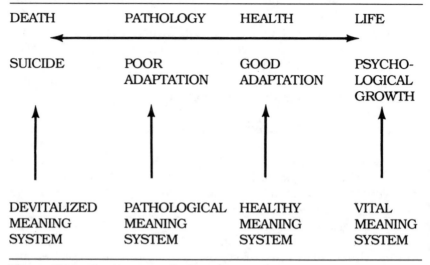

DEATH	PATHOLOGY	HEALTH	LIFE

SUICIDE	POOR ADAPTATION	GOOD ADAPTATION	PSYCHO-LOGICAL GROWTH

DEVITALIZED MEANING SYSTEM	PATHOLOGICAL MEANING SYSTEM	HEALTHY MEANING SYSTEM	VITAL MEANING SYSTEM

Figure 15.1. Continuum of adaptation and meaning.

existence" (p. 4). This is comparable to the proposition of May and Yalom (1984) regarding the automatic creation of meaning from one's experience. In this book the argument has been that the schema of the person represents the meaning-making organizer of one's experiences.

Traumatic events short-circuit the formative process, and result in psychic numbing, "an incapacity to feel or to confront certain kinds of experience, due to the blocking or absence of inner forms or imagery that can connect with such experience" (Lifton, 1973, p. 4). This form of desensitization creates a roadblock to meaning. According to Lifton, the appearance of psychic numbing suggests the termination of the formative process or what he referred to as the process of creating viable inner forms. In other words, an impairment exists in the most essential mental function of symbol formation or symbolization necessary for the establishment of meaning.

The discussion in the previous section regarding the ability of the processes of authorization, routinization and dehumanization to inhibit the arousal of dissonance during combat suggests that "blocking" of the psychoformative process is actually incorporated into warfare training and is necessary for survival. Feeling, thinking, and making sense of things is discouraged and the unquestionable obeying of orders is encouraged (Clewell, 1987; Eisenhart, 1975; Kelman, 1973). Anecdotal reports of how combatants helped one another "cope" with the tragedies of war, such as the loss of a fellow comrade, portray one combatant saying to another "It don't mean nothin' man, it don't mean nothin'."

While short-circuiting the "formative process" during combat is necessary for survival, veterans with PTSD continue to operate in this survival mode years after their war experience. Via psychic numbing, their ability to symbolize and find meaning in their lives is impaired. According to Parson (1986), the absence of a vital meaning system accounts for the "death equivalents of powerlessness, isolation, emptiness, and apathy observed in many Vietnam veterans" (p. 19).

Adaptation and Values

A significant part of this deteriorative process is the loss of a value system. According to May and Yalom (1984) a direct relationship exists between the meaning system and values; a hierarchy of values is generated from one's meaning system. "Values provide us with a blueprint for life conduct; values tell us not only why we live but how to live" (May & Yalom, 1984, p. 370). Thus, if one's meaning system is shattered, a destruction will occur of the value system as well. The following quote from a veteran is a poignant example of life without meaning and values:

> I don't know what is right, or who is right. My own values got shot out of me in the Nam; and I lost faith in people and in society. I don't seem to believe in anybody. I used to go to church before Vietnam; now I don't go anymore. I do have a lovely family—a delightful wife and a son. I feel for them. I am unable to give my son values, because I don't have any for myself. So, I just fake it. But how do you fake values? You can't. You either have them or you don't. I just keep on having these morbid thoughts about death all the time. I seem to be more dying than living. What is the purpose of life? With the death of my

four good buddies in Vietnam, I wanted to join them. I just didn't care anymore. Maybe I still feel that way; I don't know. This scares me; it scares my wife. I just don't seem to give a damn about anything: I mean about anything, man. (Parson, 1986, p. 19-20)

According to McKay, Davis, and Fanning (1981), moral values provide guidelines for distinguishing between right and wrong, for making judgements of moral responsibility, and engaging in ethical behavior such as being honest, keeping agreements, and not harming others. They stated further that, "the only real test of your values is whether you act on them" (McKay et al., 1981, p. 175). Actions are unchangeable and reflect your commitment to your beliefs. "Actions are real in a way that opinions and statements are not. Your actions define your immutable history" (McKay et al., 1981, p. 175).

For the young men who went to fight in Vietnam, the values of freedom and courage were foremost and overrode moral inhibitions against injuring others. For the remainder of their lives they are faced (through reexperiencing) with actions and experiences that are unchangeable. For example, Clewell noted that in war the veil of innocence is stripped away, one's capability to destroy can no longer be denied, and the soldier "may be horrified to discover the self-righteousness such malevolent action seems to produce. Killing can be a psychological 'high,' flying in the face of a person's value system . . . . [and] this knowledge creates intense moral pain" (1987, p. 117).

How can a moral value system be maintained in the face of knowledge that one has engaged in behavior that is in violation of those values and that similar actions could be repeated in the future? What meaning and usefulness would such a value system have? Where can the individual in moral pain turn for answers to such questions?

According to Wick (1985), the issue of values falls in the "no-man's-land between psyche and soul"; neither the psychotherapist nor the clergy have been willing to incorporate this issue into their work. The danger of this is that "serious value problems readily turn into existential problems and, without help, present or ensuing experiences of despair tend to be followed by destructive actions" (Wick, 1985, p. 13). As an example of this "no-man's-land", Wick presented the case of John, a Vietnam veteran, who "after his experience with the pastoral and the mental health professionals . . . vowed never to see a priest or a psychotherapist again" (1985, p. 14).

During his tour, John sought out advice from a chaplain when the pain from the conflict between his values and his behavior and the war in general became intolerable. The chaplain told him to "Kill as many as you can," (Wick, 1985, p. 15). After he returned home his moral pain continued and a psychiatrist referred him to a priest who told him he had previously dealt with felons and murderers, but never with anybody who had killed more than two people. "You are a mass murderer. I cannot help you. You have to get professional help" (Wick, 1985, p. 16). The priest sent him back to the psychiatrist. Wick explained that John was reared with the belief that killing was bad. However, in the military this behavior was justified and considered good. After his return, the values changed again and he was considered a murderer (Wick, 1985).

Adaptation and Antinomy

The institution and subsequent revocation of the authorization to destroy and kill and the traitorous reinterpretation of brave and courageous behavior as sin has been discussed by Denton (1989) and Mahedy (1983) as well. According to Wick, the psychological conflict that arises within the veteran is a "moral antinomy." The definition of antinomy is very similar to the definition of cognitive dissonance discussed previously. **Antinomy** is a legal term referring to a paradox created by, a contradiction in the law (e.g., use of coercion to enforce democracy), or between two equally binding laws or principles, or by an authoritative contradiction (e.g., two priests within the same church). It also arises when there is an authority-change, either suddenly or over time in values that were thought to be stable (e.g., abortion is murder, then is legal; killing in war is moral, then is immoral). Wick (1985) explained that a moral antinomy may have little or no effect on one's value system "if the value discrepancy is judged to be trivial and of no existential relevance", or it may result in a complete collapse of one's value system "if the value clashes are perceived as major and if the person has a major existential investment in the value(s) involved" (p. 18).

In summary, a no-man's land exists, a state of conflict devoid of meaning and values, that combat veterans like John have fallen into. Both clergy and psychotherapists have been ill-equipped to adequately address the needs of clients with moral value problems. The difficulty in dealing with these issues arises from the fact that such problems have not been well defined and are therefore difficult to integrate into religious and psychological frameworks (Wick, 1985). This inadequacy erects a roadblock to the search for meaning and the reestablishment of a value system.

According to Marin (1981), instead of confronting this inadequacy we cover it up with lies. One way this is done is by manipulating language. For example, Kelman (1973) pointed out that although individuals in Vietnam knew what they were doing, euphemisms such as "protective reaction," "pacification," and "forced urbanization and modernization," allowed them to "avoid confrontation" with the "true meaning" of their actions (p. 48). Marin (1981) also commented on the use of language as a tool to obscure rather than clarify.

> One notices again and again the ways in which various phrases and terms are used to empty the vets' experience of moral content, to defuse and bowdlerize it. Particularly in the early literature, one feels a kind of madness at work. Repugnance toward killing and the refusal to kill are routinely called 'acute combat reaction,' and the effects of slaughter and atrocity are called 'stress,' as if the clinicians describing the vets are talking about an executive's overwork or a hysterical housewife's blood pressure. Nowhere in the literature is one allowed to glimpse what is actually occurring: the real horror of the war and its effect on those who fought it. (p. 72)

Marin took this issue a step further and argued that the sequelae of Vietnam has been encompassed and defined as a psychological disorder, a very narrowing perspective, which eliminates or extricates much of the meaning from the experience. In agreement with Marin, Mahedy (1983) stated "By now their rage, moral pain and loss of faith have been almost completely contained within the psychiatric construct 'post-traumatic stress disorder'" (p. 65).

In summary, the roadblock to meaning that veterans with combat-related PTSD face, begins with psychic numbing, which Lifton (1973) described as "a process of desymbolization and deformation" (p. 10). In this process, the original moral value system is shattered and replaced with a new value system in which killing is justified. After the war, moral antinomy occurs when this new value system is no longer supported by authority. The previous value system cannot be readopted because of the irrevocable actions during war. Although psychic numbing continues post-war, combat veterans struggle in vain to make sense and find meaning because as human beings this is what they are naturally inclined to do. But as Wick and others (Clewell, 1987) pointed out, often no person or place is available, to turn to, to answer the moral questions that arise in this process. Their experience is reduced to a psychological disorder.

The proposal here is that the reexperiencing symptomatology characteristic of PTSD is the manifestation of this ongoing and relentless struggle to make sense of one's experiences, to resolve the moral antinomy and to establish a moral value system. The reexperiencing symptomatology characteristic of PTSD may reflect the inherent need for actualization of the formative process. Clearly without meaning no goal, purpose, or direction exists in life. For veterans with PTSD, the goal, purpose, and direction in life becomes finding meaning. According to Frankl (1984), "suffering ceases to be suffering at the moment it finds a meaning" (p. 117). How can that meaning be found or created?

MEANING AND REEXPERIENCING

Clewell (1987, p. 125) stated that "to go on with life, the combatant must come to a recognition of some meaning and purpose from the traumatic stresses of warfare." But how can this recognition be achieved? According to Heimberg (1985), "the very cruelty of war is the randomness with which it impacts upon the innocent bystander" (p. 417). For many

Vietnam veterans, the experience of war still does not fit into a "recognizable pattern"; they are left in a maze of endless circles, trying to make sense out of chaos. Carlson and Hocking's (1988) statement about the national Vietnam War Memorial reflects simultaneously, the universality and the individuality of this struggle for meaning:

> The Memorial makes a compelling, though ambiguous, statement about the war. The seemingly endless list of the dead, rising on a granite wall from a gash cut in the ground, conveys the idea that something terribly wrong has happened. Thousands of people have died in a war; what did they die for, what does it mean? The Memorial refuses to answer the questions it raises. It thus calls out to the visitor to create his or her own answers. (pp. 206-207)

Thus, unlike other national memorials or symbols, such as the Flag, the Statue of Liberty, or the Liberty Bell, the meaning of the Vietnam memorial is not revealed. Paradoxically, it may symbolize the meaninglessness of war more than anything else.

Trying to make sense of "WAR", trying to find meaning and purpose in "WAR" may very well be a fruitless pursuit, if not an impossible pursuit. However, the important point is that neither war nor combat per se is what is traumatic, but rather the specific discrete events that occur in combat (Keane, 1985). Moreover, the individual's unique subjective perception of the specific traumatic events leads to symptom formation and the development of PTSD or a positive adjustment and psychological growth (Breslau & Davis, 1987; Heimberg, 1985; Hendin, Pollinger, Singer, & Ulman, 1981; Krystal, 1984; Rundell et al., 1989).

In other words, two individuals, exposed to the same traumatic event, may have very different emotional and psychological reactions to the event as a result of their unique individual perceptions and meaning systems (Hendin et al., 1981). In sum, one person may be traumatized and the other may be able to cope effectively depending on each person's unique interpretations of the event. Rather than searching for the meaning of "WAR" from a global perspective, a more important goal would be to search for meaning associated with personal experiences occurring within the context of war. Although many have acknowledged the importance of meaning in resolving traumatic conflicts, few have actually elaborated upon what meaning can be found in the traumatic combat experiences of veterans (Carlson & Hocking, 1988; Hendin et al., 1981). Meaning remains at a very abstract conceptual level. *The clues to the meaning of those personal experiences can be found in the reexperiencing symptomatology of PTSD.* Reexperiencing symptomatology are generally viewed as unwanted, persistent, disturbing remnants of a traumatic experience that need to be eliminated. However, another view of reexperiencing symptomatology is that of an active, adaptive process of meaning creation. The suggestion has been (Williams, 1983; Wilmer, 1982a, 1982b, 1986a, 1986b) that reexperiencing of trauma is an adaptive mechanism that can lead to resolution of the psychic trauma and healing of emotional wounds. The process by which this occurs involves finding meaning in the experience (Hendin & Haas, 1984). The intrusive thoughts and images, nightmares, and reliving in the form of flashbacks or dissociated states of consciousness are a living record. As unwanted and painful as they may be, they contain the meaning of events that have shattered central organizing fantasies (Ulman & Brothers, 1988), that undergo repeated representations in active memory (Horowitz, 1986), that maintain a potentiation of the threat arousal node in the cognitive network (Chemtob, Roitblat, Hamada, Carlson, & Twentyman, 1988) and result in cognitive dissonance that defies reduction. Clinical efforts at immediate suppression and elimination of reexperiencing symptoms (e.g., via pharmacotherapy, flooding, desensitization), without first understanding their purpose based on a sound theoretical model, may be a disservice comparable to simplifying the horror of war to a psychological disorder.

REFERENCES

Aronson, E. (1961). The effect of effort on the attractiveness of rewarded and unrewarded stimuli. *Journal of Abnormal and Social Psychology, 63,* 375-380.

Aronson, E. (1968). Dissonance theory: Progress and problems. In R. P. Abelson, E. Aronson, W. J. McGuire, T. M. Newcomb, M. J. Rosenberg, & P. H. Tannenbaum (Eds.), *Theories of cognitive consistency: A sourcebook* (pp. 5- 27). Chicago: Rand McNally.

Aronson, E. (1969). The theory of cognitive dissonance: A current perspective. In L. Berkowitz (Ed.), *Advances in experimental social psychology* (Vol. 4, pp. 1-34). New York: Academic.

Aronson, E. (1972). *The social animal.* San Francisco: Freeman.

Aronson, E. (1978). The theory of cognitive dissonance: A current perspective. In L. Berkowitz (Ed.), *Cognitive theories in social psychology,* (pp. 181-214). New York: Academic.

Aronson, E. (1989). Analysis, synthesis, and the treasuring of the old. *Personality and Social Psychology Bulletin, 15*(4), 508-512.

Axsom, D. (1989). Cognitive dissonance and behavior change in psychotherapy. *Journal of Experimental Psychology, 25*(3), 234-252.

Berkowitz, L., & Devine, P. G. (1989). Research traditions, analysis, and synthesis in social psychological theories: The case of dissonance theory. *Personality and Social Psychology Bulletin, 15*(4), 493-507.

Bleich, A., Garb, R., & Kottler, M. (1986). Treatment of prolonged combat reaction. *British Journal of Psychiatry, 148,* 493-496.

Bourne, P. G. (1970). Military psychiatry and the Viet Nam experience. *American Journal of Psychiatry, 127*(4), 481- 488.

Brehm, S. S. (1967). *The application of social psychology to clinical practice.* Washington, DC: Hemisphere.

Brende, J. O., & Benedict, B. D. (1980). The Vietnam combat delayed stress response syndrome: Hypnotherapy of "dissociative symptoms." *American Journal of Clinical Hypnosis, 23*(1), 34-40.

Breslau, N., & Davis, G. C. (1987). Posttraumatic stress disorder: The stressor criterion. *Journal of Nervous and Mental Disease, 175*(5), 255-264.

Carlson, A. C., & Hocking, J. E. (1988). Strategies of redemption at the Vietnam Veterans' Memorial. *Western Journal of Speech Communication, 52*(3), 203-215.

Chemtob, C., Roitblat, H. L., Hamada, R. S., Carlson, J. G., & Twentyman, C. T. (1988). A cognitive action theory of post-traumatic stress disorder. *Journal of Anxiety Disorders, 2*(3), 253-275.

Clewell, R. D. (1987). Moral dimensions in treating combat veterans with posttraumatic stress disorder. *Bulletin of the Menninger Clinic, 51*(1), 114-130.

Davis, K., & Jones, E. E. (1960). Changes in interpersonal perception as a means of reducing cognitive dissonance. *Journal of Abnormal and Social Psychology, 61*, 402-410

Deeken, M. G., & Bridenbaugh, R. H. (1987). Depression and nightmares among Vietnam veterans in a military psychiatry outpatient clinic. *Military Medicine, 152*(11), 590-591.

Denton, D. D. (1989). Excursions into the warrior's psyche: Confessional implications for the healing arts. *Counseling and Values, 33*(3), 230-233.

Eisenhart, R. W. (1975). You can't hack it little girl: A discussion of the covert psychological agenda of modern combat training. *Journal of Social Issues, 31*(4), 13-23.

Fairbank, J. A., & Brown, T. A. (1987). Current behavioral approaches to the treatment of posttraumatic stress disorder. *Behavior Therapist, 10*(3), 57-64.

Festinger, L. (1957). *A theory of cognitive dissonance.* Stanford: Stanford University Press.

Frankl, V. E. (1984). *Man's search for meaning: An introduction to logotherapy* (rev. ed., Part one I. Lasch Trans.). New York: Simon & Shuster. (Original work published 1946).

Glass, D. C. (1964). Changes in liking as a means of reducing cognitive discrepancies between self-esteem and aggression. *Journal of Personality, 32*, 531-549.

Heimberg, R. G. (1985). What makes traumatic stress traumatic? *Behavior Therapy, 16*, 417-428.

Hendin, H., & Haas, A. P. (1984). Combat adaptations of Vietnam veterans without posttraumatic stress disorders. American *Journal of Psychiatry, 141*(8), 956-960.

Hendin, H., Pollinger, A., Singer, P., & Ulman, R. B. (1981). Meanings of combat and the development of posttraumatic stress disorder. *American Journal of Psychiatry, 138*(11), 1490-1493.

Horowitz, M. J. (1986). *Stress response syndromes* (2nd ed.). Northvale, NJ: Jason Aronson.

Keane, T. M. (1985). Defining traumatic stress: Some comments on the current terminological confusion. *Behavioral Therapy, 16*(4), 419-423.

Kelman, H. C. (1973). Violence without moral restraint: Reflections on the dehumanization of victims and victimizers. *Journal of Social Issues, 29*(4), 25-61.

Krystal, H. (1984). Psychoanalytic views on human emotional damages. In B. A. van der Kolk (Ed.), *Post-traumatic stress disorder: Psychological and biological sequelae* (pp. 1-28). Washington, DC: American Psychiatric Association.

Langner, H. P. (1971). The making of a murderer. American *Journal of Psychiatry, 127*(7), 950-953.

Lifton, R. J. (1973). The sense of immortality: On death and the continuity of life. *American Journal of Psychoanalysis, 33*, 3-15.

Mahedy, W. P., (1983). 'It don't mean nothin': The Vietnam experience. *The Christian Century, 100*(3), 65-68.

Marin, P. (1981, November). Living in moral pain. *Psychology Today*, pp. 68-80.

May, R. (1974). *Love and will.* New York: Norton.

May, R., & Yalom, I. (1984). Existential psychotherapy. In R. J. Corsini (Ed.), *Current psychotherapies* (3rd ed., pp. 354-391). Itasca, IL: F. E. Peacock.

McKay, M., Davis, M., & Fanning, P. (1981). Values clarification. In M. McKay et al., *Thoughts and Feelings: The art of cognitive stress intervention* (pp. 159-178). Richmond, CA: New Harbinger.

Parson, E. R. (1986). Life after death: Vietnam veteran's struggle for meaning and recovery. *Death Studies, 10*(1), 11-26.

Peralme, L. (1991). *Empirical and theoretical analysis of reexperiencing of trauma in combat veterans.* Unpublished manuscript, Florida State University, Department of Psychology, Tallahassee.

Rundell, J. R., Ursano, R. J., Holloway, H. C., & Silberman, E. K. (1989). Psychiatric responses to trauma. *Hospital and Community Psychiatry, 40,* (1), 68-74.

Scher, S. J., & Cooper, J. (1989). Motivational basis of dissonance: The singular role of behavioral consequences. *Journal of Personality and Social Psychology, 56*(6), 899-906.

Shatan, C. F. (1974). Through the membrane of reality: "Impacted grief" and perceptual dissonance in Vietnam combat veterans. *Psychiatric Opinion, 11*(6), 6-15.

Stretch, R. H. (1986). Post-traumatic stress disorder among Vietnam and Vietnam era veterans. In C. R. Figley (Ed.), Trauma and its wake: Vol. II. *Traumatic stress theory, research, and intervention* (pp. 156-192). New York: Brunner/Mazel.

Taylor, S. E. (1989). *Positive illusions: Creative self-deception and the healthy mind.* New York: Basic Books.

Tick, E. (1987). The face of horror. *Psychotherapy Patient, 3*(2), 101-120.

Ulman, R. B., & Brothers, D. (1988). *The shattered self: A psychoanalytic study of trauma.* Hillsdale, NJ: The Analytic Press .

West, S. G., & Wicklund, R. A. (1980). Cognitive dissonance theory. In S. G. West & R. A. Wicklund (Eds.), *A primer of social psychological theories* (pp. 68-80). Monterey, CA: Brooks/Cole.

Wick, E. (1985) Lost in the no-man's-land between psyche and soul. *Psychotherapy Patient, 1,* 13-24.

Wicklund, R. A., & Brehm, J. W. (1976). *Perspectives on cognitive dissonance.* Hillsdale, NJ: Erlbaum.

Williams, C. C. (1983). The mental foxhole: The Vietnam veteran's search for meaning. *American Journal of Orthopsychiatry, 53*(1), 4-17.

Wilmer, H. A. (1982a). Dream seminar for chronic schizophrenic patients. *Psychiatry, 45,* 351-360.

Wilmer, H. A. (1982b). Vietnam and madness: Dreams of schizophrenic veterans. *Journal of The American Academy of Psychoanalysis*, *10*(1), 47-65.

Wilmer, H. A. (1986a). Combat nightmares: Toward a therapy of violence. *Spring*, 120-139.

Wilmer, H. A. (1986b). The healing nightmare: A study of the war dreams of Vietnam combat veterans. *Quadrant*, *19*(1), 47-62.

Yalom, I. (1981). *Existential psychotherapy*. New York: Basic Books.

EPILOGUE

There is a temptation at the end to say "where to begin." Hopefully this book cycled between the rubber boundaries of psychotherapy that contain both drudgery and vision, both science and art. We attempted to remain "centered" on those easily discussed therapy polarities; immediacy versus transference, insight versus action, abstraction versus detail, and subjective versus objective. Our effort especially was to respect options on psychotherapy's epistemic scales; not to excessively codify and not to excessively create. There are no absolute "visions" here. Our realm is adequacy. We are presented with a problem and a craft, where, as professionals, we have just enough skills and technology to allow for effectiveness—to cause no harm, to soothe, to challenge, to help along the way—but not enough to result in permanent change. Emersed in our conceptual base camp is the conviction that this victim may not be cured but s/he will be affected. As psychotherapists then, we become fully alive companions to our clients, using the wisdom of subjectivity, and fully professional practitioners, using the flabby rubrics of our science. There is a good deal of skepticism in even the most "professional" of us *and* a good deal of hope in even the hard-core pessimists among us. Our craft and task are messy, but there is a noble messiness

We have weaved *woven* a story that begins with a position; the person organizes and perseverates his/her life and trauma makes this more so. The task of the professional caregiver is to study the former and free up the latter. The victim can conquer only what can be known and assimilated. In this effort the victim is to become what he/she was previously plus some new understanding. It is our job to move along this "new understanding." The professional task is to punctuate the right dimensions of the person and to extract the "correct" resource frames from a stuck person and to move these along. *The business of this book has been to know how the victim treats his/her inner life, to respect this intrapsychic zone, to reframe this interiority so as to resonate across all levels of the person, and to surface the immense significance of this operation for human choice.* These tasks evolve from and are confirmed by the person, not the professional.

Our model of psychotherapy emphasizes joining, knowing, and doing. Above all, we have extended the information-processing model in one important way, making it constructionist. The information processing map of the mind tends to ignore the agency of the person. Our position has been that the collection of data is more than a cybernetic loop where hardware needs oiling and software needs correction: that the individual actively creates reality and demonstrates this repeatedly. Therefore, interventions (from this expanded view of information-processing) emphasize the phenomenological and on-going struggle of the person, the decentering by the client (being a participant-observer), the therapeutic relationship, and the whole person integration of the trauma experience. It is hoped that this sense of the paradigmatic humanness was communicated. If the trauma victim does anything well, s/he fears moving beyond what is defined as safety (in relationships, jobs, tasks, life). Our model of psychotherapy disrupts this instinct of self-preservation and creates a dialogue for new options. "Vows begin when hope dies."

We have *four post-scripts* that should have been integrated into our musings. They emphasize the person of the professional: the *victim professional,* the *ethicist professional,* the *linking object professional,* and the *improvisational professional.* The commitment in this Epilogue, however, is not to extend beyond two paragraphs for each: they must be taken further by each of us. First, we remind the homunculus in all of us that we know trauma. It is the whispering sounds of change present in "everyman"; the homunculus of each of us has had to act and we know this activity (victim professional). Second, the canons of our discipline are swankily paraded about by our professional organizations, but they ultimately depend on our own moral character. The "hard boundaries" are provided by ethics (and science); the "soft boundaries" by our person.

The professional as ethician is addressed. Third, termination; how do professionals emphasize the "goings" in the "comings and goings" of care? We have described how the goal of therapy is agency and self-care, but "the good spectator also creates" (Swiss Proverb). An effort at a lasting perspective needs to be given (linking object professional). Finally, every act of therapy is a treasure hunt into the victim for tools of change. This can best be done by a centered and free therapist, an improvisational therapist, who opens the authentic mystery of the person within a covenant of care.

Humanization of Trauma

No one escapes trauma. It is the human struggle of manageability; placing pain in perspective for me. In Chapter 12 we discussed bereavement, *the transit from losing what we have to having what we lost, the movement from resentment to integration.* This mandates that each victim re-appraise self, reassess meaning. The human concerns of how am I different because of this trauma, what lessons in loving have I learned, what lessons in living have I been taught, and what can I create of me, are stopped. Normally, these are negotiated until there is a new charge in life. PTSD victims cannot move beyond the "barrier of pain." PTSD victims, run afoul; they hit the grief barrier and get lost in it (constant pain, stuck in the past or the lost self, what "was" can't make it to "is") or avoid the grief barrier by suppression, postponement, or inhibition (act out, regress, numb, and avoid). These victims adapt by developing PTSD; the living record of the relentless but stuck struggle for meaning. Victims never realize that meaning is to be found in the life that was lived and is not to be lived in the tragedy that occurred.

Each professional knows this process in self. The factors that take each of us to point B and beyond are varied but include an understanding of the self, one's history, and current life situation. Each has evolved an awareness and engagement with his/her own schema, personality and symptoms. Soon, a restructuring of both affective and cognitive components starts to feel right, to mitigate pain, and to serve up compassion. Forgiveness rewards awareness and change. How easy it is to get caught in the "crazy making" of the experience; how the guided injections of time, mourning, and self validation (with help of another) reduce the riddle of finality or hurt. We do this to ourselves and as professionals often guide its process with others. We can use this self knowledge; we need to trust it more (Fleming & Robinson, 1990, see Chapter 12).

Ethics: Self as Moral Agent

Ethics is the art-science of health care professions that represents thinking about moral ends. It concerns itself with what is the "fitting thing" to do in this case. *Ethics is based on the application of principles (extant codes or paradigms of moral reflection) and on the person of the professional (the moral character, moral skills, and moral meaning of the care provider).* This combination forces action, punches values, frightens beliefs and always leaves moral traces. This distinction is important because, while the profession runs on an ethics espousing a formalistic coding of rights and wrongs, a principle ethics is never enough. The moral character of the professional must make a move. In any clinical decision the person of the professional is always implied. Moral authority is always different from an exercise of clinical wisdom or power. One can even argue that the more important the ethical issue, the more moral principles are irreconcilable, the more messy the process and the greater the level of involvement of the person of the professional.

If the conscious moral schemas of cooperation of the professional are central to clinical decisions, then an understanding of these is logical. How therefore, the individual professional deliberates on clinical/ethical issues (the interface of personal and professional) is critical. This process involves not just the parsing apart of ethical problem solving (stages of moral meaning), but also a reflective process on self— where do I get stuck, how do I request help, what ought I (not my profession) to do. This self reflective process extends beyond the ethics of justice (hard line principles) to ethics of care (concern for human welfare), the covenant we addressed in Chapter 7. Ethical deliberation in this sense then, is not a question of right or wrong; rather it is the conscious engagement assessing the internal workings of what the process was like and was a fair hearing of care provided. For professionals who work with trauma victims, there arise hundreds of occasions when something more is asked—the extension of care for various reasons. Having this open set, not predisposed to classify or objectify, reduces the polygraph lines of typical distance-therapies and provides rooting. Nowhere then, are the clinical decisions of victims more vibrant and real than in this ethical reframe. And, nowhere is the person of the professional more engaged.

The Never Ending Story

A highly respected writer on PTSD, John Wilson, wrote that recovery from PTSD is a lifelong process (Wilson, 1989; see Chapter 6). Current trends in the health care professions point to the schizophrenic emphases on one session psychotherapy (a head strong focus on solution) versus intermittent psychotherapy throughout the life cycle, a resource across time. Both, of course, can and do apply. And, they have a common thread; a resolution or commitment in the now to alter one's views or ways (or both) and to stay this course. Somehow the clinician must access the motivation agents of the schema to invite and continue change; a personal and compelling reference is touched that requires the patient to eavesdrop on a future self and like this exercise.

PTSD victims do not forget. The reality of psychotherapy is that people return for multiple episodes of therapy. The healthy PTSD victim views psychotherapy as part of the balanced life—an option for retooling when there are problems (or needs for growth). Clearly this view dovetails with the known needs of victims— supportive social system available after treatment, empowered problem solving focus, ability to cope in stress situations, and a personalized relapse prevention model— all aftercare activities. But there is one more issue here. The adult developmentalists (e.g., Erikson, Vaillant, Gould, Levinson, etc.) assume that one's personality continues to grow and develop through the life cycle. At various points in life, challenges "ascend"—inner needs meet cultural demands at a particular age period. At this time there is a "teachable moment" that punctuates the on-going life course. These transition points are most stressed by "deviant developmental pacing;" anxiety or depression that come from moving too fast in life (thereby requiring an external focus) or too slow (thereby requiring an internal focus—schemas). *What is central here is that PTSD victims will recapitulate their person and their trauma at all life cycle points and will need assistance. The "cure" model of care does not apply.* Again, the bottom line is that the therapist must be prepared to be a staple in the victim's life, a linking object that empowers.

Improvisional Therapy

The lesson in the first post script, humanization of trauma, is to trust self; the lesson here is to use self. We come to psychotherapy "at the ready." Our profession mandates this. "Good" therapy comes, however, not in how-to versions but in a performance made real by its inefficiency, its lack of ready-made recipes, its unthinking rule-following. Tyler and Tyler (1990) say:

> a therapeutic encounter thus becomes a conversation in which therapist and client respond to one another without benefit of a script or even of a narrative. The therapist does not control or guide the conversation into appropriate plots of pathology or along proper story lines of sickness, but lets it seek its own ways along multiple paths and through many openings. The therapist is not the "master of talk," the "overlord of the word" managing the discourse and dictating its final meaning. The therapist does not stand outside of the circle of participants, pronouncing the "last word" to another audience. In a conversation, everyone has equal rights to the role of distanced outsider. (pg. xi)

We are strengthened by our theories and victims of them. There is no need to belabor this point. But, the experience of the change process may be equally served in a reliance on our therapist self and on our self comprehension, that personal admixture of professional and person. As humans, we are very much like our clients. As professionals, even our theories which seem so defining and voluntary are really self directed autobiographies. The action point in therapy is now; the stance of two open people, one absent the pain of being stuck and one required to wrestle with the pain of being stuck. As improvisational therapists we may give ourselves permission to go beyond our boundaries, to become more of what we want, to challenge well-formed problems, to help clients make us better, to be intellectually and humanly (and clinically) curious, and above all to remain unsettled in our knowing. Conviction in self knowing is in this way dangerous: the professional should have a robust faith, but not be a believer. Better professionals extend themselves and build their own "meaning questions" to know humanness, challenge stasis, and provide a vision. They challenge their own therapeutic resources, question the need for structure in therapy, ask themselves what themes intrigue them, mull over their "best questions," struggle to know what to do when stuck, open up when asking for help, validate and isolate idiosyncratic moments, and reach for a sense of play. The growing professional extends self and doesn't mind. As little has worked to date in this field, this effort may be most important.

As in high school Latin we ended each semester with the idiom, *termatus est*—it is ended. Every ending of course is also a beginning; in this case a temporary and pyrrhic victory over chaos.

REFERENCES

Tyler, S., & Tyler, M. (1990). Forward. In B. Keeney's *Improvisational therapy: A guide for creative clinical strategies.* New York: Guilford.

Wilson, J. (1989). *Traumatic transformation and healing: An integrative approach to theory, research and post-traumatic therapy.* New York: Brunner/Mazel.

BIOGRAPHIES

ASSOCIATE AUTHORS

Richard W. Bagge, *M.D.*, at the time of the writing of this book was an assistant Professor in the Department of Psychiatry and Health Behavior at the Medical College of Georgia and director of the Psychiatric Outpatient Clinic. He is currently working with a mission organization and will be stationed in Nairobi, Kenya working with expatriates.

Patrick A. Boudewyns, *Ph.D.*, is the Chief, Psychology Service at the VA Medical Center in Augusta, GA and is a Professor (Psychology) in the Department of Psychiatry & Health Behavior at the Medical College of Georgia. He is also a Professor of Social Work at the University of Georgia. Dr. Boudewyns has published numerous data-based articles on treatment outcome for anxiety disorders. He has also published several articles and has edited a book in the area of behavioral medicine. He is presently the principal investigator or co-investigator on several Va (Merit Review) grants in the areas of post-traumatic stress disorder for combat veterans and treatment for cocaine abuse. He is the first author with Robert Shipley of a book entitled *Flooding and Implosive Therapy: Direct Therapeutic Exposure in Clinical Practice* (New York: Plenum, 1983).

Jeffrey M. Brandsma, *Ph.D.*, is a Professor of Psychiatry and Health Behavior at the Medical College of Georgia and Training Director for the Clinical Psychology Residency. He is a Fellow of A.P.A., A.P.S., A.S.P.P.B., and the Georgia Psychological Association. He remains a member and past President of the State Board of Examiners of Psychologists for the State of Georgia. He has written many different kinds of papers in the field of psychotherapy ranging from outcome research, theoretical articles, and a book on Provocative Therapy. He has served as a consultant to the Veterans Administration Hospital and also to the Fort Gordon Army Hospital in Augusta, Georgia for the last seven years.

Matthew J. Friedman, M.D., Ph.D., is a Professor of Psychiatry and Pharmacology at Dartmouth Medical School who, since 1989, has served as Executive Director of the V.A.'s National Center for PTSD. The National Center is a five part consortium mandated by Congress to carry out a broad range of multidisciplinary activities in research, education, and training. Dr. Friedman's recent work and writing on PTSD have focused on neurobiology, clinical psychopharmacology, dual diagnosis, chronicity, risk factors, cross cultural issues, and treatment.

Brett T. Litz, Ph.D., is the Deputy Director for Education and Training at the National Center for Post-Traumatic Stress Disorder, Behavioral Science Division, Boston Department of Veterans Affairs Medical Center, and an assistant professor in psychiatry at Tufts University School of Medicine. Dr. Litz has published in the area of information processing in PTSD and the assessment of PTSD.

Cynthia A. Gerrard, Ph.D., is a clinical psychologist at the Augusta Veterans Affairs Hospital, where she works extensively with veterans suffering from Post Traumatic Stress Disorder in both individual and group therapy as well as assessment. She also serves as an Assistant Clinical Professor in the Department of Psychiatry and Health Behavior, School of Medicine, Medical College of Georgia. She is active in professional organizations and is President of the Augusta Psychological Association (19921993). Previously, she worked at City Hospital Center, Elmhurst, New York and had a limited private practice. Her doctorate is from Fordham University.

Diana Hearst, Ph.D., is the Director of the rape and crime victims program at the Medical College of Pennsylvania at the College of Eastern Pennsylvania Psychiatric Institute, and an instructor in the Department of Psychiatry.

Lynn Peralme, M.A., is a clinical psychology doctoral candidate at the Florida State University. She is a currently cocoordinator of a treatment outcome study of combat-related PTSD at the Augusta Veterans Affairs Medical Center. She has been a member of the International Society for Traumatic Stress Studies since 1986 and was an editorial assistant for the *Journal of Traumatic Stress* from 1989-1991.

Francine Shapiro, Ph.D., is a Research Associate at the Mental Research Institute in Palo Alto, CA. She also servers as a member of the Editorial Advisory Group of the *Journal of Traumatic Stress.* Dr. Shapiro is the originator of Eye Movement Desensitization and Reprocessing (EMDR). She has made presentations on EMDR at numerous conferences, including the 1989, 1990, and 1991 national conferences of the Association for the Advancement of Behavior Therapy and the International Society for Traumatic Stress Studies. Her articles on EMDR have been published in the *Journal of Traumatic Stress,* the *Journal of Behavior Therapy and Experimental Psychiatry,* and the *Behavior Therapist.*

Edwin V. Sperr, Ph.D., is Director of the PTSD Treatment Program at the Augusta VA Medical Center. He is also an assistant professor at the Medical College of Georgia in the Department of Psychiatry and Health Behavior. He received his Ph.D. in Clinical Psychology from Florida State University in 1972. He has presented workshops on stress and PTSD and has had articles published in such journals as the *Journal of Traumatic Stress, Journal of Psychosomatic Research* and *Clinical Psychology.*

Mary Summers, Ph.D., is a geropsychologist at the Augusta VAMC and is currently principal investigator of a grant examining PTSD among elderly combat veterans. She is also assistant clinical professor at the MCG and a faculty member on the Georgia Consortium on the Psychology of Aging.

SUBJECT INDEX

A

B

C

K

Kindling, definition 29

L

Lacuna 5
Life review
    for the elderly patient 659-63
    functions of, *Table* 661
Lifeline 164, *Table* 172-3
Life-style 160-75
    elements, *Table* 162
    paradigm, *Figure* 157
    Sc+P+(B)+Sy, *Figure* 157
Life-style (LS) 2, 151-99
    parts of the person 151-99
Life-style analysis (LSA) 154,
    163-75, *Table* 165-71
LS=Sc+P+(B)+Sy 10-3
LSA
    use, *Table* 351
Lysis 480

M

Management
    stress in PTSD 587-628
MCMI 322
MCMI or MCMI-II 334
Meaning
    adaptation 700-3, *Figure* 702
    reexperiencing 707-9
Measurement
    beliefs 244-8
    clinical interview 249-54
    paper and pencil scales 254-9
    procedural questions 265-7
    psychophysiological 259-60
    questions, other 267-70
    recommendation 260-1, 263-4
    stressor 198-9
    symptoms 198-9
Memories, 196-8, *Figure* 197
    effects 439
    of the experience 528
    ratings of, *Figure* 197
    storage of traumatic 439

    systems, *Table* 575
    traumatic 528
Message
    impact 394
    working 393
Millon Clinical Multiaxial Inventory
    (MCMI) 232-40, *Table* 233, 235,
    236-40
Misalliance 401-3
*Mississippi Scale for Combat Related
    PTSD* (Miss-10) 256, *Table* 257-8
MMPI and *MMPI-2* 255
MMPI-PTSD scale 255
Model
    See Sc+P+(B)+Sy
    alcoholism is primary 56
    comorbid 56-7
    etiological 42-45, *Figure* 44
    health care 51-3, *Figure* 52
    illness 51-3, *Figure* 52
    medication 56
    Millon 231-2
    person/event interaction
        106-10
    post-traumatic stress disorder
        423-41
    redecision therapy 181
    Sc+P+(B)+Sy 205-77
    simple trauma 5-8, *Figure* 6
    stress management 587-93
    treatment 314-65, *Table* 316
Models
    health care 51-3, *Figure* 52
    illness 51-3, *Figure* 52
    post-traumatic stress disorder
        423-41
Moderators 59-67
    known 63-5
Modification 5
Modifiers and Perceived Stress Scale
    (MAPS) 259

N

National Vietnam Veteran
    Readjustment Study (NVVRS)
    40,70
    statistical data, *Table* 71
Node 508

psychotherapy 301-14
range of symptoms 53-9, *Table*
55
relation to other anxiety disorder
45-8
relationship to anxiety disorder
at later life 647-51
stressor 94-102
symptoms found in, *Table* 571
symptoms in older victim group,
Table 642-3
theoretical perspectives 93-140
traumatic grief 569-84
treatment 523-66
treatment by hypnotherapy
612-22
Post-traumatic therapy (PTT) 305
Potential
psychotherapy 301
Private logic
beliefs 185-8
Procedure
EMDR 510-4
Procedures and Interventions, *Table*
395
Process
cognitive 158
debriefing 536-7
destructuring and restructuring
137-9, *Figure* 138
schema and symptom, *Table*
350-3
Processing
See information processing
abnormal 577
normal 576
schematic 425-6
Professional
ethicist 716
improvisational 716
linking object 716
victim 716
Propositions ix-xii
Psychoeducation 593-600
Psychology
existential 699-700
Psychotherapy 73-8, 301-14
See therapy
approach 9
avoidance

dimensions of 293-301
labor intensive 325-7
never ending story 719-20
PTSD 301-14
potential 301
problems of outcome research
303-5
results 78
tensions in, *Table* 295
with the elderly 652-68

Q

Questions
on measurement 267-70
procedural 265-7

R

Rational Emotive Therapy 187
Reconstruction 5
Recovery styles 276
Redecision therapy model 181
Reduction
dissonance 681-709
Reexperiencing
definition 37
existential perspectives on
combat 683-709
from a dissonance perspective
689-9
meaning 707-9
Reinterpretation 5
Relapse prevention (RP) 622-7, *Table*
625-6
facts, chain, and post-treatment
problems, *Table* 625-6
treatment strategies 623-24, 627
Relationship
development 17-8
duplex 413
in therapy 327-33
meta tasks 392-412
therapeutic 383-416
therapist-patient using DTE
530-1
Reminiscence Therapy
process, *Table* 662

T

U

Unhook 394-7
Unhooking 328-31, 349

V

Validity of cognition (VOC) 503
Values
    adaptation 703-5
Victim
    role in treatment 15-9
Victimization
    vicarious 406-8

Voices
    internal 604-6

W

War Zone Stress inventory (WZS) 96
War Zone Stressor Scale (WZS) 259
Ways of Coping-Revised 265
Well-being
    dimensions, *Table* 669
Work
    detective 528-9, 536-9

NAME INDEX

A

Abelson, R. P. 710

Abrahamson, O. 125, 146, 210, 217, 284

Abrams, J. 505, 521

Abueg, F. 367, 374

Adams, H. 82, 279, 376

Adler, A. iii, 2, 154, 156, 160, 188, 189, 199, 292, 295, 296, 347, *Table* 297

Alarcon, G. S. 646, 678

Albrecht, B. 458, 493

Albrecht, J. 54, 76, 80, 228, 234, 235, 240, 273, 277, 281, 505, 520, 523, 525, 566

Aldwin, C. 635, 671

Alexander, F. 296, 374

Alford, J. 186, 187, 199, 607, 628

Alington, E. E. 263, 283

Allain, A. 99, 149

Allen, I. 64, 88

Allender, J. R. 657, 678

Allport, G. 224

Altman, B. 37, 88, 260, 285

Alvarez, W. 259, 281

American Psychiatric Association 31, 79, 94, 140, 570, 584, 640, 671

Anchin, J. C. 375, 377, 418

Anderson, B. 592, 629

Anderson, D. 251, 255, 287

Anderson, P. 39, 91, 251, 255, 287, 452, 497

Andreasen, N. C. 106, 140

Andreski, P. 64, 69, 81

Andrews, G. 103, 140

Ansbacher, H. L. 160, 162, 176, 185, 199, 200

Apfel, D. J. 487, 491

Arieti, S. 201

Arkowitz, H. 143, 280, 494

Armstrong, K. 367, 374

Arnoff, A. 677

Aronson, E. 685, 686, 690, 691, 692, 695, 696, 697, 699, 709, 710

Atkinson, R. M. 366, 374

Auerhahn, N. C. 454, 491

Autry, J. 194, 201

Axsom, D. 685, 710

B

Bagge, R. W. 569

Baltes, P. 634, 671

Bamford, C. 657, 671

Bandler, R. 620, 621, 629

Bandura, A. 393, 418

Baraga, E. 452, 494

Bargh, J. A. 134, 149, 425, 441

Barlow, D. H. 41, 42, 44, 79, 85, 100, 140, 251, 279, 427, 441, 525, 551, 552, 555, 566, 567

Barlow, O. 588, 628

Barry, J. 665, 674

Bartholow, J. 640, 676

Bartlett, G. S. 640, 672

Baum, A. 101, 140

Bauman, M. 658, 674

Baumeister, R. F. 358, 374

Bear, M. 647, 671

Beardslee, W. R. 78 80, 651, 671

Bebenishty, R. 63, 90

Beck, A. 12, 23, 110, 131, 140, 141, 155, 156, 157, 174, 181, 185, 191, 193, 197, 200, 207, 213, 216, 217, 224, 244, 247, 277, 294, 347, 374, 427, 441, 604, 605, 610, 628

Beck, J. C. 638, 676

Beebe, G. W. 633, 671

Bell, W. 314, 379

Bender, M. E. 115, 145, 431, 442, 511, 520

Benedek, E. P. 63, 80

Benedict, B.D. 692, 693, 710

Bengston, V. L. 635, 671, 675

Bennett, C. H. 453, 491

Benyakar, M. 111, 135, 137, 141, 215, 277

Bergler, E. 455, 491

Canino, G. 45, 90
Cantor, N. 425, 441, 442
Card, J. J. 66, 72, 81
Cardena, E. 272, 286
Carlson, A. C. 708, 709, 710
Carlson, E. 61, 90
Carlson, J. G. 111, 141, 423, 441, 448, 491, 604, 629, 709, 711,
Carroll, E. M. 54, 83, 105, 142
Carson, R.C. 328, 375
Carter, J. 634, 672
Cashdan, S. 328, 375, 394, 418
Caspi, A. 663, 673
Cath, C. 652, 672
Cath, S. 652, 672
Catherall, D. 181, 200, 311, 328, 375, 386, 387, 388, 418, 454, 470, 491
Cauble, A. 630
Cerny, J. 251, 279
Chafetz, P. 634, 672
Chambless, D. L. 193, 200
Charney, D. 195, 204, 250, 264, 278, 288, 452, 491, 646, 678
Chavoya, G.A. 647, 675
Chemtob, C. 111, 116, 119, 141, 423, 429, 441, 448, 491, 604, 629, 709, 711
Chiriboga, D. 637, 673
Chivalisz, K. 358, 376
Choca, J. 229, 232, 241, 278
Chodoff, P. 453, 491
Christensen, H. 103, 140
Christenson, R. M. 651, 672
Christianson, S. 38, 81
Chu, J. 408, 411, 418
Cicchetti, D. 271, 286
Claiborn, J. M. 34, 88, 114, 148
Clark, M. S. 425, 442
Clarkin, J. 194, 200, 293, 374
Cleary, P. D. 640, 672
Clewell, R. D. 476, 484, 485, 491, 496, 703, 707, 711
Clum, G.A. 524, 567
Cohen, M. 460, 492
Cohen, R. 276, 278
Connell, M. M. 65, 88
Cooper, A. 144
Cooper, J. 685, 713
Cooper, N. A. 524, 567

Corbishley, A. 657, 671
Corbishley, M. A. 657, 678
Corcoran, J. R. 58, 83
Corey, T. 263, 283
Corradi, R. B. 106, 149
Corsini, R. J. 712
Coryell, W. 84, 280, 315, 374, 381
Costa, P. 192, 202, 225, 243, 279, 284, 638, 672
Coveman, J. 419
Craig, R. 201
Craske, M. G. 551, 555, 566, 567
Crits-Christoph, P. 324, 378
Crocker, J. 425, 443
Crossman, I. 596, 631
Curtis, J. 652, 677
Cytrynbaum, S. 137, 138, 141
Czekala, J. 452, 494

D

Daldrup, R. J. 448, 489, 492
Dancu, C. 592, 629
Dasberg, H. 111, 141, 215, 277
Davanloo, H. 394, 375
Davidson, J. 45, 46, 56, 58, 59, 64, 69, 81, 94, 141, 270, 279, 309, 375, 451, 492, 573, 584, 672
Davidson, L. 101, 140
Davidson, P. O. 630
Davidson, S. M. 630
Davies, R. 657, 678
Davis, G. C. 37, 39, 64, 69, 80, 81, 87, 708, 710
Davis, H. 228, 234, 235, 240, 246, 256, 258, 281, 322, 377, 452, 458, 493, 593, 658, 674
Davis, K. 690, 711
Davis, M. 704, 712
De la Penna, A. 127, 142
Deale, S. 366, 374
Decoufle, P. 28, 80, 105, 141
Deeken, M. G. 694, 711
DeFazio, V. 511, 520
deJong, J. B. 34, 37, 88, 114, 148, 260, 285
DeLongis, A. 635, 641, 663, 675
Denny, N. 63, 82
Denton, D. D. 705, 711
deShazer, S. 318, 375

Devine, P.G. 684, 685, 710
Dewey, J. 292, 375
Diamond, A. 511, 520
Dibner, S. c. 634, 672
Dickman, H. R. 639, 641, 679
DiClemente, C. C. 294, 379, 398, 419
DiGuiseppe, R. 263, 283
Dimsdale, J. 491
DiNardo, P. A. 251, 279
Dinkmeyer, D. C. 163, 200
Doghramji, K. 38, 85
Dohrenwend, B. P. 102, 142, 640, 672
Dohrenwend, B. S. 143, 640, 672
Donahoe, C. P. 105, 142, 259, 280
Dondershine, E. 612, 614, 631
Dondershine, H. 27, 89, 363, 380
Donovan, D. M. 105, 147
Donovan, J. 348, 375
Dorr, C. 672
Dreikurs, R. 181, 185, 200
Dunn, D. 635, 668, 677
Dunn, P. 369, 381
Dye, C. 634, 672
Dye, E. 9, 23, 60, 82, 185, 200, 215, 279, 304, 375,
Dyregrov, A. 367, 375

E

Early, E. 356, 375, 403, 409, 418
Ebersole, P. 668, 673
Egendorf, A. 69, 82
Eiler, J. 645, 679
Eisdorfer, C. 94, 142
Eisen, S. 106, 149
Eisenhart, R. W. 691, 703, 711
Eisler, R. 567
Ekblad, S. vii
Elder, L. 663, 673
Eldridge, G. 57, 82
Eliott, R. 464, 492
Ellenberger, H. 160. 200
Elliott, A. 50, 88
Elliott, G. R. 94, 142
Elliott, T. R. 58, 83
Ellis, A. 185, 187, 200, 207, 245, 263, 279, 283, 604, 605, 629

Emery, G. 131, 140, 174, 185, 200, 216, 217, 224, 277, 427, 441, 604, 605, 628
Emery, P. 107, 142, 210, 231, 279
Emery, V. 107, 142, 210, 231, 279
Emmelkamp, P. G. M. 203
Emmons, R. 151, 203, 378, 673, 676
Engel, G. L. 614, 629, 667, 673
Engle, D. 448, 492
Epstein, S. 30, 58, 76, 82, 111, 112, 125, 134, 139, 142 215, 279, 464, 492, 589, 629
Erickson, K. 64, 82
Erikson, E. 178, 201, 659, 673
Ervin, F. R. 487, 495
Eth, S. 268, 279, 408, 409, 418
Ettedgui, E. 106, 142
Everett, D. 675
Everly, G. 354, 376, 588, 589, 601, 602, 608, 628, 629, 666, 673

F

Fairbank, J. 31, 37, 40, 46, 65, 70, 72, 74, 82, 85, 86, 89, 91, 96, 114, 115, 142, 145, 146, 250, 251, 255, 256, 259, 278, 282, 283, 286, 304, 309, 376, 430, 431, 442, 511, 520, 524, 567, 603, 629, 640, 675, 675, 701, 711
Fallon, J. H., Jr. 262, 281
Falsettie, G. 639, 677
Fanning, P. 704, 712
Fava, J. 294, 379
Feldman, L. 212, 284
Felstein, E. 186, 187, 199
Fenichel, O. 458, 492
Festinger, L. 685, 711
Fielding, J. 671
Fields, R. 639, 677
Figley, C. R. 72, 78, 82, 84, 86, 88, 105, 142, 143, 144, 145, 266, 281, 282, 309, 376, 381, 388, 418, 419, 442, 494, 520, 631, 713
First, M. 51, 83, 243, 286, 608, 631
Fisher, L. 57, 86
Fisher, S. 659, 674
Fisk, M. 637, 673

Fiske, S. T. 425, 442
Fitterberg, J. M. 46, 82, 603, 629
Fitzpatrick, D. 65, 87, 348, 359, 378
Fleming, B. 131, 143
Fleming, S. 76, 82, 580, 584
Flores, F. 216, 287
Foa, E. B. 45, 47, 58, 59, 66, 75, 81, 82, 83, 89, 94, 110, 112, 116, 118, 141, 142, 143, 203, 207, 270, 279, 311, 313, 356, 376, 423, 427, 428, 431, 432-3, 442, 448, 451, 492, 573, 584, 592, 593, 629, 649, 653, 655, 673, 676
Folkman, S. 72, 84, 266, 281, 597, 600, 604, 630
Fontana, A. 526, 567, 644, 677
Ford, C. V. 487, 495
Forfar, C. S. 54, 83, 255, 279
Forgue, D. F. 34, 37, 88, 114, 148, 260, 285
Forsythe, A. 46, 81
Fox, R. 461, 492
Foy, D. W. 42, 47, 54, 83, 105, 109, 142, 259, 280
Fozard, J. 637, 673
Frances, A. 51, 83, 144, 227, 287
Frank, E. 592, 629
Frank, R. G. 58, 83
Frank, S. 151, 203, 378, 673, 676
Frankl, V. E. 76, 83, 180, 200, 556, 567, 667, 673, 707, 711
Franks, C. M. 202
Frederick, C. J. 60, 83
Freedy, J. R. 77, 83
Freeman, A. 110, 131, 141, 131, 143, 155, 156, 157, 181, 191, 193, 197, 200, 207, 216, 224, 244, 247, 277, 280, 347, 374, 494, 610, 628
Frelstein, E. 607, 628
French, T. 296, 374
Freud, S. 2, 143, 453, 455, 458, 492, 580, 585
Fried, L. 51, 52, 83
Friedman, B. 585

Friedman, C. T. H. 487, 495
Friedman, J. J. 29, 83
Friedman, L. 461, 495
Friedman, M. J. v, vi, vii, 66, 89, 127, 128, 143, 191, 201, 303, 367, 374, 376, 431, 442
Fullerton, C. 677
Funari, D. 232, 286
Futterman, S. 633, 673
Fyer, M. 227, 287

G

Galanter, M. 379
Gallagher, D. 657, 673, 678
Gallers, J. 259, 280
Gallops, M. S. 40, 86, 363, 377
Gambrill, E. 13, 23
Ganaway, G. 364, 376
Garb, R. 570, 585, 699, 710
Garfield, S. L. 83
Garmezy, N. 75, 83
Garwood, G. 358, 376
Gatz, M. 652, 673
Gelder, M. 42, 84, 270, 280, 315, 376
Gendli, E. 361, 376
George, L. 648, 671
Gerardi, R. J. 34, 87, 100, 114, 141, 143, 146, 231, 248, 255, 260, 266, 278, 280, 283, 284
Gerrard, C. 445
Gerrity, E. T. 74, 90
Getzel, G. 461, 495
Gibbon, M. 243, 286, 608, 631
Gibbs, M. 64, 84
Giles, T. R. 193, 201
Gill, M. 333, 376
Giller, E. L. 28, 87, 197, 203
Gilligan, S. 148
Giometti, V. 284
Girelli, C. G. 354, 380
Girelli, S. 592, 631
Glass, D. C. 690, 711
Gleser, G. 110, 143
Glover, H. 259, 280, 463, 493
Goderez, B. I. 454, 493

Gold, F. S. 105, 106, 143, 149
Gold, M. 56, 87
Goldberg, J. 106, 149, 244, 245, 280
Goldberger, L. 87, 378
Goldfarb, J. 259, 280
Goldfried, M. R. 404, 418, 425, 443
Golding, J. 46, 81
Goldstein, A. P. 83
Goldstein, G. 639, 674
Goldstein, K. 640, 672
Goldstein, R. L. 640, 672
Goleman, D. 5, 23, 221, 223, 280
Gordon, J. 622, 630
Goryell, W. 376
Goulding, M. 181, 201
Goulding, R. 181, 201
Grace, M. 110, 143, 598, 603, 629
Grandy, D. A. 34, 40, 91
Gratton, C. 195, 201
Green, B. L. 34, 37, 67, 68, 84, 96, 113, 143, 250, 280, 598, 603, 629, 644, 674
Greenberg, J. 291, 369, 380, 382
Greenberg, L. S. 142, 247, 285, 376, 447, 448, 449, 450, 475, 488, 492, 493, 494, 496
Greenberg, M. 28, 29, 90
Greenberg, R. 659, 674
Greinberg, G. 375
Grenberg, L. S. 426, 442
Grendlin, E. 489, 492
Grinberg, L. 458, 460, 493
Grinder, J. 620, 629
Grinker, R. R. 452, 459, 460, 461, 463, 466, 477, 493
Grove, W. M. 226, 280
Gunderson, J. G. 227, 280
Gurian, B. 648, 649, 674
Gushurst, R. S. 174, 201
Gusman, F. 231, 277, 367, 374
Gut, E. 459, 493

H

Haas, A. P. 39, 61, 84, 463, 467, 479, 493, 603, 629, 686, 692, 709, 711

Hadley, S. 194, 201
Hadzi-Pavolovic, D. 103, 140
Haley, S. A. 452, 493
Haley, W. E. 646, 678
Hamada, R. S. 111, 141, 423, 441, 448, 491, 604, 629, 709, 711
Hamblin, D. 657, 671
Hamilton, V. 427, 442
Hammarberg, M. 255, 280
Hammett, E. 46, 81
Hansen, D. J. 46, 82, 603, 629
Hare, N. A. 525, 553, 556, 567
Harel, Z. 99, 144, 203, 283, 379, 630
Harris, M. 227, 287
Harrison, W. R. 65, 74, 80, 84, 255, 262, 281, 282, 487, 494, 524, 567
Hartman, C. 206, 281
Harvey, J. 358, 376
Hassinger, M. 645, 679
Hayman, P. 78, 89
Healy, J. M. 82, 142, 279, 492, 629
Hearst, D. vi
Heimberg, R. G. 707, 708, 711
Heitler, S. 48, 84
Heller 151, 201
Helzer, J. E. 53, 54, 72, 84, 108, 109, 143
Henderson, R. G. 366, 374
Hendin, H. 39, 61, 84, 105, 143, 231, 281, 463, 466, 467, 479, 493, 603, 629, 686, 692, 709, 711, 712
Herman, C. P. 443
Herman, J. L. v, vii, 50, 84
Hersen, M. 201, 567
Hersov, L. 75, 83
Herz, L. R. 37, 88, 260, 285, 646, 676
Hess, P. 668, 673
Higgins, E. T. 436, 442, 443
Hiley-Young, B. 195, 201
Hillesland, D. 322, 377, 658, 674
Himadi, W. 251, 279
Hobfoll, S. 72, 77, 84, 266, 281
Hocking, F. 108, 144
Hocking, J. E. 709, 710
Hogan, R. A. 540, 567
Holloway, H. C. 700, 713
Holmstrom, L. L. 60, 81
Horney, K. 185, 201

Horowitz, M. J. 2, 15, 23, 40, 84, 110, 111, 112, 116, 119, 120, 121, 144, 185, 195, 201, 202, 231, 256, 259, 281, 287, 304, 305, 307, 313, 358, 376, 377, 424, 427, 442, 448, 493, 603, 629, 698, 709, 712
Hough, R. L. 31, 37, 72, 86, 91, 96, 146, 250, 251, 256, 259, 282, 283, 286, 640, 675
Houscamp, B. M. 42, 83
Houts, P. S. 640, 672
Howard, G. 665, 666, 674
Howes, J. G. 82, 204, 231, 250, 282, 285, 291, 300, 373, 377, 379, 380, 419
Hughes, C. 592, 629
Hughes, D. 648, 671
Hunt, T. 612, 614, 631
Hutter, C. K. 354, 380, 592, 631
Hyer, L. iii-vi, 46, 54, 56, 65, 74, 76, 80, 84, 85, 108, 114, 141, 147, 174, 195, 201, 217, 228, 231, 232, 234, 235, 240, 245, 246, 255, 256, 258, 260, 262, 265, 273, 277, 278, 281, 282, 303, 322, 356, 377, 383, 414, 415, 418, 445, 452, 458, 471, 487, 493, 494, 505, 520, 523, 524, 525, 556, 566, 567, 587, 633, 639, 641, 645, 646, 674, 649, 650, 656, 658, 665, 674, 678

I

Iacono, C. 451, 497
Ingram, R. E. 424, 442, 443
Inman, D. J. 38, 85
Izard, C. 448, 459, 494

J

Jackson, D. 226, 283
Jacobs, M. 656, 674
Jacobsberg, L. 227, 287
James, E. 464, 492
Janoff-Bulman, R. 111, 112, 125, 134, 135, 144, 215, 217, 225, 276, 282, 284, 311, 377, 386, 419, 432, 439, 442, 474, 494

Jaransen, J. M. vi, vii
Jarrell, M. P. 77, 83
Jarvik, L. F. 649, 674
Jassani, A. 107, 142, 210, 279
Jay, J. 93, 144
Jelinek, J. M. 56, 85
Jensen, C. 35, 36, 87
Johnson, D. W. 419
Johnson, F. 648, 652, 675
Johnson, J. L. 78, 87
Jones, E. E. 585, 690, 711
Jones, J. C. 41, 85
Jordan, B. 31, 72, 86, 91, 251, 256, 259, 286 640, 675
Jordan, C. G. 354, 380, 592, 631
Jordan, H. W. 231, 282
Jordan, K. 37, 86, 96, 146, 250, 283
Juba, M. 39, 91, 251, 255, 287, 452, 497

K

Kadushin, C. 69, 82, 109, 141
Kagan, J. 494
Kahana, B. 99, 144, 203, 283, 379, 600, 629, 630
Kahana, E. 99, 144, 600, 629
Kahn, M. 18, 23, 327, 377, 401, 419
Kaloupek, D. 250, 263, 278, 283, 430, 443, 452, 491
Kaltreider, M. 231, 281
Kaltreider, N. 110, 144
Kapp, F. 402, 409, 420
Kardiner, A. 196, 201, 633, 675
Kasl, S. 100, 144
Kastenbaum, R. 652, 675

Katz, I. 649, 653, 676
Katzman, R. A. 634, 675
Kaylor, J. A. 69, 85, 105, 144
Keane, T. 34, 46, 54, 57, 59, 74, 75, 85, 86, 87, 100, 108, 111, 112, 114, 115, 116, 122, 127, 142, 144, 145, 146, 195, 202, 231, 248, 250, 255, 256, 259, 266, 278, 280, 282, 283, 284, 423, 426, 427, 430, 431, 436, 442, 443, 448, 452, 491,

494, 495, 511, 520, 524, 567, 639, 647, 671, 675, 708, 712
Kelly, W. E. 628, 678
Kelman, H. C. 687, 688, 690, 692, 703, 706, 712
Kendall, P. 49, 85, 359, 377, 424, 442, 673
Kenderdine, S. 74, 89, 303, 380
Kern, R. 181, 201
Kierkegaard, S. 523
Kiesler, D. 328, 331, 375, 377, 393, 418, 419
Kihlstrom, J. F. 425, 441, 442
Kilburg, R. R. 634, 678
Kilpatrick, D. G. 50, 89, 111, 145, 354, 381, 592, 631
King, D. 34, 51, 52, 69, 83, 85, 96, 104, 144, 145
King, G. 436, 442
King, L. A. 34, 69, 85, 96, 105, 144, 145
Kingsbury, S. 275, 282, 612, 630
Kinney, L. 38, 86, 196, 202
Kirkish, P. 657, 671
Klauminzer, G. 250, 278, 452, 491
Kleber, R. J. 305, 306, 375, 397, 418
Kluckholn, C. 8, 23
Kluznik, H. 639, 675
Knight, B. 652, 653, 675
Kohut, H. 111, 145
Kolb, L. 46, 85, 86, 100, 111, 112, 114, 127, 141, 143, 145, 146, 197, 202, 260, 271, 278, 282, 588, 630
Koretzky, M. B. 255, 282
Kormos, H. R. 28, 86
Kosten, T. 28, 87
Kottler, J. 656, 675
Kottler, M. 77, 90, 314, 381, 699, 710
Kowalski, J. 50, 89
Kozak, M. 116, 142, 207, 279, 311, 313, 356, 376, 427, 431, 442, 448, 492, 655, 673
Kramer, M. 38, 86, 196, 202
Krantz, S. 657, 678
Krasner, L. 83
Kraus, A. 226, 282
Kraus, G. 106, 113, 150, 195, 204, 645, 678

Kreitler, H. 449, 494
Kreitler, S. 449, 494
Krishnan, R. R. 46, 81
Kruedelbrach, D. 324, 378
Krupnick, J. 110, 144, 195, 202, 231, 281
Krystal, H. 111, 113, 146, 185, 202, 453, 454, 494, 708, 712
Kucala, T. 39, 91, 251, 255, 287, 452, 497
Kudler, H. S. 56, 81, 309, 375, 644, 672
Kuhne, A. 452, 494
Kulka, R. 31, 37, 53, 57, 70, 71, 72, 86, 91, 96, 106, 146, 250, 251, 256, 259, 282, 283, 286, 640, 675
Kutz, I. 111, 141, 215, 277
Kuypers, J. A. 635, 675

L

L'Abate, L. 355, 377
Lamparski, D. M. 647, 675
Lang, P. J. 42, 46, 86, 116, 146, 426, 427, 443, 448, 494
Langbaum, R. 664, 675
Langer, E. J. 666, 667, 675
Langner, H. P. 692, 712
Lasko, N. B. 646, 676
Laub, D. 454, 491
Laube, J. 83
Laufer, R. S. 40, 69, 82, 86, 215, 283, 363, 377
Lazarus, R. 448, 449, 466, 494, 597, 600, 601, 604, 630 635, 641, 663, 675
Leaf, R. 131, 143, 224, 263, 280, 283
Lebowitz, B. 674, 671, 676, 677
Lebowitz, L. 462, 496
Lefkowitz, R. 322, 377, 658, 674
Lehrer, P. 378, 419
Leonard, A. 110, 143
Lepper-Green, B. 72, 84, 266, 281
Lerer, B. 570, 585
Lesser, I. M. 487, 494, 495
Levant, R. F. 380
Levenson, A. 657, 671

Levenson, M. 635, 671
Leventhal, H. 154, 202, 445, 495
Levinson, D. 637, 676
Levis, D. J. 524, 525, 529, 553, 556, 567, 568
Lewin, K. 20
Lewis, M. I. 659, 672
Lichtenstein, E. 623, 628
Lifton, R. J. 28, 34, 86, 111, 113, 134, 146, 185, 202, 215, 283, 313, 377, 463, 486, 495, 570, 585, 701, 702, 707, 712
Lindy, J. 34, 67, 68, 84, 110, 113, 143, 454, 471, 485, 486, 495, 598, 603, 629
Links, P. S. 227, 280
Linn, M. W. 96, 146, 259, 283
Lipke, H. 505, 520
Lipkin, J. O. 231, 283
Lipps, O. 232, 285
Little, D. 314, 379
Litz, B. T. vi, 57, 86, 100, 111, 116, 122, 146, 195, 202, 259, 263, 266, 283, 423, 426, 427, 436, 443, 448, 495, 511, 520
Litz, G. 248, 254, 283
Livesley, W. 226, 283
Lockhart, E. W. 231, 282
Lodden, F. 51, 52, 83
Loftus, E. 38, 81
Lohr, N. 460, 492
Lombardi, D. N. 163, 202
Loo, C. 48, 86
Love, L. 671
Luborsky, L. 324, 378
Lundin, T. 260, 285
Lyons, J. A. 34, 49, 58, 75, 76, 87, 96, 105, 146, 231, 248, 255, 284, 311, 378, 539, 567, 603, 630, 639, 640, 651, 671, 676

M

MacKay, P. W. 105, 147
MacLeod, C. 425, 443
Magraw, R. 639, 675

Mahedy, W. P. 705, 707, 712
Maher, A. 295, 363, 378
Mahone, C. 186, 187, 199, 607, 628
Mahoney, M. C. 2, 23, 73, 76, 87, 111, 146, 152, 153, 175, 188, 202, 229, 284, 291, 367, 368, 378, 450, 495
Malas, K. L. 271, 285
Malloy, P. F. 255, 282
Maltbie, A. A. 651, 672
Manaco, V. 57, 86
Mangine, W. 37, 81
Manifold, V. 39, 91, 251, 255, 287, 452, 497
Mann, J. 294, 378
Manning, D. 227, 287
Manton, M. 369, 381
Marchione, K. 271, 284
Marhoefer-Dvorak, S. 354, 380, 592, 631
Marin, P. 706, 707, 712
Markus, H. 177, 202, 203
Marlatt, G. 622, 623, 628, 630
Marmar, C. 31, 37, 72, 86, 91, 96, 110, 144, 146, 231, 250, 251, 256, 259, 281, 282, 283, 286, 640, 675
Marmar, W. 367, 374
Marquis, J. 505, 520
Marsella, A. J. vi, vii
Martin, J. 1, 383, 445, 487, 495, 640, 672
Martin, R. S. 106, 149
Marx, B. 57, 86, 263, 283
Maser, J. D. 443
Mason, J. 28, 87
Mass, R. 263, 283

Masters, C. R. 77, 83
Masters, R. 461, 495
Matheny, K. 181, 201
Mathews, A. 425, 443
May, R. 699, 701, 702, 712
Mays, D. T. 193, 202
McAdams, D. 357, 358, 378, 664, 665, 676
McCann, C. 2, 125, 146, 210, 217, 284
McCann, L. 110, 111, 112, 123, 124, 125, 126, 141, 146, 185, 202, 215, 264, 267, 284, 342, 302, 311, 339,

356, 362, 367, 368, 378, 406, 407, 419, 424, 432, 443, 464, 465, 468, 474, 495
McCarthy, P. 649, 653, 676
McCaughey, B. 677
McConatha, D. 665, 674
McCormick, J. 653, 678
McCormick, R. 324, 378
McCrae, R. 192, 202, 225, 243, 279, 284, 638, 672
McCranie, E. 56, 74, 80, 85, 109, 147, 524, 567
McCubbin, H. 630
McDermott, J. J. 292, 375
McDermott, W. 232, 284
McDougall, J. 487, 495
McDuff, D. R. 78, 87
McEntyre, W. 232, 285
McEvoy, L. 54, 84
McFall, M. E. 35, 36, 87, 104, 147, 271, 285
McFarland, R. 232, 285
McFarlane, A. C. 35, 63, 87, 103, 106, 147, 603, 630
McGuire, W. J. 710
McKay, M. 704, 712
McKinnon, J.A. 638, 678
Meek, C. 87, 94, 100, 147, 375, 418, 419
Meichenbaum, D. 65, 72, 84, 87, 130, 147, 187, 202, 266, 281, 311, 348, 359, 378, 400, 419, 587, 589, 591, 593, 604, 624, 630
Melges, F. T. 573, 578, 580, 581, 583, 585
Mellman, T. A. 39, 87
Mellon, J. 324, 378
Melton, M. 195, 201
Meredith, K. 657, 671
Metter, J. 637, 673
Michaelson, C. 635, 676
Michaelson, R. 635, 676
Michels, R. 419
Michelson, L. K. 271, 284
Mikulincer, M. 34, 63, 90, 91
Milgram, A. 72, 84, 266, 281
Miller, D. J. 639, 674
Miller, N. 56, 87, 677
Miller, P. 82, 204, 285, 380, 419, 567

Miller, W. R. 323, 379
Miller-Perrin, C. 58, 87
Millon, T. iii, 2, 3, 23, 110, 147, 155, 159, 189, 193, 202, 203, 231, 234, 241, 284, 292, 295, 299, 322, 379, 610, 630
Miner, J. 648, 649, 674
Mischel, W. 206, 284
Mitchell, J. 367, 375
Modlin, C. 409, 419
Monroe, S. M. 65, 88
Moore, L. 658, 674
Moos, R. 600, 628
Mora, C. 259, 282, 639, 671
Moretti, M. 212, 284
Morgan, H. J. 276, 284
Morrow, J. 103, 147
Mosak, H. H. 161, 163, 185, 203
Mosnaim, A. vii, 87, 148, 380, 630
Mowrer, O. 114, 115, 147, 458, 484, 495, 524, 568
Mt. Zion Psychotherapy Research Group 325, 336, 380, 381
Mueser, K. T. 363, 379
Muff, A. M. 74, 90
Murburg, M. 35, 36, 87
Murdock, C. 47, 82
Murdock, T. 66, 89, 432, 433, 442, 592, 593, 629
Murphy, S. 83
Murray, H. 8, 23

N

Nace, E. P. 56, 88
Nadler, W. 295, 378
Nagy, L. 250, 278, 452, 491
Nardi, C. 77, 90, 314, 381
Nathan, P. 309, 380
Needleman, J. 229, 285
Neimoff, R. 672
Neisser, V. 38, 88
Nesselroade, J. 151, 203
Nettler, G. 18, 23
Neugarten, B. L. 676
Neumann, D. A. 42, 83
Newcomb, T. M. 710
Newman, F. 135, 136, 148
Nichols, C. 182, 183, 203

Polster, M. 489, 496
Poon, L. 141
Popkin, S. 652, 673
Porter, C. 177, 203
Potter, R. 657, 671
Prabucki, K. 101, 110, 150
Pretzer, J. 131, 143
Price, G. 471, 496
Price, J. 640, 676
Price, S. 231, 277
Prigatano, G. P. 127, 148
Prochaska, J. 294, 295, 379, 398, 419
Prout, M. 41, 45, 55, 74, 88, 113, 148, 261, 285, 303, 379, 612, 613, 631
Pruyser, P. W. 485, 496
Puk, G. 505, 520
Pumpian-Mindlin, E. 633, 673
Putnam, F. 273, 278
Pynoos, R. S. 408, 409, 418

Q

Quadagno, J. 629
Quarantelli, E. L. 85, 88
Quiana, N. 107, 142, 210, 279

R

Rabin, A. 151, 203, 378, 673, 677
Rabin, L. 676
Rabkin, J. G. 108, 148
Rado, S. 455, 460, 496
Rahe, A. 61, 90
Rangell, L. 60, 88
Raphael, B. 260, 285
Realmuto, G. 640, 676
Reich, J. 106, 148, 227, 280
Renneberg, B. 193, 200
Resick, P. A. 111, 145, 354, 380, 424, 432, 443, 592, 631
Resnick, H. 50, 89, 106, 148, 377
Resnick, P. 592, 631
Reveille, J. D. 646, 678
Riba, M. vii
Rice, L. N. 247, 285, 312, 380
Richmond, J. S. 638, 676

Riggs, D. 47, 66, 82, 89, 432, 433, 442, 592, 593, 629
Robert, J. 232, 285
Robinowitz, R. 54, 63, 82, 88, 314, 379
Robins, L. N. 53, 84
Robinson, P. 76, 82, 404, 419, 580, 584
Rodin, J. 666, 667, 675, 677
Roitblat, H. L. 111, 141, 423, 442, 448, 491, 604, 629, 709, 711
Rollnick, S. 323, 379
Rosen, J. 639, 677
Rosenbaum, M. 244, 285, 398, 419
Rosenberg, M. J. 710
Rosenberg, S. 66, 89, 232, 285
Rosencheck, R. 309, 380, 526, 567, 644, 677
Rosenman, S. 462, 496
Rosner, T. 99, 144
Ross, M. R. 651, 672
Rossi, E. 129, 148
Roszell, D. K. 271, 285
Roth, S. 9, 23, 60, 82, 135, 136, 148, 185, 200, 215, 278, 304, 375, 462, 496
Rothbart, G. 69, 82
Rothbaum, B. 47, 66, 82, 83, 89, 110, 143, 655, 673
Rothstein, M. 325, 347, 366, 380, 404, 419
Rounsaville, B. 271, 286
Rozynko, V. 27, 89, 363, 380
Rubin, T. I. 667, 677
Rueger, D. B. 54, 83
Rundell, J. R. 700, 708, 713
Rush, A. J. 193, 203
Russell, D. 649, 674
Rustin, S. 511, 520
Rutter, M. 83
Ryan, D. A. 308, 381
Ryan, J. 232, 285
Ryff, C. 635, 668, 669, 677

S

Sacks, M. 144
Safran, J. 110, 142, 148, 187, 196, 203, 207, 221, 247, 267, 285, 286,

T

Thompson, L. W. 657, 673, 678
Tichner, J. 313, 381
Tick, E. 683, 686, 713
Tilleskjor, C. 452, 497
Titchener, J. 402, 409, 420
Touze, J. 273, 277
Trigos, G. 105, 143
True, W. 106, 149
Tulving, E. 574, 575, 585
Tuma, A. H. 443
Turco, R. N. 570, 585, 594, 631
Turkat, I. 192, 204, 290, 316, 317, 381, 608, 631
Turner, S. M. 193, 201, 204
Twentyman, C. T. 111, 141, 423, 441, 448, 491, 604, 629, 709, 711
Tyler, M. 720, 721
Tyler, S. 720, 721

U

Uddo-Crane, M. 99, 149
Uleman, J. S. 149
Ulman, R. B. 105, 125, 134, 143, 149, 196, 204, 466, 493, 708, 709, 712, 713
Urbanczyk, S. 273, 287
Ursano, R. J. 61, 90, 677, 700, 713

V

Vallis, M. 325, 347, 366, 380
Vallis, T. 82 159, 204, 285, 380, 419, 584
van Denburg, E. 229, 241, 278
van der Hart, O. 453, 497, 570, 572, 573, 585, 594, 631
van der Kolk, B. 28, 29, 72, 84, 90, 111, 127, 142, 150, 266, 281, 453, 458, 497, 588, 599, 631, 712
Van Dyke, C. 638, 678
van Kammen, D. 28, 90, 639, 674, 677
Van Kampen, M. 452, 497
Van Valkenburg, C. 639, 675
VandenBos, G. R. 634, 652, 673, 678
Vassar, P. 452, 497
Vauenargues 423

Velicur, W. 294, 379
ver Ellen, P. 28, 90
Verbosky, S. J. 308, 381
Vermilyea, B. B. 251, 279
Vermilyea, J. A. 251, 279
Veronen, L. 106, 111, 145, 148, 354, 381, 592, 631
Voltaire, F. 587

W

Wachtel P. L. 208, 287
Waddell, M. 251, 279
Wadner, D. 137, 138, 141
Wagner, N. 640, 676
Waid, L. 273, 287
Wakefield, D. 51, 83
Walker, A. 116, 129, 150
Walker, C. 650, 674
Walker, J. I. 651, 672
Wallace, E. 414, 415, 418
Wallerstein, R. 110, 144, 231, 281
Walsh, W. 66, 89
Walter, J. L. 296, 381
Warheit, G. T. 640, 672
Washton, A. 626, 632
Watson, C. 39, 40, 91, 249, 251, 255, 287, 452, 497
Watson, D. 673
Watts, F. N. 425, 443
Weisaeth, L. 63, 91, 260, 285
Weisenberg, M. 34, 91
Weiss, D. 31, 37, 72, 86, 91, 96, 146, 250, 251, 256, 259, 282, 283, 286, 287, 640, 675
Weiss, J. 325, 336, 349, 380, 381
Weiss, R. S. 571, 585
Weissman, A. 245, 287
Wellerman, F. 653, 678
Wells, R. 284
West, D. 592, 629
West, S. G. 685, 688, 697, 713
Wheale, C. 658, 674
Wheatley, R. 61, 90
Whelan, J. 675
Whitbourne, S. K. 209, 287, 636, 678
Wick, E. 704, 705, 706, 713
Wicklund R. A. 685, 688, 691, 697, 713

Widiger, T. 51, 83, 227, 287
Wilk, C. 137, 138, 141
Williams, C. C. 687, 709, 713
Williams, J. 608, 631
Williams, J. B. 243, 250, 271, 278, 286
Williams, J. M. 425, 427, 443
Williams, T. 56, 85, 454, 497, 634, 671
Wilmer, H. A. 196, 204, 709, 713, 714
Wilmer, N. C. 110, 144, 231, 256, 281, 287, 603, 629, 719, 721
Wilson, G. 623, 628
Wilson, J. 116, 129, 150
Wilson, J. P. 34, 67, 68, 84, 91, 101, 106, 107, 108, 110, 113, 116, 117, 143, 144, 150, 195, 203, 204, 210, 231, 244, 283, 287, 310, 366, 378, 381, 409, 420, 630, 647, 678
Winchun, G. 374
Wine, P. R. 639, 671
Winfrey, L. P. 425, 443
Winograd, T. 216, 287
Winokur, G. 84, 280, 315, 318, 376, 381
Wolf, M. 87, 630
Wolfe, B. E. 525, 552, 566
Wolfe, J. 34, 87, 111, 145, 195, 204, 231, 263, 264, 283, 284, 288 305, 382, 646, 678
Wolfe, M. E. vii, 148, 380
Wolman, B. 199
Wolpe, J. 503, 505, 521
Wonderlich, S. A. 58, 83
Woods, G. 65, 70, 82, 217, 228, 232, 234, 235, 240, 245, 256, 273, 279, 281, 309, 376, 322, 377, 458, 493

Woods, M. G. 46, 54, 74, 80, 85, 109, 147, 174, 201, 246, 255, 256, 258, 262, 281, 282, 303, 377, 452, 487, 493, 494, 524, 567, 658, 674
Woolfolk, R. L. 34, 40, 91, 378, 419
Worden, J. W. 581, 585
Worthington, E. R. 105, 150
Wotman, S. R. 358, 374
Wright, L. 658, 674
Wurtele, S. 58, 87

Y

Yalom, I. 699, 700, 701, 702, 703, 714
Yee, P. 610, 632
Yehuda, R. 197, 203
Yost, E. B. 657, 678
Young, D. E. 193, 201
Young, J. 110, 150, 152, 204, 213, 222, 241, 288, 334, 382
Young, R. R. 193, 201, 600, 629
Young, S. 487, 495

Z

Zanna, M. P. 443
Zaponc, R. 494
Zarit, S. 645, 646, 679
Zeig, J. 148
Zeiss, R. A. 639, 641, 679
Zigelbaum S. D. 231, 287
Zilberg, N. J. 638, 678
Zimering, R. T. 74, 85, 114, 115, 145, 259, 282, 378, 430, 431, 442, 511, 520, 524, 567, 673, 676, 677

ABOUT
THE AUTHOR

Lee A. Hyer is a clinical psychologist and Associate Professor of Psychiatry and Health Behavior at the Medical College of Georgia. He received his doctorate at Lehigh University and has had extensive postdoctoral training, including the Alfred Adler Institute in New York City and the New Jersey Academy of Group Psychotherapy. In addition he had a multiyear postdoctoral fellowship at the Center of Aging and Human Development at Duke University Medical Center. His research interests revolve around the necessary musings of psychological and psychiatric residents. Currently, he is monitoring two grants in the assessment and treatment of trauma problems.